CONTEXTUALIZING AESTHETICS:
From Plato to Lyotard

Gene H. Blocker
Ohio University

Jennifer M. Jeffers
University of South Dakota

Wadsworth Publishing Company
I(T)P® An International Thomson Publishing Company

Belmont, CA • Albany, NY • Bonn • Boston • Cincinnati • Detroit • Johannesburg • London • Madrid
Melbourne • Mexico City • New York • Paris • Singapore • Tokyo • Toronto • Washington

Philosophy Editor: Peter Adams
Assistant Editor: Kerri Abdinoor
Production: Matrix Productions Inc.
Editorial Assistant: Kelly Bush
Marketing Manager: Dave Garrison
Print Buyer: Stacey Weinberger
Permissions Editor: Robert Kauser
Interior Designer: Polly Christensen
Cover Designer: Stephen Rapley
Copy Editor: Victoria Nelson

Cover: (front) Robert Goldstrom, *Woman Looking at a Painting,* The Newborn Group; (back) Barnett Newman, *Be I,* Artists Rights Society/ photo by Lars Larson, Ohio Learning Resources. Barnett Newman has extended into painting the long and continuing philosophical discussion of "the sublime," from Longinus, through Burke, Kant, and Lyotard—a major theme of this book.
Compositor: R&S Book Composition
Printer: Transcontinental

Printed in Canada
1 2 3 4 5 6 7 8 9 10

For more information, contact Wadsworth Publishing Company, 10 Davis Drive, Belmont, California 94002, or electronically at http://www.wadsworth.com

International Thomson Publishing Europe
Berkshire House
168-173 High Holborn
London, WC1V 7AA, United Kingdom

International Thomson Editores
Seneca, 53
Colonia Polanco
11560 México D.F. México

Nelson ITP, Australia
102 Dodds Street
South Melbourne
3205 Victoria, Australia

International Thomson Publishing Asia
60 Albert Street, #15-01
Albert Complex
Singapore 189969

Nelson Canada
1120 Birchmount Road
Scarborough, Ontario
Canada M1K 5G4

International Thomson Publishing Japan
Hirakawa-cho Kyowa Building, 3F
2-2-1 Hirakawa-cho, Chiyoda-ku
Tokyo 102, Japan

International Thomson Publishing
   Southern Africa
Building 18, Constantia Square
138 Sixteenth Road, P.O. Box 2459
Halfway House, 1685 South Africa

Library of Congress Cataloging-in-Publication Data
Contextualizing aesthetics: from Plato to Lyotard/
   Jennifer Jeffers and Gene Blocker, editors.
        p.   cm.
      Includes bibliographical references and index.
      ISBN 0-534-52821-X
      1. Aesthetics.   I. Jeffers, Jennifer M.   II. Blocker, H. Gene.
   BH39.C6664   1998
   111′.85—dc21
                                        98-6704

For Basil

Contents

Preface

In this book we try to bring together different areas of aesthetics that are usually kept apart in separate anthologies—the classics of the history of aesthetics (Plato, Aristotle, Kant, Schopenhauer, etc.), mid-twentieth-century Anglo-American analytic aesthetics, and recent (late twentieth-century) Continental, mainly French and German, post-structuralist theory. We think the time is right to bring philosophical aesthetics back into a broader cultural interest in the fine arts.

In the first half of the twentieth-century aesthetics (the philosophy of art) was widely perceived as having an intimate connection with literature and the fine arts. Aesthetics was understood as providing a theoretical foundation for the study and practice of literature and the fine arts, guiding and channeling the critical and art historical discussion of the arts (including literature). Textbooks on aesthetics were used by departments of English, philosophy, modern languages, art history, and fine arts, in courses on art and literary criticism. Works on aesthetics were also used in courses on the history, analysis, and assessment of culture and taste. Leading aesthetics writers, such as John Dewey, Suzanne Langer, Roger Fry, Benedetto Croce, and Monroe Beardsley, were widely read by artists, art critics, and art historians as well as educated laypersons. But that began to change in midcentury, when aesthetics became increasingly a professional academic field of specialization. As it was brought into the arena of technical, professional philosophy, aesthetics ceased to be of much interest or relevance, and indeed even to be comprehensible to anyone who was not a professional philosopher.

The increasing specialization of academic aesthetics (as a technical discipline by professional philosophers writing for other professional philosophers) has also had the effect of detaching and isolating the philosophical study of art and literature from the broader social context in which art and literature exist. In the spirit of specialization, the tendency has been to leave economic issues to the economists, cultural history to the sociologists and historians, and ethnic and gender issues to the political arena, whereas those actively engaged in the arts tend to see art and literature as embedded in a broad social context and look for theories to help explicate the complex inter-weaving of art and economics and politics and cultural history.

The heyday of American and British aesthetics was reached by the mid-1960s, when analytic philosophers became very technical in their use of language, causing many readers, including university instructors of courses on art, literature, and cultural criticism, to become discouraged by reading contemporary aesthetics texts produced by analytic philosophers. At the same time the Continental philosophical scene was thriving, as Jacques Derrida, Michel Foucault, Gilles Deleuze, and Jean-François Lyotard were just then coming to the fore of the French intellectual scene after the long reign of Jean-Paul Sartre, the neo-Hegelians, and the Marxists. By the mid-1970s, French theory was all the rage in American language and anthropology departments and the new and emerging fields of media studies, communications, and cultural studies across the country. Continental philosophy, including the German hermeneutical philosophers Hans-Georg Gadamer and Jürgen Habermas, could account for—and were willing to deal with—the postwar environment and our rapidly changing technologi-cal, increasingly global, world community. And so, the breach between Continental and analytic aesthetics from the 1970s through the 1980s and now, at the end of the 1990s, has not been rectified, and perhaps is more intractable than ever.

Despite their broader interests in the wider context in which art emerges, Conti-nental writers have also proved as difficult for those not trained in Continental philo-sophical traditions as analytic philosophy had been in its own way. And so the need continues to bridge the gap, not only between aestheticians on either side of the En-glish Channel, but between the aestheticians on one side and those more directly in-volved with the arts on the other. Our goal in this book is to bridge this dual gap, to provide a way of bringing aestheticians and others interested in the arts in a variety of other ways into a fruitful dialogue on the role of art in today's world.

Although philosophy of art does not account for all of the disputes between Conti-nental and analytic philosophers, we would like our text to be a starting point, at least, in the *recontextualization* of all branches of aesthetics, and to propose a discourse that begins to rectify the breach not only between contemporary Continental and analytic philosophers, but also between philosophers and the wider art and literary public. By encouraging such a dialogue, both Continental and analytic aestheticians may be able to reenter the wider public debate over art and culture that they occupied and even led in the first half of this century.

But the biases that keep philosophers apart and that keep philosophers of art out of the public debate are not biases we think are shared by you. We think you have a right to know all sides of this ongoing debate so you can make up your own minds. That is why we have included in this book selections from the history of aesthetics (Part I); from analytic aesthetics (Part II); and from contemporary Continental literary theory and from commentators on art and culture from outside philosophy (Part III). The criterion we set for the success of this book is that it make a significant contribution to a wide range of college courses crisscrossing many disciplines of philosophy of art, lit-erary theory, art and/or literary criticism, cultural history, and comparative arts.

Indeed, our text is itself the attempt of one analytically trained philosopher and one Continentally trained theorist to see similarities and make connections, as well as to ap-preciate and affirm differences. It is not so much a matter of rejecting one set of ideas in favor of another, but rather of continuously reinterpreting ideas from the past in light of a changing social context. Each period of aesthetics (even those that histori-cally predate or postdate the high point of the eighteenth- and nineteenth-century in-terest in theories of aesthetic experience) is of interest and has important insights to be understood in the larger context of the history of ideas—a history that must be con-stantly reinterpreted and recontextualized. An interesting example of this need for continual reinterpretation is Lyotard's analysis of the postmodern sublime (Part III), which is a reinterpretation of the Kantian notion of the sublime (Part I), which is, in turn, a reinterpretation of Burke's theory of the sublime (Part I), deriving at last from Longinus' Greek text of the second century (Part I).

To accomplish these goals, we have cast our net as widely as possible in search of di-verse approaches to the arts—from literary theorists like Paul de Man to art historians such as Rosalind Krauss and Meyer Shapiro to cultural materialists like Tony Bennett and Fredric Jameson to the philosophers Martin Heidegger and George Dickie to cul-tural critics Theodor Adorno and Robert Venturi; and in the process our discussion of art ranges from painting to poetry to architecture to music, including reproductions of many artworks specifically discussed by our authors.

We do not imagine that everyone who uses this book will read it from cover to cover, and in fact there are many ways to read this book and many ways to organize various university courses in aesthetics, philosophy of art, art theory, and the like, using our book. For those concerned primarily with the history of ideas, a quarter or semester course can be successfully organized around Part I with selected portions from Parts II and III. Those more concerned with current trends in the arts and theorizing about the arts, on the other hand, will more likely choose one or two readings from Part I and, for some historical context, one or two readings from Part II, but concentrate mainly on Part III. Those centered in the mainstream of Anglo-American analytic philosophy will probably prefer Plato, Aristotle, Hume, and Kant from Part I, focusing mainly on Part II (and perhaps one or two readings from Part III for contrast in philosophical style and methodology). Still another approach is from a literary theory or art historical perspective, leaning less on the philosophers and built mainly on Part III, but including perhaps Hegel and Nietzsche from Part I. Finally, instructors interested in letting their students judge for themselves the full range of positions and approaches in these essentially and eternally contested debates will want to do as much from each of the three parts as time permits.

We also recognize the need for flexibility and diversity in the use of our introductory material. We believe the texts stand by themselves and we have not tried to speak for or "explain" what these authors have already ably said in their own way. Certainly our introductory remarks, whether introducing the book, or each of the three parts of the book, or the various sections within each of these parts, are not intended as a substitute for students coming to grips with the primary sources on their own. Rather, what we have tried to provide is some historical and cultural background and context to situate the texts in the history of ideas.

In addition to books listed in our Bibliography at the end of the book, there are many CD-ROMS and Internet resources and sound libraries for exposure to and enjoyment of works of art. The complete Getty collection, for example, which is now housed in the new hilltop museum and gallery in Los Angeles, is now available on the World Wide Web. A few of the numerous CD-ROMS currently available are:

Great Paintings: Renaissance to Impressionism
Digital Collections, Inc.
Alameda, CA, 1995

Microsoft Art Gallery
The National Gallery of London
Microsoft, 1993

Exploring Modern Art
The Tate Gallery of London
ATTICA Cybernetics, Inc.
London, 1994

Of particular interest for sources on art criticism, philosophy of art, literary theory, and aesthetics is *Infotrac,* an online library of over 600 current scholarly and popular publications, which we think will prove an invaluable tool for students working on research papers, whether because of smaller libraries or simply the convenience of working at home (and at times when the library may not be open).

We would like to thank our students at University of South Dakota and Ohio University, who have willingly acted as our human guinea pigs as we tested our reader in the classroom. We are also grateful to the University of South Dakota and Ohio University for their clerical and research support. We thank the following individuals for their careful reviews of the book: James Anderson, University of Wisconsin, Madison; Steven Crowell, Bryn Mawr College; Angela Curran, Bucknell University; Timothy Davis, Essex Community College; Helen Elam, State University of New York at Albany; Michael Jones, Western Carolina University; David Michael Levin, Northwestern University; Diane Michelfelder, Utah State University; Linda Patrik, Union College; Michael H. Reed, Eastern Michigan University; and Joanne B. Waugh, University of South Florida. Finally, we wish to thank Peter Adams and Kerri Abdinoor of Wadsworth Publishing Company for their encouragement, patience and advice in guiding us through the many steps and stages in the production of this book.

Introduction

As the title suggests, this book recognizes the fact that theories of art and art itself exist within a context—philosophical, cultural, class and gender specific—from which it emerges and without which it does not exist. The cliché "no man is an island" is no less pertinent in the history of ideas. Philosophers and art theorists today can no more escape the influence of past philosophers and theorists than they can remain isolated and untouched by current trends in popular culture, the arts, electronic media, and other areas of broad social change. This book is organized around the historical theme of the tradition of the aesthetic (aesthetic experience and the aesthetic attitude) and what comes before and after it—that is, three periods of the "pre-aesthetic," the "aesthetic," and the "postaesthetic." A closely related way of putting this would be in terms of "premodern," "modern," and "postmodern" art and culture. The idea here is based on the assumption that art and culture and *theories* of art and culture are inseparably and organically linked together—and moreover that this is not a static or eternal pattern but one that is constantly changing historically over time.

Aesthetics (as the study of art and beauty), aesthetic experience (the proper way to approach and experience art and beauty), and modern art ("art for art's sake") all arose together at approximately the same time as expressions of *modernist* culture—a period lasting somewhere between the Renaissance and the middle of the twentieth century. *Aesthetics* is the name of the philosophical study (investigation or science) of art and natural beauty. It is a relatively new branch of philosophy that arose in the early eighteenth century (early 1700s) in England and Germany, over two thousand years after the beginnings of other branches of Western philosophy (which began in Greece around 600 B.C.E.).

Aesthetics as the study of art and beauty is closely related to the concept of aesthetic experience. Indeed, aesthetics arose as an investigation of aesthetic experience. As one of the early aestheticians, Alexander Baumgarten (1714–1762), put it, humans experience the world in one of two fundamentally different ways—logically and aesthetically. *Logical experience* is the most common and ordinary way in which we see and experience and think about things by classifying them in practically useful ways—"that is a thorn; it will prick your finger if you touch it." *Aesthetic experience*, by contrast, is looking at things for their own sake—just for the fun of it, as when we enjoy looking at a rose, watching a sunset, taking a leisurely walk in the park, looking at seashells or colorful birds or flowers, and, of course, enjoying works of art. The main question for that branch of philosophy known as aesthetics was: What is the nature of aesthetic experience? How does aesthetic experience differ from other sorts of experience?

Beauty and art were therefore defined in terms of aesthetic experience and not the other way round. You do not have an aesthetic experience because the object is beautiful or because it is a work of art, but just the reverse—it is beautiful because you are looking at it aesthetically; it is art because it has been made to be looked at aesthetically. The same object, a flower, for example, could be viewed nonaesthetically, identified as part of a botany midterm exam, for example, or a summer job planting flowers in the city park. And a work of art can also be seen in nonaesthetic ways, as in packing an expensive oil painting for shipment overseas, or repairing a damaged piece of sculpture. By the same token, an oil smear in a puddle of water could be beautiful or a piece of driftwood could become a work of art if they are viewed and approached aesthetically.

Art and beauty, therefore, according to the eighteenth-century aesthetics investigation into aesthetic experience, are subjective and psychological. They do not exist objectively as properties of objects, but only as human ways of perceiving objects. Nonetheless, art and beauty can be universally *perceived* in the same way by all people, just as colors that are subjective and psychological sensations, that only exist "in the mind," are nonetheless virtually the same for all people (that is, subjective but universal). Only humans and certain other animals experience the colors of objects, but because our sense organs are similar, our experiences, though subjective, are roughly similar. And even though white as the appropriate color for a wedding gown and black for funeral attire is culturally relative (red being the appropriate color for a wedding dress in China and white for funeral garments in Japan), anyone raised in a Western culture will perceive white as "right" for weddings and black for funerals. So even though aesthetic qualities are subjective and psychological (and sometimes culturally relative), existing only "in the minds" of observers, they are nonetheless universal, or potentially universal, for all humans (or at least for all people raised similarly in the same culture).

What we call art, or more properly fine art, is therefore, according to the eighteenth- and nineteenth-century tradition of the aesthetic, those objects made by humans to be enjoyed aesthetically. In that sense, objects made by people before the emergence of aesthetic experience are not really art, though we today will see them and think of them as art. The early Paleolithic Europeans who produced the famous cave paintings of prehistoric bison did not, so far as we know, make them simply to be viewed, as modern artists do, but for ritual, ceremonial, and religious purposes (located as they were in dark, virtually inaccessible interiors of the cave complex and so available to very few people, probably only the high priests or shamans). In the same way, ancient Native Americans or Africans made wood carvings as religious objects (homes for gods to temporarily occupy, for example). Although today we enjoy these objects as works of fine art, they were not so appreciated by the people who originally made and used them. We might call this *art-before-art* (in the preaesthetic, or premodern period). What we call *works of art,* by contrast, are objects made primarily to be enjoyed aesthetically, *as* art, and not as religious icons.

So, art created as art, aesthetic experience, and aesthetics as the study of aesthetic experience are notions that all arose together at about the same time. These human ways of interpreting the world have not always existed since the dawn of human society and not even since the beginning of Western civilization (beginning as far back as 1000 B.C.E.), or even philosophy (beginning in the sixth century B.C.E.) or even the beginning of the Christian era (around 400 C.E.). It is a relatively new development—only after the pre-aesthetic, or premodern period of art-before-art do we find the aesthetic, modern period of art (for its own sake).

This would be the end of our story were it not for the recent phenomenon called *postmodern* that we are now in (and have been since shortly after the middle of the twentieth century). If aesthetic experience and aesthetics and fine art arose with and as part of the modern period, then the postmodern period we have now entered would seem in some sense or other to have gone *beyond* art and the aesthetic. But *how* exactly is not at all clear.

In this book we will look at the precursors to the modern period of aesthetic interest in fine art and its evolution into the modern era of aesthetic appreciation, moving finally to attempts of artists and art theorists to move beyond the modern into the postmodern.

Aesthetics, then, is a branch of philosophy concerned with art and beauty; in other words, aesthetics is simply the philosophy of art. Philosophy is often thought of today as a kind of systematic reflection of our ordinary commonsense intuitions and deep-seated, unconscious beliefs and assumptions. But this means that aesthetics is a reflection on ideas we already have about art, artists, aesthetic experience, and so on, as these ideas have gradually filtered down since the Renaissance into our ordinary way of looking at things. In other words, if aesthetics is a branch of philosophy and philosophy is a reflection of our ordinary commonsense intuitions, then, in a sense, we already know (all of us, all of *you*) what aesthetic, art, and artists are (and what words like *aesthetic, art,* and *artist* mean).

But these commonsense intuitions may be so deeply engrained and internalized within us—so much a part of our normal outlook, assumed and taken for granted—that it is difficult for us to see them. It is precisely because all of us humans have a certain blindness to points of view other than our own that we can only see one perspective at a time (we can only inhabit one place at any given time). Yet it is possible for us humans to imaginatively and sympathetically view the world in other ways, and if we can open up new ways of seeing the world—if we can see the artwork from other points of view—we can enlarge our knowledge of the world and eventually of ourselves. That is why shifting contexts is so important. We need to ask ourselves: How can we fully experience the artwork if we can only see it from our own particular, habitual way of seeing art and the world? How can we enlarge our perspective? Perhaps this is possible only by way of contrast. Without a contrast (real or imagined), our own ways of seeing things will always seem natural, normal and obviously right, perhaps the *only* ways to see things, and therefore invisible to us as one perspective among many. With that in mind, let us consider for a moment a contrasting point of view.

Most big city art museums have rooms devoted to African art and pre-Columbian American art. Many people collect, buy, and sell these objects as artworks, and beautifully illustrated art books have been written on them. But consider for a moment where these objects come from and how they were originally used by the people who made them. Many of the ceramic pieces from Mexico and Central America are grave goods; that is, they were made to accompany the dead into an afterlife. Much the same is true of works from ancient China and Egypt. Everything we need in this life was made available to the dead for their use in an afterlife, except that people or goods needed were fashioned in the form of miniature ceramic or wooden replicas or effigies—small figurines of musicians, guards, servants, horses, and so on. The only (living) people to ever see these objects were the people who made them, the family members who purchased them, and the priest who cast whatever magical spells were required to make them come to life and perform in the "land of the dead" (that is, to make these little ceramic and wooden figurines play music, serve food, and so on).

Only forty or fifty years ago, West Africa farmers could not begin their annual planting until the high priests had initiated a ceremonial dance by masked performers in the fields reenacting the original farming techniques given the people by their gods. But today these same wooden masks are displayed in art museums, described in art books, and bought and sold in Europe and North America as works of art. (Although the *first* Europeans who saw them in the late eighteenth and early nineteenth century saw them as false religious idols and accordingly destroyed as many of them as they could. Only later, beginning around 1904, did European artists, including Picasso, begin thinking of these same objects as works of fine art—and even started imitating them in their own art.)

But what *are* these wooden and ceramic objects, really? Are they works of art? Were they made by artists? Were they meant to be aesthetically appreciated? Even before we study the *history* of these concepts (work of art, artist, aesthetic appreciation) to learn when and how they first appeared, the precise way in which they were defined and defended, and so on, we already have some idea what these words mean. Even though today we look at these objects as works of fine art, the people who originally made and used them did not (or at least this was not their primary purpose). These objects were not used aesthetically but for religious, ceremonial purposes; they didn't have to be beautiful for people to look at but just to be sufficiently representational (of a musician, for example) to perform their ritual function (to play music beyond the grave, to call forth the agricultural gods, to chase away the evil spirits, and so on). The people who made them were not expressing their own individual feelings, attitudes, and beliefs, but conforming to the traditional pattern (form) required by the religious traditions of that particular society. And certainly the objects were not made to be looked at and admired—obviously not in the case of the grave goods, but neither in the case of the African masks, which are stored away out of sight most of the time and are only brought out once a year to be seen during the planting ceremony.

This gives us a fairly accurate idea—by way of contrast—of what is meant by the "aesthetic attitude" and the "aesthetic experience" of "works of fine art" made by "artists." These are objects made for no other purpose than (or at least whose *main* purpose is) to be viewed aesthetically—that is, to be enjoyed just for the pleasure and satisfaction of looking at and listening to them. Consider in your own case: Why do you listen to music? What do you get out of it? Aesthetic experience of works of art, in other words, is nonutilitarian, where *utilitarian* means making and using something for some ulterior motive (that is, for some other reason). If someone has made a sandwich, we don't just look at it—we eat it. If someone has made a burglar alarm, we don't set it off just to hear how it sounds—in fact, we hope it *won't* go off. This means that we do not listen to music with any expectation of personal gain (beyond the pleasure of the experience itself), as opposed to listening to a lecture in your accounting class (from which you hope to gain something—a good grade on the next test, leading to a good grade in the class, leading to a degree, and a job, a house in the 'burbs with a BMW in the garage . . . and so on). But after class you go back home and listen to music—why? And the people who make these works of art are not just skilled craftspersons. We think of them as artists who have something important to say or express. Artists who just say the same things over and over again, or those who just say what other artists have already been saying for a long time, we tend to think are not as good as artists who have something new to say and new ways of saying it.

And what are they "saying," what are they "telling" us? Think about it. It's very hard to put into words, isn't it? Somehow the people we think of as artists, or at least those we think of as great artists, are expressing or saying something that can't be said in some more ordinary way through the ordinary use of language. The musicians we love are expressing how things feel to them, how things in general seem to be; they are relating a kind of mood, we might say, or a point of view. Well, what *is* this overall mood or point of view? To find out, you just have to listen to the music. The artist has expressed this unique perspective in and only in her music. The "meaning" or "message" is there for anyone who bothers to listen from an aesthetic point of view. It's all right there in the music, we feel like saying; just listen.

But now going back to our contrast with pre-Columbian American ceramic grave goods and the masks used in West African planting ceremonies, we can see that people have not always looked at things in this ("aesthetic," "fine art") way. As natural as this may seem to us, it is not the only way; it is not universal, not a permanent part of human nature. It appears at a certain point in the history of certain cultures and may just as easily disappear later and be replaced by another way of looking at things. Being able to recognize that these views are subjective shows that indeed contexts *do* shift and change over time and from culture to culture.

These ideas of aesthetic enjoyment and fine art and artist arose in what we call the modern period—roughly from the end of the seventeenth century through the middle of the twentieth century. If, as we said earlier, philosophy is the reflection of our ordinary, commonsense intuitions, then we can easily formulate from our reflections here the main points of modernist aesthetics.

1. Aesthetic experience is nonutilitarian.
2. Aesthetic experience is detached from ordinary self-interested pursuits (i.e., is disinterested).
3. Works of art are made to be viewed aesthetically—and so just to be enjoyed (for no other purpose).
4. Everyone can appreciate art just by adopting the aesthetic point of view (it is universal in all human beings).
5. Artists see things in a unique way and creatively find innovative ways of communicating that vision to us.
6. Artists, or at least the great artists, show us how to look at the world, how to understand ourselves, who we are, and what our world is like.
7. Works of art (or at least great works of art) express these unusual ideas of artists.
8. Great works of art must be innovative and creative, expressing new ideas in new ways.
9. The history of art is the history of these great innovations by these great artists (the first one to do this, the first one to do that, etc.).
10. Art is not hard to understand—it just requires that we adopt the aesthetic point of view.

Traditionally, these views express, more or less, the modern period of the aesthetic simply by articulating what have now become our commonsense intuitions. What we hope you come to realize as you read the selections in this book is that this so-called commonsensical view of the world is simply *one* way of viewing the world—one that seems natural and normal and perhaps even inevitable to us but that is only one human way of looking at things. Although modernist aesthetics is deeply engrained in our attitude toward the arts and culture even at the beginning of the twenty-first century, you will become aware as you read this book that this view is only "common" relative to our particular culture and the era in which we happen to live. The Greeks (especially Plato) had no notion of "art for art's sake," and many philosophers and theorists on art in the past (Nietzsche, for example) and present (Foucault, for instance) do not believe that art and aesthetic experience can or should be distanced or detached from the broader social context in which we live.

Indeed, there is an interesting history of the rise and fall of this set of intertwined modernist concepts (aesthetic, fine art, artist). The story begins with Thomas Hobbes's (1588–1679) claim that all human perception and action is "self interested." Everything you do, Hobbes said, is selfishly motivated. If you help your grandmother, it is because you expect some reward, or because you are afraid your parents will punish you if you don't, or just to feel good.

Many people opposed this idea of Hobbes's because it seemed to imply that it was impossible to love God or to do good or to love someone or to enjoy art or natural beauty without expecting to gain something in return. If Hobbes was right, then what many people regarded as the most important things in life—that is, genuinely heartfelt spontaneous religious, moral, aesthetic feelings—were impossible. So in reaction philosophers began exploring the idea that some human actions were "*dis*interested"—that is, were not done for any ulterior motive, but enjoyed and appreciated for their own sake. And one large subset of such disinterested actions were those associated with art and natural beauty.

This reaction begins with Anthony Ashley Cooper (Earl of Shaftesbury, 1671–1713) in Britain around the turn of the eighteenth century, who said we can love things for themselves—a good wine, a beautiful sunset, a handsome bird, a painting, a piece of music. But, of course, people can love and enjoy many different things, some good, some bad. What should guide us in our disinterested love? How can we be sure we are loving the *right* things, those things that *deserve* to be loved? If we ask, in this whole class of things we love in a disinterested way (God, goodness, art and beauty), how we know what we should like and what we should not like, we have to say it is just a matter of taste, a kind of inner sensation, or feeling, or sixth sense—it is not something one can learn from a book; it is not a question of acquiring intellectual or scientific information.

Of course, we may not at first like the best things (the best wines, the best music, the best paintings), and so our taste may need to be developed and improved. But even in that case we do not improve our taste—say, in music—by learning academically (memorizing) what the experts say is good music—we have to actually come to *like* this music ourselves, and like it better than other sorts of music. Good taste is not knowing what is good but actually *liking it best*. Imagine trying to explain to someone who doesn't understand why a certain musical CD you like is good. It's a matter of refining the feelings, not learning a new set of facts. It's like trying to explain to someone who's never tasted one how a mango tastes.

In the 1750s the German thinker Alexander Baumgarten pursued this idea by dividing all human thought into two broad categories—logic and aesthetic. Logic is our intellectual, cognitive, rational way of looking at, exploring, and explaining things; aesthetic is our intuitive, sensual way of knowing things by the "feel" of them (this is the root of the word *aesthetic,* as we can see in the term *anaesthetic,* "no feeling"). After Baumgarten, the British, mostly the Scots, worked on the idea of good taste as a kind of refined sensibility available to anyone who would adopt the detached, disinterested aesthetic point of view. And still later, at the very end of the eighteenth century, the German philosopher Immanuel Kant synthesized the work of the British taste theorists and the German attempts to define the aesthetic as differentiated from the logical, and Kant's efforts pretty well defined and stabilized the tradition of the aesthetic attitude for the next hundred and fifty years.

Now that we have a little better idea of what is meant by the aesthetic attitude in the modern period, we can ask whether, at the end of the twentieth century and the beginning of the twenty-first, we are still in the modernist period or are moving beyond that into a postmodern phase? It is always difficult to understand the period we are actually living in (hard to see the forest for the trees, as we say). But there seems little doubt that *something* is going on—some fundamental changes in our society, our general culture, in the arts, and in our theories of the arts.

One way to understand many recent developments in art, art criticism, and theories about art and art criticism is to see them as *rejections* of various claims of modernist aesthetics. Modernist aesthetics claims, for example, that the basis of aesthetic appreciation is universal in all human beings. Not so, say some postmodernists. Art is understood within socially constructed art conventions and these differ widely from culture to culture. The claim that aesthetics is universal, say the postmodernists, is simply a way of trying to privilege your own art and put down the art of everyone else. "Universal" really just means "the way *we* see and do it." Hence these modernist claims are really very ethnocentric and Eurocentric, putting our culture above everyone else's.

When we shift our context from modern to postmodern, we see a series of traditional propositions simply nullified by contemporary views and practices. For example, modernist aesthetics claims that anyone can adopt the aesthetic attitude. Not so, says the postmodernist; the aesthetic attitude is simply the perspective of well-educated, usually white males and is very different from the point of view of poor, uneducated, disenfranchised, nonwhite, Third World, females. Modernist aesthetics claims to be autonomous and detached from politics. Not so, say the postmodernists; all art reflects the cultural assumptions, values, "ideologies" of a particular society, European art supporting the politics of the powerful—again, rich, well-educated, white (imperialist, colonialist) males. Modernist aesthetics claims that works of art are creative expressions of the particular point of view of the individual artist, showing us new ways of seeing things, revealing ourselves and our world in a new light, and so on. Not so, say the postmodernists; art merely reflects the already existing power politics of a particular society; far from being innovative, art merely supports the existing power relations.

Modernist aesthetics claims that there is a canon of great artists who led the way in creative innovations. Not so, say the postmodernists; there is no canon of great art or artists—this is just a way of privileging those artists who support the existing power elite, a way of keeping them in power and those out of power permanently out of power (women, blacks, nonEuropeans, colonized peoples). Modernist aesthetics claims there is a historical development in art in a single progressive direction. Not so, say the postmodernists; that is just another way to privilege the contributions of certain artists and belittle the contributions of others.

Of course, it is always hard to judge the outcome of the period of history we are actually living in. It may be too soon to tell whether all these counterclaims against modernist aesthetics will be proved true or at least become widely accepted, and, even if they are, it is still too soon to tell whether postmodernism will simply replace modernist aesthetics by a postmodern aesthetics or whether postmodernism will do away with aesthetics altogether (in which case we would say that aesthetics rose and fell with modernism—that is, we could actually *date* both aesthetics and modernism somewhere between 1710 and 1960). Nonetheless, as you will see from the contemporary readings in Part III (from the 1980s and 1990s), philosophers of art and art theorists are certainly moving away from the detached aesthetic gaze of art for art's sake and toward an understanding of art as embedded in a broader social context. One clear difference we can observe, in other words, during the past twenty-five years, and a clear indication of a move from the modern into the postmodern, is the effort to understand art and literature, not as isolated from, but as integral parts of the larger political, economic, technological context in which we find ourselves.

The most interesting issue in this ongoing debate is whether art merely reflects the existing politics of the status quo or whether art can create new ways of looking at things that may challenge the status quo. Does art have its own voice, can it generate its own point of view, or is it merely the expression, symptom, reflex of a larger political system? This is the question of aesthetic detachment and artistic autonomy—if art is merely a part of a larger social context, then it has no autonomous voice of its own and merely speaks for the powers that be; but if, on the other hand, art, though arising from the broader social context, can create within the artwork itself an independent perspective or point of view that can challenge the status quo, that can show us alternative perspectives, other ways of seeing and doing things, then the modernist aesthetics may continue on for some time, though perhaps in a weakened, diluted, modified form.

At the beginning of our discussion we said that it is hard for us to be aware of our own assumptions and perspectives. It is like a bias or prejudice—it is easy to see in other people, but very difficult to see in ourselves (as in the West African proverb, "A skunk has no nose"). So, in this case, postmodern writers argue that while artists may imagine they are expressing their own unique individual points of view, ones that they think are at odds with the values of the larger society, they are in fact simply a *part* of that larger society and are unknowingly expressing the dominant, mainstream view of those in power. The main idea here was stated long ago by Karl Marx (in the 1840s–60s). Even if I want to rebel against society and embrace the idea that the individual has a right to be free from all restraints to do as he or she pleases—even that, Marx (and now postmodernists) say, is really just a reflection of the values of the dominant capitalist middle class.

According to Marx (Part III, section D), when the middle class was forming in Europe at the end of the Middle Ages, it had to overcome the values, laws, and customs ("ideology") of the feudal aristocracy in which tradespeople and craftspeople were under the control of the landed gentry. They were not free to move where they liked, to engage in whatever business they preferred, to invest or accumulate money as they chose, to educate their children as they wished. But gradually this small class of merchants and craftspersons grew larger, settled in larger towns (Paris, London) and, as their wealth increased, so did their power, challenging finally the wealth and power of the aristocracy. The values of the middle class capitalists were very different from those of the declining aristocracy. The new values that supported the middle class included the leveling idea of the basic "equality" among all people (or at least among all middle class people, and especially equality between the middle class and the aristocracy), along with the idea of the "rights" of the individual to go wherever and do whatever would make money, along with the right to keep that money and pass it on to their children.

This ideological analysis is very different from the idealized account offered by Enlightenment philosophers like John Locke and Thomas Jefferson, who held that these basic human rights and freedoms are an inalienable part of human nature, the natural birthright of every human, and therefore universal in all people at all times. Marx argued, on the contrary, that ideas of "freedom," "individualism," "individual rights," "equality" are *not* universal with all people at all times, embedded in human nature, but arose historically precisely with the rise of the middle class as a way of defending their interests against the upper classes (and later against the lower working classes). According to this Marxist perspective, different historical periods have their own values—that is, values that support and defend the dominant power structure within that particular society—and art and philosophy are used to support the dominant value system. In a feudal society, for example, individual "rights" and "equality" would be completely inappropriate and out of place, undermining the feudal value that each person and each class should know and accept its proper place in harmonious interaction with others in a complex hierarchical social order.

From this Marxist perspective, all art and all philosophy spring from an ideological or political motivation. Let's look again at the debate between Hobbes and Shaftesbury on disinterested experience as an ideological debate. Hobbes was writing at a time of great political and religious turmoil. Many people had begun to challenge the rights of monarchs to rule them; at the same time, with the rise of Protestantism, many felt capable of receiving the divine spirit into their hearts directly, without the intermediary of duly appointed priests or other religious experts. In general, we may regard this as the beginning of the modern idea of individualism, in which many people began to feel that they had as much "right" to decide what was morally, politically or religiously good as anyone else.

Hobbes found this trend very troubling because it seemed to encourage extremists and fanatics, saying to them, in effect, "If in your heart you think you are right to rebel against the existing government or established church or traditional moral customs, then go ahead—no one has any greater right to decide these things than you." Hobbes used the new scientific theories emerging at that time in an attempt to silence and control these rebellious individualists. Scientifically, Hobbes argued, goodness (whether of art, social policy, or customs) is not an objective property of physical objects, but is merely the power of objects to arouse feelings of desire or aversion within us. Good is simply what we call those things we desire and want; bad is what we call those things we hate and want to avoid. All love and desire is, therefore, self-interested. Goodness is neither an objective property of things in the physical world nor is it a universal desire among all human beings; it is strictly relative to each individual's feelings and desires.

For that reason, Hobbes argued, political rebels and religious fanatics are wrong to think they have some special access to the truth. In matters of taste (about what is religiously, morally, or aesthetically correct), no one has any better knowledge than anyone else. But if everyone is allowed to go his or her own way, won't we soon end up with chaos and anarchy? And if so, then how can we decide what is best, or at least come to some common agreement within a given society? Only by selecting an absolute ruler to decide for us, Hobbes said. The only alternative is complete chaos and anarchy, a horrible state in which Hobbes tells us life is "nasty, brutish and short." So in this way Hobbes used the scientific theory of his day regarding self-interested desires to support his conservative political agenda, rejecting the rights of individuals to decide for themselves when it is legitimate to try to overthrow the government.

Shaftesbury (as Cooper is generally known) agreed with Hobbes that it was dangerous to encourage rebellious individualists (each of whom thinks he or she has discovered a special Truth to which everyone else is blind), but he opposed Hobbes's political support of the absolute right of the monarchy to decide everything for us. Shaftesbury argued instead that there is a universal standard of good (in art, morals, and religion) known by a special faculty of mind possessed by every human but needing to be developed and refined, one that is capable of perceiving how things harmoniously fit together. Goodness is not a property of physical objects and is not therefore capable of being perceived through ordinary sense perception. Goodness is rather a kind of harmonious interrelationship of parts within an organic whole that all humans have the innate capacity to apprehend.

For Shaftesbury, therefore, unlike Hobbes, there was an absolute standard of moral and aesthetic right and wrong, capable of being understood by everyone, to which even the king must be held accountable. So, while in Hobbes's "Social Contract" we give the monarch absolute right to decide everything for us without any challenge or restraint or prospect for appeal, Shaftesbury sets certain limits on the power of the sovereign. In this way what first appear as the concerns of morality or aesthetics turn out upon closer inspection to be politically, or "ideologically," inspired. Indeed, any art or philosophy or religious doctrine can be analyzed "ideologically"; all art can be said to be, in one way or another, political.

In a similar way, postmodernists often argue that even the Romantic idea of the artist following his or her own idiosyncratic bent, opposing society, rejecting crass middle-class capitalist values—even this, strange as it may seem, is really just a way of supporting the middle-class capitalist market economy. Many people living in Third World, underdeveloped countries today regard the ideal of liberal democracy—the rights of the individual to be free to pursue his or her own interests so long as he or she does not interfere with the equal right of others—as something typically American or Western. Suppose you claim to reject the values of your own society; you say you want to strike out on your own, to find your own values, to find what is right for you—you are totally opposed to any attempts by your society to force you into some straightjacket. But many people in other parts of the world will simply see this as a typical American attitude. "You are *all* individualists; you are *all* antisocial; you *all* claim equality and the right to be different!" Ironically, it is the Western tradition to be antitraditional. The social value we share is that of individualism; we are culturally conditioned to demand freedom!

Something like this is the challenge thrown at the artist by postmodern theory: "Try as you like to do your own thing and to speak with your own voice, you are a product of your society and whether you like it or not (or realize it or not) you are just a patsy supporting and defending the very society you claim to be trying to overthrow or radically change!" Contemporary artists have responded to this challenge in many ways, sometimes playfully mocking the idea of cultural absorption by exemplifying and thereby gently contradicting it.

By now the astute reader will have noticed that aesthetic modernism coincides precisely with the rise of capitalist, free market middle class society. But if modernism is about to be supplanted by postmodernism, does that mean that we are nearing the end of the capitalist, free market, democratic society? Or is something else going on? Something that has less to do with economics and more to do with enormous changes in mass media and communications. In the middle of the nineteenth century Hegel (Part I, section B) talked about the "death of art." Perhaps it is art, rather than aesthetic consciousness or theories of art, that is changing. Or perhaps the changes we are witnessing *begin* with art and only later filter down into other areas of our common culture. Do artists any longer define the world for us? Do we any longer look to artists to show us the way into the future—to define for us who we are, what the world is or will be like? Does anyone any longer have the time to really look at or listen to art? How can art function in the age of the sound bite and channel and internet surfing?

Of course, we respect the art of the past, but who are the "great artists" of today—who sets the pace which we look to for answers, for vision? Perhaps that is what has changed. Is there a place for "high art," "fine art" in our present age? Or will the only contemporary art of real interest be environmental, socially situated, electronically interactive art—rather than the art of the art galleries, private collections, and art museums? If this is the new art and the new role for art in our contemporary society, how will attitudes towards art and theories of art arise to meet this new challenge? Who has the answers? In times of rapid change, even the smartest and most sensitive people are trying to discover the answers—if indeed there are any "answers" to be had. In the end you will have to decide these issues for yourselves; in this book we can only provide you with some of the background information and tools you will need to engage in this complex debate.

Part I

History

A. The Ancient (Greek and Roman) Period

PLATO AND ARISTOTLE HAVE BOTH HAD AN ENORMOUS INFLUENCE on the long history of aesthetics, as they have had in most areas of philosophy. Although aesthetics as an independent study and separate branch of philosophy did not exist before the eighteenth century, ancient and medieval philosophers discussed many issues related to art and beauty that influenced and continue to influence modern aesthetics.

Like all movements in the history of ideas, new ideas do not spring up suddenly, but generally have a long gestation period of gradual evolution. Since we consider the Greeks and Romans to be our cultural forebears, we tend to see their notions of art as very similar to our own, but in fact the modern sense of the aesthetic appreciation of art for art's sake had not yet fully developed. The Greek and Roman idea of art lies somewhere between what we are calling the pre-aesthetic and the aesthetic (or the pre-modern and the modern). The root of the English word *art* simply means anything that does not appear in "nature" but that is made by people (a tree comes from "nature," for example, while a wooden axe handle comes from "art"). This is the sense in which we still speak of an *artifact,* or of something's being *artificial,* or the sense in which we speak of medicine or cooking as an art and not a science.

Toward the end of the medieval period (somewhere between the thirteenth and the fifteenth centuries) a distinction was drawn among the ordinary arts, the liberal arts, and the fine arts. The *ordinary arts* included such skills as stone masonry, while the *fine arts* included more representational and expressive skills, such as stone sculpture (the *liberal arts* included history and philosophy, which are still included in the Arts division of most universitys' College of Arts and Sciences—but excluding painting, sculpture, printmaking, and ceramics, which are housed in the School of Fine Arts.) From this notion of the fine arts eventually derived our modern sense of art as the "high art" of oil painting, for example, but excluding crafts like carpentry. As we will see, this division of the arts has come under attack in the postaesthetic or postmodern period during the latter half of the twentieth century as being snobbish and elitist, and many people today consider making a ceramic teapot or a quilt, or a handmade rocking chair an art form (and the teapot, quilt, and rocking chair themselves works of art) no less "high" than oil painting or classical music.

The Greek and Romans had still not yet devised any special terminology to differentiate fine art from the broader category of any humanly made artifact, but were nonetheless well on their way to treating certain artifacts in ways which resemble the modern aesthetic way of dealing with what we call "fine art." The Greeks and Romans apparently differentiated the representational arts (pictures and statues and stories that are about people and events) from the nonrepresentational arts, like a ceramic storage pot, even though they didn't have different terms or theories to mark this distinction. They also recognized and honored famous artists, for example, just as we do, and although most of their art still had religious or ceremonial or other functional connotations, it was evolving toward a more purely aesthetic enjoyment, art for art's sake.

Also, despite the lack of a distinct terminology for fine art, and despite the lack of any independent discipline or branch of learning for investigating fine art and its appreciation, the Greek and Roman philosophers, in the midst of discussing other issues (found in many different books), did raise many important issues of concern to aestheticians today—questions of beauty, creativity, and the like. In this sense we can find the roots of many modern aesthetic concerns with fine art and aesthetic experience in the ancient philosophers, especially Plato and Aristotle, but also Longinus.

Plato's influence was especially great in the Renaissance and continuing until the end of the seventeenth century, but in the more recent period (through the first half of the twentieth century) Aristotle has been the dominant figure. The revival of interest in Longinus' notion of the sublime at the beginning of the eighteenth century was of major importance in the formulation of the modern distinction between the beautiful and the sublime, which in turn helped explain and justify the Romantic art movement beginning at the end of the eighteenth century, and, as we will see in Part III, has also inspired a postmodern trend in terms of a new reading of sublimity. How precisely have Plato, Aristotle, and Longinus been important to modern aesthetics?

Plato

In dialogues concerned with a variety of issues, Plato raises many issues of interest to aestheticians today—in *Symposium* and *Phaedrus* Plato discusses the love of beauty; in other dialogues he talks about the abstract patterns (circles and the like) reflected in our perceptual experience, which later aestheticians have related to the formal characteristics of artworks, and in other dialogues, like the *Ion,* Plato raises the issue whether artists rationally know what they are doing or are merely inspired or possessed by forces outside their control; and in many dialogues Plato himself writes metaphorically and about metaphor, a practice that has had a great influence on subsequent discussions of allegorical and/or metaphorical painting and poetry.

But probably Plato's greatest contribution to the discussion of art has been his analysis of the representational function of art, the idea of art as the "imitation of nature." Rather than inventing new concepts, philosophers often reflect on, analyze, and try to clarify and refine concepts that are already widely in use at the time. So Plato analyzes the popular idea of his day that art "imitates" reality. When we study the history of ancient Greek art, we can see quite clearly that it was the generation just before Plato (that is, around 500 B.C.E.) that Greek art reached the pinnacle of its highly "realistic," "naturalistic" phase.

For Plato art is to be judged, not by standards internal to itself, but by *non*aesthetic, *non*artistic criteria, that is, by realistic, moralistic, educational, and political standards. In their artworks poets talk about and artists represent people riding horses, for example, but unless this is represented accurately (showing the precise way saddles and bridles are made and the exact way horses actually run and jump), then, Plato insists, the artist has, in a sense, deceived us. And by making the works as realistic as artists were attempting to do in Plato's day, artists also trick us, Plato points out, into mistaking the painting for the real object. According to the historian Durius (fourth century B.C.E.), Appelles painted a horse so lifelike that real horses tried to get friendly with the painted horse, and in a contest with Parrhasius, Zeuxis painted grapes so realistically that birds tried to eat them; but—not to be outdone—when Zeuxis then went to pull the curtain from Parrhasius' painting, he discovered that the curtain was only painted on the canvas—and so the prize went to Parrhasius! These stories, though surely apocryphal, nonetheless indicate the pride that the Greeks of Plato's day took in the highly illusionistic art of that time.

Plato worried that we may be giving artists too much power over our lives, giving them credit for understanding many things which they know nothing about. Today Plato would have similar worries about moral philosophers who say that novelists are our best guide to moral knowledge. Certainly, Plato would argue, these novelists can give the illusion that they understand social and psychological reality very well, but do they really? After all, they are merely story tellers. Granted they can spin a good yarn, what makes us think they know anything about life? Wouldn't we be better off turning to the social scientists—sociologists, psychologists, historians?

Part of Plato's concern is to put as much of our lives as possible on a firm scientific basis. This is one of the themes of the *Cratylus*. Like many aspects of culture, language seems to many people to be purely conventional. Why do we call cats *cats,* and not *stac,* and why do we spell it *c-a-t,* and not *k-o-d-t*? If language is to represent the world accurately, as Plato insisted it should, then don't we need some better, more scientific basis for assigning words to ideas and objects—something better than mere tradition and convention? Although much of the discussion is playful, the problem of language's ability to accurately represent reality is a perennial concern of philosophers. Outside Plato's dialogue Cratylus is famous as one of the Greek skeptics who argued that we can never know anything since language cannot capture reality or communicate ideas. Physical objects are constantly changing, he said, whereas words are relatively static. Cratylus' teacher Heraclitus once said, "You can't step twice in the same river," to which Cratylus replied, "You can't step once in the same river." Pointing, we say, "That's the Wabash River," but halfway through the sentence the river (or at least the water) is different. So how can language capture reality? And, even if it could, how can language then communicate ideas from one person to another? While you and I both refer to the same object by the same word, your idea may be very different from mine. And if that is so, how can we be said to live in a common world? One of the features of postaesthetic, postmodern thinking is a renewed worry about the possibility of language's accuracy in representing reality and of our being able to live in a common, shared world. This is one reason *Cratylus* is becoming a popular dialogue (see the Derrida essay in Part III) among art critics and theorists.

Knowledge, according to Plato, can only come from a philosophical grasp of the essential nature of the underlying causes of things, which Plato regarded as immaterial, abstract, and eternal principles, laws, patterns, or "Forms." The ordinary perceptual knowledge of a saddlemaker or a boatbuilder is at best a pale reflection of this genuine philosophical knowledge; these people know in a practical sense *how* things work but they don't know in a scientific sense *why.* Since the artist doesn't even understand how saddles or boats are actually made, he or she can only copy what these objects *look like.* The artist therefore knows even less than skilled craftspersons, who themselves lack the philosophical knowledge of the underlying reality involved in their craft. The artist, Plato argues, is therefore *twice* removed from truth and reality—below the crafts-person, who at least has some ordinary working knowledge of things, but who nonetheless falls below (is once removed from) the philosopher, who understands the underlying principles, causes, laws, and reasons that things work as they do.

philosopher	Form of Bed
craftsperson	actual bed (copy of Form of Bed)
artist	painting of a bed (copy of an actual bed, a copy of a copy)

In this schema we can see the three levels of knowledge and reality, and the sense in which the craftsperson is *once* removed from the top (the philosopher's grasp of the Form of Bed), whereas the poor artist is *twice* removed—right on the bottom!

Such artistic ignorance would be harmless were it not for the enormous rhetorical force that art has. What worried Plato (and what worries many people today) is the great emotional power art has over us, including its ability to make us think that life is just like what is represented in art. Instead of learning from life itself (or at least from scientific accounts of life), Plato worried that we will get all our ideas from art itself (and that these ideas are likely to be highly inaccurate). In Cervantes's sixteenth-century story, Don Quixote knows nothing about love except what he has read in ro-mantic love stories and so makes a perfect fool of himself in real life.

Similarly, many people today wonder if music videos, television dramas, or movies of sex and violence are good for young people to watch. From Plato's point of view, these works claim to "imitate" reality, like someone holding up a mirror to the world (to use Plato's famous image), and this is very dangerous since many people will de-velop attitudes about how to settle arguments (with force) or how to treat women (as submissive sex objects) by viewing these videos and movies. This gives artists entirely too much power to control our social attitudes, and therefore, Plato argues, the artists must be censored and their work controlled by more knowledgeable experts.

What is dangerous about art, Plato felt, is its irrational, emotional hold on us. In-stead of leading us to look at things rationally, philosophically, or scientifically, art, es-pecially music, encourages us to judge things and to view the world emotionally. We can imagine what Plato would think of rap, hip-hop, and hard metal rock music today. Given this great power of art to influence our attitudes and behavior, Plato thought that this force should at least be harnessed for social good. Educationalists, Plato thought, should use music and fiction to emotionally instill in young people the proper attitudes toward disciplined behavior and proper habits of social harmony. Music and fiction that contributed to this socially useful end should be allowed and in-deed encouraged, but any music or fiction that led toward slovenly lack of discipline, social alienation, or rebellion must be firmly outlawed.

Here we see a perennial theme in the history of aesthetics—the idea that certain kinds of art can strengthen and encourage morality, whereas other kinds of art are likely to encourage licentious immorality. Art that encourages morality is art that emphasizes balance and proportion, thereby training young people to fit harmoniously into society and to take their proper place with good grace, whereas art that emphasizes unre-strained emotion will encourage young people to become rebellious misfits. In this way a longstanding and ongoing tradition was established between the alliance of the "good" and the "beautiful"—both of which were interpreted in terms of the harmonious balance of different, often opposing forces (as we saw briefly in the Introduction in discussing Shaftesbury's notion of beauty as "a kind of harmonious inter-relationship of parts within an organic whole.")

Aristotle

Although Aristotle studied under Plato (his father sent him to Plato's "Academy" when Aristotle was around seventeen), his aesthetic theories could hardly be more different from Plato's. As Aristotle once said, "Plato is dear; but truth is dearer."

Without attacking his teacher directly, Aristotle refutes point by point almost every assertion Plato makes about art. When Plato says that the emotion expressed in art, especially music and drama, is dangerous, Aristotle points out how the "cathartic" release of emotion in the imaginary space of the theater is actually healthy. When Plato says that the artist must accurately describe precisely how things actually happen, Aristotle says the artist need only describe how things *usually* happen, *might* have happened, or how they are generally *thought* to have happened. Where Plato rejects any depiction in art of falsity or absurd impossibilities, Aristotle allows this if they "serve the end of poetry itself." Where Plato criticized the artist for not being rational, Aristotle says the good playwright constructs an intricate web of logical probabilities. Where Plato criticized the artist for not being sufficiently philosophical, Aristotle defends poetry as being more philosophical than history.

For Plato, knowledge can only come from an intellectual grasp of the essential nature of things, which he conceived as abstract immaterial patterns or Forms existing apart from physical objects; for Aristotle, the essential nature or "form" of a thing cannot exist apart from that physical object. Aristotle agrees with Plato that there *is* a human nature, for example, but for Aristotle this only exists *in* particular human beings—that is, as the essence or nature that every person possesses, the inner force that causes the fetus to develop as a human rather than a dog or a cat. Therefore, for Aristotle, but not for Plato, one could come to have genuine knowledge of the essential nature of things by studying the physical objects themselves, and there is no reason in principle, Aristotle thought, why such knowledge of universals could not come from artists as well as from scientists or philosophers—all of whom are abstracting from their experience the common nature or essence of many different particular entities.

In very general terms, we can say that while Plato made art subservient to nonartistic functions (of morality and politics, for example), Aristotle is appreciated today for his efforts to give art a measure of autonomy, isolating art, more or less, from morality and politics, and thereby defending the artist against Plato's censorship. Aristotle therefore seems to us today a forerunner or "father" of the modern notion of a detached aesthetic interest in art for art's sake, although Aristotle himself would not have accorded art and aesthetic experience nearly so much autonomy as theorists did in the eighteenth and nineteenth centuries. In the first half of the twentieth century (in what was then called New Criticism) Aristotle was seen as a pioneer in the attempt to find a peculiarly aesthetic domain for art and the experience of beauty. A work of art is not to be judged by standards or criteria pertinent to some *other* domain *outside* art— whether morality, religion, science, or politics. Art must be judged on its own terms, by its own standards—*l'art pour l'art*, art for art's sake. From this recent (and there-fore anachronistic) perspective Plato seems more old fashioned and conservative, try-ing to keep Greek culture closer to what we are calling the pre-aesthetic or premodern notion of art as subservient to other societal functions. Today, however (still anachro-nistically), we can see the pendulum swinging away from Aristotelian artistic autonomy toward a more Platonic integration of art into a larger social, political, and economic contextual whole—as we move into the uncharted waters many call postmodern and which we prefer to call postaesthetic. Though currently out of fashion, formalism, art for art's sake, and New Criticism nonetheless all lean heavily on Aristotle's *Poetics*.

Specifically, Aristotle's notion of aesthetic and artistic autonomy expresses itself in three main areas. First, Aristotle insists that when we talk about art, we must concen-trate on the art object itself—and not on the thoughts or feelings of the artist that the art work is said to express, nor on the external reality that the artwork represents or im-itates. For Aristotle, a work of art is a kind of humanly constructed object that has its own special character that must be studied and analyzed, just as we study and analyze natural objects.

According to Aristotle, everything in the world belongs to some definite *kind* of thing (snakes, frogs, butterflies, and so on), and the scientific study of these things is the study of the "essence" or "nature" of each of these kinds (or species). Aristotle's father was a medical doctor and many of his examples are drawn from biology. So, for example, when we study Monarch butterflies, we are interested in the main features of this *species* as a whole (and not the individual butterflies we happen to catch in our net for observation). The essential form of a Monarch butterfly, as a natural object, is in-nate within the butterfly, actually inside the biological material the butterfly is made of (today we would say it is in the genetic code of the DNA within the chromosomes of each cell of the butterfly).

Similarly, in the case of works of art, we should investigate the essential nature of each *kind* of artwork, except in this case, Aristotle says, the "form" or essential nature of works of art of a particular kind is not something *natural* and *inherent* in the mate-rial stuff the artwork is made of, but something imposed on it by human beings from the outside. A work of art is thus an *artificial* and not a *natural* object. While the wood from which a carving of a man or woman has been made has the essential char-acteristics of the wood of that particular species of tree (hard or soft, dark or light in color, fine or coarse-grained, and so on), there is nothing within the wood to make it grow into a sculpture of a man or woman. Only the artist can impose this form on the material. (This is that broad "nature-versus-art" distinction we discussed earlier. The word *poetics* in ancient Greek did not refer to that special form of literature we call "poetry" but meant "something made by people," and so could include bricks, paper, boats, saddles, as well as paintings, plays, and sculpture.)

But Aristotle nonetheless insists that we must understand a work of art, like a nat-ural species, as belonging to a particular kind or genre of artworks, and that it is the kind or genre that defines its essential nature. Just as we look at a particular Monarch butterfly as an example of its species, so we must examine each work of art as a mem-ber of a particular *kind* of art work, with its own history, traditions, and so on. That means we cannot talk about art in general, but only of kinds of art—tragic drama, comic theater, lyric poetry, epic poetry, Italian opera, symphonic music, and so on. Nor can we talk about an individual work of art in isolation from the kind or genre to which it belongs. Each of these genres will have its own defining character and ideal paradigm in terms of which we judge individual members of the same kind.

Like Plato, Aristotle continued to clarify the popular notion in his day that art is the "imitation of nature" (and this is Aristotle's way of differentiating ships from paintings—both are made by people, but some arts, like painting, are representational, while other arts, like shipbuilding, are not). But Aristotle tries to refine this common assumption in a way that allows us to distinguish between different kinds or genres of art. As he says, each art genre can be distinguished by differences in the "object, manner, and means" of its imitation. So, for example, what is imitated or represented (the object imitated) in tragedy is different from what is represented (the object imitated) in comedy. Tragedy represents people who are on the whole above average (morally and in social standing), while comedy generally represents people who are average or slightly below average. And while both tragedy and epic poetry (such as the *Iliad* or the *Odyssey*) use the same *means* of imitation (i.e., language rather than the painterly *means* of lines and shapes and colors), they nonetheless differ in the *manner* of their imitation or representation. Tragedy uses a dramatic manner of direct discourse, in which characters speak for themselves (e.g., MARY: "I'd rather do it myself"), while epic poetry uses a narrative manner of indirect discourse, in which the narrator of the epic poem often speaks for the characters (e.g., "As usual, rather than asking someone for help, Mary would rather just do it herself.")

In the *Poetics* Aristotle gives us an example in his celebrated analysis of Greek tragedy. He is not talking about all works of art, nor even of all dramatic plays, and certainly not about modern (e.g., Shakespearean) tragedy, but only of that kind of tragedy that developed in Greece from the sixth through the fourth centuries B.C.E. Aristotle traces this historical development from its earliest stages to its full maturity. Only by examining many examples of mature Greek tragedy can we gain some idea of what a Greek tragedy should be like; only then can we extract the standards by which to judge a particular Greek tragedy (the example Aristotle selects is Sophocles's *Oedipus Rex*).

Had Aristotle lived in the middle of the nineteenth century he would have approached the genre of lyric poetry in a similar manner; and had he lived toward the end of the nineteenth century this is how he would have analyzed the modern novel (neither of which genres existed in Aristotle's day). Like Greek tragedy, each of these genres has its own history, and we don't know what the ideal "shape" or "form" of the novel or lyric poem will be until that genre reaches the stage of its mature development—in the early nineteenth century, in the case of lyric poetry, or the later nineteenth century, in the case of the novel. Aristotle once said, "One swallow does not make a summer" (where by *swallow* he meant a bird, not a sip), a rough American translation of which might be, "It ain't over till it's over." We can't tell what a baseball game or a particular summer will be like until it is almost over; we don't know what a person's life is like until that person has reached maturity and done most of the things that person is going to do. Each work of art must be understood and judged as good of its kind: Given the fully developed form of the novel, is this a good novel? Given the fully developed form of lyric poetry, is this a good lyric poem?

Second, Aristotle has given us what is still probably the clearest statement of the organic unity of a work of art. Though the specific character of each art genre is unique, all works of art, as humanly constructed objects, aim at an organic unity of many parts into a single whole. Looking at a work of art as a humanly constructed artifact, Aristotle investigates precisely how the art work is constructed: What are the formal characteristics that make this art work the unique work of art that it is? Again, the analogy is with the living organism.

Just as the parts of a living organism all work together in harmony—the stomach to motivate us to look for food, the eye to spot the berries, the legs to transport us to the berry patch, the hands to grab the berries, the mouth to gobble them up, the stomach . . . etc.—so each part of a good work of art must similarly fit harmoniously together with all the others, ideally so that no part could be either added or subtracted or moved from one place to another without destroying the whole. Everything that is needed to complete the whole is there and nothing is there that is not required, and all those necessary parts are in the precise order and arrangement necessary for the whole to function as a single unity. Think of a poem—according to Aristotle, if you change one word, or add one word or drop one word or change the order of any of the words, you have destroyed the unity of the poem—in effect you have created a different poem. *That* poem, the original poem, can only be said in that precise way, and its "meaning," emotional impact, is the product of just those words in just that order.

Finally, Aristotle has defined realism as relative and internal to the artwork. A work is realistic only within the story or play or poem or painting (as when someone today says that the story of *The Hobbit* is "very realistic")—not, as Plato thought, by comparison with some external reality (as though someone today might complain that, after all, hobbits don't exist). Therefore Aristotle argued that we should not use the same standards in judging what happens in the story as we use to judge events in real life, outside the story. What is believable in real life might seem quite arbitrary in a story, and vice versa, what is highly unlikely in real life (such as the appearance of a ghost) could be made to seem very believable in a story (as in Henry James's novel *The Turn of the Screw*). And it is also for this reason that Aristotle argued that the emotional response to the artistic "imitation" of an object in a work of art is different from the emotional response to the objects that the artwork "imitates" as they exist outside the art work. For one thing, Aristotle pointed out how most people enjoy the imitation of something that in real life they find boring or uninteresting, and for another, he noted that in a tragedy we enjoy a dramatic enactment of events we would be horrified and hate to see in real life. Hence Plato's worry that our emotional response to events portrayed in art will be the same as that to events observed in real life is deflected in Aristotle, shielding the artist from this criticism as well.

Longinus

Another influential text of the Greek and Roman period is Longinus' work on the idea of the sublime. First attributed to the third-century Roman writer Cassius Longinus, *Peri Hupsous* (*On the Sublime*) is now thought to be the work of an unknown Greek author of the first century. The book was not written as a text in aesthetics or the philosophy of art, but rather as a manual for rhetoric, or public speaking. Despite its antiquity, the work had little influence in European thought until Nicolas Boileau's French translation in 1674 and Edmund Burke's discussion of the "The Sublime and the Beautiful" in 1757, after which the sublime became a key concept for defining the budding Romantic art of the time (beginning in the late eighteenth and early nineteenth century).

In this short book Longinus contrasts the emotional power of the sublime with "what is reasonable" and "merely agreeable"; that is, the sublime is neither logical nor beautiful but emotionally powerful. And that emotional power, Longinus tells us, is instantly conveyed, "with the vividness of a lightning-flash," like falling in love. But if so, then how, Longinus wonders, can such a thing be taught? Plato had attacked the idea of artistic inspiration; since art is not the product of rational, planned thought but just comes to the artist, overpowering him, Plato found it highly dangerous. Later this idea appears as the interpretation of artistic activity as the "second Creation" (God's being the first). Much later (late eighteenth and early nineteenth centuries) this idea resurfaces as the modern notion of "genius," and still later as the Romantic doctrine of "talent," and finally in the twentieth century as the Freudian unconscious. Throughout this long history, the question is: Can artistic creativity be taught (and if so, how), or is it simply something we are (or are not) born with?

As a professional teacher of rhetoric, Longinus argues that creativity can be taught and developed, at least partially. Of the five "principal sources" of the sublime that he lists, the first two (in order of importance) he admits are "god-given" while the last three can be taught and learned. This is a restatement of the old problem of a kind of aesthetic control the artist exerts over her craft that is nevertheless *not* the kind of rational, scientific control that Plato demands of the artist. Is the artist "possessed" by alien (or perhaps unconscious) powers, or does the artist know what she is doing? This old problem is still not fully solved.

But we must distinguish the true from the false sublime, the brilliant from the merely flashy, Longinus warns us. But how can we tell what is really sublime? The test of what is truly sublime, he says, is whatever is approved by the "noble" and "elevated" person. But how do we recognize the "noble" and "elevated" person? If we say this is the person who produces the truly sublime, then we are obviously arguing in a circle (the genuinely sublime is what is recognized by the noble and the noble are those who recognize the truly sublime). Longinus also mentions the test of universality—that is, the truly sublime is what everyone enjoys as sublime. But does everyone agree on what is really sublime, any more than everyone today can agree on what is the best music or the best movies? And if we say that not everyone knows the genuinely sublime but only the experts, then we must define who are the "experts." If we say they are the "noble" and "elevated" (i.e., highly educated) people, then we are right back where we started. Later (Part I, section B) we will recognize this as the eighteenth-century problem of taste. Who can really discriminate the best music, the best paintings, the best wines? The experts, we say. But who are the experts? Those who discriminate the best music, paintings, wines. Again, we seem to be arguing in a vicious circle.

The sublime, Longinus says, must suggest or point to a great deal beyond what is actually said, that is, it must be "pregnant in suggestion." Later (Part I, section B) we will see how Kant, and still later (Part III, section E) Lyotard, develops this aspect of the sublime. Another point Longinus raises that will seem familiar to us today is the question whether the person pursuing lofty emotional grandeur is to be faulted for minor technical flaws in her work. Is it a fault of Louis Armstrong that he fluffs a few notes in *Potato Head Blues,* or is this rather a sign of his sublime greatness—focusing on the larger issues and oblivious to trivial details?

Finally, where does this capacity for sublimity come from, Longinus asks? It is a unique capacity of our human nature, he says, "from the first implanted in our souls an invincible yearning for all that is great, all that is diviner than ourselves." This is the one constant theme through all the many twists and turns in the two-thousand-year evolution of the notion of the sublime—from Longinus to Lyotard.

The Republic

PLATO

WE MUST COME TO an understanding about the mimetic art—whether the poets, in narrating their stories, are to be allowed by us to imitate, and if so, whether in whole or in part, and if the latter, in what parts; or should all imitation be prohibited?

You mean, I suspect, to ask whether tragedy and comedy shall be admitted into our State?

Perhaps, I said; but there may be more than this in question: I really do not know as yet, but whither the argument may blow, thither we go.

And go we will, he said.

Then, Adeimantus, let me ask you to consider whether our guardians should or should not be fond of imitation; or rather, has not this question been decided by the rule already laid down that one man can only do one thing well, and not many; and that one who grasps at many will altogether fail of gaining much reputation in any?

Certainly.

And this is equally true of imitation; no one man can imitate many things as well as he would imitate a single one?

He cannot.

Then the same person will hardly be able to play a serious part in life, and at the same time to be an imitator and imitate many other parts as well. . . .

If then we adhere to our original notion and bear in mind that our guardians, released from every other business, are to dedicate themselves wholly to the maintenance of the freedom of the State, making this their craft and engaging in no work which does not bear on this end, then they ought not to practice or even imitate anything else; if they imitate at all, they should imitate from youth upward only those characters which are suitable to their profession—the courageous, temperate, holy, free, and the like; but they should not depict or be skilful at imitating any kind of illiberality or baseness, lest the fruit of imitation should be reality. Did you never observe how imitations, beginning in early youth and continuing far into life, at length grow into habits and become a second nature, affecting body, voice, and mind? . . .

I answered: Of the harmonies I know nothing, but would have you leave me one which can render the note or accent which a brave man utters in warlike action and in stern resolves; and when his cause is failing, and he is going to wounds or death or is overtaken by disaster in some other form, at every such crisis he meets the blows of fortune with firm step and a determination to endure; and an opposite kind for times of peace and freedom of action, when there

From The Dialogues of Plato, *3rd ed., trans. B. Jowett (Oxford: Oxford University Press, 1892).*

is no pressure of necessity, and he is seeking to persuade God by prayer, or man by instruction and admonition, or when on the other hand he is expressing his willingness to yield to the persuasion or entreaty or admonition of others. And when in this manner he has attained his end, I would have the music show him not carried away by his success, but acting moderately and wisely in all circumstances, and acquiescing in the event. These two harmonies I ask you to leave; the strain of necessity and the strain of freedom, the strain of the unfortunate and the strain of the fortunate, the strain of courage and the strain of temperance; these, I say, leave. . . .

Then let us now finish the purgation, I said. Next in order to harmonies, rhythms will naturally follow, and they should be subject to the same rules, for we ought not to seek out complex systems of meter, and a variety of feet, but rather to discover what rhythms are the expressions of a courageous and harmonious life; and when we have found them, we shall adapt the foot and the melody to words having a like spirit, not the words to the foot and melody. To say what these rhythms are will be your duty—you must teach me them, as you have already taught me the harmonies.

But, indeed, he replied, I cannot tell you. I know from observation that there are some three principles of rhythm out of which metrical systems are framed, just as in sounds there are four notes out of which all the harmonies are composed. But of what sort of lives they are severally the imitations I am unable to say.

Then, I said, we must take Damon into our counsels; and he will tell us what rhythms are expressive of meanness, or insolence, or fury, or other unworthiness, and what are to be reserved for the expression of opposite feelings. . . .

But it does not require much analysis to see that grace or the absence of grace accompanies good or bad rhythm.

None at all.

And also that good and bad rhythm naturally assimilate to a good and bad style; and that harmony and discord in like manner follow style; for

our principle is that rhythm and harmony are regulated by the words, and not the words by them.

Just so, he said, they should follow the words.

And will not the words and the character of the style depend on the temper of the soul?

Yes.

And everything else on the style?

Yes.

Then beauty of style and harmony and grace and good rhythm depend on simplicity—I mean the true simplicity of a rightly and nobly ordered mind and character, not that other simplicity which is only a euphemism for folly?

Very true, he replied.

And if your youth are to do their work in life, must they not make these graces and harmonies their perpetual aim?

They must.

And surely the art of the painter and every other creative and constructive art are full of them—weaving, embroidery, architecture, and every kind of manufacture; also nature, animal and vegetable—in all of them there is grace or the absence of grace. And ugliness and discord and inharmonious motion are nearly allied to ill words and ill nature, as grace and harmony are the twin sisters of goodness and self-restraint and bear their likeness.

That is quite true, he said.

But shall our superintendence go no further, and are the poets only to be required by us to express the image of the good in their works, on pain, if they do anything else, of expulsion from our State? Or is the same control to be extended to other artists, and are they also to be prohibited from exhibiting the opposite forms of vice and intemperance and meanness and deformity in sculpture and building and the other creative arts; and is he who cannot conform to this rule of ours to be prevented from practising his art in our State, lest the taste of our citizens be corrupted by him? We would not have our guardians grow up amid images of moral deformity, as in some noxious pasture, and there browse and feed upon many a baneful herb and flower day by day, little by little, until they silently gather a festering mass of corruption in their own soul. Let us rather search for artists who are gifted to discern the true nature of the beautiful and graceful; then will our youth dwell in a land of health, amid fair sights and sounds, and receive the good in everything; and beauty, the effluence of fair works, shall flow into the eye and ear, like a health-giving breeze from a purer region, and insensibly draw the soul from earliest years into likeness and sympathy with the beauty of reason.

There can be no nobler training than that, he replied.

And therefore, I said, Glaucon, musical training is a more potent instrument than any other, because rhythm and harmony find their way into the inward places of the soul, on which they mightily fasten, imparting grace, and making the soul of him who is rightly educated graceful, or of him who is ill-educated ungraceful; and also because he who has received this true education of the inner being will most shrewdly perceive omissions or faults in art and nature, and with a true taste, while he praises and rejoices over and receives into his soul the good, and becomes noble and good, he will justly blame and hate the bad, now in the days of his youth, even before he is able to know the reason why; and when reason comes he will recognize and salute the friend with whom his education has made him long familiar.

Yes, he said, I quite agree with you in thinking that it is for such reasons that they should be trained in music.

Just as in learning to read, I said, we were satisfied when we knew the letters of the alphabet, few as they are, in all their recurring combinations; not slighting them as unimportant whether they occupy a space large or small, but everywhere eager to make them out, because we knew we should not be perfect in the art of reading until we could do so:

True—

And as we recognize the reflection of letters in water, or in a mirror, only when we know the let-

ters themselves, the same art and study giving us the knowledge of both:

Exactly—

Even so, as I maintain, neither we nor the guardians, whom we say that we have to educate, can ever become musical until we and they know the essential forms of temperance, courage, liberality, magnanimity, and their kindred, as well as the contrary forms, in all their combinations, and can recognize them and their images wherever they are found, not slighting them either in small things or great, but believing them all to be within the sphere of one art and study.

Most assuredly.

And when nobility of soul is observed in harmonious union with beauty of form, and both are cast from the same mold, that will be the fairest of sights to him who has an eye to see it?

Of the many excellences which I perceive in the order of our State, there is none which upon reflection pleases me better than the rule about poetry.

To what do you refer?

To our refusal to admit the imitative kind of poetry, for it certainly ought not to be received; as I see far more clearly now that the parts of the soul have been distinguished.

What do you mean?

Speaking in confidence, for you will not denounce me to the tragedians and the rest of the imitative tribe, all poetical imitations are ruinous to the understanding of the hearers, unless as an antidote they possess the knowledge of the true nature of the originals.

Explain the purport of your remark.

Well, I will tell you, although I have always from my earliest youth had an awe and love of Homer which even now makes the words falter on my lips, for he seems to be the great captain and teacher of the whole of that noble tragic company; but a man is not to be reverenced more than the truth, and therefore I will speak out.

Very good, he said.

Listen to me, then, or rather, answer me.

Put your question.

Can you give me a general definition of imitation? for I really do not myself understand what it professes to be. . . .

Well then, shall we begin the inquiry at this point, following our usual method: Whenever a number of individuals have a common name, we assume that there is one corresponding idea or form: —do you understand me?

I do.

Let us take, for our present purpose, any instance of such a group; there are beds and tables in the world—many of each, are there not?

Yes.

But there are only two ideas or forms of such furniture—one the idea of a bed, the other of a table.

True.

And the maker of either of them makes a bed or he makes a table for our use, in accordance with the idea—that is our way of speaking in this and similar instances—but no artificer makes the idea itself: how could he?

Impossible.

And there is another artificer—I should like to know what you would say of him.

Who is he?

One who is the maker of all the works of all other workmen.

What an extraordinary man!

Wait a little, and there will be more reason for your saying so. For this is the craftsman who is able to make not only furniture of every kind, but all that grows out of the earth, and all living creatures, himself included; and besides these he can make earth and sky and the gods, and all the things which are in heaven or in the realm of Hades under the earth.

He must be a wizard and no mistake.

Oh! you are incredulous, are you? Do you mean that there is no such maker or creator, or that in one sense there might be a maker of all these things but in another not? Do you see that there is a way in which you could make them all yourself?

And what way is this? he asked.

An easy way enough; or rather, there are many ways in which the feat might be quickly and easily accomplished, none quicker than that of turning a mirror round and round—you would soon enough make the sun and the heavens, and the earth and yourself, and other animals and plants, and furniture and all the other things of which we were just now speaking, in the mirror.

Yes, he said; but they would be appearances only.

Very good, I said, you are coming to the point now. And the painter too is, as I conceive, just such another—a creator of appearances, is he not?

Of course.

But then I suppose you will say that what he creates is untrue. And yet there is a sense in which the painter also creates a bed? Is there not?

Yes, he said, but here again, an appearance only.

And what of the maker of the bed? were you not saying that he too makes, not the idea which according to our view is the real object denoted by the word bed, but only a particular bed?

Yes, I did.

Then if he does not make a real object he cannot make what *is*, but only some semblance of existence; and if any one were to say that the work of the maker of the bed, or of any other workman, has real existence, he could hardly be supposed to be speaking the truth.

Not, at least, he replied, in the view of those who make a business of these discussions.

No wonder, then, that his work too is an indistinct expression of truth.

No wonder.

Suppose now that by the light of the examples just offered we inquire who this imitator is?

If you please.

Well then, here we find three beds: one existing in nature, which is made by God, as I think that we may say—for no one else can be the maker?

No one, I think.

There is another which is the work of the carpenter?

Yes.

And the work of the painter is a third?

Yes.

Beds, then, are of three kinds, and there are three artists who superintend them: God, the maker of the bed, and the painter?

Yes, there are three of them. . . .

Shall we, then, speak of God as the natural author or maker of the bed?

Yes, he replied; inasmuch as by the natural process of creation He is the author of this and of all other things.

And what shall we say of the carpenter—is not he also the maker of a bed?

Yes.

But would you call the painter an artificer and maker?

Certainly not.

Yet if he is not the maker, what is he in relation to the bed?

I think, he said, that we may fairly designate him as the imitator of that which the others make.

Good, I said; then you call him whose product is third in the descent from nature, an imitator?

Certainly, he said.

And so if the tragic poet is an imitator, he too is thrice removed from the king and from the truth; and so are all other imitators.

That appears to be so.

Then about the imitator we are agreed. And what about the painter?—Do you think he tries to imitate in each case that which originally exists in nature, or only the creations of artificers?

The latter.

As they are or as they appear? you have still to determine this.

What do you mean?

I mean to ask whether a bed really becomes different when it is seen from different points of view, obliquely or directly or from any other point of view? Or does it simply appear different, without being really so? And the same of all things.

Yes, he said, the difference is only apparent.

Now let me ask you another question: Which is the art of painting designed to be—an imitation of things as they are, or as they appear—of appearance or of reality?

Of appearance, he said.

Then the imitator is a long way off the truth, and can reproduce all things because he lightly touches on a small part of them, and that part an image. For example: A painter will paint a cobbler, carpenter, or any other artisan, though he knows nothing of their arts; and, if he is a good painter, he may deceive children or simple persons when he shows them his picture of a carpenter from a distance, and they will fancy that they are looking at a real carpenter.

Certainly.

And surely, my friend, this is how we should regard all such claims: whenever any one informs us that he has found a man who knows all the arts, and all things else that anybody knows, and every single thing with a higher degree of accuracy than any other man—whoever tells us this, I think that we can only retort that he is a simple creature who seems to have been deceived by some wizard or imitator whom he met, and whom he thought all-knowing, because he himself was unable to analyze the nature of knowledge and ignorance and imitation.

Most true.

And next, I said, we have to consider tragedy and its leader, Homer; for we hear some persons saying that these poets know all the arts; and all things human; where virtue and vice are concerned, and indeed all divine things too; because the good poet cannot compose well unless he knows his subject, and he who has not this knowledge can never be a poet. We ought to consider whether here also there may not be a similar illusion. Perhaps they may have come across imitators and been deceived by them; they may not have remembered when they saw their works that these were thrice removed from the truth, and could easily be made without any knowledge of the truth, because they are appearances only and not realities? Or, after all, they may be in the right, and good poets do really know the things about which they seem to the many to speak so well?

The question, he said, should by all means be considered.

Now do you suppose that if a person were able to make the original as well as the image, he would seriously devote himself to the image-making branch? Would he allow imitation to be the ruling principle of his life, as if he had nothing higher in him?

I should say not.

But the real artist, who had real knowledge of those things which he chose also to imitate, would be interested in realities and not in imitations; and would desire to leave as memorials of himself works many and fair; and, instead of being the author of encomiums, he would prefer to be the theme of them.

Yes, he said, that would be to him a source of much greater honour and profit.

Now let us refrain, I said, from calling Homer or any other poet to account regarding those arts to which his poems incidentally refer: we will not ask them, in case any poet has been a doctor and not a mere imitator of medical parlance, to show what patients have been restored to health by a poet, ancient or modern, as they were by Asclepius; or what disciples in medicine a poet has left behind him, like the Asclepiads. Nor shall we press the same question upon them about the other arts. But we have a right to know respecting warfare, strategy, the administration of States and the education of man, which are the chiefest and noblest subjects of his poems, and we may fairly ask him about them. "Friend Homer," then we say to him, "if you are only in the second remove from truth in what you say of virtue, and not in the third—not an image maker, that is, by our definition, an imitator—and if you are able to discern what pursuits make men better or worse in private or public life, tell us what State was ever better governed by your help? . . .

Is there any city which he might name?

I think not, said Glaucon; not even the Homerids themselves pretend that he was a legislator.

Well, but is there any war on record which was carried on successfully owing to his leadership or counsel?

There is not.

Or is there anything comparable to those clever improvements in the arts, or in other operations, which are said to have been due to men of practical genius. . . .

There is absolutely nothing of the kind.

But, if Homer never did any public service, was he privately a guide or teacher of any? Had he in his lifetime friends who loved to associate with him, and who handed down to posterity an Homeric way of life, such as was established by Pythagoras who was especially beloved for this reason and whose followers are to this day conspicuous among others by what they term the Pythagorean way of life?

Nothing of the kind is recorded of him. . . .

But can you imagine, Glaucon, that if Homer had really been able to educate and improve mankind—if he had been capable of knowledge and not been a mere imitator—can you imagine, I say, that he would not have attracted many followers, and been honoured and loved by them? . . . And is it conceivable that the contemporaries of Homer, or again of Hesiod, would have allowed either of them to go about as rhapsodists, if they had really been able to help mankind forward in virtue? Would they not have been as unwilling to part with them as with gold, and have compelled them to stay at home with them? Or, if the master would not stay, then the disciples would have followed him about everywhere, until they had got education enough?

Yes, Socrates, that, I think, is quite true.

Then must we not infer that all these poetical individuals, beginning with Homer, are only imitators, who copy images of virtue and the other themes of their poetry, but have no contact with the truth? The poet is like a painter who, as we have already observed, will make a likeness of a cobbler though he understands nothing of cobbling; and his picture is good enough for those who know no more than he does, and judge only by colors and figures.

Quite so.

In like manner the poet with his words and phrases may be said to lay on the colors of the several arts, himself understanding their nature only enough to imitate them; and other people, who are as ignorant as he is, and judge only from his words, imagine that if he speaks of cobbling, or of military tactics, or of anything else, in meter and harmony and rhythm, he speaks very well—such is the sweet influence which melody and rhythm by nature have. For I am sure that you know what a poor appearance the works of poets make when stripped of the colors which art puts upon them, and recited in simple prose. You have seen some examples?

Yes, he said.

They are like faces which were never really beautiful, but only blooming, seen when the bloom of youth has passed away from them?

Exactly.

Come now, and observe this point: The imitator or maker of the image knows nothing, we have said, of true existence; he knows appearances only. Am I not right?

Yes.

Then let us have a clear understanding, and not be satisfied with half an explanation.

Proceed.

Of the painter we say that he will paint reins, and he will paint a bit?

Yes.

And the worker in leather and brass will make them?

Certainly.

But does the painter know the right form of the bit and reins? Nay, hardly even the workers in brass and leather who make them; only the horseman who knows how to use them—he knows their right form.

Most true.

And may we not say the same of all things?

What?

That there are three arts which are concerned with all things: one which uses, another which makes, a third which imitates them?

Yes.

And the excellence and beauty and rightness of every structure, animate or inanimate, and of every action of man, is relative solely to the use for which nature or the artist has intended them.

True.

Then beyond doubt it is the user who has the greatest experience of them, and he must report to the maker the good or bad qualities which develop themselves in use; for example, the flute-player will tell the flute-maker which of his flutes is satisfactory to the performer; he will tell him how he ought to make them, and the other will attend to his instructions?

Of course.

So the one pronounces with knowledge about the goodness and badness of flutes, while the other, confiding in him, will make them accordingly?

True.

The instrument is the same, but about the excellence or badness of it the maker will possess a correct belief, since he associates with one who knows, and is compelled to hear what he has to say; whereas the user will have knowledge?

True.

But will the imitator have either? Will he know from use whether or not that which he paints is correct or beautiful? or will he have right opinion from being compelled to associate with another who knows and gives him instructions about what he should paint?

Neither.

Then an imitator will no more have true opinion than he will have knowledge about the goodness or badness of his models?

I suppose not.

The imitative poet will be in a brilliant state of intelligence about the theme of his poetry?

Nay, very much the reverse.

And still he will go on imitating without knowing what makes a thing good or bad, and may be expected therefore to imitate only that which appears to be good to the ignorant multitude?

Just so.

Thus far then we are pretty well agreed that the imitator has no knowledge worth mentioning of what he imitates. Imitation is only a kind of play or sport, and the tragic poets, whether they write in iambic or in heroic verse, are imitators in the highest degree?

Very true.

And now tell me, I conjure you—this imitation is concerned with an object which is thrice removed from the truth?

Certainly.

And what kind of faculty in man is that to which imitation makes its special appeal?

What do you mean?

I will explain: The same body does not appear equal to our sight when seen near and when seen at a distance?

True.

And the same objects appear straight when looked at out of the water, and crooked when in the water; and the concave becomes convex, owing to the illusion about colors to which the sight is liable. Thus every sort of confusion is revealed within us; and this is that weakness of the human mind on which the art of painting in light and shadow, the art of conjuring, and many other ingenious devices impose, having an effect upon us like magic.

True.

And the arts of measuring and numbering and weighing come to the rescue of the human understanding—there is the beauty of them—with the result that the apparent greater or less, or more or heavier, no longer have the mastery over us, but give way before the power of calculation and measuring and weighing?

Most true.

And this, surely, must be the work of the calculating and rational principle in the soul?

To be sure.

And often when this principle measures and certifies that some things are equal, or that some are greater or less than others, it is, at the same time, contradicted by the appearance which the objects present?

True.

But did we not say that such a contradiction is impossible—the same faculty cannot have contrary opinions at the same time about the same thing?

We did; and rightly.

Then that part of the soul which has an opinion contrary to measure can hardly be the same

with that which has an opinion in accordance with measure?

True.

And the part of the soul which trusts to measure and calculation is likely to be the better one?

Certainly.

And therefore that which is opposed to this is probably an inferior principle in our nature?

No doubt.

This was the conclusion at which I was seeking to arrive when I said that painting or drawing, and imitation in general, are engaged upon productions which are far removed from truth, and are also the companions and friends and associates of a principle within us which is equally removed from reason, and that they have no true or healthy aim.

Exactly.

The imitative art is an inferior who from intercourse with an inferior has inferior offspring.

Very true.

And is this confined to the sight only, or does it extend to the hearing also, relating in fact to what we term poetry?

Probably the same would be true of poetry.

Do not rely, I said, on a probability derived from the analogy of painting; but let us once more go directly to that faculty of the mind with which imitative poetry has converse, and see whether it is good or bad.

By all means.

We may state the question thus:—Imitation imitates the actions of men, whether voluntary or involuntary, on which, as they imagine, a good or bad result has ensued, and they rejoice or sorrow accordingly. Is there anything more?

No, there is nothing else.

But in all this variety of circumstances is the man at unity with himself—or rather, as in the instance of sight there was confusion and opposition in his opinions about the same things, so here also is there not strife and inconsistency in his life? Though I need hardly raise the question again, for I remember that all this has been already admitted; and the soul has been acknowledged by us to be full of these and ten thousand similar oppositions occurring at the same moment?

And we were right, he said.

Yes, I said, thus far we were right; but there was an omission which must now be supplied.

What was the omission?

Were we not saying that a good man, who has the misfortune to lose his son or anything else which is most dear to him, will bear the loss with more equanimity than another?

Yes, indeed.

But will he have no sorrow, or shall we say that although he cannot help sorrowing, he will moderate his sorrow?

The latter, he said, is the truer statement.

Tell me: will he be more likely to struggle and hold out against his sorrow when he is seen by his equals, or when he is alone in a deserted place?

The fact of being seen will make a great difference, he said.

When he is by himself he will not mind saying many things which he would be ashamed of any one hearing, and also doing many things which he would not care to be seen doing?

True.

And doubtless it is the law and reason in him which bids him resist; while it is the affliction itself which is urging him to indulge his sorrow?

True.

But when a man is drawn in two opposite directions, to and from the same object, this, as we affirm, necessarily implies two distinct principles in him?

Certainly.

One of them is ready to follow the guidance of the law?

How do you mean?

The law would say that to be patient under calamity is best, and that we should not give way to impatience, as the good and evil in such things are not clear, and nothing is gained by impatience; also, because no human thing is of serious importance, and grief stands in the way of that which at the moment is most required.

What is most required? he asked.

That we should take counsel about what has happened, and when the dice have been thrown, according to their fall, order our affairs in the way which reason deems best; not, like children who have had a fall, keeping hold of the part struck and wasting time in setting up a howl, but always accustoming the soul forthwith to apply a remedy, raising up that which is sickly and fallen, banishing the cry of sorrow by the healing art.

Yes, he said, that is the true way of meeting the attacks of fortune.

Well then, I said, the higher principle is ready to follow this suggestion of reason?

Clearly.

But the other principle, which inclines us to recollection of our troubles and to lamentation, and can never have enough of them, we may call irrational, useless, and cowardly?

Indeed, we may.

Now does not the principle which is thus inclined to complaint, furnish a great variety of materials for imitation? Whereas the wise and calm temperament, being always nearly equable, is not easy to imitate or to appreciate when imitated, especially at a public festival when a promiscuous crowd is assembled in a theatre. For the feeling represented is one to which they are strangers.

Certainly.

Then the imitative poet who aims at being popular is not by nature made, nor is his art intended, to please or to affect the rational principle in the soul; but he will appear rather to the lachrymose and fitful temper, which is easily imitated?

Clearly.

And now we may fairly take him and place him by the side of the painter, for he is like him in two ways: first, inasmuch as his creations have an inferior degree of truth—in this, I say, he is like him; and he is also like him in being the associate of an inferior part of the soul; and this is enough to show that we shall be right in refusing to admit him into a State which is to be well ordered, because he awakens and nourishes this part of the soul, and by strengthening it impairs the reason. As in a city when the evil are permitted to wield power and the finer men are put out of the way, so in the soul of each man, as we shall maintain, the imitative poet implants an evil constitution, for he indulges the irrational nature which has no discernment of greater and less, but thinks the same thing at one time great and at another small—he is an imitator of images and is very far removed from the truth.

Exactly.

But we have not yet brought forward the heaviest count in our accusation:—the power which poetry has of harming even the good (and there are very few who are not harmed), is surely an awful thing?

Yes, certainly, if the effect is what you say.

Hear and judge: The best of us, as I conceive, when we listen to a passage of Homer or one of the tragedians, in which he represents some hero who is drawling out his sorrows in a long oration, or singing, and smiting his breast—the best of us, you know, delight in giving way to sympathy, and are in raptures at the excellence of the poet who stirs our feelings most.

Yes, of course I know.

But when any sorrow of our own happens to us, then you may observe that we pride ourselves on the opposite quality—we would fain be quiet and patient; this is considered the manly part, and the other which delighted us in the recitation is now deemed to be the part of a woman.

Very true, he said.

Now can we be right in praising and admiring another who is doing that which any one of us would abominate and be ashamed of in his own person?

No, he said, that is certainly not reasonable.

Nay, I said, quite reasonable from one point of view.

What point of view?

If you consider, I said, that when in misfortune we feel a natural hunger and desire to relieve our sorrow by weeping and lamentation, and that this very feeling which is starved and suppressed in our own calamities is satisfied and delighted by the poets;—the better nature in each of us, not having been sufficiently trained by reason or habit, allows the sympathetic element to break loose because the sorrow is another's; and the spectator fancies that there can be no disgrace to himself in praising and pitying any one who while professing to be a brave man, gives way to untimely lamentation; he thinks that the pleasure is a gain, and is far from wishing to lose it by rejection of the whole poem. Few persons ever reflect, as I should imagine, that the contagion must pass from others to themselves. For the pity which has been nourished and strengthened in the misfortunes of others is with difficulty repressed in our own.

How very true!

And does not the same hold also of the ridiculous? There are jests which you would be ashamed to make yourself, and yet on the comic stage, or indeed in private, when you hear them, you are greatly amused by them, and are not at all disgusted at their unseemliness;—the case of pity is repeated;—there is a principle in human nature which is disposed to raise a laugh, and this, which you once restrained by reason because you were afraid of being thought a buffoon, is now let out again; and having stimulated the risible faculty at the theatre, you are betrayed unconsciously to yourself into playing the comic poet at home.

Quite true, he said.

And the same may be said of lust and anger and all the other affections, of desire and pain and pleasure, which are held to be inseparable from every action—in all of them poetry has a like effect; it feeds and waters the passions instead of drying them up; she lets them rule, although they ought to be controlled if mankind are ever to increase in happiness and virtue.

I cannot deny it.

Therefore, Glaucon, I said, whenever you meet with any of the eulogists of Homer declaring that he has been the educator of Hellas, and that he is profitable for education and for the ordering of human things, and that you should take him up again and again and get to know him and regulate your whole life according to him, we may love and honour those who say these things—they are excellent people, as far as their lights extend; and we are ready to acknowledge that Homer is the greatest of poets and first of tragedy writers; but we must remain firm in our conviction that hymns to the gods and praises of famous men are the only poetry which ought to be admitted into our State. For if you go beyond this and allow the honeyed Muse to enter, either in epic or lyric verse, not law and the reason of mankind, which by common consent have ever been deemed best, but pleasure and pain will be the rulers in our State.

That is most true, he said.

And now since we have reverted to the subject of poetry, let this our defense serve to show the reasonableness of our former judgment in sending away out of our State an art having the tendencies which we have described; for reason constrained us. But that she may not impute to us any harshness or want of politeness, let us tell her that there is an ancient quarrel between philosophy and poetry; of which there are many proofs, such as the saying of "the yelping hound howling at her lord," or of one "mighty in the vain talk of fools," and "the mob of sages circumventing Zeus," and the "subtle thinkers who are beggars after all"; and there are innumerable other signs of ancient enmity between them. Notwithstanding this, let us assure the poetry which aims at pleasure, and the art of imitation, that if she will only prove her title to exist in a well-ordered State we shall be delighted to receive her—we are very conscious of her charms; but it would not be right on that account to betray the truth. I dare say, Glaucon, that you are as much charmed by her as I am, especially when she appears in Homer?

Yes, indeed, I am greatly charmed.

Shall I propose, then, that she be allowed to return from exile, but upon this condition only—that she make a defense of herself in some lyrical or other meter?

Certainly.

And we may further grant to those of her defenders who are lovers of poetry and yet not poets the permission to speak in prose on her behalf: let them show not only that she is pleasant but also useful to States and to human life, and we will listen in a kindly spirit; for we shall surely be the gainers if this can be proved, that there is a use in poetry as well as delight?

Certainly, he said, we shall be the gainers.

If her defense fails, then, my dear friend, like other persons who are enamored of something, but put a restraint upon themselves when they think their desires are opposed to their interests, so too must we after the manner of lovers give her up, though not without a struggle. We too are inspired by that love of such poetry which the education of noble States had implanted in us, and therefore we shall be glad if she appears at her best and truest; but so long as she is unable to make good her defense, this argument of ours shall be a charm to us, which we will repeat to ourselves while we listen to her strains; that we may not fall away into the childish love of her which captivates the many. At all events we are well aware that poetry, such as we have described, is not to be regarded seriously as attaining to the truth; and he who listens to her, fearing for the safety of the city which is within him, should be on his guard against her seductions and make our words his law.

Yes, he said, I quite agree with you.

Yes, I said, my dear Glaucon, for great is the issue at stake, greater than appears, whether a man is to be good or bad. And what will any one be profited if under the influence of honor or money or power, aye, or under the excitement of poetry, he neglect justice and virtue?

Cratylus

PLATO

Hermogenes: Suppose that we make Socrates a party to the argument.

Cratylus: If you please.

Hermogenes: I should explain to you, Socrates, that our friend Cratylus has been arguing about names. He says that they are natural and not conventional—not a portion of the human voice which men agree to use—but that there is a truth or correctness in them, which is the same for Hellenes as for barbarians. . . . I have often talked over this matter, both with Cratylus and others, and cannot convince myself that there is any principle of correctness in names other than convention and agreement. Any name which you give, in my opinion, is the right one, and if you change that and give another, the new name is as correct as the old—we frequently change the names of our slaves, and the newly imposed name is as good as the old. For there is no name given to anything by nature; all is convention and habit of the users. Such is my view. But if I am mistaken I shall be happy to hear and learn of Cratylus; or of anyone else.

Socrates: I dare say that you may be right, Hermogenes. Let us see—your meaning is that the name of each thing is only that which anybody agrees to call it?

Hermogenes: That is my notion.

Socrates: Whether the giver of the name be an individual or a city?

Hermogenes: Yes.

Socrates: Well, now, let me take an instance. Suppose that I call a man a horse or a horse a man. You mean to say that a man will be rightly called a horse by me individually, and rightly called a man by the rest of the world, and a horse again would be rightly called a man by me and a horse by the world—that is your meaning?

Hermogenes: He would, according to my view.

Socrates: But how about truth, then? You would acknowledge that there is in words a true and a false?

Hermogenes: Certainly. . . .

Socrates: And the name of anything is that which anyone affirms to be the name?

Hermogenes: Yes.

Socrates: And will there be so many names of each thing as everybody says that there are? And will they be true names at the time of uttering them?

Hermogenes: Yes, Socrates, I can conceive no correctness of names other than this. You give one name, and I another, and in different cities and countries there are different names for the same things. Hellenes differ from barbarians in their use of names, and the several Hellenic tribes from one another.

Socrates: But would you say, Hermogenes, that the things differ as the names differ? And are they relative to individuals, as Protagoras tells us? For he says that man is the measure of all things, and that things are to me as they appear to me, and that they are to you as they appear to you. Do you agree with him, or would you say that things have a permanent essence of their own?

Hermogenes: There have been times, Socrates, when I have been driven in my perplexity to take refuge with Protagoras, not that I agree with him at all. . . .

Socrates: But if Protagoras is right, and the truth is that things are as they appear to anyone, how can some of us be wise and some of us foolish?

Hermogenes: Impossible.

Socrates: And if, on the other hand, wisdom and folly are really distinguishable you will allow, I think, that the assertion of Protagoras can

From The Dialogues of Plato, *3rd ed., trans. B. Jowett (Oxford: Oxford University Press, 1892).*

hardly be correct. For if what appears to each man is true to him, one man cannot in reality be wiser than another.

Hermogenes: He cannot.

Socrates: But if . . . things are not relative to individuals . . . they must be supposed to have their own proper and permanent essence; they are not in relation to us, or influenced by us, fluctuating according to our fancy, but they are independent, and maintain to their own essence the relation prescribed by nature.

Hermogenes: I think, Socrates, that you have said the truth. . . .

Socrates: And this holds good of all actions?

Hermogenes: Yes.

Socrates: And speech is a kind of action?

Hermogenes: True.

Socrates: And will a man speak correctly who speaks as he pleases? Will not the successful speaker rather be he who speaks in the natural way of speaking, and as things ought to be spoken, and with the natural instrument? Any other mode of speaking will result in error and failure.

Hermogenes: I quite agree with you.

Socrates: And is not naming a part of speaking? For in giving names men speak.

Hermogenes: That is true.

Socrates: And if speaking is a sort of action and has a relation to acts, is not naming also a sort of action?

Hermogenes: True.

Socrates: And we saw that actions were not relative to ourselves, but had a special nature of their own?

Hermogenes: Precisely.

Socrates: Then the argument would lead us to infer that names ought to be given according to a natural process, and with a proper instrument, and not at our pleasure; in this and no other way shall we name with success.

Hermogenes: I agree.

Socrates: But again, that which has to be cut has to be cut with something?

Hermogenes: Yes. . . .

Socrates: And that which has to be named has to be named with something?

Hermogenes: True.

Socrates: What is that with which we . . . name?

Hermogenes: A name.

Socrates: Very good. Then a name is an instrument?

Hermogenes: Certainly. . . .

Socrates: Regarding the name as an instrument, what do we do when we name?

Hermogenes: I cannot say.

Socrates: Do we not give information to one another, and distinguish things according to their natures?

Hermogenes: Certainly we do.

Socrates: Then a name is an instrument of teaching and of distinguishing natures. . . . And the teacher will use the name well—and well means like a teacher?

Hermogenes: Yes.

Socrates: And when the weaver uses the shuttle, whose work will he be using well?

Hermogenes: That of the carpenter.

Socrates: And is every man a carpenter, or the skilled only?

Hermogenes: Only the skilled.

Socrates: And when the piercer uses the awl, whose work will he be using well?

Hermogenes: That of the smith.

Socrates: And is every man a smith, or only the skilled?

Hermogenes: The skilled only.

Socrates: And when the teacher uses the name, whose work will he be doing?

Hermogenes: There again I am puzzled. . . .

Socrates: . . . The teacher, when he gives us a name, does the work of the legislator?

Hermogenes: I agree.

Socrates: And is every man a legislator, or the skilled only?

Hermogenes: The skilled only.

Socrates: Then, Hermogenes, not every man is able to give a name, but only a maker of names, and this is the legislator, who of all skilled artisans in the world is the rarest.

Hermogenes: True.

Socrates: And how does the legislator make names? And to what does he look? . . . When a man has discovered the instrument which is naturally adapted to each work, he must express this natural form, and not others which he fancies, in the material, whatever it may be, which he employs. For example, he ought to know how to put into iron the forms of awls adapted by nature to their several uses?

Hermogenes: Certainly. . . .

Socrates: Then, as to names, ought not our legislator also to know how to put the true natural name of each thing into sounds and syllables, and to make and give all names with a view to the ideal name, if he is to be a namer in any true sense? And we must remember that different legislators will not use the same syllables. For neither does every smith, although he may be making the same instrument for the same purpose, make them all of the same iron. The form must be the same, but the material may vary, and still the instrument may be equally good of whatever iron made, whether in Hellas or in a foreign country—there is no difference.

Hermogenes: Very true.

Socrates: And the legislator, whether he be Hellene or barbarian, is not therefore to be deemed by you a worse legislator, provided he gives the true and proper form of the name in whatever syllables—this or that country makes no matter.

Hermogenes: Quite true.

Socrates: But who then is to determine whether the proper form is given to the shuttle, whatever sort of wood may be used? The carpenter who makes, or the weaver who is to use them?

Hermogenes: I should say, he who is to use them, Socrates. . . .

Socrates: And who will be best able to direct the legislator in his work, and will know whether the work is well done, in this or any other country? Will not the user be the man?

Hermogenes: Yes.

Socrates: And this is he who knows how to ask questions?

Hermogenes: Yes.

Socrates: And how to answer them?

Hermogenes: Yes.

Socrates: And him who knows how to ask and answer you would call a dialectician?

Hermogenes: Yes, that would be his name. . . .

Socrates: Then, Hermogenes, I should say that this giving of names can be no such light matter as you fancy, or the work of light or chance persons. And Cratylus is right in saying that things have names by nature; and that not every man is an artificer of names, but he only who looks to the name which each thing by nature has, and is able to express the true forms of things in letters and syllables.

Hermogenes: I cannot answer you, Socrates, but I find a difficulty in changing my opinion all in a moment, and I think that I should be more readily persuaded, if you would show me what this is which you term the natural fitness of names.

Socrates: My good Hermogenes, I have none to show. Was I not telling you just now—but you have forgotten—that I knew nothing, and was I not proposing to share the inquiry with you? But now that you and I have talked over the matter, a step has been gained, for we have discovered that names have by nature a truth, and that not every man knows how to give a thing a name.

Hermogenes: Very good.

Socrates: And what is the nature of this truth or correctness of names? That, if you care to know, is the next question.

Hermogenes: Certainly, I care to know. . . .

Socrates: There is reason, I think, in calling the lion's whelp a lion, and the foal of a horse a horse; I am speaking only of the ordinary course of nature, when an animal produces after his kind, and not of extraordinary births. If contrary to nature a horse have a calf, then I should not call that a foal but calf; nor do I call any inhuman birth a man, but only a natural birth. And the same may be said of trees and other things. Do you agree with me?

Hermogenes: Yes, I agree.

Socrates: Very good. But you had better watch me and see that I do not play tricks with you. For on the same principle the son of a king is to be called a king. And whether the syllables of the name are the same or not the same makes no difference, provided the meaning is retained; nor does the addition or subtraction of a letter make any difference so long as the essence of the thing remains in possession of the names and appears in it. . . .

Hermogenes: I believe you are right.

Socrates: And may not the same be said of a king? A king will often be the son of a king, the good son or the noble son of a good or noble sire, and similarly the offspring of every kind, in the regular course of nature, is like the parent, and therefore has the same name. Yet the syllables may be disguised until they appear different to the ignorant person, and he may not recognize them, although they are the same, just as any one of us would not recognize the same drugs under different disguises of color and smell, although to the physician, who regards the power of them, they are the same, and he is not put out by the addition. And in like manner the etymologist is not put out by the addition or transposition or subtraction of a letter or two, or indeed by the change of all the letters, for this need not interfere with the meaning. . . .

Hermogenes: Yes.

Socrates: The same names, then, ought to be assigned to those who follow in the course of nature?

Hermogenes: Yes.

Socrates: And what of those who follow out of the course of nature, and are prodigies? For example, when a good and religious man has an irreligious son, he ought to bear the name not of his father, but of the class to which he belongs, just as in the case which was before supposed of a horse foaling a calf.

Hermogenes: Quite true.

Socrates: Then the irreligious son of a religious father should be called irreligious?

Hermogenes: Certainly.

Socrates: He should not be called Theophilus (beloved of God) or Mnesitheus (mindful of God), or any of these names—if names are correctly given, his should have an opposite meaning.

Hermogenes: Certainly, Socrates.

Socrates: Again, Hermogenes, there is Orestes (the man of the mountains), who appears to be rightly called, whether chance gave the name, or perhaps some poet who meant to express the brutality and fierceness and mountain wilderness of his hero's nature.

Hermogenes: That is very likely, Socrates.

Socrates: And his father's name is also according to nature.

Hermogenes: Clearly.

Socrates: Yes, for as his name, so also is his nature. Agamemnon (admirable for remaining) is one who is patient and persevering in the accomplishment of his resolves, and by his virtue crowns them, and his continuance at Troy with all the vast army is a proof of that admirable endurance in him which is signified by the name Agamemnon. I also think that Atreus is rightly called, for his murder of Chrysippus and his exceeding cruelty to Thyestes are damaging and destructive to his reputation. . . . Then let us proceed, and where would you have us begin, now that we have got a sort of outline of the inquiry? Are there any names which witness of themselves that they are not given arbitrarily, but have a natural fitness? The names of heroes and of men in general are apt to be deceptive because they are often called after ancestors with whose names, as we were saying, they may have no business, or they are the expression of a wish, like Eutychides (the son of good fortune), or Sosias (the Savior), or Theophilus (the beloved of God), and others. But I think that we had better leave these, for there will be more chance of finding correctness in the names of immutable essences—there ought to have been more care taken about them when they were named, and perhaps there may have been some more-than-human power at work occasionally in giving them names.

Hermogenes: I think so, Socrates. . . .

Socrates: Yes, very likely. . . . For we should remember that if a person goes on analyzing names into words, and inquiring also into the elements out of which the words are formed, and keeps on always repeating this process, he who has to answer him must at last give up the inquiry in despair.

Hermogenes: Very true.

Socrates: And at what point ought he to lose heart and give up the inquiry? Must he not stop when he comes to the names which are the elements of all other names and sentences? For these cannot be supposed to be made up of other names. . . . But if we take a word which is incapable of further resolution, then we shall be right in saying that we have at last reached a primary element, which need not be resolved any further.

Hermogenes: I believe you to be in the right.

Socrates: And suppose the names about which you are now asking should turn out to be primary elements. Must not their truth or law be examined according to some new method? . . . Suppose that we had no voice or tongue, and wanted to communicate with one another. Should we not, like the deaf and dumb, make signs with the hands and head and the rest of the body?

Hermogenes: There would be no choice, Socrates.

Socrates: We should imitate the nature of the thing; the elevation of our hands to heaven would mean lightness and upwardness; heaviness and downwardness would be expressed by letting them drop to the ground; if we were describing the running of a horse, or any other animal, we should make our bodies and their gestures as like as we could to them.

Hermogenes: I do not see that we could do anything else.

Socrates: We could not, for by bodily imitation only can the body ever express anything.

Hermogenes: Very true.

Socrates: And when we want to express ourselves, either with the voice, or tongue, or mouth, the expression is simply their imitation of that which we want to express?

Hermogenes: It must be so, I think.

Socrates: Then a name is a vocal imitation of that which the vocal imitator names or imitates?

Hermogenes: I think so.

Socrates: Nay, my friend, I am disposed to think that we have not reached the truth as yet.

Hermogenes: Why not?

Socrates: Because if we have we shall be obliged to admit that the people who imitate sheep, or cocks, or other animals, name that which they imitate.

Hermogenes: Quite true.

Socrates: Then could I have been right in what I was saying?

Hermogenes: In my opinion, no. But I wish that you would tell me, Socrates, what sort of an imitation is a name?

Socrates: In the first place, I should reply, not a musical imitation, although that is also vocal, nor, again, an imitation of what music imitates; these, in my judgment, would not be naming. Let me put the matter as follows. All objects have sound and figure, and many have color?

Hermogenes: Certainly

Socrates: But the art of naming appears not to be concerned with imitations of this kind. The arts which have to do with them are music and drawing?

Hermogenes: True.

Socrates: Again, is there not an essence of each thing, just as there is a color, or sound? And is there not an essence of color and sound as well as of anything else which may be said to have an essence?

Hermogenes: I should think so.

Socrates: Well, and if anyone could express the essence of each thing in letters and syllables, would he not express the nature of each thing?

Hermogenes: Quite so.

Socrates: The musician and the painter were the two names which you gave to the other imitators. What will this imitator be called?

Hermogenes: I imagine, Socrates, that he must be the namer, or name giver, of whom we are in search.

Socrates: If this is true, then I think that we are in a condition to consider the names "stream," "to go," "retention," about which you were asking, and we may see whether the namer has grasped the nature of them in letters and syllables in such a manner as to imitate the essence or not.

Hermogenes: Very good.

Socrates: But are these the only primary names, or are there others?

Hermogenes: There must be others.

Socrates: So I should expect. But how shall we further analyze them, and where does the imitator begin? Imitation of the essence is made by syllables and letters. Ought we not, therefore, first to separate the letters, just as those who are beginning rhythm first distinguish the powers of elementary and then of compound sounds, and when they have done so, but not before, proceed to the consideration of rhythms?

Hermogenes: Yes.

Socrates: Must we not begin in the same way with letters—first separating the vowels, and then the consonants and mutes, into classes, according to the received distinctions of the learned, also the semivowels, which are neither vowels nor yet mutes, and distinguishing into classes the vowels themselves? And when we have perfected the classification of things, we shall give their names, and see whether, as in the case of letters, there are any classes to which they may be all referred, and hence we shall see their natures, and see, too, whether they have in them classes as there are in the letters. And when we have well considered all this, we shall know how to apply them to what they resemble, whether one letter is used to denote one thing, or whether there is to be an admixture of several of them, just as, in painting, the painter who wants to depict anything sometimes uses purple only, or any other color, and sometimes mixes up several colors, as his method is when he has to paint flesh color or anything of that kind—he uses his colors as his figures appear to require them. And so, too, we shall apply letters to the expression of objects, either single letters when required, or several letters, and so we shall form syllables, as they are called, and from syllables make nouns and verbs, and thus, at last, from the combinations of nouns and verbs arrive at language, large and fair and whole. And as the painter made a

figure, even so shall we make speech by the art of the namer or the rhetorician, or by some other art. Not that I am literally speaking of ourselves, but I was carried away—meaning to say that this was the way in which not we, but the ancients formed language, and what they put together we must take to pieces in like manner, if we are to attain a scientific view of the whole subject. And we must see whether the primary, and also whether the secondary elements are rightly given or not, for if they are not, the composition of them, my dear Hermogenes, will be a sorry piece of work, and in the wrong direction.

Hermogenes: That, Socrates, I can quite believe.

Socrates: Well, but do you suppose that you will be able to analyze them in this way? For I am certain that I should not.

Hermogenes: Much less am I likely to be able.

Socrates: Shall we leave them, then? Or shall we seek to discover, if we can, something about them, according to the measure of our ability, saying by way of preface, as I said before of the gods, that of the truth about them we know nothing, and do but entertain human notions of them. And in this present inquiry, let us say to ourselves, before we proceed, that the higher method is the one which we or others who would analyze language to any good purpose must follow, but under the circumstances, as men say, we must do as well as we can. What do you think?

Hermogenes: I very much approve.

Socrates: That objects should be imitated in letters and syllables, and so find expression, may appear ridiculous, Hermogenes, but it cannot be avoided—there is no better principle to which we can look for the truth of first names. Deprived of this, we must have recourse to divine help, like the tragic poets, who in any perplexity have their gods waiting in the air, and must get out of our difficulty in like fashion, by saying that "the gods gave the first names, and therefore they are right." This will be the best contrivance, or perhaps that other notion may be even better still, of deriving them from some barbarous people, for the barbarians are older than we are, or we may say that antiquity has cast a veil over them, which is the same sort of excuse as the last, for all these are not reasons but only ingenious excuses for having no reasons concerning the truth of words. And yet any sort of ignorance of first or primitive names involves an ignorance of secondary words, for they can only be explained by the primary. Clearly then the professor of languages should be able to give a very lucid explanation of first names, or let him be assured he will only talk nonsense about the rest. Do you not suppose this to be true?

Hermogenes: Certainly, Socrates.

Socrates: My first notions of original names are truly wild and ridiculous, though I have no objection to imparting them to you if you desire, and I hope that you will communicate to me in return anything better which you may have.

Hermogenes: Fear not. I will do my best.

Socrates: In the first place, the letter *r* appears to me to be the general instrument expressing all motion. . . . Now the letter *r,* as I was saying, appeared to the imposer of names an excellent instrument for the expression of motion, and he frequently uses the letter for this purpose. . . . And there is another class of letters, *sh* and *s,* of which the pronunciation is accompanied by great expenditure of breath; these are used in the imitation of such notions as shivering, seething, to be shaken, shock, and are always introduced by the giver of names when he wants to imitate what is windy. . . . Thus did the legislator, reducing all things into letters and syllables, and impressing on them names and signs, and out of them by imitation compounding other signs. That is my view, Hermogenes, of the truth of names, but I should like to hear what Cratylus has more to say. . . . Have we not been saying that the correct name indicates the nature of the thing? Has this proposition been sufficiently proved?

Cratylus: Yes, Socrates, what you say, as I am disposed to think, it quite true.

Socrates: Names, then, are given in order to instruct?

Cratylus: Certainly.

Socrates: And naming is an art, and has artificers?

Cratylus: Yes.

Socrates: And who are they?

Cratylus: The legislators, of whom you spoke at first.

Socrates: And does this art grow up among men like other arts? Let me explain what I mean. Of painters, some are better and some worse?

Cratylus: Yes.

Socrates: The better painters execute their works, I mean their figures, better, and the worse execute them worse. And of builders also, the better sort build fairer houses, and the worse build them worse.

Cratylus: True.

Socrates: And among legislators, there are some who do their work better and some worse?

Cratylus: No, there I do not agree with you.

Socrates: Then you do not think that some laws are better and others worse?

Cratylus: No, indeed.

Socrates: Or that one name is better than another?

Cratylus: Certainly not.

Socrates: Then all names are rightly imposed?

Cratylus: Yes, if they are names at all.

Socrates: Well, what do you say to the name of our friend Hermogenes, which was mentioned before—assuming that he has nothing of the nature of Hermes in him, shall we say that this is a wrong name, or not his name at all?

Cratylus: I should reply that Hermogenes is not his name at all, but only appears to be his, and is really the name of somebody else, who has the nature which corresponds to it.

Socrates: And if a man were to call him Hermogenes, would he not be even speaking falsely? For there may be a doubt whether you can call him Hermogenes, if he is not.

Cratylus: What do you mean?

Socrates: Are you maintaining that falsehood is impossible? For if this is your meaning I should answer that there have been plenty of liars in all ages.

Cratylus: Why, Socrates, how can a man say that which is not—say something and yet say nothing? For is not falsehood saying the thing which is not?

Socrates: Your argument, friend, is too subtle for a man of my age. But I should like to know whether you are one of those philosophers who think that falsehood may be spoken but not said?

Cratylus: Neither spoken nor said.

Socrates: Nor uttered nor addressed? For example, if a person, saluting you in a foreign country, were to take your hand and say, Hail, Athenian stranger, Hermogenes, son of Smicrion—these words, whether spoken, said, uttered, or addressed, would have no application to you but only to our friend Hermogenes, or perhaps to nobody at all?

Cratylus: In my opinion, Socrates, the speaker would only be talking nonsense.

Socrates: Well, but that will be quite enough for me, if you will tell me whether the nonsense would be true or false, or partly true and partly false, which is all that I want to know.

Cratylus: I should say that he would be putting himself in motion to no purpose, and that his words would be an unmeaning sound like the noise of hammering at a brazen pot.

Socrates: But let us see, Cratylus, whether we cannot find a meeting point, for you would admit that the name is not the same with the thing named?

Cratylus: I should.

Socrates: And would you further acknowledge that the name is an imitation of the thing?

Cratylus: Certainly.

Socrates: And you would say that pictures are also imitations of things, but in another way?

Cratylus: Yes.

Socrates: I believe you may be right, but I do not rightly understand you. Please to say, then, whether both sorts of imitation—I mean both pictures or words—are not equally attributable and applicable to the things of which they are the imitation.

Cratylus: They are.

Socrates: First look at the matter thus. You may attribute the likeness of the man to the man, and of the woman to the woman, and so on?

Cratylus: Certainly.

Socrates: And conversely you may attribute the likeness of the man to the woman, and of the woman to the man?

Cratylus: Very true.

Socrates: And are both modes of assigning them right, or only the first?

Cratylus: Only the first.

Socrates: That is to say, the mode of assignment which attributes to each which belongs to it and is like it?

Cratylus: That is my view.

Socrates: Now then, as I am desirous that we being friends should have a good understanding about the argument, let me state my view to you. The first mode of assignment, whether applied to figures or to names, I call right, and when applied to names only, true as well as right, and the other mode of giving and assigning the name which is unlike, I call wrong, and in the case of names, false as well as wrong.

Cratylus: That may be true, Socrates, in the case of pictures; they may be wrongly assigned. But not in the case of names—they must be always right.

Socrates: Why, what is the difference? May I not go to a man and say to him, This is your picture, showing him his own likeness, or perhaps the likeness of a woman, and when I say show, I mean bring before the sense of sight.

Cratylus: Certainly.

Socrates: And may I not go to him again, and say, This is your name? For the name, like the picture, is an imitation. May I not say to him, This is your name? And may I not then bring to his sense of hearing the imitation of himself, when I say, This is a man, or of a female of the human species, when I say, This is a woman, as the case may be? Is not all that quite possible?

Cratylus: I would fain agree with you, Socrates, and therefore I say, granted.

Socrates: That is very good of you, if I am right,

which need hardly be disputed at present. But if I can assign names as well as pictures to objects, the right assignment of them we may call truth, and the wrong assignment of them falsehood. Now if there be such a wrong assignment of names, there may also be a wrong or inappropriate assignment of verbs, and if of names and verbs then of the sentences, which are made up of them. What do you say, Cratylus?

Cratylus: I agree, and think that what you say is very true.

Socrates: And further, primitive nouns may be compared to pictures, and in pictures you may either give all the appropriate colors and figures, or you may not give them all—some may be wanting—or there may be too many or too much of them—may there not?

Cratylus: Very true.

Socrates: And he who gives all gives a perfect picture or figure, and he who takes away or adds also gives a picture or figure, but not a good one.

Cratylus: Yes.

Socrates: In like manner, he who by syllables and letters imitates the nature of things, if he gives all that is appropriate will produce a good image, or in other words a name, but if he subtracts or perhaps adds a little, he will make an image but not a good one; whence I infer that some names are well and others ill made.

Cratylus: That is true.

Socrates: Then the artist of names may be sometimes good, or he may be bad?

Cratylus: Yes.

Socrates: And this artist of names is called the legislator?

Cratylus: Yes.

Socrates: Then like other artists the legislator may be good or he may be bad; it must surely be so if our former admissions hold good.

Cratylus: Very true, Socrates, but the case of language, you see, is different. For when by the help of grammar we assign the letters *a* or *e*, or any other letters, to a certain name, then, if we add, or subtract, or misplace a letter, the name which is written is not only written wrongly, but not written at all, and in any of these cases becomes other than a name.

Socrates: But I doubt whether your view is altogether correct, Cratylus.

Cratylus: How so?

Socrates: I believe that what you say may be true about numbers, which must be just what they are, or not be at all. For example, the number ten at once becomes other than ten if a unit be added or subtracted, and so of any other number, but this does not apply to that which is qualitative or to anything which is represented under an image. I should say rather that the image, if expressing in every point the entire reality, would no longer be an image. Let us suppose the existence of two objects. One of them shall be Cratylus, and the other the image of Cratylus, and we will suppose, further, that some god makes not only a representation such as a painter would make of your outward form and color, but also creates an inward organization like yours, having the same warmth and softness, and into this infuses motion, and soul, and mind, such as you have, and in a word copies all your qualities, and places them by you in another form. Would you say that this was Cratylus and the image of Cratylus, or that there were two Cratyluses?

Cratylus: I should say that there were two Cratyluses.

Socrates: Then you see, my friend, that we must find some other principle of truth in images, and also in names, and not insist that an image is no longer an image when something is added or subtracted. Do you not perceive that images are very far from having qualities which are the exact counterpart of the realities which they represent?

Cratylus: Yes, I see.

Socrates: But then how ridiculous would be the effect of names on things, if they were exactly the same with them! For they would be the doubles of them, and no one would be able to determine which were the names and which were the realities.

Cratylus: Quite true.

Socrates: Then fear not, but have the courage to admit that one name may be correctly and another incorrectly given, and do not insist that the name shall be exactly the same with the thing, but allow the occasional substitution of a wrong letter, and if of a letter also of a noun in a sentence, and if of a noun in a sentence also of a sentence which is not appropriate to the matter, and acknowledge that the thing may be named, and described, so long as the general character of the thing which you are describing is retained. And this, as you will remember, was remarked by Hermogenes and myself in the particular instance of the names of the letters.

Cratylus: Yes, I remember.

Socrates: Good, and when the general character is preserved, even if some of the proper letters are wanting, still the thing is signified—well, if all the letters are given, not well, when only a few of them are given. I think that we had better admit this, lest we be punished like travelers in Aegina who wander about the street late at night, and be likewise told by truth herself that we have arrived too late. Or if not, you must find out some new notion of correctness of names, and no longer maintain that a name is the expression of a thing in letters or syllables, for if you say both, you will be inconsistent with yourself.

Cratylus: I quite acknowledge, Socrates, what you say to be very reasonable.

Socrates: Then as we are agreed thus far, let us ask ourselves whether a name rightly imposed ought not to have the proper letters.

Cratylus: Yes.

Socrates: And the proper letters are those which are like the things?

Cratylus: Yes.

Socrates: Enough then of names which are rightly given. And in names which are incorrectly given, the greater part may be supposed to be made up of proper and similar letters, or there would be no likeness, but there will be likewise a part of which is improper and spoils the beauty and formation of the word. You would admit that?

Cratylus: There would be no use, Socrates, in my quarreling with you, since I cannot be satisfied that a name which is incorrectly given is a name at all.

Socrates: Do you admit a name to be the representation of a thing?

Cratylus: Yes, I do.

Socrates: But do you not allow that some nouns are primitive, and some derived?

Cratylus: Yes, I do.

Socrates: Then if you admit that primitive or first nouns are representations of things, is there any better way of framing representations than by assimilating them to the objects as much as you can? Or do you prefer the notion of Hermogenes and of many others, who say that names are conventional, and have a meaning to those who have agreed about them, and who have previous knowledge of the things intended by them, and that convention is the only principle? And whether you abide by our present convention, or make a new and opposite one, according to which you call small great and great small—that, they would say, makes no difference, if you are only agreed. Which of these two notions do you prefer?

Cratylus: Representation by likeness, Socrates, is infinitely better than representation by any chance sign.

Socrates: Very good, but if the name is to be like the thing, the letters out of which the first names are composed must also be like things. Returning to the image of the picture, I would ask how anyone could ever compose a picture which would be like anything at all, if there were not pigments in nature which resembled the things imitated, and out of which the picture is composed.

Cratylus: Impossible.

Socrates: No more could names ever resemble any actually existing thing, unless the original elements of which they are compounded bore some degree of resemblance to the objects of which the names are the imitation. And the original elements are letters?

Cratylus: Yes.

Socrates: Let me now invite you to consider

what Hermogenes and I were saying about sounds. Do you agree with me that the letter *r* is expressive of rapidity, motion, and hardness? Were we right or wrong in saying so?

Cratylus: I should say that you were right.

Socrates: And that *l* was expressive of smoothness, and softness, and the like?

Cratylus: There again you were right.

Socrates: And yet, as you are aware, that which is called by us *skloratas,* is by the Eretrians called *skloratar* [hard].

Cratylus: Very true.

Socrates: But are the letters *r* and *s* equivalents, and is there the same significance to them in the termination *r,* which there is to us in *s,* or is there no significance to one of us?

Cratylus: Nay, surely there is a significance to both of us.

Socrates: In so far as they are like, or in so far as they are unlike?

Cratylus: In so far as they are like.

Socrates: Are they altogether alike?

Cratylus: Yes, for the purpose of expressing motion.

Socrates: And what do you say of the insertion of the *l*? For that is expressive not of hardness but of softness.

Cratylus: Why, perhaps the letter *l* is wrongly inserted, Socrates, and should be altered into *r,* as you were saying to Hermogenes, and in my opinion rightly, when you spoke of adding and subtracting letters upon occasion.

Socrates: Good, but still the word is intelligible to both of us. When I say *skloratas* [hard], you know what I mean.

Cratylus: Yes, my dear friend, and the explanation of that is custom.

Socrates: And what is custom but convention? When I utter a sound which I understand, and

you know that I understand the meaning of the sound—this is what you are saying?

Cratylus: Yes.

Socrates: And if when I speak you know my meaning, there is an indication given by me to you?

Cratylus: Yes.

Socrates: This indication of my meaning may proceed from unlike as well as from like. . . . But if this is true, then you have made a convention with yourself, and the correctness of a name turns out to be convention, since letters which are unlike are indicative equally with those which are like, if they are sanctioned by custom and convention. And even supposing that you distinguish custom from convention ever so much, still you must say that the signification of words is given by custom and not by likeness; for custom may indicate by the unlike as well as by the like. But as we are agreed thus far, Cratylus, for I shall assume that your silence gives consent, then custom and convention must be supposed to contribute to the indication of our thoughts. For suppose we take the instance of number. How can you ever imagine, my good friend, that you will find names resembling every individual number, unless you allow that which you term convention and agreement to have authority in determining the correctness of names? I quite agree with you that words should as far as possible resemble things, but I fear that this dragging in of resemblance, as Hermogenes says, is a shabby thing, which has to be supplemented by the mechanical aid of convention with a view to correctness. For I believe that if we could always, or almost always, use likenesses, which are perfectly appropriate, this would be the most perfect state of language, as the opposite is the most imperfect.

The Poetics

ARISTOTLE

OUR SUBJECT BEING POETRY, I propose to speak not only of the art in general but also of its species and their respective capacities; of the structure of plot required for a good poem; of the number and nature of the constituent parts of a poem; and likewise of any other matters in the same line of inquiry. Let us follow the natural order and begin with the primary facts.

Epic poetry and Tragedy, as also Comedy, Dithyrambic poetry, and most flute-playing and lyre-playing, are all, viewed as a whole, modes of imitation. But at the same time they differ from one another in three ways, either by a difference of kind in their means, or by differences in the objects, or in the manner of their imitations.

Just as color and form are used as means by some, who (whether by art or constant practice) imitate and portray many things by their aid, and the voice is used by others; so also in the above-mentioned group of arts, the means with them as a whole are rhythm, language, and harmony—used, however, either singly or in certain combinations. A combination of harmony and rhythm alone is the means in flute-playing and lyre-playing, and any other arts there may be of the same description, e.g. imitative piping. Rhythm alone, without harmony, is the means in the dancer's imitations; for even he, by the rhythms of his attitudes, may represent men's characters, as well as what they do and suffer. There is further an art which imitates by language alone, without harmony, in prose or in verse, and if in verse, either in some one or in a plurality of meters. This form of imitation is to this day without a name. We have no common name for a mime of Sophron or Xenarchus and a Socratic Conversation; and we should still be without one even if

the imitation in the two instances were in trimeters or elegiacs or some other kind of verse—though it is the way with people to take on "poet" to the name of a meter, and talk of elegiac-poets and epic-poets, thinking that they call them poets not by reason of the imitative nature of their work, but indiscriminately by reason of the meter they write in. Even if a theory of medicine or physical philosophy be put forth in a metrical form, it is usual to describe the writer in this way; Homer and Empedocles, however, have really nothing in common apart from their meter; so that, if the one is to be called a poet, the other should be termed a physicist rather than a poet. . . . There are, lastly, certain other arts, which combine all the means enumerated, rhythm, melody, and verse, e.g. Dithyrambic and Nomic poetry, Tragedy and Comedy; with this difference, however, that the three kinds of means are in some of them employed together, and in others brought in separately, one after the other. These elements of difference in the above arts I term the means of their imitation.

The objects the imitator represents are actions, with agents who are necessarily either good men or bad—the diversities of human character being nearly always derivative from this primary distinction, since the line between virtue and vice is one dividing the whole of mankind. It follows, therefore, that the agents represented must be either above our own level of goodness, or beneath it, or just such as we are; in the same way as, with the painters, the personages of Polygnotus are better than we are, those of Pauson worse, and those of Dionysius just like ourselves. It is clear that each of the above-mentioned arts will admit of these differences, and that it will become a

From The Oxford Translation of Aristotle *(ed. W. D. Ross), trans. Ingram Bywater (Oxford: Clarendon Press, 1920).*

separate art by representing objects with this point of difference. Even in dancing, flute-playing, and lyre-playing such diversities are possible; and they are also possible in the nameless art that uses language, prose or verse without harmony, as its means; Homer's personages, for instance, are better than we are; Cleophon's are on our own level; and those of Hegemon of Thasos, the first writer of parodies, and Nicochares, the author of the *Diliad,* are beneath it. . . . This difference it is that distinguishes Tragedy and Comedy also; the one would make its personages worse, and the other better, than the men of the present day.

A third difference in these arts is in the manner in which each kind of object is represented. Given both the same means and the same kind of object for imitation, one may either (1) speak at one moment in narrative and at another in an assumed character, as Homer does; or (2) one may remain the same throughout, without any such change; or (3) the imitators may represent the whole story dramatically, as though they were actually doing the things described.

As we said at the beginning, therefore, the differences in the imitation of these arts come under three heads, their means, their objects, and their manner.

So that as an imitator Sophocles will be on one side akin to Homer, both portraying good men; and on another to Aristophanes, since both present their personages as acting and doing. This in fact, according to some, is the reason for plays being termed dramas, because in a play the personages act the story. . . .

So much, then, as to the number and nature of the points of difference in the imitation of these arts.

It is clear that the general origin of poetry was due to two causes, each of them part of human nature. Imitation is natural to man from childhood, one of his advantages over the lower animals being this, that he is the most imitative creature in the world, and learns at first by imitation. And it is also natural for all to delight in works of imitation. The truth of this second point is shown by experience: though the objects themselves may be painful to see, we delight to view the most realistic representations of them in art, the forms for example of the lowest animals and of dead bodies. The explanation is to be found in a further fact: to be learning something is the greatest of pleasures not only to the philosopher but also to the rest of mankind, however small their capacity for it; the reason of the delight in seeing the picture is that one is at the same time learning—gathering the meaning of things, e.g. that the man there is so-and-so; for if one has not seen the thing before, one's pleasure will not be in the picture as an imitation of it, but will be due to the execution or coloring or some similar cause. Imitation, then, being natural to us—as also the sense of harmony and rhythm, the meters being obviously species of rhythms—it was through their original aptitude, and by a series of improvements for the most part gradual on their first efforts, that they created poetry out of their improvisations.

Poetry, however, soon broke up into two kinds according to the differences of character in the individual poets; for the graver among them would represent noble actions, and those of noble personages; and the meaner sort the actions of the ignoble. The latter class produced invectives at first, just as others did hymns and panegyrics. We know of no such poem by any of the pre-Homeric poets, though there were probably many such writers among them; instances, however, may be found from Homer downwards, e.g., his *Margites,* and the similar poems of others. . . . The result was that the old poets became some of them writers of heroic and others of iambic verse. Homer's position, however, is peculiar: just as he was in the serious style the poet of poets, standing alone not only through the literary excellence, but also through the dramatic character of his imitations, so too he was the first to outline for us the general forms of Comedy by producing not a dramatic invective, but a dramatic picture of the Ridiculous; his *Margites* in fact stands in the same relation to our comedies as the *Iliad* and *Odyssey* to our tragedies. As soon, however, as Tragedy and Comedy appeared in the field, those naturally drawn to the one line of poetry became writers of comedies instead of iambs, and those naturally drawn to the other, writers of tragedies instead of epics, because these new modes of art were grander and of more esteem than the old.

If it be asked whether Tragedy is now all that it need be in its formative elements, to consider that, and decide it theoretically and in relation to the theatres, is a matter for another inquiry.

It certainly began in improvisations—as did also Comedy; the one originating with the authors of the Dithyramb, the other with those of the phallic songs, which still survive as institutions in many of our cities. And its advance after that was little by little, through their improving on whatever they had before them at each stage. It was in fact only after a long series of changes that the movement of Tragedy stopped on its attaining to its natural form. (1) The number of actors was first increased to two by Aeschylus, who curtailed the business of the Chorus, and made the dialogue, or spoken portion, take the leading part in the play. (2) A third actor and scenery were due to Sophocles. (3) Tragedy acquired also its magnitude. Discarding short stories and a ludicrous diction through its passing out of its satyric stage, it assumed, though only at a late point in its progress, a tone of dignity; and its meter changed then from trochaic to iambic. The reason for their original use of the trochaic tetrameter was that their poetry was satyric [lecherous, like the half-man, half-goat Greek deity] and more connected with dancing than it now is. As soon, however, as a spoken part came in, nature herself found the appropriate meter. The iambic, we know, is the most speakable of meters, as is shown by the fact that we very often fall into it in conversation, whereas we rarely talk hexameters, and only when we depart from the speaking tone of voice. (4) Another change was a plurality of episodes or acts. As for the remaining matters, the superadded embellishments and the account of their introduction, these must be taken as said, as it would probably be a long piece of work to go through the details.

As for Comedy, it is (as has been observed) an imitation of men worse than the average; worse, however, not as regards any and every sort of fault, but only as regards one particular kind, the Ridiculous, which is a species of the Ugly. The Ridiculous may be defined as a mistake or deformity not productive of pain or harm to others; the mask, for instance, that excites laughter, is something ugly and distorted without causing pain.

Though the successive changes in Tragedy and their authors are not unknown, we cannot say the same of Comedy; its early stages passed unnoticed, because it was not as yet taken up in a serious way. It was only at a late point in its progress that a chorus of comedians was officially granted by the archon; they used to be mere volunteers. It had also already certain definite forms at the time when the record of those termed comic poets begins. Who it was who supplied it with masks, or prologues, or a plurality of actors and the like, has remained unknown. The invented Fable, or Plot, however, originated in Sicily with Epicharmus and Phormis; of Athenian poets Crates was the first to drop the Comedy of invective and frame stories of a general and nonpersonal nature, in other words, Fables or Plots.

Epic poetry, then, has been seen to agree with Tragedy to this extent, that of being an imitation of serious subjects in a grand kind of verse. It differs from it, however, (1) in that it is in one kind of verse and in narrative form; and (2) in its length—which is due to its action having no fixed limit of time, whereas Tragedy endeavors to keep as far as possible within a single circuit of the sun, or something near that. This, I say, is another point of difference between them, though at first the practice in this respect was just the same in tragedies as in epic poems. They differ also (3) in their constituents, some being common to both and others peculiar to Tragedy— hence a judge of good and bad in Tragedy is a judge of that in epic poetry also. All the parts of an epic are included in Tragedy; but those of

Tragedy are not all of them to be found in the Epic.

Reserving hexameter poetry and Comedy for consideration hereafter, let us proceed now to the discussion of Tragedy; before doing so, however, we must gather up the definition resulting from what has been said. A tragedy, then, is the imitation of an action that is serious and also, as having magnitude, complete in itself; in language with pleasurable accessories, each kind brought in separately in the parts of the work; in a dramatic, not in a narrative form; with incidents arousing pity and fear, wherewith to accomplish its catharsis of such emotions. Here by "language with pleasurable accessories" I mean that with rhythm and harmony or song superadded; and by "the kinds separately" I mean that some portions are worked out with verse only, and others in turn with song.

As they act the stories, it follows that in the first place the Spectacle (or stage-appearance of the actors) must be some part of the whole; and in the second Melody and Diction, these two being the means of their imitation. Here by "Diction" I mean merely this, the composition of the verses; and by "Melody," what is too completely understood to require explanation. But further: the subject represented also is an action; and the action involves agents, who must necessarily have their distinctive qualities both of character and thought, since it is from these that we ascribe certain qualities to their actions. There are in the natural order of things, therefore, two causes, Thought and Character, of their actions, and consequently of their success or failure in their lives. Now the action (that which was done) is represented in the play by the Fable or Plot. The Fable, in our present sense of the term, is simply this, the combination of the incidents, or things done in the story; whereas Character is what makes us ascribe certain moral qualities to the agents; and Thought is shown in all they say when proving a particular point or, it may be, enunciating a general truth. There are six parts consequently of every tragedy, as a whole (that is) of such or such quality, viz. a Fable or Plot, Characters, Diction, Thought, Spectacle, and Melody; two of them arising from the means, one from the manner, and three from the objects of the dramatic imitation; and there is nothing else besides these six. Of these, its formative elements, then, not a few of the dramatists have made due use, as every play, one may say, admits of Spectacle, Character, Fable, Diction, Melody and Thought.

The most important of the six is the combination of the incidents of the story. Tragedy is essentially an imitation not of persons but of action and life, of happiness and misery. All human happiness or misery takes the form of action; the end for which we live is a certain kind of activity, not a quality. Character gives us qualities, but it is in our actions—what we do—that we are happy or the reverse. In a play accordingly they do not act in order to portray the Characters; they include the Characters for the sake of the action. So that it is the action in it, i.e. its Fable or Plot, that is the end and purpose of the tragedy; and the end is everywhere the chief thing. Besides this, a tragedy is impossible without action, but there may be one without Character. The tragedies of most of the moderns are characterless—a defect common among poets of all kinds, and with its counterpart in painting in Zeuxis as compared with Polygnotus; for whereas the latter is strong in character, the work of Zeuxis is devoid of it. And again; one may string together a series of characteristic speeches of the utmost finish as regards Diction and Thought, and yet fail to produce the true tragic effect; but one will have much better success with a tragedy which, however inferior in these respects, has a Plot, a combination of incidents, in it. And again: the most powerful elements of attraction in Tragedy, the Peripeties and Discoveries, are parts of the Plot. A further proof is in the fact that beginners succeed earlier with the Diction and Characters than with the construction of a story; and the same may be said of nearly all the early dramatists. We maintain, therefore, that the first essential, the life and soul, so to speak, of Tragedy is the Plot; and that the Characters come second—compare the parallel in painting, where the most beautiful colours laid on without order will not give one the same pleasure as a simple black-and-white sketch of a portrait. We maintain that Tragedy is primarily an imitation of action, and that it is mainly for the sake of the action that it imitates the personal agents. Third comes the element of Thought, i.e. the power of saying whatever can be said, or what is appropriate to the occasion. This is what, in the speeches in Tragedy, falls under the arts of Politics and Rhetoric; for the older poets make their personages discourse like statesmen, and the modern like rhetoricians. One must not confuse it with Character. Character in a play is that which reveals the moral purpose of the agents, i.e. the sort of thing they seek or avoid, where that is not obvious—hence there is no room for Character in a speech on a purely indifferent subject. Thought, on the other hand, is shown in all they say when proving or disproving some particular point, or enunciating some universal proposition. Fourth among the literary elements is the Diction of the personages, i.e., as before explained, the expression of their thoughts in words, which is practically the same thing with verse as with prose. As for the two remaining parts, the Melody is the greatest of the pleasurable accessories of Tragedy. The Spectacle, though an attraction, is the least artistic of all the parts, and has least to do with the art of poetry. The tragic effect is quite possible without a public performance and actors; and besides, the getting-up of the Spectacle is more a matter for the costumier than the poet.

Having thus distinguished the parts, let us now consider the proper construction of the Fable or Plot, as that is at once the first and the most important thing in Tragedy. We have laid it down that a tragedy is an imitation of an action that is complete in itself, as a whole of some magnitude; for a whole may be of no magnitude to speak of. Now a whole is that which has beginning, middle, and end. A beginning is that which is not itself necessarily after anything else, and which has naturally something else after it; an end is that which is naturally after something

itself, either as its necessary or usual consequent, and with nothing else after it; and a middle, that which is by nature after one thing and has also another after it. A well-constructed Plot, therefore, cannot either begin or end at any point one likes; beginning and end in it must be of the forms just described. Again: to be beautiful, a living creature, and every whole made up of parts, must not only present a certain order in its arrangement of parts, but also be of a certain definite magnitude. Beauty is a matter of size and order, and therefore impossible either (1) in a very minute creature, since our perception becomes indistinct as it approaches instantaneity; or (2) in a creature of vast size—one, say, 1,000 miles long—as in that case, instead of the object being seen all at once, the unity and wholeness of it is lost to the beholder. Just in the same way, then, as a beautiful whole made up of parts, or a beautiful living creature, must be of some size, but a size to be taken in by the eye, so a story or Plot must be of some length, but of a length to be taken in by the memory. As for the limit of its length, so far as that is relative to public performances and spectators, it does not fall within the theory of poetry. If they had to perform a hundred tragedies, they would be timed by water-clocks, as they are said to have been at one period. The limit, however, set by the actual nature of the thing is this: the longer the story, consistently with its being comprehensible as a whole, the finer it is by reason of its magnitude. As a rough general formula, "a length which allows of the hero passing by a series of probable or necessary stages from misfortune to happiness, or from happiness to misfortune," may suffice as a limit for the magnitude of the story.

The Unity of a Plot does not consist, as some suppose, in its having one man as its subject. An infinity of things befall that one man, some of which it is impossible to reduce to unity; and in like manner there are many actions of one man which cannot be made to form one action. One sees, therefore, the mistake of all the poets who have written a *Heracleid,* a *Theseid,* or similar poems; they suppose that, because Heracles was one man, the story also of Heracles must be one story. Homer, however, evidently understood this point quite well, whether by art or instinct, just in the same way as he excels the rest in every other respect. In writing an *Odyssey,* he did not make the poem cover all that ever befell his hero—it befell him, for instance, to get wounded on Parnassus and also to feign madness at the time of the call to arms, but the two incidents had no necessary or probable connexion with one another—instead of doing that, he took as the subject of the *Odyssey,* as also of the *Iliad,* an action with a Unity of the kind we are describing. The truth is that, just as in the other imitative arts one imitation is always of one thing, so in poetry the story, as an imitation of action, must represent one action, a complete whole, with its several incidents so closely connected that the transposal or withdrawal of any one of them will disjoin and dislocate the whole. For that which makes no perceptible difference by its presence or absence is no real part of the whole.

From what we have said it will be seen that the poet's function is to describe, not the thing that has happened, but a kind of thing that might happen, i.e. what is possible as being probable or necessary. The distinction between historian and poet is not in the one writing prose and the other verse—you might put the work of Herodotus into verse, and it would still be a species of history; it consists really in this, that the one describes the thing that has been, and the other a kind of thing that might be. Hence poetry is something more philosophic and of graver import than history, since its statements are of the nature rather of universals, whereas those of history are singulars. By a universal statement I mean one as to what such or such a kind of man will probably or necessarily say or do—which is the aim of poetry, though it affixes proper names to the characters; by a singular statement, one as to what, say, Alcibiades did or had done to him. In Comedy this has become clear by this time; it is only when their plot is already made up of probable incidents that they give it a basis of proper names, choosing for the purpose any names that may occur to them, instead of writing like the old iambic poets about particular persons. In Tragedy, however, they still adhere to the historic names; and for this reason: what convinces is the possible; now whereas we are not yet sure as to the possibility of that which has not happened, that which has happened is manifestly possible, else it would not have come to pass. Nevertheless even in Tragedy there are some plays with but one or two known names in them, the rest being inventions; and there are some without a single known name, e.g. Agathon's *Antheus,* in which both incidents and names are of the poet's invention; and it is no less delightful on that account. So that one must not aim at a rigid adherence to the traditional stories on which tragedies are based. It would be absurd, in fact, to do so, as even the known stories are only known to a few, though they are a delight none the less to all.

It is evident from the above that the poet must be more the poet of his stories or Plots than of his verses, inasmuch as he is a poet by virtue of the imitative element in his work, and it is actions that he imitates. And if he should come to take a subject from actual history, he is none the less a poet for that; since some historic occurrences may very well be in the probable and possible order of things; and it is in that aspect of them that he is their poet.

Of simple Plots and actions the episodic are the worst. I call a Plot episodic when there is neither probability nor necessity in the sequence of its episodes. Actions of this sort bad poets construct through their own fault, and good ones on account of the players. His work being for public performance, a good poet often stretches out a Plot beyond its capabilities, and is thus obliged to twist the sequence of incident.

Tragedy, however, is an imitation not only of a complete action, but also of incidents arousing pity and fear. Such incidents have the very greatest effect on the mind when they occur unexpectedly and at the same time in consequence of one another; there is more of the marvellous in them then than if they happened of themselves or by mere chance. Even matters of chance seem most marvellous if there is an appearance of design as it were in them; as for instance the statue of Mitys at Argos killed the author of Mitys' death by falling down on him when a looker-on at a public spectacle; for incidents like that we think to be not without a meaning. A Plot therefore, of this sort is necessarily finer than others.

Plots are either simple or complex, since the actions they represent are naturally of this twofold description. The action, proceeding in the way defined, as one continuous whole, I call simple, when the change in the hero's fortunes takes place without Peripety or Discovery; and complex, when it involves one or the other, or both. These should each of them arise out of the structure of the Plot itself, so as to be the consequence, necessary or probable, of the antecedents. There is a great difference between a thing happening [*because* of something and merely following *after* something].

A Peripety is the change of the kind described from one state of things within the play to its opposite, and that too in the way we are saying, in the probable or necessary sequence of events; as it is for instance in *Oedipus:* here the opposite state of things is produced by the Messenger, who, coming to gladden Oedipus and to remove his fears as to his mother, reveals the secret of his birth. And in *Lynceus:* just as he is being led off for execution, with Danaus at his side to put him to death, the incidents preceding this bring it about that he is saved and Danaus put to death. A Discovery is, as the very word implies, a change from ignorance to knowledge, and thus to either love or hate, in the personages marked for good or evil fortune. The finest form of Discovery is one attended by Peripeties, like that which goes with the Discovery in *Oedipus.* There are no doubt other forms of it; what we have said may happen in a way in reference to inanimate things, even things of a very casual kind; and it is also possible to discover whether some one has done or not done something. But the form most

directly connected with the Plot and the action of the piece is the first-mentioned. This, with a Peripety, will arouse either pity or fear—actions of that nature being what Tragedy is assumed to represent; and it will also serve to bring about the happy or unhappy ending. The Discovery, then, being of persons, it may be that of one party only to the other, the latter being already known; or both the parties may have to discover themselves. Iphigenia, for instance, was discovered to Orestes by sending the letter; and another Discovery was required to reveal him to Iphigenia.

Two parts of the Plot, then, Peripety and Discovery, are on matters of this sort. A third part is Suffering; which we may define as an action of a destructive or painful nature, such as murders on the stage, tortures, woundings, and the like. The other two have been already explained.

The parts of Tragedy to be treated as formative elements in the whole were mentioned in a previous Chapter. From the point of view, however, of its quantity, i.e. the separate sections into which it is divided, a tragedy has the following parts: Prologue, Episode, Exode, and a choral portion, distinguished into Parode and Stasimon; these two are common to all tragedies, whereas songs from the stage and *Commoe* are only found in some. The Prologue is all that precedes the Parode of the chorus; an Episode all that comes in between two whole choral songs; the Exode all that follows after the last choral song. In the choral portion the Parode is the whole first statement of the chorus; a Stasimon, a song of the chorus without anapaests or trochees; a *Commos,* a lamentation sung by chorus and actor in concert. The parts of Tragedy to be used as formative elements in the whole we have already mentioned; the above are its parts from the point of view of its quantity, or the separate sections into which it is divided.

The next points after what we have said above will be these: (1) What is the poet to aim at, and what is he to avoid, in constructing his Plots? and (2) What are the conditions on which the tragic effect depends?

We assume that, for the finest form of Tragedy, the Plot must be not simple but complex; and further, that it must imitate actions arousing fear and pity, since that is the distinctive function of this kind of imitation. It follows, therefore, that there are three forms of Plot to be avoided. (1) A good man must not be seen passing from happiness to misery, or (2) a bad man from misery to happiness. The first situation is not fear-inspiring or piteous, but simply odious to us. The second is the most untragic that can be; it has no one of the requisites of Tragedy; it does not appeal either to the human feeling in us, or to our pity, or to our fears. Nor, on the other hand, should (3) an extremely bad man be seen falling from happiness into misery. Such a story may arouse the human feeling in us, but it will not move us to either pity or fear; pity is occasioned by undeserved misfortune, and fear by that of one like ourselves; so that there will be nothing either piteous or fear-inspiring in the situation. There remains, then, the intermediate kind of personage, a man not pre-eminently virtuous and just, whose misfortune, however, is brought upon him not by vice and depravity but by some error of judgement, of the number of those in the enjoyment of great reputation and prosperity; e.g. Oedipus, Thyestes, and the men of note of similar families. The perfect Plot, accordingly, must have a single, and not (as some tell us) a double issue; the change in the hero's fortunes must be not from misery to happiness, but on the contrary from happiness to misery; and the cause of it must lie not in any depravity, but in some great error on his part; the man himself being either such as we have described, or better, not worse, than that. Fact also confirms our theory. Though the poets began by accepting any tragic story that came to hand, in these days the finest tragedies are always on the story of some few houses, on that of Alcmeon, Oedipus, Orestes, Meleager, Thyestes, Telephus, or any others that may have been involved, as either agents or sufferers, in some deed of horror. The theoretically best tragedy, then, has a Plot of this description. The critics, therefore, are wrong

who blame Euripides for taking this line in his tragedies, and giving many of them an unhappy ending. It is, as we have said, the right line to take. The best proof is this: on the stage, and in the public performances, such plays, properly worked out, are seen to be the most truly tragic; and Euripides, even if his execution be faulty in every other point, is seen to be nevertheless the most tragic certainly of the dramatists. After this comes the construction of Plot which some rank first, one with a double story (like the *Odyssey*) and an opposite issue for the good and the bad personages. It is ranked as first only through the weakness of the audiences; the poets merely follow their public, writing as its wishes dictate. But the pleasure here is not that of Tragedy. It belongs rather to Comedy, where the bitterest enemies in the piece (e.g. Orestes and Aegisthus) walk off good friends at the end, with no slaying of any one by any one.

The tragic fear and pity may be aroused by the Spectacle; but they may also be aroused by the very structure and incidents of the play—which is the better way and shows the better poet. The Plot in fact should be so framed that, even without seeing the things take place, he who simply hears the account of them shall be filled with horror and pity at the incidents; which is just the effect that the mere recital of the story in *Oedipus* would have on one. To produce this same effect by means of the Spectacle is less artistic, and requires extraneous aid. Those, however, who make use of the Spectacle to put before us that which is merely monstrous and not productive of fear, are wholly out of touch with Tragedy; not every kind of pleasure should be required of a tragedy, but only its own proper pleasure.

The tragic pleasure is that of pity and fear, and the poet has to produce it by a work of imitation; it is clear, therefore, that the causes should be included in the incidents of his story. Let us see, then, what kinds of incident strike one as horrible, or rather as piteous. In a deed of this description the parties must necessarily be either friends, or enemies, or indifferent to one another. Now when enemy does it on enemy, there is nothing to move us to pity either in his doing or in his meditating the deed, except so far as the actual pain of the sufferer is concerned; and the same is true when the parties are indifferent to one another. Whenever the tragic deed, however, is done within the family—when murder or the like is done or mediated by brother on brother, by son on father, by mother on son, or son on mother—these are the situations the poet should seek after. The traditional stories, accordingly, must be kept as they are, e.g. the murder of Clytaemnestra by Orestes and of Eriphyle by Alcmeon. At the same time even with these there is something left to the poet himself; it is for him to devise the right way of treating them. Let us explain more clearly what we mean by "the right way." The deed of horror may be done by the doer knowingly and consciously, as in the old poets, and in Medea's murder of her children in Euripides. Or he may do it, but in ignorance of his relationship, and discover that afterwards, as does Oedipus in Sophocles. Here the deed is outside the play; but it may be within it, like the act of Alcmeon in Astydamas, or that of Telegonus in *Ulysses Wounded*. A third possibility is for one meditating some deadly injury to another, in ignorance of his relationship, to make the discovery in time to draw back. These exhaust the possibilities, since the deed must necessarily be either done or not done, and either knowingly or unknowingly.

The worst situation is when the personage is with full knowledge on the point of doing the deed, and leaves it undone. It is odious and also (through the absence of suffering) untragic; hence it is that no one is made to act thus except in some few instances, e.g. Haemon and Creon in *Antigone*. Next after this comes the actual perpetration of the deed mediated. A better situation than that, however, is for the deed to be done in ignorance, and the relationship discovered afterwards, since there is nothing odious in it, and the Discovery will serve to astound us. But the best of all is the last; what we have in *Cresphontes*, for example, where Merope, on the point of slaying her son, recognizes him in time; in *Iphigenia*, where sister and brother are in a like position; and in *Helle*, where the son recognizes his mother, when on the point of giving her up to her enemy.

This will explain why our tragedies are restricted (as we said just now) to such a small number of families. It was accident rather than art that led the poets in quest of subjects to embody this kind of incident in their Plots. They are still obliged, accordingly, to have recourse to the families in which such horrors have occurred.

On the construction of the Plot, and the kind of Plot required for Tragedy, enough has now been said.

In the Characters there are four points to aim at. First and foremost, that they shall be good. There will be an element of character in the play, if (as has been observed) what a personage says or does reveals a certain moral purpose; and a good element of character, if the purpose so revealed is good. Such goodness is possible in every type of personage, even in a woman or a slave, though the one is perhaps an inferior, and the other a wholly worthless being. The second point is to make them appropriate. The Character before us may be, say, manly; but it is not appropriate in a female Character to be manly, or clever. The third is to make them like the reality, which is not the same as their being good and appropriate, in our sense of the term. The fourth is to make them consistent and the same throughout; even if inconsistency be part of the man before one for imitation as presenting that form of character, he should still be consistently inconsistent. We have an instance of baseness of character, not required for the story, in the Menelaus in *Orestes;* of the incongruous and unbefitting in the lamentation of Ulysses in *Scylla,* and in the (clever) speech of Melanippe; and of inconsistency in *Iphigenia at Aulis,* where Iphigenia the suppliant is utterly unlike the later Iphigenia. The right thing, however, is in the Characters just as in the incidents of the play to endeavor always after the necessary or the probable; so that whenever such-and-such a personage says or does such-and-such a thing, it shall be the necessary or probable outcome of his character; and whenever this incident follows on that, it shall be either the necessary or the probable consequence of it. From this one sees (to digress for a moment) that the Denouement also should arise out of the plot itself, and not depend on a stage-artifice, as in *Medea,* or in the story of the (arrested) departure of the Greeks in the *Iliad.* The artifice must be reserved for matters outside the play—for past events beyond human knowledge, or events yet to come, which require to be foretold or announced; since it is the privilege of the Gods to know everything. There should be nothing improbable among the actual incidents. If it be unavoidable, however, it should be outside the tragedy, like the improbability in the *Oedipus* of Sophocles. But to return to the Characters. As Tragedy is an imitation of personages better than the ordinary man, we in our way should follow the example of good portrait-painters, who reproduce the distinctive features of a man, and at the same time, without losing the likeness, make him handsomer than he is. The poet in like manner, in portraying men quick or slow to anger, or with similar infirmities of character, must know how to represent them as such, and at the same time as good men, as Agathon and Homer have represented Achilles. . . .

The Plot and Characters having been discussed, it remains to consider the Diction and Thought. As for the Thought, we may assume what is said of it in our Art of Rhetoric, as it belongs more properly to that department of inquiry. The Thought of the personages is shown in everything to be effected by their language—in every effort to prove or disprove, to arouse emotion (pity, fear, anger, and the like), or to maximize or minimize things. It is clear, also, that their mental procedure must be on the same lines in their actions likewise, whenever they wish them to arouse pity or horror, or to have a look of importance or probability. The only difference is that with the act the impression has to be made without explanation; whereas with the spoken word it has to be produced by the speaker, and result from his language. What, indeed, would be the good of the speaker, if things appeared in the required light even apart from anything he says. . . .

The perfection of Diction is for it to be at once clear and not mean. The clearest indeed is that made up of the ordinary words for things, but it is mean, as is shown by the poetry of Cleophon and Sthenelus. On the other hand the Diction becomes distinguished and non-prosaic by the use of unfamiliar terms, i.e. strange words, metaphors, lengthened forms, and everything that deviates from the ordinary modes of speech.—But a whole statement in such terms will be either a riddle or a barbarism, a riddle, if made up of metaphors, a barbarism, if made up of strange words. The very nature indeed of a riddle is this, to describe a fact in an impossible combination of words (which cannot be done with the real names for things, but can be with their metaphorical substitutes); e.g. "I saw a man glue brass on another with fire," and the like. The corresponding use of strange words results in a barbarism.—A certain admixture, accordingly, of unfamiliar terms is necessary. These, the strange word, the metaphor, the ornamental equivalent, etc., will save the language from seeming mean and prosaic, while the ordinary words in it will secure the requisite clearness. What helps most, however, to render the Diction at once clear and non-prosaic is the use of the lengthened, curtailed, and altered forms of words. Their deviation from the ordinary words will, by making the language unlike that in general use, give it a non-prosaic appearance; and their having much in common with the words in general use will give it the quality of clearness. It is not right, then, to condemn these modes of speech, and ridicule the poet for using them, as some have done; e.g. the elder Euclid, who said it was easy to make poetry if one were to be allowed to lengthen the words in the statement itself as much as one likes. . . . The proper use of them is a very different thing. To realize the difference one should take an epic verse and see how it reads when the normal words are introduced. The same should be done too with the strange word, the metaphor, and the rest; for one has only to put the ordinary words in their place to see the truth of what we are saying. The same iambic, for instance, is found in Aeschylus and Euripides, and as it stands in the former it is a poor line; whereas Euripides, by the change of a single word, the substitution of a strange for what is by usage the ordinary word, has made it seem a fine one. . . .

It is a great thing, indeed, to make a proper use of these poetical forms, as also of compounds and strange words. But the greatest thing by far is to be a master of metaphor. It is the one thing that cannot be learnt from others: and it is also a sign of genius, since a good metaphor implies an intuitive perception of the similarity in dissimilars. . . .

Let this, then, suffice as an account of Tragedy, the art imitating by means of action on the stage.

As for the poetry which merely narrates, or imitates by means of versified language (without action), it is evident that it has several points in common with Tragedy.

The construction of its stories should clearly be like that in a drama; they should be based on a single action, one that is a complete whole in itself, with a beginning, middle, and end, so as to enable the work to produce its own proper pleasure with all the organic unity of a living thing. Nor should one suppose that there is anything like them in our usual histories. A history has to deal not with one action, but with one period and all that happened in that to one or more persons, however disconnected the several events may have been. Just as two events may take place at the same time, e.g. the sea-fight off Salamis and the battle with the Carthaginians in Sicily, without converging to the same end, so too of two consecutive events one may sometimes come after the other with no one end as their common issue. Nevertheless most of our epic poets, one may say, ignore the distinction.

Herein, then, to repeat what we have said before, we have a further proof of Homer's marvellous superiority to the rest. He did not attempt to deal even with the Trojan war in its entirety, though it was a whole with a definite beginning and end—through a feeling apparently that it was too long a story to be taken in one view, or if not that, too complicated from the variety of incident in it. As it is, he has singled out one section of the whole; many of the other incidents, however, he brings in as episodes, using the Catalogue of the Ships, for instance, and other episodes to relieve the uniformity of his narrative. As for the other epic poets, they treat of one man, or one period; or else of an action which, although one, has a multiplicity of parts in it. This last is what the authors of the *Cypria* and *Little Iliad* have done. And the result is that, whereas the *Iliad* or *Odyssey* supplies materials for only one, or at most two tragedies, the *Cypria* does that for several and the *Little Iliad* for more than eight. . . .

Besides this, Epic poetry must divide into the same species as Tragedy; it must be either simple or complex, a story of character or one of suffering. Its parts, too, with the exception of Song and Spectacle, must be the same, as it requires Peripeties, Discoveries, and scenes of suffering just like Tragedy. Lastly, the Thought and Diction in it must be good in their way. All these elements appear in Homer first; and he has made due use of them. His two poems are each examples of construction, the *Iliad* simple and a story of suffering, the *Odyssey* complex (there is Discovery throughout it) and a story of character. And they are more than this, since in Diction and Thought too they surpass all other poems.

There is, however, a difference in the Epic as compared with Tragedy, (1) in its length, and (2) in its meter. (1) As to its length, the limit already suggested will suffice: it must be possible for the beginning and end of the work to be taken in in one view—a condition which will be fulfilled if the poem be shorter than the old epics, and about as long as the series of tragedies offered for one hearing. For the extension of its length epic poetry has a special advantage, of which it makes large use. In a play one cannot represent an action with a number of parts going on simultaneously; one is limited to the part on the stage and connected with the actors. Whereas in epic poetry the narrative form makes it possible for one to describe a number of simultaneous incidents; and these, if germane to the subject, increase the body of the poem. This then is a gain to the Epic, tending to give it grandeur, and also variety of interest and room for episodes of diverse kinds. Uniformity of incident by the satiety it soon creates is apt to ruin tragedies on the stage. (2) As for its meter, the heroic has been assigned it from experience; were any one to attempt a narrative poem in some one, or in several, of the other meters, the incongruity of the thing would be apparent. The heroic in fact is the gravest and weightiest of meters—which is what makes it more tolerant than the rest of strange words and metaphors, that also being a point in which the narrative form of poetry goes beyond all others. The iambic and trochaic, on the other hand, are meters of movement, the one representing that of life and action, the other that of the dance. Still more unnatural would it appear, if one were to write an epic in a medley of meters, as Chaeremon did. Hence it is that no one has ever written a long story in any but heroic verse; nature herself, as we have said, teaches us to select the meter appropriate to such a story.

Homer, admirable as he is in every other respect, is especially so in this, that he alone among epic poets is not unaware of the part to be played by the poet himself in the poem. The poet should say very little in his own person, as he is no imitator when doing that. Whereas the other poets are perpetually coming forward in person, and say but little, and that only here and there, as imitators, Homer after a brief preface brings in forthwith a man, a woman, or some other Character—no one of them characterless, but each with distinctive characteristics.

The marvellous is certainly required in Tragedy. The Epic, however, affords more opening for the improbable, the chief factor in the marvellous, because in it the agents are not vis-

ibly before one. The scene of the pursuit of Hector would be ridiculous on the stage—the Greeks halting instead of pursuing him, and Achilles shaking his head to stop them; but in the poem the absurdity is overlooked. The marvellous, however, is a cause of pleasure, as is shown by the fact that we all tell a story with additions, in the belief that we are doing our hearers a pleasure.

Homer more than any other has taught the rest of us the art of framing lies in the right way. I mean the use of paralogism. Whenever, if A is or happens, a consequent, B, is or happens, men's notion is that, if the B is, the A also is—but that is a false conclusion. Accordingly, if A is untrue, but there is something else, B, that on the assumption of its truth follows as its consequent, the right thing then is to add on the B. Just because we know the truth of the consequent, we are in our minds led on to the erroneous inference of the truth of the antecedent. Here is an instance, from the *Bath-story* in the *Odyssey*.

A likely impossibility is always preferable to an unconvincing possibility. The story should never be made up of improbable incidents; there should be nothing of the sort in it. If, however, such incidents are unavoidable, they should be outside the piece, like the hero's ignorance in *Oedipus* of the circumstances of Laius' death; not within it, like the report of the Pythian games in *Electra,* or the man's having come to Mysia from Tegea without uttering a word on the way, in *The Mysians.* So that it is ridiculous to say that one's Plot would have been spoilt without them, since it is fundamentally wrong to make up such Plots. If the poet has taken such a Plot, however, and one sees that he might have put it in a more probable form, he is guilty of absurdity as well as a fault of art. Even in the *Odyssey* the improbabilities in the setting-ashore of Ulysses would be clearly intolerable in the hands of an inferior poet. As it is, the poet conceals them, his other excellences veiling their absurdity. Elaborate Diction, however, is required only in places where there is no action, and no Character or Thought to be revealed. Where there is Character or

Thought, on the other hand, an over-ornate Diction tends to obscure them.

As regards Problems and their Solutions, one may see the number and nature of the assumptions on which they proceed by viewing the matter in the following way. (1) The poet being an imitator just like the painter or other maker of likenesses, he must necessarily in all instances represent things in one or other of three aspects, either as they were or are, or as they are said or thought to be or to have been, or as they ought to be. (2) All this he does in language, with an admixture, it may be, of strange words and metaphors, as also of the various modified forms of words, since the use of these is conceded in poetry. (3) It is to be remembered, too, that there is not the same kind of correctness in poetry as in politics, or indeed any other art. There is, however, within the limits of poetry itself a possibility of two kinds of error, the one directly, the other only accidentally connected with the art. If the poet meant to describe the thing correctly, and failed through lack of power of expression, his art itself is at fault. But if it was through his having meant to describe it in some incorrect way (e.g. to make the horse in movement have both right legs thrown forward) that the technical error (one in a matter of, say, medicine or some other special science), or impossibilities of whatever kind they may be, have got into his description, his error in that case is not in the essentials of the poetic art. These, therefore, must be the premises of the Solutions in answer to criticisms involved in the Problems.

As to the criticisms relating to the poet's art itself. Any impossibilities there may be in his descriptions of things are faults. But from another point of view they are justifiable, if they serve the end of poetry itself—if (to assume what we have said of that end) they make the effect of either that very portion of the work or some other portion more astounding. The Pursuit of Hector is an instance in point. If, however, the poetic end might have been as well or better attained without sacrifice of technical correctness in such matters, the impossibility is not to be justified, since

the description should be, if it can, entirely free from error. One may ask, too, whether the error is in a matter directly or only accidentally connected with the poetic art; since it is a lesser error in an artist not to know, for instance, that the hind has no horns, than to produce an unrecognizable picture of one.

If the poet's description be criticized as not true to fact, one may urge perhaps that the object ought to be as described—an answer like that of Sophocles, who said that he drew men as they ought to be, and Euripides as they were. If the description, however, be neither true nor of the thing as it ought to be, the answer must be then, that it is in accordance with opinion. The tales about Gods, for instance, may be as wrong as Xenophanes thinks, neither true nor the better thing to say; but they are certainly in accordance with opinion. Of other statements in poetry one may perhaps say, not that they are better than the truth, but that the fact was so at the time; e.g. the description of the arms: "their spears stood upright, butt-end upon the ground"; for that was the usual way of fixing them then, as it is still with the Illyrians. As for the question whether something said or done in a poem is morally right or not, in dealing with that one should consider not only the intrinsic quality of the actual word or deed, but also the person who says or does it, the person to whom he says or does it, the time, the means, and the motive of the agent—whether he does it to attain a greater good, or to avoid a greater evil.

The question may be raised whether the epic or the tragic is the higher form of imitation. It may be argued that, if the less vulgar is the higher, and the less vulgar is always that which addresses the better public, an art addressing any and every one is of a very vulgar order. It is a belief that their public cannot see the meaning, unless they add something themselves, that causes the perpetual movements of the performers—bad flute-players, for instance, rolling about, if quoit-throwing is to be represented, and pulling at the conductor, if Scylla is the subject of the piece. Tragedy, then, is said to be an art of this order—to be in fact just what the later actors were in the eyes of their predecessors; for Mynniscus used to call Callippides "the ape," because he thought he so overacted his parts; and a similar view was taken of Pindarus also. All Tragedy, however, is said to stand to the Epic as the newer to the older school of actors. The one, accordingly, is said to address a cultivated audience, which does not need the accompaniment of gesture; the other, an uncultivated one. If, therefore, Tragedy is a vulgar art, it must clearly be lower than the Epic.

The answer to this is twofold. In the first place, one may urge (1) that the censure does not touch the art of the dramatic poet, but only that of his interpreter; for it is quite possible to overdo the gesturing even in an epic recital, as did Sosistratus, and in a singing contest, as did Mnasitheus of Opus. (2) That one should not condemn all movement, unless one means to condemn even the dance, but only that of ignoble people—which is the point of the criticism passed on Callippides and in the present day on others, that their women are not like gentlewomen. (3) That Tragedy may produce its effect even without movement or action in just the same way as Epic poetry; for from the mere reading of a play its quality may be seen. So that, if it be superior in all other respects, this element of inferiority is no necessary part of it.

In the second place, one must remember (1) that Tragedy has everything that the Epic has (even the epic meter being admissible), together with a not inconsiderable addition in the shape of the Music (a very real factor in the pleasure of the drama) and the Spectacle. (2) That its reality of presentation is felt in the play as read, as well as in the play as acted. (3) That the tragic imitation requires less space for the attainment of its end; which is a great advantage, since the more concentrated effect is more pleasurable than one with a large admixture of time to dilute it—consider the *Oedipus* of Sophocles, for instance, and the effect of expanding it into the number of lines of the *Iliad*. (4) That there is less unity in the imitation of the epic poets, as is proved by the fact that any one work of theirs supplies matter for several tragedies; the result being that, if they take what is really a single story, it seems curt when briefly told, and thin and waterish when on the scale of length usual with their verse. In saying that there is less unity in an epic, I mean an epic made up of a plurality of actions, in the same way as the *Iliad* and *Odyssey* have many such parts, each one of them in itself of some magnitude; yet the structure of the two Homeric poems is as perfect as can be, and the action in them is as nearly as possible one action. If, then, Tragedy is superior in these respects, and also, besides these, in its poetic effect (since the two forms of poetry should give us, not any or every pleasure, but the very special kind we have mentioned), it is clear that, as attaining the poetic effect better than the Epic, it will be the higher form of art.

On the Sublime

LONGINUS

THE SUBLIME, wherever it occurs, consists in a certain loftiness and excellence of language, and . . . it is by this, and this only, that the greatest poets and prosewriters have gained eminence. . . . A lofty passage does not convince the reason of the reader, but takes him out of himself.

From Longinus: On the Sublime, *trans. H. L. Havell (London: Macmillan & Co., 1890).*

That which is admirable ever confounds our judgment, and eclipses that which is merely reasonable or agreeable. To believe or not is usually in our own power; but the Sublime, acting with an imperious and irresistible force, sways every reader whether he will or no. Skill in invention, lucid arrangement and disposition of facts, are appreciated not by one passage, or by two, but gradually manifest themselves in the general structure of a work; but a sublime thought, if happily timed, illumines an entire subject with the vividness of a lightning-flash, and exhibits the whole power of the orator in a moment of time. . . .

The first question which presents itself for solution is whether there is any art which can teach sublimity or loftiness in writing. For some hold generally that there is mere delusion in attempting to reduce such subjects to technical rules. "The Sublime," they tell us, "is born in a man, and not to be acquired by instruction; genius is the only master who can teach it. The vigorous products of nature are weakened and in every respect debased, when robbed of their flesh and blood by frigid technicalities." But I maintain that the truth can be shown to stand otherwise in this matter. Let us look at the case in this way; Nature in her loftier and more passionate moods, while detesting all appearance of restraint, is not wont to show herself utterly wayward and reckless; and though in all cases the vital informing principle is derived from her, yet to determine the right degree and the right moment, and to contribute the precision of practice and experience, is the particular province of scientific method. The great passions, when left to their own blind and rash impulses without the control of reason, are in the same danger as a ship let drive at random without ballast. Often they need the spur, but sometimes also the curb. The remark of Demosthenes with regard to human life in general—that the greatest of all blessings is to be fortunate, but next to that and equal in importance is to be well advised—for good fortune is utterly ruined by the absence of good counsel—may be applied to literature, if we substitute genius for fortune, and art for counsel. Then, again (and this is the most important point of all), a writer can only learn from art when he is to abandon himself to the direction of his genius. . . .

It is proper to observe that in human life nothing is truly great which is despised by all elevated minds. . . . Now let us apply this principle to the Sublime in poetry or in prose; let us ask in all cases, is it merely a specious sublimity? is this gorgeous exterior a mere false and clumsy pageant, which if laid open will be found to conceal nothing but emptiness? for if so, a noble mind will scorn instead of admiring it. It is natural to us to feel our soul uplifted by the true Sublime, and in a sort of generous exultation to be filled with joy and pride, as though we ourselves had originated the ideas which we read. If then any work, on being repeatedly submitted to the judgment of an acute and cultivated critic, fails to dispose his mind to lofty ideas; if the thoughts which it suggests do not extend beyond what is actually expressed; and if, the longer you read it, the less you think of it—there can be here no true sublimity, when the effect is not sustained beyond the mere act of perusal. But when a passage is pregnant in suggestion, when it is hard, nay impossible, to distract the attention from it, and when it takes a strong and lasting hold on the memory, then we may be sure that we have lighted on the true Sublime. In general we may regard those words as truly noble and sublime which always please and please all readers. For when the same book always produces the same impression on all who read it, whatever be the difference in their pursuits, their manner of life, their aspirations, their ages, or their language, such a harmony of opposites gives irresistible authority to their favorable verdict.

I shall now enumerate the five principal sources from which almost all sublimity is derived, assuming, of course, the preliminary gift on which all these depend, namely, command of language. The first and the most important is (1) grandeur of thought. The second is (2) a vigorous and spirited treatment of the passions. These two conditions of sublimity depend mainly on natural endowments, whereas those which follow derive assistance from Art. The third is (3) a certain artifice in the employment of figures, which are of two kinds, figures of thought and figures of speech. The fourth (4) dignified expression, which is subdivided into (a) the proper choice of words, and (b) the use of metaphors and other ornaments of diction. The fifth cause of sublimity, which embraces all those preceding, is (5) majesty and elevation of structure. . . .

Of all these five conditions of the Sublime the most important is the first, that is, a certain lofty cast of mind. Therefore, although this is rather natural than acquired, nevertheless it will be well for us in this instance to train up our souls to sublimity, and make them as it were ever big with noble thoughts. How, it may be asked, is this to be done? I have hinted elsewhere in my writings that sublimity is, so to say, the image of greatness of soul. Hence a thought in its naked simplicity, even though unuttered, is sometimes admirable by the sheer greatness of soul implied. Thus, the silence of Ajax in the underworld is great, and grander than anything he could have said. It is absolutely essential, then, first of all to settle the question whence this grandeur of conception arises; and the answer is that true eloquence can be found only in those whose spirit is generous and aspiring. For those whose whole lives are wasted in paltry and illiberal thoughts and habits cannot possibly produce any work worthy of the lasting reverence of mankind. It is only natural that their words should be full of sublimity whose thoughts are full of majesty. Hence sublime thoughts belong properly to the loftiest minds. . . .

But supposing now that we assume the existence of a really unblemished and irreproachable writer. Is it not worth while to raise the whole question whether in poetry and prose we should prefer sublimity accompanied by some faults, or a style which never rising above moderate excellence never stumbles and never requires correction? and again, whether the first place in literature is justly to be assigned to the more numerous, or the loftier excellences? For these are questions proper to an inquiry on the Sublime, and urgently demanding settlement.

I know, then, that the largest intellects are far from being the most exact. A mind always intent on correctness is apt to be dissipated in trifles; but in great affluence of thought, as in vast material wealth, there must needs be an occasional neglect of detail. And is it not inevitably so? Is it not by risking nothing, by never aiming high, that a writer of low or middling powers keeps generally clear of faults and secure of blame? whereas the loftier walks of literature are by their very loftiness perilous? I am well aware, again, that there is a law by which in all human productions the weak points catch the eye first, by which their faults remain indelibly stamped on the memory, while their beauties quickly fade away. Yet, though I have myself noted not a few faulty passages in Homer and in other authors of the highest rank, and though I am far from being partial to their failings, nevertheless I would call them not so much willful blunders as oversights which were allowed to pass unregarded through that contempt of little things, that "brave disorder" which is natural to an exalted genius; and I still think that the greater excellences, though not everywhere equally sustained, ought always to be voted to the first place in literature, if for no other reason, for the mere grandeur of soul they evince. . . .

What truth, then, was it that was present to those mighty spirits of the past, who, making whatever is greatest in writing their aim, thought it beneath them to be exact in every detail? Among many others especially this, that it was not in nature's plan for us her chosen children to be creatures base and ignoble—no, she brought us into life, and into the whole universe, as into some great field of contest, that we should be at once spectators and ambitious rivals of her mighty deeds, and from the first implanted in our souls an invincible yearning for all that is great, all that is diviner than ourselves. Therefore even the whole world is not wide enough for the soaring range of human thought, but man's mind often overleaps the very bounds of space. When we survey the whole circle of life, and see it abounding everywhere in what is elegant, grand, and beautiful, we learn at once what is the true end of man's being. And this is why nature prompts us to admire, not the clearness and usefulness of a little stream, but the Nile, the Danube, the Rhine, and far beyond all the Ocean; not to turn our wandering eyes from the heavenly fires, though often darkened, to the little flame kindled by human hands, however pure and steady its light; not to think that tiny lamp more wondrous than the caverns of Aetna, from whose raging depths are hurled up stones and whole masses of rock, and torrents sometimes come pouring from earth's center of pure and living fire.

To sum the whole: Whatever is useful or needful lies easily within man's reach; but he keeps his homage for what is astounding.

B. The Modern (18th- and 19th-Century) Period

Earlier we noted that aesthetics proper begins in the eighteenth century, first with the British taste theorists in the early part of the century and later with the German attempts to define aesthetic experience. The two traditions come together at the very end of the eighteenth century in Kant's *Critique of Judgment,* and this was followed by the post-Kantian developments (Hegel, Schopenhauer, and, in response to Schopenhauer, Nietzsche) of the nineteenth century. It is to these important developments, the mainstay of the aesthetic tradition, that we now turn, starting with the British taste theorists.

On your birthday a good friend gives you a large framed painting in Day-Glo colors on black velvet of the young Elvis Presley. Will you hang it up? (And if so, where? in your living room or in the closet?) What's the problem? Not only do you not like it, but you also worry that other people will think it's awful and that that will somehow make you look bad (showing that you don't have good taste in paintings). Or suppose you have invited the parents of your "significant other" to your apartment for supper. They have served for many years as U.S. Embassy personnel in France, Austria, and now Belgium. Your favorite wine happens to be Strawberry Ripple. This is the one you really like, but will you serve it? Probably not. Why not? This is the problem of taste. Although you like it, you nonetheless worry it will not meet some more "objective" criteria (of the wine connoisseurs, or experts). They are all convinced that Strawberry Ripple wine is terrible and moreover that those who like such wines suffer from incredibly bad taste. Finally, suppose a friend introduces you to a kind of music that you never really liked before, but then you find that the more you listen to and learn about this music, the more you come to like it—that is, you have come to like what the experts like. Not just that you *know* what the experts like and why, but, more interestingly, that you yourself have gradually come to prefer this kind of music as well. Later you may even be a little embarrassed to look over your first CD purchases.

The practical problem of taste is the problem of how to reconcile two seemingly opposite components—what you like and what is truly ("objectively") good. The first component in taste is simply your liking the look, sound, or taste of something (paintings, music, wines, etc.). That is, when you see or hear or sip any one of these things, you enjoy it, it gives you pleasure, and you prefer it to others. But the second component is the question of whether this painting or music or wine is really good—that is, whether it is *worthy* of being liked and preferred, and whether you are *correct* in liking it. The practical problem of taste is how to put these two questions together: How can I like what I should like (what is really good, and objectively better)?

That is the *practical* problem of taste. The *theoretical* (philosophical) problem of taste is how we know and can tell what is really better, what is truly good. Suppose I were asked to host a weekly radio jazz program and for the entire hour I featured the big band sound of Lawrence Welk. People would think I didn't know much about big band jazz and that I didn't have very good taste in jazz. It seems clearly an objective and universal opinion, at least among jazz buffs, that Duke Ellington is much better than Lawrence Welk. On the other hand, big band jazz experts often disagree among themselves on whether Artie Shaw or Duke Ellington created better big band jazz. And there seems no way to resolve or settle such a disagreement. And even if we can agree that Duke Ellington is better than Lawrence Welk, it is hard to say precisely *why* it is better, that is, what exactly makes it better.

In matters of taste we are dealing with *sensual* preferences, that is, the likes and dislikes of our five senses—how things look, sound, and taste—and not with the question of whether these things are logically, scientifically, politically, religiously, or morally correct. And this makes it seem like we are looking for empirical criteria—that is, visual, auditory features of objects that will tell us which are really good. Suppose you go to the farmer's market to buy tomatoes. You want to buy the best-tasting ones, but how can you tell which ones will taste best? You might reason that the reddest tomatoes are generally the sweetest, and since it is easy to visually pick out the reddest ones, you have succeeded in finding an empirical criterion for tomato excellence (at least as regards sweetness). By analogy, we might therefore think that we could find empirical criteria or standards of beauty simply by comparing a number of clearly recognized good paintings with an equal number of clearly recognized bad paintings. (Perhaps we can trust the museum curators of major big city art museums, along with the most authoritative books on art history, to have selected the best paintings.) And, on the other side, we might turn to the annual World's Worst Painting contest held each year in the United States (the Elvis Presley painting mentioned earlier took third prize in 1994). Lining up these paintings, we look for those features we can actually see with our own eyes that all the good paintings have and all the bad paintings lack.

But when we actually attempt such an experiment, we see immediately that it is far more problematic than we first supposed. It is very hard to name features that are both sufficiently observable and also sufficiently universal, applying to all good paintings (and no bad paintings). Suppose I notice that the good paintings are all symmetrical (the left side is the mirror image of the right side). That would certainly be an easily observable criterion (like the redness of the tomatoes); if the left side mirrors the right side, then it is symmetrical, and if it is symmetrical, then it is a good (beautiful) painting. But are all good paintings symmetrical and are all symmetrical paintings good? No; so our criterion fails the test of sufficient generality.

But if we propose a criterion that is sufficiently universal, then it fails to be sufficiently empirically observable. Suppose we propose that all good (beautiful) paintings are well balanced, or harmonious, or integrated. In this case, we might be able to say that indeed all good paintings are balanced and all balanced paintings are good, but now, if we try to use this property of paintings as an empirical criterion for good and bad paintings, how can we tell whether a painting is balanced or not? This is not as easily observable a property as symmetry was. We can't just look and see whether a painting is balanced in the same way we can look and see whether it is done in colors or only in black and white.

From the early seventeenth century, British philosophers argued that all knowledge was ultimately grounded in sense experience. When a child is first born, John Locke said, she knows nothing until she begins to gain sense impressions from the outside world. Only when these sense impressions have been grouped together in the mind in various ways can the child be said to know something about the world. From the beginning these British empiricist philosophers recognized that most properties do not exist in the object just as we perceived them. If the object itself is made up of atoms, which are themselves made up of neutrons, protons, and electrons, we cannot say that these real objects (the atoms, or the electrons) are themselves actually red or blue, or sweet or sour, or hot or cold. Rather, these real objects have the ability to cause in normal human beings the sense experiences of red, blue, sweet, sour, hot, and cold. "If a tree falls in the forest, does it make a sound if there is no one there to hear it?" No; without the conscious mind, there would be no sounds, colors, tastes, or smells. None of these properties exists in the object as we perceive them. They are *relational* properties, meaning that they cause the same sensations in all normal human observers. Any normal observer looking at an indigo-dyed dress will see it as blue. Strictly speaking, therefore, we really should say that the indigo-dyed dress has the property to cause normal people to have the sense experience we call "blue," but that's rather long-winded. As a convenient shorthand device we just say, "The dress is blue."

Since taste is a sensual matter (of how things look, sound, and taste), we might expect beauty to also be a similarly relational property. The problem with matters of taste is that *not* all normal observers see beauty in the same things. Some people think Strawberry Ripple wine is good; others think it is awful. Some people think the black velvet Elvis Presley is wonderful; others think it is not. Even among the experts some prefer the Ellington band to the Shaw group, while others prefer Shaw to Ellington. And very few European music experts will be able to distinguish good from mediocre or bad Tibetan music; similarly, Tibetans will have a hard time judging European music that they never heard before.

Going back to our earlier statement of the problem of taste, we can say that the problem is that while not everyone agrees (sees the same thing), we still feel like saying that everyone *ought to* or is *capable of* agreeing. The Strawberry Ripple wine lover can be wine educated; the taste of the Lawrence Welk fan can be improved. Everyone is capable of seeing the difference between beauty and ugliness, though not all actually do. Why? What is it that blocks their correct vision? Taste theorists usually mention both positive and negative factors. Negative factors include lack of exposure or faulty sense organs (like a color-blind person), and personal bias and prejudice may also get in the way. Positive factors include education and acculturation.

But if we take into account "positive" factors like acculturation, then aren't we really saying that taste is *not* universal in all people but relative—at least culturally relative? I cannot discriminate good from bad Tibetan music because I was not brought up in that society and culture, and even within the society and culture I was brought up in there are still unresolved and apparently unresolvable disagreements, even among the experts, about the relative merits of the Beatles and the Stones, Shaw and Ellington, Impressionist and Expressionist paintings, and so on. Aren't we then saying, in effect, that matters of taste are either relative to the individual or at best relative to the particular society and culture in question? At most we can only say that for very obvious cases (Ellington over Welk) taste is relative to a particular culture and more or less universal within that culture but not outside it. All other disagreements over matters of taste seem to be irresolvable, even within the same culture.

So why not abandon the search for a standard of taste and just admit that it is all relative? "There is no disputing over matters of taste"; "beauty is in the eye of the beholder." That certainly makes me feel a lot better as I sip a glass of ice-cold strawberry wine admiring my black velvet painting of Elvis and listening to a well-worn recording of the famous champagne music of Lawrence Welk. The problem is that we still haven't entirely gotten rid of that old worry that our likes and dislikes (our taste) may be incorrect. Although I frankly much prefer watching the Simpsons to any Shakespeare play, I can't help worrying that there may be something wrong with me—that a Shakespeare play is really better than an episode of the Simpsons (though I couldn't tell you why). And you may be worrying about the dinner party you are hosting this evening for your soon-to-be European-savvy, ambassadorial, globetrotting in-laws.

This, then, is the "problem of taste." Much of our everyday behavior and everyday attitudes seem to imply or demand an objective, universal standard of taste, but when we look at the matter more closely we find no empirical criteria are truly universal in all people, or even "normal" people, in the same way that redness in tomatoes is a pretty good crosscultural indicator of sweetness. At most, we find within particular societies and cultures, for limited periods of time, reasonably well accepted standards of excellence, but even these can be challenged and do indeed change and in any case cannot decide between any but the most obvious cases (Ellington over Welk, but not Ellington over Shaw).

The problem of taste is a "problem" in the sense that it forces us into the awkward dilemma that though our everyday attitudes and behavior and ways of speaking seem to imply some such objective or universal standard or criterion, when we actually look for such a standard we simply can't find any! Late eighteenth-century Scottish philosopher, David Hume expresses this dilemma very clearly without really solving it. Indeed, it is hard to see how the issue can be solved empirically. Using an empiricist model of ordinary sense perception, British aestheticians were led to look for an observable (*empirical*) criterion of beauty on the analogy with redness as a criterion of sweetness in tomatoes or smiling as a standard of friendliness in a face. If we say that certain objects look beautiful, the taste theorists reasoned, then there must be certain visible marks and features by which we know how and when and where to correctly apply the word "beauty."

Thus, British empiricists found it natural to treat beauty as just another empirical concept. If we say that the tree is beautiful, that the lake is beautiful, that the young child is beautiful, and that the painting is beautiful, then we seem to be applying a general empirical concept to these many different objects in much the same way we say, when we are doing the dishes, that the water and the dishes and our hands are all wet. So, we are led to ask, what empirical, observable property tells us that an object is beautiful (that is, possesses the empirical property which all beautiful things have in common, by virtue of which we know they are beautiful)?

But posing the question in this way, as natural (or inevitable) as it may seem (or seemed in the early eighteenth century), simply leads us on a wild goose chase. There is no such empirical property! As we saw earlier, no proposed empirical property is sufficiently general (to include all and only beautiful things) and no sufficiently general property (e.g., balanced, harmonious) is empirically observable. All the British taste theorists were able to do was to speculate on why this elusive universal "standard of taste" is actually shared by so few people—sometimes, they said, it is because people are poorly educated, or have damaged sense organs, or are unwilling or unable to take a "disinterested," "unbiased" look at an object.

Presumably, if we could all overcome these aesthetic liabilities, we would all find the same things beautiful. But is that really true, and how could we ever find out? Notice how speculative, indeed, how unempirical this approach is. Suppose you like the Stones while I prefer the Beatles. If there is a universal standard of beauty, why don't we agree? I may say that you are biased, that you not listening to the Beatles in a "disinterested" way. But you can say exactly the same of me. How could we ever prove empirically which of us was right? Or suppose you have better taste in Italian opera than I do because you are more familiar with it, while I have better taste than you in Chinese Song Dynasty "bird and flower" paintings because I have been studying this kind of painting for a long time. But what does that prove? Does it prove that your greater exposure to and education in Italian opera (and mine in Chinese painting) has uncovered an existing but hidden universal standard of taste, or does it merely show that this exposure and education has given each of us a limited cultural expertise which we didn't have before? Unfortunately, this is a very unempirical empiricism!

As we will see, eighteenth-century German philosopher, Immanuel Kant takes a very different approach to this problem. And we can also contrast the approach of the British taste theorists with that of Plato and Aristotle which we examined in the previous section (Part I, section A). Like the British taste theorists, Plato also sought a universal standard of beauty, but unlike them he rejected any *empirical* criterion and opted instead for an intellectually apprehensible Form of Beauty. Aristotle, you remember, did not look for a universal criterion of beauty, crossculturally valid for all people in all cultures at all times. Aristotle was only interested in the culturally defined traits of excellence in particular art genres. Like the British taste theorists, Aristotle also asks an empirical question, but a much more limited and modest one—not what do all beautiful art works have in common, but what are the standards accepted by most educated people of a given culture for judging the best examples of mature works of a particular art genre within that culture.

Although eighteenth-century English political philosopher, Edmund Burke discussed the problem of taste, he is equally important for his distinction of the beautiful and the sublime. Although the notion of the sublime was introduced by Longinus in the first century, it held no place of importance in European aesthetics until the seventeenth and especially the eighteenth century, due in large part to Burke. The main feature of the sublime, according to Burke, is that it presents a terrifying, fearsome object from which we are however in no real danger. Just as the beautiful object is one we love and long for, so the sublime object is one which we dread and fear—but in either case only in a "virtual" or pretend way. Through disinterestedness we are sufficiently detached and distanced from the object that it does not actually or literally pose any threat to us. Although the storm is raging outside, we are safely tucked in bed; walking along the beach, we admire the power of the waves crashing against the rocks although they pose no immediate danger to us. One reason for the revival of the old idea of the sublime was that it helped explain the new Romantic art cropping up at the time, art that was not so much "beautiful," as it was "awesome," "powerful," "disturbing," "moving," and "profound."

Kant is most important in the history of aesthetics for defining aesthetic experience in terms of a subjective universality of taste and for laying the foundations for the position later known as formalism (the formalist Clement Greenberg, for example, used Kant's theoretical formalist analysis to defend the then new American Abstract Expressionist art movement of the 1950s). More recently, renewed interest in the eighteenth-century notion of the sublime has brought Kant's aesthetics once more into prominence.

In his work on aesthetic judgment, Kant synthesized the work of British taste theorists of the early eighteenth century and the German attempts in the mid-eighteenth century to define "aesthetic experience." As we saw, British taste theorists were concerned with the problem how there could be normative standards of taste when people seemed so often to disagree in matters of taste. The German problem of aesthetic experience was how best to characterize the essential nature of our intuitive and sensuous experience of objects of natural and artistic beauty. The early eighteenth-century German philosopher, Alexander Baumgarten, for example, divided all human experience into two distinct realms; a cognitive, discursive, analytic kind of experience that he called *logic* and a more intuitive, sensuous and direct kind of experience called *aesthetic* (from the Greek term meaning "feeling," the root of which we find in words like *anaesthesia,* meaning "no feeling").

Kant combined these two concerns by developing the theory that aesthetic experience is essentially a kind of pleasure derived from an aesthetic judgment of taste—we experience aesthetic pleasure in the judgment that the beautiful object seems suited to accommodate our perceptive faculties (or more precisely, the judgment that "the form of an object is as though designed to accommodate the free play of our cognitive faculties"). Kant was also able in his theory to provide an account of the distinction widely recognized since Burke between the aesthetic experience of *beauty* and the aesthetic experience of the *sublime*. Beauty was the older eighteenth-century Enlightenment notion of a pleasurably self-contained, well-ordered, organic whole, ideally found in classical (and neoclassical) art. Sublimity was the newer late eighteenth-century notion of the excitement of something beyond control, bursting its bounds, suggesting notions of the infinite, numinous and all powerful—ideally found in the budding Romantic art of the time.

Kant's aesthetic theory is part of a larger effort to synthesize the major strands in the rest of his philosophy, in particular his earlier work in the *Critique of Pure Reason* and the *Critique of Practical Reason*. These two critiques had established a kind of dualism between the "realm of nature," in which deterministic causality operates, and the "realm of freedom," in which moral freedom and autonomy prevail. In the *Critique of Pure Reason* Kant had established that the necessary conditions for any human experience is the conformity of sense experience to the Categories of human understanding. This meant that all human experience must be filtered and ordered through these human concepts, including causal necessity. We can therefore know, for example, prior to any actual experience, that everything we human beings experience will be subject to causal necessity.

But, by the same token, the *Critique of Pure Reason* also limits the concepts of the understanding, in particular causal necessity, to sense experience. Beyond that, these cognitive concepts cannot claim any jurisdiction, and therefore it follows that we cannot cognitively know reality (using the concepts of the understanding). The concepts of the understanding only apply to objects as they appear to us in sense experience and not as they are in reality, as they are in themselves. As Kant argued in the *Critique of Practical Reason,* morality, which also lies outside sense experience, is not subject to causal determinism (which Kant recognized would make morality impossible). Throughout his writing, Kant maintains a "critical" separation among these spheres of influence—appearances (*phenomena*) and reality (*noumena*), scientific causality and morality. Nonetheless, the gap remaining between these two distinct realms created an uncomfortable dualism with which Kant was increasingly unhappy. For example, although morality for Kant was defined in terms of the agent's intention (in the realm of freedom), the act itself nonetheless must be performed in the space-time world of causal necessity (the realm of nature). How are these two connected?

The third critique, the *Critique of Judgment,* was written late in Kant's career to provide a bridge between the first two critiques. Always the master of architectonic, Kant reasoned that since the three cognitive faculties, understanding, reason, and judgment, should govern or regulate the operations of the three basic mental faculties, cognition, desire, and feeling, and furthermore since the cognitive faculties of understanding and reason had already, in the earlier critiques, been assigned the control over cognition and desire, respectively, it seemed logical to conclude that the cognitive faculty legislating over feeling (i.e., pleasure) should be judgment, and so the *Critique of Judgment* concerns judgments of feeling (i.e., pleasure), especially aesthetic judgments of taste (the first part of the third critique) and teleological judgments in biology (the second part of the third critique).

Mental faculties	*Cognitive faculties*	*Critiques*
cognition	understanding	*of Pure Reason*
desire	reason	*of Practical Reason*
feeling	judgment	*of Judgment*

But, of course, in a sense, judgment had already been dealt with in the first critique—judgments such as "That is a horse" are straightforward cognitive judgments of the understanding. But these are *determinate* judgments, Kant said, in which an object is judged to fall under a given concept. There is another kind of judgment, Kant argues, namely, *reflective* judgments, in which no concept is given and the sense faculties are, as it were, "searching" for a concept without ever finally finding one. This is the domain of aesthetic judgment, according to Kant. In the aesthetic judgment of beauty there is a pleasurable recognition that the form of the perceived object seems to be designed to accommodate the "free play" of our cognitive faculties—suggesting meaning, intimating a conceptual closure always just beyond our grasp.

Where the free play is between imagination and understanding, the judgment is one of beauty; where the free play is between imagination and reason, the judgment is one of sublimity. Since Kant had already established the idea in earlier critiques that understanding is the faculty that orders sense experience and reason deals with matters outside sense experience, such as morality, religion, and ideas of the world as a whole, Kant was able to provide a richer explanation of the distinction already in use between two distinct areas of aesthetic pleasure—beauty and sublimity. Later we will see in Lyotard's "postmodern sublime" a new interpretation of this Kantian idea, itself traceable to Longinus, that sublimity is something that lies beyond the grasp of the rule-like, logical, conceptual mind—whether this means something mystical, religious, irrational, divinely inspired, subconscious, or just free is the part of the notion of sublimity that is constantly changing.

By separating desire (in the second critique) from feeling (in the third critique) Kant is also able to provide a richer explanation for the already well-established idea that aesthetic experience is "disinterested." "Interested" experiences are precisely those in which I desire to *possess* something, and my judgment that it is good or likable is just the judgment that I want to *have* this object. Aesthetic judgments, on the other hand, from Shaftesbury through Burke and Baumgarten, were said to be disinterested, in that the pleasure of the experience is not to acquire the object, but to enjoy the experience of it for its own sake. Whereas Hobbes had claimed that *all* experience is self-interested, Shaftesbury and others objected that there were certain kinds of human experience, including aesthetic experience, which were *not* interested in this sense. Kant could now provide an explanation for this psychological insight—the realm of morality in which desire conforms to the dictates of reason (don't do anything you can't universalize) is quite distinct from the realm of feeling over which judgment rules.

When Kant says that the judgment of beauty is the judgment that the form of the object is *as though* designed to accommodate the free play of the cognitive faculties, he is thinking primarily of judgments of natural beauty and not of works of art. If we assume a scientific, deterministic picture of the natural world, then it can only be a fortunate accident, a lucky serendipity, that the formal properties of seashells, birds, and flowers are of precisely the sort to please us aesthetically. It is "as though" they were designed explicitly for this end, though of course we know that they were not. Kant's analysis obviously works less well in the case of works of art, since these were indeed actually designed by the artist (and not "as though" designed) to give us aesthetic pleasure.

In his account of aesthetic experience as a judgment of *feeling* (and not of *objects*), Kant made it clear that aesthetic judgments of taste were strictly subjective (that is, a judgment that an object is designed to cause us pleasure) but were nonetheless *universally* subjective—that in an aesthetic judgment of taste one had a right to presume agreement from others, though in fact such agreement was seldom actually forthcoming.

The basis of the subjective universality of judgments of taste is precisely the universality of the cognitive faculties, and this provides the basis later for formalism. To be universal, the judgment must refer to universal human faculties, and these, Kant holds, can only be the cognitive faculties (understanding and reason), and not faculties of sense (which he acknowledges are relative to each person). But the cognitive faculties are not utilized in aesthetic judgments in the ordinary way of classifying objects, since this would mean that the aesthetic judgment of beauty was simply a branch of theoretical understanding ("That is a picture of a horse," "That one is of a woman and her young child"), which Kant rightly denies.

But this means that aesthetic judgments must not include sense qualities of objects nor must they include the recognition of subject matter in art. The pleasure in sense qualities would not be universal, and the recognition of subject matter is simply the ordinary classifying understanding of cognition that for Kant is distinct from aesthetics. All that is left, therefore, is the bare form of the object, the kind of thing generally capable of being understood but for which there is no concept—only a kind of invitation for the cognitive faculties to enjoy engaging with one another in a "free"—that is, undetermined—manner. Unlike theoretical cognition, which strictly controls our sense experience and to which sense experience must rigidly conform, the structure of music, for example, suggests something we feel we can almost cognitively grasp, and so we utilize our cognitive faculties in pleasurably searching for, comparing, constructing, anticipating structures, and so on, but without ever reaching any definite "conclusion."

Aesthetic judgments, then, are not objective, for Kant, in the sense that they do not assert a property, such as beauty, of an object, nor are they conceptual in the sense that they do not subsume an object under a general concept, such as beauty. Beauty is not a concept, Kant insists, as Francis Hutcheson (1694–1746) thought it was in his definition of beauty as "uniformity amidst variety," which can be theoretically mastered and then correctly attributed to this or that object. (Suppose I am training young art critics just to look for the "uniformity amidst variety"—will this produce good art critics? Why or why not?) Beauty is the pleasurable experience of the accommodation of certain objects (or rather their form) to our cognitive faculties. The judgment of beauty is therefore subjective in the sense in which "that is painful" is subjective, that is, in describing the capacity of the object to produce a subjective response.

At the same time, however, the judgment is universal, applicable for all people. This is not to say that the judgment is universally endorsed by all people, which it is not, but only that it is judged to be universal for all people. Since the pleasure I feel is one that I recognize as the pleasure that springs from the accommodation of the form of an object to human cognition in general, and not just to my particular mental equipment, I judge that the pleasure should be experienced by anyone. When I say, "This is beautiful," and not merely that "I like it," I am judging the form of the object to pleasurably accommodate the cognitive faculties of any human, and I therefore expect others to agree with me—though, of course, I am often disappointed in real life.

In one way Kant's position has been severely challenged by many contemporary aestheticians who deny any universality of taste, but in another way his position has perhaps been vindicated. Insofar as contemporary aestheticians urge us to refrain from making aesthetic judgments of taste—that is, asserting that one work of art is better than another—they seem to affirm Kant's view that the very act of asserting or judging in matters of taste presupposes that one opinion is correct and the other is incorrect, and that therefore in making such assertions we expect, or demand, agreement (and *not* getting it generally starts an argument!). By backing away from such assertions or judgments, many contemporary writers seem to agree with Kant that if you don't think there is any basis for agreement, if you think taste is truly relative and you don't want to privilege your own response over someone else's, then you had better not express yourself on works of art in the form of assertions or judgments, for, as Kant pointed out, that will only imply that you are being judgmental. As we will see later, contemporary writers are also finding a renewed interest in Kant's notion of the sublime.

For at least a hundred years following Kant's *Critique of Judgment,* European aesthetics was Kantian in one form or another. Although each new Kantian development was distinct from every other, they shared certain common features. Neo-Kantians tended to reject Kant's "critical" stance of acknowledging an external reality on the one hand while denying any cognitive knowledge of it on the other. The long and short of this "critical" posture of Kant's was that we could never know reality, the thing-in-itself, and that was simply too hard for the followers of Kant to swallow. Neo-Kantians argued in various ways that reality could be understood through human reason.

Two of the most important neo-Kantian developments, those of Georg W. F. Hegel and Arthur Schopenhauer, appeared at about the same time (in Germany in the early nineteenth century). Hegel and Schopenhauer took neo-Kantianism in very different directions, Schopenhauer interpreting reality as a blind, unconscious will, the will to live, which human beings could understand and overcome through a kind of mystical, aesthetic experience, and Hegel interpreting reality as a thoroughly rational cosmic mind that humans could understand through reason.

What is of lasting importance in Hegel's philosophy of art? One of the most important ideas modern aesthetics has derived from Hegel is the idea of the "identity of form and content" ("the medium is the message"), the idea that in art what you say cannot be separated from how you say it. This presupposes a *cognitive* theory of art, that art expresses and articulates a view of the world but in a sensual format. In art, according to this view, the concrete sensual artwork expresses an imperceptible, transcendent reality. And that particular idea of reality cannot be expressed or understood in any other way than the precise way it has been expressed in that single work of art. According to this theory, the artist doesn't know what she is going to say until she has actually "said" it in the medium of art. Indeed, art is where ideas first come to be expressed (articulated, formulated). Only later can one state the idea in abstract, intellectual, cognitive terms and be able to say, in ordinary language, what ideas the art work has expressed.

According to Hegel, there is a natural evolution or development of ideas from their first embodiment in art to their cognitive formulation in science and everyday life. And just as animals radically change in the evolutionary process, from fish to amphibians to lizards to mammals, for example, so ideas become transformed as they evolve from their expression in art to their cognitive formulations in science and philosophy. To take an idea that has already been intellectually formulated and then try to dress it up in a work of art could therefore only produce a very mediocre and inferior artwork—a kind of propaganda or cliché of what was "oft thought but ne're so well expressed," something the American critic Cleanth Brooks dubbed the "sugar-coated pill." And it is for reasons of this sort that T. S. Eliot once said that a poem is untranslatable—to translate a poem presupposes that the same idea (content) can be expressed in different words (form), which Hegel says is impossible.

One problem with this idea, however, is that while Hegel thinks the content of art is purely ideal and spiritual, the actual making of an art work is nonetheless a physical activity (stretching the canvas, mixing the pigments, applying the paints, framing the canvas, and so on). For Hegel (and neo-Hegelians), artistic creativity is therefore a two-stage process—first to imaginatively create in one's mind a new aesthetic form-content intuition, and then to physically craft that idea in paint or stone or words on paper. Hegel also develops and expands the nineteenth-century Romantic idea of "genius" that we saw in Kant—also associated with the theory of creative imagination.

Hegel is the first aesthetician to limit aesthetics to philosophy of art (separating it from the analysis of our experience of natural beauty that previous aestheticians had considered an integral part of aesthetics). This is because Hegel considers art a representational product of the human mind, not just an "imitation" of the natural world as we already understand it, but an expression and formulation of a human view of reality, which natural objects can never be. A tree is a part of the world; a painting of a tree is a human interpretation of the world. Only expressions of mind, like art and philosophy, are concerned with "truth."

According to Hegel, reality is essentially mental or spiritual—not physical. Metaphysically, some philosophers (known as materialists) have argued that reality is essentially physical and others (called dualists), that reality is both physical and mental, while still others, idealists, like Hegel, argue that reality is essentially mental or spiritual. What appears to us as physical objects is just that, a mental appearance, a sense idea in our minds, like the objects in a dream. As the Irish idealist philosopher George Berkeley put it, "to be is to be perceived"—though, unlike Berkeley, Hegel does not regard reality simply as the ideas in someone's mind but rather as the mental activity of the cosmic "world soul."

Hegel sees the world as an evolving consciousness. Before the appearance of humans, nature or reality is not aware of itself. Only with people does reality become conscious of itself, although this evolves slowly over long periods of time. In Hegel's analysis everything in the world evolves in stages of three—thesis, antithesis, and synthesis in Hegel's famous theory of *dialectics*. The *thesis* evolves into its opposite, the *antithesis,* and the tension between the thesis and antithesis evolves into a *synthesis* of the two. Once a synthesis is reached, it then becomes the thesis in a new dialectical move toward its antithesis and resolution in a new synthesis (which then becomes a new thesis, and so on). In this case (philosophy of art), the first stage (the thesis) is art; that is, art is the stage when humans first begin to express in a sensuous medium and perceptible form ideas about the underlying spiritual reality of the universe. This in turn evolves into religion (its rational, cognitive antithesis), which finally evolves into philosophy (the synthesis of the two). So art eventually turns into philosophy, resulting, as Hegel says, in the "death of art" (that is, the "birth" of philosophy is simultaneously the "death" of art).

And art itself evolves through three stages—symbolical, classical, and romantic. When Hegel talks about symbolical art, he is thinking primarily of so-called "primitive art" of archaic and nonWestern peoples. By classical art he has in mind Greek and Roman and eighteenth-century neoclassical European art, while "Romantic art" refers to the kind of art that first appeared in Europe in Hegel's own lifetime, that is, at the end of the eighteenth and beginning of the nineteenth century. In the symbolical stage (the thesis), artists are only dimly aware of the abstract ideas they are trying to express in a sensuous form. As Hegel says, at this early stage the artistic "form" is not fully adequate to the ideal "content" of art. In symbolic art we might, for example, express the idea of courage by the image of a lion. The image of a lion, according to Hegel, is an "inadequate" expression of courage in the sense that the lion signifies more than courage (to a zoologist or a hunter or a gamekeeper, for example), while there are obviously many other ways to express the idea of courage besides the image of a lion.

Gradually, Hegel says, artists strive to find images that are more adequate to the content they express, images, that is, that ideally could only signify that particular content (or, to put it the other way round, images that ideally provide the *only* way in which that particular idea can be understood). As the ideal content becomes clearer to artists, the artistic form becomes more and more suited to the ideal content, at which point symbolical art becomes (that is, evolves into, and is replaced by) classical art (the antithesis), in which form and content are interchangeable and inseparable. There is no higher art than this, according to Hegel's ideal in classical art of the identity of artistic form and content, but the evolution of thought nonetheless continues, and so people gradually become more interested in the Ideal content of the art than in the artistic form in which that content appears. This eventually leads to Romantic art, in which the ideal content is gradually separated from the artistic form. But taken to an extreme, this can only lead to an interest in the ideas themselves, quite apart from their sensual embodiment in artistic form, and this means that art finally evolves into philosophy, or pure thought.

In Part II we will discover that the British and American analytic aestheticians' criticism in the 1950s and 1960s of traditional aesthetics was in fact very largely an attack on neo-Hegelian (neo-idealist) aesthetics of the 1920s and 1930s. And still later (Part III, section D) we will see the enormous debt of twentieth-century cultural materialists to Karl Marx and Marx's debt, in turn, to Hegel. As Marx once said, he took Hegel's main idea and turned it "right side up." While Hegel was an idealist, arguing that the physical world was the product of ideas, Marx found this formulation "upside down" and claimed instead that all our ideas about ourselves (whether in religion or philosophy or art) were the product of an ever-evolving material reality. More specifically, Marx argued that the "social superstructure" (art, philosophy, religion, etc.) was the product of the "economic substructure." Clearly, Hegel has had a tremendous influence on nineteenth- and twentieth-century thought—including aesthetics.

The reading we have selected from Hegel's writings are actually from his lecture notes for a philosophy of art course he once offered as a university teacher. (Interestingly, Hegel and Schopenhauer tried to offer their philosophy courses at the same time at the same university. In German universities at that time professors were paid according to how many students attended their lectures. Since Hegel was a very popular lecturer, Schopenhauer lost out in his ill-timed competition with Hegel!) In his lecture notes Hegel raises the interesting problem of how we can scientifically study art. That is, how can we scientifically study something that is primarily a mode of escape, relaxation, and enjoyment and that is based, as Plato said, on illusionistic deception? As

Hegel points out, there is a long tradition of scholars who felt the need to defend art against philosophy, science, morality, and religion, all of which seem serious and of practical benefit, as opposed to art that has seemed to many a superficial luxury concerned with play, enjoyment, pleasure, and above all semblance (appearance, deception) and thus not to be taken seriously. Also, as Hegel says, our approach to art is a matter of feeling and not of theoretical or scientific knowledge. How can you scientifically or philosophically analyze something as sensual as music? In addition, far from demanding or wanting some scientific or philosophical rules for how works of art are produced, most people believe very strongly that art is the product of human creativity and inventiveness—where there are no rules—so again, how can there be a science of art where there are no rules? And finally, as Plato said long ago, science deals with intellectual abstractions and generalities whereas art is concerned with concrete sense particulars. In short, how can there be a science of art?

Nonetheless, despite all of these gratifications, art properly understood, Hegel tells us, is of a kind with philosophy and religion—that is, they are all expressions of the mind of man searching for the truth about reality. For Hegel, reality, although mental and spiritual, is not abstract but concrete. Unlike Plato, who held that concrete objects of sense experience were less fully real than the immaterial ideas of perfect Beauty or Justice, Hegel sees reality as the contextual integration of concrete particulars—the whole world as an enormous contextual whole. Think of the world as the incredibly rich texture of sense ideas in the evolving "mind" of the "world soul." In such a vision, art is no mere illusion or appearance but something capable of revealing the truth of reality.

While art is not concerned with abstract, conceptual thought, neither is it interested in sense particulars (birds, flowers, trees, etc.) for their own sake. Instead, art is interested in sense particulars for what they symbolically connote, suggest, intimate, or point to *beyond* themselves (a flower symbolizing, for example, beauty, youth, fertility, and sexual passion). So, while art may not be as highly developed a form of thought about reality as we find in philosophy or religion, it nonetheless, when understood correctly, is interested in indicating, pointing to, or, we might say, imaginatively symbolizing these higher spiritual truths that are also revealed in philosophy and religion. For Hegel, art is to be understood as an early stage in the gradual evolution of human thought.

Schopenhauer accepted Kant's critical limitation of cognitive understanding to what appears to us in sense perception. We cannot cognitively understand things as they exist in and of themselves but only as they appear to our particular sense modalities (the five senses as enjoyed by humans). Like Hegel, Schopenhauer also adopted much of Kant's terminology—distinguishing reason from understanding, and will from cognition, as well as the alignment of reason with will and understanding with cognition. But by introducing elements of Indian thought and biology, Schopenhauer gave this terminological framework a very different meaning from what Kant had intended.

Europeans had not known much about Indian or Chinese thought until the end of the eighteenth and the beginning of the nineteenth centuries. Schopenhauer is one of the first European philosophers not only to read translations of the great Eastern texts (the Hindu *Upanishads* and certain Buddhist texts in particular), but also to incorporate what he understood of their thought into his own neo-Kantian philosophy—which he also combined in a very unusual way with certain biological insights of his day.

The notion of *will,* traceable to Plato and Aristotle, originally meant what we might call volition or will power. Psychologically, we not only desire something and think about how best to get it; we can also decide to "go for it" (or not to). Beginning in the early nineteenth century, however, will came to be associated with what we would now call "unconscious" or "subconscious" motivation. Suppose your grandmother asked you to take three unwanted kittens down to the river and drown them. Of course, you wouldn't want to do this, but suppose you did. You can imagine how the kittens, small as they are, would put up a terrific fight to live. Something like this is what Schopenhauer, following the biological thinking of his day, means by the "will to live." The kittens are not thinking about why they want to continue living; at some level, deeper than any conscious thought, the kittens simply have an instinctual drive to survive. The same applies to human beings. In Jack London's novel *Martin Eden,* the main character of the same name tries to commit suicide by drowning. After carefully thinking it through, he comes to the firm decision to end his life; he dives into the water, swimming deeper and deeper beneath the surface. But suddenly, against his conscious decision, he desperately scrambles to the surface for air—a powerful unconscious, biological will to live, very much like that of the kittens. From this biological perspective, much of our desire to control our own lives consciously and rationally—to choose our goals and move firmly toward them—and our sense that this is who we are and what we are in fact doing at least most of the time, is simply an illusion. To make sure that the species survives, "Mother Nature" has built into each of us (programmed into us) an overwhelming desire to live, to succeed, and to have sex—any of our ancestors without these basic drives simply didn't make the evolutionary cut!

And this is where the interesting connection with Indian Hinduism and Buddhism comes in. Both these Indian thought systems encourage us to overcome these powerful human and biological/animal drives to succeed, survive, procreate—and however powerful these instinctual drives undoubtedly are, Indian thought systems claim to have worked out ways of transcending them. As humans we are capable of seeing through the illusion Nature has programmed inside us and, realizing that it is an illusion, to reject it (that is, not to be ruled or controlled by it). Within the Indian tradition the way to achieve such an insight is known as *yoga,* similar in many ways to what is known within Western traditions as a mystical sense of being at one with the whole world. Instead of thinking of myself, as I usually do, as an individual ego anxious to live and succeed and procreate, it is possible, at least occasionally, to perceive myself as simply a part of the larger universe. If we call the egoistic instinct to live and procreate *will,* then we can understand Schopenhauer's mystical philosophy as the renunciation of will.

But what has this got to do with aesthetics? A lot. For now Schopenhauer interprets disinterested aesthetic experience as the kind of mystical experience in which it is actually possible, at least momentarily, to go beyond one's individual will to live (i.e., ego) to a sense of being part of the entire universe. Imagine you are watching a highly engrossing movie. Don't you find that, at least momentarily and partially, you stop thinking about yourself and your needs and for a time simply get lost in the film, maybe also losing all sense of time? Or listening to music that you really like? Of course, you haven't entirely forgotten about yourself. Should a fire break out or a child in the seat behind you start pouring soda pop down the back of your neck, you will have enough will to move! But to a certain extent, because of the "disinterestedness," "distance" and "detachment" of aesthetic experience, as Kant himself had described it, we do become less conscious of ourselves and our ego needs and drives as we appreciate works of art and objects of natural beauty.

So, according to Schopenhauer, we can understand the world in one of two different ways, the world as it appears to us in our cognitive representations of it and as it really is in itself, that is, as the driving force or will behind the universe—as Schopenhauer expresses it in the title of his most important book, from which the reading in this section comes, *The World as Representation and as Will*. Following Kant, Schopenhauer holds that most of our everyday common sense, as well as our philosophical and scientific perceptions and theories are "representations" of the world from a utilitarian, self-interested human perceptual and cognitive standpoint. But, going beyond Kant, Schopenhauer also holds that there are grades or levels of representation—that is, that some representations reveal more of reality than others. Kant had shown how limited our cognitive representations of the world are; Schopenhauer argues that artistic representations reveal reality far more adequately.

By aesthetically detaching us, at least momentarily, from practical, self-interested concerns, art can penetrate beyond the everyday representation of things, representing instead universal Ideas of reality itself. In everyday perception a tree, for example, is perceived as a three-dimensional object that we cognitively classify as the biological entity known as an elm tree (which we can use for shade, firewood, soil erosion control, etc.), but in the detachment of aesthetic experience that we find in art the tree can represent (or symbolize) ideas of stability, permanence, or the link between heaven and earth. We are still representing the world to ourselves through a sensual intermediary—seeing the link between heaven and earth through the representation (or symbol) of the tree, but we are no longer tied to the pragmatic, utilitarian, functional aspect of mundane perception and cognition (shade, firewood, etc.). Art, in other words, achieves a higher grade or level of representation. In music, however, which is not representational at all, Schopenhauer thinks we are able to grasp the will itself (that is, ultimate reality) directly, without the intermediary of any representation.

Friedrich Nietzsche has exerted a major influence in contemporary aesthetics, art theory and culture studies. Indeed, following Nietzsche's death at the beginning of this century, different generations of scholars, including Martin Heidegger and Gilles Deleuze (in Part III, section B), have found his writings foundational, though for very different reasons and for very different projects. One reason for Nietzsche's many-faceted influence is his radical, revolutionary critique of the foundations of mainstream Western thought. Another reason is traceable to his elusive, aphoristic style, which naturally lends itself to diverse interpretations. As we will see in Part III, the most recent reading of Nietzsche focuses on his radical reinterpretation of truth as an expression of and subservient to the will to live.

Nietzsche accepts Schopenhauer's concept of will as the life-affirming "will to power," but instead of attempting to deny, overcome, and reject this natural, biological impulse, as Schopenhauer does, Nietzsche embraces it as the source of all human value, including the value of truthfulness and especially of aesthetic value. For Nietzsche, art flows from "accumulated and surging will-power" arising out of psychological states of "ecstasy" (states of intoxication and elation). This exuberant will to live is not bad, as Schopenhauer claims, but good. In this sense, art is both an expression of and a contributor to a life-affirming, biologically vigorous, healthy, strong (powerful) will to live.

Under this will to live strongly, people impose their will on things, "idealizing" natural objects and events, transforming them into a more positive, life-affirming image. We humans have the power to create (construct) our own world (or at least our image or interpretation of the world) by emphasizing, exaggerating, and reinforcing ("accentuating") the positive factors and playing down the negative forces we find in "real life."

Art does not therefore "imitate" reality, as Plato and Aristotle and many others have said, but enriches it, adding to reality some of the fullness ("abundance") of the artist's own overflowing will to live and to flourish, the "will to strength and power." In that sense art does not copy reality but improves, idealizes, and "transforms" it. Indeed, art may even *falsify* nature to make it better. And in this way art, according to Nietzsche, is opposed to the pursuit of truth, at least as that has been understood in traditional Western philosophy and science. Art, according to Nietzsche, is the "good will to illusion," transforming reality into a more beautiful—that is, stronger, more life-affirming—human construction than scientific truth would allow. Through art we therefore create our own human world, a world constructed in our own image to better reflect a robust, vigorous, life-affirming human optimism. The "joyful wisdom," as Nietzsche titles his book, is precisely not to let the world get us down but instead to take responsibility for our own creative construction of a life-affirming vision of the world. It is up to us whether to accept the sickly life-denying defeatism of the rationalist philosophers or the robust, flourishing life-affirming and ecstatic vision of the passionate artist.

Art is therefore fundamentally opposed by the fearful, cautious, pessimistic life-denying "anti-artist." For Nietzsche the anti-art, anti-life culprit is always Greek rationality (the idea of truth for truth's sake) and Christianity. "Turn the other cheek," "the meek shall inherit the earth" is for Nietzsche a kind of "slave morality" that tries to glorify and valorize all the life-denying forces our human biology is geared up to suppress. For Nietzsche rational philosophy has conspired with Christianity to undermine the real source of human value—our innate love of life ("sucking its blood and making it thinner"). Whatever supports that will to live and love of life (above all, art and music) is good and should be encouraged; whatever denies it (rationality, most philosophy, including Plato and Schopenhauer, and above all Christianity) should be exposed for what it really is and soundly defeated.

For late twentieth-century writers, such as Deleuze, Foucault, and Lyotard, it is this aspect of Nietzsche's thought that has seemed so promising. All human values, including the value of truth, are to be judged by a higher standard of their value to the flourishing of life. We do not judge a theory by whether it is true or not; rather, we judge the value of truthfulness itself by whether it increases or decreases our love and zest for life.

For Nietzsche, all truth and beauty is therefore relative to humans. They are biological expressions and supports of the will to live vigorously and strongly. The physically and mentally strong and healthy person sees and embraces as true the world as "overflowing with beauty." Beauty is an extension and projection of this joyful zest for living. The artist projects his or her overflowing will to live on to the world, thereby "humanizing" the world.

Thus, the source of beauty for us humans is the excess energy of the robust, healthy, vigorous, and life-affirming person, and by the same token, the source of all ugliness is the weak, timid, overly cautious, life-denying person. Traced to its biological roots, ugliness is a sign of disease, fatigue, and exhaustion, while beauty is a sign of life-affirming strength and robust health.

Schopenhauer therefore got it precisely backwards when he interpreted art as the great rejection of the life force, the will to live and flourish. Art, according to Nietzsche, is the expression and instigator of a life-affirming will to power. Despite Schopenhauer's rejection of Christianity in favor of Hindu concepts, all Schopenhauer has really done, Nietzsche tells us, is to reinterpret the Christian renunciation of life in a new, quasi-Eastern manner.

Schopenhauer is therefore wrong to think of beauty as an escape from Nature's trap. Plato was closer to the truth, Nietzsche maintains, when he traces the initial stimulus in the pursuit of beauty to the sexual desire for the body of a beautiful young person. Nonetheless, Nietzsche opposed the attempts of traditional philosophers, including Plato, to subordinate art to morality. *L'Art pour l'art*, "Art for art's sake" should mean, "Let morality go to the devil"! Yet the fact that art does not have a moral purpose does not mean that it has no purpose whatever. For Nietzsche art has a profound biological purpose. Art celebrates and strengthens the will to live and flourish, the "will to power"—the strong, healthy, optimistic Yes to life. Even tragedy should not be seen as the resignation of human weakness in the face of Nature's ultimate triumph over us, but as the joyous celebration of human courage in the face of even the worst of life's terrors.

Nietzsche accepts Plato's idea of the quarrel between poetry and prose—that is, between art and philosophy, passion and reason—but whereas Plato sides with prose, philosophy and reason, Nietzsche takes the side of poetry, passion, and art.

Later (in Part III, section B) we will see how Deleuze interprets Nietzsche as providing an even more radical critique than Kant of cognitive, scientific, intellectual understanding. Kant argued, in effect, that our cognitive apparatus was only equipped to help us make sense of phenomena, that is, things as they appear to humans through the five senses—not as they really are in themselves. According to Deleuze, Nietzsche carries this critique a step further, arguing that philosophy, science, and the search for truth must ultimately be judged by their contribution to our biological life. According to this interpretation, Nietzsche is attempting a radically new definition of truth. The old, traditional, rationalist conception of truth (as the correspondence of thought to reality, however painful, demeaning, or demoralizing that might turn out to be) is life denying and life defeating; against this Nietzsche proposes a completely new definition and conception of truth, a *pragmatic* conception according to which truth is a life-affirming value, a higher truth supporting that view of the world which strengthens the flourishing and vigor of life. Only by enriching our lives can truth be valued; otherwise not. By the old rationalist standard, says Nietzsche, art is the "good will to *illusion*," but by the new pragmatic standard art is valued for its new pragmatic "truthfulness."

The Sublime and Beautiful

EDMUND BURKE

ON A SUPERFICIAL VIEW, we may seem to differ very widely from each other in our reasonings, and no less in our pleasures: but notwithstanding this difference, which I think to be rather apparent than real, it is probable that the standard both of reason and Taste is the same in all human creatures. For if there were not some principles of judgment as well as of sentiment common to all mankind, no hold could possibly be taken either on their reason or their passions, sufficient to maintain the ordinary correspondence of life. It appears indeed to be generally acknowledged, that with regard to truth and falsehood there is something fixed. We find people in their disputes continually appealing to certain tests and standards which are allowed on all sides, and are supposed to be established in our common nature. But there is not the same obvious concurrence in any uniform or settled principles which relate to Taste. It is even commonly supposed that this delicate and aerial faculty, which seems too volatile to endure even the chains of a definition, cannot be properly tried by any test, nor regulated by any standard. There is so continual a call for the exercise of the reasoning faculty, and it is so much strengthened by perpetual contention, that certain maxims of right reason seem to be tacitly settled amongst the most ignorant. The learned have improved on this rude science, and reduced those maxims into a system. If Taste has not been so happily cultivated, it was not that the subject was barren, but that the labourers were few or negligent; for to say the truth, there are not the same interesting motives to impel us to fix the one, which urge us to ascertain the other. And after all, if men differ in their opinion concerning such matters, their difference is not attended with the same important consequences, else I make no doubt but that the logic of Taste, if I may be allowed the expression, might very possibly be as well digested, and we might come to discuss matters of this nature with as much certainty, as those which seem more immediately within the province of mere reason. And indeed it is very necessary at the entrance into such an enquiry, as our present, to make this point as clear as possible; for if Taste has no fixed principles, if the imagination is not affected according to some invariable and certain laws, our labour is like to be employed to very little purpose; as it must be judged an useless, if not an absurd undertaking, to lay down rules for caprice, and to set up for a legislator of whims and fancies.

The term Taste, like all other figurative terms, is not extremely accurate: the thing which we understand by it, is far from a simple and determinate idea in the minds of most men, and it is therefore liable to uncertainty and confusion. I have no great opinion of a definition, the celebrated remedy for the cure of this disorder. For when we define, we seem in danger of circumscribing nature within the bounds of our own notions, which we often take up by hazard, or embrace on trust, or form out of a limited and partial consideration of the object before us, instead of extending our ideas to take in all that nature comprehends, according to her manner of combining. We are limited in our enquiry by the strict laws to which we have submitted at our setting out. . . .

I mean by the word Taste no more than that faculty, or those faculties of the mind which are affected with, or which form a judgment of the works of imagination and the elegant arts. This

From A Philosophical Enquiry into the Origin of Our Ideas of the Sublime and the Beautiful *(London: J. Dodsley, 1770)*

Edmund Burke: The Sublime and Beautiful67

is, I think, the most general idea of that word, and what is the least connected with any particular theory. And my point in this enquiry is to find whether there are any principles, on which the imagination is affected, so common to all, so grounded and certain, as to supply the means of reasoning satisfactorily about them. And such principles of Taste, I fancy there are; however paradoxical it may seem to those, who on a superficial view imagine, that there is so great a diversity of Tastes both in kind and degree, that nothing can be more indeterminate.

All the natural powers in man, which I know, that are conversant about external objects, are the Senses; the Imagination; and the Judgment. And first with regard to the senses. We do and we must suppose, that as the conformation of their organs are nearly, or altogether the same in all men, so the manner of perceiving external objects is in all men the same, or with little difference. We are satisfied that what appears to be light to one eye, appears light to another; that what seems sweet to one palate, is sweet to another; that what is dark and bitter to this man, is likewise dark and bitter to that; and we conclude in the same manner of great and little, hard and soft, hot and cold, rough and smooth; and indeed of all the natural qualities and affections of bodies. If we suffer ourselves to imagine, that their senses present to different men different images of things, this sceptical proceeding will make every sort of reasoning on every subject vain and frivolous, even that sceptical reasoning itself, which had persuaded us to entertain a doubt concerning the agreement of our perceptions. But as there will be very little doubt that bodies present similar images to the whole species, it must necessarily be allowed, that the pleasures and the pains which every object excites in one man, it must raise in all mankind, whilst it operates naturally, simply, and by its proper powers only; for if we deny this, we must imagine, that the same cause operating in the same manner, and on subjects of the same kind, will produce different effects, which would be highly absurd. Let us first consider this point in the sense

of Taste, and the rather as the faculty in question has taken its name from that sense. All men are agreed to call vinegar sour, honey sweet, and aloes bitter; and as they are all agreed in finding these qualities in those objects, they do not in the least differ concerning their effects with regard to pleasure and pain. They all concur in calling sweetness pleasant, and sourness and bitterness unpleasant. Here there is no diversity in their sentiments; and that there is not appears fully from the consent of all men in the metaphors which are taken from the sense of Taste. A sour temper, bitter expressions, bitter curses, a bitter fate, are terms well and strongly understood by all. And we are altogether as well understood when we say, a sweet disposition, a sweet person, a sweet condition, and the like. It is confessed, that custom, and some other causes, have made many deviations from the natural pleasures or pains which belong to these several Tastes; but then the power of distinguishing between the natural and the acquired relish remains to the very last. A man frequently comes to prefer the Taste of tobacco to that of sugar, and the flavour of vinegar to that of milk; but this makes no confusion in Tastes, whilst he is sensible that the tobacco and vinegar are not sweet, and whilst he knows that habit alone has reconciled his palate to these alien pleasures. Even with such a person we may speak, and with sufficient precision, concerning Tastes. But should any man be found who declares, that to him tobacco has a Taste like sugar, and that he cannot distinguish between milk and vinegar; or that tobacco and vinegar are sweet, milk bitter, and sugar sour, we immediately conclude that the organs of this man are out of order, and that his palate is utterly vitiated. We are as far from conferring with such a person upon Tastes, as from reasoning concerning the relations of quantity with one who should deny that all the parts together were equal to the whole. We do not call a man of this kind wrong in his notions, but absolutely mad. Exceptions of this sort in either way, do not at all impeach our general rule, nor make us conclude that men have various principles concerning the relations of quantity, or Taste of things. So that when it is said, Taste cannot be disputed, it can only mean, that no one can strictly answer what pleasure or pain some particular man may find from the Taste of some particular thing This indeed cannot be disputed; but we may dispute, and with sufficient clearness too, concerning the things which are naturally pleasing or disagreeable to the sense. But when we talk of any peculiar or acquired relish, then we must know the habits, the prejudices, or the distempers of this particular man, and we must draw our conclusion from those.

This agreement of mankind is not confined to the Taste solely. The principle of pleasure derived from sight is the same in all. Light is more pleasing than darkness. Summer, when the earth is clad in green, when the heavens are serene and bright, is more agreeable than winter, when every thing makes a different appearance. I never remember that any thing beautiful, whether a man, a beast, a bird, or a plant, was ever shewn, though it were to an hundred people, that they did not all immediately agree that it was beautiful, though some might have thought that it fell short of their expectation, or that other things were still finer. I believe no man thinks a goose to be more beautiful than a swan, or imagines that what they call a Friezland hen excels a peacock. It must be observed too, that the pleasures of the sight are not near so complicated, and confused, and altered by unnatural habits and associations, as the pleasures of the Taste are; because the pleasures of the sight more commonly acquiesce in themselves; and are not so often altered by considerations which are independent of the sight itself. But things do not spontaneously present themselves to the palate as they do to the sight; they are generally applied to it, either as food or as medicine; and from the qualities which they possess for nutritive or medicinal purposes, they often form the palate by degrees, and by force of these associations. . . .

Thus the pleasure of all the senses, of the sight, and even the Taste, that most ambiguous of the senses, is the same in all, high and low, learned and unlearned.

Besides the ideas, with their annexed pains and pleasures, which are presented by the sense; the mind of man possesses a sort of creative power of its own; either in representing at pleasure the images of things in the order and manner in which they were received by the senses, or in combining those images in a new manner, and according to a different order. This power is called Imagination; and to this belongs whatever is called wit, fancy, invention, and the like. But it must be observed, that this power of the imagination is incapable of producing any thing absolutely new; it can only vary the disposition of those ideas which it has received from the senses. Now the imagination is the most extensive province of pleasure and pain, as it is the region of our fears and our hopes, and of all our passions that are connected with them; and whatever is calculated to affect the imagination with these commanding ideas, by force of any original natural impression, must have the same power pretty equally over all men. For since the imagination is only the representative of the senses, it can only be pleased or displeased with the images from the same principle on which the sense is pleased or displeased with the realities; and consequently there must be just as close an agreement in the imaginations as in the senses of men. A little attention will convince us that this must of necessity be the case.

But in the imagination, besides the pain or pleasure arising from the properties of the natural object, a pleasure is perceived from the resemblance, which the imitation has to the original; the imagination, I conceive, can have no pleasure but what results from one or other of these causes. And these causes operate pretty uniformly upon all men, because they operate by principles in nature, and which are not derived from any particular habits or advantages. . . .

Now as the pleasure of resemblance is that which principally flatters the imagination, all men are nearly equal in this point, as far as their knowledge of the things represented or compared extends. The principle of this knowledge is very much accidental, as it depends upon experience and observation, and not on the strength or weakness of any natural faculty; and it is from this difference in knowledge that what we commonly, though with no great exactness, call a difference in Taste proceeds. A man to whom sculpture is new, sees a barber's block, or some ordinary piece of statuary; he is immediately struck and pleased, because he sees something like an human figure; and entirely taken up with this likeness, he does not at all attend to its defects. No person, I believe, at the first time of seeing a piece of imitation ever did. Some time after, we suppose that this novice lights upon a more artificial work of the same nature; he now begins to look with contempt on what he admired at first; not that he admired it even then for its unlikeness to a man, but for that general though inaccurate resemblance which it bore to the human figure. What he admired at different times in these so different figures, is strictly the same; and though his knowledge is improved, his Taste is not altered. Hitherto his mistake was from a want of knowledge in art, and this arose from his inexperience; but he may be still deficient from a want of knowledge in nature. For it is possible that the man in question may stop here, and that the masterpiece of a great hand may please him no more than the middling performance of a vulgar artist; and this not for want of better or higher relish, but because all men do not observe with sufficient accuracy on the human figure to enable them to judge properly of an imitation of it. . . .

In poetry, and other pieces of imagination, the same parity may be observed. It is true, that one man is charmed with Don Bellianis, and reads Virgil coldly; whilst another is transported with the Eneid, and leaves Don Bellianis to children. These two men seem to have a Taste very different from each other; but in fact they differ very little. In both these pieces, which inspire such opposite sentiments, a tale exciting admiration is told; both are full of action, both are passionate, in both are voyages, battles, triumphs, and continual changes of fortune. The admirer of Don Bellianis perhaps does not understand the refined language of the Eneid, who it if was degraded into the style of the Pilgrim's Progress,

might feel it in all its energy, on the same principle which made him an admirer of Don Bellianis.

In his favourite author he is not shocked with the continual breaches of probability, the confusion of times, the offences against manners, the trampling upon geography; for he knows nothing of geography and chronology, and he has never examined the grounds of probability. . . .

So far then as Taste belongs to the imagination, its principle is the same in all men; there is no difference in the manner of their being affected, nor in the causes of the affection; but in the *degree* there is a difference, which arises from two causes principally; either from a greater degree of natural sensibility, or from a closer and longer attention to the object. To illustrate this by the procedure of the senses in which the same difference is found, let us suppose a very smooth marble table to be set before two men; they both perceive it to be smooth, and they are both pleased with it, because of this quality. So far they agree. But suppose another, and after that another table, the latter still smoother than the former, to be set before them. It is now very probable that these men, who are so agreed upon what is smooth, and in the pleasure from thence, will disagree when they come to settle which table has the advantage in point of polish. Here is indeed the great difference between Tastes, when men come to compare the excess or diminution of things which are judged by degree and not by measure. Nor is it easy, when such a difference arises, to settle the point, if the excess or diminution be not glaring. If we differ in opinion about two quantities, we can have recourse to a common measure, which may decide the question with the utmost exactness; and this I take it is what gives mathematical knowledge a greater certainty than any other. But in things whose excess is not judged by greater or smaller, as smoothness and roughness, hardness and softness, darkness and light, the shades of colours, all these are very easily distinguished when the difference is any way considerable, but not when it is minute, for want of some common measures which perhaps may never come to be discovered. In these nice cases, supposing the acuteness of the sense equal, the greater attention and habit in such things will have the advantage. In the question about the tables, the marble polisher will unquestionably determine the most accurately. But notwithstanding this want of a common measure for settling many disputes relative to the senses and their representative the imagination, we find that the principles are the same in all, and that there is no disagreement until we come to examine into the preeminence or difference of things, which brings us within the province of the judgment.

So long as we are conversant with the sensible qualities of things, hardly any more than the imagination seems concerned; little more also than the imagination seems concerned when the passions are represented, because by the force of natural sympathy they are felt in all men without any recourse to reasoning, and their justness recognized in every breast. Love, grief, fear, anger, joy, all these passions have in their turns affected every mind; and they do not affect it in an arbitrary or casual manner, but upon certain, natural and uniform principles. But as many of the works of imagination are not confined to the representation of sensible objects, nor to efforts upon the passions, but extend themselves to the manners, the characters, the actions, and designs of men, their relations, their virtues and vices, they come within the province of the judgment, which is improved by attention and by the habit of reasoning. All these make a very considerable part of what are considered as the objects of Taste; and Horace sends us to the schools of philosophy and the world for our instruction in them. Whatever certainty is to be acquired in morality and the science of life; just the same degree of certainty have we in what relates to them in works of imitation. Indeed it is for the most part in our skill in manners, and in the observances of time and place, and of decency in general, which is only to be learned in those schools to which Horace recommends us, that what is called Taste by way of distinction, consists; and which is in reality no other than a more refined judgment. On the whole it appears to me, that what is called

Taste, in its most general acceptation, is not a simple idea, but is partly made up of a perception of the primary pleasures of sense, of the secondary pleasures of the imagination, and of the conclusions of the reasoning faculty, concerning the various relations of these, and concerning the human passions, manners and actions. All this is requisite to form Taste, and the ground-work of all these is the same in the human mind; for as the senses are the great originals of all our ideas, and consequently of all our pleasures, if they are not uncertain and arbitrary, the whole ground-work of Taste is common to all, and therefore there is a sufficient foundation for a conclusive reasoning on these matters.

Whilst we consider Taste, merely according to its nature and species, we shall find its principles entirely uniform; but the degree in which these principles prevail in the several individuals of mankind, is altogether as different as the principles themselves are similar. For sensibility and judgment, which are the qualities that compose what we commonly call a *Taste*, vary exceedingly in various people. From a defect in the former of these qualities, arises a want of Taste; a weakness in the latter, constitutes a wrong or a bad one. . . .

The cause of a wrong Taste is a defect of judgment. And this may arise from a natural weakness of understanding (in whatever the strength of that faculty may consist) or, which is much more commonly the case, it may arise from a want of proper and well-directed exercise, which alone can make it strong and ready. Besides that ignorance, inattention, prejudice, rashness, levity, obstinacy, in short, all those passions, and all those vices which pervert the judgment in other matters, prejudice it no less in this its more refined and elegant province. These causes produce different opinions upon every thing which is an object of the understanding, without inducing us to suppose, that there are no settled principles of reason. And indeed on the whole one may observe, that there is rather less difference upon matters of Taste among mankind, than upon most of those which depend upon the naked reason; and that men are far better agreed on the excellence of a description in Virgil, than on the truth or falsehood of a theory of Aristotle.

A rectitude of judgment in the arts which may be called a good Taste, does in a great measure depend upon sensibility; because if the mind has no bent to the pleasures of the imagination, it will never apply itself sufficiently to works of that species to acquire a competent knowledge in them. But, though a degree of sensibility is requisite to form a good judgment, yet a good judgment does not necessarily arise from a quick sensibility of pleasure; it frequently happens that a very poor judge, merely by force of a greater complexional sensibility, is more affected by a very poor piece, than the best judge by the most perfect; for as every thing new, extraordinary, grand, or passionate is well calculated to affect such a person, and that the faults do not affect him, his pleasure is more pure and unmixed; and as it is merely a pleasure of the imagination, it is much higher than any which is derived from a rectitude of the judgment; the judgment is for the greater part employed in throwing stumbling blocks in the way of the imagination, in dissipating the scenes of its enchantment, and in tying us down to the disagreeable yoke of our reason. . . .

Before I leave this subject I cannot help taking notice of an opinion which many persons entertain, as if the Taste were a separate faculty of the mind, and distinct from the judgment and imagination; a species of instinct by which we are struck naturally, and at the first glance, without any previous reasoning with the excellencies, or the defects of a composition. So far as the imagination and the passions are concerned, I believe it true, that the reason is little consulted; but where disposition, where decorum, where congruity are concerned, in short wherever the best Taste differs from the worst, I am convinced that the understanding operates and nothing else; and its operation is in reality far from being always sudden, or when it is sudden, it is often far from being right. Men of the best Taste by consideration, come frequently to change these early and precipitate judgments which the mind from its aversion to neutrality and doubt loves to form on the spot. It is known that the Taste (whatever it is) is improved exactly as we improve our judgment, by extending our knowledge, by a steady attention to our object, and by frequent exercise. . . . Whatever is fitted in any sort to excite the ideas of pain, and danger, that is to say, whatever is in any sort terrible, or is conversant about terrible objects, or operates in a manner analogous to terror, is a source of the *sublime;* that is, it is productive of the strongest emotion which the mind is capable of feeling. I say the strongest emotion, because I am satisfied the ideas of pain are much more powerful than those which enter on the part of pleasure. . . . When danger or pain press too nearly, they are incapable of giving any delight, and are simply terrible; but at certain distances, and with certain modifications, they may be, and they are delightful, as we every day experience. . . .

The passion caused by the great and sublime in *nature,* when those causes operate most powerfully, is Astonishment; and astonishment is that state of the soul, in which all its motions are suspended, with some degree of horror. In this case the mind is so entirely filled with its object, that it cannot entertain any other, nor by consequence reason on that object which employs it. Hence arises the great power of the sublime, that far from being produced by them, it anticipates our reasonings, and hurries us on by an irresistible force. Astonishment, as I have said, is the effect of the sublime in its highest degree; the inferior effects are admiration, reverence and respect.

No passion so effectually robs the mind of all its powers of acting and reasoning as fear. For fear being an apprehension of pain or death, it operates in a manner that resembles actual pain. Whatever therefore is terrible, with regard to sight, is sublime too, whether this cause of terror, be endued with greatness of dimensions or not; for it is impossible to look on any thing as trifling, or contemptible, that may be dangerous. There are many animals, who though far from being large, are yet capable of raising ideas of the sublime, because they are considered as objects of terror. As serpents and poisonous animals of almost all kinds. And to things of great dimensions, if we annex an adventitious idea of terror, they become without comparison greater. A level plain of a vast extent on land, is certainly no mean idea; the prospect of such a plain may be as extensive as a prospect of the ocean; but can it ever fill the mind with any thing so great as the ocean itself? This is owing to several causes, but it is owing to none more than this, that the ocean is an object of no small terror. Indeed terror is in all cases whatsoever, either more openly or latently the ruling principle of the sublime. . . . To make any thing very terrible, obscurity seems in general to be necessary. When we know the full extent of any danger, when we can accustom our eyes to it, a great deal of the apprehension vanishes. Every one will be sensible of this, who considers how greatly night adds to our dread, in all cases of danger, and how much the notions of ghosts and goblins, of which none can form clear ideas, affect minds, which give credit to the popular tales concerning such sorts of beings. Besides these things which *directly* suggest the idea of danger, and those which produce a similar effect from a mechanical cause, I know of nothing sublime which is not some modification of power. And this branch rises as naturally as the other two branches, from terror, the common stock of every thing that is sublime. The idea of power at first view, seems of the class of these indifferent ones, which may equally belong to pain or to pleasure. But in reality, the affection arising from the idea of vast power, is extremely remote from that neutral character. For first, we must remember, that the idea of pain, in its highest degree, is much stronger than the highest degree of pleasure; and that it preserves the same superiority through all the subordinate gradations. From hence it is, that where the chances for equal degrees of suffering or enjoyment are in any sort equal, the ideas of the suffering must always be prevalent. And indeed the ideas of pain, and above all of death, are so very affecting, that whilst we remain in the presence of whatever is

supposed to have the power of inflicting either, it is impossible to be perfectly free from terror. . . .

Greatness of dimension, is a powerful cause of the sublime. This is too evident, and the observation too common, to need any illustration; it is not so common, to consider in what ways greatness of dimension, vastness of extent, or quantity, has the most striking effect. For certainly, there are ways, and modes, wherein the same quantity of extension shall produce greater effects than it is found to do in others. Extension is either in length, height, or depth. Of these the length strikes least; an hundred years of even ground will never work such an effect as a tower an hundred yards high, or a rock or mountain of that altitude. I am apt to imagine likewise, that height is less grand than depth; and that we are more struck at looking down from a precipice, than at looking up at an object of equal height, but of that I am not very positive. A perpendicular has more force in forming the sublime, than an inclined plane; and the effects of a rugged and broken surface seem stronger than where it is smooth and polished. It would carry us out of our way to enter in this place into the cause of these appearances; but certain it is they afford a large and fruitful field of speculation. However, it may not be amiss to add to these remarks upon magnitude; that, as the great extreme of dimension is sublime, so the last extreme of littleness is in some measure sublime likewise; when we attend to the infinite divisibility of matter, when we pursue animal life into these excessively small, and yet organized beings, that escape the nicest inquisition of the sense, when we push our discoveries yet downward, and consider those creatures so many degrees yet smaller, and the still diminishing scale of existence, in tracing which the imagination is lost as well as the sense, we become amazed and confounded at the wonders of minuteness; nor can we distinguish in its effect this extreme of littleness from the vast itself. For division must be infinite as well as addition; because the idea of a perfect unity can no more be arrived at, than that of a compleat whole to which nothing may be added.

Another source of the sublime, is *infinity;* if it does not rather belong to the last. Infinity has a tendency to fill the mind with that sort of delightful horror, which is the most genuine effect, and truest test of the sublime. There are scarce any things which can become the objects of our senses that are really, and in their own nature infinite. But the eye not being able to perceive the bounds of many things, they seem to be infinite, and they produce the same effects as if they were really so. We are deceived in the like manner, if the parts of some large object are so continued to any indefinite number, that the imagination meets no check which may hinder its extending them at pleasure.

Another source of greatness is *Difficulty.* When any work seems to have required immense force and labour to effect it, the idea is grand. . . .

Magnificence is likewise a source of the sublime. A great profusion of things which are splendid or valuable in themselves, is *magnificent.* The starry heaven, though it occurs so very frequently to our view, never fails to excite an idea of grandeur. This cannot be owing to any thing in the stars themselves, separately considered. The number is certainly the cause. The apparent disorder augments the grandeur, for the appearance of care is highly contrary to our ideas of magnificence. Besides, the stars lie in such apparent confusion, as makes it impossible on ordinary occasions to reckon them. This gives them the advantage of a sort of infinity. In works of art, this kind of grandeur, which consists in multitude, is to be very cautiously admitted; because, a profusion of excellent things is not to be attained, or with too much difficulty. . . .

It is my design to consider beauty as distinguished from the sublime; and in the course of the enquiry, to examine how far it is consistent with it. But previous to this, we must take a short review of the opinions already entertained of this quality; which I think are hardly to be reduced to any fixed principles; because men are used to talk of beauty in a figurative manner, that is to say, in a manner extremely uncertain, and indeterminate. By beauty I mean, that quality or those qualities in bodies by which they cause love, or some passion similar to it.

I confine this definition to the merely sensible qualities of things, for the sake of preserving the utmost simplicity in a subject which must always distract us, whenever we take in those various causes of sympathy which attach us to any persons or things from secondary considerations, and not from the direct force which they have merely on being viewed. I likewise distinguish love, by which I mean that satisfaction which arises to the mind upon contemplating any thing beautiful, of whatsoever nature it may be, from desire or lust; which is an energy of the mind, that hurries us on to the possession of certain objects, that do not affect us as they are beautiful, but by means altogether different. We shall have a strong desire for a woman of no remarkable beauty; whilst the greatest beauty in men, or in other animals, though it causes love, yet excites nothing at all of desire. Which shews that beauty, and the passion caused by beauty, which I call love, is different from desire, though desire may sometimes operate along with it; but it is to this latter that we must attribute those violent and tempestuous passions, and the consequent emotions of the body which attend what is called love in some of its ordinary acceptations, and not to the effects of beauty merely as it is such. . . .

Beauty is a thing much too affecting not to depend upon some positive qualities. And, since it is no creature of our reason, since it strikes us without any reference to use, and even where no use at all can be discerned, since the order and method of nature is generally very different from our measures and proportions, we must conclude that beauty is, for the greater part, some quality in bodies, acting mechanically upon the human mind by the intervention of the senses. We ought therefore to consider attentively in what manner those sensible qualities are disposed, in such things as experience we find beautiful, or which excite in us the passion of love or some correspondent affection. . . .

The most obvious point that presents itself to us in examining any object, is its extent or quantity. And what degree of extent prevails in bodies, that are held beautiful, may be gathered from the usual manner of expression concerning it. I am told that in most languages, the objects of love are spoken of under diminutive epithets. . . . A great beautiful thing, is a manner of expression scarcely ever used; but that of a great ugly thing, is very common. There is a wide difference between admiration and love. The sublime, which is the cause of the former, always dwells on great objects, and terrible; the latter on small ones, and pleasing; we submit to what we admire, but we love what submits to us; in one case we are forced, in the other we are flattered into compliance. In short, the ideas of the sublime and the beautiful stand on foundations so different, that it is hard, I had almost said impossible, to think of reconciling them in the same subject, without considerably lessening the effect of the one or the other upon the passions. So that attending to their quantity, beautiful objects are comparatively small. . . .

The next property constantly observable in such objects is *Smoothness*. A quality so essential to beauty, that I do not now recollect any thing beautiful that is not smooth. In trees and flowers, smooth leaves are beautiful; smooth slopes of earth in gardens; smooth streams in the landscape; smooth coats of birds and beasts in animal beauties; in fine women, smooth skins; and in several sorts of ornamental furniture, smooth and polished surfaces. A very considerable part of the effect of beauty is owing to this quality; indeed the most considerable. For take any beautiful object, and give it a broken and rugged surface, and however well formed it may be in other respects, it pleases no longer. . . . For indeed any ruggedness, any sudden projection, any sharp angle, is in the highest degree contrary to that idea.

But as perfectly beautiful bodies are not composed of angular parts, so their parts never continue long in the same right line.

They vary their direction every moment, and they change under the eye by a deviation contin-

ually carrying on, but for whose beginning or end you will find it difficult to ascertain a point. The view of a beautiful bird will illustrate this observation. Here we see the head increasing insensibly to the middle, from whence it lessens gradually until it mixes with the neck; the neck loses itself in a larger swell, which continues to the middle of the body, when the whole decreases again to the tail; the tail takes a new direction; but it soon varies its new course; it blends again with the other parts; and the line is perpetually changing, above, below, upon every side. In this description I have before me the idea of a dove; it agrees very well with most of the conditions of beauty. It is smooth and downy; its parts are (to use that expression) melted into one another; you are presented with no sudden protuberance through the whole, and yet the whole is continually changing.

An air of robustness and strength is very prejudicial to beauty. An appearance of *delicacy*, and even of fragility, is almost essential to it. Whoever examines the vegetable or animal creation, will find this observation to be founded in nature. It is not the oak, the ash, or the elm, or any of the robust trees of the forest, which we consider as beautiful; they are awful and majestic; they inspire a sort of reverence. It is the delicate myrtle, it is the orange, it is the almond, it is the jessamine, it is the vine, which we look on as vegetable beauties. It is the flowery species, so remarkable for its weakness and momentary duration, that gives us the liveliest idea of beauty, and elegance.

It is no small bar in the way of our enquiry into the cause of our passions, that the occasion of many of them are given, and that their governing motions are communicated at a time when we have not capacity to reflect on them; at a time of which all sort of memory is worn out of our minds. For besides such things as affect us in various manners according to their natural powers, there are associations made at that early season, which we find it very hard afterwards to distinguish from natural effects. Not to mention the unaccountable antipathies which we find in many persons, we all find it impossible to remember when a steep became more terrible than a plain; or fire or water more dreadful than a clod of earth; though all these are very probably either conclusions from experience, or arising from the premonitions of others; and some of them impressed, in all likelihood, pretty late. But as it must be allowed that many things affect us after a certain manner, not by any natural powers they have for that purpose, but by association; so it would be absurd on the other hand, to say that all things affect us by association only; since some things must have been originally and naturally agreeable or disagreeable, from which the others derive their associated powers; and it would be, I fancy, to little purpose to look for the cause of our passions in association, until we fail of it in the natural properties of things.

Of the Standard of Taste

DAVID HUME

THE GREAT VARIETY OF TASTE, as well as of opinion, which prevails in the world, is too obvious not to have fallen under every one's observation. Men of the most confined knowledge are able to remark a difference of taste in the narrow circle of their acquaintance, even where the persons have been educated under the same government, and have early imbibed the same prejudices. But those, who can enlarge their view to contemplate distant nations and remote ages, are still more surprised at the great inconsistence and contrariety. We are apt to call *barbarous* whatever departs widely from our own taste and apprehension: But soon find the epithet of reproach retorted on us. And the highest arrogance and self-conceit is at last startled, on observing an equal assurance on all sides, and scruples, amidst such a contest of sentiment, to pronounce positively in its own favour.

As this variety of taste is obvious to the most careless enquirer; so will it be found, on examination, to be still greater in reality than in appearance. The sentiments of men often differ with regard to beauty and deformity of all kinds, even while their general discourse is the same. There are certain terms in every language, which import blame, and others praise; and all men, who use the same tongue, must agree in their application of them. Every voice is united in applauding elegance, propriety, simplicity, spirit in writing; and in blaming fustian, affectation, coldness, and a false brilliancy: But when critics come to particulars, this seeming unanimity vanishes; and it is found, that they had affixed a very different meaning to their expressions. In all matters of opinion and science, the case is opposite: The difference among men is there oftener found to lie in generals than in particulars; and to be less in reality than in appearance. An explanation of the terms commonly ends the controversy; and the disputants are surprized to find, that they had been quarrelling, while at bottom they agreed in their judgment.

Those who found morality on sentiment, more than on reason, are inclined to comprehend ethics under the former observation, and to maintain, that, in all questions, which regard conduct and manners, the difference among men

From T. H. Greene and T. H. Grose, eds., Essays Moral, Political, and Literary *by David Hume (Edinburgh, Cadell, Donaldson, and Creech, 1777).*

is really greater than at first sight it appears. It is indeed obvious, that writers of all nations and all ages concur in applauding justice, humanity, magnanimity, prudence, veracity; and in blaming the opposite qualities. Even poets and other authors, whose compositions are chiefly calculated to please the imagination, are yet found, from Homer down to Fenelon, to inculcate the same moral precepts, and to bestow their applause and blame on the same virtues and vices. This great unanimity is usually ascribed to the influence of plain reason; which, in all these cases, maintains similar sentiments in all men, and prevents those controversies, to which the abstract sciences are so much exposed. So far as the unanimity is real, this account may be admitted as satisfactory: But we must also allow that some part of the seeming harmony in morals may be accounted for from the very nature of language. The word *virtue,* with its equivalent in every tongue, implies praise; as that of *vice* does blame: And no one, without the most obvious and grossest impropriety, could affix reproach to a term, which in general acceptation is understood in a good sense; or bestow applause, where the idiom requires disapprobation. . . .

The merit of delivering true general precepts in ethics is indeed very small. Whoever recommends any moral virtues, really does no more than is implied in the terms themselves. That people, who invented the word *charity,* and used it in a good sense, inculcated more clearly and much more efficaciously, the precept, *be charitable,* than any pretended legislator or prophet, who should insert such a *maxim* in his writings. Of all expressions, those, which, together with their other meaning, imply a degree either of blame or approbation, are the least liable to be perverted or mistaken.

It is natural for us to seek a *Standard of Taste;* a rule, by which the various sentiments of men may be reconciled; at least, a decision afforded, confirming one sentiment, and condemning another.

There is a species of philosophy, which cuts off all hopes of success in such an attempt, and rep-

resents the impossibility of ever attaining any standard of taste. The difference, it is said, is very wide between judgment and sentiment. All sentiment is right; because sentiment has a reference to nothing beyond itself, and is always real, wherever a man is conscious of it. But all determinations of the understanding are not right; because they have a reference to something beyond themselves, to wit, real matter of fact; and are not always conformable to that standard. Among a thousand different opinions which different men may entertain of the same subject, there is one, and but one, that is just and true; and the only difficulty is to fix and ascertain it. On the contrary, a thousand different sentiments, excited by the same object, are all right: Because no sentiment represents what is really in the object. It only marks a certain conformity or relation between the object and the organs or faculties of the mind; and if that conformity did not really exist, the sentiment could never possibly have being. Beauty is no quality in things themselves: It exists merely in the mind which contemplates them; and each mind perceives a different beauty. One person may even perceive deformity, where another is sensible of beauty; and every individual ought to acquiesce in his own sentiment, without pretending to regulate those of others. To seek the real beauty, or real deformity, is as fruitless an enquiry, as to pretend to ascertain the real sweet or real bitter. According to the disposition of the organs, the same object may be both sweet and bitter; and the proverb has justly determined it to be fruitless to dispute concerning tastes. It is very natural, and even quite necessary, to extend this axiom to mental, as well as bodily taste; and thus common sense, which is so often at variance with philosophy, especially with the sceptical kind, is found, in one instance at least, to agree in pronouncing the same decision.

But though this axiom, by passing into a proverb, seems to have attained the sanction of common sense; there is certainly a species of common sense which opposes it, at least serves to modify and restrain it. Whoever would assert an equality of genius and elegance between Ogilby and Milton, or Bunyan and Addison, would be thought to defend no less an extravagance, than if he had maintained a mole-hill to be as high as Teneriffe, or a pond as extensive as the ocean. Though there may be found persons, who give the preference to the former authors, no one pays attention to such a taste; and we pronounce without scruple the sentiment of these pretended critics to be absurd and ridiculous. The principle of the natural equality of tastes is then totally forgot, and while we admit it on some occasions, where the objects seem near an equality, it appears an extravagant paradox, or rather a palpable absurdity, where objects so disproportioned are compared together.

It is evident that none of the rules of composition are fixed by reasoning *a priori,* or can be esteemed abstract conclusions of the understanding, from comparing those habitudes and relations of ideas, which are eternal and immutable. Their foundation is the same with that of all the practical sciences, experience; nor are they any thing but general observations, concerning what has been universally found to please in all countries and in all ages. Many of the beauties of poetry and even of eloquence are founded on falsehood and fiction, on hyperboles, metaphors, and an abuse or perversion of terms from their natural meaning. To check the sallies of the imagination, and to reduce every expression to geometrical truth and exactness, would be the most contrary to the laws of criticism; because it would produce a work, which, by universal experience, has been found the most insipid and disagreeable. But though poetry can never submit to exact truth, it must be confined by rules of art, discovered to the author either by genius or observation. If some negligent or irregular writers have pleased, they have not pleased by their transgressions of rule or order, but in spite of these transgressions: They have possessed other beauties, which were conformable to just criticism; and the force of these beauties has been able to overpower censure, and give the mind a satisfaction superior to the disgust arising from

the blemishes. Ariosto pleases; but not by his monstrous and improbable fictions, by his bizarre mixture of the serious and comic styles, by the want of coherence in his stories, or by the continual interruptions of his narration. He charms by the force and clearness of his expression, by the readiness and variety of his inventions, and by his natural pictures of the passions, especially those of the gay and amorous kind: And however his faults may diminish our satisfaction, they are not able entirely to destroy it. Did our pleasure really arise from those parts of his poem, which we denominate faults, this would be no objection to criticism in general: It would only be an objection to those particular rules of criticism, which would establish such circumstances to be faults, and would represent them as universally blameable. If they are found to please, they cannot be faults; let the pleasure, which they produce, be ever so unexpected and unaccountable.

But though all the general rules of art are founded only on experience and on the observation of the common sentiments of human nature, we must not imagine, that, on every occasion, the feelings of men will be comfortable to these rules. Those finer emotions of the mind are of a very tender and delicate nature, and require the concurrence of many favourable circumstances to make them play with facility and exactness, according to their general and established principles. The least exterior hindrance to such small springs, or the least internal disorder, disturbs their motion, and confounds the operation of the whole machine. When we would make an experiment of this nature, and would try the force of any beauty or deformity, we must choose with care a proper time and place, and bring the fancy to a suitable situation and disposition. A perfect serenity of mind, a recollection of thought, a due attention to the object; if any of these circumstances be wanting, our experiment will be fallacious, and we shall be unable to judge of the catholic and universal beauty. The relation, which nature has placed between the form and the sentiment, will at least be more obscure; and it will require greater accuracy to trace and discern it. We shall be able to ascertain its influence not so much from the operation of each particular beauty, as from the durable admiration, which attends those works, that have survived all the caprices of mode and fashion, all the mistakes of ignorance and envy.

The same Homer, who pleased at Athens and Rome two thousand years ago, is still admired at Paris and at London. All the changes of climate, government, religion, and language, have not been able to obscure his glory. Authority or prejudice may give a temporary vogue to a bad poet or orator; but his reputation will never be durable or general. When his compositions are examined by posterity or by foreigners, the enchantment is dissipated, and his faults appear in their true colours. On the contrary, a real genius, the longer his works endure, and the more wide they are spread, the more sincere is the admiration which he meets with. Envy and jealousy have too much place in a narrow circle; and even familiar acquaintance with his person may diminish the applause due to his performances: But when these obstructions are removed, the beauties, which are naturally fitted to excite agreeable sentiments, immediately display their energy; and while the world endures, they maintain their authority over the minds of men.

It appears then, that, amidst all the variety and caprice of taste, there are certain general principles of approbation or blame, whose influence a careful eye may trace in all operations of the mind. Some particular forms or qualities, from the original structure of the internal fabric, are calculated to please, and others displease; and if they fail of their effect in any particular instance, it is from some apparent defect or imperfection in the organ. A man in a fever would not insist on his palate as able to decide concerning flavours; nor would one, affected with the jaundice, pretend to give a verdict with regard to colours. In each creature, there is a sound and defective state; and the former alone can be supposed to afford us a true standard of taste and sentiment. If, in the sound state of the organ, there be an entire or a considerable uniformity of sentiment among men, we may thence derive an idea of the perfect beauty; in like manner as the appearance of objects in day-light, to the eye of a man in health, is denominated their true and real colour, even while colour is allowed to be merely a phantasm of the senses.

Many and frequent are the defects in the internal organs which prevent or weaken the influence of those general principles, on which depends our sentiment of beauty or deformity. Though some objects, by the structure of the mind, be naturally calculated to give pleasure, it is not to be expected, that in every individual the pleasure will be equally felt. Particular incidents and situations occur, which either throw a false light on the objects, or hinder the true from conveying to the imagination the proper sentiment and perception.

One obvious cause, why many feel not the proper sentiment of beauty, is the want of that *delicacy* of imagination, which is requisite to convey a sensibility of those finer emotions. This delicacy every one pretends to: Every one talks of it; and would reduce every kind of taste or sentiment to its standard. But as our intention in this essay is to mingle some light of the understanding with the feeling of sentiment, it will be proper to give a more accurate definition of delicacy, than has hitherto been attempted. And not to draw our philosophy from too profound a source, we shall have recourse to a noted story in *Don Quixote*.

It is with good reason, says Sancho to the squire with the great nose, that I pretend to have a judgment in wine: This is a quality hereditary in our family. Two of my kinsmen were once called to give their opinion of a hogshead, which was supposed to be excellent, being old and of a good vintage. One of them tastes it; considers it; and after mature reflection pronounces the wine to be good, were it not for a small taste of leather, which he perceived in it. The other, after using the same precautions, gives also his verdict in favour of the wine; but with the reserve of a taste of iron, which he could easily distinguish.

You cannot imagine how much they were both ridiculed for their judgment. But who laughed in the end? On emptying the hogshead, there was found at the bottom, an old key with a leathern thong tied to it.

The great resemblance between mental and bodily taste will easily teach us to apply this story. Though it be certain that beauty and deformity, more than sweet and bitter, are not qualities in objects, but belong entirely to the sentiment, internal or external; it must be allowed, that there are certain qualities in objects, which are fitted by nature to produce those particular feelings. Now as these qualities may be found in a small degree, or may be mixed and confounded with each other, it often happens, that the taste is not affected with such minute qualities, or is not able to distinguish all the particular flavours, amidst the disorder, in which they are presented. Where the organs are so fine, as to allow nothing to escape them; and at the same time so exact as to perceive every ingredient in the composition: This we call delicacy of taste, where we employ these terms in the literal or metaphorical sense. Here then the general rules of beauty are of use; being drawn from established models, and from the observation of what pleases or displeases, when presented singly and in a high degree: And if the same qualities, in a continued composition and in a smaller degree, affect not the organs with a sensible delight or uneasiness, we exclude the person from all pretensions to this delicacy. To produce these general rules or avowed patterns of composition is like finding the key with the leathern thong; which justified the verdict of Sancho's kinsmen, and confounded those pretended judges who had condemned them. Though the hogshead had never been emptied, the taste of the one was still equally delicate, and that of the other equally dull and languid: But it would have been more difficult to have proved the superiority of the former, to the conviction of every by-stander. In like manner, though the beauties of writing had never been methodized, or reduced to general principles; though no excellent models had ever

been acknowledged; the different degrees of taste would still have subsisted, and the judgment of one man been preferable to that of another; but it would not have been so easy to silence the bad critic, who might always insist upon his particular sentiment, and refuse to submit to his antagonist. But when we show him an avowed principle of art; when we illustrate this principle by examples, whose operation, from his own particular taste, he acknowledges to be conformable to the principle; when we prove, that the same principle may be applied to the present case, where he did not perceive or feel its influence: He must conclude, upon the whole, that the fault lies in himself, and that he wants the delicacy, which is requisite to make him sensible of every beauty and every blemish, in any composition or discourse.

It is acknowledged to be the perfection of every sense or faculty, to perceive with exactness its most minute objects, and allow nothing to escape its notice and observation. The smaller the objects are, which become sensible to the eye, the finer is that organ, and the more elaborate its make and composition. A good palate is not tried by strong flavours; but by a mixture of small ingredients, where we are still sensible of each part, notwithstanding its minuteness and its confusion with the rest. In like manner, a quick and acute perception of beauty and deformity must be the perfection of our mental taste; nor can a man be satisfied with himself while he suspects, that any excellence or blemish in a discourse has passed him unobserved. In this case, the perfection of the man, and the perception of the sense or feeling, are found to be united. A very delicate palate, on many occasions, may be a great inconvenience both to a man himself and to his friends: But a delicate taste of wit or beauty must always be a desirable quality; because it is the source of all the finest and most innocent enjoyments, of which human nature is susceptible. In this decision the sentiments of all mankind are agreed. Wherever you can ascertain a delicacy of taste, it is sure to meet with approbation; and the best way of ascertaining it is to appeal to those models and principles, which have been established by the uniform consent and experience of nations and ages.

But though there be naturally a wide difference in point of delicacy between one person and another, nothing tends further to encrease and improve this talent, than *practice* in a particular art, and the frequent survey or contemplation of a particular species of beauty. When objects of any kind are first presented to the eye or imagination, the sentiment, which attends them, is obscure and confused; and the mind is, in a great measure, incapable of pronouncing concerning their merits or defects. The taste cannot perceive the several excellences of the performance; much less distinguish the particular character of each excellency, and ascertain its quality and degree. If it pronounce the whole in general to be beautiful or deformed, it is the utmost that can be expected; and even this judgment, a person, so unpractised, will be apt to deliver with great hesitation and reserve. But allow him to acquire experience in those objects, his feeling becomes more exact and nice: He not only perceives the beauties and defects of each part, but marks the distinguishing species of each quality, and assigns it suitable praise or blame. A clear and distinct sentiment attends him through the whole survey of the objects; and he discerns that very degree and kind of approbation or displeasure, which each part is naturally fitted to produce. The mist dissipates, which seemed formerly to hang over the object: The organ acquires greater perfection in its operations; and can pronounce, without danger of mistake, concerning the merits of every performance. In a word, the same address and dexterity, which practice gives to the execution of any work, is also acquired by the same means, in the judging of it.

So advantageous is practice to the discernment of beauty, that, before we can give judgment on any work of importance, it will even be requisite, that that very individual performance be more than once perused by us, and be surveyed in different lights with attention and deliberation. There is a flutter or hurry of thought which attends the first perusal of any piece, and which confounds the genuine sentiment of beauty. The relation of the parts is not discerned: The true

characters of style are little distinguished: The several perfections and defects seem wrapped up in a species of confusion, and present themselves indistinctly to the imagination. Not to mention, that there is a species of beauty, which, as it is florid and superficial, pleases at first; but being found incompatible with a just expression either of reason or passion, soon palls upon the taste, and is then rejected with disdain, at least rated at a much lower value.

It is impossible to continue in the practice of contemplating any order of beauty, without being frequently obliged to form *comparisons* between the several species and degrees of excellence, and estimating their proportion to each other. A man, who has had no opportunity of comparing the different kinds of beauty, is indeed totally unqualified to pronounce an opinion with regard to any object presented to him. By comparison alone we fix the epithets of praise or blame, and learn how to assign the due degree of each. The coarsest daubing contains a certain lustre of colours and exactness of imitation, which are so far beauties, and would affect the mind of a peasant or Indian with the highest admiration. The most vulgar ballads are not entirely destitute of harmony or nature; and none but a person familiarized to superior beauties, would pronounce their numbers harsh, or narration uninteresting. A great inferiority of beauty gives pain to a person conversant in the highest excellence of the kind, and is for that reason pronounced a deformity: As the most finished object, with which we are acquainted, is naturally supposed to have reached the pinnacle of perfection, and to be entitled to the highest applause. One accustomed to see, and examine, and weigh the several performances, admired in different ages and nations, can only rate the merits of a work exhibited to his view, and assign its proper rank among the productions of genius.

But to enable a critic the more fully to execute this undertaking, he must preserve his mind free from all *prejudice,* and allow nothing to enter into his consideration, but the very object which is submitted to his examination. We may observe, that every work of art, in order to produce its due effect on the mind, must be surveyed in a certain point of view, and cannot be fully relished by persons, whose situation, real or imaginary, is not conformable to that which is required by the performance. An orator addresses himself to a particular audience, and must have a regard to their particular genius, interests, opinions, passions, and prejudices; otherwise he hopes in vain to govern their resolution, and inflame their affections. Should they even have entertained some prepossessions against him, however unreasonable, he must not overlook this disadvantage; but, before he enters upon the subject, must endeavour to conciliate their affection, and acquire their good graces. A critic of a different age or nation, who should peruse this discourse, must have all these circumstances in his eye, and must place himself in the same situation as the audience, in order to form a true judgment of the oration. In like manner, when any work is addressed to the public, though I should have a friendship or enmity with the author, I must depart from this situation; and considering myself as a man in general, forget, if possible, my individual being and my peculiar circumstances. A person influenced by prejudice, complies not with this condition, but obstinately maintains his natural position, without placing himself in that point of view, which the performance supposes. If the work be addressed to persons of a different age or nation, he makes no allowance for their peculiar views and prejudices; but, full of the manners of his own age and country, rashly condemns what seemed admirable in the eyes of those for whom alone the discourse was calculated. If the work be executed for the public, he never sufficiently enlarges his comprehension, or forgets his interest as a friend or enemy, as a rival or commentator. By this means, his sentiments are perverted; nor have the same beauties and blemishes the same influence upon him, as if he had imposed a proper violence on his imagination, and had forgotten himself for a moment. So far his taste evidently departs from the true standard; and of consequence loses all credit and authority.

It is well known, that in all questions, submitted to the understanding, prejudice is destructive of sound judgment, and perverts all operations of the intellectual faculties: It is no less contrary to good taste; nor has it less influence to corrupt our sentiment of beauty. It belongs to *good sense* to check its influence in both cases; and in this respect, as well as in many others, reason, if not an essential part of taste, is at least requisite to the operations of this latter faculty. In all the nobler productions of genius, there is a mutual relation and correspondence of parts; nor can either the beauties or blemishes be perceived by him, whose thought is not capacious enough to comprehend all those parts, and compare them with each other, in order to perceive the consistence and uniformity of the whole. Every work of art has also a certain end or purpose, for which it is calculated; and is to be deemed more or less perfect, as it is more or less fitted to attain this end. The object of eloquence is to persuade, of history to instruct, of poetry to please by means of the passions and the imagination. These ends we must carry constantly in our view, when we peruse any performance; and we must be able to judge how far the means employed are adapted to their respective purposes. Besides every kind of composition, even the most poetical, is nothing but a chain of propositions and reasonings; not always, indeed, the justest and most exact, but still plausible and specious, however disguised by the colouring of the imagination. The persons introduced in tragedy and epic poetry, must be represented as reasoning, and thinking, and concluding, and acting, suitably to their character and circumstances; and without judgment, as well as taste and invention, a poet can never hope to succeed in so delicate an undertaking. Not to mention, that the same excellence of faculties which contributes to the improvement of reason, the same clearness of conception, the same exactness of distinction, the same vivacity of apprehension, are essential to the operations of true taste, and are its infallible concomitants. It seldom, or never happens, that a man of sense, who has experience in any art, cannot judge of its beauty; and it is no less rare to meet with a man who has a just taste without a sound understanding.

Thus, though the principles of taste be universal, and, nearly, if not entirely the same in all men; yet few are qualified to give judgment of any work of art, or establish their own sentiment as the standard of beauty. The organs of internal sensation are seldom so perfect as to allow the general principles their full play, and produce a feeling correspondent to those principles. They either labour under some defect, or are vitiated by some disorder; and by that means, excite a sentiment, which may be pronounced erroneous. When the critic has no delicacy, he judges without any distinction, and is only affected by the grosser and more palpable qualities of the object: The finer touches pass unnoticed and disregarded. Where he is not aided by practice, his verdict is attended with confusion and hesitation. Where no comparison has been employed, the most frivolous beauties, such as rather merit the name of defects, are the objects of his admiration. Where he lies under the influence of prejudice, all his natural sentiments are perverted. Where good sense is wanting, he is not qualified to discern the beauties of design and reasoning, which are the highest and most excellent. Under some or other of these imperfections, the generality of men labour; and hence a true judge in the finer arts is observed, even during the most polished ages, to be so rare a character: Strong sense, united to delicate sentiment, improved by practice, perfected by comparison, and cleared of all prejudice, can alone entitle critics to this valuable character; and the joint verdict of such, wherever they are to be found, is the true standard of taste and beauty.

But where are such critics to be found? By what marks are they to be known? How distinguish them from pretenders? These questions are embarrassing; and seem to throw us back into the same uncertainty, from which, during the course of this essay, we have endeavoured to extricate ourselves.

But if we consider the matter aright, these are questions of fact, not of sentiment. Whether any particular person be endowed with good sense and a delicate imagination, free from prejudice, may often be the subject of dispute, and be liable to great discussion and enquiry; but that such a character is valuable and estimable will be agreed in by all mankind. Where these doubts occur, men can do no more than in other disputable questions, which are submitted to the understanding: They must produce the best arguments, that their invention suggests to them; they must acknowledge a true and decisive standard to exist somewhere, to wit, real existence and matter of fact; and they must have indulgence to such as differ from them in their appeals to this standard. It is sufficient for our present purpose, if we have proved, that the taste of all individuals is not upon an equal footing, and that some men in general, however difficult to be particularly pitched upon, will be acknowledged by universal sentiment to have a preference above others.

But in reality the difficulty of finding, even in particulars, the standard of taste, is not so great as it is represented. Though in speculation, we may readily avow a certain criterion in science and deny it in sentiment, the matter is found in practice to be much more hard to ascertain in the former case than in the latter. Theories of abstract philosophy, systems of profound theology, have prevailed during one age: In a successive period, these have been universally exploded: Their absurdity has been detected: Other theories and systems have supplied their place, which again gave place to their successors: And nothing has been experienced more liable to the revolutions of chance and fashion than these pretended decisions of science. The case is not the same with beauties of eloquence and poetry. Just expressions of passion and nature are sure, after a little time, to gain public applause, which they maintain for ever. . . .

Though men of delicate taste be rare, they are easily to be distinguished in society, by the soundness of their understanding and the superiority of their faculties above the rest of mankind. The ascendant, which they acquire, gives a prevalence to that lively approbation, with which they receive any productions of genius, and renders it generally predominant. Many men, when left to themselves, have but a faint and dubious perception of beauty, who yet are capable of relishing any fine stroke, which is pointed out to them. Every convert to the admiration of the real poet or orator is the cause of some new conversion. And though prejudices may prevail for a time, they never unite in celebrating any rival to the true genius, but yield at last to the force of nature and just sentiment. Thus, though a civilized nation may easily be mistaken in the choice of their admired philosopher, they never have been found long to err, in their affection for a favorite epic or tragic author.

But notwithstanding all our endeavours to fix a standard of taste, and reconcile the discordant apprehensions of men, there still remain two sources of variation, which are not sufficient indeed to confound all the boundaries of beauty and deformity, but will often serve to produce a difference in the degrees of our approbation or blame. The one is the different humours of particular men; the other, the particular manners and opinions of our age and country. The general principles of taste are uniform in human nature: Where men vary in their judgments, some defect or perversion in the faculties may commonly be remarked; proceeding either from prejudice, from want of practice, or want of delicacy; and there is just reason for approving one taste, and condemning another. But where there is such a diversity in the internal frame or external situation as is entirely blameless on both sides, and leaves no room to give one the preference above the other; in that case a certain degree of diversity in judgment is unavoidable, and we seek in vain for a standard, by which we can reconcile the contrary sentiments.

A young man, whose passions are warm, will be more sensibly touched with amorous and tender images, than a man more advanced in years, who takes pleasure in wise, philosophical reflections concerning the conduct of life and modera-

tion of the passions. . . . Vainly would we, in such cases, endeavour to enter into the sentiments of others, and divest ourselves of those propensities, which are natural to us. We choose our favourite author as we do our friend, from a conformity of humour and disposition. Mirth or passion, sentiment or reflection; whichever of these most predominates in our temper, it gives us a peculiar sympathy with the writer who resembles us.

One person is more pleased with the sublime; another with the tender; a third with raillery. One has a strong sensibility to blemishes, and is extremely studious of correctness: Another has a more lively feeling of beauties, and pardons twenty absurdities and defects for one elevated or pathetic stroke. The ear of this man is entirely turned towards conciseness and energy; that man is delighted with a copious, rich, and harmonious expression. Simplicity is affected by one; ornament by another. Comedy, tragedy, satire, odes, have each its partisans, who prefer that particular species of writing to all others. It is plainly an error in a critic, to confine his approbation to one species or style of writing, and condemn all the rest. But it is almost impossible not to feel a predilection for that which suits our particular turn and disposition. Such preferences are innocent and unavoidable, and can never reasonably be the object of dispute, because there is no standard, by which they can be decided.

For a like reason, we are more pleased, in the course of our reading, with pictures and characters, that resemble objects which are found in our own age or country, than with those which describe a different set of customs. It is not without some effort, that we reconcile ourselves to the simplicity of ancient manners, and behold princesses carrying water from the spring, and kings and heroes dressing their own victuals. We may allow in general, that the representation of such manners is no fault in the author, nor deformity in the piece, but we are not so sensibly touched with them. For this reason, comedy is not easily transferred from one age or nation to another. . . .

The Critique of Judgment

IMMANUEL KANT

THE JUDGMENT OF TASTE is not a judgment of knowledge, and is consequently not scientific but aesthetic; by which I mean that it is a judgment for which the ground can only be subjective. All our ideas, even those of sensation, can, however, refer to objects (and then they signify a reality corresponding to an empirical idea), except only those which refer to the feelings of pleasure and pain. Here nothing is indicated in the object, but we have a feeling of ourselves as we are affected by the idea. . . .

The satisfaction connected with our idea of the existence of an object is called interest. This satisfaction is therefore always also related to the faculty of desire, either as affecting it or as necessarily connected with what affects it. But when the question is whether a thing be beautiful, we do not want to know whether anything depends or can depend, for us or for anybody else, on the existence of the object, but only how we estimate it in mere contemplation. . . .

Everything which pleases us through our reason when we simply conceive of it is *good*. What thus pleases us only as a means to something else we call useful or *good for something;* other things which please us for their own sake we call *good in themselves*. Both always imply the conception of a purpose, and consequently the relation of our reason to an act, or possible act, of will, and therefore a satisfaction in the existence of an object or an act, that is to say, some sort of interest.

To deem anything good I must always know what sort of thing it ought to be; I must have a conception of it. To find beauty in a thing, this is not necessary. Flowers, arabesques, decorative intertwining of lines in what is called foliation, mean nothing and depend on no definite conception, and yet please us. . . .

Of all these three kinds of satisfaction, we may say that the satisfaction of taste in the beautiful is the only one that is disinterested and free. . . .

Taste is the faculty of estimating an object or a type of idea in respect of satisfaction or dissatisfaction without any interest. The object of such satisfaction is called *beautiful*.

A thing of which every one recognizes that his own satisfaction in its beauty is without any interest, must be estimated by him to afford a ground of satisfaction for all men. For since his satisfaction does not depend upon any inclination of his own (nor upon any other conscious interest), and since he feels himself absolutely free in the satisfaction which he accords to the object, he can find no private peculiarity, affecting him alone, as the cause of his satisfaction; and consequently he must regard the satisfaction as caused by something which he can presuppose in every other man. So he must think he has reason for attributing a like satisfaction to every man. Hence he will speak of beauty as if it were a quality of the object, and as if his judgment were scientific—that is, constituted a knowledge of the object by conceptions of it—though it is only aesthetical. . . . So a claim to subjective universality must be implied in the judgment of taste. . . .

A man says the *thing* is beautiful; he does not merely expect the assent of others to his judgment of satisfaction because they have agreed with him before; he *demands* it of them. He blames them when they judge differently, and denies their taste. . . .

From Philosophies of Beauty from Socrates to Robert Bridges, *ed. and trans. E. F. Carritt (Oxford: Clarendon Press, 1931).*

If we estimate objects merely by conceptions, all idea of beauty is lost. So there can be no rule by which anybody can be compelled to recognize anything as beautiful. No one allows his judgment on the beauty of a coat, a house, a flower, to be coerced by reasons or principles. He wants to have the thing before him, just as if his satisfaction were sensuous; yet, if he then calls it beautiful, he claims to have the universal voice on his side, whereas sensation is private and decides nothing beyond the satisfaction of the man who has it. . . .

If the pleasure in a given object came first and only the universal communicability of the pleasure were to be attributed to the idea of the object by the judgment of taste, we should have a contradiction. For such a pleasure would be nothing but mere pleasantness of sensation, and so could naturally only have private validity, as depending immediately on our perception of the object.

Consequently it is the universal communicability of our state of mind, in having the idea, which must occasion in our minds the judgment of taste and be a condition of it; and the pleasure in the thing must be the result of this. But nothing can be universally communicated except knowledge, and ideas so far as they belong to knowledge. For only so far are ideas objective, and only so have they a common point of reference in which the ideas of all men are bound to agree. Now when we have to think that what makes us judge our idea to be universally communicable is merely subjective—is in fact no conception of the object—it can be nothing but the state of mind consisting in the mutual relation of our faculties for forming ideas, so far as these faculties employ a perception for purposes of knowledge in general.

The faculties of knowledge brought into play by the idea are in such a case in free play, because no definite conception of the object's nature confines them to any particular principle of knowledge. So the state of mind in having such an idea must be a feeling of the free play of our faculties for ideas in using a perception for purposes of

knowledge in general. Now for any idea of an *object,* and so for knowledge in general, there are required *Imagination* to combine the manifold apprehended and *Understanding* to afford a conception which can unify the ideas. This state of the free play of our faculties of knowledge in the idea of an object must be one that can be shared universally; for knowledge (being the distinction of an object, with which all perceptions, to whomever they belong, must agree) is the only kind of idea that is valid for every man. . . .

This merely subjective (aesthetic) estimation of the object, or of our idea of it, precedes our pleasure in it, and occasions this pleasure in the harmony of our faculties of knowledge. And the universal, though subjective, validity of that satisfaction which we connect with the idea of the object which we call beautiful, is effected solely by the universality in men of these subjective conditions for estimating objects. . . .

In a judgment of taste we impute, as necessary, to everybody the pleasure we feel ourselves; as if the beauty we ascribe to a thing were to be considered a property following from the conception of it; though beauty, apart from relation to our feeling, is itself nothing. . . .

So far as the faculty of desire can be stimulated to activity by conceptions, that is by a purpose, it is called the will. But a thing or a state of mind or an action is said to be adapted to purpose, though its possibility does not necessarily presuppose a purpose. This is so whenever we can only explain or understand the thing's possibility by supposing it to be brought about by a final cause, or in other words to have been devised by a will according to the idea of some principle. The adaptation, then, can be without a purpose, so far as we do not attribute the thing's arrangement to a will, though we could only give any intelligible account of its possibility by so attributing it. . . .

Any purpose, regarded as the cause of our pleasure, implies an interest to occasion our judgment about the pleasing object. So it can be no purpose of ours which occasions the judgment of taste [which is without interest]. Nor can the judgment of taste be occasioned by any idea of an objective purpose (that is, of the object's possibility depending on design) or by any conception of the good. For it is an aesthetic, not a scientific judgment, and so involves no conception of the thing's character nor of its possibility through causes within or without itself, but only the relation set up between our faculties for forming ideas. . . . So the occasion for a judgment of taste can be nothing but a seeming adaptation in our idea of an object, without any purpose either objective or belonging to ourselves. And a seeming adaptation is the merely general form of adaptation in our perception of objects, so far as we are aware of it. This effects the satisfaction, which we estimate as universally communicable though we are using no conception; and that is the occasion of a judgment of taste. . . .

A mere color, for instance the green of a lawn, and a mere tone (as distinguished from sound and noise), for instance that of a violin, are by most people called beautiful in themselves, though both seem to depend upon the mere matter [as opposed to form] of our ideas, namely simple sensations, and so only to deserve the name of pleasant or charming. We may, however, note here that the sensations of color and tone have the claim to be counted beautiful, so far, but so far only, as they are *pure*. For purity is a character of their form and also the only character of these ideas which can certainly be universally appreciated. . . .

In painting, sculpture, and indeed all the arts of form such as architecture and gardening, so far as these are fine arts, the essential thing is the design. And herein it is not what pleases the senses, but what satisfies us by its form that fundamentally concerns taste. . . .

The form of all sensible objects, both of those that are external, and also indirectly of those that are internal, is either shape or play. The latter is either play of shapes in space (pantomime and dance) or mere play of sensations in time. The charm of color or the pleasant tone of the instrument may be added, but in shape the design, and

in play the composition, are the proper objects of pure judgments of taste. . . .

Emotion, a feeling in which pleasure is aroused only through a momentary check and ensuing stronger outflow of our vital force, has nothing to do with beauty. But sublimity, which involves the feeling of emotion, demands a criterion other than that on which taste relies. The pure judgment of taste is occasioned neither by charm, nor emotion. . . .

The formal element in the idea of a thing, that is the harmonizing of its multifarious constituents into a unity, without any thought what this unity ought to be, indicates by itself absolutely no objective adaptation; for, since we do not consider this unity as the end which the thing ought to fulfil, there remains nothing but the adaptation of ideas in our mind. This announces indeed a certain adaptation of our mental condition and a fitness therein to picture a presented shape, but not the perfection of any object. For the object is not thought of as serving any purpose.

There are two different kinds of beauty: free beauty (*pulchritudo vaga*), and merely dependent beauty (*pulchritudo adhaerens*). The former does not presuppose any conception of what the thing ought to be; the latter does, and presupposes also the thing's conformity to it. . . . Greek decorative designs, foliation for margins or on wallpapers, and so on, mean nothing in themselves; they represent nothing of which we have any definite conception and are free beauties. We can also count as belonging to the same class what in music are called Fantasies, or compositions without theme, and in fact all music without words. . . . But the beauty of mankind, whether man, woman, or child, of a horse and of a building, whether church, palace, arsenal, or summer-house, presupposes a purpose which settles what the thing ought to be (that is, a conception of its ideal) and is consequently only dependent beauty. Just as we saw that to combine what is sensuously pleasant with beauty, which should properly consist in form only, prevents a pure judgment of taste, so also, we now see, does the combination of the good with beauty. . . . Properly, perfection gains nothing through beauty, nor beauty through perfection; but when we compare our perception of an object with our conception of what it ought to be, since we cannot help combining the idea at the same time with our own feeling about it, the whole faculty of forming ideas of things profits by the harmony of the two mental states. . . .

By this distinction we can adjust many differences between critics of beauty, by pointing out that one is emphasizing free and the other dependent beauty.

There can be no objective rule of taste to determine by conceptions what is to be beautiful. . . .

The beautiful agrees with the sublime in this, that both please us in themselves, and that neither presupposes a judgment of sense nor yet a scientific judgment (about the nature of an object) but a reflective judgment. Consequently the satisfaction in neither depends on a sensation, as that in the pleasant does, nor yet on a definite conception, as does that in the good. . . . But there are important and obvious differences between them. The beautiful in nature belongs to the form of a thing, which consists in having boundaries; the sublime, on the other hand, can be found even in a formless thing, so far as in it or by occasion of it we find an idea of boundlessness and yet attach to it the thought of a whole. So the beautiful seems to be taken as representing some quite indefinite conception of the understanding, the sublime as representing a similar conception of the reason. So our satisfaction in beauty is connected with the idea of quality, that of sublimity with one of quantity. And they are clearly different in kind. Beauty brings with it directly a feeling of vital stimulus, and so can be united with charm and play of imagination. But our feeling for the sublime is only an indirect pleasure, since it is produced by the experience of a momentary check to our vital powers, which are thereby stimulated immediately to a correspondingly stronger outflow. Consequently, as an emotion, it seems to be no play of our imagination but its serious employment. So it cannot be united with charm.

And as the mind is not merely attracted by the object, but also, alternately, repelled, our satisfaction in sublimity implies less a positive pleasure than admiration or respect, and might well be called a negative pleasure.

The fundamental and most important difference between the sublime and the beautiful is, however, as follows. (In the first instance we naturally consider only the sublimity of natural things, for in art sublimity is conditioned by agreement with nature). The independent beauty of nature has a fitness of form, whereby the thing seems, as it were, intended for our judgment, and so becomes in itself an object of satisfaction. On the contrary, whatever arouses in us, by its mere perception and without reasoning, the feeling of sublimity, may have a form that seems very ill-fitted to our judgment, unsuited to our powers of perception, and, as it were, doing violence to our imagination; and yet it will be judged all the more sublime.

We at once see from this that we generally express ourselves incorrectly when we call any natural thing sublime, though we can quite properly call many such things beautiful. For how can we designate with a term of approval that which we apprehend as in its nature chaotic? We can only say that the thing serves to present to us a sublimity which is to be found in the mind. For the sublime proper can be embodied in no sensible form. . . .

The analysis of sublimity involves a division, which was not needed by that of beauty, into the Mathematical and the Dynamic sublime. The feeling of sublimity is characterized by an emotion connected with our estimation of the object; whereas taste for beauty must find and maintain the mind in calm contemplation. But since the sublime pleases us, this emotion must be estimated as if it were adapted. Consequently the emotion is related, through the imagination, either to the faculty of knowledge or to that of desire. In either relation we only estimate the perception as adapted to the faculty, not to any end or interest. So what is really the suitability of an emotion to our faculty of knowledge is ascribed to the object as something mathematically affecting our imagination, but its suitability to our faculty of desire as doing so dynamically. So the object can be found sublime in either of these two ways. . . .

The [mathematical] sublime is that in comparison with which everything else is small. . . . Thus considered, nothing which can be an object of the senses is to be called sublime. Our imagination strives for a progress to infinity, but our reason demands a complete totality as an idea to be realized. So the very fact that our power of measuring sensible objects is inadequate to this idea, awakes the feeling of a power in us superior to sense. It is the use which we naturally make of certain objects to arouse this feeling, when we judge about them, that is absolutely great, though the object of sense is not; and any other use is comparatively trivial. So not the object should be called sublime, but rather the state of mind caused by an idea which excites our reflective faculty of judgment. So we can add to our previous formulas for explaining sublimity this: a thing is sublime, if the mere power of thinking it is evidence of a mental power surpassing all standards of sense. . . .

Examples of mathematical sublimity in nature for mere intuition are afforded by all instances where we are given not so much a larger numerical conception as a large unit to be a standard of measurement for the imagination. A tree, which is itself measured by the height of a man, gives us a standard for measuring a mountain; and if this were a mile high it could serve as the unit for the number expressing the earth's diameter, so as to make the latter intuitable. The earth's diameter serves as a standard for the known planetary system, that again for the milky way; and the immeasurable host of milky way systems, which are called nebulae, and which presumably in their turn compose a system of the same kind, forbids us to expect any limit here. . . .

When we estimate nature as being dynamically sublime, our idea of it must be fearful. . . . We can, however, consider an object as fearful without fearing it, if we so estimate it that we imagine circumstances in which we might choose to resist it, and that then all resistance would be perfectly vain. . . . A man in a state of fear is as incapable of judging nature to be sublime as one possessed by longing or appetite is of judging about beauty . . . Bold, overhanging rocks which seem to threaten us, storm-clouds piled up in heaven and moving on their way with lightnings and thunders, volcanoes with all their destructive might, hurricanes leaving a wake of devastation, the boundless ocean in its anger, a high waterfall in a mighty river:—such things reduce our power of resistance to impotence as compared with their might. But the sight of them is attractive in proportion to their fearfulness so long as we find ourselves in security, and we readily call such things sublime because they elevate the powers of our souls above their wonted level and discover in us a faculty for resistance of quite a different kind, which encourages us to measure ourselves against the apparent omnipotence of nature. . . . Nature is not aesthetically estimated to be sublime so far as it excites fear, but because it calls up in us the power, which is beyond nature, to regard all that we care for—wealth, health, life itself—as small. Thus we come to regard the might of nature, on which for all these things we are utterly dependent, as nevertheless, in relation to us and our personality, a power beneath which we need not bend if the maintenance of our highest principles were at stake. So nature is here called elevated or sublime just because she elevates the imagination to picture situations in which the mind can realize the proper sublimity of its own destiny as surpassing nature itself. . . .

The charms of beautiful nature which are to be met with in such plenty, fused in her beautiful forms, belong either to the modifications of light (in coloring) or of sound (in tones). For these are the only sensations which afford not only mere sense-feeling but reflection upon the form of these affections of our senses; and consequently contain, as it were, a language which nature speaks to us and which seems to have an inward meaning. So the whiteness of lilies seems to affect the mind with ideas of innocence; and, following the order of the seven colors from red to violet, we get the ideas of (I) Sublimity, (2) Courage, (3) Candor, (4) Friendliness, (5) Modesty, (6) Constancy, (7) Tenderness. . . .

The following contradiction arises about the principle of taste:

(I) *Thesis*. The judgments of taste cannot depend on conceptions, for otherwise we could argue about them, that is to say, give conclusive proofs.

(2) *Antithesis*. The judgments of taste must depend on conceptions, for otherwise, however much they differed, we could not even quarrel about them, that is to say, demand that other people should necessarily agree with us. [We do not make this demand about mere sensations.] . . .

All contradiction disappears if we say that the judgment of taste does depend on a conception, but only on a general conception of some reason for the seeming adaptation of nature to our powers of judgment. From such a conception nothing could be learned or proved about the nature of an object, since no particular object can be *known* to exemplify such a conception. . . .

[On an empirical or sensationalist theory of taste] the object of aesthetic satisfaction would be merely pleasant, but on a rationalist theory (if the judgment depended on definite conceptions) it would be merely good. So beauty would be shuffled out of the world, and all that would be left would be a particular name given perhaps to a certain mixture of these two kinds of satisfaction. But we have shown that there are grounds of satisfaction other than empirical, and therefore consistent with the rationalist principle, although they cannot be grasped as definite conceptions.

Such rationalist principles of taste must further be distinguished according as they take the apparent adaptation [of art and nature to our faculties] to be really designed or only accidental. . . .

One fact positively proves that, as the ground of our aesthetic judgments, we assume only an apparent adaptation of beautiful nature, to the exclusion of any explanation which asserts its real adaptation to our perceptive faculties. I mean the fact that, whenever we estimate beauty, we do not seek any criterion from experience, but judge for ourselves aesthetically whether the thing is beautiful. This could not be if we assumed a designed adaptation of nature, for then we should have to learn from nature what we had to find beautiful, and the judgment of taste would have to bow to experience. But such an estimation does not depend on what nature is or even on how it is in fact adapted to us, but on how we look at it. If nature had produced its forms for our satisfaction, that would in the end be an objective design in nature, not a merely apparent suitability to us resting on the free play of our imagination; it would be a grace done to us by nature, whereas in fact we confer one upon her. In beautiful art it is even easier to recognize that the adaptation can only be known as apparently designed. . . . The fact that the beauties of art by their nature must be considered as products not of scientific understanding, but of genius, plainly shows that, even on a rationalistic theory, it is only apparent and not necessarily real design which accounts for our satisfaction. . . .

Now I say that the beautiful is the symbol of the morally good; and only from this point of view (which every man naturally takes and thinks it the duty of others to take) do we claim that all men should agree about the pleasure it gives. . . . In the faculty of taste the judgment does not find itself, as in judging by experience, constrained by empirical laws; it legislates for itself on the objects of so pure a satisfaction, just as reason legislates autonomously on the faculty of desire in morality. And owing to this capacity in ourselves and to the capacity in external nature to harmonize therewith, the judgment finds in itself a reference to something in us and also outside us, which is neither physical necessity nor moral freedom but is allied to the supersensible [though intelligible] conditions of freedom. In this supersensuous reality, the theoretical faculty [of judgment] and the practical faculty [of moral reason] are mutually and mysteriously interwoven. . . .

Even common understanding pays respect to this analogy, and we often call beautiful objects of nature or art by names which imply a moral estimate. We call trees and buildings majestic or dignified and meadows smiling or gay; even colors are called pure, chaste, tender, because they arouse feelings analogous to those aroused by moral judgments. Taste facilitates a gradual transition from sensuous charm to an habitual interest in morality, since it exhibits the imagination as at once free and adapted to conform to the understanding, and so accustoms us to find a satisfaction that is free from sensuous allurement even in the objects of sense.

Aesthetics

GEORG W. F. HEGEL

THE BEAUTY OF ART is a beauty that has not only been born of the mind or spirit but born again of it. . . .

Everything that is beautiful is only really beautiful as partaking in something higher [namely mind] and being produced thereby. In this sense natural beauty manifests itself as only a reflection of the beauty which properly belongs to the mind—as an imperfect and incomplete manifestation whose essential reality is contained in the mind. . . .

Very serious purposes have been ascribed to art, and it has been recommended as a matchmaker between sense and reason or duty and inclination, and as able to reconcile those elements which clash in so harsh a conflict. To which one may reply that—however respectable the purposes thus ascribed to art—reason and duty are not the gainers by the efforts of such a go-between; since, by the essential purity of their nature, they are incapable of being so compromised, they cannot suffer anything less pure than themselves. Further, art itself is not thus made any more worthy of scientific treatment, for it is made to serve two masters; serious aims, no doubt, on the one hand, but, on the other, laziness and frivolity. In short, if this were art's service, instead of being an end, art could only appear a means. And, to consider the nature of such service, it would still be a contemptible character in art that, if it is really to serve serious ends and produce important results, its only means for doing so is illusion. For beauty lives in seeming. . . .

Only when it has attained its appropriate freedom is fine art really art; it cannot fulfil its highest function till it has established itself in the same sphere with religion and philosophy and has become simply one of the ways of expressing, or presenting to consciousness, the divine, the deepest interests of man, the most comprehensive spiritual truths. . . . This character art shares with philosophy and religion, but there is this difference: that art expresses even what is highest by sensuous form, and so brings it nearer to natural appearances, to our senses and feeling. . . .

The universal and absolute need from which art, in its general character, springs, originates in the fact that man is a *thinking* consciousness; that is, that he makes explicit to himself, by means of his own nature, what he is and what the world is. Natural things are simply there, and that is the

From Philosophies of Beauty from Socrates to Robert Bridges, *ed. and trans. E. F. Carritt (Oxford: Clarendon Press, 1931).*

end of it; man, being a mind, gives himself a double existence, since he not only, like natural things, is, but also realizes his own existence, perceives himself, has ideas of himself, thinks himself; and only by this active realization of himself is he a mind. Man attains this self-consciousness in a twofold way. First *theoretically,* so far as he has to bring his inmost self before consciousness—every movement of the human heart, every storm that sways it. In general he has to contemplate himself, to picture himself, to fix before himself what thought discovers as his essential character; he has to recognize only himself both in all that is called up in him and in all that he assimilates from without. Secondly man realizes himself through *practical* activity, since he has the impulse to express himself, and so again to recognize himself, in things that are at first simply presented to him as externally existent. He attains this end by altering external things and impressing on them the stamp of his own inner nature, so that he rediscovers his own character in them. Man does this in order that he may profit by his freedom to break down the stubborn indifference of the external world to himself, and may enjoy in the countenance of nature only an outward embodiment of himself. . . .

The material or sensible element in a work of art only has any claim to its place so far as it exists for the mind of man; not in virtue of its own materiality. . . . The interest in art is distinguished from the practical interest of desire by the fact that it leaves its objects alone in their independence, while desire adapts them, or even destroys them, for its own purposes. Conversely, artistic contemplation differs from the theoretical contemplation of the scientific intelligence in cherishing an interest for the objects in their individuality; it does not busy itself in reducing them to universal thoughts and conceptions. Hence it follows that, though the sensuous material must indeed be present in a work of art, it need only appear as a superficial semblance of matter. . . . The demand for realism, as such is not fundamental or primary in art. So, although the representation of external nature is an essential element in art, actual nature does not prescribe the rule; nor is imitation of outward appearances for their own sake the end of art. So we have still to ask: What, then, is the subject-matter of the arts and with what end must it be presented? Here there at once rises to the mind the common view that it is the function and purpose of art to stir our senses, our feeling, our emotions with everything which can find a place in the human soul. Art must realize for us the famous saying *Nihil humani a me alienum puto.* . . . Art does indeed possess this formal character of being able to beautify every possible subject-matter by engaging our contemplation and our feelings. . . . But the very heterogeneity of this subject prevents us from resting content with this merely formal characteristic of art. The rationality which permeates this motley chaos challenges us to recognize the emergence and actual attainment of some all-embracing purpose in these contradictory elements. . . . A very little reflection, then, suggests to us the consideration that the end of art lies in its capacity and function of mitigating the passions. . . . And even if art confined itself to the task of presenting images of the passions to our contemplation, though it should thereby flatter them, yet even in that there is already a kind of mitigation. For by that means man at least becomes aware of what before he merely was. Now for the first time man contemplates his impulses and instincts; and whereas formerly they hurried him along without reflection, he now sees them externalized, and begins, so soon as they are presented to him as objects, to achieve freedom from them. Thus it may often happen to an artist, overtaken by grief, that he can mitigate the intensity of his private feeling by the expression of it. Some comfort is to be found even in tears. The man who at first was utterly concentrated and sunk in grief, at least thus externalizes, in however physical a way, what before was pent within him. Far greater is the relief by expression of inner feeling in words, forms, tones, and shapes. . . .

But this definition of art, that it should guide and educate our crude passions, remained purely formal and general, so that a further question had to be asked about the specific nature and essential aim of this education. . . .

If the end of art is confined to didactic utility, then its other side, that of delight, entertainment, satisfaction, is implied to be unessential and to have its justification only in the profit of the lesson which it accompanies. . . .

If we still continue to speak of an end, we must, to begin with, guard against the perverse interpretation of our question about the *end* as being really one about the *use*. . . . Against this we must maintain that art has the function of revealing truth in the form of sensuous artistic shapes and of presenting to us the reconciliation of the contradiction [between sense and reason, between what is and what ought to be, between desire and duty]. Consequently it contains its end in itself, in this very revelation and presentation. . . .

Division of the Subject. Since we have spoken of art as issuing from the absolute spiritual reality, and have assigned as its end the sensuous presentation of that absolute itself, we must now proceed with our summary to show, at least in outline, how the particular divisions of art originate from this notion of artistic beauty in general as being the representation of absolute reality. For this purpose we must try to give some general idea of this notion. As already said, the subject-matter of art is the spiritual reality and its form is the sensuous, plastic image. Art has to reconcile these two sides in an independent whole of mutually necessary parts. (1) The first condition for this is that the subject-matter to be represented in art should be intrinsically capable of such representation. Otherwise we only get an artificial combination, where some subject-matter which is naturally incapable of sensuous plastic expression is forced into that form, and an essentially prosaic material struggles for an apt expression to which it is fundamentally unsuited. (2) The second condition, which follows from the first, is that the subject-matter of art shall not be essentially abstract. . . . (3) Thirdly, if a genuine and therefore concrete subject-matter is to receive an adequate sensuous form, the latter

must be a no less fully concrete and individual thing. This concreteness of the two elements in art, the subject and the presentation, is just the point in which they can harmonize and interpenetrate. The natural human body, for instance, is a concrete object of sense which is capable of expressing adequately the concrete mind or spirit. We must reject the idea that it is only a coincidence when some natural object is used as a significant form. Art adopts such form not just because it is to hand nor because nothing else is to hand; the definiteness of subject-matter implies the possibility of external actualization, in fact of sensuous expression. On the other hand, in order that this should be possible, this concrete object of sense in which an essentially spiritual subject-matter figures itself, is in its turn essentially spiritualized. The outward form by which the subject-matter becomes [an] object of perception or imagination has no purpose except its appeal to our heart and mind. Although the sensuous shape bestowed by art is not, from this point of view, accidental, on the other hand it is not the highest method of apprehending the concrete spiritual reality. Thought is higher than any sensuously concrete representation. Relatively, thought is abstract; but in order to be true and rational it must not be one-sided but concrete thought. . . . The Greek gods, as contrasted with the Christian God, exemplify the difference between a subject-matter whose adequate form is sensuous artistic representation and one whose very nature essentially demands a form which is higher and more spiritual. The Greek god is no abstraction but an individual, to whom a bodily form is not alien; the Christian God likewise is concrete personality, but personality purely spiritual, that must be known as spirit and in spirit. He is present to us therefore essentially by inward knowledge and not by external natural form, which can only represent him imperfectly and not in the full depth of our conception of him. But it is the function of art to present ultimate reality to our immediate perception in sensuous shape and not in the form of thought or pure spirit merely. And the value of this representation depends on the correspondence and unity between these two elements. Consequently the greatness and excellence of art in achieving its ideal will depend upon the degree of intimacy with which this form and subject-matter are fused and united.

Our scientific survey, then, must found its classification of art upon the degree of truth attained; that is, upon the degree to which mind has achieved a plastic form adequate to its ideal. For before mind attains a true conception of its absolute essence it must pass through a series of stages, a series which can be deduced from that conception. And to these stages in the development of a subject-matter which mind thus supplies to itself there answers an exactly corresponding series of types of art, in which the mind, by its artistic activity, becomes aware of itself. This evolution of the artistic spirit has itself from its own nature two sides. First, there is a universal spiritual development, wherein the series of different conceptions of the universe, different ways of regarding God, man, and nature as a whole, express themselves artistically. Secondly, these inner developments of art have to find for themselves actual external realizations in sensuous media; and these make up the necessary distinctions of art, that is to say, the particular arts. The distinction of different types of art being a distinction in the universal nature of mind, it is impossible for any one type to be confined to a single medium, and each sensuous medium also can be variously applied. But since the sensuous medium, as well as the mind, is potentially rational, each sensuous medium has an especially close and subtle correspondence with one of the different spiritual types of art. . . .

Any subject-matter whatever can, so far as its own nature goes, be adequately represented, but it cannot merely thereby lay claim to ideal artistic beauty. The very representation of such a chance subject will, indeed, appear defective when compared with the ideal. Here may opportunely be suggested, what can only be proved later, that imperfection in a work of art need not always be attributed merely to lack of skill in the artist, but

that imperfection of form may arise from imperfection of subject. For instance, the idols and artistic representations of divinity among the Chinese, Indians, and Egyptians remained formless, or achieved only a false and vicious definiteness of form, never true beauty, because their mythological ideas, which were the mental subject-matter of this art, were still vague or falsely definite, and not the true subject matter of art. . . .

So now that we have discussed artistic beauty in its essential nature, we must observe how the realm of beauty differentiates itself into diverse species. This affords us, as the second part of our treatise, the doctrine of the types of art.

These forms owe their birth to the various ways of conceiving the ultimate reality [which is to be their subject-matter]; from these varieties arise the differences of form in which they are expressed. Types of art, then, are nothing but the various relations of subject-matter to form, relations which arise out of the very nature of spiritual reality. . . . We have to consider three such relations.

At first the ultimate reality which is conceived as the subject-matter of artistic presentation is something itself vague and indistinct, or endowed with false and inappropriate distinctness. It is indistinct as not being yet endowed with that individuality which is a condition of artistic beauty; this abstractness and one-sidedness leave the outward manifestation arbitrary and incomplete. This first form of art is rather a mere straining after embodiment than a capacity for actual representation. No true form has yet been found for the spiritual reality itself, these are only wrestlings and strivings towards one. This type of art may be generally described as the *Symbolic*. Here the abstract conception of spiritual reality finds an alien embodiment in natural sensible matter, with which artistic representation starts and to which it remains, at this stage, confined. Natural objects of perception are at first left as they are, but invested with a significance as embodiments of absolute spiritual reality, in virtue of which embodiment they are given the function of expressing it, and have to be interpreted as if they actually presented it to our senses. This implies, no doubt, that natural objects really have an element in virtue of which they are capable of representing a universal meaning. But as complete adequacy is not yet possible, the relation between the two can only be limited and artificial, as when, for instance, strength is indicated by a lion.

Another consequence of this artificial relation between the spiritual reality and the natural object is to make us aware of the gulf between them. When the spiritual reality, which has no other physical thing to express it, expatiates in all these shapes, and seeks to express itself in them with that impatience of limitation or definition which still belongs to it, it finds none of them adequate to itself. So it proceeds to exaggerate the shapes and appearances of nature to an unlimited monstrosity like its own. . . .

Owing to this inadequacy of the two sides to each other, the relation of the spiritual reality to its objectification becomes one of contrast; for the former, as something inward, despises any such externalization. As being the inward universal import of this host of inadequate forms, it elevates itself above them all as *Sublime*. In this sublimity, natural objects and the human form and its experiences are no doubt accepted and tolerated as they are; but they are recognized as inadequate to a meaning which is exalted above all things in heaven or earth.

These features determine the general character of the primitive artistic pantheism of the East, which either embodies the deepest meaning in the most trivial objects or violently distorts natural appearances to express its theory of life. Hence this form of art either becomes bizarre, grotesque, and tasteless, or contemptuously contrasts the infinite, though abstract, freedom of what is spiritually real with the ephemeral nothingness of all actual appearances. In this way the import can never be fully embodied in the expression; and in spite of every effort and struggle, the inadequacy of the form to the spiritual reality remains insuperable. This may be taken as the first type of art, the Symbolic with its yearning, and its turbid, enigmatic sublimity.

In the second type, which we will call the *Classical*, the defect which beset the symbolic on both its sides is overcome. Symbolic imagery is imperfect because on the one side ultimate reality is only thought of with artificial definitions or quite indefinitely; and on the other, for that very reason, the union of import and imagery must remain imperfect and, itself, merely abstract. The classical type of art, as the correction of this double failure, is the natural and adequate embodiment of the spiritual reality in the form peculiarly and essentially appropriate to it, so that the two unite in a perfect and natural harmony. So in the classical type for the first time we get the production and apprehension of the perfect ideal, now realized in fact. . . .

The peculiarity of the subject-matter of classical art is that it is itself concrete reality, that is to say concrete mind; for only mind is truly individual or self-contained. We have then to look among natural things for one which naturally corresponds to the essential character of mind. . . . Now if ultimate reality as mind and, indeed, mind definitely individualized, is to manifest itself in temporal appearances, it has as its natural form the human shape. Personification and anthropomorphism have been freely blamed as a degradation of the spiritual; but art, if it is to make mind apprehensible to sense, must rise to such anthropomorphism, for it is only in its body that mind is adequately manifest to the senses. . . .

The forms of the human body in classical art are treated no longer as mere objects presented to the senses, but only as the presentation and natural image of mind; for which reason they must be freed from all the deficiencies of what is merely material and from the accidental limitations of natural appearance. But just as the imagery must be thus purified if it is to express within its four corners a subject-matter suitable to it, so, too, its spiritual subject-matter must be of a kind which can be fully expressed in the natural human form, and which does not surpass the possibilities of sensuous bodily expression. Only so can the harmony of imagery and import be complete. Consequently mind is at this stage immediately limited to the particular human mind, as opposed to what is, without qualification, absolute and eternal, which can only express itself or announce its presence as pure spirituality. This limitation is fatal to classical art in its turn and necessitates the transition to a third and higher type, the Romantic.

The *Romantic* type of art rises above the complete identification of ultimate reality with its external manifestation, and returns, though at a higher level, to that distinction and opposition of the two sides which symbolic art had failed to overcome. Classical art in fact reached the perfection of sensuous presentation, and if it has any defect it is a defect inherent in art, a limitation in its very nature. This defect arises because art in general presents mind, whose essence is infinite concrete universality, as an object in sensuous concrete form, and classical art presents the complete fusion of spiritual and sensuous as a harmony. But mind cannot be represented in its true essence by any such fusion. . . . Christianity represents God not as an individual separate spirit but as absolute in spirit and in truth. Consequently it sacrifices sensuous, spatial presentation and finds a more inward and spiritual way of embodying its meaning. . . . Similarly romantic art is the passing of art beyond its proper nature, though still retaining the form of art and working within its limits. . . . Such art, in conformity with its new subject-matter, addresses itself no longer to mere sensuous perception but to something more subjective and inward, which can identify itself more intimately with such a subject-matter:—to the inner soul and feeling. . . . The inner life is the subject of romantic art and has to be represented as such. . . . It celebrates its triumph over the body and manifests that triumph in bodily things themselves, so that the sensuous appearance is degraded and despised.

Yet this form of art, like all others, needs some sensuous form of expression. Because mind has retired into itself and withdrawn from direct unity with the external world, the material sensuous form is treated, as it was in symbolic art, as something unessential and superficial. . . .

We find once more, then, the characteristics of symbolic art, mutual indifference, inade-quacy, and separation between the spiritual meaning and the images; but with an essential difference. In symbolic art the defective conception of ultimate reality involved a defectiveness of imaging it. In romantic art this reality has to be presented as mind and soul made perfect, and consequently disdains any intimate union with external things. . . .

The third division of our subject, assuming the notion of the ideal and of the universal types of art established in the first two, has to trace out their realization in definite sensuous materials. . . .

Each type of art attains its specific character in a specific sensible material and realizes itself completely in the technique appropriate to that material. Yet these types being differentiations of *all* art, cannot be confined to realizing themselves each in a particular art, but are found actualizing themselves, though not so characteristically, in other arts also. Conversely, each particular art belongs properly to one of the general types of art and produces works appropriate thereto, yet each also, in its own way, illustrates all the types of art. . . .

The material of *architecture* is just physical matter as a heavy mechanical mass, and its forms are merely the forms of inorganic nature arranged symmetrically by the abstract relations of understanding. In such material and forms the ideal cannot, as concrete mind, be realized, and so the work produced stands over against the spiritual meaning as something external to it, not permeated by it, but only in an artificial relation to it. Consequently the symbolic type of art is the fundamental principle of architecture. . . . The import of architecture can be more or less clearly embodied in its material and forms, according as this import, which is the aim of the work, is more or less developed and distinct, and free from obscurity and superficiality. Architecture can even go so far in this direction as to create an adequate artistic embodiment of this import in its forms and material, but then it has passed its natural limits and is tending to the stage of sculpture, which is the grade above it. . . .

In *sculpture,* the inner life of mind, which architecture could only dimly indicate, actually embodies itself in the sensuous form and its physical material, and the two sides so inform each other that neither overweights its fellow. Consequently the fundamental principle of this art is the classical type. Here the sensuous form expresses nothing except spirit as such, and conversely no spiritual import is completely expressible by sculpture which cannot be completely presented to our intuition in bodily form. In sculpture the mind should stand before us in undifferentiated unity, as untroubled and not divided against itself; what breathes life into the form is spiritual individuality.

A yet higher import than that expressed by sculpture is mind not only in its ultimate reality, but as it actually manifests itself differentiated in individual spirits or souls. Here we have no longer the serene repose of a god . . . but every kind of subjective emotion and activity in the passions, actions, and experiences of living men. In short the wide realm of human feeling, will, and failure is made the subject of artistic representation. To suit such a subject the sensuous element in art has to appear as similarly differentiated and also as itself akin to the experience of our own minds. Colors, sounds, and sounds used merely as signs of perceptions and ideas, afford such materials, and so we get *painting, music,* and *poetry* as the ways of embodying such an import. . . . These arts get their principle from the romantic type of art. It is a group of arts, not one, that is adequate to manifest most appropriately the romantic type, because that type is the least abstract.

The next art after sculpture is *painting.* . . . Every feeling, idea, and aim that can arise in man's heart and everything that he can realize in action compose the varied subject-matter of painting. The whole realm of individual fact from the highest reach of soul to the most insignificant fact of nature has its place here; not even unconscious nature is excluded in its various scenes and aspects so long as some hint of mind relates it to our thought and feeling.

The second art which goes to realize the romantic type, along with and in contrast to paint-ing, is *music.* The material it works with, though still sensuous, is yet more differentiated and mental. Painting acknowledges and expressly counterfeits the spatial coexistence of unorganically connected parts. But music spiritualizes the sensuous by transcending this extension of parts in undivided unity. . . . In musical tones the whole scale of our feelings and passions, not yet defined in their object, can echo and reverberate. So, just as sculpture stood between the extremes of architecture and the romantic arts, so music forms the central point of these romantic arts, midway between the one-sided materialism of painting and the one-sided intellectuality of poetry. Like architecture, music sets over against subjective feelings its own intelligible measurable relations. . . .

The characteristic of *poetry* is its power of subduing the sensuous element, against which music and painting had already rebelled, to mind and ideas. Sound, the only sensuous material it retains, is now no longer feeling *in* sound, but a symbol without value of its own, and a symbol no longer of indefinite feelings with their graduated shades, but of completely concrete ideas. So sound becomes words. . . . The sensuous element which in music was inseparably fused with the spiritual is here consciously distinguished from what it imports . . . so that the sound may be replaced by mere letters, the visible and the audible alike being degraded to mere indications of spirit. So, properly speaking, the material with which poetry works is poetical ideas or images. And since imagination is common to all the arts, poetry enters into them all and has a place of its own in each. Poetry is the universal art of the mind, no longer of mind confined for its self-realization to external sensuous materials, but free to expatiate in the imaginary space and time of its own ideas and feelings. But it is at this very stage that art transcends itself. It sacrifices the reconciliation and union of sensuous things with mind and passes from the poetry of imagination to the prose of thought.

The World as Will and Idea

ARTHUR SCHOPENHAUER

In the First Book the world was explained as mere *idea,* object for a subject. In the Second Book we considered it from its other side, and found that in this aspect it is *will,* which proved to be simply that which this world is besides being idea. In accordance with this knowledge we called the world as idea, both as a whole and in its parts, the *objectification of will,* which therefore means the will become object, i.e. idea. . . .

Knowledge, now, as a rule, remains always subordinate to the service of the will, as indeed it originated for this service, and grew, so to speak, to the will, as the head to the body. In the case of brutes this subjection of knowledge to the will can never be abolished. . . . This human excellence is exhibited in the highest degree by the Apollo of the Belvedere; the head of the God of the Muses, with eyes fixed on the far distance, stands so freely on his shoulders that it seems wholly delivered from the body, and no more subject to its cares.

If, raised by the power of the mind, a man relinquishes the common way of looking at things, gives up tracing, under the guidance of the forms of the principle of sufficient reason, their relations to each other, the final goal of which is always a relation to his own will; if he thus ceases to consider the where, the when, the why, and the whither of things, and looks simply and solely at the *what;* if, further, he does not allow abstract thought, the concepts of the reason, to take possession of his consciousness, but, instead of all this, gives the whole power of his mind to perception, sinks himself entirely in this, and lets his whole consciousness be filled with the quiet contemplation of the natural object actually present, whether a landscape, a tree, a mountain, a build-

ing, or whatever it may be; inasmuch as he *loses* himself in this object (to use a pregnant German idiom), i.e., forgets even his individuality, his will, and only continues to exist as the pure subject, the clear mirror of the object, so that it is as if the object alone were there, without any one to perceive it, and he can no longer separate the perceiver from the perception, but both have become one, because the whole consciousness is filled and occupied with one single sensuous picture; if thus the object has to such an extent passed out of all relation to something outside it, and the subject out of all relation to the will, then that which is so known is no longer the particular thing as such; but it is the *Idea,* the eternal form, the immediate objectivity of the will at this grade; and, therefore, he who is sunk in this perception is no longer individual, for in such perception the individual has lost himself; but he is *pure,* will-less, painless, timeless *subject of knowledge.* . . .

Whoever now has, after the manner referred to, become so absorbed and lost in the perception of nature that he only continues to exist as the pure knowing subject, becomes in this way directly conscious that, as such, he is the condition, that is, the supporter, of the world and all objective existence; for this now shows itself as dependent upon his existence. Thus he draws nature into himself, so that he sees it to be merely an accident of his own being. In this sense Byron says—

Are not the mountains, waves, and skies, a part
Of me and of my soul, as I of them?

The common mortal, that manufacture of Nature which she produces by the thousand

From The World as Will and Idea, *trans. R. B. Haldane and J. Kemp (London: Routledge & K. Paul, 1883).*

every day, is, as we have said, not capable, at least not continuously so, of observation that in every sense is wholly disinterested, as sensuous contemplation, strictly so called, is. He can turn his attention to things only so far as they have some relation to his will, however indirect it may be. Since for this purpose, which never demands anything but the knowledge of relations, the abstract conception of the thing is sufficient, and for the most part even better adapted for use, the ordinary man does not linger long over the mere perception, does not fix his attention long on one object, but in all that is presented to him hastily seeks merely the concept under which it is to be brought, as the lazy man seeks a chair; and then it interests him no further. This is why he is so soon done with everything, with works of art, objects of natural beauty, and indeed everywhere with the truly significant contemplation of all the scenes of life. He does not linger; only seeks to know his own way in life, together with all that might at any time become his way. Thus he makes topographical notes in the widest sense; over the consideration of life itself as such he wastes no time. The man of genius, on the other hand, whose excessive power of knowledge frees it at times from the service of will, dwells on the consideration of life itself, strives to comprehend the Idea of each thing, not its relations to other things; and in doing this he often forgets to consider his own path in life, and therefore for the most part pursues it awkwardly enough. While to the ordinary man his faculty of knowledge is a lamp to lighten his path, to the man of genius it is the sun which reveals the world. . . .

Aesthetic pleasure is one and the same whether it is called forth by a work of art or directly by the contemplation of nature and life. The work of art is only a means of facilitating the knowledge in which this pleasure consists. That the Idea comes to us more easily from the work of art than directly from nature and the real world, arises from the fact that the artist, who knew only the Idea, no longer the actual, has reproduced in his work the pure Idea, has abstracted it from the actual, omitting all disturb-

ing accidents. The artist lets us see the world through his eyes. That he has these eyes, that he knows the inner nature of things apart from all their relations, is the gift of genius, is inborn; but that he is able to lend us this gift, to let us see with his eyes, is acquired, and is the technical side of art. . . .

In the aesthetical mode of contemplation we have found *two inseparable constituent parts*— the knowledge of the object, not as individual thing but as Platonic Idea, that is, as the enduring form of this whole species of things; and the self-consciousness of the knowing person, not as individual, but as *pure will-less subject of knowledge*. The condition, under which both these constituent parts appear always united, was found to be the abandonment of the method of knowing which is bound to the principle of sufficient reason, and which, on the other hand, is the only kind of knowledge that is of value for the service of the will and also for science. Moreover, we shall see that the pleasure which is produced by the contemplation of the beautiful arises from these two constituent parts, sometimes more from the one, sometimes more from the other, according to what the object of the aesthetical contemplation may be.

All *willing* arises from want, therefore from deficiency, and therefore from suffering. The satisfaction of a wish ends it; yet for one wish that is satisfied there remain at least ten which are denied. Further, the desire lasts long, the demands are infinite; the satisfaction is short and scantily measured out. But even the final satisfaction is itself only apparent; every satisfied wish at once makes room for a new one; both are illusions; the one is known to be so, the other not yet. No attained object of desire can give lasting satisfaction, but merely a fleeting gratification; it is like the alms thrown to the beggar, that keeps him alive to-day that his misery may be prolonged till the morrow. Therefore, so long as our consciousness is filled by our will, so long as we are given up to the throng of desires with their constant hopes and fears, so long as we are the subject of willing, we can never have lasting happiness nor peace. It is essentially all the same whether we pursue or flee, fear injury or seek enjoyment; the care for the constant demands of the will, in whatever form it may be, continually occupies and sways the consciousness; but without peace no true well-being is possible. The subject of willing is thus constantly stretched on the revolving wheel of Ixion, pours water into the sieve of the Danaids, is the ever-longing Tantalus.

But when some external cause or inward disposition lifts us suddenly out of the endless stream of willing, and delivers knowledge from the slavery of the will, the attention is no longer directed to the motives of willing, but comprehends things free from their relation to the will, and thus observes them without personal interest, without subjectivity, purely objectively, and gives itself entirely up to them so far as they are ideas, but not in so far as they are motives. Then all at once the peace which we were always seeking, but which always fled from us on the former path of the desires, comes to us of its own accord, and it is well with us. It is the painless state which Epicurus prized as the highest good and as the state of the gods; we are for the moment set free from the miserable striving of the will; we keep the Sabbath of the penal servitude of willing; the wheel of Ixion stands still.

But this is just the state which I described above as necessary for the knowledge of the Idea, as pure contemplation, as sinking oneself in perception, losing oneself in the object, forgetting all individuality, surrendering that kind of knowledge which follows the principle of sufficient reason, and comprehends only relations; the state by means of which at once and inseparably both the perceived particular thing is raised to the Idea of its whole species, and the knowing individual to the pure subject of will-less knowledge, and as such they are both taken out of the stream of time and all other relations. It is then all one whether we see the sun set from the prison or from the palace.

Inward disposition, the predominance of knowing over willing, can produce this state under any circumstances. This is shown by those admirable Dutch artists who directed this purely objective perception to the most insignificant objects, and established a lasting monument of their objectivity and spiritual peace in their pictures of *still life*, which the aesthetic beholder does not look on without emotion; for they present to him the peaceful, still frame of mind of the artist, free from will, which was needed to contemplate such insignificant things so objectively, to observe them so attentively, and to repeat this perception so intelligently; and as the picture enables the onlooker to participate in this state, his emotion is often increased by the contrast between it and the unquiet frame of mind, disturbed by vehement willing, in which he finds himself. In the same spirit, landscape-painters, and particularly Ruisdael, have often painted very insignificant country scenes, which produce the same effect even more agreeably.

Lastly, it is this blessedness of will-less perception which casts an enchanting glamor over the past and distant, and presents them to us in so fair a light by means of self-deception. For as we think of days long gone by, days in which we lived in a distant place, it is only the objects which our fancy recalls, not the subject of will, which bore about with it then its incurable sorrows just as it bears them now; but they are forgotten, because since then they have often given place to others. Now, objective perception acts with regard to what is remembered just as it would in what is present, if we let it have influence over us, if we surrendered ourselves to it free from will. Hence it arises that, especially when we are more than ordinarily disturbed by some want, the remembrance of past and distant scenes suddenly flits across our minds like a lost paradise. The fancy recalls only what was objective, not what was individually subjective, and we imagine that the objective stood before us then just as pure and undisturbed by any relation to the will as its image stands in our fancy now; while in reality the relation of the objects to our will gave us pain then just as it does now. We can deliver ourselves from all suffering just as well through present objects as through distant ones whenever we raise ourselves to a purely objective contemplation of them and so are able to bring about the illusion that only the objects are present and not we ourselves. Then, as the pure subject of knowledge, freed from the miserable self, we become entirely one with these objects, and, for the moment, our wants are as foreign to us as they are to them. The world as idea alone remains, and the world as will has disappeared. . . .

Sight, unlike the affections of the other senses, cannot, in itself, directly and through its sensuous effect, make the *sensation* of the special organ agreeable or disagreeable; that is, it has no immediate connexion with the will. . . . In the case of hearing this is to some extent otherwise; sounds can give pain directly, and they may also be sensuously agreeable, directly and without regard to harmony or melody. Touch, as one with the feeling of the whole body, is still more subordinated to this direct influence upon the will; and yet there is such a thing as a sensation of touch which is neither painful nor pleasant. But smells are always either agreeable or disagreeable, and tastes still more so. Thus the last two senses are most closely related to the will, and therefore they are always the most ignoble, and have been called by Kant the subjective senses. The pleasure which we experience from light is in fact only the pleasure which arises from the objective possibility of the purest and fullest perceptive knowledge, and as such it may be traced to the fact that pure knowledge, freed and delivered from all will, is in the highest degree pleasant, and of itself constitutes a large part of aesthetic enjoyment. . . .

All these reflections are intended to bring out the subjective part of aesthetic pleasure; that is to say, that pleasure so far as it consists simply of delight in perceptive knowledge as such, in opposition to will. And as directly connected with this, there naturally follows the explanation of that disposition or frame of mind which has been called the sense of the *sublime*.

We have already remarked above that the transition to the state of pure perception takes place most easily when the objects bend themselves to it, that is, when by their manifold and yet definite and distinct form they easily become representatives of their Ideas, in which beauty, in the objective sense, consists. This quality belongs preeminently to natural beauty, which thus affords even to the most insensible at least a fleeting aesthetic satisfaction.

When we say that a thing is *beautiful,* we thereby assert that it is an object of our aesthetic contemplation, and this has a double meaning; on the one hand it means that the sight of the thing makes us *objective,* that is to say, that in contemplating it we are no longer conscious of ourselves as individuals, but as pure will-less subjects of knowledge; and on the other hand it means that we recognize in the object, not the particular thing, but an Idea; and this can only happen, so far as our contemplation of it is not subordinated to the principle of sufficient reason, does not follow the relation of the object to anything outside it (which is always ultimately connected with relations to our own will), but rests in the object itself . . . Since, on the one hand, every given thing may be observed in a purely objective manner and apart from all relations; and since, on the other hand, the will manifests itself in everything at some grade of its objectivity, so that everything is the expression of an Idea; it follows that everything is also *beautiful.* . . .

Sometimes the possession of special beauty in an object lies in the fact that the Idea itself which appeals to us in it is a high grade of the objectivity of will, and therefore very significant and expressive. Therefore it is that man is more beautiful than all other objects, and the revelation of his nature is the highest aim of art. Human form and expression are the most important objects of plastic art, and human action the most important object of poetry. Yet each thing has its own peculiar beauty, not only every organism which expresses itself in the unity of an individual being, but also everything unorganized and formless, and even every manufactured article. For all these reveal the Ideas through which the will objectifies itself at its lowest grades, they give, as it were, the deepest resounding bass-notes of nature. Gravity, rigidity, fluidity, light, and so forth, are the Ideas which express themselves in rocks, in buildings, in waters. . . .

In aesthetic contemplation (in the real, or through the medium of art) of the beauty of nature in the inorganic and vegetable worlds, or in works of architecture, the pleasure of pure willless knowing will predominate, because the Ideas which are here apprehended are only low grades of the objectivity of will, and are therefore not manifestations of deep significance and rich content. On the other hand, if animals and man are the objects of aesthetic contemplation or representation, the pleasure will consist rather in the comprehension of these Ideas, which are the most distinct revelation of will; for they exhibit the greatest multiplicity of forms, the greatest richness and deep significance of phenomena, and reveal to us most completely the nature of will, whether in its violence, its terribleness, its satisfaction or its aberration (the latter in tragic situations), or finally in its change and self-surrender, which is the peculiar theme of Christian painting; as the Idea of the will enlightened by full knowledge is the object of historical painting in general, and of the drama. . . .

We all recognize human beauty when we see it, but in the true artist this takes place with such clearness that he shows it as he has never seen it, and surpasses nature in his representation; this is only possible because *we ourselves are* the will whose adequate objectification at its highest grade is here to be judged and discovered. Thus alone have we in fact an anticipation of that which nature (which is just the will that constitutes our own being) strives to express. . . .

Music is as *direct* an objectification and copy of the whole *will* as the world itself, nay, even as the Ideas, whose multiplied manifestation constitutes the world of individual things. Music is thus by no means like the other arts, the copy of the Ideas, but the *copy of the will itself,* whose objectivity the Ideas are. This is why the effect of music is so much more powerful and penetrating than that of the other arts, for they speak only of shadows, but it speaks of the thing itself. Since, however, it is the same will which objecti-

fies itself both in the Ideas and in music, though in quite different ways, there must be, not indeed a direct likeness, but yet a parallel, an analogy, between music and the Ideas whose manifestation in multiplicity and incompleteness is the visible world. . . .

It does not, therefore, express this or that particular and definite joy, this or that sorrow, or pain, or horror, or delight, or merriment, or peace of mind; but joy, sorrow, pain, horror, delight, merriment, peace of mind *themselves* to a certain extent in the abstract, their essential nature, without accessories, and therefore without their motives. Yet we completely understand them in this extracted quintessence. Hence it arises that our imagination is so easily excited by music, and now seeks to give form to that invisible yet actively moved spirit-world which speaks to us directly, and clothe it with flesh and blood, i.e. to embody it in an analogous example. . . .

The pleasure we receive from all beauty, the consolation which art affords, the enthusiasm of the artist, which enables him to forget the cares of life—the latter an advantage of the man of genius over other men, which alone repays him for the suffering that increases in proportion to the clearness of consciousness, and for the desolate loneliness among men of a different race—all this rests on the fact that the in-itself of life, the will, existence itself, is, as we shall see farther on, a constant sorrow, partly miserable, partly terrible; while, on the contrary, as idea alone, purely contemplated, or copied by art, free from pain, it presents to us a drama full of significance. This purely knowable side of the world, and the copy of it in any art, is the element of the artist. He is chained to the contemplation of the play, the objectification of will; he remains beside it, does not get tired of contemplating it and representing it in copies; and meanwhile he bears himself the cost of the production of that play, i.e. he himself is the will which objectifies itself, and remains in constant suffering. That pure, true, and deep knowledge of the inner nature of the world becomes now for him an end in itself: he stops there. Therefore it does not become to him a quieter of the will, as, we shall see in the next book, it does in the case of the saint who has attained to resignation: it does not deliver him for ever from life, but only at moments, and is therefore not for him a path out of life, but only an occasional consolation in it, till his power, increased by this contemplation and at last tired of the play, lays hold of the real.

Art and the Will to Power

FRIEDRICH NIETZSCHE

CONCERNING THE PSYCHOLOGY of the artist. For art to be possible at all—that is to say, in order that an aesthetic mode of action and of observation may exist, a certain preliminary physiological state is indispensable: *ecstasy.* This state of ecstasy must first have intensified the susceptibility of the whole machine: otherwise, no art is possible. All kinds of ecstasy, however differently produced, have this power to create art, and above all the state dependent upon sexual excitement—this most venerable and primitive form of ecstasy. The same applies to that ecstasy which is the outcome of all great desires, all strong passions; the ecstasy of the feast, of the arena, of the act of bravery, of victory, of all extreme action; the ecstasy of cruelty; the ecstasy of destruction; the ecstasy following upon certain meteorological influences, as for instance that of springtime, or upon the use of narcotics; and finally the ecstasy of will, that ecstasy which results from accumulated and surging will-power.—The essential feature of ecstasy is the feeling of increased strength and abundance. Actuated by this feeling a man gives of himself to things, he *forces* them to partake of his riches, he does violence to them—this proceeding is called *idealizing.* Let us rid ourselves of a prejudice here: idealizing does not consist, as is generally believed, in a suppression or an elimination of detail or of unessential features. A stupendous *accentuation* of the principal characteristics is by far the most decisive factor at work, and in consequence the minor characteristics vanish.

In this state a man enriches everything from out his own abundance: what he sees, what he wills, he sees distended, compressed, strong, overladen with power. He transfigures things until they reflect his power—until they are stamped with his perfection. This compulsion to transfigure into the beautiful is—Art. Everything—even that which he is not—is nevertheless to such a man a means of rejoicing over himself; in Art man rejoices over himself as perfection.—It is possible to imagine a contrary state, a specifically anti-artistic state of the instincts—a state in which a man impoverishes, attenuates, and draws the blood from everything. And, truth to tell, history is full of such anti-artists, of such creatures of low vitality who have no choice but to appropriate everything they see and to suck its blood and make it thinner. This is the case with the genuine Christian, Pascal for instance. There is no such thing as a Christian who is also an artist. . . . Let no one be so childish as to suggest Raphael or any homeopathic Christian of the nineteenth century as an objection to this statement: Raphael said Yea, Raphael *did* Yea—consequently Raphael was no Christian.

From The Twilight of the Idols, *trans. Anthony M. Ludorici, and* The Joyful Wisdom, *trans. Thomas Common, in Oscar Levy, ed.,* The Complete Works of Friedrich Nietzsche *(London: T. N. Foulis, 1909–11).*

What is the meaning of the antithetical concepts *Apollonian* and *Dionysian* which I have introduced into the vocabulary of Aesthetic, as representing two distinct modes of ecstasy?—Apollonian ecstasy acts above all as a force stimulating the eye, so that it acquires the power of vision. The painter, the sculptor, the epic poet are essentially visionaries. In the Dionysian state, on the other hand, the whole system of passions is stimulated and intensified, so that it discharges itself by all the means of expression at once, and vents all its power of representation, of imitation, of transfiguration, of transformation, together with every kind of mimicry and histrionic display at the same time. The essential feature remains the facility in transforming, the inability to refrain from reaction (—a similar state to that of certain hysterical patients, who at the slightest hint assume any role). It is impossible for the Dionysian artist not to understand any suggestion; no outward sign of emotion escapes him, he possesses the instinct of comprehension and of divination in the highest degree, just as he is capable of the most perfect art of communication. He enters into every skin, into every passion: he is continually changing himself. Music as we understand it today is likewise a general excitation and discharge of the emotions; but, notwithstanding this, it is only the remnant of a much richer world of emotional expression, a mere residuum of Dionysian histrionism. For music to be made possible as a special art, quite a number of senses, and particularly the muscular sense, had to be paralyzed (at least relatively: for all rhythm still appeals to our muscles to a certain extent): and thus man no longer imitates and represents physically everything he feels, as soon as he feels it. Nevertheless that is the normal Dionysian state, and in any case its primitive state. Music is the slowly attained specialization of this state at the cost of kindred capacities. . . .

Beautiful and Ugly:—Nothing is more relative, let us say, more restricted, than our sense of the beautiful. He who would try to divorce it from the delight man finds in his fellows, would immediately lose his footing. "Beauty in itself," is simply a word, it is not even a concept. In the beautiful, man postulates himself as the standard of perfection; in exceptional cases he worships himself as that standard. A species has no other alternative than to say "yea" to itself alone, in this way. Its lowest instinct, the instinct of self-preservation and self-expansion, still radiates in such sublimities. Man imagines the world itself to be overflowing with beauty—he forgets that he is the cause of it all. He alone has endowed it with beauty. Alas! and only with human all-too-human beauty! Truth to tell man reflects himself in things, he thinks everything beautiful that throws his own image back at him. The judgment "beautiful" is the "vanity of his species." . . . A little demon of suspicion may well whisper into the sceptic's ear: is the world really beautified simply because man thinks it beautiful? He has only humanized it—that is all. But nothing, absolutely nothing proves to us that it is precisely man who is the proper model of beauty. Who knows what sort of figure he would cut in the eyes of a higher judge of taste? He might seem a little odd. . . .

Nothing is beautiful; man alone is beautiful: all aesthetic rests on this piece of ingenuousness, it is the first axiom of this science. And now let us straightway add the second to it: nothing is ugly save the degenerate man—within these two first principles the realm of aesthetic judgments is confined. From the physiological standpoint, everything ugly weakens and depresses man. It reminds him of decay, danger, impotence; he literally loses strength in its presence. The effect of ugliness may be gauged by the dynamometer. Whenever man's spirits are downcast, it is a sign that he scents the proximity of something "ugly." His feeling of power, his will to power, his courage and his pride—these things collapse at the sight of what is ugly, and rise at the sight of what is beautiful. In both cases an inference is drawn; the premises to which are stored with extraordinary abundance in the instincts. Ugliness is understood to signify a hint and a symptom of degeneration: that which reminds us however remotely of degeneracy, impels us to the judgment "ugly." Every sign of exhaustion, of gravity, of age, of fatigue; every kind of constraint, such as cramp, or paralysis; and above all the smells, colors and forms associated with decomposition and putrefaction, however much they may have been attenuated into symbols—all these things provoke the same reaction which is the judgment "ugly." A certain hatred expresses itself here: what is it that man hates? Without a doubt it is the *decline of his type*. In this regard his hatred springs from the deepest instincts of the race: there is horror, caution, profundity and far-reaching vision in this hatred—it is the most profound hatred that exists. On its account alone Art is profound.

Schopenhauer.—Schopenhauer, the last German who is to be reckoned with (—who is a European event like Goethe, Hegel, or Heinrich Heine, and who is not merely local, national), is for a psychologist a case of the first rank: I mean as a malicious though masterly attempt to enlist on the side of a general nihilistic depreciation of life, the very forces which are opposed to such a movement—that is to say, the great self-affirming powers of the "will to live," the exuberant forms of life itself. He interpreted Art, heroism, genius, beauty, great sympathy, knowledge, the will to truth, and tragedy, one after the other, as the results of the denial, or of the need of the denial, of the "will"—the greatest forgery, Christianity always excepted, which history has to show. Examined more carefully, he is in this respect simply the heir of the Christian interpretation; except that he knew how to approve in a Christian fashion (i.e., nihilistically) even of the great facts of human culture, which Christianity completely repudiates. (He approved of them as paths to "salvation," as preliminary stages to "salvation," as *appetizers* calculated to arouse the desire for "salvation.")

Let me point to one single instance. Schopenhauer speaks of beauty with melancholy ardor—why in sooth does he do this? Because in beauty he sees a bridge on which one can travel further, or which stimulates one's desire to travel further. According to him it constitutes a momentary emancipation from the "will"—it lures to eternal salvation. He values it more particularly as a deliverance from the "burning core of the will" which is sexuality—in beauty he recognises the negation of the procreative instinct. Singular Saint! Someone contradicts thee; I fear it is Nature. Why is there beauty of tone, color, aroma, and of rhythmic movement in Nature at all? What is it forces beauty to the fore? Fortunately, too, a certain philosopher contradicts him. No less an authority than the divine Plato himself (thus does Schopenhauer call him), upholds another proposition: that all beauty lures to procreation—that this precisely is the chief characteristic of its effect, from the lowest sensuality to the highest spirituality.

Plato goes further. With an innocence for which a man must be Greek and not "Christian," he says that there would be no such thing as Platonic philosophy if there were not such beautiful boys in Athens: it was the sight of them alone that set the soul of the philosopher reeling with erotic passion, and allowed it no rest until it had planted the seeds of all lofty things in a soil so beautiful. He was also a singular saint!—One scarcely believes one's ears, even supposing one believes Plato. At least one realises that philosophy was pursued differently in Athens; above all, publicly. Nothing is less Greek than the cobweb-spinning with concepts by an anchorite, *amor intellectualis dei* after the fashion of Spinoza. Philosophy according to Plato's style might be defined rather as an erotic competition, as a continuation and a spiritualization of the old agonal gymnastics and the conditions on which they depend. . . . What was the ultimate outcome of this philosophic eroticism of Plato's? A new artform of the Greek *Agon*, dialectics.—In opposition to Schopenhauer and to the honor of Plato, I would remind you that all the higher culture and literature of classical France, as well, grew up on the soil of sexual interests. In all its manifestations you may look for gallantry, the senses, sexual competition, and "woman," and you will not look in vain.

L'Art pour l'Art.—The struggle against a purpose in art is always a struggle against the moral tendency in art, against its subordination to morality. *L'art pour l'art* means, "let morality go to the devil!"—But even this hostility betrays the preponderating power of the moral prejudice. If art is deprived of the purpose of preaching morality and of improving mankind, it does not by any means follow that art is absolutely pointless, purposeless, senseless, in short *l'art pour l'art*—a snake which bites its own tail. "No purpose at all is better than a moral purpose!"—thus does pure passion speak. A psychologist, on the other hand, puts the question: what does all art do? does it not praise? does it not glorify? does it not select? does it not bring things into prominence? In all this it strengthens or weakens certain valuations. Is this only a secondary matter? an accident? something in which the artist's instinct has no share? Or is it not rather the very prerequisite which enables the artist to accomplish something? . . . Is his most fundamental instinct concerned with art? Is it not rather concerned with the purpose of art, with life? with a certain desirable kind of life? Art is the great stimulus to life: how can it be regarded as purposeless, as pointless, as *l'art pour l'art*?—There still remains one question to be answered: Art also reveals much that is ugly, hard and questionable in life—does it not thus seem to make life intolerable?—And, as a matter of fact, there have been philosophers who have ascribed this function to art. According to Schopenhauer's doctrine, the general object of art was to "free one from the Will"; and what he honored as the great utility of tragedy, was that it "made people more resigned."—But this, as I have already shown, is a pessimistic standpoint; it is the "evil eye": the artist himself must be appealed to. What is it that the soul of the tragic artist communicates to others? Is it not precisely his fearless attitude towards that which is terrible and questionable? This attitude is in itself a highly desirable one; he who has once experienced it honours it above everything else. He communicates it. He must communicate, provided he is an artist and a genius in the art of communication. A courageous and free spirit, in the presence of a mighty foe, in the presence of a sublime misfortune, and face to face with a problem that inspires horror—this is the triumphant attitude which the tragic artist selects and which he glorifies. The martial elements in our soul celebrate their Saturnalia in tragedy; he who is used to suffering, he who looks out for suffering, the heroic man, extols his existence by means of tragedy—to him alone does the tragic artist offer this cup of sweetest cruelty. . . .

Prose and Poetry.—Let it be observed that the great masters of prose have almost always been poets as well, whether openly, or only in secret and for the "closet"; and in truth one only writes good prose *in view of poetry!* For prose is an uninterrupted, polite warfare with poetry; all its charm consists in the fact that poetry is constantly avoided and contradicted; every abstraction wants to have a gibe at poetry, and wishes to be uttered with a mocking voice; all dryness and coolness is meant to bring the amiable goddess into an amiable despair; there are often approximations and reconciliations for the moment, and then a sudden recoil and a burst of laughter; the curtain is often drawn up and dazzling light let in just while the goddess is enjoying her twilights and dull colors; the word is often taken out of her mouth and chanted to a melody while she holds her fine hands before her delicate little ears:—and so there are a thousand enjoyments of the warfare, the defeats included, of which the unpoetic, the so-called prose-men know nothing at all:—they consequently write and speak only bad prose! *Warfare is the father of all good things,* it is also the father of good prose! . . .

Our Ultimate Gratitude to Art.—If we had not approved of the Arts and invented this sort of cult of the untrue, the insight into the general untruth and falsity of things now given us by science—an insight into delusion and error as conditions of intelligent and sentient existence—would be quite unendurable. *Honesty* would have disgust and suicide in its train. Now, however, our honesty has a counterpoise which helps us to escape such consequences:—namely, Art, as the *good-will* to illusion. We do not always restrain our eyes from rounding off and perfecting in imagination: and then it is no longer the eternal imperfection that we carry over the river of Becoming—for we think we carry a *goddess,* and are proud and artless in rendering this service. As an aesthetic phenomenon existence is still *endurable* to us; and by Art, eye and hand and above all the good conscience are given to us, *to be able* to make such a phenomenon out of ourselves. We must rest from ourselves occasionally by contemplating and looking down upon ourselves, and by laughing or weeping *over* ourselves from an artistic remoteness: we must discover the *hero,* and likewise the *fool,* that is hidden in our passion for knowledge; we must now and then be joyful in our folly, that we may continue to be joyful in our wisdom! And just because we are heavy and serious men in our ultimate depth, and are rather weights than men, there is nothing that does us so much good as the *fool's cap and bells:* we need them in presence of ourselves—we need all arrogant, soaring, dancing, mocking, childish and blessed Art, in order not to lose the *free dominion over things* which our ideal demands of us. It would be *backsliding* for us, with our susceptible integrity, to lapse entirely into morality, and actually become virtuous monsters and scarecrows, on account of the overstrict requirements which we here lay down for ourselves. We ought also to *be able* to stand *above* morality, and not only stand with the painful stiffness of one who every moment fears to slip and fall, but we should also be able to soar and play above it! How could we dispense with Art for that purpose, how could we dispense with the fool?—And as long as you are still *ashamed* of yourselves in any way, you still do not belong to us!

Part II

The Analytic Critique of the Aesthetic

AROUND 1950, THE FIRST MAJOR CRACKS in the two-hundred-year-old tradition of the aesthetic began to appear—both in the British and American English-speaking movement known as analytic aesthetics, and also in various French and German movements of Continental Europe. In Part II we will examine the first of these two—the English-speaking movement of analytic aesthetics. This school began not as a movement within aesthetics, but as a major turn within philosophy itself. In fact, aesthetics was rather late in coming on board the analytic train. Philosophy has always been torn between its more logical and scientific side and its more poetic and religious side—as William James put it, its tough-minded and its tender-hearted traditions. One way to see the rise of analytic aesthetics is to view it as the swing of the pendulum away from the tender-hearted neo-Hegelian idealism of the nineteenth and early twentieth centuries toward a more rigorous, tough-minded, sciencelike, logically accurate, and precise reorientation of philosophy.

This pendulum has been swinging back and forth for centuries. Plato referred to what was already the "ancient quarrel between philosophy and poetry." Although Plato tried to place philosophy on a more scientific footing, the Renaissance Platonists saw Plato as an allegorical and mystical poet. Kant tried in the middle of the eighteenth century to align philosophy with the positive successes of the natural sciences, thereby restricting philosophy to what human reason could more realistically hope to accomplish and giving up its unverifiable metaphysical pretensions. But as we saw in the last section (Part I, section B), that only created the momentum in Schopenhauer and Hegel for the opposite swing of the pendulum toward a more ambitious search for ultimate reality beyond the reach of the natural sciences.

Like other "back-to-science" movements of philosophy, analytic philosophy is characterized by the attempt to make philosophy more logically, conceptually precise and exact and to avoid more ambitious speculative metaphysical generalizations concerning the nature of ultimate reality, generalizations that may simply be beyond the capacity of ordinary human reason. What is peculiar to the analytic movement is its emphasis on language analysis as the proper tool of philosophy. What methodologies are available to philosophers in their search for the truth? They cannot employ empirical methods, for these are the tools of the natural sciences. They cannot appeal to mystical intuitions or divine inspiration, for these are the traditional appeals of religion, poetry, and mythology. What is left for the philosopher? According to the analytic philosophers, only the logical relations among words, beliefs, and theories. Thus another name for analytic philosophy is *linguistic philosophy* or the *philosophy of language*.

In her article "Letting the Sunshine In," Anita Silvers presents the history of analytic aesthetics. Like many philosophers trained in the United States in the early 1960s, Silvers herself studied and became part of what is known as *analytic aesthetics*. During the first half of the twentieth century, aesthetics in the English-speaking world had followed the neo-Hegelian—that is, neo-Idealist—aesthetics of the early twentieth century Italian philosopher, Benedetto Croce and the early twentieth century British philosopher, Robin G. Collingwood. Beginning around 1950, British and American philosophers shifted to what is known as analytic or linguistic philosophy. Analytic philosophy is primarily interested in "analyzing" the concepts (words and ideas) we use in describing the world—but not the world itself. Historians might talk about historical causes, for example, but analytic philosophers wondered if the word *cause* functioned in historical studies in the same way it did in the writings of the physical scientists (e.g., physicists), who also talk about "causes." The analytic philosopher's concern was not what causes cancer, for example, but what the word *cause* means (hence the label "linguistic philosophy" or "philosophy of language"). Analytic philosophers thus wanted to talk about talk—that is, talk about talk about the world—and analytic philosophy was therefore also known as a second order investigation. Where *first-order* investigations, such as history, talked about the world, *second order* (i.e., philosophical) investigations talked about the way the first-order historians (and others) talked about the world, with analytic philosophy thus becoming a kind of super talk (talk about talk). In Part III you will want to compare this analytic emphasis on language with that of the poststructuralists Jacques Derrida and Paul de Man.

The purpose of this analysis of words and concepts (such as causality) was to clarify otherwise confusing words and ideas—not to discover new facts about the world, but simply to clarify the way we already think and talk about the world. As Anita Silvers notes in "Letting the Sunshine In" (the "sunshine," from the lyrics of a popular song of the 1960s, being the clarification introduced by analytic philosophy), aesthetics was slow to join the new movement of analytic philosophy, first because aesthetics traditionally spilled over beyond the confines of philosophy proper into art history, art criticism, culture studies, psychology, sociology, and so on, and second because its "tender" idealist orientation was diametrically opposed to the rigorously logical and systematic program of philosophical analysis.

The question Silvers asks is whether analytic aesthetics succeeded in clarifying aesthetics (did it in fact "let the sunshine in"?). Although long associated herself with the analytic movement in aesthetics, Silvers points out several serious problems in the program to clarify aesthetics. First, since the analytic aestheticians were not trying to change existing first-order practices of art historians and art critics, but only to clarify confusions arising from the way they talked about art, analytic aesthetics could do nothing to correct or otherwise intervene in blunders and errors within art history and art criticism themselves. Second, she points out that although analytic aestheticians did succeed in clearing away some of the confusions embedded in art critical talk, they were themselves very confusing and hard to understand.

And this confusion led to another problem, that whereas older aestheticians, such as Croce, were widely read by artists, art historians, and art critics, the new analytic aesthetics was read by virtually no one but other analytic aestheticians. Thus, because of the analytic movement, aesthetics had far less influence on the art public outside philosophy than before! Finally, Silvers traces these problems within the analytic movement to its very foundations, their refusal to talk about the "world," that is, in the case of aesthetics, the refusal of analytic aesthetics, at least in the beginning, to talk about art itself—what artists, critics, museums, collectors were actually doing. As she points out, this did not apply to all analytic aestheticians, and she singles out Margaret Macdonald, Nelson Goodman, and Arthur Danto for special praise precisely because they broke away from the more rigid demands of analytic philosophy in order to talk about the "world"—what Danto calls the "art world."

In Part II we will look at four areas of analytic aesthetics: in section A, the analytic critique of the concept of aesthetic experience; in section B, the analytic critique of the definition of art; in section C, the analytic critique of the metaphysical status of the work of art; and in section D, the analytic critique of the expression theory of art.

Letting the Sunshine In: Has Analysis Made Aesthetics Clear?

ANITA SILVERS

IN THE MIDDLE of the twentieth century, some analytic philosophers set out to rescue aesthetics from dreariness. Although it would be an exaggeration to think of them as a self-conscious movement, as were the logical positivists of the Vienna Circle, it is not difficult to reconstruct the program to which they generally adhered in their attempt to rescue and enliven aesthetics. The body of work which I take to announce and to exemplify the program was published in a period of about fifteen years, from 1946 through 1962, in England and America. Much fine work in philosophical aesthetics was done subsequently, some more and some less obviously addressed to the issues raised by the program and responsive to the program's standards and objectives. But in reconstructing the theses characteristic of the program, it is not necessary to examine more than a representative sample of the exemplary, influential work done during this fifteen-year post war period.

In fact, the program succeeded in some respects, and aesthetics seems less dreary today. Ironically, what dreariness remains is blamed by some on the very techniques which the analysts promoted. When the analytic aestheticians sought to cleanse their domain of obscurity, the charge goes, they failed to recognize that the activities they promoted were drearier than those they sought to extirpate.

With probably only one single exception, that being Wimsatt and Beardsley's "The Intentional Fallacy," historians and critics of the arts treated the work of the analytic aestheticians at best as irrelevant, but sometimes as malevolent. Of course, the concern that such negative reactions provokes depends on whether philosophical aesthetics is expected to make a positive impact on art studies. Nevertheless, the failure of the analytic program to influence art studies contrasts not only with the profound influence of those whom the analytic aestheticians sought to reform—for instance, Wordsworth, Tolstoi, and Bell—but also with the influence attained by their programmatic successors like Nelson Goodman (on arts education), Arthur Danto (on postmodern art criticism), and Jacques Derrida (on literary theory). Nevertheless, it might be said that analytic aesthetics provided reforms from which more substantive developments could evolve. In this essay, I want to explore whether the reforms of the analytic aestheticians were beneficial, or whether their program was defective at its core.

Did the analytic program revive aesthetics? Did it succeed on its own terms? Did it at least initiate reforms from which more substantive im-

From The Journal of Aesthetics and Art Criticism *46 (1987), Special Issue. Reprinted by permission of* The American Society for Aesthetics.

provements evolved? Or was it nothing more than a sterile interlude? Resolving these questions is of more than mere historical interest, for the failure of a philosophical program can be as instructive as its success. By discovering how such a program was meant to operate and what it was meant to achieve, and then by observing what promoted and what impeded it, philosophy gains a firmer grasp of its own purpose and philosophers are aided in perfecting their craft.

To reconstruct the program of analytic aesthetics, I rely on three sources: the collection of essays titled *Aesthetics and Language* [William Elton, ed.], the collection of essays edited by Joseph Margolis and titled *Philosophy Looks at the Arts,* and a report by Arnold Isenberg titled "Analytical Philosophy and the Study of Art." The earliest essay is Beardsley and Wimsatt's "The Intentional Fallacy," originally published in 1946 and included in Margolis; the most recent is Charles Stevenson's "On the Reasons That Can Be Given for the Interpretation of a Poem," which appeared for the first time in the Margolis collection in 1962. The full text of the Isenberg report has never been published, although excerpts from it appear in the posthumous collection of Isenberg's writings. . . .

In diagnosing the causes of dreariness in aesthetics, the source writings converge in advocating the reformation of aesthetic as guided by three theses. Although these are related to each other, none entails any of the others. Here is the first and most general directive.

1. Aesthetics must be reformed by replacing its typically obscure and confused ideas with clear ones.

How is this thesis applied? W. B. Gallie, for instance, demonstrates the method he proposes by analyzing Wordsworth's *Preface to the 1815 Edition of the Lyrical Ballads* to expose what he thinks of as contradictions and confusions. Gallie assesses the *Preface* (and the *Essay Supplementary* of the same year) as "great"; nevertheless he applies his "logical tools" to reveal how Wordsworth gets himself "into a muddle." He does not, however, blame Wordsworth as much as pity him. That is, Gallie diagnoses the contradictions into which he

thinks Wordsworth falls as faults resulting from Wordsworth's lack of logical sophistication in treating the complex aesthetic phenomena he was aesthetically sensitive enough to recognize. Wordsworth's observations are valuable, Gallie admits, but their value is obscured by Wordsworth's apparently contradicting himself by suggesting both that the processes of imaginative abstraction necessarily falsify and also provide us with new truths.

Isenberg sounds a similar note by saying,

> The best thing that philosophy can do for the art studies is to bring some clarity to those issues with which modern criticism is rife—which have arisen "naturally," as it were, out of recent aesthetic preoccupations.

Subsequently, Isenberg analyzes a passage of criticism of *Hamlet* and comments:

> Broad remarks about the fundamental purpose of criticism, narrow rules of thumb which have been useful to the author in his work, a few objections to prevailing practices among contemporaries, a few intelligent suggestions as to paths of thought that deserve to be opened up, some ideas of theses that belong *in* the field rather than in an essay about it, some inconclusive examples (often minutely analyzed) which are supposed to prove general principles about the distinction between creativity and criticism or the relation of art and knowledge or the bearing of historical erudition upon critical judgment—all these are scrambled together with a fine disregard for logical order and coherence. . . .
>
> The same topics, in the hands of persons trained in logical analysis, could be treated with unexampled clarity and rigor.

Deploring confusion and advocating the increased clarity afforded by applying logical tools lead analytic aesthetics to a second characteristic thesis.

2. Aesthetics must be reformed by prohibiting the practice of generalizing insights gained from experience of particular artworks and then expecting the generalizations to function as rules in aesthetic arguments.

This message runs throughout. It is an outcome of the injunction to be clear. Of the murky phenomena of aesthetic discourse, the analytic aestheticians find the field's unrequited enchantment with formulating rules among the most obscure. Noticing that what passes for aesthetic rules or principles systematically falls short of success, they suspect that to argue aesthetically by appealing to generalizations is to masquerade.

In "Logic and Appreciation," Stuart Hampshire concludes,

> when in Aesthetics one moves from the particular to the general, one is travelling in the wrong direction.

And, in "Arguments Used By Criticism of the Arts," Margaret Macdonald writes:

> But to attempt to legislate for art is to invite successful infringement of any law, as the "Unities" showed. Criticism is, therefore, I suggest, an indefinite set of devices for "presenting" not "proving" the merits of works of art. It has none of the stability of logical truth, scientific method, legal and moral law.

In "Critical Communication," Arnold Isenberg writes:

> Is it reasonable to expect better evaluations of art after a thousand years of criticism than before? . . . I think we have already numerous passages which are not to be corrected or improved upon. And if this opinion is right, then it could not be the case that the validation of critical judgments waits upon the discovery of aesthetic laws. . . . We are not more fully convinced in our own judgment because we know its explanation; and we cannot hope to convince an imaginary opponent by appeal to this explanation, which by hypothesis does not hold for him.

And in "The Interpretation of a Poem," Charles Stevenson writes,

> The inconclusiveness of the reasons mentioned (and they are inconclusive even when used collectively) suggests that they are not premises in an argument that is strictly deductive.

The formulation of the various versions of this thesis are developed by the analytic aestheticians in the process of clarifying the way aesthetic discourse actually functions. In his or her own way, each notes how claims which typically might be taken as aesthetic principles, or as resting on aesthetic principles, never enjoy results compatible with their functioning as major or minor premises in sound arguments. Where someone proposes to generalize from the properties which seem responsible for value or meaning in the case of one work or one small group of works of art, the generalization fails to create conclusive conviction when applied beyond the initial case. Although some proportion of failure, even a high one, could pass without remark, the categorical inability of aesthetic debate to achieve the force of sound argument indicates to the aesthetic analysts that aesthetics is systematically and profoundly confused.

A special source of confusion lies in what analytic aesthetics takes as the traditional cause of misguided generalization—the desire to be definitive about art. This diagnosis leads to a third characteristic thesis, the only one of the three addressed not to aesthetic discourse only but also to art itself.

3. Aesthetics must be reformed by recognizing that art admits of no essential properties.

The most influential of the essays pursuing this thesis is Morris Weitz's "The Role of Theory in Aesthetics." Here is a sketch of the position to which so many of Weitz's successors felt called upon to respond.

> Theory has been central in aesthetics and is still the preoccupation of the philosophy of art. Its main avowed concern remains the determination of the nature of art which can be formulated into a definition of it. . . .
>
> In this essay I want to plead for the rejection of this problem. I want to show that theory—in the requisite classical sense—is *never* forthcoming in aesthetics, and that we would do much better as philosophers to supplant the question, "What is the nature of art?" by other questions, the answers to which will provide us with all the understanding of the arts there can be. . . . Aesthetic theory—all of it—is wrong in principle in thinking that a correct theory is possible because it radically misconstrues the logic of the

concept of art. Its main contention that "art" is amenable to real or any kind of true definition is false.

And in "The Dreariness of Aesthetics," J. A. Passmore remarks:

> Woolliness of this sort seems to have a natural habitat in certain fields. . . . Why should these particular fields be thus distinguished by so fine an array of empty formulae? . . .
>
> The woolliness of education, of sociology, of metaphysics, is understandable, then, as arising out of the attempt to impose a spurious unity on things, the spuriousness being reflected in the emptiness of the formulae in which that unity is described. We can easily understand the passions which lie behind this anxiety to reconcile. But why should the same sort of thing happen in aesthetics?

What justifies the program's directions for reform? In general, the analysis starts with an observation that form apparently does not fulfill function. The development of the second thesis, prohibiting generalizations which take the form of rules, provides a good illustration of how this process works.

In formulating this position, Isenberg and Macdonald contend that, although critical discourse contains expressions that have the form of major premises, these expressions do not function successfully in that capacity. Then it is assumed that the mismatch of function and form results in dysfunction, which in turn explains why aesthetics seems incapable of escaping dreary futility. Thus, Macdonald, Isenberg, and others rely on their readers agreeing with them that not only has there never been a successful categorical principle of art, but also that no sophisticated person expects there to be such. They deplore aesthetics' history of pursuing such principles—a kind of activity which to them is not merely futile, but, worse, is patently so.

Having noted that expressions possessing the form of aesthetic rules or principles fail to perform according to form, it remains for contributors to the program both to explain why and to recommend an appropriate remedy. Different ways of accounting for this phenomenon are offered. These typically are claims about how critical discourse functions. For instance, in "The Use of 'Good' in Aesthetic Discourse" Helen Knight appeals to what we do and do not say.

> One picture is good for one sort of thing, and another for something quite different. . . . We praise the brightness and clarity of an Impressionist painting, but do not condemn a Rembrandt for lacking those qualities. It is clear that we look for something different in each case. . . . And how do we praise a realistic picture? We say that the artist has caught the exact pose, the kind of thing one might see at any moment. And the very banality of that pose (in the case of Degas) is a merit. But we do not condemn Botticelli because we fail to meet his goddesses and nymphs as we walk through the street. On the contrary, we praise him for imagination of the ideal. And we praise him for his flowing rhythm, but do not condemn Byzantine art for being rigid, nor Cezanne for being ponderous.

Within the program of analytic aesthetics, the futility of proposing categorical rules for judging or understanding art is not explained in terms of the nature of art, or of aesthetic experience. Earlier philosophers who arrived at analogous conclusions, such as Kant, Collingwood, or Dewey, were inclined to appeal to ontological or epistemological considerations to support and inform their opposition to aesthetic rules. But, of the analytic aestheticians, it is Margaret Macdonald, I think, who forges furthest beyond appealing simply to "what we say and do" when we talk about art when she insists that:

> It is often said that a great artist is reinterpreted in every age and no doubt by some of these interpretations he would be much astonished. Yet even the apparently bizarre interpretations are often illuminating. It seems to follow that interpretation is partly subjective invention, but about this there could be endless argument of the sort that would hardly be necessary about the description of a chair or horse, except perhaps in extreme borderline cases. Certainly, the critic claims to be interpreting the work, not supplying his own fancies. But the work is what

it is interpreted to be, though some interpretations may be rejected. There seems to be no work apart from *some* interpretation. . . .

Compare this with Paul Ziff's approach in "Art and the 'Object of Art'" in the same volume [*Aesthetics and Language*], wherein Ziff proposes to dissolve such claims by showing that the seemingly incompatible attributions which lead some philosophers to accord special status to art objects should be explained not epistemologically or ontologically, but, instead, by noticing that we employ these attributions in different discourses suited for and used in quite different contexts. Ziff proposes that so-called incompatible attributions can be treated by understanding that the discourses in which they are embedded belong to different families that are, if not incommensurable, then at least disassociated from each other. Consequently, these attributions are not inconsistent with each other, and one need not save appearances by explaining that art objects are illusory or otherwise ontologically mysterious.

To what extent does the sort of account favored by the analysts explain why aesthetic discourse is dysfunctional? Since the most typical stratagem of the analytic aestheticians is to draw attention to actual practice and to speculate cautiously on what such practice can and cannot achieve, their explanations tend to lay the blame for confusion on the doorstep of inflated expectations. We are tricked by attending to the form of expressions rather than to their use, they say. As a result, we expect aesthetic discourse to function more powerfully than it can do.

On the program of analytic aesthetics, such mistakes must be rectified once their cause has been clarified. But revealing a source of an error does not necessarily disclose its remedy. And the technique used by the analytic aestheticians to diagnose aesthetics' problems creates a particular puzzle about where the solution lies.

To dispel obscurity, we are directed to observe practice carefully, to lower our expectations, and not to seek results beyond what actual practice has shown it can attain. On this program, then,

existing practice sets the standard. But if existing practice is the standard, and existing practice is also obscure, against what standard should existing practice be reformed?

Here, the analytic program's most general directive appears to take precedence. If, in practice, aesthetic discourse is beclouded because form and function typically are mismatched, clarity must be imposed rigorously. To dispel confusion, either the form of the discourse should change to suit its functions, or its functions must be revised to more appropriately make use of its form.

But to urge such change must be to advocate that practice be changed. That is what the theses which constitute the analytic aestheticians' program advise. Presumably, this advice derives either from considerations internal to practice, or else from grounds logically prior to, or more fundamental than, practice itself. We also can presume that the source of the program's directives ultimately affects how serviceable the advice they offer turns out to be.

It is typical of analytic aesthetics that the reasons given for reforming practice are considerations drawn from practice itself. Passmore addresses the issue characteristically. His whistle-blowing is motivated by the suspicion that dreariness engulfs aesthetic discourse just when those who engage in the discourse distort it by imposing inappropriate models.

> . . . it seems to me possible at least that the dullness of aesthetics arises from the attempt to construct a subject where there isn't one. . . . perhaps the truth is that there is no aesthetics and yet there [is] . . . literary criticism, . . . music criticism, etc.

But how to identify the appropriate model? Weitz suggests that criticism works by favorably recasting features which previously have been considered either as unimportant or as defects of the discourse.

> But what makes them—these honorific definitions—so supremely valuable is not their disguised linguistic recommendations; rather it is the *debates* over the reasons for changing the

criteria of the concept of art which are built into the definitions. In each of the great theories of art, whether correctly understood as honorific definitions or incorrectly accepted as real definitions, what is of the utmost importance are the reasons proffered in the arguments for the respective theory, that is, the reasons given for the chosen or preferred criterion of excellence and evaluation. It is this perennial debate over these criteria of evaluation which makes the history of aesthetic theory the important study it is. . . . Thus, the role of the theory is not to define anything but to use the definitional form, almost epigrammatically, to pin-point a crucial recommendation to turn our attention once again to the plastic elements in painting.

Isenberg adopts the same approach. He tries to explain why we think we are giving critical reasons when we actually are not giving critical reasons at all. He proposes that the critic uses the locutions we call reasons to direct perception of works of art.

I have perhaps overstressed the role of the critic as teacher, *i.e.* as one who affords *new* perceptions and with them new values. . . . it often happens that there are qualities in a work of art which are, so to speak, neither perceived nor ignored but felt or endured. . . . Suppose it is only a feeling of monotony, a slight oppressiveness, which comes to us from the style of some writer. A critic then refers to his "piled-up clauses, endless sentences, repetitious diction." This remark shifts the focus of our attention and brings certain qualities which had been blurred and marginal into distinct consciousness.

In his report to the Rockefeller Foundation, Isenberg addresses the question of reform systematically. He justifies the reform of aesthetics and provides detailed commentary about who should do it and how it should be done. . . .

What is to be reformed, and how is the reform to be effected? Isenberg begins by recommending that philosophers and critics should acquire expertise in each other's fields.

I believe we may say that the best work in the field is to be done, if it is done at all, by young

and unknown people. These people will appear if and when graduate students become convinced that aesthetics is worth studying. Analytically minded students of philosophy nowadays try to learn something about sciences such as mathematics or psychology. When they believe that criticism and art history also deserve their attention, when students of literature come to feel that they must go far into logic and philosophy, there will be some prospect of advances in aesthetics. . . . The subject, analytical aesthetics, remains largely to be created. . . .

So we must turn to rigorously trained philosophers, whose education and interests need only be broadened.

For logical analysts, however, the danger lies in lack of familiarity with the concrete subject-matter and its problems, leading to an excessive abstractness. Even today there are some good ideas in theoretical aesthetics which are ignored by critics and historians because of their forbidding dryness, their apparent lack of relevance to practical pursuits. A thorough acquaintance with the rich though incoherent reflections of men working in the mines are the corrective to this philosophical remoteness.

What remains unclear from this and other comments is why Isenberg is so confident in the above passages, and others, that criticism can advance toward truth, greater objectivity, precision, generality, and comprehensiveness. The latter objectives are noteworthy in view of the position he takes earlier in "Critical Communication.". . .

How realistic is it to expect that scholars in other fields will value philosophers' telling them what to do? I think that Isenberg's expectation here is mediated by his belief that analytic philosophy does not impose prescriptions on other disciplines but, instead, merely clarifies those disciplines' own preferred methods. This is the status he accords Hempel's hypothetico-deductive model. . . .

It is important to notice that whatever recommendations for reform philosophers make, on Isenberg's view here the advice is to be drawn from considerations internal to the structure of critical practice itself. On its least virile interpretation, the program is not to change critical practice, but merely to aid the practitioners in sorting their practices out.

In the Rockefeller report, Isenberg speculates on the beneficial results which could be expected from well-trained philosophers of good taste reviewing and criticizing key masterworks of aesthetic discourse. To better grasp the thrust of this program, it is illuminating to follow the speculation through and explore what would occur if the directives of analytic aesthetics were implemented. Would this improve the discourse by rendering it less obscure? What, for instance, would be the result of reforming art studies as the program's second thesis directs? Would eliminating the purported mismatch between form and function eliminate some dysfunctional dimensions of aesthetic discourse and make it more successful?

Suppose we erased the generalizations "flung out" by Goethe, Coleridge, De Quincey, and Valery from their critical writings? What remains are these writers' insights about particular works of art. Suppose, as Urmson does, we correct A. E. Housman's poetics by pointing out that Housman's own examples do not support his contention that being moved by thrilling utterances makes a situation aesthetic? What remains are the examples themselves, which Urmson appropriates as confirmation of his own account of what makes a situation aesthetic. Suppose, as Gallie does, we explicate Wordsworth's 1815 *Preface* so as to obtain a more rigorous theory of the imagination. What remains of Wordsworth's varied but perhaps inconsistent examples of imaginative activity (subtracting properties from an object, endowing an object with properties that do not inhere in it, consolidating discrete entities into a unity and separating a thing into discrete elements, framing comparisons of expression and effect) is Gallie's summation that, unlike mathematical abstraction, poetic abstractions are inexplicit, indefinite, and vague.

In all these cases, it seems to me, clarifying criticism results only in impoverishing it. Goethe,

Coleridge, De Quincey, Valery, and Housman no longer have theories at all after their work has been clarified. Their brilliance illuminates nothing beyond the illustrations they give. And the illustrations illustrate nothing beyond themselves. On the other hand, Wordsworth's theory no longer is illuminated by the brilliance of the illustrations, since on Gallie's showing these illustrations do not all drive uniformly in the same logical direction.

To strip, or not to strip, criticism of components which fall short of being clear. What is gained, and what, if anything, is lost? It should be noted that successful analysis need not make the critical writings easier to understand, as philosophical accounts that are clear to philosophers are not necessarily clear to anyone else.

Moreover, eliminating all but the critics' discussions of individual works could restrict interest in the criticism to those acquainted with the particular works discussed. For example, Reynolds's *Discourses* command some interest from those unacquainted with the paintings Reynolds names because he generalizes, and consequently his views apply to other paintings that these readers might have seen. Remove the theories and general remarks, inadequate though they may be, and one is left with remarks one recognizes as penetrating only if one has encountered the subjects of the remarks, a condition which the audience to whom Reynolds's lectures were directed might have found difficult to satisfy.

It is hard to see how methodological clarification of the kind exemplified by these analyses of Isenberg, Gallie, and Urmson advances criticism intellectually, since none of the revisions reform anything other than their immediate object. It is also hard to see why improving criticism logically should make it less rather than more dreary. . . .

Despite the obscure and perhaps self-contradictory methodology which, on the standards of the analytic program, mars Wordsworth's *Preface,* his poetics surely would be more rather than less dreary if purged of the language he chooses to convey and instill rational conviction. What is true of Wordsworth's *Preface* is true also of the treatises of Aristotle, Reynolds, Tolstoi, and Bell, to take some influential examples. Each provides an apologia which expands appreciation of a certain sort of artwork by arguing (whether the argument succeeds is not at issue here) that the distinguishing properties of that kind of work resemble (or have evolved out of) those found in admired predecessor works. The analytic aestheticians would have it that this form of aesthetics is illegitimate. But to eliminate or radically revise art studies that are among the most influential in the field, and perhaps to carry out such reforms on most instances of study in the field, comes perilously close to just what Isenberg warned analytic aesthetics was unauthorized to do: reform critical practice from the ground up.

What went wrong with the program should now be more transparent. Analytic aesthetics violated one of its own rules, and in doing so, exacerbated the dreariness it was meant to reduce. By limiting the grounds for reforming practice to considerations internal to aesthetic discourse, the analysts argued from form to function, but then also from function to form. Consequently, they obscured their own procedure. They appealed to practice to demonstrate that the argument forms found in traditional aesthetics do not fulfill their supposed functions. To account for the persistence of these forms, they offered explanations in terms of alternative functions, consistent with the continued use of the forms. Thus, the tactic they adopted identified the presence of the traditional forms as the source of confusion. But, because form obscures function, the program's commitment to illumination required that the misleading forms be cleared away.

Why should clearing up confusion leave aesthetics duller than before? The answer, I think, is that the analysts misjudged the relation between function and form. If form follows function, it is equally so that function depends on form. There is a vast difference between being formally equipped to fulfill a function but regularly failing to fulfill it, and not being equipped to fulfill it at all. To illustrate by analogy, a student might have formal training in geometry but nevertheless always encounter defeating conditions and always flunk the exam. In respect to having potential to

pass the exam, such a student is situated differently from a student who never has learned geometry, even though the two students are indistinguishable in respect to having failed the exam. Whereas in traditional aesthetics, defeating conditions may stand between form and function, form still may serve as an enabling condition of function. If this is so, then clearing out forms that provoke confusion and logical blunders cannot help but have a reductive impact on function. The price of eliminating confusion in aesthetics seems to be the constriction of critical force and scope.

It might be objected here that this is all to the good because practices doomed to fail to function should not be retained. But this objection conflates failing to have an orientation with failing to meet a necessary condition. That is, for an activity to be functional, it need not necessarily attain its goal; it may suffice that the activity is goal-oriented.

To illustrate, suppose the function of an apprentice's activity is to acquire his master's skill, but the apprentice always fails to do so. Possibly, revising the training program will provide for success, although it is unlikely that useful reforms can be grounded in considerations internal to the inadequate practices. On the other hand, the world may be such that no one can ever equal the master's hand. If such is the case, is the program a failure? Only if drawing near to the goal has no value at all. Only if approximating the goal is completely insufficient. Imposition of such severe conditions for retaining practices seems implicit in the analytic aestheticians' procedures, but this standard may be so rigorous that complex, sophisticated human activities should not be held to it.

To decide whether to impose such a strict standard in aesthetics, we need to know whether (in practice) benefits accrue from using forms whose functions may never be fulfilled. The question is not whether the forms themselves make an irreplaceable contribution to aesthetics, but rather whether the functions these forms serve, however unsuccessfully, are integral to aesthetic discourse. To address this question requires departing from the procedures of analytic aesthetics. To decide how important it is to retain or eliminate any function of traditional aesthetics, we cannot restrict ourselves, as most of the analytic aestheticians did, to considerations internal to aesthetic discourse. We must go further than to ask, "Is the discourse coherent and clear?" Whether or not it is useful to retain any function as a goal, even if we are systematically frustrated in reaching it, depends on the benefits or drawbacks of pursuing it in the world. Consequently, to make this decision, we must advance beyond the analytic aestheticians' program and seek grounds logically prior to aesthetic discourse.

Outside of, and prior to, aesthetics is at least a world, and at most a multiplicity of worlds. This provides the subject matter of aesthetics. To explore what methods will permit aesthetics to function most productively demands not only views about how aesthetic discourse operates, but also a theory of semantics, a philosophical account of the relations between aesthetic discourse and its world(s).

Analytic aesthetics benefited the field by focusing on the methodology of studying art. But the program did not acknowledge that getting clear about methodology is not the same as getting a methodology for studies which are clear. If the world with which a methodology deals is disordered and confused, then the studies it produces should reflect this state of affairs. If that world does not enjoy clearly delineated entities and conclusive outcomes, then what we learn about it is clear and conclusive only at the risk of being misleading.

With a few exceptions such as Margaret Macdonald, the analytic aestheticians did not reveal what they thought the world of art was like. Possibly, some of them avoided having such thoughts, fearing to be drawn into speculation.

But in detouring around the world, they also missed opportunities to talk about art itself and to illustrate their work with remarks enlightened by the piercing brilliance Isenberg praised.

Why this was so, I have argued, is attributable to a defect in the analysts' procedure. But considering this flaw from a historical perspective may also provide some light. An unacknowledged ontological boundary seems to circumscribe the thinking of most of them. . . .

What prevents these analytic aestheticians from stepping beyond phenomenological boundaries to think of art not only as existing in experience but also as situated in a world? In the preface to his third (substantially revised) edition of *Philosophy Looks at the Arts,* Joseph Margolis describes analytic aesthetics as "a general mode of working that departed abruptly but penetratingly from the then-dominant idealist tradition." While this is so, I think it also may be the case that analytic aesthetics' departure from idealism was not abrupt and clean enough to impel the program to achieve its goals.

In the mid-1960s, work in aesthetics which directly engaged questions about worlds began to appear. In 1964, Arthur Danto published "The Artworld," initiating a major and influential project in which Danto tells us about how the artworld makes art. In 1968, Nelson Goodman published *The Languages of Art,* initiating a major and influential project in which Goodman tell us about how art makes worlds. With their expertise in art and their philosophical talent, Danto and Goodman fulfill Isenberg's programmatic recommendation to integrate insightful commentary on art with rigorous philosophical argument. These contemporary aestheticians exemplify how aesthetics has brightened up because its practitioners turn their lights on the world.

A. The Analytic Critique of Aesthetic Experience

Let us examine in detail how this new focus of analytic aesthetics affected the question of aesthetic experience. From the eighteenth through the mid-twentieth century aesthetics could be defined as the investigation of aesthetic experience. What are the essential features of our experience of objects of natural beauty and works of fine art? From the psychological or phenomenological perspective of the audience—that is, the observers of natural beauty and the consumers and appreciators of fine art—the question is, are there any characteristics of such experiences that are unique to aesthetic experience, that are present in all aesthetic experiences and not present in any nonaesthetic experiences? And if so, what are those features? Although opinions varied over the centuries, most answers took what became the traditional form of the three D's—distance, disinterestedness, and detachment. As Kant said, the love of beauty is not the desire to possess the object nor is it the desire for any ulterior end beyond the immediate experience itself.

Nonetheless, despite a certain general agreement on the broad outlines of the disinterested nature of aesthetic experience, the theory actually contained a number of different and overlapping ideas that were never completely reconciled. Kant had emphasized the point that a disinterested enjoyment is not to possess the object. Other aestheticians said that aesthetic experience is disinterested in the sense that we disengage (becoming detached) from practical concerns. And still others argued that aesthetic experience is distanced, detached, and disinterested in the sense that we focus on the appearance or semblance of the sensory appearance of the object and not on what the object really is. Not that these interpretations of the three Ds are totally at variance with one another. Clearly, they overlap in significant ways. If I concentrate on the sensory appearance (e.g., the play of light on the surface of the water), I am not primarily concerned with what the object really is (e.g., water) and therefore I am not concerned with the practical ramifications of the object (e.g., a refreshing swim, irrigating my garden, putting out a fire, flooding my home, etc.), nor do I wish to possess it (e.g., to take a drink of water). Nonetheless, these connections were never satisfactorily harmonized (or really even noticed).

The theory remained, then, rather vague and open ended. As such, it became a prime target of analytic aesthetics. Beginning in the mid-1950s, analytic aesthetics (Joseph Margolis's first edition of *Philosophy Looks at the Arts* in 1962 and William Elton's anthology *Aesthetics and Language* in 1954) sought to bring the "wooly," interdisciplinary field of aesthetics firmly within the new program of "conceptual clarification" inaugurated by analytic philosophy. From the perspective of analytic philosophy, early twentieth-century aesthetics was plagued by half-digested psychological, neo-Hegelian (that is, idealist), Romantic and literary "essentialist" generalizations (see Part II, section B), which analytic aesthetics vowed to clean up—and among the early tasks of clarification was the notion of aesthetic experience.

At first some aestheticians, such as Eliseo Vivas, Jerome Stolnitz, and Monroe Beardsley, tried to rectify the concept of aesthetic experience, weeding out extraneous notions and logically tightening up the remaining core. In the mid-1960s, however, George Dickie declared this effort a waste of time. There is no aesthetic experience, Dickie announced; the long tradition of aesthetic experience is simply a "myth." Beardsley and Stolnitz nonetheless continued to defend and refine the concept to make it more acceptable to its critics, but it was a losing battle.

At the heart of this mid-1960s debate is the psychological and phenomenological question of whether one can look at the same object from several perspectives or points of view, regarding it now from a practical point of view (which reveals the utilitarian aspect, or *intentional object*) and now from an aesthetic point of view (which reveals an aesthetic aspect, the so-called *aesthetic object* as its correlative intentional object). No, replied Dickie, when you shift gears in this way, you are simply turning attention from one object to a different object, not to a different aspect of the same object. In the theater you are focusing on the play *Othello,* but then you begin to worry whether your spouse is being unfaithful to you—but, according to Dickie, this response is not to be analyzed as your first attending to the aesthetic aspect of the play and then shifting to a more personal and self-interested aspect—no, it is just that you are first paying attention to the play and then paying attention to your marital situation.

The Aesthetic Point of View

MONROE C. BEARDSLEY

THERE HAS BEEN a persistent effort to discover the uniquely aesthetic component, aspect, or ingredient in whatever is or is experienced. Unlike some other philosophical quarries, the object of this chase has not proved as elusive as the snark, the Holy Grail, or Judge Crater—the hunters have returned not empty-handed, but overburdened. For they have found a rich array of candidates for the basically and essentially aesthetic:

aesthetic experience   aesthetic objects
aesthetic value   aesthetic concepts
aesthetic enjoyment   aesthetic situations
aesthetic satisfaction

Confronted with such trophies, we cannot easily doubt that there *is* something peculiarly aesthetic to be found in our world or our experience; yet its exact location and its categorial status remain in question. This is my justification for conducting yet another raid on the ineffable, with the help of a different concept, one in the contemporary philosophical style.

When the conservationist and the attorney for Con Edison argue their conflicting cases before a state commission that is deciding whether a nuclear power plant shall be built beside the Hudson River, we can say they do not merely disagree; they regard that power plant from different points of view. When the head of the Histadrut Publishing House refused to publish the novel *Exodus* in Israel, he said: "If it is to be read as history, it is inaccurate. If it is to be read as literature, it is vulgar." And Maxim Gorky reports a remark that Lenin once made to him:

'I know nothing that is greater than [Beethoven's] *Appassionata*. I would like to listen to it every day. A marvelous, superhuman music. I always say with pride—a naive pride perhaps: What miracles human beings can perform!' Then screwing his eyes [Lenin] added, smiling sadly, "But I can't listen to music too often; it affects your nerves. One wants to say stupid nice things and stroke on the head the people who can create such beauty while living in this vile hell. And now you must not stroke anyone on the head: you'll have your hands beaten off. You have to hit them on the head without mercy, though our ideal is not to use violence against anyone. Hmm, hmm,—an infernally cruel job we have.'

In each of these examples, it seems plausible to say that one of the conflicting points of view is a peculiarly aesthetic one: that of the conservationist troubled by threats to the Hudson's scenic beauty; that of the publisher who refers to

From Contemporary Philosophic Thought *3 (1970). Reprinted by permission of the publisher.*

reading *Exodus* "as literature"; that of Lenin, who appears to hold that we ought to adopt the political (rather than the aesthetic) point of view toward Beethoven's sonata, because of the unfortunate political consequences of adopting the aesthetic point of view.

If the notion of the aesthetic point of view can be made clear, it should be useful from the philosophical point of view. The first philosophical use is in mediating certain kinds of dispute. To understand a particular point of view, we must envision its alternatives. Unless there can be more than one point of view toward something the concept breaks down. Consider, for example, the case of architecture. The classic criteria of Vitruvius were stated tersely by Sir Henry Wotton in these words: "Well-building hath three conditions: Commodity, Firmness, and Delight." Commodity is function: that it makes a good church or house or school. Firmness is construction: that the building holds itself up. Suppose we were comparing a number of buildings to see how well built they are, according to these "conditions." We would find some that are functionally effective, structurally sound, and visually attractive. We would find others—old wornout buildings or new suburban shacks—that are pretty poor in each of these departments. But also we would find that the characteristics vary independently over a wide range; that some extremely solid old bank buildings have Firmness (they are knocked down at great cost) without one obvious and notable kind, and we judge it in relation to that kind, the "point of view" terminology is unnecessary. We wouldn't ordinarily speak of considering music from a musical point of view, because it wouldn't occur to us that someone might regard it from a political point of view. In the same way, it would be natural to speak of considering whiskey from a medical point of view but not of considering penicillin from a medical point of view. This shows that the "point of view" terminology is implicitly rejective: it is a device for setting aside considerations advanced by others (such as that the bridge will fall) in order to focus attention on the set of consider-

ations that *we* wish to emphasize (such as that the sweep and soar of the bridge are a joy to behold).

The "point of view" terminology, however, is more elastic than the "good of its kind" terminology. To consider a bridge or music or sculpture as an aesthetic object is to consider it from the aesthetic point of view, but what about a mountain, a sea shell, or a tiger? These are neither musical compositions, paintings, poems nor sculptures. A sea shell cannot be *good* sculpture if it is not sculpture at all. But evidently we can adopt the aesthetic point of view toward these things. In fact, some aesthetic athletes (or athletic aesthetes) have claimed the ability to adopt the aesthetic point of view toward anything at all—toward *The Story of O* (this is what Elliot Fremont-Smith has called "beyond pornography"), toward a garbage dump, toward the murders of three civil rights workers in Philadelphia, Mississippi. (This claim has been put to a severe test by some of our more far-out sculptors.) Perhaps even more remarkable is the feat recently performed by those who viewed the solemn installation of an "invisible sculpture" behind the Metropolitan Museum of Art. The installation consisted in digging a grave-size hole and filling it in again. "It is really an underground sculpture," said its conceiver, Claes Oldenburg. "I think of it as the dirt being loosened from the sides of a certain section of Central Park." The city's architectural consultant, Sam Green, commented on the proceedings:

> This is a conceptual work of art and is as much valid as something you can actually see. Everything is art if it is chosen by the artist to be art. You can say it is good art or bad art, but you can't say it isn't art. Just because you can't see a statue doesn't mean that it isn't there.

This, of course, is but one of countless examples of the current tendency to stretch the boundaries of the concept of "art."

The second philosophical use of the notion of the aesthetic point of view is to provide a broad concept of art that might be helpful for certain purposes. We might say:

> A work of art (in the broad sense) is any perceptual or intentional object that is deliberately regarded from the aesthetic point of view.

Here, "regarding" would have to include looking, listening, reading, and similar acts of attention, and also what I call "exhibiting"—picking up an object and placing it where it readily permits such attention, or presenting the object to persons acting as spectators. What, then, is the aesthetic point of view? I propose the following:

> To adopt the aesthetic point of view with regard to X is to take an interest in whatever aesthetic value X may possess.

I ask myself what I am doing in adopting a particular point of view, and acting toward an object in a way that is appropriate to that point of view; and, so far as I can see, it consists in searching out a corresponding value in the object, to discover whether any of it is present. Sometimes it is to go farther: to cash in on that value, to realize it, to avail myself of it. All this searching, seeking and, if possible, realizing, I subsume under the general phrase "taking an interest in." To listen to Beethoven's *Appassionata* with pleasure and a sense that it is "marvelous, superhuman music," is to seek—and find—aesthetic value in it. To read the novel *Exodus* "as literature," and be repelled because it is "vulgar" is (I take it) to seek aesthetic value in it but not find very much of it. And when Geoffrey Scott makes his distinction between different ways of regarding a building, and between that "constructive integrity in fact" which belongs under Firmness, and that "constructive vividness in appearance" which is a source of architectural Delight, he adds that "their value in the building is of a wholly disparate kind"; in short, the two points of view, the engineering and the aesthetic, involve two kinds of value.

This proposed definition of "aesthetic point of view" will not, as it stands, fit all of the ordinary uses of this phrase. There is a further complication. I am thinking of a remark by John Hightower, executive director of the New York State Council on the Arts, about the council's aim to "encourage some sort of aesthetic standards." He said, "There are lots of laws that unconsciously inhibit the arts. Architecture is the most dramatic example. Nobody has looked at the laws from an aesthetic point of view." And I am thinking of a statement in the *Yale Alumni Magazine* that the Yale City Planning Department was undertaking "a pioneering two-year research project to study highway environment from an aesthetic point of view." I suppose the attention in these cases was not on the supposed aesthetic value of the laws or of the present "highway environment," but rather in the aesthetic value that might be achieved by changes in these things. Perhaps that is why these examples speak of "*an* aesthetic point of view," rather than "*the* aesthetic point of view." And we could, if we wish, make use of this verbal distinction in our broadened definition:

> To adopt *an* aesthetic point of view with regard to X is to take an interest in whatever aesthetic value that X may possess *or that is obtainable by means of X.*

I have allowed the phrase "adopting the aesthetic point of view" to cover a variety of activities. One of them is judging:

> To judge X from the aesthetic point of view is to estimate the aesthetic value of X.

Those who are familiar with Paul Taylor's treatment of points of view in his book *Normative Discourse* will note how the order I find in these concepts differs from the one he finds. His account applies only to judging, which makes it too narrow to suit me. It also has, I think, another flaw. He holds that:

> Taking a certain point of view is nothing but adopting certain canons of reasoning as the framework within which value judgments are to be justified; the canons of reasoning define the point of view. . . . We have already said that a value judgment is a moral judgment if it is made from the moral point of view.

Thus we could ask of Taylor, What is an aesthetic value judgment? He would reply, It is one made from the aesthetic point of view. And which are those? They are the ones justified by appeal to certain "canons of reasoning," and more particularly the "rules of relevance." But which are the aesthetic rules of relevance? These are the rules "implicitly or explicitly followed by people" in using the aesthetic value-language—that is, in making judgments of aesthetic value. Perhaps I have misunderstood Taylor's line of thought here, but the path it seems to trace is circular. I hope to escape this trap by breaking into the chain at a different point.

I define "aesthetic point of view" in terms of "aesthetic value." And while I think this step is by no means a trivial one, it is not very enlightening unless it is accompanied by some account of aesthetic value. I don't propose to present a detailed theory on this occasion, but I shall extend my chain of definitions to a few more links, and provide some defense against suspected weaknesses. What, then, is aesthetic value?

> The aesthetic value of an object is the value it possesses in virtue of its capacity to provide aesthetic gratification.

There are three points about this definition that require some attention.

First, it will be noted that this is not a definition of "value." It purports to distinguish *aesthetic* value from other kinds of value in terms of a particular capacity. It says that in judging the total value of an object we must include that part of its value which is due to its capacity to provide aesthetic gratification.

The second point concerns "aesthetic gratification." My earliest version of this capacity-definition of "aesthetic value" employed the concept of aesthetic experience. I am still not persuaded that this concept must be abandoned as hopeless, but it needs further elaboration in the face of the criticism coming from George Dickie, whose relentless attack on unnecessarily multiplied entities in aesthetics has led him to skepticism about whether there is such a thing as aesthetic experience. I have tried working with the concept of aesthetic enjoyment instead, and

that may be on the right track. For the present occasion, I have chosen a term that I think is somewhat broader in scope, and perhaps therefore slightly less misleading

Again, however, the term "aesthetic gratification" is not self-explanatory. It seems clear that one kind of gratification can be distinguished from another only in terms of its intentional object: that is, of the properties that the pleasure is taken *in,* or the enjoyment is enjoyment *of.* To discriminate aesthetic gratification—and consequently aesthetic value and the aesthetic point of view—we must specify what it is obtained from. I offer the following:

> Gratification is aesthetic when it is obtained primarily from attention to the formal unity and/or the regional qualities of a complex whole, and when its magnitude is a function of the degree of formal unity and/or the intensity of regional quality.

The defense of such a proposal would have to answer two questions. First, is there such a type of gratification? I think there is, and I think that it can be distinguished from other types of gratification, though it is often commingled with them. Second, what is the justification for calling this type of gratification "aesthetic"? The answer to this question would be more complicated. Essentially, I would argue that there are certain clear-cut exemplary cases of works of art—that is, poems, plays, musical compositions, etc.—that must be counted as works of art if anything is. There is a type of gratification characteristically and preeminently provided by such works, and this type of gratification is the type I have distinguished above. Finally, this type of gratification (once distinguished) has a paramount claim to be denominated "aesthetic"—even though there are many other things that works of art can do to you, such as inspire you, startle you, or give you a headache.

If this line of argument can be made convincing, we find ourselves with what might be called primary *marks* of the aesthetic: it is the presence in the object of some notable degree of unity and/or the presence of some notable intensity of regional quality that indicates that the enjoyments or satisfactions it affords are aesthetic—insofar as those enjoyments or satisfactions are afforded by these properties. I shall return to these marks a little later, and show the sort of use I think can be made of them.

But before we come to that, we must consider the third point about the capacity-definition of "aesthetic value"—and this is the most troublesome of them all.

The term "capacity" has been chosen with care. My view is that the aesthetic value of an object is not a function of the actual degree of gratification obtained from it. It is not an average, or the mean degree of gratification obtained from it by various perceivers. It is not a sum, or the total gratification obtained from it in the course of its existence. All these depend in part on external considerations, including the qualifications of those who happen to resort to libraries, museums, and concerts, and the circumstances of their visits. I am thinking in terms of particular exposures to the work—a particular experience of the music of the poem, of the painting—and of the degree of aesthetic gratification obtained on each occasion. Aesthetic value depends on the highest degree obtainable under optimal circumstances. Thus my last definition should be supplemented by another one:

> The amount of aesthetic value possessed by an object is a function of the degree of aesthetic gratification it is capable of providing in a particular experience of it.

My reason for holding this view is that I want to say that a critical evaluation is a judgment of aesthetic value, and it seems clear to me that estimating capacities is both the least and the most we can ask of the critical evaluator. I take it that when a literary critic, for example, judges the goodness of a poem (from the aesthetic point of view), and is prepared to back up his judgment with reasons, he must be saying something about the relationship of the poem to the experiences of actual or potential readers. The question is,

What is this relationship? When a critic says that a poem is good, he is hardly ever in a position to predict the gratification that particular readers or groups of readers will receive from it. Moreover, he is usually not in a position to generalize about tendencies, to say, for instance, that readers of such-and-such propensities, preferences, or preparations will probably be delighted by the poem. If the critic has at his disposal the information required to support such statements, he is of course at liberty to say such things as: "This would have appealed to President Kennedy," or "This is an ideal Christmas gift for your friends who love mountain climbing." But when he simply says, "This is a good poem," we must interpret him as saying something weaker (though still significant) about the capacity of the work to provide a notable degree of aesthetic gratification. For *that* is a judgment he should be able to support, if he understands the poem.

The question, however, is whether the capacity-definition of "aesthetic value" is too weak, as a report of what actually happens in art criticism. I can think of three difficulties that have been or could be raised. They might be called (1) the unrecognized masterpiece problem, (2) the LSD problem, and (3) the Edgar Rice Burroughs problem. Or, to give them more abstract names, they are (1) the problem of falsification, (2) the problem of illusion, and (3) the problem of devaluation.

(1) Some people are troubled by one consequence of the capacity-definition—that objects can possess aesthetic value that never has been and never will be realized, such as the "gems of purest ray serene the dark unfathomed caves of ocean bear." This ought not to trouble us, I think. It is no real paradox that many objects worth looking at can never be looked at. But there is another kind of aesthetic inaccessibility in the highly complicated and obscure work that no critic can find substantial value in, though it may still be there. In Balzac's short story, "Le Chef-d'oeuvre inconnu," the master painter works in solitude for years, striving for the perfection of his greatest work; but in his dedication and delu-

sion he overlays the canvas with so many brush strokes that the work is ruined. When his fellow artists finally see the painting, they are appalled by it. But how can they be sure that the painting doesn't have aesthetic value, merely because they have not found any? The capacity to provide aesthetic gratification of a high order may still be there, though they are not sharp or sensitive enough to take advantage of it.

If my proposed definition entailed that negative judgments of aesthetic value cannot even in principle be justified, then we would naturally mistrust it. But of course this consequence is not necessary. What does follow is that there is a certain asymmetry between negative and affirmative judgments, with respect to their degree of confirmation; but this is so between negative and affirmative existential statements in general. The experienced critic may have good reason in many cases not only for confessing that he finds little value in a painting, but for adding that very probably no one ever will find great value in it.

(2) If aesthetic value involves a capacity, then its presence can no doubt be sufficiently attested by a single realization. What a work *does* provide, it clearly *can* provide. And if my definition simply refers to the capacity, without qualification, then it makes no difference under what conditions that realization occurs. Now take any object you like, no matter how plain or ugly—say a heap of street sweepings awaiting the return of the street cleaner. Certainly we want to say that it is lacking in aesthetic value. But suppose someone whose consciousness is rapidly expanding under the influence of LSD or some other hallucinogenic drug happens to look at this heap and it gives him exquisite aesthetic gratification. Then it has the capacity to do so, and so it has high aesthetic value. But then perhaps every visual object has high aesthetic value, and all to about the same degree—if the reports may be trusted.

I cannot speak authoritatively of the LSD experience, but I gather that when a trip is successful, the object, however humble, may glow with unwonted intensity of color and its shapes assume an unexpected order and harmony. In short, the experience is illusory. This is certainly suggested by the most recent report I have run across. Dr. Lloyd A. Grumbles, a Philadelphia psychiatrist,

> said that while listening to Beethoven's *Eroica*, particularly the third movement, he felt simultaneously "insatiable longing and total gratification.". . . Dr. Grumbles said he also looked at prints of Picasso and Renoir paintings and realized, for the first time, "they were striving for the same goal."

Now you *know* he was under the influence of LSD.

This example suggests a modification of the definition given earlier:

> The aesthetic value of X is the value that X possesses in virtue of its capacity to provide aesthetic gratification when *correctly experienced*.

(3) The problem of devaluation can perhaps be regarded as a generalization of the LSD problem. When I was young I was for a time an avid reader of the Martian novels of Edgar Rice Burroughs. Recently when I bought the Dover paperback edition and looked at them again, I found that I could hardly read them. Their style alone is enough to repel you, if you really pay attention to it.

The problem is this: if on Monday I enjoy a novel very much, and thus know that it has the capacity to provide gratification, then how can I ever reverse the judgment and say the novel lacks that capacity? If the judgment that the novel is a good one is a capacity-judgment, it would seem that downward reevaluations (that is, devaluations) are always false—assuming that the original higher judgment was based on direct experience. There is no problem about upward reevaluations: when I say on Tuesday that the novel is better than I thought on Monday, this means that I have discovered the novel to have a greater capacity than I had realized. But how can we explain the lowering of an aesthetic evaluation and still maintain that these evaluations are capacity-judgments?

Some cases of devaluation can no doubt be taken care of without modifying the definition of "aesthetic value." The devaluation may be due to a shift in our value grades caused by enlargement of our range of experience. I might think that *Gone with the Wind* is a great novel, because it is the best I have read, but later I might take away that encomium and give it to *War and Peace*. Or the devaluation may be due to the belated recognition that my previous satisfaction in the work was a response to extra-aesthetic features. I now realize that my earlier enjoyment of detective stories was probably caused only in small part by their literary qualities, and was much more of a game-type pleasure.

But setting these cases aside, there remain cases where on perfectly sound and legitimate grounds I decide that the work, though it has provided a certain level of aesthetic gratification, is in fact not really that good. I have overestimated it. Evidently the definition of "aesthetic value" must be modified again. One thing we might do is insert a stipulation that the work be a reliable or dependable source of gratification: flukes don't count. We need not change the judgment into a straight tendency-statement. But we might insist that the enjoyment of the novel must at least be a repeatable experience. Something like this notion seems to underlie the frequent claim that our first reactions to a new work of art are not wholly to be trusted, that we should wait awhile and try it again; that we should see whether we can find at least one other person to corroborate our judgment; or that only posterity will be in a position to know whether the work is great.

I grant that all these precautions are helpful—indeed, they enable us to avoid the two sources of error mentioned a moment ago: having an inadequately formulated set of grading terms, and confusing aesthetic with nonaesthetic gratification. But I think it ought to be possible for a person, after a single experience of a work, to have excellent grounds for thinking it good and for commending it to others. And I think he would be justified in pointing out that he has found a potential source of aesthetic gratification that lies ready to be taken advantage of—even though he does not yet know how readily, how easily, how conveniently, or how frequently recourse may be had to it. Thus my escape from the difficulty is to revise the definition of "aesthetic value" again so as to stipulate that it is the value of the whole work that is in question:

> The aesthetic value of X is the value that X possesses in virtue of its capacity to provide aesthetic gratification *when correctly and completely experienced.*

The youth who was carried away by the adventures of Thuvia and the green men of Mars and the other denizens of that strange planet may well have gotten greater aesthetic gratification than the elderly person who returned to them after so many years. For the youth was fairly oblivious to the faults of style, and he filled in the flat characterizations with his own imagination, giving himself up unself-consciously to the dramatic events and exotic scenery. But, though he was lucky in a way, his judgment of the *whole* work was not to be trusted.

We saw earlier that the notion of a point of view plays a particular role in focusing or forwarding certain disputes by limiting the range of relevant considerations. We invoke the aesthetic point of view when we want to set aside certain considerations that others have advanced—as that a poem is pornographic, or that a painting is a forgery—or that (as Jacques Maritain remarks) "A splendid house without a door is not a good work of architecture." But the person whose considerations are thus rejected may feel that the decision is arbitrary, and enter an appeal, in the hope that a higher philosophical tribunal will rule that the lower court erred in its exclusions. How do we know whether being pornographic, or being a forgery, or lacking a door, is irrelevant from the aesthetic point of view? I propose this answer:

> A consideration about an object is relevant to the aesthetic point of view if and only if it is a fact about the object that affects the degree to which the marks of aesthetic gratification (formal unity and intensity of regional quality) are present in the object.

Thus: Is the fact that a painting is a forgery relevant to a judgment of it from the aesthetic point of view? No; because it has no bearing on its form or quality. Is the fact that a painting is a seascape relevant? Sometimes. It is when the subject contributes to, or detracts from, its degree of unity or its qualitative intensity. Is the biography of the composer relevant? According to a writer in *The Music Review:*

> It is a well-known fact that knowledge of the circumstances surrounding the composition of a work enhances the audience's appreciation. . . . It is because of this that program notes, radio comments, and music appreciation courses are in such demand. To secure such knowledge is one of the important tasks of musical research.

Now, I'm not sure that this "well-known fact" is really a fact, but let us assume that it is. Does it follow that information about the circumstances of composition is relevant to consideration of the work from an aesthetic point of view? We can imagine this sort of thing:

> It was a cold rainy day in Vienna, and Schubert was down to his last crust of bread. As he looked about his dingy garret, listening to the rain that beat down, he reflected that he could not even afford to feed his mice. He recalled a sad poem by Goethe, and suddenly a melody sprang into his head. He seized an old piece of paper, and began to write feverishly. Thus was "Death and the Maiden" born.

Now even if everyone, or *nearly* everyone, who reads this program note finds that it increases his appreciation of the song, a condition of appreciation is not necessarily a condition of value. From this information—say, that it was raining—nothing can be inferred about the specifically aesthetic character of the song. (It is relevant, of course, that the words and music match each other in certain ways; however, we know that not by biographical investigation but by listening to the song itself.)

Here is one more example. In a very interesting article "On the Aesthetic Attitude in Romanesque Art," Meyer Shapiro has argued that:

> Contrary to the general belief that in the Middle Ages the work of art was considered mainly as a vehicle of religious teaching or as a piece of craftsmanship serving a useful end, and that beauty of form and color was no object of contemplation in itself, these texts abound in aesthetic judgments and in statements about the qualities and structure of the work. They speak of the fascination of the image, its marvelous likeness to physical reality, and the artist's wonderful skill, often in complete abstraction from the content of the object of art.

Shapiro is inquiring whether medieval people were capable of taking the aesthetic point of view in some independence of the religious and technological points of view. He studies various texts in which aesthetic objects are described and praised, to elicit the grounds on which this admiration is based, and to discover whether these grounds are relevant to the aesthetic point of view. Form and color, for example, are clearly relevant, and so to praise a work for its form or color is to adopt the aesthetic point of view. And I should think the same can be said for "the fascination of the image"—by which Shapiro refers to the extraordinary interest in the grotesque figures freely carved by the stonecutters in Romanesque buildings. These centaurs, chimeras, two-headed animals, creatures with feet and the tail of a serpent, etc., are the images deplored by Saint Bernard with an ambivalence like that in Lenin's remark about Beethoven:

> In the cloister, under the eyes of the brethren who read there, what profit is there in those ridiculous monsters, in that marvelous and deformed beauty, in that beautiful deformity?

But what of Shapiro's other points—the image's "marvelous likeness to physical reality, and the artist's wonderful skill"?

If a person admires skill in depiction, he is certainly not taking a religious point of view—but is he taking the aesthetic point of view? I should think not. No doubt when he notices the accuracy of depiction, reflects on the skill required to achieve it, and thus admires the artist, he may be placed in a more favorable psychological posture toward the work itself. But this contributes to the conditions of the experience; it does not enter into the experience directly, as does the perception of form and color, or the recognition of the represented objects as saints or serpents. So I would say that the fact that the medieval writer admired the skill in depiction is *not* evidence that he took the aesthetic point of view, though it is evidence that he took *an* aesthetic point of view, since skill was involved in the production of the work.

There is one final problem that may be worth raising and commenting upon briefly—although it is not at all clear to me how the problem should even be formulated. It concerns the justification of adopting the aesthetic point of view, and its potential conflicts with other points of view. On one hand, it is interesting to note that much effort has been spent (especially during recent decades) in getting people to adopt the aesthetic point of view much more firmly and continuously than has been common in our country. The conservationists are trying to arouse us to concern for the preservation of natural beauties, instead of automatically assuming that they have a lower priority than any other interest that happens to come up—such as installing power lines, or slaughtering deer, or advertising beer. And those who are concerned with "education of the eye," or "visual education," are always developing new methods of teaching the theory and practice of good design, the aim being to produce people who are aware of the growing hideousness of our cities and towns, and who are troubled enough to work for changes.

But the effort to broaden the adoption of the aesthetic point of view sometimes takes another form. According to its leading theoretician, the "Camp sensibility" is characterized by the great range of material to which it can respond: "Camp is the consistently aesthetic experience of the world," writes Susan Sontag. "It incarnates a victory of style over content, of aesthetics over morality, of irony over tragedy."

Here is an extreme consequence of trying to increase the amount of aesthetic value of which

we can take advantage. But it also gives rise to an interesting problem, which might be called "the dilemma of aesthetic education." The problem is pointed up by a cartoon I saw not long ago (by David Gerard), showing the proprietor of a junkyard named "Sam's Salvage" standing by a huge pile of junked cars, and saying to two other men: "Whattya mean it's an ugly eyesore? If I'd paid Picasso to pile it up, you'd call it a work of art."

The central task of aesthetic education, as traditionally conceived, is the improvement of taste, involving the development of two dispositions: (1) the capacity to obtain aesthetic gratification from increasingly subtle and complex aesthetic objects that are characterized by various forms of unity—in short, the response to beauty in one main sense; and (2) an increasing dependence on objects beautiful in this way (having harmony, order, balance, proportion) as sources of aesthetic satisfaction. It is this impulse that is behind the usual concept of "beautification"— shielding the highways from junkyards and billboards, and providing more trees and flowers and grass. As long as the individual's aesthetic development in this sense is accompanied by increasing access to beautiful sights and sounds, it is all to the good. His taste improves; his aesthetic pleasures are keener, and when he encounters unavoidable ugliness, he may be moved to eliminate it by labor or by law. On the other hand, suppose he finds that his environment grows uglier, as the economy progresses, and that the ugliness becomes harder to escape. Second, suppose he comes to enjoy another kind of aesthetic value, one that derives from intensity of regional quality more than formal fitness. And third, suppose he comes to realize that his aesthetic gratification is affected by the demands he makes upon an object—especially because the intensity of its regional qualities partly depends on its symbolic import. For example, the plain ordinary object may be seen as a kind of symbol, and become expressive (i.e., assume a noteworthy quality) if the individual attends to it in a way that invites these features to emerge. Suddenly, a whole new field of aesthetic gratification opens up. Trivial objects, the accidental, the neglected, the meretricious and vulgar, all take on new excitement. The automobile graveyard and the weed-filled garden are seen to have their own wild and grotesque expressiveness as well as symbolic import. The kewpie doll, the Christmas card, the Tiffany lampshade, can be enjoyed aesthetically, not for their beauty but for their bizarre qualities and their implicit reflection of social attitudes. This is a way of transfiguring reality, and though not everything can be transfigured, perhaps, it turns out that much can.

What I mean by the dilemma of aesthetic education is this: that we are torn between conflicting ways of redirecting taste. One is the way of love of beauty, which is limited in its range of enjoyment, but is reformist by implication, since it seeks a world that conforms to its ideal. The other is the way of aestheticizing everything—of taking the aesthetic point of view wherever possible—and this widens enjoyment, but is defeatist, since instead of eliminating the junkyard and the slum it tries to see them as expressive and symbolic. The conflict here is analogous to that between the social gospel and personal salvation in some of our churches—though no doubt its consequences are not equally momentous. I don't suppose this dilemma is ultimately unresolvable, though I cannot consider it further at the moment. I point it out as one of the implications of the tendency (which I have been briefly exploring) to extend the aesthetic point of view as widely as possible.

But there is another weighty tradition opposed to this expansion. Lenin and Saint Bernard stand witness to the possibility that there may be situations in which it is morally objectionable to adopt the aesthetic point of view. A man who had escaped from Auschwitz commented on Rolf Hochmuth's play: "*The Deputy* should not be considered as a historical work or even as a work of art, but as a moral lesson." Perhaps he only meant that looking for historical truth or artistic merit in *The Deputy* is a waste of time. But he may also have meant that there is something blameworthy about anyone who is capable of contemplating those terrible events from a purely historical or purely aes-

thetic point of view. Renata Adler, reporting in *The New Yorker* on the New Politics Convention that took place in Chicago on Labor Day weekend, 1967, listed various types of self-styled "revolutionaries" who attended, including "the aesthetic-analogy revolutionaries, who discussed riots as though they were folk songs or pieces of local theatre, subject to appraisal in literary terms ('authentic,' 'beautiful')." That is carrying the aesthetic point of view pretty far.

This possibility has not gone unnoticed by imaginative writers—notably Henry James and Henrik Ibsen. The tragedy of Mrs. Gereth, in *The Spoils of Poynton,* is that of a woman who could not escape the aesthetic point of view. She had a "passion for the exquisite" that made her prone "to be rendered unhappy by the presence of the dreadful [and] she was condemned to wince wherever she turned." In fact, the things that troubled her most—and she encountered them everywhere, but nowhere in more abundance than the country house known as Waterbath—were just the campy items featured by Miss Sontag: "trumpery ornament and scrapbook art, with strange excrescences and bunchy draperies, with gimcracks that might have been keepsakes for maid-servants [and even] a souvenir from some centennial or other Exhibition." The tragedy of the sculptor, Professor Rubek, in *When We Dead Awaken,* is that he so utterly aestheticized the woman who loved him and who was his model that she was not a person to him. As she says, "The work of art first—then the human being." It may even be—and I say this with the utmost hesitation, since I have no wish to sink in these muddy waters—that this is the theme of Antonioni's film, *Blow-Up:* the emptiness that comes from utter absorption in an aesthetic point of view of a photographer to whom every person and every event seems to represent only the possibility of a new photographic image. In that respect, Antonioni's photographer is certainly worse than Professor Rubek.

The mere confrontation of these two vague and general social philosophies of art will not, of course, take us very far in understanding the possibilities and the limitations of the aesthetic point of view. I leave matters unresolved, with questions hanging in the air. Whatever resolution we ultimately find, however, will surely incorporate two observations that may serve as a pair of conclusions.

First, there are occasions on which it would be wrong to adopt the aesthetic point of view, because there is a conflict of values and the values that are in peril are, in that particular case, clearly higher. Once in a while you see a striking photograph or film sequence in which someone is (for example) lying in the street after an accident, in need of immediate attention. And it is a shock to think suddenly that the photographer must have been on hand. I don't want to argue ethics of news photography, but if someone, out of the highest aesthetic motives, withheld first aid to a bleeding victim in order to record the scene, with careful attention to lighting and camera speed, then it is doubtful that that picture could be so splendid a work of art as to justify neglecting so stringent a moral obligation.

The second conclusion is that there is nothing—no object or event—that is *per se* wrong to consider from the aesthetic point of view. This, I think, is part of the truth in the art-for-art's-sake doctrine. To adopt the aesthetic point of view is simply to seek out a source of value. And it can never be a moral error to realize value—barring conflict with other values. Some people seem to fear that a serious and persistent aesthetic interest will become an enervating hyperaestheticism, a paralysis of will like that reported in advanced cases of psychedelic dependence. But the objects of aesthetic interest—such as harmonious design, good proportions, intense expressiveness—are not drugs, but part of the breath of life. Their cumulative effect is increased sensitization, fuller awareness, a closer touch with the environment and concern for what it is and might be. It seems to me very doubtful that we could have too much of these good things, or that they have inherent defects that prevent them from being an integral part of a good life.

The Myth of the Aesthetic Attitude

GEORGE DICKIE

SOME RECENT ARTICLES have suggested the unsatisfactoriness of the notion of the aesthetic attitude and it is now time for a fresh look at that encrusted article of faith. This conception has been valuable to aesthetics and criticism in helping wean them from a sole concern with beauty and related notions. However, I shall argue that the aesthetic attitude is a myth and while, as G. Ryle has said, "Myths often do a lot of theoretical good while they are still new," this partic-

ular one is no longer useful and in fact misleads aesthetic theory.

There is a range of theories which differ according to how strongly the aesthetic attitude is characterized. This variation is reflected in the language the theories employ. The strongest variety is Edward Bullough's theory of physical distance, recently defended by Sheila Dawson. The central technical term of this theory is "distance" used as a verb to denote an action which either

From The American Philosophical Quarterly *1 (1964). Reprinted by permission of the publisher and the author.*

constitutes or is necessary for the aesthetic attitude. These theorists use such sentences as "He distanced (or failed to distance) the play." The second variety is widely held but has been defended most vigorously in recent years by Jerome Stolnitz and Eliseo Vivas. The *central* technical term of this variety is "disinterested" used either as an adverb or as an adjective. This weaker theory speaks not of a special kind of action (distancing) but of an ordinary kind of action (attending) done in a certain way (disinterestedly). These first two versions are perhaps not as different as my classification suggests. However, the language of the two is different enough to justify separate discussions. My discussion of this second variety will for the most part make use of Jerome Stolnitz's book, which is a through, consistent, and large-scale version of the attitude theory. The weakest version of the attitude theory can be found in Vincent Tomas' statement "If looking at a picture and attending closely to how it looks is not really to be in the aesthetic attitude, then what on earth is?" In the following I shall be concerned with the notion of *aesthetic* attitude and this notion may have little or no connection with the ordinary notion of an *attitude*.

Psychical distance, according to Bullough, is a psychological process by virtue of which a person *puts* some object (be it a painting, a play, or a dangerous fog at sea) "out of gear" with the practical interests of the self. Miss Dawson maintains that it is "the beauty of the phenomenon, which captures our attention, puts us out of gear with practical life, and forces us, if we are receptive, to view it on the level of aesthetic consciousness."

Later she maintains that some persons (critics, actors, members of an orchestra, and the like) "distance deliberately." Miss Dawson, following Bullough, discusses cases in which people are unable to bring off an act of distancing or are incapable of being induced into a state of being distanced. She uses Bullough's example of the jealous ("underdistanced") husband at a performance of *Othello* who is unable to keep his attention on the play because he keeps thinking of his own wife's suspicious behavior. On the other hand, if "we are mainly concerned with the technical details of its [the play's] presentation, then we are said to be over-distanced." There is, then, a species of action—distancing—which may be deliberately done and which initiates a state of consciousness—being distanced.

The question is: Are there actions denoted by "to distance" or states of consciousness denoted by "being distanced"? When the curtain goes up, when we walk up to a painting, or when we look at a sunset are we ever induced into a state of being distanced either by being struck by the beauty of the object or by pulling off an act of distancing? I do not recall committing any such special actions or of being induced into any special state, and I have no reason to suspect that I am atypical in this respect. The distance-theorist may perhaps ask, "But are you not usually oblivious to noises and sights other than those of the play or to the marks on the wall around the painting?" The answer is of course—"Yes." But if "to distance" and "being distanced" simply mean that one's attention is focused, what is the point of introducing new technical terms and speaking as if these terms refer to special kinds of acts and states of consciousness? The distance-theorist might argue further, "But surely you put the play (painting, sunset) 'out of gear' with your practical interests?" This question seems to me to be a very odd way of asking (by employing the technical metaphor "out of gear") if I attended to the play rather than thought about my wife or wondered how they managed to move the scenery about. Why not ask me straight out if I paid attention? Thus, when Miss Dawson says that the jealous husband underdistanced *Othello* and that the person with a consuming interest in techniques of stagecraft over-distanced the play, these are just technical and misleading ways of describing two different cases of inattention. In both cases something is being attended to, but in neither case is it the action of the play. To introduce the technical terms "distance," "under-distance," and "over-distance" does nothing but send us chasing after phantom acts and states of consciousness.

Miss Dawson's commitment to the theory of distance (as a kind of mental insulation material necessary for a work of art if it is to be enjoyed aesthetically) leads her to draw a conclusion so curious as to throw suspicion on the theory.

> One remembers the horrible loss of distance in *Peter Pan*—the moment when Peter says "Do you believe in fairies? . . . If you believe, clap your hands!" the moment when most children would like to slink out of the theatre and not a few cry—not because Tinkerbell may die, but because the magic is gone. What, after all, should we feel like if Lear were to leave Cordelia, come to the front of the stage and say, "All the grown-ups who think that she loves me, shout 'Yes.'"

It is hard to believe that the responses of any children could be as theory-bound as those Miss Dawson describes. In fact, Peter Pan's request for applause is a dramatic high point to which children respond enthusiastically. The playwright gives the children a momentary chance to become actors in the play. The children do not at that moment lose or snap out of a state of being distanced because they never had or were in any such thing to begin with. The comparison of Peter Pan's appeal to the hypothetical one by Lear is pointless. *Peter Pan* is a magical play in which almost anything can happen, but *King Lear* is a play of a different kind. There are, by the way, many plays in which an actor directly addresses the audience (*Our Town, The Marriage Broker, A Taste of Honey*, for example) without causing the play to be less valuable. Such plays are unusual, but what is unusual is not necessarily bad; there is no point in trying to lay down rules to which every play must conform independently of the kind of play it is.

It is perhaps worth noting that Susanne Langer reports the reaction she had as a child to this scene in *Peter Pan*. As she remembers it, Peter Pan's appeal shattered the illusion and caused her acute misery. However, she reports that all the other children clapped and laughed and enjoyed themselves.

The second way of conceiving of the aesthetic attitude—as the ordinary action of attending done in a certain way (disinterestedly)—is illustrated by the work of Jerome Stolnitz and Eliseo Vivas. Stolnitz defines "aesthetic attitude" as "disinterested and sympathetic attention to and contemplation of any object of awareness whatever, for its own sake alone." Stolnitz defines the main terms of his definition: "disinterested" means "no concern for any ulterior purpose"; "sympathetic" means "accept the object on its own terms to appreciate it"; and "contemplation" means "perception directed toward the object in its own right and the spectator is not concerned to analyze it or ask questions about it."

The notion of disinterestedness, which Stolnitz has elsewhere shown to be seminal for modern aesthetic theory, is the key term here. Thus, it is necessary to be clear about the nature of disinterested attention to the various arts. It can make sense to speak, for example, of listening disinterestedly to music only if it makes sense to speak of listening interestedly to music. It would make no sense to speak of walking *fast* unless walking could be done *slowly*. Using Stolnitz' definition of "disinterestedness," the two situations would have to be described as "listening with no ulterior purpose" (disinterestedly) and "listening with an ulterior purpose" (interestedly). Note that what initially appears to be a perceptual distinction—listening in a certain way (interestedly or disinterestedly)—turns out to be a motivational or an intentional distinction—listening for or with a certain purpose. Suppose Jones listens to a piece of music for the purpose of being able to analyze and describe it on an examination the next day and Smith listens to the same music with no such ulterior purpose. There is certainly a difference between the motives and intentions of the two men: Jones has an ulterior purpose and Smith does not, but this does not mean Jones's *listening* differs from Smith's. It is possible that both men enjoy the music or that both be bored. The attention of either or both may flag and so on. It is important to note that a person's motive or intention is different from his action (Jones's listening to the music, for example). There is only one way to *listen* to (to attend to) music, although the listening may be more or less attentive and there may be a variety of motives, intentions, and reasons for doing so and a variety of ways of being distracted from the music.

In order to avoid a common mistake of aestheticians—drawing a conclusion about one kind of art and assuming it holds for all the arts—the question of disinterested attention must be considered for arts other than music. How would one look at a painting disinterestedly or interestedly? An example of alleged interested viewing might be the case in which a painting reminds Jones of his grandfather and Jones proceeds to muse about or to regale a companion with tales of his grandfather's pioneer exploits. Such incidents would be characterized by attitude-theorists as examples of using a work of art as a vehicle for associations and so on, i.e., cases of interested attention. But Jones is not looking at (attending to) the painting at all, although he may be facing it with his eyes open. Jones is now musing or attending to the story he is telling, although he had to look at the painting at first to notice that it resembled his grandfather. Jones is not now looking at the painting interestedly, since he is not now looking at (attending to) the painting. Jones's thinking or telling a story about his grandfather is no more a part of the painting than his speculating about the artist's intentions is and, hence, his musing, telling, speculating, and so on cannot properly be described as attending to the painting interestedly. What attitude-aestheticians are calling attention to is the occurrence of irrelevant associations which distract the viewer from the painting or whatever. But distraction is not a special kind of attention, it is a kind of inattention.

Consider now disinterestedness and plays. I shall make use of some interesting examples offered by J. O. Urmson, but I am not claiming that Urmson is an attitude-theorist. Urmson never speaks in his article of aesthetic attitude but rather of aesthetic satisfaction. In addition to aesthetic satisfaction, Urmson mentions economic, moral, personal, and intellectual satisfactions. I think the attitude-theorist would consider these last four kinds of satisfaction as "ulterior purposes" and, hence, cases of interested attention. Urmson considers the case of a man in the audience of a play who is delighted. It is discovered that his delight is *solely* the result of the fact that there is a full house—the man is the impresario of the production. Urmson is right in calling *this* impresario's satisfaction economic rather than aesthetic, although there is a certain oddness about the example as it finds the impresario sitting *in the audience*. However, my concern is not with Urmson's examples as such but with the attitude theory. This impresario is certainly an interested party in the fullest sense of the word, but is his behavior an instance of interested attention as distinct from the supposed disinterested attention of the average citizen who sits beside him? In the situation as described by Urmson it would not make any sense to say that the impresario is attending to the play at all, since his *sole* concern at the moment is the till. If he can be said to be attending to anything (rather than just thinking about it) it is the size of the house. I do not mean to suggest that an impresario could not attend to his play if he found himself taking up a seat in a full house; I am challenging the sense of disinterested attention. As an example of personal satisfaction Urmson mentions the spectator whose daughter is in the play. Intellectual satisfaction involves the solution of technical problems of plays and moral satisfaction the consideration of the effects of the play on the viewer's conduct. All three of these candidates which the attitude-theorist would propose as cases of interested attention turn out to be just different ways of being distracted from the play and, hence, not cases of interested attention to the play. Of course, there is no reason to think that in any of these cases the distraction or inattention must be total, although it could be. In fact, such inattentions often occur but are so fleeting that nothing of the play, music, or whatever is missed or lost.

The example of a playwright watching a rehearsal or an out-of-town performance with a view to rewriting the script has been suggested to me as a case in which a spectator is certainly attending to the play (unlike our impresario) and attending in an interested manner. This case is unlike those just discussed but is similar to the earlier case of Jones (not Smith) listening to a particular piece of music. Our playwright—like Jones, who was to be examined on the music—has ulterior motives. Furthermore, the playwright, unlike an ordinary spectator, can change the script after the performance or during a rehearsal. But how is our playwright's *attention* (as distinguished from his motives and intentions) different from that of an ordinary viewer? The playwright might enjoy or be bored by the performance as any spectator might be. The playwright's attention might even flag. In short, the kinds of things which may happen to the playwright's attention are no different from those that may happen to an ordinary spectator, although the two may have quite different motives and intentions.

For the discussion of disinterested-interested reading of literature it is appropriate to turn to the arguments of Eliseo Vivas, whose work is largely concerned with literature. Vivas remarks that "By approaching a poem in a nonaesthetic mode it may function as history, as social criticism, as diagnostic evidence of the author's neuroses, and in an indefinite number of other ways." Vivas further notes that according to Plato "the Greeks used Homer as an authority on war and almost anything under the sun," and that a certain poem "can be read as erotic poetry or as an account of a mystical experience." The difference between reading a poem *as* history or whatever (reading it nonaesthetically) and reading it aesthetically depends on how *we* approach or read it. A poem "does not come self-labelled," but presumably is a poem only when it is read in a certain way—when it is an object of aesthetic experience. For Vivas, being an aesthetic object means being the object of the aesthetic attitude. He defines the aesthetic experience as "an experience of rapt attention which involves the intransitive apprehension of an object's immanent meanings and values in their full presentational immediacy." Vivas maintains that his definition "helps me understand better what I can and

what I cannot do when I read *The Brothers* [*Karamazov*]" and his definition "forces us to acknowledge that *The Brothers Karamazov* can hardly be read as art. . . ." This acknowledgment means that we probably cannot intransitively apprehend *The Brothers* because of its size and complexity.

"Intransitive" is the key term here and Vivas' meaning must be made clear. A number of passages reveal his meaning but perhaps the following is the best. "Having once seen a hockey game in slow motion, I am prepared to testify that it was an object of pure intransitive experience [attention]—for I was not *interested* in which team won the game and no external factors mingled with my interest in the beautiful rhythmic flow of the slow-moving men." It appears that Vivas' "intrinsic attention" has the same meaning as Stolnitz's "disinterested attention," namely, "attending with no ulterior purpose." Thus, the question to ask is "How does one attend to (read) a poem or any literary work transitively?" One can certainly attend to (read) a poem for a variety of different purposes and because of a variety of different reasons, but can one attend to a poem transitively? I do not think so, but let us consider the examples Vivas offers. He mentions "a type of reader" who uses a poem or parts of a poem as a spring-board for "loose, uncontrolled, relaxed day-dreaming, woolgathering rambles, free from the contextual control" of the poem. But surely it would be wrong to say such musing is a case of transitively attending to a poem, since it is clearly a case of not attending to a poem. Another supposed way of attending to a poem transitively is by approaching it "as diagnostic evidence of the author's neuroses." Vivas is right if he means that there is no critical point in doing this since it does not throw light on the poem. But this is a case of *using* information gleaned from a poem to make inferences about its author rather than attending to a poem. If anything can be said to be attended to here it is the author's neuroses (at least they are being thought about). This kind of case is perhaps best thought of as a rather special way of getting distracted from a poem. Of course, such "biographical" distractions might be insignificant and momentary enough so as scarcely to distract attention from the poem (a flash of insight or understanding about the poet). On the other hand, such distractions may turn into dissertations and whole careers. Such an interest may lead a reader to concentrate his attention (when he does read a poem) on certain "informational" aspects of a poem and to ignore the remaining aspects. As deplorable as such a sustained practice may be, it is at best a case of attending to certain features of a poem and ignoring others.

Another way that poetry may allegedly be read transitively is by reading it as history. This case is different from the two preceding ones since poetry often *contains* history (makes historical statements or at least references) but does not (usually) contain statements about the author's neuroses and so on nor does it contain statements about what a reader's free associations are about (otherwise we would not call them "*free associations*"). Reading a poem as history suggests that we are attending to (thinking about) historical events by way of attending to a poem—the poem is a time-telescope. Consider the following two sets of lines:

> *In fourteen hundred and ninety-two*
> *Columbus sailed the ocean blue.*

> *Or like stout Cortez when with eagles eyes*
> *He star'd at the Pacific—and all his men*
> *Look'd at each other with a wild surmise—*
> *Silent, upon a peak in Darien.*

Someone might read both of these raptly and not know that they make historical references (inaccurately in one case)—might this be a case of intransitive attention? How would the above reading differ—so far as attention is concerned—from the case of a reader who recognized the historical content of the poetic lines? The two readings do not differ as far as attention is concerned. History is a part of these sets of poetic lines and the two readings differ in that the first fails to take account of an aspect of the poetic lines (its historical content) and the second does not fail to do so. Perhaps by "reading as history" Vivas means "reading *simply* as history." But even this mean-

ing does not mark out a special kind of attention but rather means that only a single aspect of a poem is being noticed and that its rhyme, meter, and so on are ignored. Reading a poem as social criticism can be analyzed in a fashion similar to reading as history. Some poems simply are or contain social criticism, and a complete reading must not fail to notice this fact.

The above cases of alleged interested attending can be sorted out in the following way. Jones listening to the music and our playwright watching the rehearsal are both attending with ulterior motives to a work of art, but there is no reason to suppose that the attention of either is different in kind from that of an ordinary spectator. The reader who reads a poem as history is simply attending to an aspect of a poem. On the other hand, the remaining cases—Jones beside the painting telling of his grandfather, the gloating impresario, daydreaming while "reading" a poem, and so on—are simply cases of not attending to the work of art.

In general, I conclude that "disinterestedness" or "intransitiveness" cannot properly be used to refer to a special kind of attention. "Disinterestedness" is a term which is used to make clear that an action has certain kinds of motives. Hence, we speak of disinterested findings (of boards of inquiry), disinterested verdicts (of judges and juries), and so on. Attending to an object, of course, has its motives but the attending itself is not interested or disinterested according to whether its motives are of the kind which motivate interested or disinterested action (as findings and verdicts might), although the attending may be more or less close.

I have argued that the second way of conceiving the aesthetic attitude is also a myth, or at least that its main content—disinterested attention—is; but I must now try to establish that the view misleads aesthetic theory. I shall argue that the attitude-theorist is incorrect about (1) the way in which he wishes to set the limits of aesthetic relevance; (2) the relation of the critic to a work of art; and (3) the relation of morality to aesthetic value.

Since I shall make use of the treatment of aesthetic relevance in Jerome Stolnitz's book, let me make clear that I am not necessarily denying the relevance of the specific items he cites but disagreeing with his criterion of relevance. His criterion of relevance is derived from his definition of "aesthetic attitude" and is set forth at the very beginning of his book. This procedure leads Monroe Beardsley in his review of the book to remark that Stolnitz's discussion is premature. Beardsley suggests "that relevance cannot be satisfactorily discussed until after a careful treatment of the several arts, their dimensions and capacities."

First, what is mean by "aesthetic relevance?" Stolnitz defines the problem by asking the question: "Is it ever 'relevant' to the aesthetic experience to have thoughts or images or bits of knowledge which are not present within the object itself?" Stolnitz begins by summarizing Bullough's experiment and discussion of single colors and associations. Some associations absorb the spectator's attention and distract him from the color and some associations "fuse" with the color. Associations of the latter kind are aesthetic and the former are not. Stolnitz draws the following conclusion about associations:

> If the aesthetic experience is as we have described it, then whether an association is aesthetic depends on whether it is compatible with the attitude of "disinterested attention." If the association reenforces the focusing of attention upon the object, by "fusing" with the object and thereby giving it added "life and significance," it is genuinely aesthetic. If, however, it arrogates attention to itself and away from the object, it undermines the aesthetic attitude.

It is not clear how something could *fuse* with a single color, but "fusion" is one of those words in aesthetics which is rarely defined. Stolnitz then makes use of a more fruitful example, one from I. A. Richards' *Practical Criticism*. He cites the responses of students to the poem which begins:

Between the erect and solemn trees
I will go down upon my knees;
I shall not find this day
So meet a place to pray.

The image of a rugby forward running arose in the mind of one student-reader on reading the third verse of this poem. A cathedral was suggested to a second reader of the poem. The cathedral image "is congruous with both the verbal meaning of the poem and the emotions and mood which it expresses. It does not divert attention away from the poem." The rugby image is presumably incongruous and diverts attention from the poem.

It is a confusion to take compatibility with disinterested attention as a criterion of relevance. If, as I have tried to show, *disinterested attention* is a confused notion, then it will not do as a satisfactory criterion. Also, when Stolnitz comes to show why the cathedral image is, and the rugby image is not relevant, the criterion he actually uses is *congruousness with the meaning of the poem,* which is quite independent of the notion of disinterestedness. The problem is perhaps best described as the problem of relevance to a poem, or more generally, to a work of art, rather than aesthetic relevance.

A second way in which the attitude theory misleads aesthetics is its contention that a critic's relationship to a work of art is different in kind from the relationship of other persons to the work. H. S. Langfeld in an early statement of this view wrote that we may "slip from the attitude of aesthetic enjoyment to the attitude of the critic." He characterizes the critical attitude as "intellectually occupied in coldly estimating . . . merits" and the aesthetic attitude as responding "emotionally to" a work of art. At the beginning of his book in the discussion of the aesthetic attitude, Stolnitz declares that if a percipient of a work of art "has the purpose of passing judgment upon it, his attitude is not aesthetic." He develops this line at a later stage of his book, arguing that appreciation (perceiving with the aesthetic attitude) and criticism (seeking for reasons to support an evaluation of a work) are (1) distinct and (2) "psychologically opposed to each other." The critical attitude is questioning, analytical, probing for strengths and weakness, and so on. The aesthetic attitude is just the opposite: "It commits our allegiance to the object freely and unquestioningly"; "the spectator 'surrenders' himself to the work of art." "Just because the two attitudes are inimical, whenever criticism obtrudes, it reduces aesthetic interest." Stolnitz does not, of course, argue that criticism is unimportant for appreciation. He maintains criticism plays an important and necessary role in preparing a person to appreciate the nuances, detail, form, and so on of works of art. We are quite right, he says, thus to read and listen perceptively and acutely, but he questions, "Does this mean that we must analyze, measure in terms of value-criteria, etc., *during* the supposedly aesthetic experience?" His answer is "No" and he maintains that criticism must occur "*prior* to the aesthetic encounter," or it will interfere with appreciation.

How does Stolnitz know that criticism will always interfere with appreciation? His conclusion sounds like one based upon the observations of actual cases, but I do not think it is. I believe it is a logical consequence of his definition of aesthetic attitude in terms of disinterested attention (no ulterior purpose). According to his view, to appreciate an object aesthetically one has to perceive it with no ulterior purpose. But the critic has an ulterior purpose—to analyze and evaluate the object he perceives—hence, in so far as a person functions as a critic he cannot function as an appreciator. But here, as previously, Stolnitz confuses a perceptual distinction with a motivational one. If it were possible to *attend* disinterestedly or interestedly, then perhaps the critic (as percipient) would differ from other percipients. But if my earlier argument about attending is correct, the critic differs from other percipients only in his motives and intentions and not in the way in which he attends to a work of art.

Of course, it might just be a fact that the search for reasons is incompatible with the appreciation of art, but I do not think it is. Several years ago I participated in a series of panel discussions of films. During the showing of each film we were to discuss, I had to take note of various aspects of the film (actor's performance, dramatic development, organization of the screen-plane and screen-space at given moments, and so on) in order later to discuss the films. I believe that this practice not only helped educate me to appreciate subsequent films but that it en-

hanced the appreciation of the films I was analyzing. I noticed and was able to appreciate things about the films I was watching which ordinarily out of laziness I would not have noticed. I see no reason why the same should not be the case with the professional critic or any critical percipient. If many professional critics seem to appreciate so few works, it is not because they are critics, but perhaps because the percentage of good works of art is fairly small and they suffer from a kind of combat fatigue.

I am unable to see any significant difference between "perceptively and acutely" attending to a work of art (which Stolnitz holds enhances appreciation) and searching for reasons, so far as the experience of a work of art is concerned. If I attend perceptively and acutely, I will have certain standards and/or paradigms in mind (not necessarily consciously) and will be keenly aware of the elements and relations in the work and will evaluate them to some degree. Stolnitz writes as if criticism takes place and then is over and done with, but the search for and finding of reasons (noticing this fits in with that, and so on) is continuous in practiced appreciators. A practiced viewer does not even have to be looking for a reason, he may just notice a line or an area in a painting, for example, and the line or area becomes a reason why he thinks the painting better or worse. A person may be a critic (not necessarily a good one) without meaning to be or without even realizing it.

There is one final line worth pursuing. Stolnitz' remarks suggest that one reason he thinks criticism and appreciation incompatible is that they compete with one another for time (this would be especially bad in the cases of performed works). But seeking and finding reasons (criticism) does not compete for time with appreciation. First, to seek for a reason means to be ready and able to notice something and to be thus ready and able as one attends does not compete for time with the attending. In fact, I should suppose that seeking for reasons would tend to focus attention more securely on the work of art. Second, finding a reason is an achievement, like winning a race. (It takes time to run a race but not to win it.) Consider the finding of the following reasons. How much time does it take to "see" that a note is off key (or on key)? How long does it take to notice that an actor mispronounces a word (or does it right)? How much time does it take to realize that a character's action does not fit his already established personality? (One is struck by it.) How long does it take to apprehend that a happy ending is out of place? It does not take time to find any of these reasons or reasons in general. Finding a reason is like coming to understand—it is done in a flash. I do not mean to suggest that one cannot be mistaken in finding a reason. What may appear to be a fault or a merit (a found reason) in the middle of a performance (or during one look at a painting and so forth) may turn out to be just the opposite when seen from the perspective of the whole performance (or other looks at the painting).

A third way in which the attitude theory misleads aesthetic theory is its contention that aesthetic value is always independent of morality. This view is perhaps not peculiar to the attitude theory, but it is a logical consequence of the attitude approach. Two quotations from attitude-theorists will establish the drift of their view of morality and aesthetic value.

> We are either concerned with the beauty of the object or with some other value of the same. Just as soon, for example, as ethical considerations occur to our mind, our attitude shifts.

> Any of us might reject a novel because it seems to conflict with our moral beliefs . . . When we do so . . . We have *not* read the book aesthetically, for we have interposed moral . . . responses of our own which are alien to it. This disrupts the aesthetic attitude. We cannot then say that the novel is *aesthetically* bad, for we have not permitted ourselves to consider it aesthetically. To maintain the aesthetic attitude, we must follow the lead of the object and respond in concert with it.

This conception of the aesthetic attitude functions to hold the moral aspects and the *aesthetic* aspects of the work of art firmly apart. Presumably, although it is difficult to see one's way clearly here, the moral aspects of a work of art cannot be an object of aesthetic attention because aesthetic attention is by definition disinterested and the moral aspects are somehow practical (interested). I suspect that there are a number of confusions involved in the assumption of the incompatibility of aesthetic attention and the moral aspects of art, but I shall not attempt to make these clear, since the root of the assumption—disinterested attention—is a confused notion. Some way other than in terms of the aesthetic attitude, then, is needed to discuss the relation of morality and aesthetic value.

David Pole in a recent article has argued that the moral vision which a work of art may embody is *aesthetically* significant. It should perhaps be remarked at this point that not all works of art embody a moral vision and perhaps some kinds of art (music, for example) cannot embody a moral vision, but certainly some novels, some poems, and some films and plays do. I assume it is unnecessary to show how novels and so on have this moral aspect. Pole notes the curious fact that while so many critics approach works of art in "overtly moralistic terms," it is a "philosophical commonplace . . . that the ethical and the aesthetic modes . . . form different categories." I suspect that many philosophers would simply say that these critics are confused about their roles. But Pole assumes that philosophical theory "should take notice of practice" and surely he is right. In agreeing with Pole's assumption I should like to reserve the right to argue in specific cases that a critic may be misguided. This right is especially necessary in a field such as aesthetics because the language and practice of critics is so often burdened with ancient theory. Perhaps *all* moralistic criticism is wrong but philosophers should not rule it out of order at the very beginning by use of a definition.

Pole thinks that the moral vision presented by a particular work of art will be either true or false (perhaps a mixture of true and false might occur). If a work has a false moral vision, then something "is lacking within the work itself. But to say that is to say that the [work] is internally incoherent; some particular aspect must jar with what—on the strength of the rest—we claim a right to demand. And here the moral fault that we have found will count as an aesthetic fault too." Pole is trying to show that the assessment of the moral vision of a work of art is just a special case of coherence or incoherence, and since everyone would agree that coherence is an aesthetic category, the assessment of the moral vision is an aesthetic assessment.

I think Pole's conclusion is correct but take exception to some of his arguments. First, I am uncertain whether it is proper to speak of a moral vision being true or false, and would want to make a more modest claim—that a moral vision can be judged to be acceptable or unacceptable. (I am not claiming Pole is wrong and my claim is not inconsistent with his.) Second, I do not see that a false (or unacceptable) moral vision makes a work incoherent. I should suppose that to say a work is coherent or incoherent is to speak about how its parts fit together and this involves no reference to something outside the work as the work's truth or falsity does.

In any event, it seems to me that a faulty moral vision can be shown to be an aesthetic fault independently of Pole's consideration of truth and coherence. As Pole's argument implies, a work's moral vision is a *part* of the work. Thus, any statement—descriptive or evaluative—about the work's moral vision is a statement about the *work;* and any statement about a *work* is a critical statement and, hence, falls within the aesthetic domain. To judge a moral vision to be morally unacceptable is to judge it defective and this amounts to saying that the work of art has a defective part. (Of course, a judgment of the acceptability of a moral vision may be wrong, as a judgment of an action sometimes is, but this fallibility does not make any difference.) Thus, a work's moral vision may be an aesthetic merit or defect just as a work's degree of unity is a merit or defect. But what justifies saying that a moral vision is a part of a work of art? Perhaps "part" is not quite the right word but it serves to make

the point clear enough. A novel's moral vision is an essential part of the novel and if it were removed (I am not sure how such surgery could be carried out) the novel would be greatly changed. Anyway, a novel's moral vision is not like its covers or binding. However, someone might still argue that even though a work's moral vision is defective and the moral vision is part of the work, that this defect is not an *aesthetic* defect. How is "aesthetic" being used here? It is being used to segregate certain aspects or parts of works of art such as formal and stylistic aspects from such aspects as a work's moral vision. But it seems to me that the separation is only nominal. "Aesthetic" has been selected as a name for a certain sub-set of characteristics of works of art. I certainly cannot object to such a stipulation, since an underlying aim of this essay is to suggest the vacuosness of the term "aesthetic." My concern at this point is simply to insist that a work's moral vision is a part of the work and that, therefore, a critic can legitimately describe and evaluate it. I would *call* any defect or merit which a critic can legitimately point out an aesthetic defect or merit, but what we call it does not matter.

It would, of course, be a mistake to judge a work solely on the basis of its moral vision (it is only one part). The fact that some critics have judged works of art in this way is perhaps as much responsible as the theory of aesthetic attitude for the attempts to separate morality from the aesthetic. In fact, such criticism is no doubt at least partly responsible for the rise of the notion of the aesthetic attitude.

If the foregoing arguments are correct, the second way of conceiving the aesthetic attitude misleads aesthetic theory in at least three ways.

In answer to a hypothetical question about what is seen in viewing a portrait with the aesthetic attitude, Tomas in part responds, "If looking at a picture and attending closely to how it looks is not really to be in the aesthetic attitude, then what on earth is?" I shall take this sentence as formulating the weakest version of the aesthetic attitude. (I am ignoring Tomas' distinction between appearance and reality. . . . My remarks, thus, are not a critique of Tomas' argument; I am simply using one of his sentences.) First, this sentence speaks only of "looking at a picture," but "listening to a piece of music," "watching and listening to a play," and so on could be added easily enough. After thus expanding the sentence, it can be contracted into the general form: "Being in the aesthetic attitude is attending closely to a work of art (or a natural object)."

But the aesthetic attitude ("the hallmark of modern aesthetics") in this formulation is a great letdown—it no longer seems to say anything significant. Nevertheless, this does seem to be all that is left after the aesthetic attitude has been purged of *distancing* and *disinterestedness*. The only thing which prevents the aesthetic attitude from collapsing into simple attention is the qualification *closely*. One may, I suppose, attend to a work of art more or less closely, but this fact does not seem to signify anything very important. When "being in the aesthetic attitude" is equated with "attending (closely)," the equation neither involves any mythical element nor could it possibly mislead aesthetic theory. But if the definition has no vices, it seems to have no virtues

either. When the aesthetic attitude finally turns out to be simply attending (closely), the final version should perhaps not be called "the weakest" but rather "the vacuous version" of the aesthetic attitude.

Stolnitz is no doubt historically correct that the notion of the aesthetic attitude has played an important role in the freeing of aesthetic theory from an overweening concern with beauty. It is easy to see how the slogan, "Anything can become an object of the aesthetic attitude," could help accomplish this liberation. It is worth noting, however, that the same goal could have been (and perhaps to some extent was) realized by simply noting that works of art are often ugly or contain ugliness, or have features which are difficult to include within beauty. No doubt, in more recent times people have been encouraged *to take an aesthetic attitude toward a painting* as a way of lowering their prejudices, say, against abstract and nonobjective art. So if the notion of aesthetic attitude has turned out to have no theoretical value for aesthetics, it has had practical value for the appreciation of art in a way similar to that of Clive Bell's suspect notion of significant form.

B. The Problem of Defining Art

From the outset a central objective of analytic aesthetics was the elimination of *essentialism*, the traditional goal of philosophy, going back to Plato and Aristotle, to find the essential nature of justice, education, good, and, in aesthetics, the essence of art. In Plato's dialogues Socrates is continually demanding of his interlocutors that they tell him what is common to a group of individual things—don't give me the "bees," Socrates insists, give me the "beehive"—that is, don't give me examples of beautiful objects, tell me what beauty is in general; don't give me examples of just and unjust men and institutions, tell me what justice is in general.

What philosophers like Plato and Aristotle were after, therefore, were general definitions of terms like *justice, good, beauty,* and *art,* definitions that would name the essential features of all just, good, and beautiful things, listing the necessary and sufficient criteria by which we call them just, good, or beautiful. And this did seem to define the main task of the philosophy of art—to discover and articulate the essential nature, first of aesthetic experience and second of art: Don't just tell me that this painting and that piece of sculpture and that particular poem or novel are works of art, which I already know; tell me what art is in general—what all works of art have in common and the essential criteria by which I can judge for myself which objects are art and which are not. As the early twentieth-century English critic Clive Bell put it,

> Either all works of visual art have some common quality, or when we speak of "works of art" we gibber. Everyone speaks of "art," making a mental classification by which he distinguishes the class "works of art" from all other classes. What is the justification of this classification? . . . There must be some one quality without which a work of art cannot exist; possessing which, in the least degree, no work is altogether worthless. What is this quality?

Nonetheless, as one of the founders of analytic philosophy, Ludwig Wittgenstein, argued, it is a mistake to think that general terms (common nouns and adjectives) derive their meaning from naming general essences. It is simply not the case, Wittgenstein argued, that terms of general reference, like *dog* or *book,* denote something common to the whole class of dogs or books. The mistake, Wittgenstein claimed, is part of a larger misunderstanding about linguistic meaning, the widespread but false assumption that the meaning of a word is something that word names. If we think the meaning of the words *White House* is the building where the U.S. President lives, then what do we think the meaning of the word *house* is? Is it all the houses in the world, past, present, and future, or some feature or set of properties common to all houses (and what could that be?), or is it some immaterial, abstract Universal Houseness, as Plato thought?

According to Wittgenstein, the root of Plato's strange theory that in addition to individual physical houses, the world also contains abstract, immaterial Forms, such as the Universal Houseness, is his mistaken view of linguistic meaning. Plato was wrong, Wittgenstein thought, to think that if words like *beauty* were meaningful they must name some object, and if that object was not a concrete, particular physical object, like the White House, then *beauty* must name some abstract, general object, the Form of Beauty itself—otherwise, Plato thought, the word would be meaningless and we could no longer talk sensibly about beauty. Many terms of general reference, such as *game,* are meaningful, Wittgenstein said, without naming some feature common to all the things so designated.

There is no single feature common to all games, Wittgenstein argued—some are played by more than one person, but not all; some are very athletic, but not all; some are played with a ball, but not all; some are played by competing teams, but not all; some are played for fun, but not all, and so on. Nor do all games have to have something in common in order for the word *game* to be meaningful. Rather than being defined by some common essence, Wittgenstein claimed that groups of games form *family resemblances,* a series of overlapping commonalities that does not require any one common feature found in all games.

Although Wittgenstein himself had little to say about art and aesthetics, the American aesthetician Morris Weitz applied Wittgenstein's anti-essentialist notion of family resemblance to the concept of art. If we try to find some common feature in all works of art—clay pots, cathedrals, poems, musical operas, paintings, and so on—we will surely be frustrated and come up empty handed. In addition, Weitz thought it was dogmatic and intolerant to try to define something as creative and innovative as art. What is special about art, Weitz reasoned, is precisely its ability to constantly change and adapt to new situations. By insisting on a fixed definition of art, Weitz held, we would only be trying to limit art, pinning it down and preventing its creative evolution.

Of course, as some analytic philosophers pointed out, it might still be possible to define art without trying to pick out some set of common empirically observable features—perhaps the essence of art is simply to be creative. "Creative," in other words, might be a feature common to all works of art but not one that we can observe with our five senses. Even so, as William Kennick pointed out, defining art in terms of non-empirical properties is of little use to us in learning how to apply the word *art,* that is, how to differentiate artworks from other sorts of objects. Either we define art in terms of observable features, he said, in which case we can't seem to find any such observable features common to all works of art (as Weitz had argued), or else we define art in terms of nonempirical features (such as "creative"), in which case the definition is of no use to us in distinguishing artworks from other objects.

Imagine a huge warehouse, Kennick proposes, in which artworks are mixed with other sorts of objects. Now imagine instructing a worker to bring out all the artworks (and only the artworks). Suppose the worker asks us how to differentiate the art from the nonart objects. We might tell her that artworks are "innovative" and "creative," that they are "expressive," or "harmonious," but how is that going to help the worker? And if we try to be more specific, naming properties she can see with her own two eyes, such properties obviously won't pick out all and only works of art.

But if Weitz (following Wittgenstein) is right, then it means that art cannot be defined—and that is a serious blow to philosophers of art who for hundreds of years thought their main job was to define art! We can follow Wittgenstein's lead in discussing how the word *art* is used, pointing out the various family resemblances among various strands of art genres (some representational, others not; some expressive, others not; some innovative, others not; some beautiful, others not, etc.), but it is hopeless to attempt to define art. Other analytic philosophers, however, such as George Dickie and Arthur Danto, argued that art perhaps could be defined, though in a special and unusual way. They agreed with Weitz that art could not be defined by naming the necessary and sufficient properties of art, those empirical, observable features that all works of art shared and that were shared by no other sorts of objects. But, they argued, that is not the only way to define something.

Sometimes we define things in terms of conventional decisions made by duly appointed officials of various human communities. University students often do not know whether their instructor has a Ph.D. or not, or whether he or she is a teaching assistant, a lecturer, an assistant professor, an associate professor, or a full professor. A likely guess is that a young person is a teaching assistant and an older person is a professor, but not always or necessarily. There are no sure-fire, easily observable properties, like being female, having brown eyes, or having a pierced nose. But that doesn't mean these words (*teaching assistant, Ph.D., professor*) have no meaning; a teaching assistant is anyone who has been selected as a teaching assistant by the graduate committee of a department within a university. If they say you are a teaching assistant, then you are a teaching assistant—that's all there is to it. Similarly, if the appropriate body says that you have graduated with a major in electrical engineering, then you are a graduate with a B.S. in electrical engineering.

Similarly, Dickie and Danto argued, though in different ways, we can define a work of art as anything that authorities and experts in the art world say is a work of art. But who are these art expert authorities, and who has appointed them? Dickie and Danto are thinking primarily of well-known art critics, art museum and art gallery curators and directors, art historians, art teachers, and some prominent artists themselves. But unlike the graduate committee of the electrical engineering department of Slippery Slope University, there is no accepted group or convention that determines who these art experts are. And of course they disagree among themselves. And finally, like the poor worker in Kennick's example, this sort of institutional definition in terms of the art world doesn't help the ordinary person learn how to distinguish art from nonart.

Before 1960, most people could distinguish artworks from other sorts of objects, even though they couldn't come up with a good definition of art. But in the latter half of the twentieth century many objects which had previously not been considered works of art were put forward as artworks—an ordinary necktie, a room filled with dirt, a hole dug in the ground, a 1960 Chevy half buried in the sand, an illegal drive on an uncompleted freeway. Perhaps in these sorts of cases there is no way for any of us to tell whether these are works of art except to attend art openings, read art magazines— in short, to listen to what the experts in the art world have decided. Someone who has not followed the institutional dictates of the art world might innocently enter the gallery, try on the necktie and ask to buy it; a policeman who had not had the opportunity to take Contemporary Art 101 might simply arrest the artist performing the illegal drive on the uncompleted freeway.

What's the difference between an ordinary necktie that is not a work of art and that same necktie displayed and sold as a work of art? Just the fact that someone known as an artist (Picasso) offered the object as a work of art in an art setting (an art gallery or museum) and those in positions of authority within the art world agreed to treat it as art. But don't try this yourself. Unless you are already well known as an artist, your attempt to put yourself through college by selling your old sweat socks as artworks for five-figure sums will probably not make the art critical cut. It is a work of art if those in the art world say it is art (and in most cases they are not going to say it is unless you are already recognized as an artist—sorry). A strange definition, but a definition, nonetheless, and perhaps the best we can do given the direction taken by some contemporary art.

In section A we discussed the analytic critique of the aesthetic experience tradition. Another nail, and perhaps the final one, in the coffin of aesthetic experience was Danto's reversal of the direction in the relationship between aesthetic experience and our recognition of something as a work of art. Previously one of the mainstays of the aesthetic experience tradition had been its presumed role in defining what is a work of art. Besides objects of natural beauty, our aesthetic interests are also directed toward works of fine art. In the case of a work of art, according to the traditional view, an artist sets out deliberately to create an object likely to produce an aesthetic experience. So when we see something made by a person that seems obviously designed to arouse our aesthetic experience, we know that it is a work of art. So says the traditional theory of aesthetic experience. Danto argues, however, that it is just the reverse!

Thinking of the controversial Conceptual artworks of the 1960s—for example, the Closed Gallery (an exhibition by a well-known artist at a certain gallery at certain times of the day when that gallery was closed), 4:33 (a piece of music consisting of four minutes and thirty-three seconds of silence), Picasso's necktie, and early "found art" pieces such as Duchamp's 1917 *The Fountain* (an ordinary urinal taken from a men's room)—Danto argues that we must first recognize the piece as an artwork *before* we can have any aesthetic experience of it. Picasso's necktie and Duchamp's urinal don't arouse any aesthetic experience until we first begin to think of them as avant-garde works of art. And how do we recognize them as artworks? Obviously not just by looking—the necktie in the men's shop and the necktie as artwork are identical ("indiscernible," Danto says), as are the urinal in the men's room and the urinal that Duchamp displayed as *The Fountain*. It is only by understanding and being a part of a social, historical, institutional "art world" that we begin to think of such ordinary, utilitarian objects as works of fine art.

Later (Part III) we will discuss Martin Heidegger's theory that works of art call our attention to and make us aware of the "being" or essence of ordinary physical objects by representing them in artworks, as van Gogh does in his painting of the peasant's shoes (see p. 323). What Conceptual artists sought to do was to let these ordinary physical objects speak for themselves simply by treating them as works of art—instead of painting a picture of a pair of peasant shoes a Conceptual artist would simply display an old pair of shoes, elevating, transforming, "transfiguring" them, as Danto said, from physical objects into artworks. Echoing Hegel's claim (Part I, section B) that art eventually "dies," as it becomes philosophy, Danto writes of the new Conceptual Art as the "death of art"—a strange new kind of art that is more philosophical than aesthetic. Someone in the 1960s unfamiliar with then-current events in the art world would have continued to see the necktie simply as a necktie and not as a work of fine art (or if such a person realized that these objects were being exhibited as art, she might be puzzled or perhaps outraged to find neckties, urinals, and hat racks displayed in art galleries as works of fine art).

Danto thus undercuts the whole psychological or phenomenological base from under the tradition of aesthetic experience. It would be absurd to imagine an art critic savoring the organic interrelations of formal properties of the necktie or the urinal (though, ironically, these objects were indeed designed by commercial artists at some stage). It is not from the private vantage point of the viewer, reader, audience that we need to examine aesthetic experience, but rather from the sociological, historical, institutional framework of the art world (that is, the world of artists, critics, galleries, openings, public funding of art, buying and selling of art, state censorship of art, art education, the recent history of art, the traditions of high and low art, the distinction between arts and crafts, and so on). Later (Part III, section B) we will look at Paul Crowther's criticism of Danto's reading of the contemporary art scene.

The Artistic Enfranchisement of Real Objects: The Artworld

ARTHUR DANTO

Hamlet: Do you see nothing there?
The Queen: Nothing at all; yet all that is I see.

–Shakespeare: Hamlet, Act III, Scene IV

HAMLET AND SOCRATES, though in praise and deprecation respectively, spoke of art as a mirror held up to nature. As with many disagreements in attitude, this one has a factual basis. Socrates saw mirrors as but reflecting what we can already see; so art, insofar as mirrorlike, yields idle accurate duplications of the appearances of things, and is of no cognitive benefit whatever. Hamlet, more acutely, recognized a remarkable feature of reflecting surfaces, namely that they show us what we could not otherwise perceive— our own face and form—and so art, insofar as it is mirrorlike, reveals us to ourselves, and is, even by Socratic criteria, of some cognitive utility after all. As a philosopher, however, I find Socrates' discussion defective on other, perhaps less profound grounds than these. If a mirror image of *o* is indeed an imitation of *o*, then, if art is imitation, mirror images are art. But in fact mirroring objects no more is art than returning weapons to a madman is justice; and reference to mirrorings would be just the sly sort of counterinstance we would expect Socrates to bring forward in rebuttal of the theory he instead uses them to illustrate. If that theory requires us to class *these* as art, it thereby shows its inadequacy: "is an imitation" will not do as a sufficient condition for "is art." Yet, perhaps because artists *were* engaged in imitation, in Socrates' time and after, the insufficiency of the theory was not noticed until the invention of photography. Once rejected as a sufficient condition, mimesis was quickly discarded as even a necessary one; and since the achieve-ment of Kandinsky, mimetic features have been relegated to the periphery of critical concern, so much so that some works survive in spite of possessing those virtues, excellence in which was once celebrated as the essence of art, narrowly escaping demotion to mere illustrations.

It is, of course, indispensable in Socratic discussion that all participants be masters of the concept up for analysis, since the aim is to match a real defining expression to a term in active use, and the test for adequacy presumably consists in showing that the former analyzes and applies to all and only those things of which the latter is true. The popular disclaimer notwithstanding, then, Socrates' auditors purportedly knew what art was as well as what they liked; and a theory of art, regarded here as a real definition of "Art," is accordingly not to be of great use in helping men to recognize instances of its application. Their antecedent ability to do this is precisely what the adequacy of the theory is to be tested against, the problem being only to make explicit what they already know. It is *our* use of the term that the theory allegedly means to capture, but we are supposed able, in the words of a recent writer, "to separate those objects which are works of art from those which are not, because . . . we know how correctly to use the word 'art' and to apply the phrase 'work of art.'" Theories, on this account, are somewhat like mirror images on Socrates' account, showing forth what we already know, wordy reflections of the actual linguistic practice we are masters in.

But telling artworks from other things is not so simple a matter, even for native speakers, and these days one might not be aware he was on artistic terrain without an artistic theory to tell

From The Journal of Philosophy, *61 (1964). Reprinted by permission of* The Journal of Philosophy *and the author.*

him so. And part of the reason for this lies in the fact that terrain is constituted artistic in virtue of artistic theories, so that one use of theories, in addition to helping us discriminate art from the rest, consists in making art possible. Glaucon and the others could hardly have known what was art and what not: otherwise they would never have been taken in by mirror images.

Suppose one thinks of the discovery of a whole new class of artworks as something analogous to the discovery of a whole new class of facts anywhere, viz., as something for theoreticians to explain. In science, as elsewhere, we often accommodate new facts to old theories *via* auxiliary hypotheses, a pardonable enough conservatism when the theory in question is deemed too valuable to be jettisoned all at once. Now the Imitation Theory of Art (IT) is, if one but thinks it through, an exceedingly powerful theory, explaining a great many phenomena connected with the causation and evaluation of artworks, bringing a surprising unity into a complex domain. Moreover, it is a simple matter to shore it up against many purported counterinstances by such auxiliary hypotheses as that the artist who deviates from mimeticity is perverse, inept, or mad. Ineptitude, chicanery, or folly are, in fact, testable predications. Suppose, then, tests reveal that these hypotheses fail to hold, that the theory, now beyond repair, must be replaced. And a new theory is worked out, capturing what it can of the old theory's competence, together with the heretofore recalcitrant facts. One might, thinking along these lines, represent certain episodes in the history of art as not dissimilar to certain episodes in the history of science, where a conceptual revolution is being effected and where refusal to countenance certain facts, while in part due to prejudice, inertia, and self-interest, is due also to the fact that a well-established, or at least widely credited theory is being threatened in such a way that all coherence goes.

Some such episode transpired with the advent of post-impressionist paintings. In terms of the prevailing artistic theory (IT), it was impossible to accept these as art unless inept art: otherwise they could be discounted as hoaxes, self-advertisements, or the visual counterparts of madmen's ravings. So to get them accepted *as* art, on a footing with the *Transfiguration* (not to speak of a Landseer stag), required not so much a revolution in taste as a theoretical revision of rather considerable proportions, involving not only the artistic enfranchisement of these objects, but an emphasis upon newly significant features of accepted artworks, so that quite different accounts of their status as artworks would now have to be given. As a result of the new theory's acceptance, not only were post-impressionist paintings taken up as art, but numbers of objects (masks, weapons, etc.) were transferred from anthropological museums (and heterogeneous other places) to *musées des beaux arts,* though, as we would expect from the fact that a criterion for the acceptance of a new theory is that it account for whatever the older one did, nothing had to be transferred out of the *musée des beaux arts*—even if there were internal rearrangements as between storage rooms and exhibition space. Countless native speakers hung upon suburban mantelpieces innumerable replicas of paradigm cases for teaching the expression "work of art" that would have sent their Edwardian forebears into linguistic apoplexy.

To be sure, I distort by speaking of a theory: historically, there were several, all, interestingly enough, more or less defined in terms of the IT. Art-historical complexities must yield before the exigencies of logical exposition, and I shall speak as though there were one replacing theory, partially compensating for historical falsity by choosing one which was actually enunciated. According to it, the artists in question were to be understood not as unsuccessfully imitating real forms but as successfully creating new ones, quite as real as the forms which the older art had been thought, in its best examples, to be creditably imitating. Art, after all, had long since been thought of as creative (Vasari says that God was the first artist), and the post-impressionists were to be explained as genuinely creative, aiming, in Roger Fry's words, "not at illusion but reality."

This theory (RT) furnished a whole new mode of looking at painting, old and new. Indeed, one might almost interpret the crude drawing in Van Gogh and Cézanne, the dislocation of form from contour in Rouault and Dufy, the arbitrary use of color planes in Gauguin and the Fauves, as so many ways of drawing attention to the fact that these were *non-imitations,* specifically intended not to deceive. Logically, this would be roughly like printing "Not Legal Tender" across a brilliantly counterfeited dollar bill, the resulting object (counterfeit *cum* inscription) rendered incapable of deceiving anyone. It is not an illusory dollar bill, but then, just because it is non-illusory it does not automatically become a real dollar bill either. It rather occupies a freshly opened area between real objects and real facsimiles of real objects: it is non-facsimile, if one requires a word, and a new contribution to the world. Thus, Van Gogh's *Potato Eaters,* as a consequence of certain unmistakable distortions, turns out to be a non-facsimile of real life potato eaters; and inasmuch as these are not facsimiles of potato eaters Van Gogh's picture, as a non-imitation, had as much right to be called a real object as did its putative subjects. By means of this theory (RT), artworks re-entered the thick of things from which Socratic theory (IT) had sought to evict them; if no *more* real than what carpenters wrought, they were at least no *less* real. The Post-Impressionist won a victory in ontology.

It is in terms of RT that we must understand the artworks around us today. Thus Roy Lichtenstein paints comic-strip panels, though ten or twelve feet high. These are reasonably faithful projections onto a gigantesque scale of the homely frames from the daily tabloid, but it is precisely the scale that counts. A skilled engraver might incise *The Virgin and the Chancellor Rollin* on a pinhead, and it would be recognizable as such to the keen of sight, but an engraving of a Barnett Newman on a similar scale would be a blob, disappearing in the reduction. A *photograph* of a Lichtenstein is indiscernible from a photograph of a counterpart panel from *Steve Canyon;* but the photograph fails to capture the scale, and hence is as inaccurate a reproduction as a black-and-white engraving of Botticelli, scale being essential here as color there. Lichtensteins, then, are not imitations but *new entities,* as giant whelks would be. Jasper Johns, by contrast, paints objects with respect to which questions of scale are irrelevant. Yet his objects cannot be imitations, for they have the remarkable property that any intended copy of a member of this class of objects is automatically a member of the class itself, so that these objects are logically inimitable. Thus, a copy of a numeral just *is* that numeral: a painting of 3 is a 3 made of paint. Johns, in addition, paints targets, flags, and maps. Finally, in what I hope are not unwitting footnotes to Plato, two of our pioneers—Robert Rauschenberg and Claes Oldenburg—have made genuine beds.

Rauschenberg's bed hangs on a wall, and is streaked with some desultory house-paint. Oldenburg's bed is a rhomboid, narrower at one end than the other, with what one might speak of as a built-in perspective: ideal for small bedrooms. As beds, these sell at singularly inflated prices, but one *could* sleep in either of them: Rauschenberg has expressed the fear that someone might just climb into his bed and fall asleep. Imagine, now, a certain Testadura—a plain speaker and noted philistine—who is not aware that these are art, and who takes them to be reality simple and pure. He attributes the paintstreaks on Rauschenberg's bed to the slovenliness of the owner, and the bias in the Oldenburg bed to the ineptitude of the builder or the whimsy, perhaps, of whoever had it "custom-made." These would be mistakes, but mistakes of rather an odd kind, and not terribly different from that made by the stunned birds who pecked the sham grapes of Zeuxis. They mistook art for reality, and so has Testadura. But it was meant to *be* reality, according to RT. Can one have mistaken reality for reality? How shall we describe Testadura's error? What, after all, prevents Oldenburg's creation from being a misshapen bed? This is equivalent to asking what makes it art, and with this query we enter a domain of conceptual inquiry where native speakers are poor guides: *they* are lost themselves.

To mistake an artwork for a real object is no great feat when an artwork is the real object one mistakes it for. The problem is how to avoid such errors, or to remove them once they are made. The artwork is a bed, and not a bed-illusion; so there is nothing like the traumatic encounter against a flat surface that brought it home to the birds of Zeuxis that they had been duped. Except for the guard cautioning Testadura not to sleep on the artworks, he might never have discovered that this was an artwork and not a bed; and since, after all, one cannot discover that a bed is not a bed, how is Testadura to realize that he has made an error? A certain sort of explanation is required, for the error here is a curiously philosophical one, rather like, if we may assume as correct some well-known views of P. F. Strawson, mistaking a person for a material body when the truth is that a person *is* a material body in the sense that a whole class of predicates, sensibly applicable to material bodies, are sensibly, and by appeal to no different criteria, applicable to persons. So you cannot *discover* that a person is not a material body.

We begin by explaining, perhaps, that the paintstreaks are not to be explained away, that they are *part* of the object, so the object is not a mere bed with—as it happens—streaks of paint spilled over it, but a complex object fabricated out of a bed and some paintstreaks: a paint-bed. Similarly, a person is not a material body with—as it happens—some thoughts superadded, but is a complex entity made up of a body and some conscious states: a conscious-body. Persons, like artworks, must then be taken as irreducible to *parts* of themselves, and are in that sense primitive. Or, more accurately, the paintstreaks are not part of the real object—the bed—which happens to be part of the artwork, but are *like* the bed, part of the artwork as such. And this might be generalized into a rough characterization of artworks that happen to contain real objects as parts of themselves: not every part of an artwork A is

part of a real object R when R is part of A and can, moreover, be detached from A and seen *merely* as R. The mistake thus far will have been to mistake A for *part* of itself, namely R, even though it would not be incorrect to say that A is R, that the artwork is a bed. It is the "is" which requires clarification here.

There is an *is* that figures prominently in statements concerning artworks which is not the *is* of either identity or predication; nor is it the *is* of existence, of identification, or some special *is* made up to serve a philosophic end. Nevertheless, it is in common usage, and is readily mastered by children. It is the sense of *is* in accordance with which a child, shown a circle and a triangle and asked which is him and which his sister, will point to the triangle saying "That is me"; or, in response to my question, the person next to me points to the man in purple and says "That one is Lear"; or in the gallery I point, for my companion's benefit, to a spot in the painting before us and say "That white dab is Icarus." We do not mean, in these instances, that whatever is pointed to stands for, or represents, what it is said to be, for the *word* "Icarus" stands for or represents Icarus: yet I would not in the same sense of *is* point to the word and say "That is Icarus." The sentence "That a is b" is perfectly compatible with "That a is not b" when the first employs this sense of *is* and the second employs some other, though a and b are used nonambiguously throughout. Often, indeed, the truth of the first *requires* the truth of the second. The first, in fact, is incompatible with "That a is not b" only when the *is* is used nonambiguously throughout. For want of a word I shall designate this the *is of artistic identification;* in each case in which it is used, the a stands for some specific physical property of, or physical part of, an object; and, finally, it is a necessary condition for something to be an artwork that some part or property of it be designable by the subject of a sentence that employs this special *is*. It is an *is*, incidentally, which has near-relatives in marginal and mythical pronouncements. (Thus, one *is* Quetzalcoatl; those *are* the Pillars of Hercules.)

Let me illustrate. Two painters are asked to decorate the east and west walls of a science library with frescoes to be respectively called *Newton's First Law* and *Newton's Third Law*. These paintings, when finally unveiled, look, scale apart, as follows:

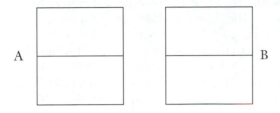

As objects I shall suppose the works to be indiscernible: a black horizontal line on a white ground, equally large in each dimension and element. *B* explains his work as follows: a mass, pressing downward, is met by a mass pressing upward: the lower mass reacts equally and oppositely to the upper one. *A* explains his work as follows: the line through the space is the path of an isolated particle. The path goes from edge to edge, to give the sense of its *going beyond*. If it ended or began within the space, the line would be curved; and it is parallel to the top and bottom edges, for if it were closer to one than to another, there would have to be a force accounting for it, and this is inconsistent with its being the path of an *isolated* particle.

Much follows from these artistic identifications. To regard the middle line as an edge (mass meeting mass) imposes the need to identify the top and bottom half of the picture as rectangles, and as two distinct parts (not necessarily as two masses, for the line could be the edge of *one* mass jutting up—or down—into empty space). If it is an edge, we cannot thus take the entire area of the painting as a single space: it is rather composed of two forms, or one form and a nonform. We could take the entire area as a single space only by taking the middle horizontal as a *line* which is not an edge. But this almost requires a three-dimensional identification of the whole picture: the area can be a flat surface which the line is *above* (*Jet-flight*), or *below* (*Submarine-path*), or

on (*Line*), or in (*Fissure*), or *through* (*Newton's First Law*)—though in this last case the area is not a flat surface but a transparent cross section of absolute space. We could make all these prepositional qualifications clear by imagining perpendicular cross sections to the picture plane. Then, depending upon the applicable prepositional clause, the area is (artistically) interrupted or not by the horizontal element. If we take the line as *through* space, the edges of the picture are not really the edges of the space: the space goes beyond the picture if the line itself does; and we are in the same space as the line is. As *B*, the edges of the picture can be *part* of the picture in case the masses go right to the edges, so that the edges of the picture are *their* edges. In that case, the vertices of the picture would be the vertices of the masses, except that the masses have four vertices more than the picture itself does: here four vertices would be part of the artwork which were not part of the real object. Again, the faces of the masses could be the face of the picture, and in looking at the picture, we are looking at these faces; but *space* has no face, and on the reading of *A* the work has to be read as faceless, and the face of the physical object would not be part of the artwork. Notice here how one artistic identification engenders another artistic identification and how, consistently with a given identification, we are *required* to give others and *precluded* from still others; indeed, a given identification determines how many elements the work is to contain. These different identifications are incompatible with one another, or generally so, and each might be said to make a different artwork, even though each artwork contains the identical real object as part of itself—or at least parts of the identical real object as parts of itself. There are, of course, senseless identifications: no one could, I think, sensibly read the middle horizontal as *Love's Labour's Lost* or *The Ascendency of St. Erasmus*. Finally, notice how acceptance of one identification rather than another is in effect to exchange one *world* for another. We could, indeed, enter a quiet poetic world by identifying the upper area with a clear and cloudless sky, reflected in the still surface of the water below, whiteness kept from whiteness only by the unreal boundary of the horizon.

And now Testadura, having hovered in the wings throughout this discussion, protests that *all he sees is paint:* a white painted oblong with a black line painted across it. And how right he really is: that is all he sees or that anybody can, we aesthetes included. So, if he asks us to show him what there is further to see, to demonstrate through pointing that this is an artwork *(Sea and Sky),* we cannot comply, for he has overlooked nothing (and it would be absurd to suppose he had, that there was something tiny we could point to and he, peering closely, say "So it is! A work of art after all!"). We cannot help him until he has mastered the *is of artistic identification* and so *constitutes* it a work of art. If he cannot achieve this, he will never look upon artworks: he will be like a child who sees sticks as sticks.

But what about pure abstractions, say something that looks just like *A* but is entitled No. 7? The 10th Street abstractionist blankly insists that there is nothing here but white paint and black, and none of our literary identifications need apply. What then distinguishes him from Testadura, whose philistine utterances are indiscernible from his? And how can it be an artwork for him and not for Testadura, when they agree that there is nothing that does not meet the eye? The answer, unpopular as it is likely to be to purists of every variety, lies in the fact that this artist has returned to the physicality of paint through an atmosphere compounded of artistic theories and the history of recent and remote painting, elements of which he is trying to refine out of his own work; and as a consequence of this his work belongs in this atmosphere and is part of this history. He has achieved abstraction through rejection of artistic identifications, returning to the real world from which such identifications remove us (he thinks), somewhat in the mode of Ch'ing Yuan, who wrote:

> Before I had studied Zen for thirty years, I saw mountains as mountains and waters as waters. When I arrived at a more intimate knowledge, I came to the point where I saw that mountains are not mountains, and waters are not waters. But now that I have got the very substance I am at rest. For it is just that I see mountains once again as mountains, and waters once again as waters.

His identification of what he has made is logically dependent upon the theories and history he rejects. The difference between his utterance and Testadura's "This is black paint and white paint and nothing more" lies in the fact that he is still using the *is* of artistic identification, so that his use of "That black paint is black paint" is not a tautology. Testadura is not at that stage. To see something as art requires something the eye cannot descry—an atmosphere of artistic theory, a knowledge of the history of art: an artworld.

Mr. Andy Warhol, the Pop artist, displays facsimiles of Brillo cartons, piled high, in neat stacks, as in the stockroom of the supermarket. They happen to be of wood, painted to look like cardboard, and why not? To paraphrase the critic of the *Times,* if one may make the facsimile of a human being out of bronze, why not the facsimile of a Brillo carton out of plywood? The cost of these boxes happens to be 2×10^3 that of their homely counterparts in real life—a differential hardly ascribable to their advantage in durability. In fact the Brillo people might, at some slight increase in cost, make their boxes out of plywood without these becoming artworks, and Warhol might make *his* out of cardboard without their ceasing to be art. So we may forget questions of intrinsic value, and ask why the Brillo people cannot manufacture art and why Warhol cannot *but* make artworks. Well, his are made by hand, to be sure. Which is like an insane reversal of Picasso's strategy in pasting the label from a bottle of Suze onto a drawing, saying as it were that the academic artist, concerned with exact imitation, must always fall short of the real thing: so why not just *use* the real thing? The Pop artist laboriously reproduces machine-made objects by hand, e.g. painting the labels on coffee cans (one can hear the familiar commendation "Entirely made by hand" falling painfully out of the guide's vocabulary when confronted by these objects). But the difference cannot consist in craft: a man who carved pebbles out of stones and carefully constructed a work called *Gravel Pile* might evoke the labor theory of value to account for the price he demands; but the question is, What makes it art? And why need Warhol *make* these things anyway? Why not just scrawl his signature across one? Or crush one up and display it as *Crushed Brillo Box* ("A protest against mechanization . . .") or simply display a Brillo carton as *Uncrushed Brillo Box* ("A bold affirmation of the plastic authenticity of industrial . . .")? Is this man a kind of Midas, turning whatever he touches into the gold of pure art? And the whole world consisting of latent artworks waiting, like the bread and wine of reality, to be transfigured, through some dark mystery, into the indiscernible flesh and blood of the sacrament? Never mind that the Brillo box may not be good, much less great art. The impressive thing is that it is art at all. But if it is, why are not the indiscernible Brillo boxes that are in the stockroom? Or *has* the whole distinction between art and reality broken down?

Suppose a man collects objects (ready-mades), including a Brillo carton; we praise the exhibit for variety, ingenuity, what you will. Next he exhibits nothing but Brillo cartons, and we criticize it as dull, repetitive, self-plagiarizing—or (more profoundly) claim that he is obsessed by regularity and repetition, as in *Marienbad*. Or he piles them high, leaving a narrow path; we tread our way through the smooth opaque stacks and find it an unsettling experience, and write it up as the closing in of consumer products, confining us as prisoners: or we say he is a modern pyramid builder. True, we don't say these things about the stockboy. But then a stockroom is not an art gallery, and we cannot readily separate the Brillo cartons from the gallery they are in, any more than we can separate the Rauschenberg bed from the paint upon it. Outside the gallery, they are pasteboard cartons. But then, scoured clean of paint, Rauschenberg's bed is a bed, just what it was before it was transformed into art. But then if we think this matter through, we discover that the artist has failed, really and of necessity, to produce a mere real object. He has produced an artwork, his use of real Brillo cartons being but an expansion of the resources available to artists, a contribution to *artists' materials,* as oil paint was, or *tuche.*

What in the end makes the difference between a Brillo box and a work of art consisting of a Brillo Box is a certain theory of art. It is the theory that takes it up into the world of art, and keeps it from collapsing into the real object which it is (in a sense of *is* other than that of artistic identification). Of course, without the theory, one is unlikely to see it as art, and in order to see it as part of the artworld, one must have mastered a good deal of artistic theory as well as a considerable amount of the history of recent New York painting. It could not have been art fifty years ago. But then there could not have been, everything being equal, flight insurance in the Middle Ages, or Etruscan typewriter erasers. The world has to be ready for certain things, the artworld no less than the real one. It is the role of artistic theories, these days as always, to make the artworld, and art, possible. It would, I should think, never have occurred to the painters of Lascaux that they were producing *art* on those walls. Not unless there were neolithic aestheticians.

IV. The artworld stands to the real world in something like the relationship in which the City of God stands to the Earthly City. Certain objects, like certain individuals, enjoy a double citizenship, but there remains, the RT notwithstanding, a fundamental contrast between artworks and real objects. Perhaps this was already dimly sensed by the early framers of the IT who, inchoately realizing the nonreality of art, were perhaps limited only in supposing that the sole way objects had of being other than real is to be sham, so that artworks necessarily had to be imitations of real objects. This was too narrow. So Yeats saw in writing "Once out of nature I shall never take/My bodily form from any natural thing." It is but a matter of choice: and the Brillo box of the artworld may be just the Brillo box of the real one, separated and united by the *is* of artistic identification. But I should like to say some final words about the theories that make artworks possible, and their relationship to one another. In so doing, I shall beg some of the hardest philosophical questions I know.

I shall now think of pairs of predicates related to each other as "opposites," conceding straight off the vagueness of this *demodé* term. Contradictory predicates are not opposites, since one of each of them must apply to every object in the universe, and neither of a pair of opposites need apply to some objects in the universe. An object must first be of a certain kind before either of a pair of opposites applies to it, and then at most and at least one of the opposites must apply to it. So opposites are not contraries, for contraries may both be false of some objects in the universe, but opposites cannot both be false; for of some objects, neither of a pair of opposites *sensibly* applies, unless the object is of the right sort. Then, if the object is of the required kind, the opposites behave as contradictories. If F and non-F are opposites, an object o must be of a certain kind K before either of these sensibly applies; but if o is a member of K, then o either is F or non-F to the exclusion of the other. The class of pairs of opposites that sensibly apply to the (o) Ko I shall designate as the class of *K-relevant predicates*. And a necessary condition for an object to be of a kind K is that at least one pair of K-relevant opposites be sensibly applicable to it. But, in fact, if an object is of kind K, at least and at most one of each K-relevant pair of opposites applies to it.

I am now interested in the K-relevant predicates for the class K of artworks And let F and non-F be an opposite pair of such predicates. Now it might happen that, throughout an entire period of time, every artwork is non-F. But since nothing thus far is both an artwork and F, it might never occur to anyone that non-F is an artistically relevant predicate. The non-F-ness of artworks goes unmarked. By contrast, all works up to a given time might be G, it never occurring to anyone until that time that something might both be an artwork and non-G; indeed, it might have been thought that G was a *defining trait* of artworks when in fact something might first have to be an artwork before G is sensibly

predicable of it—in which case non-G might also be predicable of artworks, and G itself then could not have been a defining trait of this class.

Let G be "is representational" and let F be "is expressionist." At a given time, these and their opposites are perhaps the only artrelevant predicates in critical use. Now letting "+" stand for a given predicate P and "−" for its opposite non-P, we may construct a style matrix more or less as follows:

F	G
+	+
+	−
−	+
−	−

The rows determine available styles, given the active critical vocabulary: representational expressionistic (e.g., Fauvism); representational nonexpressionistic (Ingres); nonrepresentational expressionistic (Abstract Expressionism); nonrepresentational nonexpressionist (hard-edge abstraction). Plainly, as we add artrelevant predicates, we increase the number of available styles at the rate of 2^n. It is, of course, not easy to see in advance which predicates are going to be added or replaced by their opposites, but suppose an artist determines that H shall henceforth be artistically relevant for his paintings. Then, in fact, both H and non-H become artistically relevant for *all* painting, and if his is the first and only painting that is H, every other painting in existence becomes non-H and the entire community of paintings is enriched, together with a doubling of the available style opportunities. It is this retroactive enrichment of the entities in the artworld that makes it possible to discuss Raphael and DeKooning together or Lichtenstein and Michelangelo. The greater the variety of artistically relevant predicates, the more complex the individual members of the artworld become, and the more one knows of the entire population of the artworld, the richer one's experience with any of its members.

In this regard, notice that, if there are m artistically relevant predicates, there is always a bottom row with m minuses. This row is apt to be occupied by purists. Having scoured their canvasses clear of what they regard as inessential, they credit themselves with having distilled out the essence of art. But this is just their fallacy: exactly as many artistically relevant predicates stand true of their square monochromes as stand true of any member of the Artworld, and they can *exist* as artworks only insofar as "impure" paintings exist. Strictly speaking, a black square by Reinhardt is artistically as rich as Titian's *Sacred and Profane Love*. This explains how less is more.

Fashion, as it happens, favors certain rows of the style matrix: museums, connoisseurs, and others are makeweights in the Artworld. To insist, or seek to, that all artists become representational, perhaps to gain entry into a specially prestigious exhibition, cuts the available style matrix in half. There are then $2^n/2$ ways of satisfying the requirement, and museums then can exhibit all these "approaches" to the topic they have set. But this is a matter of almost purely sociological interest: one row in the matrix is as legitimate as another. An artistic breakthrough consists, I suppose, in adding the possibility of a column to the matrix. Artists then, with greater or less alacrity, occupy the positions thus opened up: this is a remarkable feature of contemporary art, and for those unfamiliar with the matrix, it is hard, and perhaps impossible, to recognize certain positions as occupied by artworks. Nor would these things be artworks without the theories and the histories of the Artworld.

Brillo boxes enter the artworld with that same tonic incongruity the *commedia dell'arte* characters bring into *Ariadne auf Naxos*. Whatever is the artistically relevant predicate in virtue of which they gain their entry, the rest of the Artworld becomes that much the richer in having the opposite predicate available and applicable to its members. And, to return to the views of Hamlet with which we began this discussion, Brillo boxes may reveal us to ourselves as well as anything might: as a mirror held up to nature, they might serve to catch the conscience of our kings.

The Art Circle

GEORGE DICKIE

THUS FAR IN DISCUSSING the institutional nature of art I have described art's essential framework. In doing so I have concentrated on the roles of artist and public, sketchily characterizing them in terms of what those who fulfill these roles know from the past about art, its creation, and the experience of it. It may be wise at this juncture to point out the obvious fact that creating art is an intentional activity; accidents, fortuitous and not, may occur *within* the creative process, but the overall activity is not accidental. I shall continue the discussion of artist and public roles, focusing on the relation between artist and public. In creating art an artist is always involved with a public, since the object he creates is of a kind to be presented to a public. The relationship is, then, one of creating an object of a kind which is presented. Actual presentation of the created object or even being intended by its maker for presentation cannot be required, because, as noted earlier, some works of art are never presented and some are not even intended by their makers for presentation to a public. What is to be emphasized here is that the created

From The Art Circle *(New York: Haven Publications, 1984). Reprinted by permission of the author.*

object is of a *kind* which is made for presentation. Consider some cases in which works of art are *not* presented. Some works are not presented by their creators because they consider them to be practice works, not worthy of presentation. Practice works are of a kind for presentation, otherwise it would be pointless to judge one unworthy of presentation. Some works of art are not presented because their creators are uncertain of their worth. Some works of art are not presented because their creators believe the works to be too revealing about themselves. One could go on. In these kinds of cases, there is what might be called a "double intention"; there is an intention to create a thing of a kind which is presented, but there is also an intention not to actually present it. Artist and public in relation may be called, as I did on an earlier occasion, "the presentation group." A presentation group is, in fact, the minimum framework for the creation of art.

The role of artist has two central aspects. First, there is the general aspect which is characteristic of all artists, namely, the awareness that what is created for presentation is art. Second, there is the wide variety of art techniques, of which the ability to use one in some degree, enables one to create art of a particular kind. When these two aspects are taken together the wide variety of things that artists do (paint, sculpt, write, compose, act, dance, and so on) are seen to be subsumed under the description "creating an object of a kind which is presented." The role of artist may be realized in various ways. The role may be filled by a single person as is typically the case with painters. Even with painters the role of artist may be internally complex in the sense that a number of persons may be involved, as when an assistant (or assistants) aids a master. In cases of this kind there is still a single role, but it is being fulfilled by several persons. By contrast, in the performing arts it is the rule that the artist role is in fact a multiplicity of cooperative roles. For example, in the theater, the artist role encompasses the roles of playwright, director, and actors. These various roles might in a partic-

ular case be played by a single person. In such a case there is still a variety of roles, but they are being fulfilled by a single person.

The role of a member of a public also has two central aspects. First, there is the general aspect which is characteristic of all members of art publics, namely, the awareness that what is presented to them is art. The second aspect of the role of a member of a public is the wide variety of abilities and sensitivities which enable one to perceive and understand the particular kind of art with which one is presented. Some sensitivities or their opposites may be of a specific physiological kind: deafness, tone deafness, ordinary tone hearing, perfect pitch; blindness, ordinary color vision, acute color sensitivity; and so on. Such sensitivities may be sharpened by training and experience; and they may be blunted by aging, accident, or other factors. Some abilities do not have a specific physiological base and depend in a fundamental way upon one's having acquired certain information—the ability to recognize, for example. Other abilities are of a more specific sort—the intellectual ability to comprehend a number of elements as members of a whole, for example. One could go on.

At the beginning of this chapter I spoke of artist and public in relation as "the presentation group." If, however, artists create and publics perceive and understand, there is a function which lies between them and brings them together. In *Art and the Aesthetic* I characterized this function as the task of "presenter"—stage managers and their personnel, museum directors and their personnel, and the like. (There is a sense in which actors, directors, and the like are presenters, but they also participate in the artist role as well.) Also, in the earlier book, I distinguished a number of conventions (there called "secondary conventions") which are involved in the presentation of works of art to publics. A list of such conventions would be very long because of the diversity of the arts, but it is worth noting a few. One convention of theater discussed at length in the earlier book is the "nonparticipation-by-spectator" convention which functions as a rule for directing the behavior of the members of an audience. It is this conventional rule which is bent by Peter Pan's request for applause to save Tinkerbell's life and by similar devices employed in other plays. Another kind of convention is used to direct the audience's attention, for example, the curtain going up and the lights going down. Still another kind of convention of theater is the concealing of the actions of stagehands. In classical Chinese theater, however, the stagehand convention is to have the property man on stage among the actors during the performance. The two differing theatrical conventions for dealing with the same problem—the manipulation of various theatrical elements—provide an interesting and instructive contrast. In the domain of painting, it is a convention to hang paintings with their "backs" to the wall. As noted in the earlier book, we might have had the convention of hanging paintings with their "fronts" to the wall. The two actual solutions for the employment of stagehands and the way we actually hang paintings together with a conceivably different way of hanging them brings out an essential feature of conventions. Any conventional way of doing something could have been done in a different way. The failure to realize that things of the kind just mentioned are conventions can result in confused theory; for example, certain aesthetic-attitude theorists failed to see that the non-participation theater rule is a conventional rule and concluded that it is a rule derived from "aesthetic consciousness" and is written in stone. These attitude theorists are horrified by Peter Pan's request for momentary audience participation, because they think that the request violates a dictate of aesthetic consciousness. The request, however, merely amounts to the introduction of a new convention (which permits momentary audience participation) which small children, but not some aestheticians, catch on to right away.

The various arts employ many different conventions to do many different things, but there is no *primary* convention in the arts to which the above discussed conventions are secondary, as I claimed in *Art and the Aesthetic*. I wrote there of

the primary convention of theater as ". . . the understanding shared by the actors and the audience that they are engaged in a certain kind of formal activity." Of painting I wrote, "The *display* of a painting is the public aspect of the primary convention of presentation." The first thing to be remarked about these two statements is that the first fails to mention playwrights and the second fails to mention artists (painters), that is, the creators of works of art. These failures arose because the statements occurred within a discussion of the presentation of works of art to audiences, a context within which the creators of works of art do not ordinarily play a big role. Any description of what earlier I mistakenly called "the primary convention" must exhibit a role for playwrights, poets, painters, and the like.

If, however, there is no primary *convention*, there is a primary *something* within which the conventions of the kind already described have a place. What is primary is the understanding shared by all involved that they are engaged in an established activity or practice within which there is a variety of different roles: creator roles, presenter roles, and "consumer" roles. There are, as I indicated, certain conventions involved in the presenting of works of art, and there are, no doubt, conventions involved in the creating of works. The practice within which these conventions are used and observed, however, is not itself conventional. One of the reasons that the way in which stagehands are employed in traditional Western theater is conventional is that it could have been done differently, and the way in which the same task is done in classical Chinese theater clearly shows this. The practice of theater itself or painting itself, however, is not just one way of doing something which could be done in one or more other ways, although there are alternative ways of doing theater and of painting, that is, engaging in these activities using different conventions.

There are rules of very different kinds within the institution of art. There are conventional rules which derive from the various conventions employed in presenting and creating art. There are, however, the more basic rules which govern the engaging in an art activity, and these rules are not conventional. The artifact rule—if one wishes to make a work of art, one must do so by creating an artifact—is not a conventional rule, it states a condition for engaging in a certain kind of practice.

Put in a formal way, the art enterprise can be seen to be a complex of interrelated roles governed by conventional and nonconventional rules. At the end of the last chapter, I discussed the nonconventional rules involved in the creation of art. Here at the beginning of this chapter, I have discussed the conventional rules involved in the presenting and receiving of works of art together with the practice within which these conventional rules have a place.

In addition to the roles of artist, presenter, and public, which are essential for presentation, there are supplementary roles for assisting presentation which exist in a society of any complexity. Some of these roles are aimed at assisting an artist mount his work: producers, theater managers, museum directors, art dealers, and the like. Some of these roles are aimed at assisting a public locate, understand, interpret, or evaluate a work presented: newspaper reporters, critics, and the like. Some other roles revolve around the presented work at a greater distance: art historians, art theorists, and philosophers of art.

The artworld consists of the totality of roles just discussed with the roles of artist and public at its core. Described in a somewhat more structured way, the artworld consists of a set of individual artworld systems, each of which contains its own specific artist roles plus specific supplementary roles. For example, painting is one artworld system, theater is another, and so on.

There is an ambiguity inherent in the way I used the expression "the artworld" in *Art and the Aesthetic* which needs to be recognized and dealt with. I sometimes wrote there of the artworld as a system of roles, as I intend to be speaking of it here. I also wrote of "the core personnel of the artworld," and this way of speaking at least suggests that I was talking about a particular group of people involved in a person-institution. If I were to use the word "personnel" in characterizing the artworld in this book, I would want it to be understood in a metaphorical way to mean a person fulfilling a role in an *action*-institution. It is the roles I want to emphasize here and not the particular persons who play the roles. There is of course always a community of persons who fill the artworld roles and in a sense are the artworld (personnel) at a particular time, but this is another sense of "artworld."

What all of the artworld systems have in common is that each is a framework or a system for the creation of an artifact for presentation to a public. . . .

The problem, however, [of] . . . the hodgepodge aspect of the collection of artworld systems—remains. The class of works of art has a unity because each work of art is embedded in an artworld system, but what provides the unity which binds the systems themselves together? What Walton takes to be the most promising solution, as I have suggested, does not resolve the hodgepodge aspect of the class of protosystems. And, if the hodgepodge aspect of the protosystems cannot be resolved, there does not seem to be much point in trying to resolve the hodgepodge aspect of the systems "not on the list" by relating them to the protosystems. What has to be accepted is the "arbitrariness" of being an artworld system—the lack of a "crucial similarity" of the kind sought by traditional theories which would easily and obviously distinguish it from nonartworld systems. If there were such "crucial similarities" there would be no need for an institutional approach—the traditional approach would suffice.

Some may feel these results involve a vicious circularity, just as some felt that the definition of "work of art" in *Art and the Aesthetics* did. I acknowledged there that the definition was circular but argued that it was not viciously so because the circle it ran was large and contained a lot of information about the artworld. There is something to be said for this argument, but I now believe that more can and should be said about the "problem" of circularity.

Although circularity in definition and explanation is widely regarded as a grave logical fault, little or nothing seems to have been written which explores the question in any depth. No doubt the explanation for this lack is that most have thought it obvious why circularity is a fault. No doubt circularity is a fault in many cases where it occurs, but is it always a fault?

There is a philosophical ideal which underlies the noncircularity norm of definition, although it does not seem to have been articulated. The ideal goes something like this. There are basic or primitive terms which are unanalyzable and, hence, undefinable. One can learn the meaning of these primitive terms only in some nonlinguistic way: sensory experience, rational intuition, or whatever. In characterizing the ideal, the primitive terms can be represented by small letters: *a, b, c,* and *d.* The basic terms can be used to define first-level definable terms which can be represented by capital letters: *A, B, C,* and *D.* There may be second-level terms *(M, N, 0,* and *P)* which are defined in terms of first-level terms or a combination of primitive and first-level terms. There may be third-level terms which are defined by lower-level terms and so on and so on. According to the ideal, all definitions lead back to and depend on the primitive terms and the things they denote. The primitive terms are the foundations of knowledge. The ideal may not envisage a multiplicity of levels above the primitive level, but it does require a level of primitive terms and a level of defined terms.

Can this ideal of the nature of definition be realized? Has it even been attempted on any scale at all? Dictionaries, which are large-scale attempts at definition, make no attempt to isolate a set of primitive terms and are unashamedly circular. Perhaps, however, the ideal might be achieved on a more limited scale. Even if in a domain more limited than that of a dictionary, say, the language of physical objects, one could achieve a set of reductive definitions as envisaged by the ideal, it does not follow from this that such an achievement is possible for definition in any other domain.

There may be a more pragmatic ideal underlying the norm of noncircular definition, one which is a kind of shadow of the first epistemological ideal sketched just above. According to this view, words used to define other words are only primitive relative to the context in which the defining occurs. The functionally primitive terms can be defined in other contexts. On this view, epistemologically primitive terms do not have to turn up, although perhaps they might in some cases. Perhaps some sets of dictionary definitions realize the pragmatic ideal, in that although there are no epistemologically primitive terms upon which they ultimately rest, they constitute a series of definitions which contain no elements which circle back. For example, the word "saddler" is defined as "One who makes saddles," and "saddle" is defined as "A seat for a rider, to be used on the back of a horse or other animal." There does not seem to be any reason to think that the definition of "seat," "rider," "back," and so on will require the use of the words "saddler" or "saddle." Just as the possibility that some definitions might realize the epistemological ideal does not show that all definitions must, the fact that some definitions realize (or seem to realize) the pragmatic ideal does not show that all definitions must. In other words, the fact that some dictionary entries realize the pragmatic ideal does not mean that every term in the language can be made to do so. Bearing in mind these observations about the two ideals, the only way to show that a circular account of art is incorrect would be either to show that either of the ideals under the discussion can be or has been achieved quite generally or that a correct, noncircular account of art can be or has been given. Since neither of these two has been accomplished, the way is at least open for an exploration of a circular account of art.

This very way of putting it will, I suppose, send logical shudders through many, but if art is the sort of thing I think it is, the only correct account of it would have to be a circular account.

Part of, or at least attached to, the ideal of noncircular definition is the view that the role of definition is to inform someone of the meaning of an expression one is ignorant of by means of words one already knows. It is true that one does sometimes look up the definition of a highfalutin word with which one is unfamiliar, say, a word such as "penultimate." More often than not, however, one looks up the definition of a word in order to see if one really knows what it means (and usually discovers that one does) or in order to see what the exact meaning of a word is, although one knows in a general way what the word means and has no trouble in using it correctly in a wide variety of contexts.

The definitions which philosophers have given of "work of art" do not function, nor are they really intended to function, as the dictionary definition of a pedantic word such as "penultimate" functions for most of us. (This is no doubt true of the other definitions which philosopher's have given.) Virtually everyone, including even quite small children, has at least a partial understanding of the expression "work of art." Virtually everyone can recognize some things as works of art, knows how some works of art are made, and the like. Thus, virtually no one is in need of a definition of "work of art" in the way that many would be in need of a definition if they came upon an unfamiliar word such as, say, "penultimate." So a philosopher's definition of "work of art" does not and cannot function in the way a definition is supposed to function according to the ideal mentioned earlier—to inform someone of the meaning of an expression one is ignorant of by means of words one already knows. The reason it cannot so function is that anyone who has gotten to the point of reading documents on the philosophy of art will already know what the expression "work of art" means.

What philosophical definitions of "work of art" are really attempting to do is then to make clear to us in a self-conscious and explicit way what we already in some sense know. That philosopher's definitions have been so frequently misdirected testifies to the difficulty of saying precisely what we in some sense already know—a difficulty that Socrates tried to get Meno and his slave boy to appreciate. Definitions of terms such as "work of art" cannot inform us of something we are really ignorant of. Furthermore, the fear that some philosophers have of circularity in certain definitions is, I think, groundless. In any event, if a definition of "work of art" is circular, it may just be so because of the very nature of what the definition is about.

In what now follows I shall present an account of art which is clearly circular, or to put it in a better way, an account which reveals the *inflected* nature of art. By "inflected nature" I mean a nature the elements of which bend in on, presuppose, and support one another. In *Art and the Aesthetic* I attempted to define only "work of art," although I discussed the other aspects of the artworld, as I then conceived of them, in some detail. There, in defining, I focused on the "center" of what I am now calling art's essential framework—works of art themselves. I now think that each of the structural intersections of the framework requires definition, for the framework's center is not its only vital part. Consequently, I shall now, in effect, try to supply a small dictionary—a dictionary for the philosophy of art. This series of definitions is just a shorthand way of presenting in summary form the major conclusions of the previous chapters.

I shall begin with a definition of the term "artist," not because it has alphabetical priority over the other terms to be defined, but because the series of definitions seems to flow most easily from this particular source. Any of the structural intersections would, however, serve as a beginning point.

I) An artist is a person who participates with understanding in the making of a work of art.

There is nothing controversial, or even surprising, about this definition, so matters are off to a smooth start. The definition in itself is not circular, although it does cry out for a definition of "work of art" which will come along shortly. The "understanding" clause in the definition is necessary to distinguish an artist (say, a playwright or a director) from someone such as a stage carpenter who builds various stage elements. What the artist understands is the general idea of art and the particular idea of the medium he is working with. To forestall misunderstanding, let me hasten to add that a stage carpenter or the like may very well understand the art of the stage but that such knowledge is just not required for the carrying out of the function which constitutes his participation in the artistic process. This definition of "artist" also makes it clear that art-making is an intentional. activity; although elements of a work of art may have their origin in accidental occurrences which happen during the making of a work, a work as a whole is not accidental. Participating with understanding implies that an artist is aware of what he is doing.

These remarks lead naturally to the definition of "work of art."

II) *A work of art is an artifact of a kind created to be presented to an artworld public.*

Being a work of art, thus, involves having a status or position within a structure which in a way is somewhat similar to the earlier view of *Art and the Aesthetic*. According to the present view, however, the status in no way results from a conferral but rather is achieved through working in a medium within the artworld framework. Let me note here, as I did earlier, that an object need never actually be presented to an artworld public in order to be a work of art. The definition speaks only of the creation of a *kind* of thing which is presented. To forestall one possible misunderstanding, in using the word "kind" here I am not talking about genres or even larger categories such as *painting, play, poem,* or the like. The kind specified by the definition is of a larger sort, namely, an artifact of a kind to be presented. The kind in question is, of course, not to be identified with the kind *work of art,* because the kind in question is only an aspect of a work of art.

To forestall another possible objection to the definition, let me acknowledge that there are artifacts which are created for presentation to the artworld publics which are not works of art: for example, playbills. Things such as playbills are, however, parasitic or secondary to works of art. Works of art are artifacts of a primary kind in this domain, and playbills and the like which are *dependent* on works of art are artifacts of a secondary kind within this domain. The word "artifact" in the definition should be understood to be referring to artifacts of the primary kind. The definition could be explicitly reformulated: A work of art is an artifact (primary) of a kind created to be presented to an artworld public.

In the discussion following the definition of "artist," I remarked that art-making is clearly an intentional activity. In a parallel way, the definition of "work of art" implies that such objects are intentional, i.e., are the product of an intentional activity. The definition of "works of art" leads on to the notions of *public* and *artworld*.

III) *A public is a set of persons the members of which are prepared in some degree to understand an object which is presented to them.*

This definition is not only not circular in itself, it is stated in a general way and does not necessarily involve the artworld. Put otherwise, it is a formulation which characterizes all publics, not just those of the artworld. The definition of "public" is not formerly tied to the other definitions I am giving. Any actual public, however, will be necessarily tied to some particular system; for example, the artworld public is necessarily related to artists, works of art, and other things.

IV) *The artworld is the totality of all artworld systems.*

At this point it may be worth emphasizing what is perhaps implicitly clear enough, namely, that the roles of artist and public and the structure of artworld systems are herein conceived of as things which persist through time and have a history. In short, the definitions characterize an ongoing cultural enterprise. This definition of "the artworld" certainly gives the appearance of being circular in itself, although this impression is at least counteracted by remembering that the expression "all artworld systems" is short for a list which includes literary system, theater system, painting system, and so on. The circularity in itself of the definition of "the artworld" may be real or apparent, but the circularity of the whole set of definitions becomes transparent with the definition of "artworld system."

V) An artworld system is a framework for the presentation of a work of art by an artist to an artworld public.

The series of definitions has not led down strata after strata until bedrock is reached. The "final" definition, that of "artworld system," simply reaches back and employs all the previous focal terms: "artist," "work of art," "public," and "artworld." What is to be made of this blatant circularity? Conventional philosophical wisdom tells us to recoil in logical horror and to reject it as uninformative and worse. Beginning with the charge of uninformativeness, as noted earlier, in a basic sense we do not need to be informed about art—we already have a fundamental understanding of it. Conventional wisdom notwithstanding, there is a sense in which the definitions are informative; if they accurately reflect the nature of art and the relations which hold among the various elements of the artworld, then they do in a way inform us. These remarks may counter the charge of uninformativeness, but what of the charge of logical fault—the "worse" of the "uninformative and worse"? If, however, the definitions accurately mirror the inflected nature of the art enterprise, then they are not logically faulty.

I have done what I could to show, in this chapter and the one before that works of art are embedded in what I have called an *essential* framework. What the definitions I have given do, I believe, is to give the leanest possible description of that essential framework and the embedded works. What the definitions reveal, by eliminating distracting detail, is that art-making involves an intricate, co-relative structure which cannot be described in the straightforward, linear way that such activities as saddlemaking presumably can be described. In short, what the definitions reveal and thereby inform us of is the inflected nature of art. The definitions help us get clear about something with which we are already familiar but about whose nature we have not been sufficiently clear from a theoretical point of view. What the definitions describe and thus reveal is the complex of necessarily related elements which constitute the art-making enterprise.

Danto's "indistinguishable-pairs" argument and the failure of the Romantic-artist thesis show that works of art require a framework, but what shows that the framework has the inflected nature that the definitions picture it as having? Reflection on how we learn about art will, I think, reveal in what sense and why an account of art must be circular. How, then, do we learn what it is that we know about art?

We do not learn about art from the theories or definitions of philosophers; their remarks would be unintelligible if we did not already know about art. We learn about art in different ways, but we invariably do so at a tender age. Children are frequently taught about art by being shown how to make works for display: "Now draw a nice picture to take home to your mother or to put up on the board." One may be introduced to art in a more abstract, lecture-like way: "These are pictures done by some men who lived a long time ago to be put up in churches." Art instruction such as the foregoing are typically preceded by remarks which prepare a child for it; for example, "This is the way we draw a face," which helps a child come to understand representation. I do not mean to suggest by my example that a knowledge of representation is necessary for the subsequent understanding of art, but it is almost always involved in the beginnings of teaching about art—at least with Western art.

These, then, are some of the ways that we learn about art. *What* is it that such instruction teaches? We learn that a complex of interrelated things is involved in the art-enterprise: artists (oneself, other children, men who lived a long time ago), works (the nice picture, pictures of religious figures), an artworld public (mother, the other children, the teacher, people who go into churches). We also learn that special places can be set aside for the display of works (the refrigerator door at home, the board at school, the walls of a church).

Considered more abstractly, what is it that such instruction teaches us? We are taught about agent, artifact, and public all at the same time, and this is no accident for the various artworld elements do not exist independently of one another. In learning about what a poem, a painting, or a play is, we cannot fail to learn that it is an object with a past—an object which results from a human action—and that it is an object with an intended future—an object which is of a kind which is presented. When we come to know that an object is a work of art, or even just see an object as a work of art (perhaps mistakenly), we fit it into a certain kind of cultural role—the kind of role I have been trying to describe in this and previous chapters.

Perhaps a good way to round out the account of the artworld would be to consider some of the implications of the speculations of the last chapter about the origins of art. There it was speculated that the art enterprise must have evolved out of a prior activity or activities as the cumulative effect of the innovations of what I called "Romantic proto-artists." At a certain point—perhaps a rather elongated point—a prior activity ceased to be merely a single activity and became a complex one—say, religious activity plus an art form. The participants themselves (in a certain way) and some of the other elements of the prior activity metamorphosed into the kind of structure I have called "an artworld system." Given this account, one can see that the activity or role of artist, the conception of the product of this activity as a work of art, and the activity or role of public had to develop together, growing into the identifiable elements of a single integrated whole—an artworld system.

Artist, work of art, artworld, and artworld system are what I shall call "inflected concepts." I mean the expression "inflected concept" to designate a concept which is a member of a set of concepts which bend in on themselves, presupposing and supporting one another. No member of such a set can be understood apart from all the other concepts in the set. Consequently, in coming to understand a concept which is a member of such a set, one must in some degree come to understand all the other member concepts as well. There are, I suspect, other sets of inflected concepts: law, legislature, executive, and judiciary, for example. The domain of "cultural concepts" is perhaps rife with inflected sets. In any event, an account of the art enterprise requires the use of a nest of inflected concepts.

But isn't there more to be said about art? Even many of those who are in general agreement with the institutional approach may feel that there is more to the nature of art than my remarks allow. Certainly those who disagree with what I have said, but still think that art has an essential nature, will feel that there is more to that nature than the institutional theory claims. . . .

C. The Status of the Work of Art

Although we distinguish aesthetics from other branches of philosophy, in practice it is hard to keep the various branches of philosophy neatly separated. If we ask, for instance, whether the art critic really knows which works of art are better than others, we are raising epistemological problems about knowledge in general (from the branch of philosophy known as *epistemology,* or theory of knowledge). And when we wonder what sort of thing a work of art is, whether it is a physical object or merely an imaginary object existing, as the early twentieth-century English aesthetician Robin Collingwood once said, "inside our heads," we are raising a metaphysical issue about the ontological status of different sorts of things in the world. Is a number (e.g., the number 743) the same kind of thing as a grasshopper? Is a law of physics the same sort of thing as a city ordinance recently passed in Schenectady, New York? Do either of these belong to the same class of object as a brick? These questions belong to that branch of philosophy known as *metaphysics,* and as soon as we begin to wonder what sort of object is a work of art, we have slipped over into metaphysics.

Part of the agenda of analytic or linguistic philosophy was the elimination of metaphysics. Of all the traditional branches of philosophy, metaphysics was considered by analytic philosophers the worst—the most confusing, muddle headed, wooly headed, wrong headed, and utterly useless. Plato had argued that beauty was an immaterial abstract universal Form outside space and time and therefore unobservable by the five senses. Idealist philosophers (Hegel and twentieth-century neo-idealists such as Collingwood and Croce) had argued that physical objects, like the White House, exist only in our minds. For philosophers sympathetic to the successes of the natural sciences, metaphysics was an embarrassment—a kind of retrograde substitute for religion or poetry.

A major project of analytic aesthetics was therefore the clarification of the metaphysical (or ontological) status of the work of art. Earlier aestheticians had seen the difficulty in thinking of works of art simply as physical objects. A poem, piece of music, play, or novel cannot be simply identified with the piece of paper on which they are written nor with the particular performance of the play or music nor the particular reading of the poem or novel (otherwise a poem or a symphony or a play could be destroyed in a fire, which is absurd). And even more substantial artworks like a cathedral or a painting or a piece of sculpture only seem to function as art when they are looked at in the right way. To the pigeon in the park or the dog on a walk, the outdoor Picasso sculpture really isn't sculpture. Art doesn't seem to exist for dogs and cats. Even in these cases involving substantial physical objects the artwork seems to require some sort of human observer. Earlier (Part I, section A) we saw how Aristotle had observed that unlike physical objects the work of art had its "form" imposed upon it by humans so that the artwork became a human imitation or representation *of* the world and not just another physical object *in* the world. But, following Hegel, this assumption led many philosophers of art to jump to the conclusion that a work of art was therefore an imaginary entity existing "in the mind," or in some Platonic heaven. And that, say the analytic aestheticians, is equally odd and unacceptable.

Obviously, the situation is far more complex than this simplistic either/or (either it's a physical object or it exists in the mind). What is needed, the analytic aestheticians concluded, is a more careful, precise, refined, sophisticated analysis. As Wollheim notes at the beginning of his article, we naturally tend to start out thinking that works of art, or at least some of them, must be physical objects (like a grasshopper or a brick). But he very quickly shows us the difficulty in holding such a view (this is, incidentally, a very good example of analytic philosophy at work). If we say a novel is a physical object—say, the copy of Dickens's *Hard Times* I have in my library at home—then we would have to say that if a fire destroys my copy of *Hard Times,* then the fire also destroyed the novel, which is absurd. Or if we say that Beethoven's Fifth Symphony is identical with a particular performance of it, then we would be led to say equally absurd and ridiculous things—that if tonight's performance is canceled and therefore never existed, then Beethoven's Fifth Symphony is canceled (which sounds a very odd thing to say) and never existed (which is clearly false).

But if the theory is so easily refuted by such everyday examples, why did anyone ever suppose that works of art were physical objects? Perhaps because since the seventeenth-century we have tended to divide the world into two and only two categories—if something exists then it must be either a physical object (like a brick or a grasshopper) or an imaginary object (like the dragon I dreamed about last night). What else could there be? But of course there are lots of other sorts of things in the world—laws passed by a city government, numbers, biological species, past events, and so on.

But even if we admit that literary artworks (such as poems, plays, novels, short stories) and performing arts (such as music, plays, and dance) are not physical objects, why can't we say that paintings and sculpture, at least, are physical objects? Certainly they have to be physically shipped from one museum or gallery to another. Michelangelo's *Pieta* weighs several tons and was severely damaged some years ago by a deranged critic wielding a sledge hammer! Why can't we say these artworks, at least, are physical objects? Because, as Wollheim argues, we can't say the same things about artworks that we can say about their physical embodiments (which we could if they were identical). The art critic says that a painting has "great depth," but as a physical object the painting is extremely flat, indeed less than a sixteenth of an inch thick. The thing we talk about as a work of art (having "great depth") seems to be something only humans can perceive. Birds can see and feel outdoor sculpture but they do not, so far as we know, perceive these objects as works of art.

And this distinction is precisely what led Croce, Collingwood, and other Idealist aestheticians in the 1920s and 1930s to say that works of art exist only "in one's head," that is, as imaginary mental objects. But that clearly won't work, either. An artist works not just with ideas and images in her head but with stone, paint, and canvas, with words and notes written on paper.

But if a work of art is neither a physical nor a mental object, then what is it? Wollheim's suggestion is that a work of art is a "type," as in the "type–token" distinction. But what then is a type? When I empty my pockets at night, suppose I find three pennies. Each of these is a token of a single type—the copper Lincoln penny. Or my 1992 Jeep Cherokee is but one of thousands of tokens of a single type. As Wollheim points out, the way we describe the type is precisely the way we describe the token. The token penny is round, copper, with a profile bust of Abraham Lincoln on one side, and that is precisely how I would describe the type ("the copper Lincoln penny that displays a profile bust of Abraham Lincoln"). So in a similar way Wollheim wants to say that my copy of Dickens's *Hard Times* is not the novel itself but only a token of the type, which is the novel. Nonetheless, whatever I say about my copy I mean to say about the type (or at least whenever I talk about my copy as a copy of Dickens's novel—though not when I talk about my copy simply as my copy, which, unlike Dickens's *Hard Times,* is new, belongs to me, and has unfortunately been chewed up by my dog).

Judging from Anita Silvers's article, "Letting the Sunshine In," you might think that analytic aesthetics is over and done with, but in many ways it is alive and well today—though in a decidedly modified form. Silvers herself mentions the move within analytic aesthetics away from strict second-order conceptual clarification that is not concerned with the "world," to a concern with the "world" of art by analytic philosophers like Margaret Macdonald, Nelson Goodman, and Arthur Danto. Jerrod Levinson is a good example of the younger generation of aestheticians trained in the analytic tradition and continuing in that tradition in their own way.

Levinson's article follows on naturally from Wollheim's. Wollheim introduces the metaphysical problem of the ontological status of the work of art—is an artwork a physical object, an imaginary mental object, or, perhaps, as Wollheim suggests, a type of which individual copies, performances, etc. are tokens? Levinson continues this line of investigation, directing his attention to the specific case of music. Obviously, a piece of music cannot be a physical object, or even a quasiphysical object like a particular performance by a specific orchestra on a given date in a certain city. Levinson agrees with Wollheim that a piece of music is basically a kind of type, but he wonders precisely what sort of type. In particular, he rejects the idea that a musical work can be identified with the "type of type" known as a sound structure.

What's wrong with thinking of a piece of music as a sound structure? First of all, what is a sound structure? Think of a song as pattern of sounds. There are high (pitch) sounds and low (pitch) sounds; there are long sounds and short sounds; there are loud sounds and soft sounds; and there is a definite relationship among all these sounds—for example, the sounds may go up (in pitch) quickly, followed by a long, loud, high-pitch sound, ending with a descending series of sounds going down both in pitch and in volume. If you read music, you can think of a musical score (a piece of sheet music) as a way of notating this sound pattern. This, then, is the type, but what are the tokens? Obviously, all the many instances in which these sounds (notes) are played (that is, performed). In the morning you are humming the song in the shower; on the way to school you hear the song on the radio; later in the day you buy the CD and listen to it when you get home in the evening—these are all tokens of the same type (same song).

So what's wrong with saying that a piece of music is a sound structure? The main problem Levinson finds with this suggestion is that it does not take into account what Levinson regards as an essential factor in any piece of music, namely, the precise way it is supposed to be performed—not hummed, but played on violins, bassoons, and so on. What if I try to play Beethoven's Fifth Symphony on my harmonica? Beethoven did not write the music for harmonica, but for full orchestra (at least forty instruments). Levinson questions whether it is even possible to play Beethoven's Fifth Symphony on the harmonica. That is, would what I play on my harmonica be an instance (a token) of Beethoven's Fifth Symphony? Levinson wants to say no, that it would be a different piece of music. What about performing a piece on the piano that was originally written for clavichord (before pianos had been invented)—is that a different piece of music? Or transcriptions of symphonic music for guitar or brass band? Or popular sheet music arranged for small jazz band, large orchestra, or mandolin—are these tokens of the same piece of music or not?

Even if we agree with Levinson that a piece of music must be identified with the specific sounds produced by the particular instruments intended by the composer, why can't we include that within the sound structure—that is, by adding *timbre* to pitch, volume, and length of each sound. Of course, it is true that a note played on the harmonica is not the same as that same note played by a violin, or by a twenty-piece orchestral string section of violins, violas, and cellos, and this difference is usually referred to as a difference in sound timbre (the timbre of a piano playing middle C is different from the timbre of a trombone playing middle C, though these sounds are identical in pitch, volume or duration).

Even so, wouldn't it be possible to produce electronically the same sound structure, including timbre, without using those instruments? It is possible today to produce the sound of a fifty-piece orchestra playing Beethoven's Fifth Symphony in a large concert hall using only electronic keyboards in a small recording studio. If it sounds the same—that is, produces the same sound structure, including timbre—is it a recording (token) of Beethoven's Fifth Symphony or not? Apparently Levinson would insist that it is not, because Beethoven made it clear in his handwritten score that he intended his Fifth Symphony to be performed by violins, trumpets, oboes, and so on, and not on electronic keyboard. Nonetheless, the appeal of analytic aestheticians is generally to what we would ordinarily say in everyday life. Suppose I play for you an electronically produced CD that reproduces the exact same sound structure of Beethoven's Fifth Symphony, including timbre, of a full symphonic orchestra playing in a large concert hall. Are you listening to Beethoven's Fifth Symphony, or are you not?

Art and Its Objects

RICHARD WOLLHEIM

Let us begin with the hypothesis that works of art are physical objects. I shall call this for the sake of brevity the "physical-object hypothesis." Such a hypothesis is a natural starting point: if only for the reason that it is plausible to assume that things are physical objects unless they very obviously aren't. Certain things very obviously aren't physical objects. Now though it may not be obvious that works of art are physical objects, they don't seem to belong among these other things. They don't, that is, immediately group themselves along with thoughts, or periods of history, or numbers, or mirages. Furthermore, and more substantively, this hypothesis accords with many traditional conceptions of Art and its objects and what they are.

Nevertheless the hypothesis that all works of art are physical objects can be challenged. For our purposes it will be useful, and instructive, to divide this challenge into two parts: the division conveniently corresponding to a division within the arts themselves. For in the case of certain arts the argument is that there is no physical object that can with any plausibility be identified as the work of art: there is no object existing in space and time (as physical objects must) that can be picked out and thought of as a piece of music or a novel. In the case of other arts—most notably painting and sculpture—the argument is that, though there are physical objects of a standard and acceptable kind that could be, indeed generally are, identified as works of art, such identifications are wrong.

The first part of this challenge is, as we shall see, by far the harder to meet. However it is, fortunately, not it, but the second part of the challenge, that potentially raises such difficulties for aesthetics.

That there is a physical object that can be identified as *Ulysses* or *Der Rosenkavalier* is not a view that can long survive the demand that we should pick out or point to that object. There is, of course, the copy of *Ulysses* that is on my table before me now, there is the performance of *Der*

From Richard Wollheim, Art and Its Objects *(New York: Harper and Row, 1968). Reprinted with permission of the author and Cambridge University Press.*

Rosenkavalier that I will go to tonight, and both these two things may (with some latitude, it is true, in the case of the performance) be regarded as physical objects. Furthermore, a common way of referring to these objects is by saying things like "*Ulysses* is on my table," "I shall see *Rosenkavalier* tonight": from which it would be tempting (but erroneous) to conclude that *Ulysses* just is my copy of it, *Rosenkavalier* just is tonight's performance.

Tempting, but erroneous; and there are a number of very succinct ways of bringing out the error involved. For instance, it would follow that if I lost my copy of *Ulysses*, *Ulysses* would become a lost work. Again, it would follow that if the critics disliked tonight's performance of *Rosenkavalier*, then they dislike *Rosenkavalier*. Clearly neither of these inferences is acceptable.

We have here two locutions or ways of describing the facts: one in terms of works of art, the other in terms of copies, performances, etc., of works of art. Just because there are contexts in which these two locutions are interchangeable, this does not mean that there are no contexts, moreover no contexts of a substantive kind, in which they are not interchangeable. There very evidently are such contexts, and the physical-object hypothesis would seem to overlook them to its utter detriment.

But, it might be maintained, of course it is absurd to identify *Ulysses* with my copy of it or *Der Rosenkavalier* with tonight's performance, but nothing follows from this of a general character about the wrongness of identifying works of art with physical objects. For what was wrong in these two cases was the actual physical object that was picked out and with which the identification was then made. The validity of the physical-object hypothesis, like that of any other hypothesis, is quite unaffected by the consequences of misapplying it.

For instance, it is obviously wrong to say that *Ulysses* is my copy of it. Nevertheless, there is a physical object, of precisely the same order of being as my copy, though significantly not called a "copy" with which such an identification would

be quite correct. This object is the author's manuscript: that, in other words, which Joyce wrote when he wrote *Ulysses*.

On the intimate connection, which undoubtedly does exist, between a novel or a poem on the one hand and the author's manuscript on the other, I shall have something to add later. But the connection does not justify us in asserting that one just is the other. Indeed, to do so seems open to objections not all that dissimilar from those we have just been considering. The critic, for instance, who admires *Ulysses* does not necessarily admire the manuscript. Nor is the critic who has seen or handled the manuscript in a privileged position as such when it comes to judgment on the novel. And—here we have come to an objection directly parallel to that which seemed fatal to identifying *Ulysses* with my copy of it—it would be possible for the manuscript to be lost and *Ulysses* to survive. None of this can be admitted by the person who thinks that *Ulysses* and the manuscript are one and the same thing.

To this last objection someone might retort that there are cases (e.g., *Love's Labour Won*, Kleist's *Robert Guiscard*) where the manuscript is lost and the work is lost, and moreover the work is lost because the manuscript is lost. Of course there is no real argument here, since nothing more is claimed than that there are *some* cases like this. Nevertheless the retort is worth pursuing, for the significance of such cases is precisely the opposite of that intended. Instead of reinforcing, they actually diminish, the status of the manuscript. For if we now ask, When is the work lost when the manuscript is lost? the answer is, When and only when the manuscript is unique: but then this would be true for any copy of the work were it unique.

Moreover, it is significant that in the case of *Rosenkavalier* it is not even possible to construct an argument corresponding to the one about *Ulysses*. To identify an opera or any other piece of music with the composer's holograph [handwritten score], which looks the corresponding thing to do, is implausible because (for instance), whereas an opera can be heard, a holograph cannot be. In consequence it is common at that stage of the argument, when music is considered, to introduce a new notion, that of the ideal performance, and then to identify the piece of music with this. There are many difficulties here: in the present context it is enough to point out that this step could not conceivably satisfy the purpose for which it was intended; that is, that of saving the physical-object hypothesis. For an ideal performance cannot be, even in the attenuated sense in which we have extended the term to ordinary performances, a physical object.

A final and desperate expedient to save the physical-object hypothesis is to suggest that all those works of art which cannot plausibly be identified with physical objects are identical with classes of such objects. A novel, of which there are copies, is not my or your copy but is the class of all its copies. An opera, of which there are performances, is not tonight's or last night's performance, nor even the ideal performance, but is the class of all its performances. (Of course, strictly speaking, this suggestion doesn't save the hypothesis at all: since a class of physical objects isn't necessarily, indeed is most unlikely to be, a physical object itself. But it saves something like the spirit of the hypothesis.)

However, it is not difficult to think of objections to this suggestion. Ordinarily we conceive of a novelist as writing a novel, or a composer as finishing an opera. But both these ideas imply some moment in time at which the work is complete. Now suppose (which is not unlikely) that the copies of a novel or the performances of an opera go on being produced for an indefinite period: then, on the present suggestion, there is no such moment, let alone one in their creator's lifetime. So we cannot say that *Ulysses* was written by Joyce, or that Strauss composed *Der Rosenkavalier*. Or, again, there is the problem of the unperformed symphony, or the poem of which there is not even a manuscript: in what sense can we now say that these things even *exist*?

But perhaps a more serious, certainly a more interesting, objection is that in this suggestion what is totally unexplained is why the various copies of *Ulysses* are all said to be copies of *Ulysses* and nothing else, why all the performances of *Der Rosenkavalier* are reckoned performances of that one opera. For the ordinary explanation of how we come to group copies or performances as being of this book or of that opera is by reference to something else, something other than themselves, to which they stand in some special relation. (Exactly what this other thing is, or what is the special relation in which they stand to it is, of course, something we are as yet totally unable to say.) But the effect, indeed precisely the point, of the present suggestion is to eliminate the possibility of any such reference: if a novel or opera just is its copies or its performances, then we cannot, for purposes of identification, refer from the latter to the former.

The possibility that remains is that the various particular objects, the copies or performances, are grouped as they are, not by reference to some other thing to which they are related, but in virtue of some relation that holds between them: more specifically, in virtue of resemblance.

But all copies of *Ulysses,* and certainly all performances of *Der Rosenkavalier,* are not perfect matches. And if it is now said that the differences do not matter, either because the various copies or performance resemble each other in all relevant respects, or because they resemble each other more than they resemble the copies or performances of any other novel or opera, neither answer is adequate. The first answer begs the issue, in that to talk of relevant respects presupposes that we know how, say, copies of *Ulysses* are grouped together: the second answer evades the issue, in that though it may tell us why we do not, say, reckon any of the performances of *Der Rosenkavalier* as performances of *Arabella,* it gives us no indication why we do not set some of them up separately, as performances of some third opera.

However, those who are ready to concede that some kinds of works of art are not physical objects will yet insist that others are. *Ulysses* and *Der Rosenkavalier* may not be physical objects, but the *Donna Velata* [painting] and Donatello's *Saint George* [sculpture] most certainly are.

I have already suggested that the challenge to the physical-object hypothesis can be divided into two parts. It will be clear that I am now about to embark on the second part of the challenge: namely, that which allows that there are (some) physical objects that could conceivably be identified as works of art, but insists that it would be quite erroneous to make the identification.

In the Pitti there is a canvas (No. 245) 85 cm × 64 cm: in the Museo Nazionale, Florence, there is a piece of marble 209 cm high. It is with these physical objects that those who claim that the *Donna Velata* and the *Saint George* are physical objects would naturally identify them.

This identification can be disputed in (roughly) one or other of two ways. It can be argued that the work of art has properties which are incompatible with certain properties that the physical object has, alternatively it can be argued that the work of art has properties which no physical object could have: in neither case could the work of art be the physical object.

An argument of the first kind would run: We say of the *St. George* that it moves with life (Vasari). Yet the block of marble is inanimate. Therefore the *St. George* cannot be that block of marble. An argument of the second kind would run: We say of the *Donna Velata* that it is exalted and dignified (Wölfflin). Yet a piece of canvas in the Pitti cannot conceivably have these qualities. Therefore the *Donna Velata* cannot be that piece of canvas.

These two arguments, I suggest, are not merely instances of these two ways of arguing, they are characteristic instances. For the argument that there is an incompatibility of property between works of art and physical objects characteristically concentrates on the representational properties of works of art The argument that works of art have properties that physical objects could not have characteristically concentrates on the expressive properties of works of art. The terms "representational" and "expressive" are used here in a very wide fashion, which, it is hoped, will become clear as the discussion proceeds.

We might begin by considering two false views of how works of art acquire their expressiveness: not simply so as to put them behind us, but because each is in its way a pointer to the truth. Neither view requires us to suppose that works of art are anything other than physical objects.

The first view is that works of art are expressive because they have been produced in a certain state of mind or feeling on the part of the artist: and to this the rider is often attached, that it is this mental or emotional condition that they express. But if we take the view first of all with the rider attached, its falsehood is apparent. For it is a common happening that a painter or sculptor modifies or even rejects a work of his because he finds that it fails to correspond to what he experienced at the time. If, however, we drop the rider, the view now seems arbitrary or perhaps incomplete. For there seems to be no reason why a work should be expressive simply because it was produced in some heightened condition if it is also admitted that the work and the condition need not have the same character. (It would be like trying to explain why a man who has measles is ill by citing the fact that he was in contact with someone else who was also ill when that other person was not ill with measles or anything related to measles.)

However, what is probably the more fundamental objection to this view, and is the point that has been emphasized by many recent philosophers, is that the work's expressiveness now becomes a purely external feature of it. It is no longer something that we can or might observe, it is something that we infer from what we observe: it has been detached from the object as it manifests itself to us, and placed in its history, so that it now belongs more to the biography of the artist than to criticism of the work. And this seems wrong. For the qualities of gravity, sweetness, fear that we invoke in describing works of art seem essential to our understanding of them; and if they are, they cannot be extrinsic to the works themselves. They cannot be, that is, mere attributes of the experiences or activities of Masaccio, of Raphael, of Grünewald—they inhere rather in the Bràncacci frescoes, in the Granduca Madonna, in the Isenheim Altarpiece.

The second view is that works of art are expressive because they produce or are able to produce a certain state of mind or feeling in the spectator: moreover (and in the case of this view it is difficult to imagine the rider ever detached), it is this mental or emotional condition that they express. This view is open to objections that closely parallel those we have just considered.

For, in the first place, it seems clearly false. Before works even of the most extreme emotional intensity, like Bernini's *St. Teresa* or the black paintings of Goya, it is possible to remain more or less unexcited to the emotion that it would be agreed they express. Indeed, there are many theories that make it a distinguishing or defining feature of art that it should be viewed with detachment, that there should be a distancing on the part of the spectator between what the work expresses and what he experiences: although it is worth noting, in passing, that those theorists who have been most certain that works of art do not arouse emotion have also been uncertain, in some cases confused, as to how this comes about: sometimes attributing it to the artist, sometimes to the spectator; sometimes, that is, saying that the artist refrains from giving the work the necessary causal power, sometimes saying that the spectator holds himself back from reacting to this power.

However, the main objection to this view, as to the previous one, is that it removes what we ordinarily think of as one of the essential characteristics of the work of art from among its manifest properties, locating it this time not in its past but in its hidden or dispositional endowment.

We have now completed our discussion of the physical-object hypothesis, and this would be a good moment at which to pause and review the situation.

The hypothesis, taken literally, has been clearly shown to be false: in that there are arts where it is impossible to find physical objects that are even candidates for being identified with works of art. However, as far as those other arts are concerned where such physical objects can be found, the arguments against the identification—namely, those based on the fact that works of art have properties not predicable of physical objects—seemed less cogent. I have now to justify the assertion that I made at the very beginning of the discussion that it was only insofar as it related to these latter arts that the challenge to this hypothesis had any fundamental significance for aesthetics.

The general issue raised, whether works of art are physical objects, seems to compress two questions: the difference between which can be brought out by accenting first one, then the other, constituent word in the operative phrase. Are works of art *physical* objects? Are works of art physical *objects*? The first question would be a question about the stuff or constitution of works of art, what in the broadest sense they are made of: more specifically, are they mental? or physical? are they constructs of the mind? The second question would be a question about the category to which works of art belong, about the criteria of identity and individuation applicable to them: more specifically, are they universals, of which there are instances? or classes, of which there are members? are they particulars? Roughly speaking, the first question might be regarded as metaphysical, the second as logical. And, confusingly enough, both can be put in the form of a question about what kind of thing a work of art is.

Applying this distinction to the preceding discussion, we can now see that the method of falsifying the hypothesis that all works of art are physical objects has been to establish that there are some works of art that are not objects (or particulars) at all: whereas the further part of the case, which depends upon establishing that those works of art which are objects are nevertheless not physical, has not been made good. If my original assertion is to be vindicated, I am now required to show that what is of moment in aesthetics is the physicality of works of art rather than their particularity. . . .

[I want to] go back and take up an undischarged commitment: which is that of considering the consequences of rejecting the hypothesis that works of art are physical objects, insofar as those arts are concerned where there is no physical object with which the work of art could be plausibly identified. This will, of course, be in pursuance of my general aim—which has also directed the preceding discussion—of establishing that the rejection of the hypothesis has serious consequences for the philosophy of art only insofar as those arts are concerned where there *is* such an object.

I have already stated that, once it is conceded that certain works of art are not physical *objects,* the subsequent problem that arises, which can be put by asking, What sort of thing are they? is essentially a logical problem. It is that of determining the criteria of identity and individuation appropriate to, say, a piece of music or a novel. I shall characterize the status of such things by saying that they are (to employ a term introduced by Peirce) *types.* Correlative to the term "type" is the term "token." Those physical objects which (as we have seen) can out of desperation be thought to be works of art in cases where there are no physical objects that can plausibly be thought of in this way, are *tokens.* In other words, *Ulysses* and *Der Rosenkavalier* are types; my copy of *Ulysses* and tonight's performance of *Rosenkavalier* are tokens of those types. The question now arises, What is a type?

The question is very difficult, and, unfortunately, to treat it with the care and attention to detail that it deserves is beyond the scope of this essay.

We might begin by contrasting a type with other sorts of thing that it is not. Most obviously we could contrast a type with a *particular:* this I shall take as done. Then we could contrast it with other various kinds of non-particulars: with a *class* (of which we say that it has *members),* and a *universal* (of which we say that it has *instances).* An example of a class would be the class of red

things: an example of a universal would be redness: and examples of a type would be the word "red" and the Red Flag—where this latter phrase is taken to mean not this or that piece of material, kept in a chest or taken out and flown at a masthead, but the flag of revolution, raised for the first time in 1830 and that which many would willingly follow to their death.

Let us introduce as a blanket expression for types, classes, universals, the term *generic entity,* and, as a blanket expression for those things which fall under them, the term *element.* Now we can say that the various generic entities can be distinguished according to the different ways or relationships in which they stand to their elements. These relationships can be arranged on a scale of intimacy or intrinsicality. At one end of the scale we find classes, where the relationship is at its most external or extrinsic: for a class is merely made of, or constituted by, its members which are extensionally conjoined to form it. The class of red things is simply a construct out of all those things which are (timelessly) red. In the case of universals the relation is more intimate: in that a universal is present in all its instances. Redness is in all red things. With types we find the relationship between the generic entity and its elements at its most intimate: for not merely is the type present in all its tokens like the universal in all its instances, but for much of the time we think and talk of the type as though it were itself a kind of token, though a peculiarly important or preeminent one. In many ways we treat the Red Flag as though it were a red flag (cf. "We'll keep the Red Flag flying high").

It will be clear that the preceding characterization of a type and its tokens offers us a framework within which we can (at any rate roughly) understand the logical status of things like operas, ballets, poems, etchings, etc.: that is to say, account for their principles of identity and individuation.

What a Musical Work Is

JERROLD LEVINSON

WHAT *EXACTLY* DID Beethoven compose? That is the question I will begin with. Well, for one, Beethoven composed a quintet for piano and winds (flute, oboe, clarinet, horn) in E-flat, Opus 16, in 1797. But what sort of thing is it, this quintet which was the outcome of Beethoven's creative activity? What does it consist in or of? Shall we say that Beethoven composed actual *sounds*? No, for sounds die out, but the quintet has endured. Did Beethoven compose a score? No, since many are familiar with Beethoven's composition who have had no contact with its score.

Philosophers have long been puzzled about the identity or nature of the art object in nonphysical arts, e.g., music and literature. In these arts—unlike painting and sculpture—there is no particular physical "thing" that one can plausibly take to be the artwork itself. This puzzlement has sometimes led philosophers (e.g., Croce) to maintain that musical and literary works are purely mental—that they are in fact private intuitive experiences in the minds of composers and poets. But this does not seem likely, since experiences can be neither played nor read nor heard. More generally, the Crocean view puts the objectivity of musical and literary works in dire peril—they become inaccessible and unsharable. Fortunately, however, there is a way of accepting the nonphysicality of such works without undermining their objectivity.

Those familiar with recent reflection on the ontological question for works of art will know of the widespread consensus that a musical work is in fact a variety of abstract object—to wit, a structural type or kind. Instances of this type are to be found in the individual performances of the work. The type can be heard through its in-stances, and yet exists independently of its instances. I believe this to be basically correct. A piece of music is *some* sort of structural type, and as such is both nonphysical and publicly available. But *what* sort of type is it? I aim in this paper to say as precisely as I can what structural type it is that a musical work should be identified with.

The most natural and common proposal on this question is that a musical work is a *sound* structure—a structure, sequence, or pattern of sounds, pure and simple. My first objective will be to show that this proposal is deeply unsatisfactory, that a musical work is more than just a sound structure *per se*. I will do this by developing three different objections to the sound-structure view. In the course of developing these objections, three requirements or desiderata for a more adequate view will emerge. The rightness—or at least plausibility—of those requirements will, I think, be apparent at that point. My second objective will then be to suggest a structural type that does satisfy the requirements, and thus can be identified with a musical work.

At the outset, however, I should make clear that I am confining my inquiry to that paradigm of a musical work, the fully notated "classical" composition of Western culture, for example, Beethoven's Quintet for piano and winds in E-flat, Opus 16. So when I speak of a "musical work" in this paper it should be understood that I am speaking only of these paradigm musical works, and thus that all claims herein regarding musical works are to be construed with this implicit restriction.

The first objection to the view that musical works are sound structures is this. If musical works were sound structures, then musical works

From The Journal of Philosophy *77 (1980). Reprinted by permission of* The Journal of Philosophy *and the author.*

could not, properly speaking, be created by their composers. For sound structures are types of a pure sort which exist at all times. This is apparent from the fact that they—and the individual component sound types that they comprise—can always have had instances. A sound event conforming to the sound structure of Beethoven's Quintet, Opus 16 logically could have occurred in the Paleozoic era. Less contentiously, perhaps, such an event surely could have taken place in 1760—ten years before Beethoven was born. But if that sound structure was capable of being *instantiated* then, it clearly must have *existed* at that time. Beethoven's compositional activity was not necessary in order for a certain sound-structure type to exist. It was not necessary to the possibility of certain sound events occurring which would be instances of that structure. Sound structures *per se* are not created by being scored— they exist before any compositional activity. Sound structures predate their first instantiation or conception because they are possible of exemplification *before* that point. So, if composers truly create their works—i.e., bring them into existence— then musical works cannot be sound structures.

But why should we insist that composers truly create their compositions? Why is this a reasonable requirement? This question needs to be answered. A defense of the desideratum of true creation follows.

The main reason for holding to it is that it is one of the most firmly entrenched of our beliefs concerning art. There is probably no idea more central to thought about art than that it is an activity in which participants create things—these things being artworks. The whole tradition of art assumes art is creative in the strict sense, that it is a godlike activity in which the artist brings into being what did not exist beforehand—much as a demiurge forms a world out of inchoate matter. The notion that artists truly *add* to the world, in company with cake-bakers, house-builders, lawmakers, and theory-constructors, is surely a deep-rooted idea that merits preservation if at all possible. The suggestion that some artists, composers in particular, instead merely *discover* or *select* for attention entities they have no hand in

creating is so contrary to this basic intuition regarding artists and their works that we have a strong *prima facie* reason to reject it if we can. If it is possible to align musical works with indisputably creatable artworks such as paintings and sculptures, then it seems we should do so.

A second, closely related reason to preserve true creation *vis-à-vis* musical works is that some of the status, significance, and value we attach to musical composition derives from our belief in this. If we conceive of Beethoven's Fifth Symphony as existing sempiternally, before Beethoven's compositional act, a small part of the glory that surrounds Beethoven's composition of the piece seems to be removed. There is a special glow that envelops composers, as well as other artists, because we think of them as true creators. We marvel at a great piece of music *in part* because we marvel that, had its composer not engaged in a certain activity, the piece would (almost surely) not now exist; but it does exist, and we are grateful to the composer for precisely that. Ecclesiastes was wrong—there *are* ever some things new under the sun, musical compositions being among the most splendid of them—and splendid, at least in part, in virtue of this absolute newness.

I propose then that a most adequate account of the musical work should satisfy the following requirement, that of *creatability:*

> (Cre) Musical works must be such that they do *not* exist prior to the composer's compositional activity, but are *brought into* existence *by* that activity.

The second objection to the view that musical works are sound structures is this. (1) If musical works were just sound structures, then, if two distinct composers determine the same sound structure, they necessarily compose the same musical work. (2) But distinct composers determining the same sound structure in fact inevitably produce different musical works. Therefore, musical works cannot be sound structures *simpliciter*. . . .

Composers who produce identical scores in the same notational system with the same conventions of interpretation will determine the same sound structure. But the musical works they thereby compose will generally not be the same. The reason for this is that certain attributes of musical works are dependent on more than the sound structures contained. In particular, the aesthetic and artistic attributes of a piece of music are partly a function of, and must be gauged with reference to, the total musico-historical context in which the composer is situated while composing his piece. Since the musico-historical contexts of composing individuals are invariably different, then even if their works are identical in sound structure, they will differ widely in aesthetic and artistic attributes. But then, by Leibniz's law, the musical works themselves must be non-identical: if W_1 has any attribute that W_2 lacks, or *vice versa*, then $W_1 \neq W_2$.

I will not attempt to give a strict definition of musico-historical context, but will confine myself to pointing out a large part of what is involved in it. The total musico-historical context of a composer P at a time t can be said to include at least the following: (a) the whole of cultural, social, and political history prior to t, (b) the whole of musical development up to t, (c) musical styles prevalent at t, (d) dominant musical influences at t, (e) musical activities of P's contemporaries at t, (f) P's apparent style at t, (g) P's musical repertoire at t, (h) P's oeuvre at t, (i) musical influences operating on P at t. These factors contributing to the total musico-historical context might be conveniently divided into two groups, a–d and e–i. The former, which we could call the *general* musico-historical context, consists of factors relevant to anyone's composing at t; the latter, which we could call the *individual* musico-historical context, consists of factors relevant specifically to P's composing at t. In any event, all these factors operate to differentiate aesthetically or artistically musical works identical in sound structure, thus making it impossible to identify those works with their sound structures. I now provide several illustrations of this.

A work identical in sound structure with Schoenberg's *Pierrot Lunaire* (1912), but composed by Richard Strauss in 1897 would be aesthetically different from Schoenberg's work. Call it

'Pierrot Lunaire.' As a Straussian work, *Pierrot Lunaire* would follow hard upon Brahm's *German Requiem,* would be contemporaneous with Debussy's *Nocturnes,* and would be taken as the next step in Strauss's development after *Also Sprach Zarathustra.* As such it would be more *bizarre,* more *upsetting,* more *anguished,* more *eerie* even than Schoenberg's work, since perceived against a musical tradition, a field of current styles, and an oeuvre with respect to which the musical characteristics of the sound structure involved in *Pierrot Lunaire* appear doubly extreme.

This example should serve to convince the reader that there is always some aesthetic or artistic difference between structurally identical compositions in the offing in virtue of differing musico-historical contexts. Even small differences in musico-historical context—e.g., an extra work in P's oeuvre, a slight change in style dominant in P's milieu, some musical influence deleted from P's development as a composer—seem certain to induce some change in kind or degree in some aesthetic or artistic quality, however difficult it might be in such cases to pinpoint this change verbally.

I thus propose a second requirement—that of *fine individuation*—to which any acceptable theory of the musical work should conform:

(Ind) Musical works must be such that composers composing in different musico-historical contexts who determine identical sound structures invariably compose distinct musical works.

The third objection to the view that musical works are sound structures is this. If musical works were simply sound structures, then they would not essentially involve any particular means of performance. But the paradigm musical works that we are investigating in this paper, e.g., Beethoven's Quintet, Opus 16, clearly *do* involve quite specific means of performance, i.e., particular instruments, in an essential way. The instrumentation of musical works is an integral part of those works. So musical works cannot be simply sound structures *per se.* Arguments in defense of the claim that performance means are an essential component of musical works now follow.

(1) Composers do not describe pure sound patterns in qualitative terms, leaving their means of production undiscussed. Rather, what they directly specify are means of production, through which a pure sound pattern is indirectly indicated. The score of Beethoven's Quintet, Opus 16, is not a recipe for providing an instance of a sound pattern *per se*, in whatever way you might like. Rather, it instructs one to produce an instance of a certain sound pattern through carrying out certain operations on certain instruments. When Beethoven writes a middle C for the oboe, he has done more than require an oboe-like sound at a certain pitch—he has called for such a sound as emanating from that quaint reed we call an "oboe." The idea that composers of the last 300 years were generally engaged in composing pure sound patterns, to which they were usually kind enough to append suggestions as to how they might be realized, is highly implausible. Composers are familiar with tone colors only insofar as they are familiar with instruments that possess them. We do not find composers creating pure combinations of tone color, and then later searching about for instruments that can realize or approximate these aural canvases; it would obviously be pointless or at least frustrating to do so. Composers often call for complex sounds that they have never heard before and can scarcely imagine—e.g., the sound of two trombones and three piccolos intoning middle C while four saxophones and five xylophones intone the C-sharp a half-step above; it is obvious here that what is primarily composed is not a pure untethered sound but an instrumental combination.

(2) Scores are generally taken to be definitive of musical works, at least in conjunction with the conventions of notational interpretation assumed to be operative at the time of composition. It is hard to miss the fact that scores of musical works call for specific instruments in no uncertain terms. When we read in Beethoven's score the demand "clarinet" (rather, "Klarinett") we may wonder whether a clarinet of 1970 vintage and construction will do as well as one of 1800, but we have still been given a fairly definite idea of

what sort of instrument is required. There is nothing in scores themselves that suggest that instrumental specifications are to be regarded as optional—any more than specifications of pitch, rhythm, or dynamics. Nor does the surrounding musical practice of the time encourage such a way of regarding them. If we are not to abandon the principle that properly understood scores have a central role in determining the identity of musical works, then we must insist that the Quintet, Op. 16, without a clarinet is not the same piece—even if all sound-structural characteristics (including timbre) are preserved. To feel free to disregard as prominent an aspect of scores as performing means is to leave it open for someone to disregard any aspect of a score he does not wish to conform to—e.g., tempo, accidentals, accents, articulation, harmony—and claim that one nevertheless has the same work. The only way it seems one could justify regarding performing-means specifications as just optional features of scores is to simply *assume* that musical works are nothing but sound structures *per se*.

Consider a sound event aurally indistinguishable from a typical performance of Beethoven's Quintet, Opus 16, but issuing from a versatile synthesizer, or perhaps a piano plus a set of newly designed wind instruments, two hundred in number, each capable of just two or three notes. If performance means were not an integral aspect of a musical work, then there would be no question that this sound event constitutes a performance of Beethoven's Quintet, Opus 16. But there is indeed such a question. It makes perfect sense to deny that it is such a performance on the grounds that the sounds heard did not derive from a piano and four standard woodwinds. We can count something as a performance of Beethoven's Quintet, Opus 16 only if it involves the participation of the instruments for which the piece was written—or better– of the instruments that were written into the piece.

(3) To regard performing means as essential to musical works is to maintain that the sound structure of a work cannot be divorced from the instruments and voices through which that structure is fixed, and regarded as the work itself. The

strongest reason why it cannot be so divorced is that the aesthetic content of a musical work is determined not only by its sound structure, and not only by its musico-historical context, but also in part by the actual means of production chosen for making that structure audible. The character of a musical composition, e.g., Beethoven's Quintet, Opus 16 for piano and winds, is partly a function of how its sound structure relates to the potentialities of a certain instrument or set of instruments designated to produce that structure for audition. To assess that character correctly one must take cognizance not only of the qualitative nature of sounds heard but also of their source of origin. Musical compositions, by and large, have reasonably definite characters; that is to say, we can and do ascribe to them many fairly specific aesthetic qualities. But if prescribed performing forces were not intrinsic to musical compositions, then those compositions would not have the reasonably definite characters we clearly believe them to have. The determinateness of a work's aesthetic qualities is in peril if performing means are viewed as inessential so long as exact sound structure is preserved.

(4) The dependence of aesthetic attributes on assumed or understood performing forces should now be apparent. The dependence of artistic attributes is even more plain. Consider Paganini's Caprice Opus 1, No. 17. This piece surely deserves and receives the attribution "virtuosic." But if we did not conceive of the Caprice No. 17 as essentially for the violin, as inherently a *violin piece* (and not just a *violin-sounding piece*), then it would not merit that attribution. For, as executed by a computer or by some novel string instrument using nonviolinistic technique, its sound structure might not be particularly difficult to get through. . . .

I thus propose a third requirement for any account of the musical work: *inclusion of performance means:*

(Per) Musical works must be such that specific means of performance or sound production are integral to them.

If musical works are not sound structures *simpliciter,* then what are they? The type that is a musical work must be capable of being created, must be individuated by context of composition, and must be inclusive of means of performance. The third desideratum is most easily met, and will be addressed first.

I propose that a musical work be taken to involve not only a pure sound structure, but also a structure of performing means. If the sound structure of a piece is basically a sequence of sounds qualitatively defined, then the performing-means structure is a parallel sequence of performing means specified for realizing the sounds at each point. Thus a musical work consists of at least two structures. It is a compound or conjunction of a sound structure and a performing-means structure. This compound is itself just a more complex structure; call it an "S/PM" structure, for short. Beethoven's Opus 16 Quintet is at base an S/PM structure; the means of producing the sounds belonging to it are no more dispensable to its identity as a composition than the nature and order of those sounds themselves. This satisfies requirement (Per).

To satisfy the first and second requirements of adequacy we arrived at, it is necessary to realize that a musical work is not a structure of the *pure* sort at all, and thus not even a S/PM structure *simpliciter.* An S/PM structure is no more creatable or context-individuated than a sound structure is. I propose that we recognize a musical work to be a more complicated entity, namely this:

(MW) S/PM structure-as-indicated-by-X-at-t

where X is a particular person—the composer—and t is the time of composition. For the paradigmatic pieces we are concerned with, the composer typically indicates (fixes, determines, selects) an S/PM structure by creating a score. The *piece* he thereby composes is the S/PM structure-as-indicated by him on that occasion.

An S/PM structure-as-indicated-by-X-at-t, unlike an S/PM structure *simpliciter,* does not pre-exist the activity of composition and is thus capable of being created. When a composer θ composes a piece of music, he indicates an S/PM structure Ψ, but he does not bring Ψ into being. However, through the act of indicating Ψ, he does bring into being something that did not previously exist—namely, Ψ-as-indicated-by-θ-at-t_1. Before the compositional act at t_1, no relation obtains between θ and Ψ. Composition establishes the relation of indication between θ and Ψ. As a result of the compositional act, I suggest, the world contains a new entity, Ψ-as-indicated-by-θ-at-t_1. Let me call such entities *indicated structures*. And let me represent indicated structures by expressions of form "S/PM*χ*t." It is important to realize that indicated structures are entities distinct from the pure structures *per se* from which they are derived. Thus, in particular, Ψ*θ*t_1 is *not* just the structure Ψ with the accidental property of having been indicated by θ at t_1—Ψ*θ*t_1 and Ψ are strictly non-identical, though of course related. Ψ*θ*t_1, unlike Ψ, can be and is created through θ's composing. Thus requirement (Cre) is satisfied.

Indicated structures also serve to satisfy our second requirement (Ind). If musical works are indicated structures of the sort we have suggested, then two such works, Ψ*θ*t_1 and α*ϕ*t_2 are identical if (i) $\Psi = \alpha$, (ii) $\theta = \phi$, and (iii) $t_1 = t_2$. But if musical works are necessarily distinct if composed either by different people or at different times, then it certainly follows that works composed in different musico-historical contexts will be distinct, since any difference of musico-historical context from one work to another can be traced to a difference of composer or time or both. Put otherwise, musico-historical context . . . is a function of time and person; given a time and person, musico-historical context is fixed. So requirement (Ind) is satisfied. That it is satisfied by our proposal with something to spare is a matter I will return to. . . . I now endeavor to increase the reader's grasp of what indicated structures are.

Indicated structures are a different class of type from pure structures. Types of the latter class we may call *implicit* types, and those of the

former class *initiated* types. *Implicit* types include all purely abstract structures that are not inconsistent, e.g., geometrical figures, family relationships, strings of words, series of moves in chess, ways of placing five balls in three bins, etc. By calling them "implicit types" I mean to suggest that their existence is implicitly granted when a general framework of possibilities is given. For example, given that there is space, there are all the possible configurations in space; given there is the game of chess, there are all the possible combinations of allowed moves. Sound structures *simpliciter* are clearly implicit types. Given that there are sounds of various kinds, then all possible patterns and sequences of those sounds must be granted existence immediately as well. For a sound structure, in company with all pure structures, is always capable of instantiation before the point at which it is noticed, recognized, mentioned, or singled out. And thus its existence must predate that point. The same goes for a performance-means structure *simpliciter*. Given performing means (i.e., instruments) of various kinds, then all possible combinations and sequences of such means exist as well. The compound of these two, a sound/performance-means structure, thus, of course, also counts as an implicit type.

The other class of types, *initiated* types, are so called because they begin to exist only when they are initiated by an intentional human act of some kind. All those of interest can, I think, be construed as arising from an operation, like indication, performed upon a pure structure. Typically, this indication is effected by producing an exemplar of the structure involved, or a blueprint of it. In so indicating (or determining) the structure, the exemplar or blueprint inaugurates the type which is the *indicated* structure, the structure-as-indicated-by-χ-at-t. All indicated structures are, perforce, initiated types.

Initiated types include such types as the Ford Thunderbird, the Lincoln penny, the hedgehog. The Ford Thunderbird is not simply a pure structure of metal, glass, and plastic. The pure structure that is embodied in the Thunderbird has existed at *least* since the invention of plastic (1870); there could certainly have been instances of it in 1900. But the Ford Thunderbird was created in 1957; so there could not have been instances of the Thunderbird in 1900. The Ford Thunderbird is an *initiated* type; it is a metal/glass/plastic structure-as-indicated (or determined) by the Ford Motor Company on such and such a date. It begins to exist as a result of an act of human indication or determination. The instances of this type are more than just instances of a pure structure—they are instances of an indicated structure. The Lincoln penny is similarly not a pure structure, an abstract pattern *tout court,* but a structure-as-indicated, a pattern-as-denominated-by-the-U.S. Government. Objects conforming to the pattern *tout court* but existing in 100 A.D. in Imperial Rome would not be instances of the Lincoln penny. Even the hedgehog is probably best understood, not as a pure biological structure, but rather as a biological structure-as-determined-or-fixed by natural terrestrial evolution at a particular point in history. The creatures we call "hedgehogs" possess a certain structure and stand in certain causal relations to some particular creatures which came into existence at a given past date. The biological structure of the hedgehog might have been instantiated in the Mesozoic era, or on Uranus, but nothing existing at that time, or at that place, could be an instance of the hedgehog as we understand it. Musical works, as I have suggested, are indicated structures too, and thus types that do not already exist but must instead be initiated. The same is true of poems, plays, and novels—each of these is an entity more individual and temporally bound than the pure verbal structure embodied in it.

On my view, the following must all be distinguished: (a) instances of *W;* (b) instances of the sound structure of *W;* (c) instances of the S/PM structure of *W;* (d) performances of *W.* An *instance* of a musical work *W* is a sound event which conforms *completely* to the sound/performance-means structure of *W* and which exhibits the required connection to the indicative activity wherein *W*'s composer *A* creates *W.* An instance of *W* is typically produced, either directly or indirectly, from a score that can be causally traced and is intentionally related by the performer, to the act of creation of *W* by *A.* Thus, all instances of *W* are instances of *W*'s sound structure, and instances of *W*'s S/PM structure—but the reverse is not the case.

Instances are a subclass of the set of performances of a work. A *performance* of a musical work *W* is a sound event which is *intended* to instantiate *W*—i.e., represents an attempt to exemplify *W*'s S/PM structure in accordance with *A*'s indication of it—and which *succeeds to a reasonable degree.* Since one cannot instantiate a musical work—an S/PM structure-as-indicated-by-*X*-at-*t*—without intending to, because instantiating *that* demands conscious guidance by instructions, memories, or the like which one regards as deriving from *A*'s indicative act at *t*, it follows that the instances of *W* are all to be found among the performances of *W.* However, not all performances of *W* count as instances of *W;* many if not most attempts to exemplify S/PM structures fail by some margin. So these cannot count as instances of *W,* but they *are* performances—namely *incorrect* performances. (Of course, that they are strictly incorrect by no means entails that they are bad.) There are not, however, any incorrect *instances* of *W;* the *correct performances of W* are its instances, and no others.

Finally, let me note that musical works as I understand them *can* be heard in or through their performances. One *hears* an S/PM structure-as-indicated-by-*X*-at-*t* whenever one hears an instance of that S/PM structure produced by performers who, roughly speaking, are guided by *X*'s indication of the S/PM structure in question. And one *knows* precisely what musical work, i.e., structure-as-indicated, one is hearing if one knows what creative act is in effect the guiding source of the sound event being produced.

On my view of what a musical work (of the paradigm sort) is, it follows immediately that a transcription of a musical work is a distinct musical work, whether it involves alteration of the sound structure (the normal case), or *even* of just the performance-means structure. It is a virtue of my view that it gives a clear answer to this question, which is often thought to be only arbitrarily decidable. If we want such pieces to have the definite aesthetic qualities we take them to have, instrumentation must be considered inseparable from them. Thus, we need not rely, in endorsing the distinctness position on transcriptions *vis-à-vis* original works, merely on the principle of fidelity to the composer's intended instrumentation. Rather we are also constrained by higher-order considerations of preserving the aesthetic integrity of such pieces.

In conclusion, let me stress some obvious consequences of accepting the theory of the musical work that I have proposed. First, composers would retain the status of creator in the strictest sense. Second, musical composition would be revealed as necessarily personalized. Third, musical composition could not fail to be seen as a historically rooted activity whose products must be understood with reference to their points of origin. Fourth, it would be recognized that the pure sound structure of a musical work, while graspable in isolation, does not exhaust the work structurally, and thus that the underlying means of performance must be taken into account as well if the work is to be correctly assessed.

D. The Analytic Critique of the Expression Theory of Art

Another very good example of analytic aesthetics at work is the analysis of the idea that art is mainly the expression of emotion. In the history of Western art there have been three main theories of the nature of art, which follow and attempt to explain the three main kinds of Western art. When representational art was most prominent (in the ancient Greek and Roman period and later in the eighteenth-century revival of Greek and Roman art), the main theory of art was the idea that art is essentially the imitation, or representation of reality. At the end of the eighteenth century and the beginning of the nineteenth-century, when Romantic art first appeared and began to replace representational art, theories of art changed from representational to expressionistic, that is, to the new idea that art is not a copy of the external world of nature but the expression of the inner world of human emotion—the emotions mainly vented by the artist but also aroused in the audience. And finally, in the late nineteenth and early to middle twentieth century, when abstract art burst on to the scene, theorists shifted once more, this time from the idea that art expresses the artist's emotion to the formalist idea of art for art's sake, that art neither represents the external world of nature nor expresses the inner world of human emotion but "does its own thing." Today, as we witness the move from modern to postmodern art, we can expect theories of art to shift accordingly.

In the mid-1950s, when analytic aesthetics first appeared, the dominant theory of art was still the expression theory. Analytic aestheticians neither affirmed nor denied this theory but merely tried to find out what it *meant*. What, they asked, do critics and art historians *mean* when they say that art "expresses" emotion? Does this mean that a work of art is like a child throwing a tantrum? And if so, is a tantrum a work of art? If not, how does an expressive piece of music, for example, differ from a child's tantrum? Is art a kind of outpouring of emotion by the artist onto the canvas? If so, does this mean that artists paint best when they are in extreme emotional states (when they first learn that their best friend was killed in a car accident, for example, or that their girlfriend or boyfriend has just run off with their best friend)? Or are we talking about the way in which artworks—music, for example—arouse the emotions in those of us who listen to it? But if so, does sad music really make me feel sad? And if it does, why would I want to listen to it? And again, if it does, what's the difference between hearing sad music and discovering that my best friend has died or that my girlfriend or boyfriend has just left me? And finally, if art expresses emotion, how specific or identifiable an emotion can art express? Does each work of art express a different and unique emotion? Can art express the embarrassment I feel, for example, when my credit card is turned down, or my disappointment on receiving a B– for what I know is an A paper, or the vindictive pleasure I experience in seeing my rival stumble? Or is art capable of expressing only very generalized states—broadly sad or broadly happy? And in that case doesn't it follow that all works of art will express only one or two basic emotions (so that there will be thousands of artworks expressing the same thing), and is that really true?

In attempting to analyze the meaning of *expression* as the term is used in the discussion of art, analytic aestheticians tried to differentiate between the *artistic* expression of emotion and everyday sorts of emotional expression (the child throwing a tantrum, your boy/girlfriend tearing up your photograph and slamming the door as he or she storms out of the room). Perhaps, they said, artistic expression of emotion is more a discovery or investigation of emotion than the arousing or venting of emotion. In English the word *expression* can be used in several quite different senses—in one sense we say the child throwing a tantrum is expressing her emotion, but in another sense we say that the passage in the book expresses the idea that all humans are born with unalienable human rights. The first concerns the arousal and outpouring of emotional states; the second concerns the communication of ideas, including ideas about emotion, but about other things as well. A number of analytic aestheticians held that art expresses emotion, not in the sense that it arouses emotion in us as the result of an outpouring of emotion from the artist, but rather in the sense that art is an investigation, exploration, and discovery of the nature of emotion. A novel tells us what unrequited love is like. The novelist might very well be a happily married woman who was never rejected but who is exploring this theme and giving us, the readers, some sense of what this emotional experience is like. As Suzanne Langer said, a sad piece of music has the same formal structure or pattern as the psychological experience of sadness. This became known as the *cognitive* theory of emotion because it stressed what we could learn about emotion. This is one of the earliest and most well-developed topics discussed by analytic aestheticians and one that continues to be of great interest among analytic aestheticians.

Cognitive theory emphasized how art can teach us about the nature of human emotion. At the same time, however, anyone who loves art knows that music, at least, not only tells us about emotion but somehow arouses it—that it actually does make us feel sad or happy or triumphant or despondent and so on. And anyone who plays music knows that music can also vent or release emotion. And although music may be the most emotionally arousing art form, as Plato saw long ago, other art forms are also capable of arousing and venting powerful emotions—as we sometimes cry during a movie, for example, or feel elated reading a poem or the end of a novel or short story.

In her essay Jenefer Robinson tries to restore some balance in this controversial and often heated debate over what is meant by the claim that art, and in particular music, "expresses emotion." Yes, she says, music and other art forms can indeed explore and articulate emotion and as a result we can genuinely learn about emotion by enjoying works of art, but art, and especially music, can also express emotion, and a *particular* emotion, by actually arousing it.

The Expression and Arousal of Emotion in Music

JENEFER ROBINSON

THIS ESSAY IS ABOUT the relation between the expression and the arousal of emotion by music. I am assuming that music frequently *expresses* emotional qualities and qualities of human personality such as sadness, nobility, aggressiveness, tenderness, and serenity. I am also assuming that music frequently *affects* us emotionally: it evokes or arouses emotions in us. My question is whether there is any connection between these two facts, whether, in particular, music ever expresses emotion *by virtue of* arousing emotion. Of course, what it means to say that music expresses emotion is a contentious issue and I shall not be directly addressing it here, although what I say will have implications for any theory of musical expression. Nor will I be examining all the possible contexts in which music can be said to arouse emotion. My focus in this essay will be narrower. The question I shall try to answer is this: Are the grounds on which we attribute the expression of emotion to music ever to be identified with the arousal of that same emotion in listeners?

According to some theories of musical expression, the grounds on which we attribute expressive qualities to music have nothing to do with the arousal of emotion in the audience. Accord-

ing to Peter Kivy's account in *The Corded Shell*, a musical element such as a melody, a rhythm, or a chord expresses a feeling not because it arouses that feeling in anyone but for two quite different reasons. (1) It has the same "contour" as expressive human behavior of some kind and thus is "heard as expressive of something or other because heard as appropriate to the expression of something or other" (for example, the "weeping" figure of grief in Arianna's lament from Monteverdi's *Arianna*) or it contributes in a particular context to the forming of such an expressive contour (as the diminished triad in a suitable context can contribute to a *restless* quality in the music, although all by itself it does not express anything). (2) The musical element is expressive by virtue of some custom or convention, which originated in connection with some expressive contour. The minor triad, for example, is "sad" by convention, although it may have started life as part of some expressive contour.

There are many examples of musical expression for which Kivy's argument is convincing. Thus it does seem to be true that Arianna's lament mirrors the passionate speaking voice expressing grief, that Schubert's "Gretchen am Spinnrad" mirrors Gretchen's monotonous, leaden gestures

From The Journal of Aesthetics and Art Criticism *52:1 (Winter 1994). Reprinted by permission of the journal.*

at the spinning wheel and her correspondingly dejected, leaden heart, and that the "Pleni sunt coeli" from Bach's B Minor Mass maps "bodily motion and gesture . . . of tremendous expansiveness, vigor, violent motion," thus mirroring the exuberance of " 'leaping' joy." At the same time, as Renée Cox, among others, has pointed out, virtually all the musical examples in Kivy's book are examples of music with a text, and it is relatively uncontroversial that a text can specify a particular feeling or object which is characterized by the music. Moreover, when we look closely at Kivy's examples of particular emotions said to be expressed by music we find mainly varieties of joy, sorrow, and restlessness. The vast majority of musical examples in *The Corded Shell* can be characterized as expressions of either positive or negative emotion (joy or sorrow) of various sorts. Thus although what Kivy says seems to be true as far as it goes, it does not go very far, and leaves a great deal of expressiveness in music unexplained.

Kivy holds that music can express particular emotional states such as sorrow and joy, restlessness and serenity. Susanne Langer, while agreeing that emotional qualities are to be found in the *music,* rather than in the *listener,* follows Hanslick in arguing that since only the dynamic qualities of anything (including emotional states) can be expressed by music, no particular emotions can be expressed by music, but only the felt quality of our emotional life and its dynamic development:

> [There] are certain aspects of the so-called "inner life"—physical or mental—which have formal properties similar to those of music— patterns of motion and rest, of tension and release, of agreement and disagreement, preparation, fulfillment, excitation, sudden change, etc.

> [Music] reveals the rationale of feelings, the rhythm and pattern of their rise and decline and intertwining, to our minds. . . .

In contrast to Kivy's view that the words of a text supply the "fine shadings" to otherwise only grossly expressive musical meanings, Langer holds that musical meanings are inherently rich and significant yet cannot be linked to any particular words. Langer's theory emphasizes the development of structures of feeling throughout a lengthy piece of music, which Kivy ignores, but she in turn ignores the expression of particular emotional qualities which Kivy emphasizes. Both theorists have insightful things to say about musical expression but neither tells the whole story.

A very different view of musical expression has recently been presented by Kendall Walton in a paper called "What Is Abstract about the Art of Music?" Walton proposes that one important way in which music is expressive is by virtue of the fact that in listening to music we imagine ourselves introspecting, being aware of, our own feelings. As he puts it, we imagine "of our actual introspective awareness of auditory sensations" that "it is an experience of being aware of our states of mind." Thus the expressiveness of music has to do with its power to *evoke* certain imaginative emotional experiences. Moreover, Walton says that if this is right, then:

> music probably can be said to "portray particulars" in the sense that figurative paintings do, rather than simply properties or concepts. Presumably the listener imagines experiencing and identifying *particular* stabs of pain, *particular* feelings of ecstasy, *particular* sensations of well-being, etc., as in viewing a painting one imagines seeing particular things.

However, whereas one perceives the psychological states of other people, as in figurative paintings, one "introspects one's *own* psychological states. "

There are at least two problems I see with Walton's account. (1) First, suppose someone denies that this is what she does when listening to expressive music; we should be able to *explain* to her why this is what she should be doing. What reason is there why we should imagine our awareness of auditory sensations—experienced sequences of musical tones—to be an experience of our feelings and other inner states? True, there are similarities between the two: the experience of auditory sensations is an introspectible state, and so is awareness of our feelings. True, part of what we are aware of in these auditory sensations is, as Langer points out, their ebb and flow, and our feelings too have ebb and flow. But beyond these points of resemblance there seems to be little explanation *why* we should be inclined to imagine our awareness of musical sounds to be an awareness of our feelings. Imagination requires some guidance if it is not to be merely free association: I can imagine the tree at the end of the garden to be a witch because it has a witch-like appearance, but it is unclear what it would mean for me to imagine the snowdrop at my feet to be a witch if there is nothing about the snowdrop to set off my imagination. Similarly, in order for me to imagine my awareness of musical sounds to be awareness of my feelings, something in the musical sounds must guide my imagination. However, if the only points of resemblance between feelings and sounds is introspectibility and ebb and flow, then I would suggest that this is insufficient to ground an imaginative identification between the two. There are, moreover, striking *differences* between the two which would seem to preclude any such imaginative identification. In particular, whereas our feelings clearly rise up inside us (as we say), musical sounds as clearly rise up at a distance from us: even when listening to music over good earphones—when the music is experienced with peculiar immediacy—we still experience the auditory sensations as coming from an external source, such as trombones and the like. That is why although we can perhaps imagine these sounds as feelings welling up inside the *composer,* or perhaps in some *character* described by the music, it is not obvious to me that we can imagine them as feelings welling up inside ourselves.

(2) There is a second problem related to this one. I am willing to grant that there are indeed movements in music which it is appropriate to call "stabbing" or "surging." According to Walton, however, the music induces me to imagine myself feeling a particular ecstatic surge or stab of pain. He says that the music *portrays* these particulars (it picks them out or refers to them). A

number of questions need to be distinguished here. (1) Can the stab be identified as a stab of feeling rather than the stab of a dagger or some other kind of stab? (2) If the stab is a stab of feeling, can it be identified as a stab of pain rather than some other feeling such as excitement or jealousy? (3) If the stab is indeed a stab of pain, can it be identified as a stab of pain which I imagine myself experiencing rather than a stab of pain attributed to someone else, such as Othello or the composer? If the music *portrays* my imagined stab of pain, as Walton suggests, then the music must be able to distinguish my imagined stab of pain from all these other possible alternatives. Can music do this? Can music portray this particular stab of pain and no other?

If the music were accompanied by an appropriate verbal text, then perhaps it could. As we listen to the music we hear in it particular tones, rhythms, harmonic modulations, phrases, melodies, counterpoint sections, etc., etc. We might also hear particular movements that we characterize as "stabbing" or "surging." Given a particular accompanying text, we might then be able to identify the stabbing as the stabbing of Mercutio rather than a stab of pain. With a different text, we might be able to identify the stabbing as Othello's stabbing pains of jealousy rather than his stabbing pains of remorse. And so on. However, in the absence of a text, Walton suggests no good reasons for identifying the stabbing in the music (1) with a stab of feeling (rather than some other kind of stab), (2) with a stab of pain (rather than some other kind of feeling), or (3) with my imagined stab of pain (rather than yours or Othello's real or imagined pain). Walton claims earlier in his paper that musical characterization is inherently *general.* It would seem to follow that without the specification of a particular context we cannot specify that the stab is even a stab of emotion, let alone the stab of a particular emotion, let alone an *imagined* stab of *my* particular emotion. However, Walton gives us no guidance as to how a particular context could be specified. In short, although we can hear a stabbing movement in a piece of music, Walton does not show us how to tell from the music alone—without any accompanying text—what, if any, particular stabbing is occurring.

Although Walton's theory does not identify musical expression with the straightforward arousal of feelings, he does try to explain expression in terms of the arousal of *imaginary* feelings. I am not actually feeling a stab of pain as I listen to the stabbing music; I am *imagining* experiencing a stab of pain, so it would seem that the pain is an imaginary feeling. In his paper "Music and Negative Emotions," Jerrold Levinson makes a similar point. Levinson's paper deals with the problem of why people enjoy music when it evokes negative emotions such as sadness in them. While the paper does not develop a theory of musical expression, it does make certain assumptions about what often happens when people listen to music which we would characterize as sad. In particular, he assumes that it is a normal response for people to have a sadness-reaction to music.

When a person has a "deep emotional response" to music, this is "generally in virtue of the *recognition* of emotions expressed in music," but recognition then leads to a kind of empathic identification: we "end up feeling as, in imagination, the music does." Such empathic emotional responses to music consist in "something very like experience of the emotion expressed in the music" but not *exactly* like It. In both cases the physiological and affective components of emotion are present and in both cases there is cognitive content, but the "empathic" response lacks *determinate* cognitive content:

> When one hears sad music, begins to feel sad, and imagines that one is actually sad, one must, according to the logic of the concept, be imagining that there is an object for one's sadness and that one maintains certain evaluative beliefs (or attitudes) regarding it. The point, though, is that this latter imagining generally remains indeterminate.

I feel sad but my sadness has no determinate object; it is directed only to "some featureless object posited vaguely by my imagination." Levinson illustrates his view with various kinds of negative emotion: "intense grief, unrequited passion, sobbing melancholy, tragic resolve, and angry despair." Suppose, for example, that the music evokes in me an empathic response of unrequited passion. On Levinson's view, this means that I recognize unrequited passion in the music, I imagine that I am experiencing unrequited passion, and I actually experience the physiological and affective components, of unrequited passion. My imagined unrequited passion has a cognitive content which is "etiolated by comparison to that of real-life emotion"; however, since I am not really suffering the pangs of unrequited passion, and in particular there is no special person for whom I am languishing.

I am sympathetic to some of Levinson's assumptions: I think he is right to stress that the detection of emotional qualities in music has something to do with the arousal of emotion by music, and I think he is right also to stress the role of the imagination in the appreciation of emotional qualities in music. However, the theory as it stands will not do. First of all, it is far from clear that every emotional state has identifiable physiological and affective components. For example, real-life unrequited passion might on different occasions be accompanied by a great variety of inner feelings (love, grief, longing, jealousy, wretchedness, despair, self-contempt, etc., etc.). For another thing, the particular feelings I experience on a given occasion of unrequited passion may be just the same as I have felt on occasions of angry despair or intense grief. The truth of the matter is that there may be very little difference between the affective and physiological components of very different emotions: I may feel the same mixture of grief and rage when I am jealous or when I am grieving (without jealousy), I may have very similar feelings whether angrily despairing, tragically resolving, or suffering from the pangs of unrequited passion. The difference between these emotions lies not so much in their affective and physiological components as in their cognitive content. The chief difference between unrequited passion, tragic resolve, and angry despair is how I view or conceive of the situation.

But now we come to a second set of difficulties. Levinson argues that I can recognize unrequited passion (say) in the "emotion-laden gestures embodied in musical movement" and by virtue of this recognition respond empathically with feelings of unrequited passion of my own, since I identify with the music or perhaps "with the person whom we imagine owns the emotions or emotional gestures we hear in the music." However, he fails to tell us how we detect or empathically feel the unrequited passion in the music. Although we all have some idea of what *sad* music is like, I suggest that it is much less clear what a piece of music is like in which we can recognize, and hence empathize with, unrequited passion (always assuming, of course, that there is no accompanying verbal text to help us out). If I am right and there are no distinctive affective or physiological components of unrequited passion, then the obvious way to clarify the nature of music in which we can detect unrequited passion would be to specify its cognitive content. Now, Levinson claims that the cognitive content of an emotional response to music is normally "etiolated." This could mean simply that my imagined feelings of unrequited passion are not directed to any particular individual. While it is a little odd to say that one can feel unrequited passion for someone I know not whom, we can perhaps make sense of this suggestion since on Levinson's view the unrequited passion I feel empathically belongs to the music itself or to someone whom we imagine feels unrequited passion, so that we merely empathize with this imagined person's unrequited passion.

Even if we grant, however, that there need be no specific object for the unrequited passion I detect in the music and empathize with, it would seem that there must be some identifiable cognitive content, however etiolated, which is detectable in the music in order to justify the attribution of this particular emotion. I would suggest that if my response is to count as a response of unrequited passion rather than some other emotion, then I must imagine that there is someone whom I care about deeply, that this person does not care deeply about me, and that I care deeply that this person does not care deeply about me (or something of this sort). It is a serious problem for Levinson's account that he does not tell us how such conceptions can be embodied in music and hence how we can either recognize or empathize with the corresponding emotion. We find the same problem with tragic resolve and angry despair: we cannot clearly distinguish these emotional responses by their affective and physiological components alone, but only by their cognitive content. However, Levinson gives us no clue as to how their cognitive content can be recognized in or induced by music.

In a later paper, "Hope in *The Hebrides*," Levinson claims that perhaps it is possible for music to express "higher" emotional states, and that in addition to the affective and physiological components of an emotion, music might even be able to convey part, at least, of its cognitive content. He points out that emotions are normally intentional but that music can convey a general "sense of intentionality (aboutness)." He also notes that just as ordinary extramusical emotions are often individuated by their context of occurrence, it might perhaps be the case that *musical* context can play a similar role for emotions in music. When he illustrates his thesis by reference to the emotional state of hope, which he claims to be able to distinguish in Mendelssohn's *Hebrides* overture, he remarks that "perhaps some of the pure conceptual content of hope—its favorable assessment of future in relation to present"—can be suggested by the position of the hopeful passage in its musical context. Levinson does not develop this idea very far, however, and what he does say along these lines is very tentative. Certainly he gives us no clue as to how the three marks of unrequited passion that I distinguished above could be adequately conveyed by music.

Recently Levinson's view has been criticized by Peter Kivy on the grounds that the expression of emotion in music is entirely independent of the arousal of that emotion. Kivy argues that to have one's emotions aroused by a piece of music—in particular, to be moved by a piece of music—is quite distinct from perceiving a particular emotional quality in that piece. Music that is sad or expresses sadness is music with a sad expressive contour or music that is sad by convention, not music that arouses or evokes sadness. Levinson argues that a "deep emotional response" to sad music consists in the arousal of a kind of imaginative but cognitively truncated sadness. Kivy rightly attacks this claim, arguing on the one hand that sad music may or may not make me feel anything, depending on how great the music is (the "yards and yards of mournful music" written by Telemann may fail to make me feel anything much at all), and on the other hand that there are important emotions aroused by music which are full-blown, ordinary, real-life emotions, not "truncated" or "imaginary" in any sense. He illustrates his point by reference to a performance of Josquin's "Ave verum virginitas" which, he says *moves* him deeply.

When listening to the "Ave verum virginitas" I may simply be moved by "the sheer beauty of the sound as it unfolds in its ebb and flow." If my sophistication increases, however, I may also be moved by "the incomparable beauty and craftsmanship of Josquin's counterpoint" and by the fact that despite its seeming effortlessness, the music is written in a particularly difficult canonic form, "a canon at the fifth, with the voices only one beat apart." This, then, is the cognitive component of the emotion aroused by the music, my being moved by the music. It is not a truncated emotion in any way. It is a genuine emotional experience, arising out of my perception of the music and its qualities. Furthermore, this emotion might be directed at emotional, expressive qualities in the music, such as sadness, but it does not follow that the emotion *aroused by* the music is the emotion *detected in* the music. Part of what I may be moved by in a piece of music may be its sadness, but I can be moved by joyful, by energetic, and by serene music just as well, as well as

by music which does not have any marked emotional character. The expressive qualities, if any, which I detect in the music are entirely independent of the emotions I feel as I listen to the music.

Now, Kivy is certainly right to claim that when I am moved by a piece of music, my emotion may be independent of the emotional qualities, if any, that the music happens to have. When I appreciate a piece of music I may indeed be moved in the way Kivy describes. On the other hand, Kivy has not succeeded in showing that the expression of emotion by a piece of music is always and entirely unconnected to the arousal of emotion. Kivy makes this claim based on an analysis of just one emotion, "being moved," and it may well be true that we can be equally moved by music with different emotional qualities, as well as by music which has no marked emotional qualities. However, I believe that music arouses other feelings as well and that some of these may indeed be connected to the expressive qualities that music has. Furthermore, I think Kivy is wrong to insist that *all* the feelings aroused by music have to have a complex cognitive component as in his example from Josquin. It may be true that being moved by music involves complex evaluative judgments, but being moved is not the only emotional or feeling response which music can arouse.

Let me summarize the results of my discussion so far. Walton argues that expressive music evokes the imaginative experience of the emotion expressed: more precisely, music expressive of sadness, say, induces the listener to imagine herself experiencing sad feelings. Levinson similarly claims that sad music has the power to evoke a kind of truncated sadness-response: the listener feels certain symptoms of sadness, has an "indeterminate" idea that there is something or other to be sad about and imagines that she in fact feels sad. Both writers find a connection between the presence of an emotional quality in music and the arousal of that emotion in the listener's imagination. I have urged, however, that neither Walton nor Levinson has shown *how* complex feelings such as unrequited passion, stabs of pain, or even sadness can be aroused by music whether in fact or in imagination. Furthermore, Kivy is clearly right to hold that to have a deep emotional response to music is not necessarily to mirror the feelings that the music expresses.

At the same time, however, I believe that Walton and Levinson are right to stress the connection between the expression and the arousal of emotion in music, and that Kivy is quite wrong to think that his analysis of the one emotion "being moved" demonstrates that no such connection exists. In what remains of this paper I will try to sketch a more adequate account of what this connection really is.

None of the writers I have discussed in this essay has focused on the way in which music can *directly* affect our feelings. For both Walton and Levinson the arousal of feeling is imaginative and it relies on a good deal of cognitive activity on the part of the listener. For Kivy the emotion of being moved is a real emotion, not an imagined one, but it too relies on cognitive activity, such as recognizing the clever partwriting, etc. However, some music has the power to affect our feelings without much, if any cognitive mediation. In particular, music can induce physiological changes and a certain quality of inner feeling (what Levinson calls respectively the "phenomenological" and "sensational" aspects of the "affective" component in emotion). Music can make me feel tense or relaxed; it can disturb, unsettle, and startle me; it can calm me down or excite me; it can get me tapping my foot, singing along, or dancing; it can maybe lift my spirits and mellow me out.

Emotions vary in degree—and perhaps in kind—of cognitive content. At one end of the scale there is the startle response, which is an innate response, found in human neonates as well as throughout the phylogenetic scale. At the other end of the scale there is unrequited passion which, by contrast, is found only in humans with their highly developed cultural norms. What I want to suggest is that in addition to the sophisticated emotions of appreciation, which Kivy

identifies as "being moved" by certain perceived aspects of the music, there are more primitive emotions aroused by music, perhaps requiring less developed cognitive mediation. There are, after all, moments in music which make us jump or startle us. Similarly, the perception of certain rhythms may be enough—without any further cognitive mediation—to evoke tension or relaxation, excitement or calm. If the melodic and harmonic elements in a piece of music affect our emotions, this would seem to require familiarity with the stylistic norms of the piece, but no further cognitions need be required in order for us to feel soothed, unsettled, surprised, or excited by developments in the music. Certainly we need not notice that we are listening to a canon at the fifth in order for that canon to soothe us.

We have seen that to feel unrequited passion necessarily involves a certain fairly complicated conception of one's situation. By contrast, to feel disturbed or calm does not require having a conception of one's situation in this way. Music can make me feel disturbed or calm just by perceiving it (listening to it). The feeling is a result of a perception and to this extent it has "cognitive content," but it is not the full-blown cognitive content required for tragic resolve, angry despair or unrequited passion. The sense of relaxation we feel at the end of "Tristan und Isolde," for example, is the result of the long-awaited resolution, after over four hours of constant modulation without resolution. The feeling is the result of a perception, but we may not even be aware why we feel as we do: the effect of the constantly shifting harmonic pattern affects us "directly" without conscious cognitive mediation (except, of course, what is required by our understanding of Wagner's style). There is some psychological evidence (from Berlyne and others) that people seek high levels of arousal in order to have them drop afterwards: "excitement and complex, conflicting information are sought because of the 'arousal jag.'" The effect of the final Tristan chord may be partly accounted for in these terms.

Now, the feelings evoked "directly" by music explain some of the cases of musical expressiveness that the contour theory finds hard to deal with. Music that disturbs and unsettles us is disturbing, unsettling music. Modulations that surprise us are surprising. Melodies that soothe us are soothing. Furthermore, unexpected harmonic shifts excite us and are exciting; protracted stay in a harmonic area distant from the home key makes us uneasy and produces uneasy music; the return to the home key after a protracted stay in a distant harmonic area relaxes the tension in us and produces relaxing music. And so on. In short, as against Kivy's position, it seems to me that the expression of a feeling by music can sometimes be explained straightforwardly in terms of the arousal of that feeling. However, the feelings aroused "directly" by music are not stabs of pain or feelings of unrequited passion, but more "primitive" feelings of tension, relaxation, surprise, and so on. These feelings do, therefore, in a sense have an "etiolated" cognitive content, in the way that Levinson specifies in "Music and Negative Emotions," but it is not an etiolated, imaginary version of an emotion which normally has a complex cognitive content (such as unrequited passion), but rather a feeling such as surprise, which by its nature just has—or can have—a relatively simple cognitive content.

Even more interesting, however, is the way in which the simple feelings "directly" aroused by music can contribute to the imaginative expression of more complex emotions such as those discussed by Levinson. When we listen to a piece of music in a relatively familiar style, a succession of feelings is aroused in us: in a pattern typical of Classical sonata form, we may first be made to feel relaxed, then jolted into uncertainty, then made to feel uneasy for a prolonged period before experiencing relief and final release of tension. Now, something that most philosophical theorists of musical expression have either ignored or underemphasized is the fact that the musical expression of complex emotions is not a function of a few isolated measures here and there, as in Kivy's examples in *The Corded Shell*; rather it is very often a function of the large-scale formal structures of the piece as a whole. We

cannot understand the expression of complex emotions in music apart from the continuous development of the music itself None of the philosophical writers I have discussed has fully appreciated this point. Langer has indeed stressed the importance of large-scale movements of ebbing and flowing, tension and relaxation in musical expression, but she denies that any particular emotions can thereby be expressed. Levinson suggests at times that we need to look at the total musical context before we can say what particular emotions are being expressed. But he does not explore this idea very far. In order to explain how particular cognitively complex emotions can be expressed musically, we need to look at the overall structure of a piece and at the feelings aroused by the piece as it develops in time.

In his celebrated book, *Emotion and Meaning in Music,* Leonard Meyer showed how the formal structure of works in the Classical and Romantic styles could be analyzed in terms of the emotional *responses* of the practiced listener: his was a kind of "Reader-Response" or rather "Listener-Response" theory of musical structure. In order to understand a piece of music, on this view, the listener has to have her feelings aroused in a certain way. If we are experienced in the style of the piece, then we have certain expectations about the way the music will develop; in a meaningful piece of music these expectations will be either frustrated or satisfied in unexpected ways. As we listen new expectations are constantly being aroused and we are just as constantly being *surprised* by novel developments, *relieved* by delayed resolutions, made *tense* by the delays, etc., etc. In short, understanding musical structure, according to Meyer, is not just a matter of detached analysis; rather, it is impossible without the arousal of feeling in the listener.

Now, just as the formal structure of a piece of music can be understood in terms of the arousal of such feelings as uncertainty, uneasiness, relaxation, tension, relief, etc., so too can we understand the expressiveness of that piece of music in terms of the arousal of those and similar feelings.

After all, as Anthony Newcomb has put it: "Formal and expressive interpretations are in fact two complementary ways of understanding the same phenomena." Emotional expressiveness in music frequently corresponds to or mirrors its formal structure. The "direct" arousal of cognitively "simple" emotions such as being made surprised, disturbed, satisfied, relaxed, etc. is a clue not only to the formal structure of a musical piece, as Meyer showed, but also to its structure of emotional expressiveness. If a piece of music is heard as successively disturbing and reassuring, or as meandering uncertainly before moving forward confidently, or as full of obstacles which are with difficulty overcome, this is at least in part because of the way the music makes us feel. Disturbing passages disturb us: reassuring ones reassure. Passages that meander uncertainly make us feel uneasy: it is not clear where the music is going. Passages that move forward confidently make us feel satisfied: we know what is happening and seem to be able to predict what will happen next. Passages that are full of obstacles make us feel tense and when the obstacles are overcome, we feel relieved. It is important to notice that the feeling *expressed* is not always the feeling *aroused:* an uncertain, diffident passage may make me uneasy; a confident passage may make me feel reassured or relaxed.

Now, of course we are still a long way from showing how unrequited passion can be expressed by a piece of music, but we can perhaps begin to see how the development of a complex piece of music can mirror the development of a complex emotional experience, and how we can become aware of both the formal development and the corresponding emotional development by means of the relatively "simple" feelings that are *aroused* in the listener as she follows that development. As I listen to a piece which expresses serenity tinged with doubt, I myself do not have to feel serenity tinged with doubt, but the feelings I do experience, such as relaxation or reassurance, interspersed with uneasiness, alert me to the nature of the overall emotional expressiveness in the piece of music as a whole. Consider, for

example a piece of music in sonata form in which the two chief themes in their initial formulation are respectively lively and ponderous (we can suppose that the contour theory accounts for these characterizations). Now, suppose that the initially lively theme (in the major) gets gradually but relentlessly overwhelmed by the ponderous (minor) theme in such a way that the first theme is never allowed to return to its initial lively formulation but gets increasingly distorted, becomes darker and is finally heard in a truncated form in the same minor key as the ponderous theme. Such music might well make me feel increasingly nervous and tense, even disturbed, as it develops. On the view I am suggesting, the emotional experience aroused by the music is essential to the detection of the emotional expressiveness in the music itself. At the same time, the emotions aroused in me are not the emotions expressed by the music. *I* feel nervous, tense, and disturbed: the *music* expresses cheerful confidence turned to despair, or something of this sort. If this account is correct, then it shows that Kivy is wrong to suppose that expressiveness in music is just a matter of contour and convention, even if some expressive passages in music can be explained in such terms. In my example, it is not enough to spot the respective lively and ponderous contours of the initial statements of the two themes; the expressiveness of the piece as a whole can only be grasped if the listener's feelings are aroused in such a way that they provide a clue to both the formal and the expressive structure of the piece as it develops through time.

We can now see that Levinson and Walton are right to insist on a connection between the arousal and expression of emotion in music. However, neither of them has succeeded in showing how music can actually arouse, even in imagination, the complex emotional states that music sometimes expresses. In my example, I did not myself have to feel cheerful confidence turning to despair in order to detect that emotion in the music. The feelings I felt, which were evoked "directly" by the music, were less cognitively complicated, such as unease, tension, and disturbance. At the same time, we can see why Levinson is tempted to say that we empathize imaginatively with the feelings expressed by the music, for in order to detect these feelings in the music I am myself emotionally involved in listening to the music: I feel genuine feelings of unease, disturbance, and so on. Moreover, if I imagine that the themes are themselves characters in a kind of musical drama, then perhaps I can empathize with the fate of the lively theme, feeling sorrow and pity for it as I might for a character in a drama, and maybe I can even feel anger and frustration at the ponderous theme.

Walton wants to say that I imagine of my introspective awareness of auditory sensations that they are an experience of particular states of my own psyche, such as particular stabs of pain. Again we can see why Walton is tempted by this idea, since on the one hand the music does arouse feelings in me, although not usually the ones expressed, and on the other hand I may perhaps imagine that the feelings expressed by the music do belong to me. However, I think this view is more problematic than Levinson's. In my example, must I imagine of both themes that they are an experience of my own emotions? In this case my imagination must take both sides in the conflict as it were. Why cannot I identify entirely with the suffering lively theme, or even—gloatingly—entirely with the powerfully insistent ponderous theme? Why, more fundamentally, should I imagine these musical events as belonging to my own psyche at all? When I watch a performance of *King Lear* I do not imagine the drama to be taking place inside my own head; it seems to me that the same is just as true of the *King Lear* overture.

In this essay I have tried to confine my attention to the question of how the expression of emotion by music is related to the arousal of emotion in the listener. Obviously I have left many questions unanswered. In particular, I have given only a skeletal account of how music can express cognitively complex emotions such as the "cheerful confidence turning to despair" of my example. I have not attempted to show how cognitive content can get expressed by music nor whether particular emotions such as unrequited passion can be so expressed. What I *have* tried to do, however, is to indicate how such analyses might proceed. And the point I have urged above all is that any such analysis must begin with the emotions that are aroused by the music in the listener.

Part III

Continental and Contemporary Theory

A. Myths of Modernism

I N PART III OUR READINGS ARE BY INDIVIDUALS FROM DIFFERENT professions and from very differing points of view. From philosophy to art history to literary criticism to architecture, they capture what has been happening in art, literature and theoretical circles for the last thirty years. As you read in Part III, think about the changes from the modern period (Part I, section B) to the postmodern mode of the world. Suddenly—or so it would seem—our stable context for framing the world has gone awry. All the things modernism privileged are shattered (you might want to reread our Introduction to this book): the theory of the avant garde is a myth propagated by a handful of megalomaniacs; modernist universals—however fragmented—are mere constructs; and humanism's confidence in continuous social progress is laid waste by World War II and the Nazi genocide. Modernism is dead, despite furtive attempts by a few to revive it, and the postmodern world is alien, strange, and technologically frightening. And with the end of modernism comes the postmodern challenge to the eighteenth- and nineteenth-century tradition of disinterested aesthetic experience, that we examined in Part I, section B and saw challenged from a different perspective in Part II.

Gone forever are the days when anyone in academic circles could discuss art or literature from a so-called objective, neutral, or politically unmotivated position. Perhaps more than any other indicator that modernism is dead or, at least, has reached a state of no return is this problem of cultural and historical contextual perspective that pervades contemporary critical discourse. Of course, traditionalists and those who still believe in a universalized aesthetic blame postmodern theory for ruining a good thing— our ability to see "purely" (art for art's sake) or our ability to "just read" the text without all of this new historicist, cultural "theory." But, and this point may be the crucial one, the new theory may only be responding to the art, literature, and culture around it. If this is the case, then it is the art world that is demanding a new context, a new critical lens, or a new historical and cultural perspective from which to view art. Here we have the old chicken and egg problem. Which comes first? Did post–World War II artists and writers pastiche and parody modern art? Or did this all come from postmodern theory? As you read in Part III, think about the changes from the modern period to the postmodern mode of the world—both in art and in theory.

Taking our section title, "Myths of Modernism," from Rosalind Krauss's book, *The Originality of the Avant-Garde and Other Modernist Myths* appropriately sets the tone for the ideas put forth in this section. Krauss begins her introduction questioning the long-held view of formalist art historians that criticism only elucidates the intrinsic or universal meaning found in "good" art. Influenced by both structuralism and poststructuralism, Krauss would agree with Gilles Deleuze when he states that "truth is defined by the method that produces it." In other words, how we understand art or accept new artistic forms depends upon the theory or interpretative method we use to explain art.

The "Myths of Modernism" section is primarily concerned with the way traditional critics have constructed an idea of modernity and, in turn, the way more contemporary critics try to debunk or shake up this now traditional idea of modernity. With the selections from Paul de Man, Roland Barthes, and Robert Venturi we have writers expressing a need to break with traditional or modern interpretative practices; also with each of these three theorists there is an acknowledged institution (literary, artistic, and architectural) that has a vested interest in maintaining the status quo.

An art historian, Krauss began her career in the era when formalism was still the vogue and Clement Greenberg ruled the world of modern and contemporary art history debates. Krauss's problem with Greenberg is that he propagates a "myth" of the modern artist to accommodate his own interpretative biases—whether or not the artist or art in question actually fits into his paradigm. Indeed, Krauss's introduction is all about *paradigms*—patterns, examples, or theories for interpreting things around us. Krauss challenges not only Greenberg, but the entire art historical tradition that he represents and hopes to maintain. This tradition views works of art as universal, transhistorical forms that privilege the artist's intentions and the autonomy of the work of art. Influenced by structuralism and poststructuralism, Krauss no longer can buy into Greenberg's humanist and universalized art perspective. Krauss, as she herself admits near the end of the introduction, is defensive because there is tremendous resistance to her position and to postformalist interpretation from traditional art historians:

> That last essay [of the book Krauss has edited], which is extremely polemical in tone, raises the issue of the often combative posture of these texts. Perhaps the sweeping nature of the difference in our methodological bases—a difference that makes some of the questions raised by this work flatly incomprehensible to certain of my colleagues—that has encouraged that posture.

One of those colleagues, aesthetician Stanley Cavell, personifies the art object in the name of humanism—assigning an almost human status to the work of art so that the artist's "intentions" can be preserved. While the art object is not literally a person, it faces us like a person and we respond to it as we do to a person, Cavell says, because it is the "voice" of the artist, expressing her intention. This idea also feeds into the myth of modernism that Krauss finds so odious: the myth that artists such as Picasso or Rodin were geniuses (in the Romantic tradition, no less) is more the product of these artists' huge egos and public relations efforts than the brilliant originality of their work.

Resistance is a major theme of this section, not only in Paul de Man's "The Resistance to Theory," but also the resistance that traditional readers have moving "From Work to Text," as recounted by Roland Barthes, and the resistance to change from a stale modern to a postmodern architecture in Robert Venturi's *Complexity and Contradiction in Architecture*. As an expert on literary theory, de Man was asked to write an article for the Modern Language Association explaining and summing up the new field of critical theory. Humorously, the first draft of the article was rejected because de Man, basically, could not find a way to articulate—from a point of stability—literary theory. For every effort, from de Man's point of view, to stabilize and to render whole or complete this elusive field was foiled by theory itself. So de Man decided to write "The Resistance to Theory" as a way to approach the topic many in the profession resisted precisely because it could not be given easy meanings that critics could, in turn, simply plug into literature (compare the problem of defining art in Part II). Like Krauss, de Man is honest about what he describes as the real resistance to theory: the theorist's attention to the "literariness" of the text. Instead of discussing the novel's or poem's "aesthetic quality" that refers directly back to the world, the theorist discusses language. According to de Man, the work of the theorist is often misrepresented: "The most misleading representation of literariness, also the most recurrent objection to contemporary literary theory, considers it as pure verbalism, as a denial of the reality principle in the name of absolute fictions, and for reasons that are said to be ethically and politically shameful." Traditionalists reject theory because theorists use language to talk about language instead of using language to talk about "life" or the "world" from a representational perspective (compare Silvers's discussion of a similar shift from world to language in Part II). De Man seems to question traditional critics' conviction that language refers to the material world and not only to its own language or the language of other texts.

In "From Work to Text" Roland Barthes reflects on many of the same topics as de Man, such as the work's ability to refer to the "world" while the text refers to discourse on texts ("literariness" in de Man), and the statement by Barthes that no complete theory of the text is possible. Barthes makes lucid the difference between a *work* and a *text:* "the work is a fragment of substance, occupying a part of the space of books, the Text is a methodological field." In other words, the work is an object with an intrinsic worth that we fix and stabilize, while the text "practices the infinite deferment of the signified." In the last section, Barthes discusses the role of the author; Barthes's text is a "readerly" text, as he says elsewhere, not a writerly text. For Barthes's meaning is not deposited in the text by the author so that the reader can come along and read that meaning; rather, the reader *produces* meaning in her reading. This view dispels the notion of intentionality still utilized in many college literature classes. For example, have you ever been asked: "What do you think the author is trying to say?" or "Why do you think the author put that in the text?" Barthes would answer: "Who knows or cares?—the author knows no more about her text than anyone else." Lastly, Barthes's notion of the text is quite similar to Jacques Derrida's or Michel Foucault's: the text is open to "play" and cannot be forced into one meaning or a universalized meaning (like a "work" can be). Barthes develops his idea of the text in other writings; simply put, everything is a text (MTV, stop signs, your best friend, *Moby Dick*) and there is no end to reading and rereading these texts.

With our selection from *Complexity and Contradiction in Architecture* we find Robert Venturi challenging resistance to change, this time in the field of modern architecture. The most likely origin of the term *postmodern* as the successor of the *modern* is its use in architecture, from which it spread to literature and the other arts. One of the first to challenge the internationalist style of modernist architecture long synonymous with Frank Lloyd Wright and Ludwig Mies van der Rohe, Venturi plays on Mies van der Rohe's pithy tag for the sleek, uncomplicated internationalist modernist style, "Less is more," with "Less is a bore." In this excerpt Venturi touches upon three hallmarks of postmodernism: pastiche, parody, and Pop Art (perhaps the 3 Ps replacing the three Ds of aesthetic experience in Part I). *Pastiche* is a technique that literally takes a part of an older work and puts it into a different context in a new work. For example, Tom Stoppard lifts and incorporates dialogue out of Shakespeare's *Hamlet* and puts it in a new framework, *Rosencranz and Guildenstern Are Dead. Parody,* however, is the imitation in style or manner of another work—usually parody works to imitate a serious work in order to produce a sense of the ridiculous.

Venturi discusses his "both-and" approach, which is often read as a kind of pastiche; mixed in with the older style, it creates something new: "The paths of medieval forti-fication walls in European cities became boulevards in the nineteenth century; a section of Broadway is a piazza and a symbol rather than an artery to upper New York state." And, of course, this sort of pastiche is highly culturally relative and not, like modern architecture, "international"—that is, universally valid crossculturally. Meanwhile, par-ody is more often associated with pop art. So-called "honky-tonk" elements of archi-tecture or townscapes Venturi appreciates for their freshness and ability to create complexity in otherwise monotonous buildings or streets. An aspect of Pop Art, honky-tonk is often viewed as brash parody upon the less desirable aspects of our cul-ture, like the run-down, derelict "junkyard" looks of many of our decaying inner cities. But Venturi defends honky-tonk against "junkyard" accusations by stating that chaos can be interesting if is somehow *managed* chaos: "The seemingly chaotic juxtaposi-tions of honky-tonk elements express an intriguing kind of vitality and validity, and they produce an unexpected approach to unity as well."

The Originality of the Avant-Garde and Other Modernist Myths

ROSALIND E. KRAUSS

CAN IT BE ARGUED that the interest of critical writing lies almost entirely in its method? Can it be held that the content of any given evaluative statement—"this is good, important," "this is bad, trivial"—is not what serious criticism is, se-riously, read for? But rather, that such criticism is understood through the forms of its arguments, through the way that its method, in the process of constituting the object of criticism, exposes to view those choices that precede and predeter-mine any act of judgment?

When, more than twenty years ago, *Art and Culture* presented the critical work of Clement Greenberg to the generation of artists and writers who were to develop during the 1960s, it pre-sented its readers above all with a system through which to think the field of modernist art. And this system, or method—often referred to, inex-actly, as formalist—had far greater effect than the particularities of its author's taste. Greenberg, for example, did not support the work of Frank Stella, but the logic of his system and the privi-lege it gave to flatness as a pictorial essence or norm provided the conceptual framework within which Stella's first decade of production was un-derstood and, widely, acclaimed. Profoundly his-toricist, Greenberg's method conceives the field of art as at once timeless and in constant flux. That is to say that certain things, like art itself, or painting or sculpture, or the masterpiece, are

From The Originality of the Avant-Garde and Other Modernist Myths *(Cambridge, MA: The MIT Press, 1985). Reprinted by permission of the publisher.*

universal, transhistorical forms. But in the same breath it is to assert that the life of these forms is dependent upon constant renewal, not unlike that of the living organism. The historical logic of this renewal was what essays like "Collage" or "American-Type Painting" strove to discover, while always insisting as part of that logic that "modernist art develops out of the past without gap or break, and wherever it ends up it will never stop being intelligible in terms of the continuity of art."

It is this declaration of the ontic status of art, of its unbreachable, seamless continuity, that led Greenberg vigorously to deny that it is in the method rather than the content of the judgments that the interest of criticism lies. Art as a universal calls forth and is completed by judgment as another universal capacity of consciousness. There being no way to separate a judgment from its evaluative contents, he would argue that the point of criticism has everything to do with value and almost nothing to do with method.

Practically everything in *The Originality of the Avant-Garde and Other Modernist Myths* stands in contradiction to this position. Written during the decade from 1973 to 1983, these essays chart not only my own critical and intellectual development but that of a generation of American critics, although I must add, not for the most part critics concerned with the visual arts. For, during the years that *Art and Culture*'s impact was felt in a New York–based art world, other sections of American cultural and intellectual life were affected by a discourse coming from abroad and challenging the historicist premises on which almost all the critical thinking of this country had been based. That discourse was, of course, structuralism, with its later poststructuralist modifications, the analytic methods of which produced a radical inversion of the position on which *Art and Culture* depended. On the one hand, structuralism rejected the historicist model as the means to understand the generation of meaning. On the other, within the work of poststructuralism, those timeless, transhistorical forms, which had been seen as the indestructible cate-

gories wherein aesthetic development took place, were themselves opened to historical analysis and placement.

To reject the historicist model of the way the work of art comes to mean is to propose several things at once. It is first of all to substitute for the idea of the work of art as an organism (developing out of a past tradition, imbedded in the history of a given medium) the image of it as a structure. To illustrate this notion of structure, Roland Barthes liked to use the story of the Argonauts, ordered by the Gods to complete their long journey in one and the same ship—the *Argo*—against the certainty of the boat's gradual deterioration. Over the course of the voyage the Argonauts slowly replaced each piece of the ship, "so that they ended with an entirely new ship, without having to alter either its name or its form. This ship *Argo* is highly useful," Barthes continues. "It affords the allegory of an eminently structural object, created not by genius, inspiration, determination, evolution, but by two modest actions (which cannot be caught up in any mystique of creation): *substitution* (one part replaces another, as in a paradigm) and *nomination* (the name is in no way linked to the stability of the parts): by dint of combinations made within one and the same name, nothing is left of the origin: Argo is an object with no other cause than its name, with no other identity than its form."

Barthes's depiction of structure is, in a sense, a narrative rendering of Ferdinand de Saussure's definition of language as pure difference, the definition that can be seen as having initiated structuralism. Barthes's *substitution* refers to this system of differences. But his notion of *nomination* calls on that part of the definition of language that Saussure considered even more important. Observing that differences are generally the function of two positive terms that are set in comparison, Saussure insisted that, to the contrary, in the case of language "there are only differences *without positive terms*." With this definitive rejection of "positive terms" Saussure blocked the way for meaning to be understood as the outcome of a correlation between a sound (or word) and an object for which the word is the label. Rather, meaning came to be seen as the result of an entire system by which the use of that word, say, *rock,* can be deployed instead of a large set of possible alternatives or substitutions, say, *stone, boulder, pebble, crag, agate, lump of ore.* . . . The choice one makes within this system of substitutions betrays a whole array of assumptions keyed to vastly different vocabularies: of scale, of technical (geological) mastery, of picturesque emotion, of verbal precision or generality. There is a system of interrelated difference, and in order to enter this system the word *rock* cannot be tied uniquely to this lump of matter at one's feet. Meaning is not the label of a particular thing; nor is it a picture of it. Meaning, for the structuralist, is the result of a system of substitutions.

One of the methodological corollaries of this conception of meaning is that it is a function of the system at a given moment in time—the system synchronically displayed—rather than the outcome of a specific development or history. Rejecting the diachronic, or historical, study of language(s) as a way to arrive at a theory of signification, Saussure's work set a precedent for the attack on the temporal model that structuralist and poststructuralist theories have staged on a variety of fronts. Some of these can be heard in Barthes's way of accounting for the significance of the *Argo*-model, as he dismisses from its field of relevance a concept like *"origin,"* with its importance to traditional historical thinking, or concepts like "genius," "inspiration," "determination" and "evolution," by which works of art are imbedded within the conditions of their creation. For the nonstructuralist critic, whole realms of inquiry—aesthetic intention, biographical context, psychological models of creativity, or the possible existence of private worlds of allusion—are raised by these concepts, which not only imply the temporal condition of the work's generation, but call for an interpretive model based on the analogy between the work and its maker: the work's surface thought of as existing in relation to its "depth" much the way that the

exterior of the human subject is understood to relate to his internal, or true, self. By contrast, the structuralist model of substitutions and nomination does not call to mind the image of depth—substitution being able, after all, to take place by moving pieces about on a plane surface. Thus if Barthes cherishes the *Argo*-model, it is for its *shallowness.*

There is enormous resistance on the part of the formalist or historicist critic to this conception of the work of art, this refusal, in the name of method, of the idea of it as "profound." We hear this antistructuralist attitude formulated, for example, by Stanley Cavell when, as a professional aesthetician, he insists on the humanist analogy, as follows: "Objects of art not merely interest and absorb, they move us . . . we treat them in special ways, invest them with a value which normal people otherwise reserve only for other people—and with the same kind of scorn and outrage." If the human analogy can be used by the historicist to try to ground the work in the biographical matrix of its author, or to attempt to order and fix its "intentions," it can also serve the critic anxious to understand the work's formal integration. Here it functions as a kind of physicalist model, with the work's putative resemblance to the human body involving not only those conditions of surface and depth, inside and outside, that are supposedly shared by human subject and work of art but also those formal features that preserve and protect the life of the organism, such as unity, coherence, complexity within identity, and so on. Now this call for unity assumes that it is possible to draw boundaries around the aesthetic organism: starting with *this* work within its frame, and the formal decisions it manifests; moving to *this* medium, with the conditions that both unify it and separate it from other media; and continuing to *this* author and the unity or coherence of his oeuvre. The categories of such a discussion—work of art, medium, author, oeuvre—are never, themselves, seriously opened to question.

Having embraced structuralism's rejection of history as a way of getting at the way things (statements, works of art, any cultural production at all) signify, poststructuralism then turns around and submits the vehicles of that production to the test of their own histories. Like the life of the *Argo,* the autonomous or unified nature of concepts like "author," "oeuvre," or "work" tends to dissolve against the background of actual, material history. In his admiration for the *Argo*-model, Barthes called it "luminous and white," undoubtedly thinking of Mallarmé's sail. How many different *Argos,* he went on to wonder, are named by the word *Homer?* And, in further questioning the traditional view of authorship, poststructuralists ask, whose writing is specified by the name Freud? Freud's only? Or that of Abraham, Stekel, Flies? Getting closer to the field of the visual arts, we could extend this question: What does *Picasso* mean for his art—the historical personality who is its "cause," supplying the *meaning* for this or that figure (clown, satyr, minotaur) in his painting? Or were those meanings written long before Picasso selected them? And is not his art a profound meditation on pastiche, for which collage is itself an inspired structural metaphor? . . .

The first reason has to do with the model of meaning out of which the various authors of these texts were working, a model (the picture theory of meaning) that demonstrated the degree to which writers about modernist painting and sculpture were unaffected by and, probably, ignorant of the work on signification produced by structuralism. The second has to do with the effects of the relatively recent capture of art-critical writing by art history—an art history that has itself become increasingly historicist in the last several decades and is pursuing questions of origin and authorship as though no critique had ever been advanced about the methodological status of these concepts. But the very concern of Picasso's art with pastiche poses problems—from *within* his work—of "authorship," just as his operations, through collage, on the procedures of signification challenge any simplistic idea of reference.

This, then, is the crux of the contention that method is what criticism is, seriously, read for. Because those questions that could be thought to be statements of value—"the operations of pastiche are what is interesting, here"; "the representation of absence is what is best about Picasso's collage"—are in fact the product of what a given method allows one to ask or even to think of asking. . . .

[Much of this writing] is extremely polemical in tone, rais[ing] the issue of the often combative posture of these texts. Perhaps it is the sweeping nature of the difference in our methodological bases—a difference that makes some of the questions raised by this work flatly incomprehensible to certain of my colleagues—that has encouraged that posture. But it is also a result of my own sense that the art of the last hundred and thirty years, the art of modernism, is not being well served by writing that promotes the myths through which it can be consistently misread.

But of course the very experience of these *as* myths, many of them generated by modernist artists themselves or by the critical writing of their friends and associates, seems to be particularly possible from a certain vantage—that of the present—from which modernist art appears to have come to closure. It is, in fact, from within the perspective of postmodernist production that issues of copy and repetition, the reproducibility of the sign (most obviously in its photographic form), the textual production of the subject, are newly brought to light within modernism itself—revealed as the matter that a euphoric modernism sought both to signal and to repress. Postmodernist art enters this terrain (the theoretical domain of structuralist and poststructuralist analysis) openly. And it is this phenomenon, born of the last two decades, that in turn has opened critical practice, overtly, onto method.

The Resistance to Theory

PAUL DE MAN

A GENERAL STATEMENT ABOUT literary theory should not, in theory, start from pragmatic considerations. It should address such questions as the definition of literature (what is literature?) and discuss the distinction between literary and non-literary uses of language, as well as between literary and non-verbal forms of art. It should then proceed to the descriptive taxonomy of the various aspects and species of the literary genus and to the normative rules that are bound to follow from such a classification. Or, if one rejects a scholastic for a phenomenological model, one should attempt a phenomenology of the literary activity as writing, reading or both, or of the literary work as the product, the correlate of such an activity. Whatever the approach taken (and several other theoretically justifiable starting-points can be imagined) it is certain that considerable difficulties will arise at once, difficulties that cut so deep that even the most elementary task of scholarship, the delimitation of the corpus and the *état présent* of the question, is bound to end in confusion, not necessarily because the bibliography is so large but because it is impossible to fix its borderlines. Such predictable difficulties have not prevented many writers on literature from proceeding along theoretical rather than pragmatic lines, often with considerable success. It can be shown however that, in all cases, this success depends on the power of a system (philosophical, religious or ideological) that may well remain implicit but that determines an *a priori* conception of what is "literary" by starting out from the premises of the system rather than from the literary thing itself—if such a "thing" indeed exists. This last qualification is of course a real question which in fact accounts for the predictability of the difficulties just alluded to: if the condition of existence of an entity is itself particularly critical, then the theory of this entity is bound to fall back into the pragmatic. The difficult and inconclusive history of literary theory indicates that this is indeed the case for literature in an even more manifest manner than, for other verbalized occurrences such as jokes, for example, or even dreams. The attempt to treat literature theoretically may as well resign itself to the fact that it has to start out from empirical considerations.

Pragmatically speaking, then, we know that there has been, over the last fifteen to twenty years, a strong interest in something called literary theory and that, in the United States, this interest has at times coincided with the importation and reception of foreign, mostly but not always continental, influences. We also know that this wave of interest now seems to be receding as some satiation or disappointment sets in after the initial enthusiasm. Such an ebb and flow is natural enough, but it remains interesting, in this case, because it makes the depth of the resistance to literary theory so manifest. It is a recurrent strategy of any anxiety to defuse what it considers threatening by magnification or minimization, by attributing to it claims to power of which it is bound to fall short. If a cat is called a tiger it can easily be dismissed as a paper tiger; the question remains however why one was so scared of the cat in the first place. The same tactic works in reverse: calling the cat a mouse and then deriding it for its pretense to be mighty. Rather than being drawn into this polemical whirlpool, it might be better to try to call the cat a cat and to document, however briefly, the contemporary version of the resistance to theory in this country. . . .

From "The Resistance to Theory," Yale French Studies 63 (1982). Reprinted by permission of the publisher.

What is it that is being threatened by the approaches to literature that developed during the sixties and that now, under a variety of designations, make up the ill-defined and somewhat chaotic field of literary theory? These approaches cannot be simply equated with any particular method or country. Structuralism was not the only trend to dominate the stage, not even in France, and structuralism as well as semiology are inseparable from prior tendencies in the Slavic domain. In Germany, the main impulses have come from other directions, from the Frankfurt school and more orthodox Marxists, from post-Husserlian phenomenology and post-Heideggerian hermeneutics, with only minor inroads made by structural analysis. All these trends have had their share of influence in the United States, in more or less productive combinations with nationally rooted concerns. Only a nationally or personally competitive view of history would wish to hierarchize such hard-to-label movements. The possibility of doing literary theory, which is by no means to be taken for granted, has itself become a consciously reflected-upon question and those who have progressed furthest in this question are the most controversial but also the best sources of information. This certainly includes several of the names loosely connected with structuralism, broadly enough defined to include Saussure, Jakobson and Barthes as well as Greimas and Althusser, that is to say, so broadly defined as to be no longer of use as a meaningful historical term.

Literary theory can be said to come into being when the approach to literary texts is no longer based on non-linguistic, that is to say historical and aesthetic, considerations or, to put it somewhat less crudely, when the object of discussion is no longer the meaning or the value but the modalities of production and of reception of meaning and of value prior to their establishment—the implication being that this establishment is problematic enough to require an autonomous discipline of critical investigation to consider its possibility and its status. Literary history, even when considered at the furthest remove from the platitudes of positivistic historicism, is still the history of an understanding of which the possibility is taken for granted. The question of the relationship between aesthetics and meaning is more complex, since aesthetics apparently has to do with the *effect* of meaning rather than with its content *per se*. But aesthetics is in fact, ever since its development just before and with Kant, a phenomenalism of a process of meaning and understanding, and it may be naive in that it postulates (as its name indicates) a phenomenology of art and of literature which may well be what is at issue. Aesthetics is part of a universal system of philosophy rather than a specific theory. In the nineteenth-century philosophical tradition, Nietzsche's challenge of the system erected by Kant, Hegel and their successors is a version of the general question of philosophy. Nietzsche's critique of metaphysics includes, or starts out from, the aesthetic, and the same could be argued for Heidegger. The invocation of prestigious philosophical names does not intimate that the present-day development of literary theory is a by-product of larger philosophical speculations. In some rare cases, a direct link may exist between philosophy and literary theory. More frequently, however, contemporary literary theory is a relatively autonomous version of questions that also surface, in a different context, in philosophy, though not necessarily in a clearer and more rigorous form. Philosophy, in England as well as on the Continent, is less freed from traditional patterns than it sometimes pretends to believe and the prominent, though never dominant, place of aesthetics among the main components of the system is a constitutive part of this system. It is therefore not surprising that contemporary literary theory came into being from outside philosophy and sometimes in conscious rebellion against the weight of its tradition. Literary theory may now well have become a legitimate concern of philosophy but it cannot be assimilated to it, either factually or theoretically. It contains a necessarily pragmatic moment that certainly weakens it as theory but that adds a subversive element of unpredictability and makes it something of a wild card in the serious game of the theoretical disciplines.

The advent of theory, the break that is now so often being deplored and that sets it aside from literary history and from literary criticism, occurs with the introduction of linguistic terminology in the metalanguage about literature. By linguistic terminology is meant a terminology that designates reference prior to designating the referent and takes into account, in the consideration of the world, the referential function of language or, to be somewhat more specific, that considers reference as a function of language and not necessarily as an intuition. Intuition implies perception, consciousness, experience, and leads at once into the world of logic and of understanding with all its correlatives, among which aesthetics occupies a prominent place. The assumption that there can be a science of language which is not necessarily a logic leads to the development of a terminology which is not necessarily aesthetic. Contemporary literary theory comes into its own in such events as the application of Saussurian linguistics to literary texts.

The affinity between structural linguistics and literary texts is not as obvious as with the hindsight of history, it now may seem. Peirce, Saussure, Sapir and Bloomfield were not originally concerned with literature at all but with the scientific foundations of linguistics. But the interest of philologists such as Roman Jakobson or literary critics such as Roland Barthes in semiology reveals the natural attraction of literature to a theory of linguistic signs. By considering language as a system of signs and of signification rather than as an established pattern of meanings, one displaces or even suspends the traditional barriers between literary and presumably non-literary uses of language and liberates the corpus from the secular weight of textual canonization. The results of the encounter between semiology and literature went considerably further than those of many other theoretical models—philological, psychological or classically epistemological—which writers on literature in quest of such models had tried out before. The

responsiveness of literary texts to semiotic analysis is visible in that, whereas other approaches were unable to reach beyond observations that could be paraphrased or translated in terms of common knowledge, these analyses revealed patterns that could only be described in terms of their own specifically linguistic aspects. The linguistics of semiology and of literature apparently have something in common that only their shared perspective can detect and that pertains distinctively to them. The definition of this something, often referred to as literariness, has become the object of literary theory.

Literariness, however, is often misunderstood in a way that has provoked much of the confusion which dominates today's polemics. It is frequently assumed, for instance, that literariness is another word for, or another mode of, aesthetic response. The use, in conjunction with literariness, of such terms as style and stylistics, form or even "poetry" (as in "the poetry of grammar"), all of which carry strong aesthetic connotations, helps to foster this confusion, even among those who first put the term in circulation. Roland Barthes, for example, in an essay properly and revealingly dedicated to Roman Jakobson, speaks eloquently of the writer's quest for a perfect coincidence of the phonic properties of a word with its signifying function. . . . Whenever this autonomous potential of language can be revealed by analysis, we are dealing with literariness and, in fact, with literature as the place where this negative knowledge about the reliability of linguistic utterance is made available. The ensuing foregrounding of material, phenomenal aspects of the signifier creates a strong illusion of aesthetic seduction at the very moment when the actual aesthetic function has been, at the very least, suspended. It is inevitable that semiology or similarly oriented methods be considered formalistic, in the sense of being aesthetically rather than semantically valorized, but the inevitability of such an interpretation does not make it less aberrant. Literature involves the voiding, rather than the affirmation, of aesthetic categories. One of the consequences of this is that, whereas we have traditionally been accustomed to reading literature by analogy with the plastic arts and with music, we now have to recognize the necessity of a non-perceptual, linguistic moment in painting and music, and learn to *read* pictures rather than to *imagine* meaning.

If literariness is not an aesthetic quality, it is also not primarily mimetic. Mimesis becomes one trope among others, language choosing to imitate a nonverbal entity just as paronomasis "imitates" a sound without any claim to identity (or reflection on difference) between the verbal and non-verbal elements. The most misleading representation of literariness, and also the most recurrent objection to contemporary literary theory, considers it as pure verbalism, as a denial of the reality principle in the name of absolute fictions, and for reasons that are said to be ethically and politically shameful. The attack reflects the anxiety of the aggressors rather than the guilt of the accused. By allowing for the necessity of a non-phenomenal linguistics, one frees the discourse on literature from naive oppositions between fiction and reality, which are themselves an offspring of an uncritically mimetic conception of art. In a genuine semiology as well as in other linguistically oriented theories, the referential function of language is not being denied—far from it: what is in question is its authority as a model for natural or phenomenal cognition. Literature is fiction not because it somehow refuses to acknowledge "reality," but because it is not *a priori* certain that language functions according to principles which are those, or which are *like* those, of the phenomenal world. It is therefore not *a priori* certain that literature is a reliable source of information about anything but its own language.

It would be unfortunate, for example, to confuse the materiality of the signifier with the materiality of what it signifies. This may seem obvious enough on the level of light and sound, but it is less so with regard to the more general phenomenality of space, time or especially of the self; no one in his right mind will try to grow grapes by the luminosity of the word "day," but it is very difficult not to conceive the pattern of one's past and future existence as in accordance with temporal and spatial schemes that belong to fictional narratives and not to the world. This does not mean that fictional narratives are not part of the world and of reality; their impact upon the world may well be all too strong for comfort. What we call ideology is precisely the confusion of linguistic with natural reality, of reference with phenomenalism. It follows that, more than any other mode of inquiry, including economics, the linguistics of literariness is a powerful and indispensable tool in the unmasking of ideological aberrations, as well as a determining factor in accounting for their occurrence. Those who reproach literary theory for being oblivious to social and historical (that is to say ideological) reality are merely stating their fear at having their own ideological mystifications exposed by the tool they are trying to discredit. They are, in short, very poor readers of Marx's *German Ideology*.

In these all too summary evocations of arguments that have been much more extensively and convincingly made by others, we begin to perceive some of the answers to the initial question: what is it about literary theory that is so threatening that it provokes such strong resistances and attacks? It upsets rooted ideologies by revealing the mechanics of their workings; it goes against a powerful philosophical tradition of which aesthetics is a prominent part; it upsets the established canon of literary works and blurs the borderlines between literary and non-literary discourse. By implication, it may also reveal the links between ideologies and philosophy. All this is ample enough reason for suspicion, but not a satisfying answer to the question. For it makes the tension between contemporary literary theory and the tradition of literary studies appear as a mere historical conflict between two modes of thought that happen to hold the stage at the same time. If the conflict is merely historical, in the literal sense, it is of limited theoretical interest, a passing squall in the intellectual weather of the world. As a matter of fact, the arguments in favor of the legitimacy of literary theory are so compelling that it seems useless to concern oneself with the conflict at all. Certainly, none of the objections to theory presented again and again, always misinformed or based on crude misunderstandings of such terms as mimesis, fiction, reality, ideology, reference and, for that matter, relevance, can be said to be of genuine rhetorical interest.

It may well be, however, that the development of literary theory is itself overdetermined by complications inherent in its very project and unsettling with regard to its status as a scientific discipline. Resistance may be a built-in constituent of its discourse in a manner that would be inconceivable in the natural sciences and unmentionable in the social sciences. It may well be, in other words, that the polemical opposition, the systematic non-understanding and misrepresentation, the unsubstantial but eternally recurrent objections, are the displaced symptoms of a resistance inherent in the theoretical enterprise itself. To claim that this would be sufficient reason not to envisage doing literary theory would be like rejecting anatomy because it has failed to cure mortality. The real debate of literary theory is not with its polemical opponents but rather with its own methodological assumptions and possibilities. Rather than asking why literary theory is threatening, we should perhaps ask why it has such difficulty going about its business and why it lapses so readily either into the language of self-justification and self-defense or else into the overcompensation of a programmatically euphoric utopianism. Such insecurity about its own project calls for self-analysis, if one is to understand the frustrations that attend upon its practitioners, even when they seem to dwell in serene methodological self-assurance. And if these difficulties are indeed an integral part of the problem, then they will have to be, to some extent, a-historical in the temporal sense of the term. The way in which they are encountered on the present local literary scene as a resistance to the introduction of linguistic terminology in aesthetic and historical discourse about literature is only one particular version of a question that cannot be reduced to a specific historical situation and called modern, post-modern, post-classical or romantic (not even in Hegel's sense of the term), although its compulsive way of forcing itself upon us in the guise of a system of historical periodization is certainly part of its problematic nature. Such difficulties can be read in the text of literary theory at all times, at whatever historical moment one wishes to select. One of the main achievements of the present theoretical trends is to have restored some awareness of this fact. Classical, medieval and Renaissance literary theory is now often being read in a way that knows enough about what it is doing not to wish to call itself "modern."

We return, then, to the original question in an attempt to broaden the discussion enough to inscribe the polemics inside the question rather than having them determine it. The resistance to theory is a resistance to the use of language about language. It is therefore a resistance to language itself or to the possibility that language contains factors or functions that cannot be reduced to intuition. But we seem to assume all too readily that, when we refer to something called "language," we know what it is we are talking about, although there is probably no word to be found in the language that is as overdetermined, self-evasive, disfigured and disfiguring as "language." Even if we choose to consider it at a safe remove from any theoretical model, in the pragmatic history of "language," not as a concept, but as a didactic assignment that no human being can bypass, we soon find ourselves confronted by theoretical enigmas. . . .

What is meant when we assert that the study of literary texts is necessarily dependent on an act of reading, or when we claim that this act is being systematically avoided? Certainly more than the tautology that one has to have read at least some parts, however small, of a text (or read some part, however small, of a text about this text) in order to be able to make a statement about it. Common as it may be, criticism by hearsay is only rarely held up as exemplary. To stress the by no means self-evident necessity of reading implies at least two things. First of all, it implies that literature is not a transparent message in which it can be taken for granted that the distinction between the message and the means of communication is clearly established. Second, and more problematically, it implies that the grammatical decoding of a text leaves a residue of indetermination that has to be, but cannot be, resolved by grammatical means, however extensively conceived. The extension of grammar to include para-figural dimensions is in fact the most remarkable and debatable strategy of contemporary semiology, especially in the study of syntagmatic and narrative structures. The codification of contextual elements well beyond the syntactical limits of the sentence leads to the systematic study of metaphrastic dimensions and has considerably refined and expanded the knowledge of textual codes. It is equally clear, however, that this extension is always strategically directed towards the replacement of rhetorical figures by grammatical codes. This tendency to replace a rhetorical by a grammatical terminology (to speak of hypotaxis, for instance, to designate anamorphic or metonymic tropes) is part of an explicit program, a program that is entirely admirable in its intent since it tends towards the mastering and the clarification of meaning. The replacement of a hermeneutic by a semiotic model, of interpretation by decoding, would represent, in view of the baffling historical instability of textual meanings (including, of course, those of canonical texts), a considerable progress. Much of the hesitation associated with "reading" could thus be dispelled.

The argument can be made, however, that no grammatical decoding, however refined, could claim to reach the determining figural dimensions of a text. There are elements in all texts that are by no means ungrammatical, but whose semantic function is not grammatically definable, neither in themselves nor in context. Do we have to interpret the genitive in the title of Keats' unfinished epic *The Fall of Hyperion* as meaning "Hyperion's Fall," the case story of the defeat of an older by a newer power, the very recognizable story from which Keats indeed started out but from which he increasingly strayed away, or as "Hyperion Falling," the much less specific but more disquieting evocation of an actual process of falling, regardless of its beginning, its end or the identity of the entity to whom it befalls to be falling? This story is indeed told in the later fragment entitled *The Fall of Hyperion,* but it is told about a character who resembles Apollo rather than Hyperion, the same Apollo who, in the first version (called *Hyperion*), should definitely be triumphantly standing rather than falling if Keats had not been compelled to interrupt, for no apparent reason, the story of Apollo's triumph. Does the title tell us that Hyperion is fallen and that Apollo stands, or does it tell us that Hyperion and Apollo (and Keats, whom it is hard to distinguish, at times, from Apollo) are interchangeable in that all of them are necessarily and constantly falling? Both readings are grammatically correct, but it is impossible to decide from the context (the ensuing narrative) which version is the right one. The narrative context suits neither and both at the same time, and one is tempted to suggest that the fact that Keats was unable to complete either version manifests the impossibility, for him as for us, of reading his own title. One could then read the word "Hyperion" in the title *The Fall of Hyperion* figurally, or, if one wishes, intertextually, as referring not to the historical or mythological character but as referring to the title of Keats' own earlier text (*Hyperion*). But are we then telling the story of the failure of the first text as the success of the second, the Fall of *Hyperion* as the Triumph of *The Fall of Hyperion?* Manifestly, yes, but not quite, since the second text also fails to be concluded. Or are we telling the story of why all texts, as texts, can always be said to be falling? Manifestly yes, but not quite, either, since the story of the fall of the first version, as told in the second, applies to the first version only and could not legitimately be read as meaning also the fall of *The Fall of Hyperion.* The undecidability involves the figural or literal status of the proper name Hyperion as well as of the verb falling, and is thus a matter of figuration and not of grammar. In "Hyperion's Fall," the word "fall" is plainly figural, the representation of a figural fall, and we, as readers, read this fall standing up. But in "Hyperion Falling," this is not so clearly the case, for if Hyperion can be Apollo and Apollo can be Keats, then he can also be us and his figural (or symbolic) fall becomes his and our literal falling as well. The difference between the two readings is itself structured as a trope. And it matters a great deal how we read the title, as an exercise not only in semantics, but in what the text actually does to us. Faced with the ineluctable necessity to come to a decision, no grammatical or logical analysis can help us out. Just as Keats had to break off his narrative, the reader has to break off his understanding at the very moment when he is most directly engaged and summoned by the text. One could hardly expect to find solace in this "fearful symmetry" between the author's and reader's plight since, at this point, the symmetry is no longer a formal but an actual trap, and the question no longer "merely" theoretical.

This undoing of theory, this disturbance of the stable cognitive field that extends from grammar to logic to a general science of man and of the phenomenal world, can in its turn be made into a theoretical project of rhetorical analysis that will reveal the inadequacy of grammatical models of non-reading. Rhetoric, by its actively negative relationship to grammar and to logic, certainly undoes the claims of the *trivium* (and by extension, of language) to be an epistemologically stable construct. The resistance to theory is a resistance to the rhetorical or tropological dimension of language, a dimension which is perhaps more explicitly in the foreground in literature (broadly conceived) than in other verbal manifestations or—to be somewhat less vague—which can be revealed in any verbal event when it is read textually. Since grammar as well as figuration is an integral part of reading, it follows that reading will be a negative process in which the grammatical cognition is undone, at all times,

by its rhetorical displacement. The model of the *trivium* contains within itself the pseudo-dialectic of its own undoing and its history tells the story of this dialectic.

This conclusion allows for a somewhat more systematic description of the contemporary theoretical scene. This scene is dominated by an increased stress on reading as a theoretical problem or, as it is sometimes erroneously phrased, by an increased stress on the reception rather than on the production of texts. It is in this area that the most fruitful exchanges have come about between writers and journals of various countries and that the most interesting dialogue has developed between literary theory and other disciplines, in the arts as well as in linguistics, philosophy and the social sciences. A straightforward *report* on the present state of literary theory in the United States would have to stress the emphasis on reading, a direction which is already present, moreover, in the New Critical tradition of the forties and the fifties. The methods are now more technical, but the contemporary interest in a poetics of literature is clearly linked, traditionally enough, to the problems of reading. And since the models that are being used certainly are no longer *simply* intentional and centered on an identifiable self, nor *simply* hermeneutic in the postulation of a single originary, pre-figural and absolute text, it would appear that this concentration on reading would lead to the rediscovery of the theoretical difficulties associated with rhetoric. This is indeed the case, to some extent; but not quite. Perhaps the most instructive aspect of contemporary theory is the refinement of the techniques by which the threat inherent in rhetorical analysis is being avoided at the very moment when the efficacy of these techniques has progressed so far that the rhetorical obstacles to understanding can no longer be mistranslated in thematic and phenomenal commonplaces. The resistance to theory which, as we saw, is a resistance to reading, appears in its most rigorous and theoretically elaborated form among the theoreticians of reading who dominate the contemporary theoretical scene.

It would be a relatively easy, though lengthy process to show that this is so for theoreticians of reading who, like Greimas or, on a more refined level, Riffaterre or, in a very different mode, H. R. Jauss or Wolfgang Iser—all of whom have a definite, though sometimes occult influence on literary theory in this country—are committed to the use of grammatical models or, in the case of *Rezeptionsästhetik,* to traditional hermeneutic models that do not allow for the problematization of the phenomenalism of reading and therefore remain uncritically confined within a theory of literature rooted in aesthetics. Such an argument would be easy to make because, once a reader has become aware of the rhetorical dimensions of a text, he will not be amiss in finding textual instances that are irreducible to grammar or to historically determined meaning, provided only he is willing to acknowledge what he is bound to notice. The problem quickly becomes the more baffling one of having to account for the shared reluctance to acknowledge the obvious. But the argument would be lengthy because it has to involve a textual analysis that cannot avoid being somewhat elaborate; one can succinctly suggest the grammatical indetermination of a title such as *The Fall of Hyperion,* but to confront such an undecidable enigma with the critical reception and reading of Keats' text requires some space.

The demonstration is less easy (though perhaps less ponderous) in the case of the theoreticians of reading whose avoidance of rhetoric takes another turn. We have witnessed, in recent years, a strong interest in certain elements in language whose function is not only not dependent on any form of phenomenalism but on any form of cognition as well, and which thus excludes, or postpones, the consideration of tropes, ideologies, etc., from a reading that would be primarily performative. In some cases, a link is reintroduced between performance, grammar, logic, and stable referential meaning, and the resulting theories (as in the case of Ohmann) are not in essence distinct from those of avowed grammarians or semioticians. But the most astute practitioners of a speech act theory of reading avoid this relapse and rightly insist on the necessity to keep the actual performance of speech acts, which is conventional rather than cognitive, separate from its causes and effects—to keep, in their terminology, the illocutionary force separate from its perlocutionary function. Rhetoric, understood as persuasion, is forcefully banished (like Coriolanus) from the performative moment and exiled in the affective area of perlocution. Stanley Fish, in a masterful essay, convincingly makes this point. What awakens one's suspicion about this conclusion is that it relegates persuasion, which is indeed inseparable from rhetoric, to a purely affective and intentional realm and makes no allowance for modes of persuasion which are no less rhetorical and no less at work in literary texts, but which are of the order of persuasion by *proof* rather than persuasion by seduction. Thus to empty rhetoric of its epistemological impact is possible only because its tropological, figural functions are being bypassed. It is as if, to return for a moment to the model of the *trivium,* rhetoric could be isolated from the generality that grammar and logic have in common and considered as a mere correlative of an illocutionary power. The equation of rhetoric with psychology rather than with epistemology opens up dreary prospects of pragmatic banality, all the drearier if compared to the brilliance of the performative analysis. Speech act theories of reading in fact repeat, in a much more effective way, the grammatization of the *trivium* at the expense of rhetoric. For the characterization of the performative as sheer convention reduces it in effect to a grammatical code among others. The relationship between trope and performance is actually closer but more disruptive than what is here being proposed. Nor is this relationship properly captured by reference to a supposedly "creative" aspect of performance, a notion with which Fish rightly takes issue. The performative power of language can be called positional, which differs considerably from conventional as well as from "creatively" (or, in the technical sense, intentionally) constitutive. Speech act oriented theories of reading read only to the extent that they prepare the way for the rhetorical reading they avoid.

But the same is still true even if a "truly" rhetorical reading that would stay clear of any undue phenomenalization or of any undue grammatical or performative codification of the text could be conceived—something which is not necessarily impossible and for which the aims and methods of literary theory should certainly strive. Such a reading would indeed appear as the methodical undoing of the grammatical construct and, in its systematic disarticulation of the *trivium,* will be theoretically sound as well as effective. Technically correct rhetorical readings may be boring, monotonous, predictable and unpleasant, but they are irrefutable. They are also totalizing (and potentially totalitarian) for since the structures and functions they expose do not lead to the knowledge of an entity (such as language) but are an unreliable process of knowledge production that prevents all entities, including linguistic entities, from coming into discourse as such, they are indeed universals, consistently de-

fective models of language's impossibility to be a model language. They are, always in theory, the most elastic theoretical and dialectical model to end all models and they can rightly claim to contain within their own defective selves all the other defective models of reading-avoidance, referential, semiological, grammatical, performative, logical, or whatever. They are theory and not theory at the same time, the universal theory of the impossibility of theory. To the extent however that they are theory, that is to say teachable, generalizable and highly responsive to systematization, rhetorical readings, like the other kinds, still avoid and resist the reading they advocate. Nothing can overcome the resistance to theory since theory *is* itself this resistance. The loftier the aims and the better the methods of literary theory, the less possible it becomes. Yet literary theory is not in danger of going under; it cannot help but flourish, and the more it is resisted, the more it flourishes, since the language it speaks is the language of self-resistance. What remains impossible to decide is whether this flourishing is a triumph or a fall.

From Work to Text

ROLAND BARTHES

IT IS A FACT THAT over the last few years a certain change has taken place (or is taking place) in our conception of language and, consequently, of the literary work which owes at least its phenomenal existence to this same language. The change is clearly connected with the current development of (amongst other disciplines) linguistics, anthropology, Marxism and psychoanalysis (the term "connection" is used here in a deliberately neutral way: one does not decide a determination, be it

multiple and dialectical). What is new and which affects the idea of the work comes not necessarily from the internal recasting of each of these disciplines, but rather from their encounter in relation to an object which traditionally is the province of none of them. It is indeed as though the *interdisciplinarity* which is today held up as a prime value in research cannot be accomplished by the simple confrontation of specialist branches of knowledge. Interdisciplinarity is not the calm of

From Image, Music, Text, *trans. Steven Heath (New York: Farrar, Straus and Giroux, 1977). Reprinted by permission of the publisher.*

an easy security; it begins *effectively* (as opposed to the mere expression of a pious wish) when the solidarity of the old disciplines breaks down—perhaps even violently, via the jolts of fashion—in the interests of a new object and a new language neither of which has a place in the field of the sciences that were to be brought peacefully together, this unease in classification being precisely the point from which it is possible to diagnose a certain mutation. The mutation in which the idea of the work seems to be gripped must not, however, be over-estimated: it is more in the nature of an epistemological slide than of a real break. The break, as is frequently stressed, is seen to have taken place in the last century with the appearance of Marxism and Freudianism; since then there has been no further break, so that in a way it can be said that for the last hundred years we have been living in repetition. What History, our History, allows us today is merely to slide, to vary, to exceed, to repudiate. Just as Einsteinian science demands that *the relativity of the frames of reference* be included in the object studied, so the combined action of Marxism, Freudianism and structuralism demands, in literature, the relativization of the relations of writer, reader and observer (critic). Over against the traditional notion of the *work,* for long—and still—conceived of in a, so to speak, Newtonian way, there is now the requirement of a new object, obtained by the sliding or overturning of former categories. That object is the *Text.* I know the word is fashionable (I am myself often led to use it) and therefore regarded by some with suspicion, but that is exactly why I should like to remind myself of the principal propositions at the intersection of which I see the Text as standing. The word "proposition" is to be understood more in a grammatical than in a logical sense: the following are not argumentations but enunciations, "touches," approaches that consent to remain metaphorical. Here then are these propositions; they concern method, genres, signs, plurality, filiation, reading and pleasure.

1. The Text is not to be thought of as an object that can be computed. It would be futile to try to separate out materially works from texts.

In particular, the tendency must be avoided to say that the work is classic, the text avant-garde; it is not a question of drawing up a crude honours list in the name of modernity and declaring certain literary productions "in" and others "out" by virtue of their chronological situation: there may be "text" in a very ancient work, while many products of contemporary literature are in no way texts. The difference is this: the work is a fragment of substance, occupying a part of the space of books (in a library for example), the Text is a methodological field. The opposition may recall (without at all reproducing term for term) Lacan's distinction between "reality" and "the real": the one is displayed, the other demonstrated; likewise, the work can be seen (in bookshops, in catalogues, in exam syllabuses), the text is a process of demonstration, speaks according to certain rules (or against certain rules); the work can be held in the hand, the text is held in language, only exists in the movement of a discourse (or rather, it is Text for the very reason that it knows itself as text); the Text is not the decomposition of the work, it is the work that is the imaginary tail of the Text; or again, *the Text is experienced only in an activity of production*. It follows that the Text cannot stop (for example on a library shelf); its constitutive movement is that of cutting across (in particular, it can cut across the work, several works).

2. In the same way, the Text does not stop at (good) Literature; it cannot be contained in a hierarchy, even in a simple division of genres. What constitutes the Text is, on the contrary (or precisely), its subversive force in respect of the old classifications. How do you classify a writer like Georges Bataille? Novelist, poet, essayist, economist, philosopher, mystic? The answer is so difficult that the literary manuals generally prefer to forget about Bataille who, in fact, wrote texts, perhaps continuously one single text. If the Text poses problems of classification (which is furthermore one of its "social" functions), this is because it always involves a certain experience of limits (to take up an expression from Philippe Sollers). Thibaudet used already to talk—but in

a very restricted sense—of limit-works (such as Chateaubriand's *Vie de Rancé,* which does indeed come through to us today as a 'text'); the Text is that which goes to the limit of the rules of enunciation (rationality, readability, etc.). Nor is this a rhetorical idea, resorted to for some "heroic" effect: the Text tries to place itself very exactly *behind* the limit of the *doxa* (is not general opinion—constitutive of our democratic societies and powerfully aided by mass communications—defined by its limits, the energy with which it excludes, its *censorship*?). Taking the word literally, it may be said that the Text is always *paradoxical*.

3. The Text can be approached, experienced, in reaction to the sign. The work closes on a signified. There are two modes of signification which can be attributed to this signified: either it is claimed to be evident and the work is then the object of a literal science, of philology, or else it is considered to be secret, ultimate, something to be sought out, and the work then falls under the scope of a hermeneutics, of an interpretation (Marxist, psychoanalytic, thematic, etc.); in short, the work itself functions as a general sign and it is normal that it should represent an institutional category of the civilization of the Sign. The Text, on the contrary, practises the infinite deferment of the signified, is dilatory; its field is that of the signifier and the signifier must not be conceived of as "the first stage of meaning," its material vestibule, but, in complete opposition to this, as its *deferred action*. Similarly, the *infinity* of the signifier refers not to some idea of the ineffable (the unnameable signified) but to that of a *playing;* the generation of the perpetual signifier (after the fashion of a perpetual calendar) in the field of the text (better, of which the text is the field) is realized not according to an organic progress of maturation or a hermeneutic course of deepening investigation, but, rather, according to a serial movement of disconnections, overlappings, variations. The logic regulating the Text is not comprehensive (define "what the work means") but metonymic; the activity of associations, contiguities, carryings-over coincides with

a liberation of symbolic energy (lacking it, man would die); the work—in the best of cases—is *moderately* symbolic (its symbolic runs out, comes to a halt); the Text is *radically* symbolic: *a work conceived, perceived and received in its integrally symbolic nature is a text.* Thus is the Text restored to language; like language, it is structured but off-centered without closure (note, in reply to the contemptuous suspicion of the "fashionable" sometimes directed at structuralism, that the epistemological privilege currently accorded to language stems precisely from the discovery there of a paradoxical idea of structure: a system with neither close nor centre).

4. The Text is plural. Which is not simply to say that it has several meanings, but that it accomplishes the very plural of meaning: an *irreducible* (and not merely an acceptable) plural. The Text is not a co-existence of meanings but a passage, an overcrossing; thus it answers not to an interpretation, even a liberal one, but to an explosion, a dissemination. The plural of the Text depends, that is, not on the ambiguity of its contents but on what might be called the *stereographic plurality* of its weave of signifiers (etymologically, the text is a tissue, a woven fabric). The reader of the Text may be compared to someone at a loose end (someone slackened off from any imaginary); this passably empty subject strolls—it is what happened to the author of these lines, then it was that he had a vivid idea of the Text—on the side of a valley, a *oued* [French, meaning small stream] flowing down below (*oued* is there to bear witness to a certain feeling of unfamiliarity); what he perceives is multiple, irreducible, coming from a disconnected, heterogeneous variety of substances and perspectives: lights, colours, vegetation, heat, air, slender explosions of noises, scant cries of birds, children's voices from over on the other side, passages, gestures, clothes of inhabitants near or far away. All these *incidents* are half-identifiable: they come from codes which are known but their combination is unique, founds the stroll in a difference repeatable only as difference. So the Text: it can be it only in its difference (which does not mean

its individuality), its reading is semelfactive (thus rendering illusory any inductive-deductive science of texts—no "grammar" of the text) and nevertheless woven entirely with citations, references, echoes, cultural languages (what language is not?), antecedent or contemporary, which cut across it through and through in a vast stereophony. The intertextual in which every text is held, it itself being the text-between of another text, is not to be confused with some origin of the text: to try to find the "sources," the "influences" of a work, is to fall in with the myth of filiation; the citations which go to make up a text are anonymous, untraceable, and yet *already read:* they are quotations without inverted commas. The work has nothing disturbing for any monistic philosophy (we know that there are opposing examples of these); for such a philosophy, plural is the Evil. Against the work, therefore, the text could well take as its motto the words of the man possessed by demons (*Mark* 5: 9): "My name is Legion: for we are many." The plural of demoniacal texture which opposes text to work can bring with it fundamental changes in reading, and precisely in areas where monologism appears to be the Law: certain of the "texts" of Holy Scripture traditionally recuperated by theological monism (historical or anagogical) will perhaps offer themselves to a diffraction of meanings (finally, that is to say, to a materialist reading), while the Marxist interpretation of works, so far resolutely monistic, will be able to materialize itself more by pluralizing itself (if, however, the Marxist "institutions" allow it).

5. The work is caught up in a process of filiation. Are postulated: a *determination* of the work by the world (by race, then by History), a *consecution* of works amongst themselves, and a *conformity* of the work to the author. The author is reputed the father and the owner of his work: literary science therefore teaches *respect* for the manuscript and the author's declared intentions, while society asserts the legality of the relation of author to work (the "*droit d'auteur*" or "copyright," in fact of recent date since it was only really legalized at the time of the French Revolu-

tion). As for the Text, it reads without the inscription of the Father. Here again, the metaphor of the Text separates from that of the work: the latter refers to the image of an *organism* which grows by vital expansion, by "development" (a word which is significantly ambiguous, at once biological and rhetorical); the metaphor of the Text is that of the *network;* if the Text extends itself, it is as a result of a combinatory systematic (an image, moreover, close to current biological conceptions of the living being). Hence no vital "respect" is due to the Text: it can be *broken* (which is just what the Middle Ages did with two nevertheless authoritative texts—Holy Scripture and Aristotle); it can be read without the guarantee of its father, the restitution of the inter-text paradoxically abolishing any legacy. It is not that the Author may not "come back" in the Text, in his text, but he then does so as a "guest." If he is a novelist, he is inscribed in the novel like one of his characters, figured in the carpet; no longer privileged, paternal, aletheological, his inscription is ludic. He becomes, as it were, a paper-author: his life is no longer the origin of his fictions but a fiction contributing to his work; there is a reversion of the work on to the life (and no longer the contrary); it is the work of Proust, of Genet which allows their lives to be read as a text. The word "bio-graphy" re-acquires a strong, etymological sense, at the same time as the sincerity of the enunciation—veritable "cross" borne by literary morality—becomes a false problem: the *I* which writes the text, it too, is never more than a paper-*I*.

6. The work is normally the object of a consumption; no demagogy is intended here in referring to the so-called consumer culture but it has to be recognized that today it is the "quality" of the work (which supposes finally an appreciation of "taste") and not the operation of reading itself which can differentiate between books: structurally, there is no difference between "cultured" reading and casual reading in trains. The Text (if only by its frequent "unreadability") decants the work (the work permitting) from its consumption and gathers it up as play, activity,

production, practice. This means that the Text requires that one try to abolish (or at the very least to diminish) the distance between writing and reading, in no way by intensifying the projection of the reader into the work but by joining them in a single signifying practice. The distance separating reading from writing is historical. In the times of the greatest social division (before the setting up of democratic cultures), reading and writing were equally privileges of class. Rhetoric, the great literary code of those times, taught one to *write* (even if what was then normally produced were speeches, not texts). Significantly, the coming of democracy reversed the word of command: what the (secondary) School prides itself on is teaching to *read* (well) and no longer to write (consciousness of the deficiency is becoming fashionable again today: the teacher is called upon to teach pupils to "express themselves," which is a little like replacing a form of repression by a misconception). In fact, *reading,* in the sense of consuming, is far from *playing* with the text. "Playing" must be understood here in all its polysemy: the text itself *plays* (like a door, like a machine with "play") and the reader plays twice over, playing the Text as one plays a game, looking for a practice which re-produces it, but, in order that that practice not be reduced to a passive, inner *mimesis* (the Text is precisely that which resists such a reduction), also playing the Text in the musical sense of the term. The history of music (as a practice, not as an "art") does indeed parallel that of the Text fairly closely: there was a period when practising amateurs were numerous (at least within the confines of a certain class) and "playing" and "listening" formed a scarcely differentiated activity; then two roles appeared in succession, first that of the performer, the interpreter to whom the bourgeois public (though still itself able to play a little—the whole history of the piano) delegated its playing, then that of the (passive) amateur, who listens to music without being able to play (the gramophone record takes the place of the piano). We know that today post-serial music has radically altered the role of the "interpreter," who is called

on to be in some sort the co-author of the score, completing it rather than giving it "expression." The Text is very much a score of this new kind: it asks of the reader a practical collaboration. Which is an important change, for who executes the work? (Mallarmé posed the question, wanting the audience to *produce* the book). Nowadays only the critic executes the work (accepting the play on words). The reduction of reading to a consumption is clearly responsible for the "boredom" experienced by many in the face of the modern ("unreadable") text, the avant-garde film or painting: to be bored means that one cannot produce the text, open it out, *set it going*.

7. This leads us to pose (to propose) a final approach to the Text, that of pleasure. I do not know whether there has ever been a hedonistic aesthetics (eudaemonist philosophies are themselves rare). Certainly there exists a pleasure of the work (of certain works); I can delight in reading and re-reading Proust, Flaubert, Balzac, even—why not?—Alexandre Dumas. But this pleasure, no matter how keen and even when free from all prejudice, remains in part (unless by some exceptional critical effort) a pleasure of consumption; for if I can read these authors, I also know that I cannot *re-write* them (that it is impossible today to write "like that") and this knowledge, depressing enough, suffices to cut me off from the production of these works, in the very moment their remoteness establishes my modernity (is not to be modern to know clearly what cannot be started over again?). As for the Text, it is bound to *jouissance,* that is to a Pleasure without separation. Order of the signifier, the Text participates in its own way in a social utopia; before History (supposing the latter does not opt for barbarism), the Text achieves, if not the transparence of social relations, that at least of language relations: the Text is that space where no language has a hold over any other, where languages circulate (keeping the circular sense of the term).

These few propositions, inevitably, do not constitute the articulations of a Theory of the Text and this is not simply the result of the failings of the person here presenting them (who in many respects has anyway done no more than pick up what is being developed round about him). It stems from the fact that a Theory of the Text cannot be satisfied by a metalinguistic exposition: the destruction of meta-language, or at least (since it may be necessary provisionally to resort to meta-language) its calling into doubt, is part of the theory itself: the discourse on the Text should itself be nothing other than text, research, textual activity, since the Text is that *social* space which leaves no language safe, outside, nor any subject of the enunciation in position as judge, master, analyst, confessor, decoder. The theory of the Text can coincide only with a practice of writing.

Complexity and Contradiction in Architecture

ROBERT VENTURI

I LIKE COMPLEXITY AND contradiction in architecture. I do not like the incoherence or arbitrariness of incompetent architecture nor the precious intricacies of picturesqueness or expressionism. Instead, I speak of a complex and contradictory architecture based on the richness and ambiguity of modern experience, including that experience which is inherent in art. Everywhere, except in architecture, complexity and contradiction have been acknowledged, from Gödel's proof of ultimate inconsistency in mathematics to T. S. Eliot's analysis of "difficult" poetry and Joseph Albers' definition of the paradoxical quality of painting.

But architecture is necessarily complex and contradictory in its very inclusion of the traditional Vitruvian elements of commodity, firmness, and delight. And today the wants of program structure, mechanical equipment, and expression, even in single buildings in simple contexts, are diverse and conflicting in ways previously unimaginable. The increasing dimension and scale of architecture in urban and regional planning add to the difficulties. I welcome the problems and exploit the uncertainties. By embracing contradiction as well as complexity, I aim for vitality as well as validity.

Architects can no longer afford to be intimidated by the puritanically moral language of orthodox Modern architecture. I like elements which are hybrid rather than "pure," compromising rather than "clean," distorted rather than "straightforward," ambiguous rather than "articulated," perverse as well as impersonal, boring as well as "interesting," conventional rather than "designed," accommodating rather than excluding, redundant rather than simple, vestigial as well as innovating, inconsistent and equivocal rather than direct and clear. I am for messy vitality over obvious unity. I include the non sequitur and proclaim the duality.

I am for richness of meaning rather than clarity of meaning; for the implicit function as well as the explicit function. I prefer "both-and" to "either-or," black and white, and sometimes gray, to black or white. A valid architecture evokes many levels of meaning and combinations of focus: its space and its elements become readable and workable in several ways at once.

But an architecture of complexity and con-

From Complexity and Contradiction in Architecture (*New York: Museum of Modern Art, 1966). Reprinted by permission of the publisher.*

tradition has a special obligation toward the whole: its truth must be in its totality or its implications of totality. It must embody the difficult unity of inclusion rather than the easy unity of exclusion. More is not less.

Orthodox Modern architects have tended to recognize complexity insufficiently or inconsistently. In their attempt to break with tradition and start all over again, they idealized the primitive and elementary at the expense of the diverse and the sophisticated. As participants in a revolutionary movement, they acclaimed the newness of modern functions, ignoring their complications. In their role as reformers, they puritanically advocated the separation and exclusion of elements, rather than the inclusion of various requirements and their juxtapositions. As a forerunner of the Modern movement, Frank Lloyd Wright, who grew up with the motto "Truth against the World," wrote: "Visions of simplicity so broad and far-reaching would open to me and such building harmonies appear that . . . would change and deepen the thinking and culture of the modern world. So I believed." And Le Corbusier, co-founder of Purism, spoke of the "great primary forms" which, he proclaimed, were "distinct . . . and without ambiguity." Modern architects with few exceptions eschewed ambiguity.

But now our position is different: "At the same time that the problems increase in quantity, complexity, and difficulty they also change faster than before," and require an attitude more like that described by August Heckscher: "The movement from a view of life as essentially simple and orderly to a view of life as complex and ironic is what every individual passes through in becoming mature. But certain epochs encourage this development; in them the paradoxical or dramatic outlook colors the whole intellectual scene. . . . Amid simplicity and order rationalism is born, but rationalism proves inadequate in any period of upheaval. Then equilibrium must be created out of opposites. Such inner peace as men gain must represent a tension among contradictions and uncertainties. . . . A feeling for paradox allows seemingly dissimilar things to exist side by side, their very incongruity suggesting a kind of truth."

Rationalizations for simplification are still current, however, though subtler than the early arguments. They are expansions of Mies van der Rohe's magnificent paradox, "less is more." Paul Rudolph has clearly stated the implications of Mies' point of view: "All problems can never be solved. . . . Indeed it is a characteristic of the twentieth century that architects are highly selective in determining which problems they want to solve. Mies, for instance, makes wonderful buildings only because he ignores many aspects of a building. If he solved more problems, his buildings would be far less potent."

The doctrine "less is more" bemoans complexity and justifies exclusion for expressive purposes. It does, indeed, permit the architect to be "highly selective in determining which problems [he wants] to solve." But if the architect must be "committed to his particular way of seeing the universe," such a commitment surely means that the architect determines how problems should be solved, not that he can determine which of the problems he will solve. He can exclude important considerations only at the risk of separating architecture from the experience of life and the needs of society. If some problems prove insoluble, he can express this: in an inclusive rather than an exclusive kind of architecture there is room for the fragment, for contradiction, for improvisation, and for the tensions these produce. Mies' exquisite pavilions have had valuable implications for architecture, but their selectiveness of content and language is their limitation as well as their strength.

I question the relevance of analogies between pavilions and houses, especially analogies between Japanese pavilions and recent domestic architecture. They ignore the real complexity and contradiction inherent in the domestic program—the spatial and technological possibilities as well as the need for variety in visual experience. Forced simplicity results in oversimplification. In the Wiley House, for instance, in contrast to his glass house, Philip Johnson attempted to go beyond the simplicities of the elegant pavilion. He explicitly separated and articulated the enclosed "private functions" of living on a ground floor pedestal, thus separating them from the open so-cial functions in the modular pavilion above. But even here the building becomes a diagram of an oversimplified program for living—an abstract theory of either-or. Where simplicity cannot work, simpleness results. Blatant simplification means bland architecture. Less is a bore. . . .

Cleanth Brooks refers to Donne's art as "hav-ing it both ways" but, he says, "most of us in this latter day, cannot. We are disciplined in the tradi-tion either-or, and lack the mental agility—to say nothing of the maturity of attitude—which would allow us to indulge in the finer distinc-tions and the more subtle reservations permitted by the tradition of both-and." The tradition "either-or" has characterized orthodox modern architecture: a sun screen is probably nothing else; a support is seldom an enclosure; a wall is not violated by window penetrations but is to-tally interrupted by glass; program functions are exaggeratedly articulated into wings or segre-gated separate pavilions. Even "flowing space" has implied being outside when inside, and in-side when outside, rather than both at the same time. Such manifestations of articulation and clarity are foreign to an architecture of complex-ity and contradiction, which tends to include "both-and" rather than exclude "either-or."

If the source of the both-and phenomenon is contradiction, its basis is hierarchy, which yields several levels of meanings among elements with varying values. It can include elements that are both good and awkward, big and little, closed and open, continuous and articulated, round and square, structural and spatial. An architecture which includes varying levels of meaning breeds ambiguity and tension.

Most of the examples will be difficult to "read," but abstruse architecture is valid when it reflects the complexities and contradictions of content and meaning. Simultaneous perception of a multiplicity of levels involves struggles and hesitations for the observer, and makes his per-ception more vivid. . . .

Conventional elements in architecture repre-sent one stage in an evolutionary development, and they contain in their changed use and ex-pression some of their past meaning as well as their new meaning. What can be called the vesti-gial element parallels the double-functioning ele-ment. It is distinct from a superfluous element because it contains a double meaning. This is the result of a more or less ambiguous combination of the old meaning, called up by associations, with a new meaning created by the modified or new function, structural or programmatic, and the new context. The vestigial element discour-ages clarity of meaning: it promotes richness of meaning instead. It is a basis for change and growth in the city as manifest in remodeling which involves old buildings with new uses both programmatic and symbolic (like palazzi which become museums or embassies), and old street patterns with new uses and scales of movement. The paths of medieval fortification walls in Euro-pean cities became boulevards in the nineteenth century; a section of Broadway is a piazza and a symbol rather than an artery to upper New York state. The ghost of Dock Street in Philadelphia's Society Hill, however, is a meaningless vestige rather than a working element resulting from a valid transition between the old and the new. I shall later refer to the vestigial element as it ap-pears in Michelangelo's architecture and in what might be called Pop architecture.

The rhetorical element, like the double-functioning element, is infrequent in recent architecture. If the latter offends through its in-herent ambiguity, rhetoric offends orthodox Modern architecture's cult of the minimum. But the rhetorical element is justified as a valid if out-moded means of expression. An element can seem rhetorical from one point of view, but if it is valid, at another level it enriches meaning by un-derscoring. In the project for a gateway at Bourneville by Ledoux, the columns in the arch are structurally rhetorical if not redundant. Ex-pressively, however, they underscore the abstract-ness of the opening as a semicircle more than an arch, and they further define the opening as a gateway. As I have said, the stairway at the Penn-sylvania Academy of the Fine Arts by Furness is too big in its immediate context, but appropriate as a gesture towards the outside scale and a sense of entry. The Classical portico is a rhetorical entrance. The stairs, columns, and pediment are juxtaposed upon the other-scale, real entrance behind. Paul Rudolph's entrance in the Art and Architecture Building at Yale is at the scale of the city; most people use the little door at the side in the stair tower.

Much of the function of ornament is rhetorical—like the use of Baroque pilasters for rhythm, and Vanbrugh's disengaged pilasters at the entrance to the kitchen court at Blenheim which are an architectural fanfare. The rhetorical element which is also structural is rare in Modern architecture, although Mies has used the rhetorical I-beam with an assurance that would make Bernini envious.

A valid order accommodates the circumstantial contradictions of a complex reality. It accommodates as well as imposes. It thereby admits "control *and* spontaneity," "correctness *and* ease"—improvisation within the whole. It tolerates qualifications and compromise. There are no fixed laws in architecture, but not everything will work in a building or a city. The architect must decide, and these subtle evaluations are among his principal functions. He must determine what must be made to work and what it is possible to compromise with, what will give in, and where and how. He does not ignore or exclude inconsistencies of program and structure within the order.

I have emphasized that aspect of complexity and contradiction which grows out of the medium more than the program of the building. Now I shall emphasize the complexity and contradiction that develops from the program and reflects the inherent complexities and contradictions of living. It is obvious that in actual practice the two must be interrelated. Contradictions can represent the exceptional inconsistency that modifies the otherwise consistent order or they can represent inconsistencies throughout the order as a whole. In the first case, the relationship between inconsistency and order accommo-

dates circumstantial exceptions to the order, or it juxtaposes particular with general elements of order. Here you build an order up and then break it down, but break it from strength rather than from weakness. I have described this relationship as "contradiction accommodated." The relationship of inconsistency within the whole I consider a manifestation of "the difficult whole," which is discussed in the last chapter.

Mies refers to a need to "create order out of the desperate confusion of our times." But Kahn has said "by order I do not mean orderliness." Should we not resist bemoaning confusion? Should we not look for meaning in the complexities and contradictions of our times and acknowledge the limitations of systems? These, I think, are the two justifications for breaking order: the recognition of variety and confusion inside and outside, in program and environment, indeed, at all levels of experience; and the ultimate limitation of all orders composed by man. When circumstances defy order, order should bend or break: anomalies and uncertainties give validity to architecture.

Meaning can be enhanced by breaking the order: the exception points up the rule. A building with no "imperfect" part can have no perfect part, because contrast supports meaning. An artful discord gives vitality to architecture. You can allow for contingencies all over, but they cannot prevail all over. If order without expediency breeds formalism, expediency without order, of course, means chaos. Order must exist before it can be broken. No artist can belittle the role of order as a way of seeing a whole relevant to its own characteristics and context. "There is no work of art without a system" is Le Corbusier's dictum. . . .

Ironic convention is relevant both for the individual building and the townscape. It recognizes the real condition of our architecture and its status in our culture. Industry promotes expensive industrial and electronic research but not architectural experiments, and the Federal government diverts subsidies toward air transportation, communication, and the vast enterprises of war or, as they call it, national security, rather than toward the forces for the direct enhancement of life. The practicing architect must admit this. In simple terms, the budgets, techniques, and programs for his buildings must relate more to 1866 than 1966. Architects should accept their modest role rather than disguise it and risk what might be called an electronic expressionism, which might parallel the industrial expressionism of early Modern architecture. The architect who would accept his role as combiner of significant old clichés—valid banalities—in new contexts as his condition within a society that directs its best efforts, its big money, and its elegant technologies elsewhere, can ironically express in this indirect way a true concern for society's inverted scale of values.

I have alluded to the reasons why honky-tonk elements in our architecture and townscape are here to stay, especially in the important short-term view, and why such a fate should be acceptable. Pop Art has demonstrated that these commonplace elements are often the main source of the occasional variety and vitality of our cities, and that it is not their banality or vulgarity as elements which make for the banality or vulgarity of the whole scene, but rather their contextual relationships of space and scale.

Another significant implication from Pop Art involves method in city planning. Architects and planners who peevishly denounce the conventional townscape for its vulgarity or banality promote elaborate methods for abolishing or disguising honky-tonk elements in the existing landscape, or, for excluding them from the vocabulary of their new townscapes. But they largely fail either to enhance or to provide a substitute for the existing scene because they attempt the impossible. By attempting too much they flaunt their impotence and risk their continuing influence as supposed experts. Cannot the architect and planner, by slight adjustments to the conventional elements of the townscape, existing or proposed, promote significant effects? By modifying or adding conventional elements to still other conventional elements they can, by a twist of context, gain a maximum of effect through a minimum of means. They can make us see the same things in a different way.

Finally, standardization, like convention, can be another manifestation of the strong order. But unlike convention it has been accepted in Modern architecture as an enriching product of our technology, yet dreaded for its potential domination and brutality. But is it not standardization that is without circumstantial accommodation and without a creative use of context that is to be feared more than standardization itself? The ideas of order and circumstance, convention and context—of employing standardization in an undstandard way—apply to our continuing problem of standardization versus variety. Giedion has written of Aalto's unique "combination of standardization with irrationality so that standardization is no longer master but servant." I prefer to think of Aalto's art as contradictory rather than irrational—an artful recognition of the circumstantial and the contextual and of the inevitable limits of the order of standardization.

An architecture of complexity and accommodation does not forsake the whole. In fact, I have referred to a special obligation toward the whole because the whole is difficult to achieve. And I have emphasized the goal of unity rather than of simplification in an art "whose . . . truth [is] in its totality." It is the difficult unity through inclusion rather than the easy unity through exclusion. Gestalt psychology considers a perceptual whole the result of, and yet more than, the sum of its parts. The whole is dependent on the position, number, and inherent characteristics of the parts. A complex system in Herbert A. Simon's definition includes "a large number of parts that interact in a non-simple way." The difficult whole in an architecture of complexity and contradiction includes multiplicity and diversity of elements in relationships that are inconsistent or among the weaker kinds perceptually. . . .

Inherent in an architecture of opposites is the inclusive whole. The unity of the interior of the Imatra church or the complex at Wolfsburg is achieved not through suppression or exclusion but through the dramatic inclusion of contradictory or circumstantial parts. Aalto's architecture acknowledges the difficult and subtle conditions of program, while "serene" architecture, on the other hand, works simplifications.

However, the obligation toward the whole in an architecture of complexity and contradiction does not preclude the building which is unresolved. Poets and playwrights acknowledge dilemmas without solutions. The validity of the questions and vividness of the meaning are what make their works art more than philosophy. A goal of poetry can be unity of expression over resolution of content. Contemporary sculpture is often fragmentary, and today we appreciate Michelangelo's unfinished Pietàs more than his early work, because their content is suggested, their expression more immediate, and their forms are completed beyond themselves. A building can also be more or less incompleted in the expression of its program and its form.

The Gothic cathedral, like Beauvais, for instance, of which only the enormous choir was built, is frequently unfinished in relation to its program, yet it is complete in the effect of its form because of the motival consistency of its many parts. The complex program which is a process, continually changing and growing in time yet at each stage at some level related to a whole, should be recognized as essential at the scale of city planning. The incomplete program is valid for a complex single building as well.

Each of the fragmental twin churches on the Piazza del Popolo, however, is complete at the level of program but incomplete in the expression of form. The uniquely asymmetrically placed tower, as we have seen, inflects each building toward a greater whole outside itself. The very complex building, which in its open form is incomplete, in itself relates to Maki's "group form:" it is the antithesis of the "perfect single building" or the closed pavilion. As a fragment of a greater whole in a greater context this kind of building relates again to the scope of city planning as a means of increasing the unity of the complex whole. An architecture that can simulta-neously recognize contradictory levels should be able to admit paradox of the whole fragment: the building which is a whole at one level and a fragment of a greater whole at another level.

In *God's Own Junkyard* Peter Blake has compared the chaos of commercial Main Street with the orderliness of the University of Virginia. Besides the irrelevancy of the comparison, is not Main Street almost all right? Indeed, is not the commercial strip of a Route 66 almost all right? As I have said, our question is: what slight twist of context will make them all right? Perhaps more signs more contained. Illustrations in *God's Own Junkyard* of Times Square and roadtown are compared with illustrations of New England villages and arcadian countrysides. But the pictures in this book that are supposed to be bad are often good. The seemingly chaotic juxtapositions of honky-tonk elements express an intriguing kind of vitality and validity, and they produce an unexpected approach to unity as well.

It is true that an ironic interpretation such as this results partly from the change in scale of the subject matter in photographic form and the change in context within the frames of the photographs. But in some of these compositions there is an inherent sense of unity not far from the surface. It is not the obvious or easy unity derived from the dominant binder or the motival order of simpler, less contradictory compositions, but that derived from a complex and illusive order of the difficult whole. It is the taut composition which contains contrapuntal relationships, equal combinations, inflected fragments, and acknowledged dualities. It is the unity which "maintains, but only just maintains, a control over the clashing elements which compose it. Chaos is very near; its nearness, but its avoidance, gives . . . force." In the validly complex building or cityscape, the eye does not want to be too easily or too quickly satisfied in its search for unity within a whole.

Some of the vivid lessons of Pop Art, involving contradictions of scale and context, should have awakened architects from prim dreams of pure order, which, unfortunately, are imposed in the easy Gestalt unities of the urban renewal projects of establishment Modern architecture and yet, fortunately are really impossible to achieve at any great scope. And it is perhaps from the everyday landscape, vulgar and disdained, that we can draw the complex and contradictory order that is valid and vital for our architecture as an urbanistic whole.

B. Art and Postmodernity

In the Introduction to this book we discussed briefly and in very general terms some of the key distinctions between modernism and postmodernism. In this section we look specifically at several attempts to explain and defend the move from modernity to postmodernity, beginning in the 1950s. Our final selection in this section, Paul Crowther's "Postmodernism in the Visual Arts: A Question of Ends," provides an excellent introduction to postmodernism, integrating various strands of aesthetic and literary theory: the analytic perspective of Arthur Danto, several versions of modernism, contemporary art, deconstruction, postmodernism, Kant, Burke, and the sublime.

As we said in our introduction to Part III, modernism, along with the eighteenth- and nineteenth-century tradition of disinterested aesthetic experience, is under attack from all sides. In Part II we examined the Anglo-American analytic critique of the modern notion of aesthetic experience. But what has been happening since the 1950s on the continent of Europe, primarily among French thinkers?

Michel Foucault and Gilles Deleuze emerged from the French philosophical scene in the 1960s and their impact is still being assimilated inside and outside academics by writers, artists, and political and cultural leaders. Indeed, since the 1960s these thinkers have influenced the arts, humanities, and social sciences on both sides of the Atlantic. It would be difficult to underestimate their impact over the last three decades in American universities as whole disciplines were revolutionized, some changed focused and others, such as cultural studies or media studies, suddenly (or so it seemed) sprang up overnight guided by the work of these Continental theorists.

At the risk of oversimplifying each thinker's project, we may say that Foucault and Deleuze owe an enormous debt to Nietzsche's critique of truth (Part I, section B). In *The Genealogy of Morals* Nietzsche theorizes that instead of creating philosophical constructs to arrive at or lead us to an ideal (truth), we should focus on how we arrive at that truth, what that truth is, and why we need it and value it so much. Nietzsche asks us to consider: "In this connection let us glance at both the oldest and the most recent philosophers: to a man they lack all awareness that the will to truth itself needs to be justified." Nietzsche makes it clear that humans would rather make up and defend a fictitious "truth" than be without a foundational truth underlying all their endeavors: "man would sooner have the void for his purpose than be void of purpose." It is evident to Nietzsche that we need something that we hold as an eternal, independent standard, and so "truth," purpose or meaning, is actually a value. If truth is a value and not a principle or foundational principle, then truth has value only insofar as humans put value into the concept of truth or into individual or singular instances of truth.

Likewise, Deleuze and Foucault think that all truths are constructions made for certain philosophical, aesthetic, or even political ends. Truth, the idea or ideal, universals or the absolute (Hegel) are foundations that support a particular world view or system. According to Deleuze and Foucault, the moment that we rely on a system of thinking, a treatise or set of categorical principles, is the moment we stop thinking because we have thereby reduced thought, an artwork, or a literary text to a clichéd truth, idea or universal: heedless of the uniqueness or originality of the particular before us. What each philosopher develops in his own work is an attention to the particular, to the singular, and to difference. Each in his own way puts down the "logic of identity," which functions in Western thought to place the particular in an already established slot of identity. So, for example, when a new artist or writer comes along and seems to be doing something exciting and new, our first impulse, with the logic of identity, is to categorize (identify) that new artist and make her fit into a recognizable movement or school of artistic production. In this way, we only know what we already know. Foucault and Deleuze, as well as many other writers in Part III, find this impulse problematic.

Michel Foucault is concerned with the inability of Western thought to see itself as presenting anything other than the truth. Yet Foucault does not so much question the frame as he questions our ability to see at all. Foucault is most noted for his texts that ferret out the underside of history; in these texts, he shows that "official history" is just one version of the event or time period, and that for every history written there are several alternative versions. In terms of art or art history, Foucault shows us that what we see is only what we are able to see, given the constraints of the era's *episteme* (i.e., way of thinking about the world, and thought itself). So in looking at art of the past, for example, we see again and again certain conventions, such as the king and queen representing power or the throne, or other conventions of style and content. In both cases, Foucault would say that we are limited, first by our historical knowledge of conventions—both socially and painterly—and, second, by what we already know in the present. For Foucault states very clearly in *The Archeology of Knowledge* that the past is always written, or rewritten, for some purpose in the present. We only have to think of certain countries in the world that have rewritten the history of their country in accord with the current political regime: the former Soviet Union is an example. But more disturbing is not the fact that, of course, we can rewrite history, but at some point we will decide "what really happened" and record it. No. And this is Foucault's point: history is invented—we do not have access to the past and even if we did, how would we retell history so that it would not be contaminated by our own world view, language, and episteme? Indeed, supposing we *could* write history exactly as it really happened in the past, no one today would be interested—since today we have our own interests and concerns in terms of which we want to understand yesterday's news.

In any given age only certain things can be seen; Foucault states in *The Archeology* that phenomena (e.g., ways of thinking, social data, or physical conditions) are "invisible but not hidden." The problem, as with Derrida (Part III, section C), is that we do not—and cannot—know how to frame or know how to see what we do not have the ability to see. This idea may seem frustrating because it seems that we can only see our own blindnesses—which is no sight at all. Yet if we think beyond our own limitations, then we can also see—from a more positive angle—that Foucault's idea contains within it not only the potential to refashion the past, but also the ability to see the present differently. In other words, in the attempt to think beyond our inherited episteme, we are thinking something potentially new and different. Moreover, by seeing certain ways of thinking as only one way of thinking, we can see that truth is relative and relational.

In the selection from *This Is Not a Pipe,* at first it may be difficult to discern Foucault's point because he gives us an example that is so incredibly simple. The painting that is a pipe is not, of course, a pipe, but a representation of a pipe. Also, in "The Two Mysteries" we understand that "this is not a pipe," but a representation of *two* pipes. So what is the point? Foucault is toying with our own inability to see beyond the obvious and his little joke (along with Magritte's compliance) is on our Western episteme, which, in this case, goes back to Plato. In the *Republic* (see Part I) Plato is careful to create a hierarchy: the Form of the bed exists in ultimate reality (and is, hence, unknowable to ordinary human perception) and is the highest "bed," down a rung to the actual bed upon which one could sleep (which is based on the model in ultimate reality), to the lowest rung on this hierarchy—the representation of the bed by the artist (a representation of the actual bed). What Plato takes care to maintain is the authority of the original bed, the Form, because invested in the original is Truth. Where would we find a "true" bed? In ultimate reality, of course.

Foucault's subtle criticism is that the entire episteme of the West since Plato has privileged the "original" over the copy and the truth over falsity. What Magritte's paintings indicate is that there is no original pipe—and even if there were an original, we would have to have some way to designate it in our world. So one way to interpret the floating pipe in "The Two Mysteries" may be to see it as Plato's unknowable Form of pipe; yet we are immediately struck by the irony of the situation: any way to speak or to show the Form of pipe must be through representation—either in language or pictorially (Magritte does both). The pipe represented on the easel in every way represents the floating pipe—it seems to lack nothing. According to Plato, however, it lacks the truth of authenticity because it is not the original. Hence, we might also immediately be struck by the idea that this particular way of thinking in terms hierarchal models is a bit suspect. First, how can we "know" a realm of true Forms that is imperceptibly beyond space and time? Second, why should we privilege the original over the copy? Indeed, how will we know the difference? If we abandoned the hierarchical model, then it would seem that we must also abandon the model of primacy. Abandoning the episteme of primacy means that it no longer matters which is the original and which is copy.

The "overturning of Platonism" is also one of Gilles Deleuze's major philosophical projects. Deleuze employs different strategies from text to text to undermine traditional systems of thought, but in *The Logic of Sense* he focuses on undermining the Platonic hierarchy of truth. According to Deleuze, Plato himself knew that his system of Forms was vulnerable, which is part of the reason in his dialogues he continually feels the need to stress the authority of the Form—of "justice" or "virtue," for instance. The Sophists made Plato nervous because, from his perspective, they did not seek truth (the Form or universal) in their discourses, but instead only sought through rhetorical means a pragmatic and therefore to Plato a superficial truth. In others words, their truths, according to Plato, were those welded in everyday language and, hence, copies or bad copies of the Form (twice removed from the Form, as we saw in Part I); yet what is obvious to Deleuze is that Plato also welds his so-called truths in everyday (Greek) language—twice removed from ultimate reality. Plato tried to reformulate traditional Greek moral and political authority in terms of eternal, universal and absolute Forms, as a way of deflecting the Sophists' attempt to reduce morality to cultural relativism. Deleuze exposes Plato's fear that the universal or Form will not be revered, that Sophists will begin proliferating bad copies (their own practical ideas of what works), and the authority of the hierarchy will be undermined. As long as the state philosopher can maintain the hierarchy of universal truth, then the status quo in both thought and politics will be maintained.

The desire to break free from the notion of state philosophy and his uncompromising attention to difference are a couple of the reasons Deleuze is a self-proclaimed "nomad." According to Deleuze, the nomadic philosopher or thinker not only thinks outside preestablished systems of thought but also does not create his or her own system of thought. Deleuze uses the metaphor of a toolbox: certain paradigms of thought may be useful for a while; if not, abandon them and select another tool from the toolbox of philosophy. In this way, the very idea of one universal, overarching philosophy, eternally justifying a single moral and political standard, is not only archaic to Deleuze, but simply absurd and quickly rendered obsolete.

This nomadic thought spills over into Deleuze's text on the twentieth-century painter Francis Bacon, from which the following excerpt is taken. Deleuze, following Bacon, prizes "figure" over "figuration" because the figure is nonrepresentational and draws its power from the immediate impact of sheer sensation, while figuration relies on representation—on matching the identity of an object with that on the canvas (the "logic of identity"). On one hand, the sheer clash of colors on the canvas can excite our senses; on the other hand, the identification of a mountain represented in the painting may inspire us with feelings of grandeur. Deleuze also picks up on Bacon's use of the term *diagram,* a term Deleuze happens to utilize himself elsewhere, to talk about the open plane of the canvas as a place where sensation and thought happen: "The diagram is thus the operative set of lines and area, of asignifying and nonrepresentational brush strokes and daubs of color. And the operation of the diagram, its function, as Bacon says, is to 'suggest.'" With the "screaming pope" (p. 232) the suggestion of terror does not come from some aspect representationally painted. Even the figure of the pope with his straining mouth wide open is not in itself horrible but would normally represent the Holy Father surprised, for example, or in pain. Of course, we identify the figure in the painting representationally as the pope and we can see the pope's open mouth. But there is something else at work on Bacon's canvas. Deleuze states that it is a rip, an aberration, or a "catastrophe" on the canvas working against or in some way thwarting the figuration. According to Deleuze, pure abstract painting like that of Barnett Newman (p. 336) does not produce the sensation of the diagram; rather, abstract painting is like a code that one learns how to read. In contrast, Bacon's paintings retain elements of figuration, reuniting with human life or feeling just long enough to almost feel "safe," only to be violently ripped out of a normal context and thrust into a shockingly new space: the space of the diagram.

The final reading of this section, Paul Crowther's "Postmodernism in the Visual Arts: A Question of Ends," contextualizes a major question that plagues the art historian, theorist, or aesthetician at this time: Is art dead? In Hegel's dialectic (Part I), art eventually evolves into philosophy, resulting in the "birth" of philosophy and the "death" of art. In the 1960s Arthur Danto used Hegel's idea of the "death of art" to talk about radically new developments in the art of that time (1960s Conceptual Art pieces, such as an artist illegally driving on an unfinished freeway). Danto, as we read in Part II, theorizes that cinema caused art to turn away from the world—away from mimesis—and into itself, or into investigations of itself. Echoing Hegel, he maintains that art has become aesthetics, art criticism and philosophy of art! According to Danto, "the search for art's essence" ends in 1964 when Warhol displayed his *Brillo Boxes* for the first time. After the brillo boxes came soup cans and Minimal and Conceptual Art in the 1960s and 1970s, but Danto claims that all these movements were really only re-iterations from previous moves to conceptualize or reconceptualize the essence of art. The essence of art is finally that which the institution (art galleries, critics, and buyers) says it is: if pieces of driftwood washed ashore are picked up and put into an exclusive New York City art gallery and called "art," then they are indeed art. This example may seem radical, but Duchamp did basically the same thing in 1917 by putting the urinal in the art gallery and calling it *The Fountain,* so in similar ways the driftwood example is playing out a game started over eighty years ago. It would seem that Danto is correct: art has reached its endgame.

Crowther, however, disagrees with Danto by stating that the break with modernism does not mean art is dead. First and foremost, Crowther does not see contemporary art as playing or replaying modernist configurations; instead, he sees contemporary art as *post*modern—as going beyond or past the modernist project. Second, art is not dead, it is just different than before, and so it can longer be interpreted from standard modernist paradigms. According to Crowther, one thing that has not changed is that all art has a "legitimizing discourse" that in modern art "is some kind of elevating experience [aesthetic experience] embodied in its creation and reception." In postmodern art the legitimizing discourse deconstructs the very idea of a legitimizing discourse "by incorporating (in an apparently unmediated fashion) that which is most directly antithetical to high art, namely mechanically reproduced imagery; or by the thematizing (within a particular work) the inadequacy of artistic categories, and, indeed, art's inability to express the complexities and catastrophes of concrete historical experience." But, according to Crowther, this inability to express as found in Malcolm Morley's or Anselm Keifer's paintings, for example (p. 245), produces Kant's paralogical or Burke's "jolt" of the aesthetic sublime (Longinus, Burke, and Kant in Part I and Lyotard in the last section of the book), and hence the new legitimizing discourse in postmodern art.

This Is Not a Pipe

MICHEL FOUCAULT

THE FIRST VERSION, THAT of 1926 I believe: a carefully drawn pipe, and underneath it (handwritten in a steady, painstaking, artificial script, a script from the convent, like that found heading the notebooks of schoolboys, or on a blackboard after an object lesson), this note: "This is not a pipe."

The other version—the last, I assume—can be found in *Aube à l'Antipodes*. The same pipe, same statement, same handwriting. But instead of being juxtaposed in a neutral, limitless, unspecified space, the text and the figure are set within a frame. The frame itself is placed upon an easel, and the latter in turn upon the clearly visible slats of the floor. Above everything, a pipe exactly like the one in the picture, but much larger.

The first version disconcerts us by its very simplicity. The second multiplies intentional ambiguities before our eyes. Standing upright against the easel and resting on wooden pegs, the frame indicates that this is an artist's painting: a finished work, exhibited and bearing for an eventual view the statement that comments upon or explains it. And yet this naive handwriting, neither precisely the work's title nor one of its pictorial elements; the absence of any other trace of the artist's presence; the roughness of the ensemble; the wide slats of the floor—everything suggests a blackboard in a classroom. Perhaps a swipe of the rag will soon erase the drawing and the text. Perhaps it will erase only one or the other, in order to correct the "error" (drawing something that will truly not be a pipe, or else writing a sentence affirming that this indeed is a pipe). A temporary slip (a "mis-writing" suggesting a misunderstanding) that one gesture will dissipate in white dust?

But this is still only the least of the ambiguities; here are some others. There are two pipes. Or rather must we not say, two drawings of the same pipe? Or yet a pipe and the drawing of that pipe, or yet again two drawings each representing a different pipe? Or two drawings, one representing a pipe and the other not, or two more drawings yet, of which neither the one nor the other are or represent pipes? Or yet again, a drawing representing not a pipe at all but another drawing, itself representing a pipe so well that I must ask myself: To what does the sentence written in the painting relate? "See these lines assembled on the blackboard—vainly do they resemble, without the least digression or infidelity, what is displayed above them. Make no mistake; the pipe is overhead, not in this childish scrawl."

Yet perhaps the sentence refers precisely to the disproportionate, floating, ideal pipe—simple notion or fantasy of a pipe. Then we should have to read, "Do not look overhead for a true pipe. That is a pipe dream. It is the drawing within the painting, firmly and rigorously outlined, that must be accepted as a manifest truth."

But it still strikes me that the pipe represented in the drawing—blackboard or canvas, little matter—this "lower" pipe is wedged solidly in a space of visible reference points: width (the written text, the upper and lower borders of the frame); height (the sides of the frame, the easel's mounts); and depth (the grooves of the floor). A stable prison. On the other hand, the higher pipe lacks coordinates. Its enormous proportions render uncertain its location (an opposite effect to that found in *Tombeau des lutteurs*, where the gigantic is caught inside the most precise space). Is

From This Is Not a Pipe, *trans. W. Harkness (Berkeley, CA: University of California Press, 1983).*
Reprinted by permission of the publisher.

René Magritte, *La Trahison des Images,* 1935

the disproportionate pipe drawn in front of the painting, which itself rests far in back? Or indeed is it suspended just above the easel like an emanation, a mist just detaching itself from the painting—pipe smoke taking the form and roundness of a pipe, thus opposing and resembling the pipe (according to the same play of analogy and contrast found between the vaporous and the solid in the series *La Bataille de l'Argonne*)? Or might we not suppose, in the end, that the pipe floats behind the painting and the easel, more gigantic than it appears? In that case it would be its uprooted depth, the inner dimension rupturing the canvas (or panel) and slowly, in a space henceforth without reference point, expanding to infinity?

About even this ambiguity, however, I am ambiguous. Or rather what appears to me very dubious is the simple opposition between the higher pipe's dislocated buoyancy and the stability of the lower one. Looking a bit more closely, we easily discern that the feet of the easel, sup-porting the frame where the canvas is held and where the drawing is lodged—these feet, resting upon a floor made safe and visible by its own coarseness, are in fact beveled. They touch only by three tiny points, robbing the ensemble, itself somewhat ponderous, of all stability. An impending fall? The collapse of easel, frame, canvas or panel, drawing, text? Splintered wood, fragmented shapes, letters scattered one from another until words can perhaps no longer be reconstituted? All this litter on the ground, while above, the large pipe without measure or reference point will linger in its inaccessible, balloon-like immobility?

Magritte's drawing (for the moment I speak only of the first version) is as simple as a page borrowed from a botanical manual: a figure and the text that names it. Nothing is easier to recognize than a pipe, drawn thus; nothing is easier to say—our language knows it well in our place—than the "name of a pipe." Now, what lends the figure its strangeness is not the "con-

René Magritte, *Les Deux Mystères*, 1966

tradition" between the image and the text. For a good reason: Contradiction could exist only between two statements, or within one and the same statement. Here there is clearly but one, and it cannot be contradictory because the subject of the proposition is a simple demonstrative. False, then, because its "referent"—obviously a pipe—does not verify it? But who would seriously contend that the collection of intersecting lines above the text *is* a pipe? Must we say: My God, how simpleminded! The statement is perfectly true, since it is quite apparent that the drawing representing the pipe is not the pipe itself. And yet there is a convention of language: What is this drawing? Why, it is a calf, a square, a flower. An old custom not without basis, because the entire function of so scholarly, so academic a drawing is to elicit recognition, to allow the object it represents to appear without hesitation or equivocation. No matter that it is the material deposit, on a sheet of paper or a blackboard, of a little graphite or a thin dust of chalk. It does not

"aim" like an arrow or a pointer toward a particular pipe in the distance or elsewhere. It *is* a pipe.

What misleads us is the inevitability of connecting the text to the drawing (as the demonstrative pronoun, the meaning of the word *pipe*, and the likeness of the image all invite us to do here)—and the impossibility of defining a perspective that would let us say that the assertion is true, false, or contradictory.

I cannot dismiss the notion that the sorcery here lies in an operation rendered invisible by the simplicity of its result, but which alone can explain the vague uneasiness provoked. The operation is a calligram that Magritte has secretly constructed, then carefully unraveled. Each element of the figure, their reciprocal position and their relation derive from this process, annulled as soon as it has been accomplished. Behind this drawing and these words, before anyone has written anything at all, before the formation of the picture (and within it the drawing of the pipe), before the large, floating pipe has appeared—we must assume, I believe, that a calligram has formed, then unraveled. There we have evidence of failure and its ironic remains.

In its millennial tradition, the calligram has a triple role: to augment the alphabet, to repeat something without the aid of rhetoric, to trap things in a double cipher. First it brings a text and a shape as close together as possible. It is composed of lines delimiting the form of an object while also arranging the sequence of letters. It lodges statements in the space of a shape, and makes the text *say* what the dreaming *represents*. On the one hand, it alphabetizes the ideogram, populates it with discontinuous letters, and thus interrogates the silence of uninterrupted lines. But on the other hand, it distributes writing in a space no longer possessing the neutrality, openness, and inert blankness of paper. It forces the ideogram to arrange itself according to the laws of a simultaneous form. For the blink of an eye, it reduces phoneticism to a mere grey noise completing the contours of the shape; but it renders outline as a thin skin that must be pierced in order to follow, word for word, the outpouring of its internal text.

The calligram is thus tautological. But in opposition to rhetoric. The latter toys with the fullness of language. It uses the possibility of repeating the same thing in different words, and profits from the extra richness of language that allows us to say different things with a single word. The essence of rhetoric is in allegory. The calligram uses that capacity of letters to signify both as linear elements that can be arranged in space and as signs that must unroll according to a unique chain of sound. As a sign, the letter permits us to fix words; as line, it lets us give shape to things. Thus the calligram aspires playfully to efface the oldest oppositions of our alphabetical civilization: to show and to name; to shape and to say; to reproduce and to articulate; to imitate and to signify; to look and to read.

Pursuing its quarry by two paths, the calligram sets the most perfect trap. By its double function, it guarantees capture, as neither discourse alone nor a pure drawing could do. It

banishes the invincible absence that defeats words, imposing upon them, by the ruses of a writing at play in space, the visible form of their referent. Cleverly arranged on a sheet of paper, signs invoke the very thing of which they speak—from outside, by the margin they outline, by the emergence of their mass on the blank space of the page. And in return, visible form is excavated, furrowed by words that work at it from within, and which, dismissing the immobile, ambiguous, nameless presence, spin forth the web of significations that christen it, determine it, fix it in the universe of discourse. A double trap, unavoidable snare: How henceforth would escape the flight of birds, the transitory form of flowers, the falling rain?

And now Magritte's drawings. Let us begin with the first and simplest. It seems to be created from the fragments of an unraveled calligram. Under the guise of reverting to a previous arrangement, it recovers its three functions—but in order to pervert them, thereby disturbing all the traditional bonds of language and the image.

After having invaded the figure in order to reconstitute the old ideogram, the text has now resumed its place. It has returned to its natural site—below the image, where it serves to support it, name it, explain it, decompose it, insert it in the series of texts and in the pages of the book. Once more it becomes a "legend." Form itself reascends to the ethereal realm from which the complicity of letters with space had forced it for an instant to descend. Free from all discursive attachment, it can float anew in its natural silence. We return to the page, and to its old principle of distribution—but only apparently. Because the words we now can read underneath the drawing are themselves drawn—images of words the painter has set apart from the pipe, but within the general (yet still undefinable) perimeter of the picture. I must read them superimposed upon themselves. They are words drawing words; at the surface of the image, they form the reflection of a sentence saying that this is not a pipe. The image of a text. But conversely, the represented pipe is drawn by the same hand and with the same pen as the letters of the text: it extends the writing more than it illustrates it or fills its void. We might imagine it brimming with small, chaotic letters, graphic signs reduced to fragments and dispersed over the entire surface of the image. A figure in the shape of writing. The invisible, preliminary calligraphic operation intertwined the writing and the drawing: and when Magritte restored things to their own places, he took care that the shape would preserve the patience of writing and that the text remain always only a drawing of a representation.

The same for tautology. From calligraphic doubling, Magritte seemingly returns to the simple correspondence of the image with its legend. Without saying anything, a mute and adequately recognizable figure displays the object in its essence; from the image, a name written below receives its "meaning" or rule for usage. Now, compared to the traditional function of the legend, Magritte's text is doubly paradoxical. It sets out to name something that evidently does not need to be named (the form is too well known, the label too familiar). And at the moment when he should reveal the name, Magritte does so by denying that the object is what it is. Whence comes this strange game, if not from the calligram? From the calligram that says things twice (when once would doubtless do); from the calligram that shuffles what it says over what it shows to hide them from each other. For the text to shape itself, for all its juxtaposed signs to form a dove, a flower, or a rainstorm, the gaze must refrain from any possible reading. Letters must remain points, sentences lines, paragraphs surfaces or masses—wings, stalks, or petals. The text must say nothing to this gazing subject who is a viewer, not a reader. As soon as he begins to read, in fact, shape dissipates. All around the recognized word and the comprehended sentence, the other graphisms take flight, carrying with them the visible plenitude of shape and leaving only the linear, successive unfurling of meaning—not one drop of rain falling after another, much less a feather or a torn-off leaf. Despite appearances, in forming a bird, a flower, or rain,

the calligram does not say: These things *are* a dove, a flower, a downpour. As soon as it begins to do so, to speak and convey meaning, the bird has already flown, the rain has evaporated. For whoever sees it, the calligram *does not say, cannot yet say:* This is a flower, this is a bird. It is still too much trapped within shape, too much subject to representation by resemblance, to formulate such a proposition. And when we read it, the deciphered sentence ("this is a dove," "this is a rainstorm") *is not* a bird, is no longer a shower. By ruse or impotence, small matter—the calligram never speaks and represents at the same moment. The very thing that is both seen and read is hushed in the vision, hidden in the reading.

Magritte redistributed the text and the image in space. Each regains its place, but not without keeping some of the evasiveness proper to the calligram. The drawn form of the pipe is so easily recognized that it excludes any explanatory or descriptive text. Its academic schematicism says very explicitly, "You see me so clearly that it would be ridiculous for me to arrange myself so as to write: This is a pipe. To be sure, words would draw me less adequately than I represent myself." And in this sketch representing handwriting, the text in turn prescribes: "Take me for what I manifestly am—letters placed beside one another, arranged and shaped so as to facilitate reading, assure recognition, and open themselves even to the most stammering schoolboy. I do not claim to swell, then stretch, becoming first the bowl, then the stem of the pipe. I am no more than the words you are now reading." Against one another in the calligram are pitted a "not yet to say" and a "no longer to represent." In Magritte's *Pipe*, the birthplace of these negations is wholly different from the point where they are applied. The "not yet to say" returns not exactly in an affirmation, but in a double position. On the one hand, overhead, the polished, silent, visible shape, on whose proud and disdainful evidence the text is allowed to say whatever it pleases. On the other hand, below, the text, displayed according to its intrinsic law, affirms its own autonomy in regard to what it names. The

calligram's redundance rested on a relation of exclusion. In Magritte, the separation of the two
elements, the absence of letters in the drawing,
the negation expressed in the text—all of these
positively manifest two distinct positions.

But I have neglected, I fear, what is perhaps
essential to Magritte's *Pipe*. I have proceeded as
if the text said, "I (the ensemble of words you are
now reading) am not a pipe." I have gone on as
if there were two simultaneously and clearly differentiated positions within the same space: the
figure's and the text's. But I have omitted that
from one position to the other a subtle and in-
stable dependency, at once insistent and unsure,
is indicated. And it is indicated by the word
"this." We must therefore admit between the figure and the text a whole series of intersections—
or rather attacks launched by one against the
other, arrows shot at the enemy target, enterprises of subversion and destruction, lance blows
and wounds, a battle. For example, "this" (the
drawing, whose form you doubtless recognize
and whose calligraphic heritage I have just
traced) "is not" (is not substantially bound
to . . . , is not constituted by . . . , does not cover
the same material as . . .) "a pipe" (that is, this
word from your language, made up of pro-
nounceable sounds that translate the letters you
are reading). Therefore, *This is not a pipe* can be
read thus:

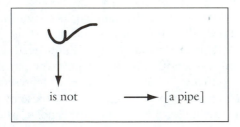

But at the same time, the text states an entirely different proposition: "This" (the statement arranging itself beneath your eyes in a line
of discontinuous elements, of which *this* is both
the signifier and the first word) "is not" (could
neither equal nor substitute for . . . , could not
adequately represent . . .) "a pipe" (one of the
objects whose possible rendering can be seen

above the text—interchangeable, anonymous,
inaccessible to any name). Then we must read:

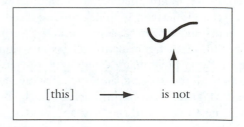

Now, on the whole it easily seems that
Magritte's statement is negated by the immediate
and reciprocal dependency between the drawing
of the pipe and the text by which the pipe can be
named. Designation and design do not overlap
one another, save in the calligraphic play hover-
ing in the ensemble's background and conjured
away simultaneously by the text, the drawing,
and their current separation. Hence the third
function of the statement: "This" (this ensemble
constituted by a written pipe and a drawn text)
"is not" (is incompatible with) "a pipe" (this
mixed element springing at once from discourse
and the image, whose ambiguous being the verbal and visual play of the calligram wants to
evoke).

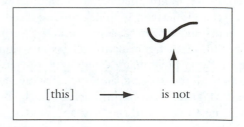

Magritte reopened the trap the calligram had
sprung on the thing it described. But in the act,
the object itself escaped. On the page of an illustrated book, we seldom pay attention to the
small space running above the words and below
the drawings, forever serving them as a common
frontier. It is there, on these few millimeters of
white, the calm sand of the page, that are established all the relations of designation, nomination, description, classification. The calligram absorbed that interstice; but once opened, it does
not restore it. The trap shattered on emptiness:

image and text fall each to its own side, of their own weight. No longer do they have a common ground nor a place where they can meet, where words are capable of taking shape and images of entering into lexical order. The slender, colorless, neutral strip, which in Magritte's drawing separates the text and the figure, must be seen as a crevasse—an uncertain, foggy region now dividing the pipe floating in its imagistic heaven from the mundane tramp of words marching in their successive line. Still it is too much to claim that there is a blank or lacuna: instead, it is an absence of space, an effacement of the "common place" between the signs of writing and the lines of the image. The "pipe" that was at one with both the statement naming it and the drawing representing it—this shadow pipe knitting the lineaments of form with the fiber of words—has utterly vanished. A disappearance that from the other side of this shallow stream the text confirms with amusement: This is not a pipe. In vain the now solitary drawing imitates as closely as possible the shape ordinarily designated by the word *pipe;* in vain the text unfurls below the drawing with all the attentive fidelity of a label in a scholarly book. No longer can anything pass between them save the decree of divorce, the statement at once contesting the name of the drawing and the reference of the text.

Nowhere is there a pipe.

On this basis, we can understand Magritte's second version of *This Is Not a Pipe.* In placing the drawing of the pipe and the statement serving as its legend on the very clearly defined surface of a picture (insofar as it is a painting, the letters are but the image of letters; insofar as it is a blackboard, the figure is only the didactic continuation of a discourse), in placing the picture on a thick, solid wood tripod, Magritte does everything necessary to reconstruct (either by the permanence of a work of art or else by the truth of an object lesson) the space common to language and the image.

Everything is solidly anchored within a pedagogic space. A painting "shows" a drawing that "shows" the form of a pipe; a text written by a zealous instructor "shows" that a pipe is really

what is meant. We do not see the teacher's pointer, but it rules throughout—precisely like his voice, in the act of articulating very clearly, "This is a pipe." From painting to image, from image to text, from text to voice, a sort of imaginary pointer indicates, shows, fixes, locates, imposes a system of references, tries to stabilize a unique space. But why have we introduced the teacher's voice? Because scarcely has he stated, "This is a pipe," before he must correct himself and stutter, "This is not a pipe, but a drawing of a pipe," "This is not a pipe but a sentence saying that this is not a pipe," "The sentence 'this is not a pipe' is not a pipe," "This is not a pipe but a sentence saying that this is not a pipe," "The sentence 'this is not a pipe' is not a pipe," "In this sentence 'this is not a pipe,' *this* is not a pipe: the painting, written sentence, drawing of a pipe—all this is not a pipe."

Negations multiply themselves, the voice is confused and choked. The baffled master lowers his extended pointer, turns his back to the board, regards the uproarious students, and does not realize that they laugh so loudly because above the blackboard and his stammered denials, a vapor has just risen, little by little taking shape and now creating, precisely and without doubt, a pipe. "A pipe, a pipe," cry the students, stamping away while the teacher, his voice sinking ever lower, murmurs always with the same obstinacy though no one is listening, "And yet it is not a pipe." He is not mistaken; because the pipe floating so obviously overhead (like the object the blackboard drawing refers to, and in whose name the text can justifiably say that the drawing is truly not a pipe) is itself merely a drawing. It is *not* a pipe. No more on the board than above it, the drawing of the pipe and the text presumed to name it find nowhere to meet and be superimposed, as the calligrapher so presumptuously had attempted to bring about.

So, on its beveled and clearly rickety mounts, the easel has but to tilt, the frame to loosen, the painting to tumble down, the words to be scattered. The "pipe" can "break": The common place—banal work of art or everyday lesson—has disappeared.

Nomad Philosophy of Art

GILLES DELEUZE

THERE ARE TWO WAYS of transcending figuration (whether illustrative or narrative): toward abstract form or toward figure. Cézanne alluded to the way toward figure by the term *sensation*. Figure is the sensible form related to sensation; it acts immediately on the nervous system which is of the flesh. Abstract form on the other hand is directed to the brain, and acts through the brain, closer to the bone. Certainly Cézanne did not invent the path of sensation in painting, but he gave it an unprecedented status. Sensation is the opposite of the facile, the ready-made, and the cliché, but also of the "sensational," the spontaneous, etc. One face of sensation is turned toward the subject (the nervous system, vital movement, "instinct," "temperament," an entire vocabulary which is common to both naturalism and Cézanne); the other face is turned toward the object ("the fact," the place, the event). Or rather, sensation has no faces at all, it is indissolubly both things, it is being-in-the-world, in the phenomenological sense. At the same time, I *become* in sensation, and something *happens* through sensation, one through the other and one in the other. And, in the last analysis, it is the same body which, being both subject and object, gives and receives sensation. As a spectator, I experience sensation only by entering the painting and by having access to the unity of the sensing and the sensed. This is Cézanne's lesson that goes beyond impressionism: sensation is not the "free" or disembodied play of light and color (impressions), rather sensation is in the body, even if this is the body of an apple. Color and sensation are in the body, and not in the sky. Sensation is that which is painted. That which is painted in the painting is the body, not insofar as

it is represented as object but insofar as it is lived as experiencing a particular sensation (what Lawrence, in discussing Cézanne, called "the being-apple [*l'être pommesque*] of the apple").

This is the general thread that links Bacon to Cézanne: *to paint sensation* or, as Bacon says, using words that closely resemble Cézanne's, to record the fact. "It's a very, very close and difficult thing to know why some paint comes across directly onto the nervous system." We might say that there are only obvious differences between these two painters: Cézanne's world as landscape and still lives, even before the portraits that are treated as landscapes; and the inverse hierarchy in Bacon, which gives up still lives and landscapes. The world of nature of Cézanne and the world as artifact for Bacon. But precisely, should not these very obvious differences be ascribed to "sensation" and "temperament," in other words, should they not be inscribed within that which links Bacon to Cézanne, or within that which is common to both? When Bacon speaks of sensation, he means two things that are very close to what Cézanne meant. Negatively, he says that form as it relates to sensation (figure) is the opposite of form as it relates to an object that the form is supposed to represent (figuration). According to Valéry's words, sensation is that which is directly transmitted and which avoids the detour and the boredom of a story to be told. And positively, Bacon continually says that sensation is that which passes from one "order" to another, from one "level" to another, or from one "domain" to another. This is why sensation is the master of deformations or rather the agent of bodily deformations. In this respect, we can make the same criticism of figurative and of ab-

From The Deleuze Reader, *trans. Constantin Boundas and Jacqueline Code (New York: Columbia University Press, 1993). Reprinted by permission of the publisher.*

stract painting: they pass through the brain, they do not act directly upon the nervous system, they do not have access to sensation, they do not liberate the figure—all of this as a result of the fact that they remain at *one and the same level*. They can bring about transformations or form but they do not achieve bodily deformations. We will have the opportunity to see exactly how much Cézannian Bacon is, even more so than if he were a disciple of Cézanne.

What does Bacon mean in his interviews when he speaks of "orders of sensation," "sensitive levels," "sensible domains," or "moving sequences"? We might initially believe that a specified sensation corresponds to each order, level, or domain: each sensation would thus be one term in a sequence or in a series. For example, Rembrandt's series of self-portraits carries us along into different sensible domains. And it is true that painting, and especially Bacon's painting, proceeds through series: series of crucifixions, series of the pope, series of portraits, series of self-portraits, series of the mouth, of the mouth which screams or smiles. . . . Moreover, the series can be one of simultaneity, as in the case of the triptychs that make at least three orders or levels coexist. The series can be closed when it has a contrasting composition, but it can be open when it is continued or continuable beyond three. All of this is true. But the point is that it would not be true if there were not something else as well which already applies to each painting, figure, or sensation.

Each painting or figure is a moving sequence or a series (and not only one term within a series). Each sensation is at diverse levels, of different orders or in several domains. Therefore, there are not sensations of different orders but, rather, different orders of one and the same sensation. It is characteristic of sensation to encompass a constitutive difference of level and a plurality of constituting domains. Every sensation and every figure is already an "accumulated" or "coagulated" sensation like a figure in limestone. Hence the irreducibly synthetic character of sensation. We can ask henceforth where this synthetic character

comes from, by virtue of which each material sensation has several levels, orders, or domains. What are these levels and what makes up their sensing and sensed unity?

A first response must obviously be rejected. That which would make up the material and synthetic unity of sensation would be the represented object, or the thing which is figured. This is theoretically impossible since figure is opposed to figuration. But even if we observe practically, as Bacon does, that something is nevertheless figured (for example, a screaming pope), this secondary figuration rests on the neutralization of every primary figuration. Bacon himself formulates this problem, which concerns the inevitable retention of a practical figuration at the moment when figure affirms its intention to break away from the figurative. We will see how he resolves this problem. In any case, Bacon has always wanted to eliminate the "sensational," that is, the primary figuration of that which provokes a violent sensation. This is what the following expression means: "I wanted to paint the scream more than the horror." When he paints the screaming pope, there is nothing that causes horror, and the curtain in front of the pope is not only a way of isolating and shielding him from view; it is rather the way in which the pope himself sees nothing and screams *in the presence of the invisible*. Being neutralized, the horror is multiplied because it is induced from the scream, and not vice versa. Certainly, it is not easy to renounce the horror, or the primary figuration. It is sometimes necessary to turn against our own instincts and to renounce our experience. Bacon carries all the violence of Ireland with him, as well as the violence of Nazism and the violence of war. He goes through the horror of the crucifixions, and especially of the fragment of crucifixion, of the head-meat or of the bleeding suitcase. But when he judges his own paintings, he turns away from all those that are too "sensational," because the figuration that subsists in them reconstitutes, albeit secondarily, a scene of horror, and from then on reintroduces a story to be told: even bullfights are too dramatic. As soon as horror is present, a

Francis Bacon, *Study after Velásquez's Portrait of Pope Innocent X*, 1953

story is reintroduced, and we botched the scream. In the last analysis, the maximum of violence will be in the sitting or crouching figures which are not undergoing any torture or brutality, to whom nothing visible is happening and which realize even better the power of the painting. The reason for this is that violence has two very different meanings: "When talking about the violence of paint, it's nothing to do with the violence of war." To the violence of that which is represented (the sensational, the cliché) the violence of sensation is opposed. The latter is identical with its direct action upon the nervous system, the levels through which it passes and the domains which it traverses: being itself figure, it owes nothing to the nature of the object which is figured. It is as in Artaud: cruelty is not what we believe, and it depends less and less on that which is represented.

A second interpretation must also be rejected, which would confuse the levels of sensation, that is, the valencies of sensation, with an ambivalence of feeling. Sylvester suggests at one moment that "since you talk about recording different levels of feeling in one image . . . you may be expressing at one and the same time a love and a hostility towards them . . . both a caress and an assault." To which, Bacon responds that this is "too logical. I don't think that's the way things work. I think it goes to a deeper thing: how do I feel I can make this image more immediately real to myself? That's all." In fact, the psychoanalytic hypothesis of ambivalence has not only the disadvantage of localizing sensation in the spectator who looks at the painting; even if we presuppose an ambivalence of figure itself, it would involve feelings that the figure would experience in relation to the represented things or in relation to a story being told. Now there are no feelings in Bacon's work. There is nothing but affects, that is, "sensations" and "instincts" according to the formula of naturalism. And sensation is that which determines the instinct at a particular moment, just as the instinct is the passage from one sensation to another, the search for the "best" sensation (not the most agreeable, but the one

that fills the flesh at a particular moment of its descent, contraction, or dilation).

There is a third, more interesting hypothesis. This is the motor hypothesis. The levels of sensation would be like arrests or snapshots of motion synthetically recomposing the movement in its continuity, speed, and violence: for example, synthetic cubism, futurism, or Duchamp's *Nude*. And it is true that Bacon is fascinated by the decompostions of movement in Muybridge and makes use of them as his material. It is also true that he obtains in his work violent movements of great intensity, such as the 180 degree turn of George Dyer's head towards Lucian Freud. And more generally, Bacon's figures are often frozen in the middle of a strange stroll: for example, *Man carrying a child* or the *Van Gogh*. The insulation of the figure, the circle and the parallelepiped, themselves become motors, and Bacon does not renounce the project that a mobile sculpture would achieve more easily: in this case, the contour or base can be moved along the armature so that the figure goes for a daily "stroll." But it is precisely the nature of this stroll that can inform us of the status of movement in Bacon's work. Never have Beckett and Bacon been closer to each other, and this is a stroll after the fashion of the strolls of Beckett's characters, who also trundle along without departing from their circle or parallelepiped. It is the stroll of the paralytic child and his mother clinging onto the edge of the balustrade in a curious race for the handicapped. It is the about-face of *The Turning Figure*. It is George Dyer's bicycle ride, which resembles closely that of Moritz's hero: "the vision was limited to the small piece of ground that he could see around him . . . the end of all things seemed to him to be at the end of his race *toward a certain point*." Therefore, even when the contour is displaced, movement is less this displacement than the amoebian exploration through which figure surrenders itself to the contour. Movement does not explain sensation; it is rather explained by the elasticity of sensation, by its *vis elastica*. According to Beckett's or Kafka's law, there is immobility beyond movement:

beyond standing up, there is sitting down, and beyond sitting down, lying down in order to be finally dissipated. The true acrobat is the one who is immobile within the circle. The large feet of the figures often do not lend themselves to walking; they are almost clubfeet (and armchairs sometimes seem to resemble shoes for clubfeet). In short, it is not movement that explains the levels of sensation; rather levels of sensation explain that which subsists of movement. And, in fact, Bacon is not exactly interested in movement, although his painting makes movement very intense and violent. But, in the last analysis, it is a movement in one place or a spasm that reveals an entirely different problem characteristic of Bacon: *the action of invisible forces on the body* (hence, the bodily deformations for which this more profound cause is responsible). In the 1973 triptych the movement of translation occurs between two spasms, between two movements of contraction in one place.

There may still be another, "phenomenological," hypothesis. The levels of sensation would really be sensible domains referring to different sensory organs; but precisely each level, each domain would have a way of referring to others, independently of their common represented object. Between a color, a taste, a touch, a smell, a noise, a weight, there would be an existential communication that would constitute the (nonrepresentative) moment of "pathos" of *the* sensation. For example, in Bacon's *Bullfights* we hear the hoofbeats of the animal; in the 1976 triptych we touch the quivering of the bird that plunges into the place where the head should be, and each time that meat is represented, we touch it, smell it, eat it, weigh it, just like in Soutine's work; and the portrait of Isabel Rawthorne causes a head to emerge to which ovals and features are added in order to widen the eyes, enlarge the nostrils, lengthen the mouth, and mobilize the skin in a joint exercise of all organs at once. It is thus the painter's task to *make us see* a kind of original unity of the senses and to make a multisensible figure appear visibly. But this operation is only possible if the sensation of a particular domain

(here, visual sensation) directly seizes a vital power that overflows all domains and traverses them. This power is rhythm, which is deeper than vision, hearing, etc. And rhythm appears as music when it invests the auditory level, and as painting when it invests the visual level.

This is the "logic of the senses" as Cézanne said, which is neither rational, nor cerebral. The ultimate then is the relation between rhythm and sensation, which places in each sensation the levels and domains through which it passes. And this rhythm runs through a painting as it runs through music. It is diastole-systole: the world that captures me by closing in on me, the "ego" that opens to the world and opens the world to itself. It is said of Cézanne that he placed a precisely vital rhythm in visual sensation. Must we say the same thing about Bacon, with his coexistence of movements when the flat tint closes on figure and when figure contracts or rather expands in order to rejoin the flat tint, to the point of merging with it? Could it be that Bacon's artificial and closed world reveals the same vital movement as Cézanne's nature? These are not empty words, when Bacon declares that he is cerebrally pessimistic, but nervously optimistic, with an optimism that only believes in life. Is this the same temperament as Cézanne's? Bacon's formula would then be figuratively pessimistic, yet figurally optimistic. . . .

We do not listen enough to what painters say. They say that the painter is *already* in the canvas. Here, he encounters all the figurative and probabilistic data that occupy and preoccupy the canvas. An entire battle occurs in the canvas between the painter and his data. There is thus preparatory work that fully belongs to painting and that nevertheless precedes the act of painting. This preparatory work may take the form of sketches, but not necessarily, and even sketches do not replace it (Bacon, like many contemporary painters, does not make sketches). This preparatory work is invisible and silent, but nevertheless very intense. Therefore, the act of painting emerges as an *après-coup* (hysteresis) in relation to this work.

What is this act of painting? Bacon defines it as follows: making marks at random (brushstrokes-lines); cleaning, sweeping, or wiping places or areas (daubs-color); throwing paint at varied angles and speeds. Now this act (or acts) presuppose that there are already figurative data on the canvas (and also within the painter's head) that are more or less virtual or more or less actual. These data will be precisely demarcated, cleaned, swept, and wiped, or covered over, by the act of painting. For example, we lengthen a mouth, we make it go from one side of the head to the other; we clean part of a head with a brush, a scrubbing brush, a sweeping brush, or a rag. This is what Bacon calls a *Diagram;* it is as if, all of a sudden, we introduce a Sahara, a Sahara region in the head; it is as if we stretched over it a rhinoceros skin seen through a microscope; it is as if we tore apart two parts of the head by means of an ocean; it is as if we changed the unit of measurement and replaced figurative units with micrometric or even cosmic units. A Sahara, a rhinoceros skin, this is the diagram suddenly stretched out. It is like a *catastrophe* happening unexpectedly to the canvas, inside figurative or probablistic data.

It is like the emergence of another world. For these marks or brushstrokes are irrational, involuntary, accidental, free, and random. They are nonrepresentative, nonillustrative, and nonnarrative. No longer are they significative or signifying: they are asignifying features. They are features of sensation, but of confused sensations (the confused sensations we bring with us when we are born, as Cézanne said). And above all, they are manual features. It is here that the painter works with a rag, brushes, scrubbing brush, or sweeping brush: it is here that he throws paint with his hands. It is as if the hand assumed an independence and passed into the service of other forces, tracing marks that no longer depend on our will or on our vision. These almost blind, manual marks reveal the intrusion of another world into the visual world of figuration. To some extent, they remove the painting from the optical organization that al-

ready governed it, and made it figurative in advance. The painter's hand is interposed in order to shake its own dependence and to break up the sovereign, optical organization: we can no longer see anything, as in a catastrophe or chaos.

This is the act of painting or the turning point of the painting. There are indeed two ways in which the painting can fail, once visually and once manually. We can remain entangled in figurative data and in the optical organization of representation, but we can also fail with the diagram, spoil it, overload it to such an extent that it is rendered inoperative (this is another way of remaining within the figurative: we will have mutilated or mistreated the cliché). The diagram is thus the operative set of lines and areas, of asignifying and nonrepresentative brushstrokes and daubs of color. And the operation of the diagram, its function, as Bacon says, is to "suggest." Or, more rigorously, it is the introduction of "possibilities of fact": an expression that resembles Wittgenstein's language. Brushstrokes and daubs of color must break away from figuration all the more since they are destined to give us figure. This is why they themselves are not sufficient; they must be "utilized": they outline possibilities of fact, but do not yet constitute a fact (pictorial fact). In order to be converted into fact, in order to evolve into figure, they must be reinjected into the visual whole; but thus, precisely, under the influence of these marks, the visual whole is no longer that of an optical organization; it would give the eye a different power, as well as an object which would no longer be figurative.

The diagram is the operative set of brushstrokes and daubs of color, lines, and areas. For example, the diagram of Van Gogh: it is the set of straight and curved cross-hatchings that raises and lowers the ground, twists the trees, makes the sky palpitate and that assumes a particular intensity from 1888 onward. We cannot only differentiate diagrams but also date the diagram of a painter, because there is always a moment when the painter confronts it more directly. The diagram is indeed a chaos, a catastrophe, but also a seed of order and of rhythm. It is a violent chaos in relation to the figurative data, but it is a seed of rhythm in relation to the new order of painting: as Bacon says, it "unlock[s] areas of sensation." The diagram completes the preparatory work and begins the act of painting. There is no painter who does not make this experiment of the chaos-seed where she no longer sees anything and risks floundering: the breakdown of visual coordinates. This is not a psychological experiment but a properly pictorial experiment, although it can have a great influence on the psychic life of a painter. Here, the painter faces the greatest dangers for her work and for herself. It is a kind of experiment always recommended by different painters: Cézanne's "abyss" or "catastrophe" and the possibility that this abyss will make room for rhythm; Paul Klee's "chaos," the vanishing "gray point," and the possibility that this gray point will "leap over itself" and open up dimensions of sensation. Of all the arts, painting is undoubtedly the only one that necessarily and "hysterically" integrates its own catastrophe and is constituted therefore as a flight forward. In the other arts, the catastrophe is only associated. But the painter moves through catastrophe, he embraces chaos and attempts to leave it behind. Where painters differ is in their manner of embracing this nonfigurative chaos, in their evaluation of the pictorial order to come, and of the relation of this order with this chaos. In this respect, we could perhaps distinguish three great paths: each one groups very different painters together but also designates a "modern" function of painting or states what painting claims to bring to "modern man" (why is there still painting today?).

Abstraction would be one of these paths, but a path that reduces the abyss or chaos, as well as the manual, to a minimum: it proposes an asceticism or spiritual salvation. By means of an intense spiritual effort, it is elevated above figurative data, but it also makes chaos a mere stream we must cross in order to discover the abstract and signifying forms. Mondrian's square emerges from the figurative (landscape) and leaps over

chaos. From this leap, it retains a kind of oscillation. Such an abstraction is essentially seen. We would like to say, about abstract painting, the same thing that Péguy said about Kantian morality: it has pure hands, but it does not have hands. Abstract forms belong to a new, purely optical space that no longer even needs to be subordinate to manual or tactile elements. They are distinguished, in fact, from uniquely geometric forms by "tension": tension is that which internalizes in the visual the manual movement that describes the form and the invisible forces that determine it. It is that which makes form a purely visual transformation. Thus, the abstract optical space no longer requires the tactile connotations that were still being organized by classical representation. But then it follows that abstract painting, on the basis of great formal oppositions, develops a symbolic *code* rather than a diagram. It replaces the diagram with a code. This code is "digital," not in the sense of manual but in the sense of a finger that counts. "Digits" are indeed units that visually group together terms in opposition. For example, according to Kandinsky, vertical-white-activity, horizontal-black-intertia, etc. Hence, there emerges a conception of binary choice that is opposed to random choice. Abstract painting has pursued extensively the development of such a properly pictorial code (Herbin's "plastic alphabet," where the distribution of forms and colors can be carried out according to the letters of a word). The code is responsible for answering the question of painting today: what is it that can save man from the abyss, that is, the external tumult and the manual chaos? This amounts to opening a spiritual state for the man of the future without hands and to giving him a pure, internal, optical space made up perhaps exclusively of the horizontal and the vertical. "Modern man seeks tranquillity because he is deafened by the outside." The hand is reduced to the finger that presses on an internal optical keyboard.

A second path, which has often been called abstract expressionism or informal art, proposes an entirely different response in the antipodes.

This time, the abyss or chaos is deployed to a maximum degree. Being a bit like a map that is as big as the country, the diagram merges with the entire painting, and the entire painting is the diagram. Optical geometry breaks down in favor of a line that is exclusively manual. The eye finds it difficult to follow. In fact, the incomparable discovery of this kind of painting is one of a line (and a daub of color) that does not form a contour, which demarcates nothing, either internal or external, either concave or convex: Pollock's line, Morris Louis's daub of color. It is the northern daub of color, the "gothic line": the line does not run from one point to another, but rather passes *between* the points, continually changes direction, and attains a power superior to *1,* becoming adequate to the entire surface. We understand that, from this point of view, abstraction remains figurative since its line still demarcates a contour. If we seek the forerunners of this new path and of this radical way of escaping the figurative, we will find them each time that an old great painter ceases painting things in order "to paint between things." Turner's last watercolors already conquer not only the forces of impressionism but also the power of an unequaled catastrophe (instead of illustrating catastrophe romantically). Is it not also one of the most phenomenal constants of painting that is isolated and selected here? For Kandinsky, there were nomadic lines without contour next to abstract geometric lines; and for Mondrian, the unequal thickness of the two sides of the square opened up a virtual diagonal without contour. But with Pollock, this brushstroke-line and color-daub reach the limit of their function: no longer the transformation of the form but rather a decomposition of the matter that yields to us its lineaments and granulations. Thus, painting becomes a catastrophe-painting and a diagram-painting at the same time. This time, it is at the closest point to catastrophe, and in absolute proximity, that modern man finds rhythm: we can easily see to what extent the response to the question of a "modern" function of painting is different from that of abstraction. Now internal

vision no longer provides infinity but rather the extension of an *all-over* manual power from one edge of the painting to the other.

In the unity of the catastrophe and the diagram, man discovers rhythm as matter and material. The painter no longer has as his instruments the paintbrush and the easel, which used to translate the subordination of the hand to the demands of an optical organization. The hand is liberated, using sticks, sponges, rags, and syringes: such is action painting, the "frenetic dance" of the painter around the painting, or rather in the painting which is not stretched onto the easel but rather nailed unstretched onto the floor. A conversion of the horizon to the ground has taken place: the optical horizon has entirely reverted to a tactile ground. The diagram expresses all painting at once, that is, the optical catastrophe and the manual rhythm. And the current evolution of abstract expressionism completes this process by actualizing what was still only a metaphor in Pollock's work: (1) the extension of the diagram to the spatial and temporal totality of the painting (displacement of the "*avant-coup*" and the "*après-coup*"); (2) the abandonment of any visual sovereignty, and even of any visual control, over the painting in the process of being created (blindness of the painter); (3) development of lines that are "more" than lines, surfaces that are "more" than surfaces or, conversely, volumes that are "less" than volumes (Carl André's plane sculptures, Ryman's fibers, Barré's laminated works, Bonnefoi's strata).

It is even more curious that the American critics, who have analyzed so extensively this abstract expressionism, have defined it by the creation of a purely and exclusively optical space, characteristic of "modern man." It seems that this is a quarrel over words, an ambiguity of words. What is meant, in fact, is that the pictorial space has lost all its imaginary, tactile referents that allowed us, in classical three-dimensional representation, to see depths and contours, forms and grounds. But these tactile referents in classical representation expressed a relative subordination of the hand to the eye, of the manual to the visual. In liberating a space that is taken (wrongly) to be purely optical, the abstract expressionists, in fact, only reveal an exclusively manual space, defined by the plane surface of the canvas, the "impenetrability" of the scene, the "gesturality" of the color. This space is imposed upon the eye as a completely foreign power in which the eye finds no peace. We are no longer confronted with tactile referents of vision, but, since it is the manual space of that which is seen, we are faced with a violent act upon the eye. We could almost say it is abstract painting that produces a purely optical space and suppresses tactile referents in favor of an eye of the mind: it suppresses the task of directing the hand that the eye retained in classical representation. But action painting does something entirely different: it overturns this classical subordination, it subordinates the eye to the hand, it imposes the hand upon the eye, and it replaces the horizon with a ground.

One of the most profound tendencies of modern painting is the tendency to abandon the easel. For the easel was a decisive element not only in the retention of a figurative appearance, not only in the relation of the painter with nature (the quest for motif), but also in the demarcation (frame and edges) and in the internal organization of the scene (depth, perspective . . .). Now what counts today is less the fact—does the painter still have an easel?—than the tendency and the diverse ways in which the tendency is realized. In the abstractions of Mondrian, the painting ceases to be an organism or an isolated organization, in order to become a division of its own surface that must create relations with the divisions of the "room" where it will be placed. It is in this sense that Mondrian's painting is by no means decorative, but rather architechtonic, and that it abandons the easel in order to become mural painting. Pollock and others explicitly impugn the easel in an entirely different manner: this time, they create "all-over" paintings by rediscovering the secret of the Gothic line (in Worringer's sense), by restoring an entire world of equal probabilities, by tracing lines that go

from one edge of the painting to the other and that begin and continue outside the frame, and by opposing the power of a mechanical repetition elevated to intuition, to organic symmetry and center. The result is no longer an easel painting; it is rather a ground painting (real horses have the ground as their only horizon). But in truth, there are many ways of breaking away from the easel: Bacon's triptych form is one of these ways, which is very different from the two previous ones; in his work, what is true of the triptychs is also true for each independent painting, which is always in some sense composed like a triptych. In the triptych, as we have seen, the edges of the three scenes no longer isolate, although they continue to separate and divide: there is a union-separation, which is Bacon's technical solution and which, in fact, affects the totality of his procedures in their difference from those of abstraction and the unformed. Are these three ways of becoming "Gothic" again?

The importance lies, in fact, in the reason Bacon did not become involved in either one of the previous paths. The severity of his reactions does not pretend to be judgmental, but rather to state what does not suit Bacon; this explains why Bacon does not take either of these paths. On one hand, he is not attracted by a kind of painting that tends to substitute a spiritual, visual code for the involuntary diagram (even if this is an exemplary attitude of the artist). The code is necessarily cerebral and misses sensation, the essential reality of the fall, that is, the direct action on the nervous system. Kandinsky defined abstract painting by "tension," but, according to Bacon, tension is that which is most lacking in abstract painting: by internalizing it in the optical form, abstract painting neutralized it. And finally, by virtue of being abstract, the code risks being a simple symbol coding of the figurative. On the other hand, Bacon is no more attracted by abstract expressionism or by the power and the mystery of the line without contour. This is because, he says, the diagram has taken over the entire painting, and its proliferation creates a veritable "mess." All the violent means of action painting—stick, brush, broom, rag, and even pastry syringe—explode in a painting-catastrophe: this time, sensation is indeed attained, but it remains in an irredeemably confused state. Bacon continually discusses the absolute necessity of preventing the diagram from proliferating, the necessity of keeping it in certain areas of the painting and in certain moments of the act of painting. He thinks that, in the domain of the irrational stroke and the line without contour, Michaux goes further than Pollock, precisely because he maintains his mastery of the diagram.

There is nothing more important for Bacon than saving contour. A line that demarcates nothing still has a contour. Blake at least knew this. The diagram should not, therefore, engulf the entire painting; it should remain limited in space and time. It should remain operative and controlled. Violent means should not be unleashed, and the necessary catastrophe should not submerge everything. The diagram is a possibility of fact—it is not the fact itself. Not all fig-

urative data should disappear, and especially, a new figuration, that of figure, should emerge from the diagram and carry sensation to the clear and the precise. Emerge from the catastrophe. . . . Even if we finish with a stream of paint afterward, it is like a localized "crack of the whip," which makes us emerge rather than sink. Could we say that the "*malerisch*" period at least extended the diagram to the entire painting? Is it not the entire surface of the painting that is lined with brushstrokes or with variations of a somber color-daub functioning as a curtain? But even so, the precision of sensation, the clarity of figure, and the rigor of contour continued to act upon the blob of color or beneath the strokes that did not erase them; it rather gave them a power of vibration and illocalization (the smiling or screaming mouth). Bacon's subsequent period returns to a random localization of strokes and cleaned areas. Thus, Bacon follows a third path, neither optical as in abstract painting, nor manual as in action painting.

Postmodernism in the Visual Arts

PAUL CROWTHER

THE QUESTION OF POSTMODERNISM in the visual arts has been dominated by a number of themes, notably the idea that art, its history, and its theory, have come to an end; and that Postmodernism is largely the product of a force external to art—namely, the market. It might be argued that, for the most part, these themes have been set forth and received with rather more enthusiasm than understanding (the works of Victor Burgin are perhaps a case in point here). However, in the writings of the philosopher and

art critic Arthur Danto, the themes are linked in a more coherent and incisive way as part of an interesting discourse concerning the end of modernity in the visual arts. In this chapter, therefore, I shall use a critique of Danto's theory as a means of answering the question of Postmodernism in the visual arts. Specifically, I will outline Danto's theory at length, and will argue that it is not philosophically decisive. . . . [Then] I will go on to offer a more plausible alternative reading of modernity and postmodernity; and . . . [lastly I]

From Critical Aesthetics and Postmodernism *(Oxford: Clarendon Press, 1993). Reprinted by permission of the publisher.*

will offer a final refutation of Danto's claim that (through being rendered posthistorical in the postmodern era) art has come to an end.

The premise of Danto's arguments concerning the end of art is that the advent of cinematography precipitated a traumatic crisis in the artworld. This crisis centred on the fact that, whilst art had always taken itself to be essentially bound with imitating the world, it was now recognized that cinematography could achieve this in a more total way. Twentieth-century Modernist art, therefore, turned towards a kind of self-interrogation. As Danto puts it, "In its great philosophical phase, from about 1905 to about 1964, modern art undertook a massive investigation into its own nature and essence. It set out to seek a form of itself so pure as art that nothing like what caused it to undertake this investigation in the first place could ever happen to it again." This interpretation is, according to Danto, confirmed by the fact that Modernist movements seem to be in perpetual conflict with each other. Again, in his words, "There have been more projected definitions of art, each identified with a different movement in art, in the six or seven decades of the modern era, than in the six or seven centuries that preceded it. Each definition was accompanied by a severe condemnation of everything else, as *not* art." On these terms, then, the discontinuity and conflict between modern movements should be taken as signifying the fact that all were involved in a search for art's essence, and that all were offering different, mutually exclusive, answers.

Now, for Danto, this search ends at a quite specific point—namely in Warhol's Pop Art, and, in particular the exhibition at the Stable Gallery in 1964 where the infamous *Brillo Boxes* were shown for the first time. Since Warhol's Boxes were ostensibly indistinguishable from real Brillo cartoons, the question of what differentiates artworks from real things was posed in the most naked and unambiguous fashion, or, as Danto has it, "its true philosophical form." And the answer emerged as follows. It is only an atmosphere of theory which differentiates artworks from other things. The essence of art does not consist in some perceptible property or set of properties, but rather in art's institutional setting. Broadly speaking, the artwork is what the artist designates as such, on the basis of some theory about art.

Now, this answer—and its reiteration in Minimal and (one presumes) Conceptual art—effectively brought the internal logic of Modernist art's quasi-philosophical questioning to fulfillment. But this created a hiatus. As Danto puts it, "the institutions of the art world continued to believe in—indeed to expect—breakthroughs, and the galleries, the collectors, the art magazines, the museums and finally the corporations that had become the major patrons of the age were also awaiting prophets and revelations." Danto's point, then, is that the radical innovations of Modernist work had by the late 1960s and 1970s found a market, and thence created a demand for art that was innovative and new. But what came next was a mere pluralism—a repetition or refinement of preceding styles (be they representational or abstract) and a willingness to accept these on their own terms, rather than on a partisan basis of mutual exclusivity. Indeed, in the terms of Danto's argument this is an entirely logical development, in so far as once Modernist art has worked through to and declared art's essence, there is nothing new for art to do. It can only rework old ground. The advent and triumph of Neo-Expressionism in the 1980s is simply a special case of this. According to Danto, "Neo-Expressionism raised, as art, no philosophical question at all, and indeed it could raise none that would not be some variant on the one raised in its perfected form by Warhol." Neo-Expressionism, then, is to be seen as an exaggerated and empty response to the art market's demand for innovation. It provides, as it were, a show of newness, but, in terms of strict artistic criteria, can only be an inflated repetition of what has gone before.

The central substantive claims of Danto's position, then, are these. In response to the usurping of its mimetic functions by cinematography, Modernist art became energized by an internal "logic" necessarily progressing towards the revelation of art's real essence—an essence that would not be assimilable in terms of other forms of communication. In Warhol's Pop Art this progression issues in its logical culmination. The essence of art is, in effect, declared as institutional. This self-congruence of art with its own essence is the culmination of art history. After it there can be nothing new in a distinctively artistic sense. On these terms, in other words, postmodern art is essentially *posthistorical*. Art, in effect, has come to an end.

Having outlined Danto's theory, I shall now make some observations concerning its strengths, and some philosophical points concerning its weaknesses. Its strength lies in two basic achievements. First, Danto has pinpointed a crucial fact—namely that in the modern epoch art practice had been taken to its logical limit. For, once what counts as art is determined by artistic intention alone—rather than by possession of specifiable phenomenal characteristics—then we have reached a point beyond which there can be no new kinds of artwork. Anything and everything is admissible in the context of artistic theory and intention. The second strength of Danto's theory is that this first point enables him to explain exactly why postmodern art is fundamentally empty and a product of market forces. Rather than simply declaring it as regressive or the result of a general cultural "slackening" (Lyotard), he provides a model wherein the origins of the slackening can be traced to art's progression towards logical exhaustion at the end of the modernist era. Postmodern art is empty because it is posthistorical.

However, whilst Danto thence offers a superficially plausible explanation of the origins and nature of Postmodernism, it is not, I think, an ultimately satisfying one. For even if we allow Danto's claim that twentieth-century Modernism consists fundamentally in a necessary progression towards the logical limit of art, there is no reason why we should regard the attainment of this limit—as Danto clearly does—as a restriction upon the creativity and historical development of

art. What is lacking here is an argument to establish that creativity and artistic advancement are necessarily connected to the having of new ideas about what counts as the essence of art. For example, we might not count something as creative and quality art unless it does embody some new and novel feature, but this feature does not have to take the form of an embodiment of new ideas about what kind of items should be counted as art. It could rather take the form of a new style of handling, or the refinement of an existing style to an optimum degree. Indeed, it is the pattern and structure of just these sorts of developments which are the key elements in the history of art. The fact that, on Danto's reading, Modernist art fixes on a particular sort of innovation bound up with quasi-philosophical questioning could simply be regarded as a kind of extended detour from the standard preoccupations of art. Indeed, the fact that this detour leads to the logical limits of art acts only as a restriction on the scope of art which is explicitly orientated towards the question of what counts as art. On these terms, in other words, the logical limit reached by Modernist art does not exhaust the possibilities of artistic creativity and advancement as such. Hence, we are not compelled on philosophical grounds to regard postmodern art as essentially posthistorical.

The second major area of difficulty raised by Danto's approach concerns his very reading of twentieth-century Modernism as a kind of quasi-philosophical endeavour. For one must ask whether there is anything which *compels* such a reading? As I interpret him, Danto might offer us two putatively compelling reasons. First, there is the fact that Modernist movements offer, in effect, different and mutually exclusive definitions of what counts as art—and hence embody rival philosophical viewpoints. Now, in relation to this, whilst it is true that the twentieth century has seen more conflicting philosophical theories of art than any other, these have generally been put forward by philosophers rather than artists. Indeed, whilst many Modernist artists have rejected the worth of traditional art in relation to modern experience, very few have claimed that it—or the work of rival modern movements—should not be regarded as art at all. What we find, rather, is a willingness to expand the field of art, rather than to restrict it to one style or one kind of artefact. Danto, in other words, wholly ignores the crucial bonds of practical and theoretical continuity which link modern movements. Now, the second reason which Danto might argue as justifying his reading of Modernism concerns the traditional supposed function of art. He claims that because the advent of cinematography finally vanquished art's mimetic function, art was led into a necessary progression towards the discovery of its essence. This, however, makes some pretty simplistic assumptions about the life which art traditionally plays in our culture. It is certainly true—as Aristotle noted—that mimesis seems to have an intrinsic fascination for human beings, but one might argue that the fascination with mimesis for its own sake has rarely been regarded as art's definitive function. Mimesis has rather been seen as a means to the end of various salutary effects—such as moral improvement, or the expression of feeling. Hence, one might see the impact of photography and cinema not as precipitating a crisis of philosophical questioning, but rather as a liberation. Artists were now free to orientate their work towards salutary effects that eluded more conventional techniques of representation.

I am arguing, then, that Danto's approach to the question of twentieth-century Modernism and Postmodernism is not philosophically decisive. In particular he overlooks possible dimensions of practical and theoretical continuity and salutary effects which might link Modernist and, indeed, postmodern movements together. In the following section of this chapter, therefore, I shall continue my critique of Danto by constructing an alternative historical interpretation which takes full account of the dimension of continuity.

Modernist art in the twentieth century has moved in two dominant directions. On the one hand, in, say, Fauvism, Futurism, Expressionism, and Surrealism, we find a revisionary approach towards representation which seeks to reappropriate it for the needs of modern experience. On the other hand, in, say, Suprematism, Neo-Plasticism, and Abstract Expressionism, we find a tendency towards purely abstract form. Now, these two tendencies are linked in two crucial respects. First, virtually all of them embody to greater or lesser degree a debt to Cézannesque and Cubist form or space. That is to say, they employ a formal vocabulary which tends to reduce form to more basic geometric shape, and/or which distributes such forms in a hyper-pictorial space, i.e. one which accentuates the two-dimensionality of the picture plans, and diminishes the sense of three-dimensional illusion. Hence, whilst Modernist movements tend in different stylistic directions, they do so on the basis of a root vocabulary derived from Cézanne and Cubism.

Now, although this vocabulary is one that departs from, and to some degree subverts, conventional forms of representation, it is not one which radically subverts the notion of high art, as such. Picasso and Braque's Cubism, for example, reappropriates and relegitimizes traditional genres such as the still life, the nude, and the portrait, in terms of an aggressive subjectivity. Indeed, even in Cubist collage—where alien physical material is incorporated into the work—such material is thoroughly mediated. Any oppositional sense of its physical reality is lost within the totality of the overall artistic composition. Again, in the case of Surrealism's dislocations of form, these do not subvert art as such, but rather draw on the precedent of Romantic and Symbolist Fantasy, in order to evoke repressed depths of subjectivity. The function of Cubist space, in other words, is not to posit an antithesis to high art but rather to refocus it in terms of a liberating affirmation of the subject.

It is this affirmative dimension which provides the second, and most important, bond between twentieth-century Modernists. It even encompasses those American Abstract Expressionists who radically break with Cubist space after 1945.

Barnett Newman, for example, declared that "Instead of making *cathedrals* out of Christ, man, or "life," we are making it out of ourselves, out of our own feelings." Compare this with the following set of statements.

> When we invented Cubism, we had no intention of inventing Cubism. We simply wanted to express what was in us.
>
> (Picasso)

> Without much intention, knowledge, or thought, I had followed an irresistible desire to represent profound spirituality, religion and tenderness.
>
> (Emil Nolde)

> We . . . create a sort of emotive ambience, seeking by intuition the sympathies and the links which exist between the exterior (concrete) scene and the interior (abstract) emotion.
>
> (Umberto Bocciono)

> The truly modern artist is aware of abstraction in an emotion of beauty . . .
>
> (Piet Mondrian)

> . . . what interests me is the intensity of a personality transposed directly into the work; the man and his vitality . . . what manner he knows how to gather sensation, emotion, into a lacework of words and sentiments.
>
> (Tristan Tzara)

On these terms, then, Newman's declaration that he and his contemporaries are making "cathedrals" of "our own feelings" is a statement that captures a profound theme running throughout Modernist art—namely that the artwork receives its ultimate authentification as a vehicle for expression of *feeling*. What *sort* of feeling is expressed here varies (as the foregoing statements show) from artist to artist. In some it is bound up with aesthetic experience and religious sentiments; in others it is linked to the artist's affective response to technological change and utopian political ideals. But what all these have in common is the view that what legitimizes modern art and gives it its worth is some kind of elevating expressive effect embodied in its creation and reception. I shall hereafter call this view the "legitimizing discourse" of art.

There are now two crucial points to be made. First (*contra* Danto), far from Modernist art movements being engaged in a kind of war between mutually exclusive definitions of art, there exists a surprising degree of continuity between them at the level of both phenomenal appearance and theoretical justification. Second, the legitimizing discourse of Modernist art also gives it continuity with more traditional idioms. For, since the Renaissance at least, the *raison d'être* of art in Western culture had been insistently tied to its elevating effects. As J.-J. David puts it, "the purpose of the arts is to serve morality and elevate the soul."

What demarcates Modernist art from such sentiments as these is the different readings of morality and elevation which it involves, and the different pictorial means which it operates. But the fundamental point is the same: art has its justification as a vehicle of—in the broadest terms—ethical and aesthetic improvement and elevation. If, therefore, we are to talk of a "logic" of modernity in the visual arts at all, it can only be in the loose sense of a *radical transformation of the existing legitimizing discourse of art*. This, however, should not be seen as a logic of "necessary" progression; neither must it be viewed as a matter wholly internal to art itself. For in Modernist art the different senses of elevation operative in the works of different artists and the means by which they are achieved are frequently enmeshed in complex responses to broader societal changes. Danto, then, is led astray in historical terms by his failure to look at the continuity of Modernist art in its sociocultural context.

There is, however, one point in the growth of Modernism which does seem more amenable to Danto's narrative. This is to be located in certain aspects of Pop Art—such as Warhol's *Brillo Boxes*—and in the development of Minimal and Conceptual art in the 1960s and 1970s. The former tendency seems to insist on collapsing the distinction between art and life, whilst the latter tendencies (respectively) seem to declare—in the most strident terms—that the minimum conditions for something being an artwork are mere objecthood, or embodying an "idea" about what counts as art. Now even if (with Danto) we view these as quasiphilosophical statements about the definition of art, they point in a rather different direction from that which Danto's interpretation would lead us to expect. For if, as I have argued, the central feature of Modernism is a radical transformation of the legitimizing discourse, then the fact that certain movements after 1960 seem to break with this carries with it the implication that we have here the beginnings of a break with modernity itself. What Danto's narrative of quasi-philosophical questioning really signifies, in other words, is not the underlying "logic" of modernity, but the transitional point at which modernity begins to pass into postmodernity. In the next section of this chapter, therefore, I will develop this interpretation by showing how the critique of the legitimizing discourse can be construed as a definitive feature of Postmodernism in the visual arts.

The key artist in understanding the transition from modern to postmodern is Malcolm Morley. In the late 1950s and early 1960s Morley was working in an Abstract Expressionist idiom much indebted to Barnett Newman. However, around 1965 he began producing works such as *S.S. Amsterdam at Rotterdam*. Now, at first sight, in utilizing imagery derived from the mass-media—in this case a commonplace postcard—it might seem that Morley is linking himself to those aspects of Pop Art which overtly celebrate the virtues of mass-culture. This, however, would be a very superficial reading. For Morley's "Super-Realism" lacks any sense of the hedonism, humour, or gentle irony which generally characterizes Pop Art's relation to its sources. The internal resources of an image such as *S.S. Amsterdam,* rather, declare it as more serious and critical through the very insistency with which it manifests its own origin in an image derived from mechanical reproduction. (Even the margin of the postcard is, in fact, worked into Morley's image.) This impression is consolidated by knowledge of how the work is created. In this (and kindred works of the late 1960s) Morley has small-scale photographic-based material blown up into poster size. He then inverts the image, divides it up into a series of grid squares, and transcribes it—one square at a time (with the rest covered up)—in acrylic paint on to a canvas. Thus the process of making the work is reduced to the level of quasi-mechanical reproduction. We have a framed picture offered in the "big" format characteristic of "high art," but whose status as high is subverted by the image's banal content. Other levels of negation are also operative. For here, a mechanically reproduced image (the postcard) is the original, whereas the high-art format painting is only a *copy* of this original. Indeed, whilst the common prejudices of the general public equate 'good' painting with verisimilitude ('it could almost be a photograph'), here the 'good' painting is achieved by quasi-mechanical reproduction, rather than the virtuoso fluency of the skilled hand.

Morley's Super-Realism, in other words, is a critical practice which highlights, questions, and thwarts our expectations of art as a "high" cultural activity. It addresses not so much the Minimalist and Conceptualist preoccupation with the minimum conditions for something to be counted as art, but rather the legitimizing discourse whereby art is justified as a vehicle of elevation and improvement. To some degree, this is anticipated in the blatant parodies of Duchamp, but in Morley's case the critical dimension is, as it were, painted into the image. We have not so much a kind of external "anti-art" as art which internalizes and displays the problematics of its own socio-cultural status.

Now, in the work of a number of other Super-Realist artists in the late 1960s and early 1970s—such as the paintings of Audrey Flack and Chuck Close or the sculptures of Duane Hanson—a broadly similar critical dimension is operative. However, the great bulk of work in this idiom has a much more superficial orientation. For, as

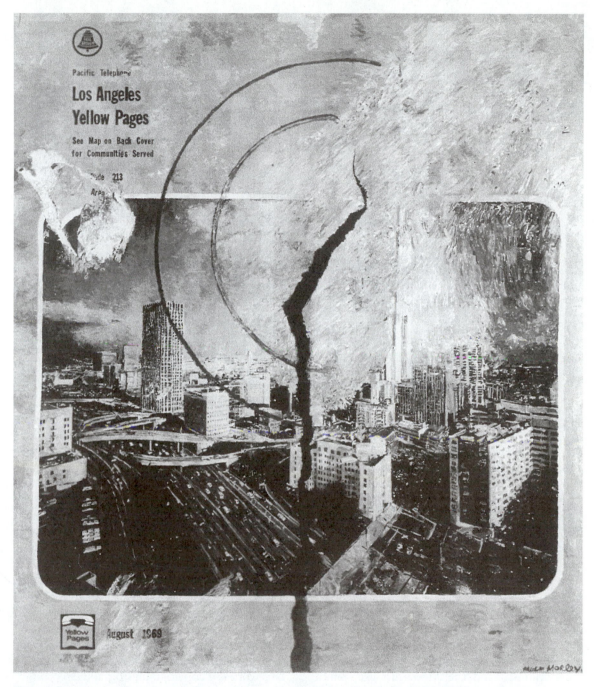

Malcolm Morley, *Pacific Telephone—Los Angeles Yellow Pages*, 1969, Louisiana Museum of Modern Art, Denmark

John Salt, *Purple Impala,* 1973

the Super-Realist tendency spread, it began to address itself to more traditional concerns and become simply a style. In the work of John Salt or Richard Estes, for example, we find close-up images of such things as cars or flashy shop frontages, which, whilst being derived from photographs, present themselves as ostensibly virtuoso performances. Super-Realism becomes the means for intricate, aesthetically dazzling compositions on the grand scale. The work of Morley and the other innovators, in other words, is reappropriated within the legitimizing discourse. Indeed, Super-Realism of this sort has overwhelming market appeal through its combining both the traditional and the Modernist exemplifications of this discourse. On the one hand, its flashy verisimilitude appeals to the traditional prejudices that art should uplift through its complexity and virtuosity; on the other hand, be-

cause such works look so much like photographs, they still seem odd—vaguely outrageous even—thus feeding on the demand for fashionable novelty and unexpectedness that is created by Modernism.

One might trace a similar pattern in relation to the development and consumption of the tendency that began to displace Super-Realism in the late 1970s—namely "Neo-Expressionism." Again, the case of Malcolm Morley proves decisive here. Around 1970 he began to ruffle the surfaces of his photographic-derived works, by working them in more broken brushstrokes. Of especial interest here is *School of Athens* (1972). This work is a copy of a photographic reproduction of Raphael's original. Raphael's work—in both content and handling—affirms art's status as a dignified and uplifting activity akin to the pursuit of those timeless essential truths which

Richard Estes, *Bus Reflections,* 1972

are the vocation of the great philosophers depicted in the painting. It is the quintessential icon of the very notion of high art itself. Morley's treatment of Raphael's work, however, makes the artistic enterprise look earthy and contingent. This is achieved not only through the disruptions effected by the loose handling, but through the fact that Morley leaves a transcriptional mistake intact in the "finished" work (namely a horizontal line of grid squares, that is manifestly asynchronous with the rest of the composition). Indeed, it becomes acutely difficult to locate Morley's *School of Athens* within the customary discourse of art history itself. Is it a copy; is it Expressionist; is it a parody; is it Surrealist; is it classicist? Perhaps all—yet none of these.

Such dislocation effects are even more manifest in Morley's more recent works. In *Day of the Locust* (1977), for example, Morley not only completely mixes up such categories as Expressionist and Surrealist, but blatantly parodies that notion of "stylistic development" which is so central to art history. Morley injects motifs drawn from his earlier work but malforms them and screws them up. One must also note a further crucial dimension to this and kindred works. Morley does not simply overload us with images of breakdown and catastrophe, but rather tangles these up in a way that makes it difficult to disentangle strands of depicted reality from strands of fiction. He does not offer an illusion of real space, but neither does he open up a surreal space of pure fantasy. We are left, rather, in a state of insecurity that seems to bear witness to painting's inadequacy in relation to articulating the complexity and/or horrors of contemporary existence. This felt inadequacy, in other words, arises from a pictorial compromisation of the legitimizing discourse. A critical dimension of this sort is to be found in other innovative "Neo-Expressionist" artists of the 1970s and 1980s, notably Anselm Kiefer, Georg Baselitz, and Philip Guston. Kiefer, for example, moves from large claustrophobic interiors that hint at unseen powers and violence, to devastated landscapes linked with symbols or inscriptions that allude more directly to catastrophe, and, in particular, the disasters of German history. In these works, the very overload of scale, catastrophic excess, and an insistence on the physical means of the medium itself, expressly thematizes painting's inadequacy in relation to life.

Now, whilst Morley, Kiefer, and others make Neo-Expressionism into a critical practice, their work created a stylistic precedent and climate which enabled less incisive, more market-orientated Neo-Expressionisms to flourish. In relation to the work of Julian Schnabel, Sandro Chia, and Francisco Clemente, for example, the term "Neo-Expressionism" is a catch-all phrase that picks out a discourse of painterly excess, and unbridled eclecticism. The overload of paint and imagery connects with its audience fundamentally at the level of private and arbitrary association. If a dimension of public or collective significance is lacking in these works, it is taken as a signifier of the artist's profundity or depth of being. The viewer is invited to compensate for his or her own lack of experience by vicarious identification with the complex signs borne by the canvas. By engaging with the work, in other words, the viewer is elevated and improved.

I am arguing, then, that there are two fundamentally different aspects to Postmodernism in the visual arts. First, in the late 1960s and 1970s, there developed a kind of art which is sceptical about the legitimizing discourse of art as a vehicle of elevation and improvement. Now, whereas radical modern movements such as Cubism and Surrealism redeploy traditional genres such as still life, and fantasy, as a means of elevating subjectivity, artists such as Morley and Kiefer radically question the affirmative discourse of high art, as such. They do so either by incorporating (in an *apparently* unmediated fashion) that which is most directly antithetical to high art—namely mechanically reproduced imagery; or by thematizing (within the particular work) the inadequacy of artistic categories, and indeed, art's inability to express the complexities and catastrophes of concrete historical experience. We have, in other words, a new form of art whose very pictorial means embody a scepticism as to the possibility of high art. By internalizing this scepticism and making it thematic within art practice, *Critical* Super-Realism and *Critical* Neo-Expressionism give art a *deconstructive* dimension. Such work embodies the same kinds of strategy which inform contemporary post structuralist approaches to discourse in general. They can, therefore, be defined as the definitive postmodern tendency. However, this deconstructive approach also created a market demand which was rapidly met by *Secondary* (uncritical) Super-Realisms and Neo-Experessionisms. These works served directly to reinvigorate the legitimizing discourse of art by tapping the traditional expectation of virtuoso performances and "profundity" and the modernist appetite for the odd and the outrageous. Now, in the latter half of the 1980s the Critical aspect of postmodern art has reached a crisis point. It is to a consideration of this phenomenon, and some broader questions, that I now turn in the final section of this chapter.

Much art practice of the late 1980s involves a kind of ironic deconstruction that recognizes and internalizes its own inevitable assimilation by the market. In the Neo-Geo abstractions of Phillip Taafe, for example, we find parodies and subversions of Modernist colour-field painting and "Op" Art. Barnett Newman's high Modernist *Who's Afraid of Red, Yellow, and Blue?* finds its riposte in Taafe's send-up "*We Are Not Afraid.*" Likewise, Peter Halley's Neo-Geo electric cell and conduit paintings parody the high-falutin claims of Rothko-style colour-field painting by stating it and containing it in terms of banal imagery drawn from the technological base of postmodern culture. Again, the "sculpture" of Jeff Koons and David Mach questions conventional notions of taste and representation, through creating assemblages of quirky and comical ingenuity. Mach's *101 Dalmatians,* for example, turns Disney's hounds loose on the domestic environment. The disturbing sense of *Obelisk* or Richard Serra's *Delineator* is here achieved through a Dalmatian balancing a washing-machine on its nose.

Now, in all these Neo-Geo paintings and sculptures a dimension of deconstruction is present, in so far as art's pretensions to elevation or improvement are called into question or shifted to the level of the humorous. But the very good humour of this strategy and the ludicrousness of its means bespeaks an overtly self-ironical and self-negating level of insight. We can deconstruct, but the legitimizing discourse and the market will still have us—so let's have fun with the whole situation while we can. This comic fatalism is of some broader significance, in so far as it marks the point where Critical Postmodernism recognizes its own limits. Any art objects set forth with internal critical intent will be assimilated by the legitimizing discourse and market forces, and redistributed in the form of a *style*. This fate is promised as soon as the attempt to criticize the legitimizing discourse of art is made internal to art itself. For here the deconstructive tendency succeeds in fulfilling the legitimizing discourse despite itself.

To see why this is so, one must invoke the experience of the sublime, in terms of its two main expositors—Kant and Burke. . . . In the Kantian version, when we encounter some phenomenon which overwhelms, or threatens to overwhelm, our imagination or emotions, this can sometimes issue in a kind of rational counterthrust. In such a case, we recognize and comprehend that which overwhelms or threatens to overwhelm us. Indeed, the very fact that a phenomenon which so manifestly defeats our sensible capacities can nev-

ertheless be articulated and thence, in a sense, contained by reason, serves to vividly affirm the extraordinary scope and resilience of rational selfhood. I would suggest that an affirmative response on something like these lines is embodied in our engagement with certain aspects of Critical Postmodernist art. Consider, for example, the overwhelming disaster motifs and dislocational effects of Critical Neo-Expressionism. These signify art's essential inadequacy in relation to expressing the complexity and immensity of the real world and its problems. However, the very fact that such a profound insight can be articulated within the idioms of art serves, paradoxically, to vivify the extraordinary scope of art itself as a mode of rational artifice. The disaster of failure to signify is, as it were, contained and redeemed by the achieved signification of this failure within the visual means of art. The artist offers an affirmative and elevating experience of a kind of artistic sublimity.

Burke's existential theory of the sublime can also be applied to the Critical dimension of postmodern art (and, indeed, avant-garde art in general). According to Burke, prolonged states of inactivity and monotony are deleterious to our organic constitution. In order to counter this, we need to experience mild shocks—which will stimulate our sensibilities, but without involving any real sense of pain or danger. Experiences of this sort are provided by such things as vast or destructive objects encountered from a position of safety, or by human artefacts which outrage or thrill us in some way. . . . The shocks and thrills provided by media news items, or such things as violent adventure films and the like, fulfil this function. It is this vein of compensatory affective response, I would suggest, which is tapped by Critical Postmodernism. In the case of Critical Super-Realism and Neo-Geo, for example, we have works which engage us fundamentally in terms of affective jolts—through thwarting of parodying expectations based on our intercourse with high art of the traditional or Modernist kinds. They have a shock or surprise value which rejuvenates and heightens our very sense of being alive. The means may be banal or ludi-crous, but in the midst of social monotony and accelerating standardization, the "whatever-will-they-do-next" aspect of artistic innovation is a life-enhancing force. Its affective jolt, indeed, may even thematize the notion that the individ-ual creator *can* resist the forces of reification to some degree—however trivial.

I am arguing, then, both that the Critical di-mension of postmodern art has ended up on a kind of comical recognition of its own limits; and that this kind of result was implicit in the very at-tempt to deconstruct art from within. Such a practice tends towards elevating experiences of the sublime in either the Kantian or Burkean modes. This interpretation raises two questions. First, is there any way in which Critical Postmod-ernism in the visual arts can avoid assimilation by the legitimizing discourse and market forces; and second, if it cannot, does this not mean that Danto is at least right in his claim that Postmod-ernism is posthistorical? Let me address the for-mer question. First, as I have already argued, in-ternalized deconstruction is assimilated by the legitimizing discourse in terms of the sublime. But what about those cases where the critique is conducted from a more external viewpoint?

A good example here is the work of the femi-nist artist Mary Kelly. In her *Post Partum Docu-ment*, Kelly seeks to break out of the patriarchal power structures which have regulated what is ad-missible as art and what is not. The work consists of a series of largely documentary displays chart-ing biographical facts about, and theoretical in-terpretations of, her relationship with her son— from earliest infancy to earliest childhood. Now, the problem with this work (and, indeed, the problem faced by "conceptual art" in general) is that the level of sensuous, essentially visual meaning is almost entirely eliminated. It might, of course, be argued that the removal of this di-mension is an extremely positive feature, in so far as it is art's sensuousness which appeals to the market and which provides the essential spectacle for the male gaze. However, on these terms, Kelly's work merely throws out the baby with the

bathwater. For to remove the appeal to distinc-tively visual meaning is to render the notion of visual art itself superfluous. Collapsing the boundary between art and documentation in this way simply eliminates art. Interestingly, however, Kelly—as is the case with most conceptual artists—is not willing to allow her *Post Partum* work to be judged as a series of theoretical state-ments, for its units are mounted so as to be hung in accordance with the presentational formats of conventional art. Thus the work takes on its de-constructive edge through the play-off between its primarily nonartistic content, and its conven-tional art format of presentation. Again, how-ever, whilst this thwarts our normal expectations as to what should be counted as art, the fact that it is mounted as an-object-for-contemplation serves to contain the shock response. We feel that this is just the avant-garde thrilling us with the outrageous and extending our horizons once more. Our sensibility is, once, more, elevated and improved.

That the legitimizing discourse should exert so profound a pull in relation to even the most (su-perficially) antithetical works is hardly surprising. For, whilst the concept "art" is a social construct of Western culture, it is not merely a construct. The reason why it needs to be constructed is to pick out the fact that certain kinds of artefacts bring about certain positive effects *through the mere contemplation of them*. It is the fact that cer-tain artefacts can be valued in this way that neces-sitates the concept "art." The legitimizing dis-course, in other words, legitimizes not just this art and that, but the very concept of "art" as such.

I shall now finally return to Danto's implicit equation between postmodern art and posthis-toricality. It will be remembered that, for Danto, the reason why this equation is justified is that Modernist art—in the form of Warhol's *Brillo Boxes*—brings about a congruence between art and the statement of its essence. Thereafter there cannot be anything artistically new—only a re-hash of old forms. Now, whilst I rehearsed the philosophical objections to this claim . . . it is worth looking at again in the light of my alternative historical account of Modernity and Post-modernity. First, I have tried to show that there is some continuity between the late Modernism of Warhol, Minimal art, and Conceptual art, and the Critical varieties of postmodern Super Realism and Neo-Expressionism. All these tendencies are energized by the philosophical implications of art. The difference between them consists in the fact that, whereas the late Modernists question the logical scope of art and take it to and beyond its limits, the Critical Postmodernists question the social reality of art (i.e. the status of the legitimizing discourse) from within. This latter fact is itself a concrete illustration of how postmodern art—working within and loosening up the limits of already established idioms (i.e. "Realism" and "Expressionism)—is authentically critical and historically innovative, rather than the mere product of market demands.

Now, of course, I also argued that whilst Critical Post-modernism shakes up and questions the legitimizing discourse, it does not escape it; but this fact in no way restricts its historical possibilities. For, as I further suggested, the legitimizing discourse is the very basis of our having a concept of art at all—indeed, it is the very basis of our interest in art's historical development. To escape the legitimizing discourse, in other words, would involve giving up art. One might expect, therefore, that future postmodern art will become less

obsessed with criticizing the legitimizing discourse, and will instead orientate itself towards new ways of exemplifying it. To some degree this process is already under way. . . .

In conclusion, then, one must concede only one major point to Danto—namely that all future art will have to work within the logical limits that were set out by late Modernism, and this will involve operating with genres and categories already defined. Even this, however, would only rule out the possibility of future authentic artistic innovation on the assumption that such innovation is sufficiently definable in negative terms, that is as simply creating something the like of which has not been created before. But, of course, this assumption is false. Historical innovation in art has always been determined in the context of creative breaks with, or refinements of, what has already been given. We do not want new artefacts that are simply unprecedented—but rather ones whose unprecedentedness casts new light on the traditions of art or on our broader relation to the lifeworld. Artistic innovation, in other words, in a complex relation between art and its past, rather than the kind of absolute philosophical break which Danto's reading makes of it. The moral is clear. Art lives . . . and will continue to do so whilstsoever artists see their world and, in particular, their discipline's history, from different viewpoints.

C. The Critique of Truth

Heidegger

Martin Heidegger is a transitional figure. In some ways he is an early postmodernist; in other ways he is the last of the moderns. As a postmodernist, Heidegger seeks to radically transform our ways of thinking and doing philosophy—to begin again at the very beginning, going all the way back, beyond Plato and Aristotle, to the oracular sayings of the pre-Socratics (Heraclitus, Parmenides, and Cratylus—the one who said "You can't step even once in the same river"). But Heidegger remains firmly planted in the modernist camp in his quest for truth, and especially in his Romantic claim that since Kant art, not science or philosophy, is the road to ultimate truth. You recall how Kant (Part I) "critically" limited what we can cognitively, intellectually know to *phenomena* (things as they appear to us), with the obvious implication that we can never know reality (*noumena*, things as they are in themselves). You also remember how this proved too much for the followers of Kant, in particular Hegel and Schopenhauer (Part I), who looked for alternative routes to truth and reality. Schopenhauer is a major spokesperson for the Romantic movement, which held that the road to truth and being was through art and poetry and not through science and cognitive philosophy. Heidegger continues in that tradition—granted that science and rational philosophy cannot give us truth and being, as Kant said, perhaps art and poetry can. As we will see in this section, postmodern thinkers tend to jettison the concept of truth in favor of human creativity—we can construct the world any way we like; we are not bound by the truth (which, as Nietzsche pointed out, is one of our creative value constructions anyway).

Like Nietzsche, Heidegger seeks a deeper truth in art than we find in science or traditional philosophy. As Aristotle noted, a work of art is an object made by a human being, and as Richard Wollheim observed (Part II), to function as art the artwork must be more than a mere physical object—it must also function as the human expression of attitudes about and a representation of the world. Heidegger develops this theme, following the phenomenological direction of his teacher Edmund Husserl. Phenomenology seeks to describe the world as human beings perceive it, not as the natural sciences describe it.

Looking at my desk, I see a ballpoint pen. I do not register sensations of color, shape, texture, size, and the like that I go on to hypothesize is a ballpoint pen. Nor do I see swirling atoms that have temporarily configured themselves into a ballpoint pen. These are just philosophical and scientific theories I have read somewhere. No, I see what I understand and take to be a ballpoint pen. For Heidegger this means that I see the object as something which functions in my human world. The pen is a tool (*Zeug*) for doing something, accomplishing one or more tasks—I need to sign some letters, correct some papers, mark a text.

This would only be true in a human world, the world as humans experience and construct it. We humans are for the most part purposive creatures, doing one thing for the sake of another. I see the pen as something I need ("equipment," a tool, basically) to correct a printed text. Heidegger exploits the implications of this pragmatic view to mean that everything in the world has multiple connections to other things, all held together by our human purposes, plans, and projects. I want to pick up the pen in order to correct the latest draft of the paper; I want to finish the paper in order to meet the deadline for the upcoming conference; and I want to participate in the conference because my job depends on it and also to achieve professional status, and I want the first because I like to eat and the second because I see this as an important goal in my life. So something as humble and mundane as a ballpoint pen is interconnected with many other things in a larger context of life as lived by me. A cat, or even a three-year-old child will not see the pen in this way—the pen will not exist in their worlds in the same way.

Only in this human way does a pen come to *be* something, that is, to have a meaningful essence, or character. *What* is that? someone asks (meaning, what kind of thing is it? what is it for? what does it do?). We answer, "A pen" (something we use to write with, or, in today's world, something we use to correct what we have printed out on a computer). Only in this human way of purposefully connecting things does a meaningful "world" appear. Without people there may be things, material stuff, but no being. The being of the pen is our sense of *what* it is (what is it? it's a pen); its essential character, for Heidegger, is its being.

Mere things aren't anything—that is, they have no essence or being—until they can occupy a place in a humanly constructed world. The pen can exist on its own, but it only exists "as a *pen*," as a recognizable instrument for writing, to be held in a certain way, within a human world. For Heidegger, then, *being* is existence revealed to humans as things of a definite sort. In a world without people, what would that thing (the pen) be? Nothing. That is, it would not be a meaningful kind of thing (would have no essence) and therefore becomes a mere thing. In some of his later writing, Heidegger distinguishes the earth from the world, whereby the *earth* is the way things exist before they are interpreted and come to occupy a place in a human *world*.

Properly interpreted, then, a single object, like the pen, can tell the story of an entire human world. We see this effect quite clearly in Heidegger's example of the peasant's shoes which van Gogh painted (see p. 323). These are not dress shoes, or dancing shoes, or running shoes, they are the shoes Heidegger says European peasants used for working in the fields in the nineteenth century. The shoes bring with them the entire contextual world of the peasant—the grinding hard work, subsistence survival, the mud and sweat and exhaustion of work in the fields (long before the days of mechanized farming). By painting a picture of the shoes, van Gogh makes us aware of this contextualized human world in a way we might otherwise overlook in the day-to-day business of life. Today we can imagine a painting of expensive Reeboks—what might this reveal about the world we live in today? Or we can compare van Gogh's painting with Andy Warhol's shoes (see p. 324).

This revelation of being (the *what* of the pen, the shoes, their essence) is what Heidegger means by truth. Truth is not a property of sentences (statements or propositions) that we describe as true if they correspond to reality and false if they do not. Truth, for Heidegger, is the revealing ("uncovering," in Greek *aletheia*) of objects as things having meaning in a human world of purposes and projects and activity, and then in artworks representing those objects as ways of calling our attention to their truth and being. Without art we might fail to notice anything very remarkable in the ballpoint pen or the shoes. Because they are tools, we would normally just use them without thinking much about them one way or the other. Here is a chair, so you sit down; here is a light switch, so you turn on the light, here are your shoes, so you put them on. Through custom and habit we cease to take any notice of such mundane things. Only in art do we recall the revelation of truth and being in something as simple and ordinary as a pair of old shoes.

Shapiro

In an interesting exchange that took place in the 1960s, art historian Meyer Shapiro takes issue with Heidegger. As we have seen throughout this book, in the history of Western thought there are two main theories of art—that art is the *representation* of reality and that art is the *expression* of the artist's feelings. Heidegger emphasizes the first and Shapiro the second. Shapiro first points out that the shoes that van Gogh painted were not peasant shoes at all, but van Gogh's own shoes—and not just any pair of shoes he owned but the pair he wore when he walked all the way from his home in Holland to the coal mine in Belgium where he went, in a failed attempt, to work as a lay minister of the Christian Gospel. Thus, according to Shapiro, the painting of the shoes does not tell us something about the world of the hardworking nineteenth-century dirt-farming peasant, but something about the artist, himself—something about the thoughts and feelings of Vincent van Gogh.

In the middle of this century there was a widespread popular interest in the life of Vincent van Gogh. We can think of Irving Stone's novel *Lust for Life,* made into a movie staring Kirk Douglas, and thousands of copies of van Gogh's letters to his brother Theo, plus many psychological studies of his tragic life, and hundreds of thousands of reproductions of his paintings. To most people growing up during this period it is well known that van Gogh failed at everything he tried and was an enormous disappointment to his family. His brother was a successful businessperson, but Vincent utterly failed when his brother gave him a chance to work for him. His father had been a successful Christian minister. But Vincent could not get the higher education necessary to enter the mainstream ministry and so turned instead to the more evangelical lay ministry, working with the poorest and most downtrodden sector of society. As many people did toward the end of the nineteenth century, van Gogh accepted a "social-consciousness" interpretation of the life of Jesus that stressed the way in which Jesus (in the *New Testament*) tried to help the poorest and weakest members of society. Taking a vow of poverty, van Gogh left his successful upper middle class Dutch family and walked for many days to his coalmining ministry. When a mine explosion killed many of the men, van Gogh spent months nursing back to health one of the miners whom everyone else had given up on. In the process, Vincent van Gogh was overwhelmed by a sense of frustration, personal failure, and spiritual anguish and, as was said at the time, "went mad." As his friend, artist Gauguin wrote later, the van Gogh family, especially brother Theo, did not want to commit him to an insane asylum and began to support him as an otherwise penniless, homeless artist. Of course, today we think of van Gogh as one of the most successful artists ever (his paintings selling in recent years in the tens of millions of dollars). But during his lifetime he never sold anything and simply lived off the money his brother, as head of the van Gogh family, sent him. In and out of mental institutions (everyone knows the story of the time he cut off part of his ear to give to a prostitute), he finally committed suicide.

For Shapiro, van Gogh's enormous but failed effort to serve Christ through helping the poor (and earn the respect of his family and respectful society) is expressed in his painting of the shoes. One thing we learn from this exchange between Heidegger and Shapiro is the very different methods of the philosopher and the art historian. Heidegger is not really concerned whose shoes these are or the details of precisely how and under what circumstances they came to be painted. Heidegger is a philosopher looking for an example to illustrate a theory he has already worked out in great detail. Shapiro, on the other hand, is an art historian, and so the details about the shoes are very important to him. He has spent years sifting through letters to and from van Gogh to determine what kind of shoes they really were and why van Gogh painted them.

Who is right in all this? Certainly, most of us would have to agree that Shapiro is right and Heidegger is wrong about the specifics of the shoes—they were not the shoes of any peasant person but van Gogh's own worn-out shoes. But that doesn't mean Heidegger's theory is completely wrong or useless—maybe he just selected a bad example (or maybe his timing was incredibly bad, writing about van Gogh when van Gogh had become such a popular icon the details of whose life were intimately known to millions of people—everyone except Heidegger, apparently). Shapiro questions whether we need an artist to call our attention to the place of the peasant shoes in the world in which they belong. Wouldn't the shoes themselves do just as well, he asks. And in that case, why bother to paint a *picture* of the shoes? But perhaps Heidegger is right on this point at least. While it is not impossible to reflect on the larger contextual meaning of a pair of shoes, most of us simply don't take the time to ponder this matter (I'm already late for work as I slip on my shoes in the morning or later in the day, meeting someone for the first time, utterly fail to notice what sort of shoes they are wearing), and therefore do need some help—some of it from artists.

Derrida

Our last selection in this section is from Jacques Derrida's *The Truth in Painting* (the title alone should be a clue), "The Parergon" and "Restitutions." Derrida first came to prominence in the United States through language departments—first French, then eventually English departments—and is most known for his self-titled method of interpretation: *deconstruction*. Although it has been thirty years since his first articles appeared (given in person at Johns Hopkins University) in the United States, Derrida is still controversial. Published in France in 1978, this selection from *The Truth in Painting* continues Derrida's critique of the logic of identity via the notion of the frame. Early in his career Derrida establishes a set of problems that he continually explores from text to text, always taking a new line of thought and opening up a new reading of an old text. The set of problems (without being overly reductive) include: the double logic at work in all texts, supplementarity, presence and absence (and other binaries that characterize thinking in the West), difference, and the context or frame of knowledge.

Using Kant's *The Critique of Judgment* Derrida wishes to explore the concept of inside and outside (binaries) in regard to the frame of art. Derrida immediately runs into several difficulties with Kant's use of the *ergon* (work) and the *parergon* (the frame). Before any discussion of art can proceed, Derrida must first understand Kant's discourse on his previous discourses. As our readings on Kant in Part I indicated, Kant wrote *The Critique of Judgment* as an answer or a bridge between his earlier texts *The Critique of Pure Reason* and *The Critique of Practical Reason*. According to Derrida, Kant has supplemented (added a center) to his previous books that originally lacked a center or a central meaning. This addition is not a problem for Derrida because we are always adding centers or attributing meaning to texts as a result of a lack. One problem for Derrida is Kant's seeming lack of awareness to acknowledge this supplement. What disturbs Derrida is that Kant takes our ability to understand what is the center and what is not (what is the ergon and what is the parergon) for granted: "The objection presupposes that one already knows what the center or the heart of the third Critique is, that one has already located its frame and the limit of its field. But nothing seems more difficult to determine." Derrida points out that it is difficult, if not impossible, to know how to frame, interpret, or contextualize Kant's discourse, and yet Kant himself expects us to do it "automatically" or "naturally."

Typically, Derrida calls into question our ability to properly frame or understand Kant, but then adds to our difficulties by showing us that with that first problem several others follow. Derrida shows that even Kant had difficulty deciding where the *ergon* stopped and the *parergon* started. So now we not only have trouble with Kant's discourse on discourse, but we also cannot decide where the discourse—which is both a work and a frame for understanding other works—on art begins and the work of the frame begins: "The relation to the understanding, which is neither certain nor essential, thus furnishes the frame of this whole discourse; and, within it, of the discourse on the frame." We have then three different levels of discourse going on: (1) the discourse on discourse; (2) discourse on art; (3) discourse on the frame—or interpretation. These discourses question the ability of the frame to present truth, "A frame is essentially constructed and therefore fragile." Derrida goes on to say that philosophy wants to manipulate the discourse or frame or interpretation so that truth is rendered, but that, basically, is impossible. What is truth? Whatever a frame or interpretation frames it to be.

Lastly, Derrida is careful not to let his own interpretation or frame reassert the truth, this one of the nonframe: "Deconstruction must neither frame nor dream of the pure and simple absence of the frame." In other words, we as humans must frame—we must always already have a perspective from which we see the world—and so we cannot simply abolish the idea of the frame because Western thought refuses to acknowledge its own frame or interpretation as being anything other than the truth. For in abolishing the frame we are, indeed, creating a new one.

As an example of the inability of most thinkers to distinguish the art object from the frame, Derrida joins the debate between Heidegger and Shapiro on the correct interpretation (frame) of van Gogh's painting of the shoes. For Heidegger, the shoes are framed in the world of the peasant; for Shapiro, the shoes are framed in the world of Vincent van Gogh. But where exactly does the painting end and the frame begin? And where exactly does the *theory* of the painting begin and its frame begin?

Derrida agrees with Shapiro that Heidegger seems to treat the painting rather naively simply as an example of a pair of real shoes—not talking about the *painting,* but apparently only wanting to talk about the significance of the actual shoes in the world and life of the nineteenth-century European peasant. It is almost embarrassing, he says, to see such a great thinker discuss a work of art so clumsily. But, Derrida warns us, perhaps Shapiro has been too hasty. First of all Heidegger makes it clear he is treating the well-known painting by van Gogh merely as an illustration of a larger philosophical point about objects in a humanly interpreted world as *Zeug,* tools or products, and he merely wants to use these well-known shoes in van Gogh's painting as an example to make that philosophical point. Art, on Heidegger's analysis, shows us or opens up for us this *Zeug* aspect of things in our world, and van Gogh's painting illustrates it, regardless of whether the original shoes belonged to a peasant woman or to van Gogh himself.

Derrida is also critical of Shapiro's own romantic and equally naive "expressionist" frame or interpretation of the painting as a revelation of the inner life of Vincent van Gogh. Surely any representational work of art reveals something about the artist who produced it as well as the world from which the subject matter represented in the artwork was drawn. Again, these frames appear as part of the painting itself. Once more, we can't avoid framing; we can only try to become more sophisticated—that is, more aware that we are doing so.

The Origin of the Work of Art

MARTIN HEIDEGGER

ORIGIN HERE MEANS THAT from and by which something is what it is and as it is. What something is, as it is, we call its essence or nature. The origin of something is the source of its nature. The question concerning the origin of the work of art asks about the source of its nature. On the usual view, the work arises out of and by means of the activity of the artist. But by what and whence is the artist what he is? By the work; for to say that the work does credit to the master means that it is the work that first lets the artist emerge as a master of his art. The artist is the origin of the work. The work is the origin of the artist. Neither is without the other. Nevertheless, neither is the sole support of the other. In themselves and in their interrelations artist and work *are* each of them by virtue of a third thing which is prior to both, namely that which also gives artist and work of art their names—art.

As necessarily as the artist is the origin of the work in a different way than the work is the origin of the artist, so it is equally certain that, in a still different way, art is the origin of both artist and work. But can art be an origin at all? Where and how does art occur? Art—this is nothing more than a word to which nothing real any longer corresponds. It may pass for a collective idea under which we find a place for that which alone is real in art: works and artists. Even if the word art were taken to signify more than a collective notion, what is meant by the word could exist only on the basis of the actuality of works and artists. Or is the converse the case? Do works and artists exist only because art exists as their origin?

Whatever the decision may be, the question of the origin of the work of art becomes a question about the nature of art. Since the question whether and how art in general exists must still remain open, we shall attempt to discover the nature of art in the place where art undoubtedly prevails in a real way. Art is present in the art work. But what and how is a work of art?

What art is should be inferable from the work. What the work of art is we can come to know only from the nature of art. Anyone can easily see that we are moving in a circle. Ordinary understanding demands that this circle be avoided because it violates logic. What art is can be gathered from a comparative examination of actual art works. But how are we to be certain that we are indeed basing such an examination on art works if we do not know beforehand what art is? And the nature of art can no more be arrived at by a derivation from higher concepts than by a collection of characteristics of actual art works. For such a derivation, too, already has in view the characteristics that must suffice to establish that what we take in advance to be an art work is one in fact. But selecting works from among given objects, and deriving concepts from principles, are equally impossible here, and where these procedures are practiced they are a self-deception.

Thus we are compelled to follow the circle. This is neither a makeshift nor a defect. To enter upon this path is the strength of thought, to continue on it is the feat of thought, assuming that thinking is a craft. Not only is the main step from work to art a circle like the step from art to work, but every separate step that we attempt circles in this circle.

In order to discover the nature of the art that really prevails in the work, let us go to the actual work and ask the work what and how it is.

From The Origin of the Work of Art, *trans. Albert Hofstadter (New York: HarperCollins Publishers, 1975).*

Works of art are familiar to everyone. Architectural and sculptural works can be seen installed in public places, in churches, and in dwellings. Art works of the most diverse periods and peoples are housed in collections and exhibitions. If we consider the works in their untouched actuality and do not deceive ourselves, the result is that the works are as naturally present as are things. The picture hangs on the wall like a rifle or a hat. A painting, e.g., the one by van Gogh that represents a pair of peasant shoes, travels from one exhibition to another. Works of art are shipped like coal from the Ruhr and logs from the Black Forest. During the First World War Hölderlin's hymns were packed in the soldier's knapsack together with cleaning gear. Beethoven's quartets lie in the storerooms of the publishing house like potatoes in a cellar.

All works have this thingly character. What would they be without it? But perhaps this rather crude and external view of the work is objectionable to us. Shippers or charwomen in museums may operate with such conceptions of the work of art. We, however, have to take works as they are encountered by those who experience and enjoy them. But even the much-vaunted aesthetic experience cannot get around the thingly aspect of the art work. There is something stony in a work of architecture, wooden in a carving, colored in a painting, spoken in a linguistic work, sonorous in a musical composition. The thingly element is so irremovably present in the art work that we are compelled rather to say conversely that the architectural work is in stone, the carving is in wood, the painting in color, the linguistic work in speech, the musical composition in sound. "Obviously," it will be replied. No doubt. But what is this self-evident thingly element in the work of art?

Presumably it becomes superfluous and confusing to inquire into this feature, since the art work is something else over and above the thingly element. This something else in the work constitutes its artistic nature. The art work is, to be sure, a thing that is made, but it says something other than the mere thing itself is, *allo agoreuei*. The work makes public something other than itself; it manifests something other; it is an allegory. In the work of art something other is brought together with the thing that is made. To bring together is, in Greek, *sumballein*. The work is a symbol.

Allegory and symbol provide the conceptual frame within whose channel of vision the art work has for a long time been characterized. But this one element in a work that manifests another, this one element that joins with another, is the thingly feature in the art work. It seems almost as though the thingly element in the art work is like the substructure into and upon which the other, authentic element is built. And is it not this thingly feature in the work that the artist really makes by his handicraft?

Our aim is to arrive at the immediate and full reality of the work of art, for only in this way shall we discover real art also within it. Hence we must first bring to view the thingly element of the work. To this end it is necessary that we should know with sufficient clarity what a thing is. Only then can we say whether the art work is a thing, but a thing to which something else adheres; only then can we decide whether the work is at bottom something else and not a thing at all.

What in truth is the thing, so far as it is a thing? When we inquire in this way, our aim is to come to know the thing-being (thingness) of the thing. The point is to discover the thingly character of the thing. To this end we have to be acquainted with the sphere to which all those entities belong which we have long called by the name of thing.

The stone in the road is a thing, as is the clod in the field. A jug is a thing, as is the well beside the road. But what about the milk in the jug and the water in the well? These too are things if the cloud in the sky and the thistle in the field, the leaf in the autumn breeze and the hawk over the wood, are rightly called by the name of thing. All these must indeed be called things, if the name is applied even to that which does not, like those just enumerated, show itself, i.e., that which does not appear. According to Kant, the whole of the world, for example, and even God himself, is a thing of this sort, a thing that does not itself appear, namely, a "thing-in-itself." In the language of philosophy both things-in-themselves and things that appear, all beings that in any way are, are called things.

Airplanes and radio sets are nowadays among the things closest to us, but when we have ultimate things in mind we think of something altogether different. Death and judgment—these are ultimate things. On the whole the word "thing" here designates whatever is not simply nothing. In this sense the work of art is also a thing, so far as it is not simply nothing. Yet this concept is of no use to us, at least immediately, in our attempt to delimit entities that have the mode of being of a thing, as against those having the mode of being of a work. And besides, we hesitate to call God a thing. In the same way we hesitate to consider the peasant in the field, the stoker at the boiler, the teacher in the school as things. A man is not a thing. It is true that we speak of a young girl who is faced with a task too difficult for her as being a young thing, still too young for it, but only because we feel that being human is in a certain way missing here and think that instead we have to do here with the factor that constitutes the thingly character of things. We hesitate even to call the deer in the forest clearing, the beetle in the grass, the blade of grass a thing. We would sooner think of a hammer as a thing, or a shoe, or an ax, or a clock. But even these are not mere things. Only a stone, a clod of earth, a piece of wood are for us such mere things. Lifeless beings of nature and objects of use. Natural things and utensils are the things commonly so called. . . .

That the thingness of the thing is particularly difficult to express and only seldom expressible is infallibly documented by the history of its interpretation indicated above. This history coincides with the destiny in accordance with which Western thought has hitherto thought the Being of beings. However, not only do we now establish

this point; at the same time we discovered a clue in this history. Is it an accident that in the interpretation of the thing the view that takes matter and form as guide attains to special dominance? This definition of the thing derives from an interpretation of the equipmental being of equipment. And equipment, having come into being through human making, is particularly familiar to human thinking. At the same time, this familiar being has a peculiar intermediate position between thing and work. We shall follow this clue and search first for the equipmental character of equipment. Perhaps this will suggest something to us about the thingly character of the thing and the workly character of the work. We must only avoid making thing and work prematurely into subspecies of equipment. We are disregarding the possibility, however, that differences relating to the history of Being may yet also be present in the way equipment *is*.

But what path leads to the equipmental quality of equipment? How shall we discover what a piece of equipment truly is? The procedure necessary at present must plainly avoid any attempts that again immediately entail the encroachments of the usual interpretations. We are most easily insured against this if we simply describe some equipment without any philosophical theory.

We choose as example a common sort of equipment—a pair of peasant shoes. We do not even need to exhibit actual pieces of this sort of useful article in order to describe them. Everyone is acquainted with them. But since it is a matter here of direct description, it may be well to facilitate the visual realization of them. For this purpose a pictorial representation suffices. We shall choose a well-known painting by van Gogh, who painted such shoes several times. But what is there to see here? Everyone knows what shoes consist of. If they are not wooden or bast shoes, there will be leather soles and uppers, joined together by thread and nails. Such gear serves to clothe the feet. Depending on the use to which the shoes are to be put, whether for work in the field or for dancing, matter and form will differ.

Such statements, no doubt correct, only explicate what we already know. The equipmental quality of equipment consists in its usefulness. But what about this usefulness itself? In conceiving it, do we already conceive along with it the equipmental character of equipment? In order to succeed in doing this, must we not look out for useful equipment in its use? The peasant woman wears her shoes in the field. Only here are they what they are. They are all the more genuinely so, the less the peasant woman thinks about the shoes while she is at work, or looks at them at all, or is even aware of them. She stands and walks in them. That is how shoes actually serve. It is in this process of the use of equipment that we must actually encounter the character of equipment.

As long as we only imagine a pair of shoes in general, or simply look at the empty, unused shoes as they merely stand there in the picture, we shall never discover what the equipmental being of the equipment in truth is. From van Gogh's painting we cannot even tell where these shoes stand. There is nothing surrounding this pair of peasant shoes in or to which they might belong—only an undefined space. There are not even clods of soil from the field or the field-path sticking to them, which would at least hint at their use. A pair of peasant shoes and nothing more. And yet—

From the dark opening of the worn insides of the shoes the toilsome tread of the worker stares forth. In the stiffly rugged heaviness of the shoes there is the accumulated tenacity of her slow trudge through the far-spreading and ever-uniform furrows of the field swept by a raw wind. On the leather lie the dampness and richness of the soil. Under the soles slides the loneliness of the field-path as evening falls. In the shoes vibrates the silent call of the earth, its quiet gift of the ripening grain and its unexplained self-refusal in the fallow desolation of the wintry field. This equipment is pervaded by uncomplaining anxiety as to the certainty of bread, the wordless joy of having once more withstood want, the trembling before the impending childbed and shivering at the surrounding menace of death. This equip-

ment belongs to the *earth,* and it is protected in the *world* of the peasant woman. From out of this protected belonging the equipment itself rises to its resting-within-itself.

But perhaps it is only in the picture that we notice all this about the shoes. The peasant woman, on the other hand, simply wears them. If only this simple wearing were so simple. When she takes off her shoes late in the evening, in deep but healthy fatigue, and reaches out for them again in the still dim dawn, or passes them by on the day of rest, she knows all this without noticing or reflecting. The equipmental quality of the equipment consists indeed in its usefulness. But this usefulness itself rests in the abundance of an essential being of the equipment. We call it reliability. By virtue of this reliability the peasant woman is made privy to the silent call of the earth; by virtue of the reliability of the equipment she is sure of her world. World and earth exist for her, and for those who are with her in her mode of being, only thus—in the equipment. We say "only" and therewith fall into error; for the reliability of the equipment first gives to the simple world its security and assures to the earth the freedom of its steady thrust.

The equipmental being of equipment, reliability, keeps gathered within itself all things according to their manner and extent. The usefulness of equipment is nevertheless only the essential consequence of reliability. The former vibrates in the latter and would be nothing without it. A single piece of equipment is worn out and used up; but at the same time the use itself also falls into disuse, wears away, and becomes usual. Thus equipmentality wastes away, sinks into mere stuff. In such wasting, reliability vanishes. This dwindling, however, to which use-things [i.e., tools, in German *Zeug*] owe their boringly obtrusive usualness, is only one more testimony to the original nature of equipmental being. The worn-out usualness of the equipment then obtrudes itself as the sole mode of being, apparently peculiar to it exclusively. Only blank usefulness now remains visible. It awakens the impression that the origin of equipment lies in a mere fabricating that impresses a form upon some matter. Nevertheless, in its genuinely equipmental being, equipment stems from a more distant source. Matter and form and their distinction have a deeper origin.

The repose of equipment resting within itself consists in its reliability. Only in this reliability do we discern what equipment in truth is. But we still know nothing of what we first sought: the thing's thingly character. And we know nothing at all of what we really and solely seek: the workly character of the work in the sense of the work of art.

Or have we already learned something unwittingly, in passing so to speak, about the work-being of the work?

The equipmental quality of equipment was discovered. But how? Not by a description and explanation of a pair of shoes actually present; not by a report about the process of making shoes; and also not by the observation of the actual use of shoes occurring here and there; but only by bringing ourselves before van Gogh's painting. This painting spoke. In the vicinity of the work we were suddenly somewhere else than we usually tend to be.

The art work let us know what shoes are in truth. It would be the worse self-deception to think that our description, as a subjective action, had first depicted everything thus and then projected it into the painting. If anything is questionable here, it is rather that we experienced too little in the neighborhood of the work and that we expressed the experience too crudely and too literally. But above all, the work did not, as it might seem at first, serve merely for a better visualizing of what a piece of equipment is. Rather, the equipmentality of equipment first genuinely arrives at its appearance through the work and only in the work.

What happens here? What is at work in the work? Van Gogh's painting is the disclosure of what the equipment, the pair of peasant shoes, *is* the truth. This entity emerges into the unconcealedness of its being. The Greeks called the unconcealedness of beings *aletheia*. We say "truth" and think little enough in using this word. If there

occurs in the work a disclosure of a particular being, disclosing what and how it is, then there is here an occurring, a happening of truth at work.

In the work of art the truth of an entity has set itself to work. "To set" means here: to bring to a stand. Some particular entity, a pair of peasant shoes, comes in the work to stand in the light of its being. The being of the being comes into the steadiness of its shining.

The nature of art would then be this: the truth of beings setting itself to work. But until now art presumably has had to do with the beautiful and beauty, and not with truth. The arts that produce such works are called the beautiful or fine arts, in contrast with the applied or industrial arts that manufacture equipment. In fine art the art itself is not beautiful, but is called so because it produces the beautiful. Truth, in contrast, belongs to logic. Beauty, however, is reserved for aesthetics.

But perhaps the proposition that art is truth setting itself to work intends to revive the fortunately obsolete view that art is an imitation and depiction of reality? The reproduction of what exists requires, to be sure, agreement with the actual being, adaptation to it; the Middle Ages called it *adaequatio:* Aristotle already spoke of *homoiosis.* Agreement with what *is* has long been taken to be the essence of truth. But then, is it our opinion that this painting by van Gogh depicts a pair of actually existing peasant shoes, and is a work of art because it does so successfully? Is it our opinion that the painting draws a likeness from something actual and transposes it into a product of artistic—production? By no means.

The work, therefore, is not the reproduction of some particular entity that happens to be present at any given time; it is, on the contrary, the reproduction of the thing's general essence. But then where and how is this general essence, so that art works are able to agree with it? With what nature of what thing should a Greek temple agree? Who could maintain the impossible view that the Idea of Temple is represented in the building? And yet, truth is set to work in such a work, if it is a work. . . .

Truth happens in the temple's standing where it is. This does not mean that something is correctly represented and rendered here, but that what is as a whole is brought into unconcealedness and held therein. To hold (*halten*) originally means to tend, keep, take care (*hüten*). Truth happens in van Gogh's painting. This does not mean that something is correctly portrayed, but rather that in the revelation of the equipmental being of the shoes, that which is as a whole—world and earth in their counterplay—attains to unconcealedness.

Thus in the work it is truth, not only something true, that is at work. The picture that shows the peasant shoes, the poem that says the Roman fountain, do not just make manifest what this isolated being as such is—if indeed they manifest anything at all; rather, they make unconcealedness as such happen in regard to what is as a whole. The more simply and authentically the shoes are engrossed in their nature, the more plainly and purely the fountain is engrossed in its nature—the more directly and engagingly do all beings attain to a greater degree of being along with them. That is how self-concealing being is illuminated. Light of this kind joins its shining to and into the work. This shining, joined in the work, is the beautiful. *Beauty is one way in which truth occurs as unconcealedness.*

We now, indeed, grasp the nature of truth more clearly in certain respects. What is at work in the work may accordingly have become more clear. But the work's now visible work-being still does not tell us anything about the work's closest and most obtrusive reality, about the thingly aspect of the work. Indeed it almost seems as though, in pursuing the exclusive aim of grasping the work's independence as purely as possible, we had completely overlooked the one thing, that a work is always a work, which means that it is something worked out, brought about, effected. If there is anything that distinguishes the work as work, it is that the work has been created. Since the work is created, and creation requires a medium out of which and in which it creates, the thingly element, too, enters into the work. This is

incontestable. Still the question remains: how does being created belong to the work? This can be elucidated only if two points are cleared up:

1. What do being created and creation mean here in distinction from making and being made?
2. What is the inmost nature of the work itself, from which alone can be gauged how far createdness belongs to the work and how far it determines the work-being of the work?

Creation is here always thought of in reference to the work. To the nature of the work there belongs the happening of truth. From the outset we define the nature of creating by its relation to the nature of truth as the unconcealedness of beings. The pertinence of createdness to the work can be elucidated only by way of a more fundamental clarification of the nature of truth. The question of truth and its nature returns again.

We must raise that question once more, if the proposition that truth is at work in the work is not to remain a mere assertion.

We must now first ask in a more essential way: how does the impulse toward such a thing as a work lie in the nature of truth? Of what nature is truth, that it can be set into work, or even under certain conditions must be set into work, in order to be *as* truth? But we defined the setting-into-a-work of truth as the nature of art. Hence our last question becomes:

What is truth, that it can happen as, or even must happen as, art? How is it that art exists at all?

Art is the origin of the art work and of the artist. Origin is the source of the nature in which the being of an entity is present. What is art? We seek its nature in the actual work. The actual reality of the work has been defined by that which is at work in the work, by the happening of truth. This happening we think of as the fighting of the conflict between world and earth. Repose occurs in the concentrated agitation of this conflict. The independence or self-composure of the work is grounded here.

In the work, the happening of truth is at work. But what is thus at work, is so *in* the work. This means that the actual work is here already presupposed as the bearer of this happening. At once the problem of the thingly feature of the given work confronts us again. One thing thus finally becomes clear: however zealously we inquire into the work's self-sufficiency, we shall still fail its actuality as long as we do not also agree to take the work as something worked, effected. To take it thus lies closest at hand, for in the word "work" we hear what is worked. The workly character of the work consists in its having been created by the artist. It may seem curious that this most obvious and all-clarifying definition of the work is mentioned only now.

The work's createdness, however, can obviously be grasped only in terms of the process of creation. Thus, constrained by the facts, we must consent after all to go into the activity of the artist in order to arrive at the origin of the work of art. The attempt to define the work-being of the work purely in terms of the work itself proves to be unfeasible.

In turning away now from the work to examine the nature of the creative process, we should like nevertheless to keep in mind what was said first of the picture of the peasant shoes and later of the Greek temple.

We think of creation as a bringing forth. But the making of equipment, too, is a bringing forth. Handicraft—a remarkable play of language—does not, to be sure, create works, not even when we contrast, as we must, the handmade with the factory product. But what is it that distinguishes bringing forth as creation from bringing forth in the mode of making? . . .

The artist is a *technites* not because he is also a craftsman, but because both the setting forth of works and the setting forth of equipment occur in a bringing forth and presenting that causes beings in the first place to come forward and be present in assuming an appearance. Yet all this happens in the midst of the being that grows out of its own accord, *phusis*. Calling art *techne* does not at all imply that the artist's action is seen in the light of craft. What looks like craft in the creation of a work is of a different sort. This doing is determined and pervaded by the nature of creation, and indeed remains contained within that creating.

What then, if not craft, is to guide our thinking about the nature of creation? What else than a view of what is to be created: the work? Although it becomes actual only as the creative act is performed, and thus depends for its reality upon this act, the nature of creation is determined by the nature of the work. Even though the work's createdness has a relation to creation, nevertheless both createdness and creation must be defined in terms of the work-being of the work. And now it can no longer seem strange that we first and at length dealt with the work alone, to bring its createdness into view only at the end. If createdness belongs to the work as essentially as the word "work" makes it sound, then we must try to understand even more essentially what so far could be defined as the work-being of the work.

In the light of the definition of the work we have reached at this point, according to which the happening of truth is at work in the work, we are able to characterize creation as follows: to create is to cause something to emerge as a thing that has been brought forth. The work's becoming a work is a way in which truth becomes and happens. It all rests on the nature of truth.

The Still Life as a Personal Object— A Note on Heidegger and van Gogh

MEYER SHAPIRO

IN HIS ESSAY ON *The Origin of the Work of Art*, Martin Heidegger interprets a painting by van Gogh to illustrate the nature of art as a disclosure of truth.

He comes to this picture in the course of distinguishing three modes of being: of useful artifacts, of natural things, and of works of fine art. He proposes to describe first, "without any philosophical theory . . . a familiar sort of equipment—a pair of peasant shoes"; and "to facilitate the visual realization of them" he chooses "a well-known painting by van Gogh, who painted such shoes several times." But to grasp "the equipmental being of equipment," we must know "how shoes actually serve." For the peasant woman they serve without her thinking about them or even looking at them. Standing and walking in the shoes, the peasant woman knows the serviceability in which "the equipmental being of equipment consists." But we,

> as long as we only imagine a pair of shoes in general, or simply look at the empty, unused shoes as they merely stand there in the picture, we shall never discover what the equipmental being of equipment in truth is. In van Gogh's painting we cannot even tell where these shoes stand. There is nothing surrounding this pair of peasant shoes in or to which they might belong, only an undefined space. There are not even clods from the soil of the field or the path through it sticking to them, which might at least hint at their employment. A pair of peasant shoes and nothing more. And yet.
>
> From the dark opening of the worn insides of the shoes the toilsome tread of the worker stands forth. In the stiffly solid heaviness of the shoes there is the accumulated tenacity of her slow trudge through the far-spreading and ever-uniform furrows of the field, swept by a raw wind. On the leather there lies the dampness and saturation of the soil. Under the soles there slides the loneliness of the field-path as the evening declines. In the shoes there vibrates the silent call of the earth, its quiet gift of the ripening corn and its enigmatic self-refusal in the fallow desolation of the wintry field. This equipment is pervaded by uncomplaining anxiety about the certainty of bread, the wordless joy of having once more withstood want, the trembling before the advent of birth and shivering at the surrounding menace of death. This equipment belongs to the *earth* and it is protected in the *world* of the peasant woman. From out of this protected belonging the equipment itself rises to its resting-in-self.

Professor Heidegger is aware that van Gogh painted such shoes several times, but he does not identify the picture he has in mind, as if the different versions are interchangeable, all disclosing the same truth. A reader who wishes to compare his account with the original picture or its photograph will have some difficulty in deciding which one to select. . . .

In reply to my question, Professor Heidegger has kindly written me that the picture to which he referred is one that he saw in a show at Amsterdam in March 1930. This is clearly de la Faille's no. 255; there was also exhibited at the same time a painting with three pairs of shoes, and it is possible that the exposed sole of a shoe in this picture, inspired the reference to the sole in the philosopher's account. But from neither of these pictures, nor from any of the others, could one properly say that a painting of shoes by van Gogh expresses the being or essence of a peasant woman's shoes and her relation to nature and work. They are the shoes of the artist, by that time a man of the town and city.

From M. L. Simmel, ed., The Reach of Mind: Essays in Memory of Kurt Goldstein (New York: Springer, 1968). Reprinted by permission of the publisher.

Heidegger has written: "The art-work told us what shoes are in truth. It would be the worst self-deception if we were to think that our description, as a subjective action, first imagined everything thus and then projected it into the painting. If anything is questionable here, it is rather that we experienced too little in contact with the work and that we expressed the experience too crudely and too literally. But above all, the work does not, as might first appear, serve merely for a better visualization of what a piece of equipment is. Rather, the equipmental being of equipment first arrives at its explicit appearance through and only in the artist's work.

"What happens here? What is at work in the work? Van Gogh's painting is the disclosure of what the equipment, the pair of peasant's shoes, *is* in truth."

Alas for him, the philosopher has indeed deceived himself. He has retained from his encounter with van Gogh's canvas a moving set of associations with peasants and the soil, which are not sustained by the picture itself. They are grounded rather in his own social outlook with its heavy pathos of the primordial and earthy. He had indeed "imagined everything and projected it into the painting." He has experienced both too little and too much in his contact with the work.

The error lies not only in his projection, which replaces a close attention to the work of art. For even if he had seen a picture of a peasant woman's shoes, as he describes them, it would be a mistake to suppose that the truth he uncovered in the painting—the being of the shoes—is something given here once and for all and is unavailable to our perception of shoes outside the painting. I find nothing in Heidegger's fanciful description of the shoes pictured by van Gogh that could not have been imagined in looking at a real pair of peasants' shoes. Though he credits to art the power of giving to a represented pair of shoes that explicit appearance in which their being is disclosed—indeed "the universal essence of things," "world and earth in their counterplay"—this concept of the metaphysical power of art remains here a theoretical idea. The example on which he

elaborates with strong conviction does not support that idea.

Is Heidegger's mistake simply that he chose a wrong example? Let us imagine a painting of a peasant woman's shoes by van Gogh. Would it not have made manifest just those qualities and that sphere of being described by Heidegger with such pathos?

Heidegger would still have missed an important aspect of the painting: the artist's presence in the work. In his account of the picture he has overlooked the personal and physiognomic in the shoes that made them so persistent and absorbing a subject for the artist (not to speak of the intimate connection with the specific tones, forms, and brush-made surface of the picture as a painted work). When van Gogh depicted the peasant's wooden sabots, he gave them a clear, unworn shape and surface like the smooth still-life objects he had set beside them on the same table: the bowl, the bottles, a cabbage, etc. In the later picture of a peasant's leather slippers, he has turned them with their backs to the viewer. His own shoes he has isolated on the ground; he has rendered them as if facing us, and so worn and wrinkled in appearance that we can speak of them as veridical portraits of aging shoes. . . .

Yet van Gogh is in some ways like the peasant; as an artist he works, he is stubbornly occupied in a task that is for him his inescapable calling, his life. Of course, van Gogh . . . has also an exceptional gift of representation; he is able to transpose to the canvas with a singular power the forms and qualities of things; but they are things that have touched him deeply, in this case his own shoes—things inseparable from his body and memorable to his reacting self-awareness. They are not less objectively rendered for being seen as if endowed with his feelings and revery about himself. In isolating his own old, worn shoes on a canvas, he turns them to the spectator; he makes of them a piece from a self-portrait, that part of the costume with which we tread the earth and in which we locate strains of movement, fatigue, pressure, heaviness—the burden of the erect body in its contact with the ground. They mark our inescapable position on the earth. To "be in someone's shoes" is to be in his predicament or his station in life. For an artist to isolate his worn shoes as the subject of a picture is for him to convey a concern with the fatalities of his social being. Not only the shoes as an instrument of use, though the landscape painter as a worker in the fields shares something of the peasant's life out-doors, but the shoes as "a portion of the self" . . . are van Gogh's revealing theme.

Gauguin, who shared van Gogh's quarters in Arles in 1888, sensed a personal history behind his friend's painting of a pair of shoes. He has told in his reminiscences of van Gogh a deeply affecting story linked with van Gogh's shoes.

"In the studio was a pair of big hob-nailed shoes, all worn and spotted with mud; he made of it a remarkable still life painting. I do not know why I sensed that there was a story behind this old relic, and I ventured one day to ask him if he had some reason for preserving with re-spect what one ordinarily throws out for the rag-picker's basket.

'My father,' he said, 'was a pastor, and at his urging I pursued theological studies in order to prepare for my future vocation. As a young pas-tor I left for Belgium one fine morning, without telling my family, to preach the gospel in the factories, not as I had been taught but as I un-derstood it myself. These shoes, as you see, have bravely endured the fatigue of that trip.'

Preaching to the miners in the Borinage, Vincent undertook to nurse a victim of a fire in the mine. The man was so badly burned and mutilated that the doctor had no hope for his recovery. Only a miracle, he thought, could save him. Van Gogh tended him forty days with lov-ing care and saved the miner's life.

Before leaving Belgium I had, in the pres-ence of this man who bore on his brow a series of scars, a vision of the crown of thorns, a vision of the resurrected Christ.

Gauguin continues:

"And Vincent took up his palette again; silently he worked. Beside him was a white canvas. I began his portrait. I too had the vision of a Jesus preaching kindness and humility.

It is not certain which of the paintings with a single pair of shoes Gauguin had seen at Arles. He described it as violet in tone in contrast to the yel-low walls of the studio. It does not matter. Though written some years later, and with some literary affectations, Gauguin's story confirms the essential fact that for van Gogh the shoes were a memorable piece of his own life, a sacred relic. . . .

Another version of Gauguin's story is in a later article that he published with the title "Na-ture Mortes" (Still Lifes) in the periodical *Essais d'Art Libre* after van Gogh's death:

"When we were together in Arles, both us of mad, in continual struggle for beautiful colors, I adored red; where could one find a perfect vermilion? He, with his yellowish brush, traced on the wall which suddenly became violet:

Je suis sain d'Esprit   [I am whole in Spirit]

Je suis le Saint-Esprit [I am the Holy Spirit]

"In my yellow-room—a small still life: violet that one. Two enormous wornout misshapen shoes. They were Vincent's shoes. Those that he took one fine morning, when they were new, for his journey on foot from Holland to Belgium. The young preacher had just finished his theo-logical studies in order to be a minister like his father. He had gone off to the mines to those whom he called his brothers, such as he had seen in the Bible, the oppressed simple laborers for the luxury of the rich.

"Contrary to the teaching of his wise Dutch professors, Vincent had believed in a Jesus who loved the poor; and his soul, deeply pervaded by charity, sought the consoling words and sacri-fice for the weak, and to combat the rich. Very decidedly, Vincent was already mad.

"His teaching of the Bible in the mines, I believed, profited the miners below and was dis-agreeable to the high authorities above ground. He was quickly recalled and dismissed, and the assembled family council, having decided he was mad, recommended confinement for his health. However, he was not locked up, thanks to his brother Theo.

"In the dark, black mine one day, chrome yellow overflowed, a terrible fiery glow of damp-fire, the dynamite of the rich who don't lack just that. The creatures who crawled at that moment grovelled in the filthy coal; they said 'adieu' to life that day, good-bye to their fellow-men without blasphemy.

"One of them horribly mutilated, his face burnt, was picked up by Vincent. 'However,' said the company doctor, 'the man is done for, unless by a miracle, or by very expensive motherly care. No, it's foolish to be concerned with him, to busy oneself with him.'

"Vincent believed in miracles, in maternal care. The madman (decidedly he was mad) sat up, keeping watch forty days, at the dying man's bedside. Stubbornly he kept the air from getting into his wounds and paid for the medicines. A comforting priest (decidedly, he was mad). The patient talked. The mad effort brought a dead Christian back to life.

"When the injured man, finally saved, went down again to the mine to resume his labors, 'You could have seen,' said Vincent, 'the martyred head of Jesus, bearing on his brow the zigzags of the Crown of Thorns, the red scars of the sickly yellow of a miner's brow.'

"'And I, Vincent, I painted him,' tracing with his yellow brush, suddenly turned violet, he cried
'I am the Holy Spirit
'I am whole in spirit
"Decidedly, this man was mad." . . .

One can describe van Gogh's painting of his shoes as a picture of objects seen and felt by the artist as a significant part of himself—he faces himself like a mirrored image—chosen, isolated, carefully arranged, and addressed to himself. Is there not in that singular artistic conception an aspect of the intimate and personal, a soliloquy, and expression of the pathos of a troubled human condition in the drawing of an ordinarily neat and in fact well-fitted, self-confident, over-protected clothed body? The thickness and heaviness of the impasto pigment substance, the emergence of the dark shoes from shadow into light, the irregular, angular patterns and surprisingly loosened curved laces extending beyond the silhouettes of the shoes, are not all these component features of van Gogh's odd conception of the shoes? . . .

While attempting to define what "the equipmental being of equipment is in truth," Heidegger ignores what those shoes meant to the painter van Gogh himself. He finds in this signed, unique painting of the shoes that the philosopher had chosen to consider as most significant a "peasant's wordless joy of having once more withstood want, the trembling before the advent of birth and the shivering at the surrounding menace of death. . . . This equipment belongs to the *earth* (his italics) and it is protected in the *world* of the peasant woman. From out of that secured belonging, the equipment itself rises to its resting-in-itself"—as if these shoes were the ones worn by the supposed peasant woman while at work in the fields. Heidegger even conjectures that his reader could imagine himself wearing these old high leather shoes and "making his way homeward with his hoe on an evening in the late fall after the last potato fires have died down." So the truth about these shoes was not only of the poor peasant woman "trembling before the advent of birth" and "the surrounding menace of death"—as if the artist's point of view were impersonal, even in placing the isolated shoes before him *unlaced* and facing the viewer, without the context of the potato field or the disarray of the laces.

Heidegger believes also that this truth is divined by him "without any philosophical theory" and would not be disclosed by any actual pair of peasant shoes alone, detached from the feet, as portrayed in a painting.

One misses in all this both a personal sense of the expression and of van Gogh's feelings of "rejection" by his own parents and by his learned teachers who had to come to doubt his fitness as a Christian preacher and missionary. These breaks are familiar to readers of van Gogh's biography and letters. . . .

The Truth in Painting

JACQUES DERRIDA

KANT EXPLAINS HIMSELF ELSEWHERE on the necessity of having recourse to dead or scholarly languages. The Greek here confers a quasi-conceptual dignity to the notion of this *hors-d'oeuvre* which however does not stand simply outside the work [*hors d'oeuvre*], also acting alongside, right up against the work (*ergon*): Dictionaries most often give "hors-d'oeuvre," which is the strictest translation, but also "accessory, foreign or secondary object," "supplement," "aside," "remainder." It is what the principal subject *must not become*, by being separated from itself: the education of children in legislation (Plato, *Laws*) or the definition of science (Plato, *Theaetetus*) *must not* be treated as *parerga*. In the search for the cause or the knowledge of principles, *one must avoid* letting the *parerga* get the upper hand over the essentials (Aristotle, *Nicomachean Ethics*). Philosophical discourse will always have been *against* the *parergon*. But what about this *against*.

A *parergon* comes against, beside, and in addition to the *ergon*, the work done [*fait*], the fact [*le fait*], the work, but it does not fall to one side, it touches and cooperates within the operation, from a certain outside. Neither simply outside nor simply inside. Like an accessory that one is obliged to welcome on the border, on board [*au bord, à bord*]. It is first of all the on (the) bo(a)rd(er) [*Il est d'abord l'à-bord*]. . . .

So, as an example among examples, the clothing on statues would have the function of a *parergon* and an ornament. This means (*das heisst*), as Kant makes clear, that which is not internal or intrinsic (*innerlich*), as an integral part to the total representation of the object but which belongs to it only in an extrinsic way as a surplus, an addition, an adjunct, a supplement.

Hors-d'oeuvres, then, the clothes of statues, which both decorate and veil their nudity. Hors-d'oeuvres stuck onto the edging of the work nonetheless, and to the edging of the represented body to the extent that—such is the argument—they supposedly do not belong to the whole of the representation. What is represented in the representation would be the naked and natural body; the representative essence of the statue would be related to this, and the only beautiful thing in the statue would be that representation; it alone would be essentially, purely, and intrinsically beautiful, "the proper object of a pure judgment of taste."

This delimitation of the center and the integrity of the representation, of its inside and its outside, might already seem strange. One wonders, too, where to have clothing commence. Where does a *parergon* begin and end. Would any garment be a *parergon*. G-strings and the like. What to do with absolutely transparent veils. And how to transpose the statement to painting. For example, Cranach's Lucretia holds only a light band of transparent veil in front of her sex: where is the *parergon*? Should one regard as a *parergon* the dagger which is not part of her naked and natural body and whose point she holds turned toward herself, touching her skin (in that case only the point of the *parergon* would touch her body, in the middle of a triangle formed by her two breasts and her navel)? A *parergon*, the necklace that she wears around her neck? The question of the representative and objectivizing essence, of its outside and its inside, of the criteria engaged in this delimitation, of the value of naturalness which is presupposed in it, and, secondarily or primarily, of the place of the human body or of its privilege in this whole

From The Truth in Painting, *trans. Geoff Bennington and Ian McLeod (Chicago: University of Chicago Press, 1987). Reprinted by permission of the publisher.*

problematic. If any *parergon* is only added on by virtue of an internal lack in the system to which it is added (as was verified in *Religion*), what is it that is lacking in the representation of the body so that the garments should come and supplement it? And what would art have to do with this? What would it give to be seen? Cause to be seen? Let us see? Let us cause to be seen? Or let itself be shown? . . .

It may appear that I am taking unfair advantage by persisting with two or three possibly fortuitous examples from a secondary subchapter; and that it would be better to go to less marginal places in the work, nearer to the center and the heart of the matter. To be sure. The objection presupposes that one already knows what is the center or the heart of the third *Critique,* that one has already located its frame and the limit of its field. But nothing seems more difficult to determine. The *Critique* presents itself as a work (*ergon*) with several sides, and as such it ought to allow itself to be centered and framed, to have its ground delimited by being marked out, with a frame, against a general background. But this frame is problematical. I do not know what is essential and what is accessory in a work. And above all I do not know what this thing is, that is neither essential nor accessory, neither proper nor improper, and that Kant calls *parergon,* for example the frame. Where does the frame take place? Does it take place? Where does it begin? Where does it end? What is its internal limit? Its external limit? And its surface between the two limits? I do not know whether the passage in the third *Critique* where the *parergon* is defined is itself a *parergon*. Before deciding what is parergonal in a text which poses the question of the *parergon,* one has to know what a *parergon* is—at least, if there is any such thing.

To the impatient objector, as s/he insists on seeing the thing itself at last: the whole analytic of aesthetic judgment forever assumes that one can distinguish rigorously between the intrinsic and the extrinsic. Aesthetic judgment *must* properly bear upon intrinsic beauty, not on finery and surrounds. Hence one must know—this is a fundamental presupposition, presupposing what is fundamental—how to determine the intrinsic—what is framed—and know what one is excluding as frame *and* outside-the-frame. We are thus *already* at the unlocatable center of the problem. And when Kant replies to our question "What is a frame?" by saying: it's a *parergon,* a hybrid of outside and inside, but a hybrid which is not a mixture or a half-measure, an outside which is called to the inside of the inside in order to constitute it as an inside; and when he gives as examples of the *parergon,* alongside the frame, clothing and column, we ask to see, we say to ourselves that there are "great difficulties" here, and that the choice of examples, and their association, is not self-evident.

The more so because, according to the logic of the supplement, the parergon is divided in two. At the limit between work and absence of work, it divides in two. And this division gives rise to a sort of pathology of the *parergon,* the forms of which must be named and classified, just as *Religion* recognized four types of parergonal misdeeds or detriments. Kant is in the process of determining "the proper object of the pure judgment of taste." But he does not simply exclude from it the parergon as such and in general. Only in certain conditions. The criterion of exclusion is here a formality.

What must we understand by formality?

The *parergon* (frame, garment, column) can augment the pleasure of taste, contribute to the proper and intrinsically aesthetic representation if it intervenes *by its form (durch seine Form)* and only by its form. If it has a "beautiful form," it forms part of the judgment of taste properly speaking or in any case intervenes directly in it. This is, if you like, the normal *parergon*. But if on the other hand it is not beautiful, purely beautiful, i.e., of a formal beauty, it lapses into *adornment* and harms the beauty of the work, it does it wrong and causes it detriment. This is analogous to the detriment or damage of *Religion*.

Now the example of this degradation of the simple *parergon* into a seductive adornment is again a frame, this time the gilded frame, the gilding of the frame done in order to recommend the painting to our attention by its attraction.

What is bad, external to the pure object of taste, is thus what seduces by an attraction; and the example of what leads astray by its force of attraction is a color, the gilding, in as much as it is nonform, content, or sensory matter. The deterioration of the *parergon,* the perversion, the adornment, is the attraction of sensory matter. As design, organization of lines, forming of angles, the frame is not at all an adornment and one cannot do without it. But in its purity, it ought to remain colorless, deprived of all empirical sensory materiality. . . .

The frame of this analytic of the beautiful, with its four moments, is thus furnished by the transcendental analytic, for the sole and bad reason that the imagination, the essential resource of the relation to beauty, is *perhaps* linked to the understanding, that there is perhaps and *still* some understanding in there. The relation to the understanding, which is neither certain nor essential, thus furnishes the frame of this whole discourse; and, within it, of the discourse on the frame. Without forcing things, but in any case in order to describe a certain forcing on Kant's part, we shall say that the whole frame of the analytic of the beautiful functions, with respect to that the content or internal structure of which is to be determined, like a *parergon;* it has all its characteristics: neither simply internal nor simply external, not falling to one side of the work as one could have said of an exergue, indispensable to *energeia* in order to liberate surplus value by enclosing labor (any market and first of all the picture market thus presupposes a process of framing: and an effective deconstructive labor cannot here do without a theory of the frame), it is called up and gathered together as a supplement from the lack—a certain "internal" indetermination—in the very thing that it comes to frame. This lack, which cannot be determined, localized, situated, *arrested* inside or outside *before the framing,* is simultaneously—still using concepts which belong, precisely, to the classical logic of the frame, here to Kant's discourse—both *product* and *production* of the frame. If one applies to it the rule defined in the "Clarification by Exam-

ples," and if it becomes in its turn an example of what it allows us to consider as an example (frame described in the frame), then one can act as though the content of the analytic of judgment were a work of art, a picture whose frame, imported from the other *Critique,* would by virtue of its formal beauty play the role of *parergon.* And if it were simply an attractive, seductive, amusing exergue, not cooperating with what is proper to the work, a pure loss of value and waste of surplus value, then it would only be adornment. But it so happens that it is this analytic of judgment itself which, in its frame, allows us to define the requirement of formality, the opposition of the formal and the material, of the pure and the impure, of the proper and the improper, of the inside and the outside. It is the analytic which *determines* the frame as *parergon,* which both constitutes it and ruins it [*l'abîme*], makes it both hold (as that which causes to hold together, that which constitutes, mounts, inlays, sets, borders, gathers, trims—so many operations gathered together by the *Einfassung*) and collapse. A frame is essentially constructed and therefore fragile: such would be the essence or truth of the frame. If it had any. But this "truth" can no longer be a "truth," it no more defines the transcendentality than it does the accidentality of the frame, merely its *parergonality.*

Philosophy wants to arraign it and can't manage. But what has produced and manipulated the frame puts everything to work in order to efface the frame effect, most often by naturalizing it to infinity, in the hands of God (one can verify this in Kant). Deconstruction must neither reframe nor dream of the pure and simple absence of the frame. These two apparently contradictory gestures are the very ones—and they are systematically indissociable—of *what* is here deconstructed.

If the operations engaged and the criteria proposed by the analytic of the beautiful depend on this parergonality; if all the value oppositions which dominate the philosophy of art (before and since Kant) depend on it in their pertinence, their rigor, their purity, their propriety, then they are affected by this logic of the *parergon* which is more powerful than that of the analytic. One could follow in detail the consequences of this infectious affection. They cannot be local. The reflective operation which we have just allowed to make itself writing on the frame or have itself written on the frame (this is—writing/written on the frame): a general law which is no longer a mechanical or teleological law of nature, of the accord or the harmony of the faculties (etc.), but a certain repeated dislocation, a regulated, irrepressible dislocation, which makes the frame in general crack, undoes it at the corners in its quoins and joints, turns its internal limit into an external limit, takes its thickness into account, makes us see the picture from the side of the canvas or the wood, etc.

To note only the first consequence of the initial forcing, see the end of the first note (another *parergon* which frames both the text and, within it as within itself, the parenthesis). Just as Kant cannot justify in all rigor the importation of the analytic of judgment, he cannot justify the *order* he follows in the application of the frame, of the four categories of the analytic of concepts. No more than with the transport of the table, i.e., the frame, does the order of exposition here manage to rationalize its interest philosophically. Its motivation hides behind the arbitrariness of philosophical decree. The exposition begins with the group of the two *mathematical* categories (*quantity and quality*). Why not begin with the two *dynamic* categories (*relation and modality*)? And why invert the order of the mathematical categories themselves, as it was followed in the original exposition (quantity before quality)? This latter reversal is explained, to be sure, by the fact that knowledge is neither the end nor the effect of the judgment of taste: quantity (here, universality) is not the *first* value of a judgment of taste. End of the note: "It is the moment of quality that I have examined first, because it is the one that the aesthetic judgment of the beautiful takes into consideration first." Why first? The priority is not prescribed by the table, by the order of judgment,

by the logic proper to the frame. Nothing in the (logical) analytic as such can account for this priority. Now if a reversal of the logical order takes place here for reasons which are not logical, why should it not continue? What is the rule or critical limit here?

Quality (the disinterested character) is the very thing that determines the formality of the beautiful object: it must be pure of all attraction, of all seductive power, it must provoke no emotion, promise no enjoyment. The *opposition* between the formal and the material, design and color (at least insofar as it is nonformal), composition and sound (at least insofar as it is nonformal), the formal *parergon* and the *parergon* for show or adornment, the opposition between the good and the bad *parergon* which in itself is neither good nor bad) thus depends on the framing of this quality, of this frame effect called quality, value of value, and with which, violently, everything seems to begin. Position: opposition: frame.

Likewise, in the "Clarification," the discourse on sound and on color is held in the angle of the two mathematical categories (quality and quantity) even as the whole analytic of the beautiful is undoing, ceaselessly and as if without wanting to, the labor of the frame.

The frame labors [*travaille*] indeed. Place of labor, structurally bordered origin of surplus value, i.e., overflowed [*débordée*] on these two borders by what it overflows, it gives [*travaille*] indeed. Like wood. It creaks and cracks, breaks down and dislocates even as it cooperates in the production of the product, overflows it and is deduc(t)ed from it. It never lets itself be simply exposed.

The analytic of the beautiful thus gives, ceaselessly undoes the labor of the frame to the extent that, while letting itself be squared up by the analytic of concepts and by the doctrine of judgment, it describes the absence of concept in the activity of taste. "The beautiful is what is represented without concept as object of a universal *Wohlgefallen*." This definition (second moment, category of quantity) derives from the qualitative definition (disinterestedness). The object of a disinterested pleasure does not depend on an empirical inclination, it therefore addresses itself to freedom and touches everyone—no matter who—where everyone can be touched. It is therefore universal. Now in explaining why this universality must be without concept, Kant exhibits in a sense the forcing—imposing an analytic of concepts on a process without concept—but he justifies his operation by an argument that one can consider to be the *constitution,* that which makes the whole edifice of the third *Critique* hold-together-and-stand-upright in the middle of its two great wings (the critique of aesthetic judgment and the critique of teleological judgment). . . .

The self-protection-*of*-the-work, of *energeia* which becomes *ergon* only as (from) *parergon:* not against free and full and pure and unfettered energy (pure act and total presence of *energeia,* the Aristotelian prime mover) but against what is *lacking* in it; not against the lack as a posable or opposable negative, a substantial emptiness, a determinable and bordered absence (still verifiable essence and presence) but against the impossibility of *arresting différance* in its contour, of arraigning the heterogeneous (*différance*) in a pose, of localizing, even in a meta-empirical way, what metaphysics calls, as we have just seen, *lack,* of making it come back, equal or similar to itself (*adaequatio-homoiosis*), to its proper place, according to a proper trajectory, preferably circular (castration as truth). Although apparently opposed—or because opposed—these two *bordering* determinations of what the parergon is working against (the operation of free energy and of pure productivity or the operation of the essential lack) are *the same* (metaphysical). That which is outside the frame (putting-into-lethargy and absolute value of the frame): naturalization of the frame. There is no natural frame. *There is* frame, but the frame *does not exist.*

The parergon—apotrope (decoration, show, parry) *of the* primary processes, of free energy, i.e., of the "theoretical fiction." So only a certain practice of theoretical fiction can work (against)

the frame, (make or let it) play (it) (against) itself. Don't forget, nonetheless, that the *content,* the *object* of this theoretical fiction (the free energy of the originary process, its pure productivity) is metaphysics, onto-theology itself. The practice of fiction always runs the risk of believing in it or having us believe in it. The *practice* of fiction must therefore guard against having metaphysical truth palmed off on it once again under the label of fiction. There is fiction and fiction. Necessity here of the angle—diagonality—where things work and play and give, and of showing up the remnants of the angle in round frames (there are such things). Hegel: spirit linked to the appearance of the round form. . . .

—What interested me, was finally to see explained from a certain angle why I had always found this passage of Heidegger's on van Gogh ridiculous and lamentable. So it really was the naïveté of what Shapiro rightly calls a "projection." One is not only disappointed when his academic high seriousness, his severity and rigor of tone give way to this "illustration" (*bildliche Darstellung*). One is not only disappointed by the consumerlike hurry toward the content of a representation, by the heaviness of the pathos, by the coded triviality of this description, which is both overloaded and impoverished, and one never knows if it's busying itself around a picture, "real" shoes, or shoes that are imaginary but outside painting; not only disappointed by the crudeness of the framing, the arbitrary and barbaric nature of the cutting-out, the massive self-assurance of the identification: "a pair of peasants' shoes," just like that! Where did he get that from? Where does he explain himself on this matter? So one is not only disappointed, one sniggers. The fall in tension is too great. One follows step by step the moves of a "great thinker," as he returns to the origin of the work of art and of truth, traversing the whole history of the West and then suddenly, at a bend in a corridor, here we are on a guided tour, as schoolchildren or tourists. Someone's gone to fetch the guide from the neighboring farm. Full of goodwill. He loves the earth and a certain type of painting when he can find himself in it [*quand il s'y retrouve*]. Giving up his usual activity he goes off to get his key while the visitors wait, slowly getting out of the coach. (There is a Japanese tourist among them, who in a moment will ask a few questions of the guide, in a stage whisper.) Then the tour begins. With his local (Swabian) accent, he tries to get the visitors going (he sometimes manages it and each time this happens he also trembles regularly, in time), he piles up the associations and immediate projections. From time to time he points out of the window to the fields and nobody notices that he's no longer talking about painting. All right. And one says to oneself that the scene, the choice of the example, the procedure of the treatment, nothing in all this is fortuitous. This casual guide is the very person who, before and after this incredible tirade, carries on with his discourse on the origin of the work of art and on truth. It's the same discourse, it has never been interrupted by the slightest digression (what all these professorial procedures with regard to the shoes are lacking in, moreover, is the sense of digression: the shoes have to make a pair and walk on the road, forwards or backwards, in a circle if pushed, but with no digressions or sidesteps allowed; now there is a link between the detachability of the step and the possibility of the digressive). I see that you are shocked, in your deference, by the scene which I have, how shall I put it

—projected.

—Then let's get back into the classroom. All that is classical, class-business, the business of pedagogy and classicity. Professor Heidegger, as Professor Shapiro says in homage to Professor Goldstein, projects a transparency. He wants to capture your interest, through this illustration, right from the beginning of his lecture. For *The Origin* was in the beginning, at a very significant date, a series of lectures delivered before a *kunstwissenschaftliche Gesellschaft* and then before a *freie deutsche Hochstift,* and shows it.

—The word "illustration" has just been uttered. And it had been several times previously. I suggest that that's where we should start, if we must begin and if we must read Shapiro's *Note* against which I intend to defend systematically, at least for the committee exercise, the cause of Heidegger (who, don't forget, also proffers, in this place where it is a question of the thing, an important discourse on the *causa*). A fair number of difficulties arise from what is translated by *illustration*. In his protocol, Shapiro uses this word which also translates [into French] "*bildliche Darstel-lung*" ("For this purpose an illustration suffices. We choose for this a famous picture by van Gogh . . ."). Shapiro opens his text—and *The Origin*—at this point (by what right?) and he writes: "In his essay on *The Origin of the Work of Art,* Martin Heidegger interprets a painting by van Gogh to illustrate the nature of art as a disclosure of truth.

"He comes to this picture in the course of distinguishing three modes of being: of useful artifacts [products], of natural things, and of works of fine art. He proposes to describe first, 'without any philosophical theory . . . a familiar sort of equipment [*Zeug:* product]—a pair of peasant shoes'; and 'to facilitate the visual realization [translating *Veranschaulichung,* intuitive sensory presentation] of them' he chooses 'a well-known painting by van Gogh, who painted such shoes several times.' But to grasp the 'equipmental being of equipment,' we must know 'how shoes actually serve.' For the peasant woman they serve without her thinking about them or even looking at them. Standing and walking in the shoes, the peasant woman knows the serviceability [*Dienlichkeit*] in which 'the equipmental being of equipment consists.' But we . . .". And Shapiro quotes these two paragraphs which you all find so ridiculous or so imprudent. Let's reread them first, in German, in French, in English.

. . . .
. . . .
. . . .

—It's done.

—Before going any further, I shall pick out from the cutting-out in Shapiro's protocol a certain number of simplifications, not to call them anything worse. They have effects on everything that follows. He simplifies matters by saying that Heidegger interprets a painting to illustrate the nature of art as the unveiling of truth. To prove this, one has no need to refer to what the following page says, i.e., (in translation first): "the work in no way served (*diente gar nicht*), as it may have seemed at first, to illustrate more clearly what a product is." What has here been translated as "illustrate" is *Veranschaulichung* this time, and not *Darstellung*, which was also translated above as illustration. *Veranschaulichung*, intuitive presentation, as it were, is what had to be facilitated by invoking the example of the picture. But it is also what *was not done,* although it seemed as though that's what was happening. Heidegger makes this quite clear: the work did not serve us to do that, did not do us this service which, all in all, we pretended to expect from it. It did better than illustrating or presenting something to sensory intuition—or worse, depending on the point of view—it showed, it made appear. Heidegger has just recalled that the work did not "serve" as *Veranschaulichung* or *Darstellung,* and he goes on to specify: "Much more is it the being-product of the product which arrives, properly (*eigens*) and only through the work, at its appearing." This appearing of the being-product does not, according to Heidegger, take place in an elsewhere which the work of art could illustrate by referring to it. It takes place properly (and only) in the work. In its very truth. This might seem to aggravate the illusion denounced by Shapiro and to place under the heading of presentation what was marked down only in the name of *re*presentation, as if Heidegger thought he could see still more directly what Shapiro reproaches him for inferring too hastily. But things are not yet so simple and we shall have to return to this.

First of all: it is not as *peasant* shoes, but as *product* (*Zeug*) or as shoes-*as-product* that the being-product manifested itself. The manifestation is that of the being-product of the product and not of this or that species of product, such as shoes. Such was the function of the *Darstellung.* It must be carefully demarcated in this passage and its stages differentiated. Heidegger is not simply, as Shapiro claims, in the process of distinguishing between three modes of being of the thing.

—Then what *is* going on when the so-called illustration intervenes?

—Heidegger has just analyzed the system of the three couples of determinations superimposed on the thing. They are connected, associated in a sort of "conceptual mechanism" (*Begriffsmechanik*) which nothing resists. Among the effects of this system, the matter/form couple and the concept of thing as informed matter have long dominated every theory of art and every aesthetics. And still do so today. From the moment he is interested here in the work of art, Heidegger insists and makes his question more precise: does this (dominant) form-matter complex have its origin in the being-thing of the thing or else in the being-work of the work and in the being-product (with the participation of man, it is understood, whence the temptation to take this matter-form complex to be the immediate structure of the thing) of the product? In other words, would it not be on the basis of the thing *as* work or as product that this *general* interpretation (or rather one that is claimed to be general) of the thing as informed matter was secretly constituted? Now reread the chapter: in the course of this questioning about the product as informed matter, the example of the pair of shoes appears at least three times *before and in the absence of the least reference to a work of art,* be it pictorial or otherwise. Twice associated with the example of the ax and the pitcher. . . .

—No. One can see *clearly, evidently,* that all that is said first in the first three paragraphs (up to the "And yet" (*Und dennoch*), an articulation or rhetorical suspension which is very unusual in

Heidegger; it must be rigorously taken into account) does not claim to say anything about the picture *itself*. The only object in view is this pair of peasants' shoes mentioned earlier. No trait specific to the picture. After the "And yet" (followed by a period and a new paragraph), the pathetic tirade (what else can you call it?) has the form of an escaping meditation. But escaping from a picture which has only been evoked and into which neither gaze nor discourse has yet penetrated, which they have not even approached or brushed with a description. Nothing has yet been said which strictly concerns the content of the picture and scarcely does it come to be named a second time than it is left again in an evasive discourse which goes beyond it. Look at it attentively: each paragraph is a new wave that pretends to brush against the object and which pulls back immediately. And yet: a light touch, a very brief contact, indeterminate enough to generate just about any discourse going beyond bounds, has left the mark of its passage in the text. So Shapiro's objection will be as light as this, and he will find only this touch to support him in his identification of the picture which he thinks Heidegger is talking about. This touch is "*Aus der dunkeln Öffnung des ausgetretenen Inwendigen des Schuhzeuges,*" "From the dark opening of the worn inside. . . ." It's vague enough, open, loose enough, for one to be able to say it, more or less, about any pair of shoes, real or not, of peasant or city dweller, and in any event, as Shapiro rightly remarks, of three paintings of shoes signed by van Gogh. But once more one can only make this into an objection by attributing to Heidegger an intention, which nothing in his text shows to be there, of describing and referring only to painted shoes, particular painted shoes, within the limits of a frame which can only be crossed in one direction: from the outside to the inside. If one ceases to attribute this intention to Heidegger, on the grounds that this question of the frame is not settled in all its implications [*portées*], then the argument can be turned around against the objector. (Let us not forget that henceforth we shall have to ask again this question of the frame,

the question of this frame, following the figure or trajectory of the *lace:* a stricture by alternate and reversible passage from inside to outside, from under to over. These laces which rise toward the collar "in" the picture or "in" the frame also form the *outline* [*le tour*] of the picture and the frame.) When Shapiro writes a little further on: "I find nothing in Heidegger's fanciful description that could not have been imagined in looking at a real pair of peasants' shoes" [Shapiro, p. 206], one can agree with him. But one can also see in this a confirmation of the fact that Heidegger was not trying to describe a picture. At least not simply, for we are still lacking even the premises of the debate, as well as the frame of the debate and the debate on the frame, on the structure (or the stricture, as we shall soon be saying) of its double limit, internal and external, its double edge.

For Shapiro did indeed pass over in silence, jumping it in his long quotation, what was inscribed on the lower edge of the "pathetic" paragraph (the third paragraph of this passage around the picture). Heidegger begins a new paragraph, as he had after "*Und dennoch,*" and he writes: "But perhaps we see all this only on the shoes in the picture (*im Bilde,* or in image)," as a picture, as an image, etc. The fact that he says "perhaps," that he pretends, at least hypothetically, to see a limit in a description constrained or contained by pictorial determinations, this simple fact clarifies the possibility of crossing the frame in both directions. So in the previous paragraph *there was a claim* to see or read *something other than or beyond* the framed picture, something other than an "image" and this picture. By saying: but perhaps we remained shut up in it as if in a projection or a subjective hallucination, Heidegger confirms fully that his project was to go beyond the picture as representation. The allusion to van Gogh did not therefore have the function attributed to it by Shapiro. The pathetic evasion.

—Heidegger would not accept these words. He would no doubt have more than one question to ask about what Shapiro calls his "pathos."

That would take us too far. And then he doesn't escape, he remains, digs himself in, stays . . .

—I meant "escape" by overflowing a pictorial limit with its collar flared out or half-turned inside out, by the crossing of the framed representation, of visible immediacy, if any such thing exists, *in* the picture. Is this overflowing the discursive operation itself, from the first word, the first articulation? Or else does it have its internal reason, in some way, *in* the pictorial structure? The question which interests me is one of those which are not thematically posed by either of the correspondents. It concerns the structure of this limit, of being-in or being-out. With regard both to the product and to the work. This is in effect the question of the supplement of *parergon* which relays or pulls along with it a certain number of other questions which I do not have the time to enumerate. From the moment that the evasion makes its takeoff from such an impoverished and indeterminate descriptive touch, any other descriptive trait (there are, so to speak, no others) would no longer concern a painting. For example (but there is no other example): "On the leather lies the rich damp earth. Under the soles. . . ." And even this "under" would push down to the underside of the canvas

—which would be the sole?

—if the canvas alone were designated. For these reasons alone, already, one cannot reproach Heidegger with getting the wrong picture, with muddling up several pictures, with describing badly or projecting into an imaginary space. He does not claim in all rigor to refer to a picture in general, or to some particular picture. . . .

—I should like to go further. No longer in order to shield Heidegger from Shapiro's verdict or to find "attenuating circumstances" for him. But to bring out, beyond Shapiro's *three demands,* a wave of supplementary identification. Supplementary since identification, like attribution, has a *supplementary* or *parergonal* structure. And

supplementary because this demand for reattachment is by definition insatiable, unsatisfied, always making a higher bid. It always starts out again, it puts more on each time. After having, in a defensive and critical mode, contested the right of agricultural property claimed by Heidegger, Shapiro passes over to the general offensive. The offensive is unleashed with the following question: does Heidegger's error (the demonstration of which is taken for granted) stem simply from a bad choice of example? No, it is rather that he was unable to analyze his own example, and even if he had been right to "see" peasant woman's shoes, he would have missed the essential thing, "the presence of the artist in his work." Here it is: "Is Heidegger's mistake simply that he chose a wrong example? Let us imagine a painting of a peasant woman's shoes by van Gogh. Would it not have made manifest just those qualities and that sphere of being described by Heidegger with such pathos? Heidegger would have missed an important aspect of the painting: the artist's presence in the work." From this moment, the reappropriation of the shoes by his own van Gogh will have no more limits, for Shapiro. At the end of the offensive, we will no longer be dealing with a detachable personal object (a personal item or a piece of the body), an object in short which would belong to van Gogh without being confused with him, even if it were a phantom member. We would be *in the presence of* van Gogh himself. The painting would manifest the "presence" of the artist himself in his "self-portrait," not only "a piece of his own life" but a nondetachable piece and one which therefore drags his whole body with it, one of those "things inseparable from his body" and even from his upright, "erect" body ("the erect body in its contact with the ground"): the step of van Gogh returning [as a ghost], *passing* into the picture. Between the body of this passerby and the shoes, between his feet and the shoes, between the two shoes themselves, in the *pair,* no more separation is possible. The real referent of the picture, the model which was so ingenuously attributed up to now to the copy, has now grown to take over the totality of the subject. The title of the picture, its legend: *Hoc est corpus meum*. One is encouraged to make this deciphering: van Gogh gives himself, gives himself to be seen, makes the sacrificial offering of his flesh in giving his shoes to be seen. And Gauguin, quoted by Shapiro in conclusion, would confirm it: he has in front of him the "vision of the resurrected Christ," "the vision of a Jesus preaching goodness and humility."

No more detachment: the shoes are no longer attached-to-van-Gogh, they *are* Vincent himself, who is undetachable from himself. They do not even figure one of his parts but his whole presence gathered, pulled tight, contracted into itself, with itself, in proximity with itself: a *parousia*.

Is it, then, a paradox or a necessity of what was called "correspondence"? Yet the moment when Shapiro seems to oppose Heidegger most radically is also the moment when his procedure most resembles that of his opposite number. How is this mediated identification produced?

So the great offensive begins at the moment when Shapiro pretends, as a tactical concession, to imagine peasant woman's shoes painted by van Gogh. In order to show that even in this case Heidegger would have missed the essential, the presence of the artist in the work, he has to rediscover the traits of Vincent in the body of the peasant woman: Vincent as a peasant woman. Better still, the peasant woman van Gogh in her/his shoes. This goes far but would be still more interesting if the protocols of this identification were different. But it matters little. It's now a question of putting a face on (into) the shoes, the face of the signatory. *Vincent van Gogh fuit hic.* What Heidegger allegedly neglected, ignored ("overlooked"), is the "personal" and the "physiognomic" aspect of these shoes. Unlike the wooden clogs which he painted at other moments (peasant clogs, clear, clean, and with no trace of wear, therefore impersonal), unlike the leather slippers (peasant slippers, seen from behind), here he shows the shoes *face-on,* coming toward us, looking at the spectator ("as if facing us"), staring at us, a star-

ing or stared-at face, with individual traits, wrinkles, a "veridical portrait of aging shoes." Somewhat as one would say "portrait of aging shoes." Somewhat as one would say "portrait of an old man," or better, to extend Shapiro's intention: *a portrait of the artist as an old thing.*

The reattachment is so tight (absolute) that it is effaced or absolved: the painted shoes are no longer only the real and really present shoes *of* real and present Vincent; they do not only come back to his feet: they *are* Vincent van Gogh from top to toe. *To shoe* equals *to be:* you should restitute the full consequences of that.

The top: that's where Vincent signed a self-portrait, and illustrated his signature, subject of the painted shoes, and if in this self-portrait he hid the feet, it would not have been in order to abandon empty (*restant*) shoes but because these shoes *are* the face of Vincent: the leather of his aged, wrinkled skin, loaded with experience and weariness, furrowed by life and above all very *familiar* (*heimlich*). If the haunted shoes are without feet, it would not be in order to remain, detached (untied), lower than the soles but to be, higher than any member, absolutely reattached: the point of attachment here is another neck. It elevates up to the face/figure, it transfigures. The transfigured shoes are in a state of levitation, they are the haloes of themselves. Don't look down any more, toward the low or the very low (the feet, the shoes, the soil, the subsoil) but once more (follow the peasant woman) look up, toward the most high, the face facing you, the Face.

We could get the impression that we're at the other pole, in relation to *The Origin*. Heidegger was pulling toward the bottom, the earth, the abyss, etc. Now toward the face of subjectivity. And yet.

And yet, despite or because of this maximal opposition, the words enter into connivance, they begin to resemble each other strangely, to send back each other's image, to be identified by more traits than one. Of course, the identification will not be complete and the correspondence will have its limits. Like any pair. And yet, when Shapiro opposes this self-portrait to Heidegger, his accent recalls that of *The Origin:* "Yet van Gogh is in many ways like the peasant; as an artist he works, he is stubbornly occupied in a persistent task that is for him his inescapable calling, his life . . . that part of the costume with which we tread the earth and in which we locate the strains of movement, fatigue, pressure, heaviness—the burden of the erect body in its contact with the ground. They mark our inescapable position on the earth."

—Yes, there is indeed this return to the earth and this concentration of a world of the artisanate in the shoes, peasants' work, etc. It is the same "pathos." But Shapiro's statements take their authorization from the analogy between the painter and the peasant. This is not the case with Heidegger.

—It's not so certain, or so simple. This analogy is of course above all a theme of van Gogh: I am a peasant, I am a cobbler, I belong to this world, and when I paint myself, so often—

—Shall we not take the fact that van Gogh so often says and paints "me" as an "attenuating circumstance" for Shapiro this time, as with the painter's "peasant" ideology for Heidegger?

—Nobody's being accused, or above all condemned, or even suspected. *There is* painting, writing, restitutions, that's all. Who among you knows van Gogh? Does anyone here know Heidegger? Goldstein? Shapiro? This square—

D. Cultural Materialism

The term *cultural materialism* is derived from, and sometimes interchangeable with, Marxism, the Frankfurt School of critical theory, and now simply the academic discipline known as "cultural studies," but this label can also be confused with "popular culture" studies or the study of medieval, Victorian, or any historical epoch. The cultural materialism that the selections here represent are definitely the first category: critics who are most concerned with the economic, political, ideological and social implications of art and aesthetic theory. All four critics—Walter Benjamin, Theodor Adorno, Tony Bennett, and Griselda Pollock—would claim Marx and the neo-Marxism of the twentieth century as influential in their work. The difference, however, between Benjamin's, Adorno's, Bennett's, and Pollock's—and especially Bennett's and Pollock's—critical projects and older, monolithic (i.e., allowing only one interpretation) Marxism is that the later critics no longer buy into an inflexible, uniform grand narrative of the progress of history, the demise of capitalism, and the impending proletariat revolution.

Instead, what each of these critics as well as many post–World War II Marxists or cultural materialists take from Marxism is Marx's attention to economic and political conditions in any given situation. They also take, some more than others, Marx's adoption of Hegel's philosophy (see Part I). There are two important concepts to understand reading cultural materialists: (1) the dialectic, and (2) the teleology of history. First, the dialectic is made up of three parts: thesis, antithesis and synthesis. For instance, there is the original position (the *thesis*), a counterposition (the *antithesis*) and then a reconciliation between the two positions (the *synthesis*). In turn, the synthesis forms a new thesis that provokes an antithesis—which then leads to a new reconciliation in the synthesis—and the process starts all over again. Hegel believed that all events in history and all ideas (the history of ideas), too, formed a web of the dialectical. Second, the word *teleology* means "doctrine of final causes" and "the study or belief that purpose exists in nature." Therefore, a teleology of history would indicate that there is an endpoint in history or a culmination and that time is moving in a purposeful way toward that endpoint or culmination. In older forms of Marxism the endpoint is, of course, the socialist revolution, but contemporary cultural materialists are less optimistic that such a revolution will ever occur. Still, cultural materialists attempt to remain faithful to these two aspects of Marxist Hegelianism, usually by employing the dialectic as a methodology and by modifying their version of the great proletariat revolution (since we have now passed beyond the industrial age into the technological age).

Our first selection, "The Work of Art in the Age of Mechanical Reproduction," was written by Walter Benjamin in the 1930s. Fleeing the Nazis in 1940, Benjamin committed suicide at the Port-Bou border; the border guards, as the story goes, were so impressed or shaken by the suicide that they allowed the rest of the fleeing party to pass into Spain. As a result of his untimely death, the bulk of Benjamin's work has been published posthumously, receiving a great deal of attention only in the last twenty years because of the originality of Benjamin's thought. Although supported by the Institute for Social Research affiliated with the University of Frankfurt, Benjamin was often criticized by his colleagues Theodor Adorno and Max Horkheimer of the Frankfurt School for being "undialectical" and writing in "materialistic categories, which by no means coincide with Marxists ones," implying that Benjamin was not a fully committed Marxist. Nevertheless, Benjamin's work was influenced by his reading of Marx and, more important, by his fascination with the material side of literature, art, and culture.

Indeed, "The Work of Art in the Age of Mechanical Reproduction" begins with Benjamin's harsh assessment of fascism's so-called theory of art, and he wants to make certain that his essay is not aligned by mistake with right-wing fascist sympathies: "The concepts which are introduced into the theory of art in what follows differ from the more familiar terms in that they are completely useless for the purposes of Fascism. They are, on the other hand, useful for the formulation of revolutionary demands in the politics of art." Benjamin eventually states that film, the new technological art form that has the capacity to influence and manipulate millions, is employed by political factions (the fascists) to give the illusion that the "masses" "have a chance to express themselves," while all other rights, including the right to expression, are taken away.

Apart from the lurking shadow of the political and an almost prophetic voice concerning humankind's immaturity in the use and application of technology, Benjamin puts forth an analysis of the fundamental change that Western culture has undergone in terms of aesthetic sensibility or appreciation and the aesthetic quality of the artwork. According to Benjamin, the original work of art carries with it a certain "aura" that comes from its singularity, from its authenticity. For example, there is only one *Mona Lisa*, no matter how many forgeries may have been painted of the famous lady in the last few hundred years and no matter how many picture postcards the Louvre in Paris sells to tourists. As we discussed earlier, the West has always privileged—going back to Plato—the authority of the original. Benjamin also discusses this tradition: "The authenticity of a thing is the essence of all that is transmissible from its beginning, ranging from its substantive duration to its testimony to the history which it has experienced. . . . And what is really jeopardized when the historical testimony is affected is the authority of the object." Benjamin believes that once the original artwork is no longer privileged because mechanical reproduction is routine, then the aura that surrounds the work is diminished. Two important and, for Benjamin, troubling events then occur. First, when the aura is diminished, or indeed completely lost, then something fundamental changes in humankind's ability to appreciate art. In other words, perception changes along with humanity's entire mode of existence. Second, the way artworks are produced and the kinds of media used to make works of art also changes as art is suddenly produced with the idea or the intention of such reproduction (copied). Benjamin's essay at once laments the past of the early modern period and foresees the future of late modernism and postmodernism.

Theodor Adorno is perhaps most widely known for his work with the senior member of the Frankfurt School, Max Horkheimer, in *The Dialectic of Enlightenment*, "written when the end of the Nazi terror was in sight." This text has been read in recent years as a forerunner to the thought of such poststructuralists as Derrida, Lyotard, and Foucault. Although some of their topics—such as the critique of methodology, power in its manifestations, and nontotalitarian practices in thought and politics—are similar, it would seem that Adorno and Horkheimer's agendas (in terms of allegiances) are quite different. Adorno, however, like Benjamin, never had any official ties to a socialist or Marxist political party beyond his affiliation with the Frankfurt School, in which he played the role of chief aesthetician.

Adorno's early training was in music, having studied with the composer Schoenberg, an innovator in atonal composition. His best-known work on art theory is *Negative Dialectics;* Adorno's *Aesthetic Theory*, excerpted here, was unfinished at the time of his death. Writing at a difficult period of art history, during the 1960s, when the margin between art and the general public was growing ever wider, Adorno takes the high road: privileging high art principles against a more traditional Marxist position of siding with the "masses." The tension between high art and a more popular stance is indicated when Adorno states: "Aesthetic identity is different, however, in one important respect: it is meant to assist and is non-identical in its struggle against the repressive identification compulsion that rules the outside world." In this statement Adorno privileges, or even "fetishizes," the work of art, placing art above empirical reality because it can tell us something about ourselves and that reality. Later he explains that "there is only one way to explain this, which is to view them as being subject to a dynamic or immanent historicity and a dialectical tension between nature and the domination of nature, a dialectic that seems to be of the same kind as the dialectic of society, or to put it more cautiously, the dialectic of art resembles the social dialectic without consciously imitating it."

Employing the dialectic as a methodological tool, Adorno manages to grant the art object a special place outside human social reality; it is a fetishized object, pure and basically untouched, though participating with, society. This paradox is one of the more basic difficulties that Marxists or cultural materialists have with implementing Marxist theory into the realm of art. On one hand, if art is untouchable, then it lies outside social and political reality (and hence outside Marxism). On the other hand, if art is a product or a manifestation of economic or political reality, then we can talk about it in terms of market forces (Why should a van Gogh be worth $35 million?), or about how bourgeois (middle class) tastes have influenced aesthetic theory for the last three hundred years.

Yet how do we go about talking about the object? It is one thing to talk about the conditions in terms of historical or contemporary political and economic reality, but it is quite another to talk about the aesthetic properties of Beethoven's Fifth Symphony or Barnett Newman's *Be I* (p. 336). And perhaps it is even more difficult to articulate why a work of art is good art or why one particular work of art is better than another from a Marxist position. Although disconcerting to the Marxists, the ability to talk about formal characteristics in art comes from a bourgeois (Burke, Kant, Schopenhauer) aesthetic tradition.

All of these various difficulties lead Tony Bennett to state that "assessed from the point of view of its yield for a socialist politics, aesthetics discourse, I want to argue, constitutes a really useless form of knowledge." Bennett feels that Marxist discourse has never been wholly adequate to the task. As he theorizes in *Outside Literature:* "Wherever the commitment to founding a Marxist aesthetic has been made, the task of developing concepts and methods appropriate to the analysis of the functioning and effects of artistic practices in the context of the historically variable social relations regulating their production and consumption has been evacuated in advance of its commencement." In other words, whenever Marxists decide to attempt aesthetic theory, they abandon—before they even begin—the formulation of a properly adequate methodology to study the economic and cultural reality in relation to the question of art.

Although a contemporary cultural materialist, Bennett sees very clearly the blindness of the previous efforts on the part of Marxists to form an aesthetic theory. What he sets out to show in the excerpt from "Really Useless 'Knowledge': A Political Critique of Aesthetics," is that aesthetic judgment or taste is actually a value and not a universal property (echoes of Nietzsche and the poststructuralists?). Bennett argues that Hume's theory of taste (Part I) relies on a rational agreement between certain members of a "drawing-room" society: "the bourgeois public maintains a united front, the illusion of a universality, in face of the masses, conducting its disagreements behind closed—and barred—doors." Likewise, Kant universalizes "the rules for valuing that are legislative within civilized society" which "accomplishes the same ideological work." In short, one must be accredited first with the proper drawing-room tastes, before one is qualified to talk about art. If this is the case, then the masses, or simply the public, will never be able to participate in aesthetic discourse or even, it seems, appreciate the kind of art found in art galleries and museums all across the country.

In the selection from her "Feminist Art Histories and Marxism," Griselda Pollock tries to reconcile Marxism with feminist art theory. As she surveys existing art histories, she finds that in their lack of broad social context most are not really histories at all, but "mere chronologies." That is, most current art histories fail to show how art evolves within a changing society. In this respect Pollock supports Marxist theory, which does provide a socialist history of art based on class struggle. But, as she points out, there is gender as well as class inequality—thus, the need to somehow combine Marxism with feminism. The problem, as she sees it, is the naive acceptance of the modernist myth (see Rosalind Krauss in Part III, section A) of the artist as a lonely, creative genius struggling against, and therefore basically outside, society (e.g., van

Gogh), which is basically a masculine stereotype. Assumed in most art history, from the very beginning, is the idea that men create art, while women merely create babies. Far more than identifying more ignored women artists from the past, the problem lies, according to Pollock, in the way art history is written. Even when we find female artists who were ignored in the past, we still tend to belittle their art as somehow more modest, softer, less heroic, less adventuresome, dealing with relatively more minor, less significant themes—in short, as essentially female and therefore inferior.

Pollock's solution? To begin to look at art in terms of the constantly changing means of "production," that is, the conditions in which things are produced in society from one period to another. If we think of the role of women in social production (in the home, the farm, the factory, and so on), we can begin to understand that the idea of women as artists has changed considerably over time. Surprisingly, perhaps, Pollock's research revealed that women were not always given such a negligible role in art history, but that this is in fact a relatively recent phenomenon. Not only were women actively involved in building the Gothic cathedrals, for instance, but they were also given their due place in historical accounts of that time. Contemporary art history, in other words, has perpetuated yet another modernist myth, presenting the exclusion of women from the art world in the most recent period as something historically eternal, static, and therefore unchangeable.

The Work of Art in the Age of Mechanical Reproduction

WALTER BENJAMIN

WHEN MARX UNDERTOOK HIS critique of the capitalistic mode of production, this mode was in its infancy. Marx directed his efforts in such a way as to give them prognostic value. He went back to the basic conditions underlying capitalistic production and through his presentation showed what could be expected of capitalism in the future. The result was that one could expect it not only to exploit the proletariat with increasing intensity, but ultimately to create conditions which would make it possible to abolish capitalism itself.

The transformation of the superstructure, which takes place far more slowly than that of the substructure, has taken more than half a century to manifest in all areas of culture the change in the conditions of production. Only today can it be indicated what form this has taken. Certain prognostic requirements should be met by these statements. However, theses about the art of the proletariat after its assumption of power or about the art of a classless society would have less bearing on these demands than theses about the developmental tendencies of art under present conditions of production. Their dialectic is no less noticeable in the superstructure than in the economy. It would therefore be wrong to underestimate the value of such theses as a weapon.

From Hannah Arendt, ed., Illuminations, *trans. Harry Zohn (New York: Schocken Books, 1969). Reprinted by permission of the publisher.*

They brush aside a number of outmoded concepts, such as creativity and genius, eternal value and mystery—concepts whose uncontrolled (and at present almost uncontrollable) application would lead to a processing of data in the Fascist sense. The concepts which are introduced into the theory of art in what follows differ from the more familiar terms in that they are completely useless for the purposes of Fascism. They are, on the other hand, useful for the formulation of revolutionary demands in the politics of art. . . .

Even the most perfect reproduction of a work of art is lacking in one element: its presence in time and space, its unique existence at the place where it happens to be. This unique existence of the work of art determined the history to which it was subject throughout the time of its existence. This includes the changes which it may have suffered in physical condition over the years as well as the various changes in its ownership. The traces of the first can be revealed only by chemical or physical analyses which it is impossible to perform on a reproduction; changes of ownership are subject to a tradition which must be traced from the situation of the original.

The presence of the original is the prerequisite to the concept of authenticity. Chemical analyses of the patina of a bronze can help to establish this, as does the proof that a given manuscript of the Middle Ages stems from an archive of the fifteenth century. The whole sphere of authenticity is outside technical—and, of course, not only technical—reproducibility. Confronted with its manual reproduction, which was usually branded as a forgery, the original preserved all its authority; not so *vis à vis* technical reproduction. The reason is twofold. First, process reproduction is more independent of the original than manual reproduction. For example, in photography, process reproduction can bring out those aspects of the original that are unattainable to the naked eye yet accessible to the lens, which is adjustable and chooses its angle at will. And photographic reproduction, with the aid of certain processes, such as enlargement or slow motion, can capture

images which escape natural vision. Secondly, technical reproduction can put the copy of the original into situations which would be out of reach for the original itself. Above all, it enables the original to meet the beholder halfway, be it in the form of a photograph or a phonograph record. The cathedral leaves its locale to be received in the studio of a lover of art; the choral production, performed in an auditorium or in the open air, resounds in the drawing room.

The situations into which the product of mechanical reproduction can be brought may not touch the actual work of art, yet the quality of its presence is always depreciated. This holds not only for the art work but also, for instance, for a landscape which passes in review before the spectator in a movie. In the case of the art object, a most sensitive nucleus—namely, its authenticity—is interfered with whereas no natural object is vulnerable on that score. The authenticity of a thing is the essence of all that is transmissible from its beginning, ranging from its substantive duration to its testimony to the history which it has experienced. Since the historical testimony rests on the authenticity, the former, too, is jeopardized by reproduction when substantive duration ceases to matter. And what is really jeopardized when the historical testimony is affected is the authority of the object.

One might subsume the eliminated element in the term "aura" and go on to say: that which withers in the age of mechanical reproduction is the aura of the work of art. This is a symptomatic process whose significance points beyond the realm of art. One might generalize by saying: the technique of reproduction detaches the reproduced object from the domain of tradition. By making many reproductions it substitutes a plurality of copies for a unique existence. And in permitting the reproduction to meet the beholder or listener in his own particular situation, it reactivates the object reproduced. These two processes lead to a tremendous shattering of tradition which is the obverse of the contemporary crisis and renewal of mankind. Both processes are intimately connected with the contemporary mass movements. Their most powerful agent is the film. Its social significance, particularly in its most positive form, is inconceivable without its destructive, cathartic aspect, that is, the liquidation of the traditional value of the cultural heritage. This phenomenon is most palpable in the great historical films. It extends to ever new positions. In 1927 Abel Gance exclaimed enthusiastically: "Shakespeare, Rembrandt, Beethoven will make films . . . all legends, all mythologies and all myths, all founders of religion, and the very religions . . . await their exposed resurrection, and the heroes crowd each other at the gate." Presumably without intending it, he issued an invitation to a far-reaching liquidation.

During long periods of history, the mode of human sense perception changes with humanity's entire mode of existence. The manner in which human sense perception is organized, the medium in which it is accomplished, is determined not only by nature but by historical circumstances as well. The fifth century, with its great shifts of population, saw the birth of the late Roman art industry and the Vienna Genesis, and there developed not only an art different from that of antiquity but also a new kind of perception. The scholars of the Viennese school, Riegl and Wickhoff, who resisted the weight of classical tradition under which these later art forms had been buried, were the first to draw conclusions from them concerning the organization of perception at the time. However far-reaching their insight, these scholars limited themselves to showing the significant, formal hallmark which characterized perception in late Roman times. They did not attempt—and, perhaps, saw no way—to show the social transformations expressed by these changes of perception. The conditions for an analogous insight are more favorable in the present. And if changes in the medium of contemporary perception can be comprehended as decay of the aura, it is possible to show its social causes.

The concept of aura which was proposed above with reference to historical objects may usefully be illustrated with reference to the aura of natural ones. We define the aura of the latter as the unique phenomenon of a distance, however close it may be. If, while resting on a summer afternoon, you follow with your eyes a mountain range on the horizon or a branch which casts its shadow over you, you experience the aura of those mountains, of that branch. This image makes it easy to comprehend the social bases of the contemporary decay of the aura. It rests on two circumstances, both of which are related to the increasing significance of the masses in contemporary life. Namely, the desire of contemporary masses to bring things "closer" spatially and humanly, which it just as ardent as their bent toward overcoming the uniqueness of every reality by accepting its reproduction. Every day the urge grows stronger to get hold of an object at very close range by way of its likeness, its reproduction. Unmistakably, reproduction as offered by picture magazines and newsreels differs from the image seen by the unarmed eye. Uniqueness and permanence are as closely linked in the latter as are transitoriness and reproducibility in the former. To pry an object from its shell, to destroy its aura, is the mark of a perception whose "sense of the universal equality of things" has increased to such a degree that it extracts it even from a unique object by means of reproduction. Thus is manifested in the field of perception what in the theoretical sphere is noticeable in the increasing importance of statistics. The adjustment of reality to the masses and of the masses to reality is a process of unlimited scope, as much for thinking as for perception.

The uniqueness of a work of art is inseparable from its being imbedded in the fabric of tradition. This tradition itself is thoroughly alive and extremely changeable. An ancient statue of Venus, for example, stood in a different traditional context with the Greeks, who made it an object of veneration, than with the clerics of the Middle Ages, who viewed it as an ominous idol. Both of them, however, were equally confronted with its uniqueness, that is, its aura. Originally the contextual integration of art in tradition found its expression in the cult. We know that the earliest art works originated in the service of a ritual—first the magical, then the religious kind. It is significant that the existence of the work of art with reference to its aura is never entirely separated from its ritual function. In other words, the unique value of the "authentic" work of art has its basis in ritual, the location of its original use value. This ritualistic basis, however remote, is still recognizable as secularized ritual even in the most profane forms of the cult of beauty. The secular cult of beauty, developed during the Renaissance and prevailing for three centuries, clearly showed that ritualistic basis in its decline and the first deep crisis which befell it. With the advent of the first truly revolutionary means of reproduction, photography, simultaneously with the rise of socialism, art sensed the approaching crisis which has become evident a century later. At the time, art reacted with the doctrine of *l'art pour l'art,* that is, with a theology of art. This gave rise to what might be called a negative theology in the form of the idea of "pure" art, which not only denied any social function of art but also any categorizing by subject matter. (In poetry, Mallarmé was the first to take this position.)

An analysis of art in the age of mechanical reproduction must do justice to these relationships, for they lead us to an all-important insight: for the first time in world history, mechanical reproduction emancipates the work of art from its parasitical dependence on ritual. To an ever greater degree the work of art reproduced becomes the work of art designed for reproducibility. From a photographic negative, for example, one can make any number of prints; to ask for the "authentic" print makes no sense. But the instant the criterion of authenticity ceases to be applicable to artistic production, the total function of art is reversed. Instead of being based on ritual, it begins to be based on another practice—politics.

Works of art are received and valued on different planes. Two polar types stand out: with one, the accent is on the cult value; with the other, on the exhibition value of the work. Artistic production begins with ceremonial objects destined to serve in a cult. One may assume that what mattered was their existence, not their being on view. The elk portrayed by the man of the Stone Age on the walls of his cave was an instrument of magic. He did expose it to his fellow men, but in the main it was meant for the spirits. Today the cult value would seem to demand that the work of art remain hidden. Certain statues of gods are accessible only to the priest in the cella; certain Madonnas remain covered nearly all year round; certain sculptures on medieval cathedrals are invisible to the spectator on ground level. With the emancipation of the various art practices from ritual go increasing opportunities for the exhibition of their products. It is easier to exhibit a portrait bust that can be sent here and there than to exhibit the statue of a divinity that has its fixed place in the interior of a temple. The same holds for the painting as against the mosaic or fresco that preceded it. And even though the public presentability of a mass originally may have been just as great as that of a symphony, the latter originated at the moment when its public presentability promised to surpass that of the mass.

With the different methods of technical reproduction of a work of art, its fitness for exhibition increased to such an extent that the quantitative shift between its two poles turned into a qualitative transformation of its nature. This is comparable to the situation of the work of art in prehistoric times when, by the absolute emphasis on its cult value, it was, first and foremost, an instrument of magic. Only later did it come to be recognized as a work of art. In the same way today, by the absolute emphasis on its exhibition value the work of art becomes a creation with entirely new functions, among which the one we are conscious of, the artistic function, later may be recognized as incidental. This much is certain: today photography and the film are the most serviceable exemplifications of this new function. . . .

For the film, what matters primarily is that the actor represents himself to the public before the camera, rather than representing someone else. One of the first to sense the actor's metamorphosis by this form of testing was Pirandello. Though his remarks on the subject in his novel *Si Gira* were limited to the negative aspects of the question and to the silent film only, this hardly impairs their validity. For in this respect, the sound film did not change anything essential. What matters is that the part is acted not for an audience but for a mechanical contrivance—in the case of the sound film, for two of them. "The film actor," wrote Pirandello, "feels as if in exile—exiled not only from the stage but also from himself. With a vague sense of discomfort he feels inexplicable emptiness: his body loses its corporeality, it evaporates, it is deprived of reality, life, voice, and the noises caused by his moving about, in order to be changed into a mute image, flickering an instant on the screen, then vanishing into silence. . . . The projector will play with his shadow before the public, and he himself must be content to play before the camera." This situation might also be characterized as follows: for the first time—and this is the effect of the film—man has to operate with his whole living person, yet forgoing its aura. For aura is tied to his presence; there can be no replica of it. The aura which, on the stage, emanates from Macbeth, cannot be separated for the spectators from that of the actor. However, the singularity of the shot in the studio is that the camera is substituted for the public. Consequently, the aura that envelops the actor vanishes, and with it the aura of the figure he portrays.

It is not surprising that it should be a dramatist such as Pirandello who, in characterizing the film, inadvertently touches on the very crisis in which we see the theater. Any thorough study proves that there is indeed no greater contrast than that of the stage play to a work of art that is completely subject to or, like the film, founded in, mechanical reproduction. Experts have long recognized that in the film "the greatest effects are almost always obtained by 'acting' as little as possible. . . ." In 1932 Rudolf Arnheim saw "the latest trend . . . in treating the actor as a stage prop chosen for its characteristics and . . . inserted at the proper place." With this idea something else is closely connected. The stage actor identifies himself with the character of his role. The film actor very often is denied this opportunity. His creation is by no means all of a piece; it is composed of many separate performances. Besides certain fortuitous considerations, such as cost of studio, availability of fellow players, décor, etc., there are elementary necessities of equipment that split the actor's work into a series of mountable episodes. In particular, lighting and its installation require the presentation of an event that, on the screen, unfolds as a rapid and unified scene, in a sequence of separate shootings which may take hours at the studio; not to mention more obvious montage. Thus a jump from the window can be shot in the studio as a jump from a scaffold, and the ensuing flight, if need be, can be shot weeks later when outdoor scenes are taken. Far more paradoxical cases can easily be construed. Let us assume that an actor is supposed to be startled by a knock at the door. If his reaction is not satisfactory, the director can resort to an expedient: when the actor happens to be at the studio again he has a shot fired behind him without his being forewarned of it. The frightened reaction can be shot now and be cut into the screen version. Nothing more strikingly shows that art has left the realm of the "beautiful semblance" which, so far, had been taken to be the only sphere where art could thrive.

The feeling of strangeness that overcomes the actor before the camera, as Pirandello describes it, is basically of the same kind as the estrangement felt before one's own image in the mirror. But now the reflected image has become separable, transportable. And where is it transported? Before the public. Never for a moment does the screen actor cease to be conscious of this fact. While facing the camera he knows that ultimately he will face the public, the consumers who constitute the market. This market, where he offers not only his labor but also his whole self, his heart and soul, is beyond his reach. During the shooting he has as little contact with it as any article made in a factory. This may contribute to that oppression, that new anxiety which, according to

Pirandello, grips the actor before the camera. The film responds to the shriveling of the aura with an artificial build-up of the "personality" outside the studio. The cult of the movie star, fostered by the money of the film industry, preserves not the unique aura of the person but the "spell of the personality," the phony spell of a commodity. So long as the movie-makers' capital sets the fashion, as a rule no other revolutionary merit can be accredited to today's film than the promotion of a revolutionary criticism of traditional concepts of art. We do not deny that in some cases today's films can also promote revolutionary criticism of social conditions, even of the distribution of property. However, our present study is no more specifically concerned with this than is the film production of Western Europe.

It is inherent in the technique of the film as well as that of sports that everybody who witnesses its accomplishments is somewhat of an expert. This is obvious to anyone listening to a group of newspaper boys leaning on their bicycles and discussing the outcome of a bicycle race. It is not for nothing that newspaper publishers arrange races for their delivery boys. These arouse great interest among the participants, for the victor has an opportunity to rise from delivery boy to professional racer. Similarly, the newsreel offers everyone the opportunity to rise from passer-by to movie extra. In this way any man might even find himself part of a work of art, as witness Vertoff's *Three Songs About Lenin* or Ivens' *Borinage*. Any man today can lay claim to being filmed. This claim can best be elucidated by a comparative look at the historical situation of contemporary literature.

For centuries a small number of writers were confronted by many thousands of readers. This changed toward the end of the last century. With the increasing extension of the press, which kept placing new political, religious, scientific, professional, and local organs before the readers, an increasing number of readers became writers—at first, occasional ones. It began with the daily press opening to its readers space for "letters to the editor." And today there is hardly a gainfully employed European who could not, in principle, find an opportunity to publish somewhere or other comments on his work, grievances, documentary reports, or that sort of thing. Thus, the distinction between author and public is about to lose its basic character. The difference becomes merely functional; it may vary from case to case. At any moment the reader is ready to turn into a writer. As expert, which he had to become willy-nilly in an extremely specialized work process, even if only in some minor respect, the reader gains access to authorship. In the Soviet Union work itself is given a voice. To present it verbally is part of a man's ability to perform the work. Literary license is now founded on polytechnic rather than specialized training and thus becomes common property.

All this can easily be applied to the film, where transitions that in literature took centuries have come about in a decade. In cinematic practice, particularly in Russia, this change-over has partially become established reality. Some of the players whom we meet in Russian films are not actors in our sense but people who portray *themselves*—and primarily in their own work process. In Western Europe the capitalistic exploitation of the film denies consideration to modern man's legitimate claim to being reproduced. Under these circumstances the film industry is trying hard to spur the interest of the masses through illusion-promoting spectacles and dubious speculations. . . .

Mechanical reproduction of art changes the reaction of the masses toward art. The reactionary attitude toward a Picasso painting changes into the progressive reaction toward a Chaplin movie. The progressive reaction is characterized by the direct, intimate fusion of visual and emotional enjoyment with the orientation of the expert. Such fusion is of great social significance. The greater the decrease in the social significance of an art form, the sharper the distinction between criticism and enjoyment by the public. The conventional is uncritically enjoyed, and the truly new is criticized with aversion. With regard to the screen, the critical and the receptive attitudes of the public coincide. The decisive reason for this is that individual reactions are predetermined by the mass audience response they are about to produce, and this is nowhere more pronounced than in the film. The moment these responses become manifest they control each other. Again, the comparison with painting is fruitful. A painting has always had an excellent chance to be viewed by one person or by a few. The simultaneous contemplation of paintings by a large public, such as developed in the nineteenth century, is an early symptom of the crisis of painting, a crisis which was by no means occasioned exclusively by photography but rather in a relatively independent manner by the appeal of art works to the masses.

Painting simply is in no position to present an object for simultaneous collective experience, as it was possible for architecture at all times, for the epic poem in the past, and for the movie today. Although this circumstance in itself should not lead one to conclusions about the social role of painting, it does constitute a serious threat as soon as painting, under special conditions and, as it were, against its nature, is confronted directly by the masses. In the churches and monasteries of the Middle Ages and at the princely courts up to the end of the eighteenth century, a collective reception of paintings did not occur simultaneously, but by graduated and hierarchized mediation. The change that has come about is an expression of the particular conflict in which painting was implicated by the mechanical reproducibility of paintings. Although paintings began to be publicly exhibited in galleries and salons, there was no way for the masses to organize and control themselves in their reception. Thus the same public which responds in a progressive manner toward a grotesque film is bound to respond in a reactionary manner to surrealism. . . .

The mass is a matrix from which all traditional behavior toward works of art issues today in a new form. Quantity has been transmuted into quality. The greatly increased mass of participants has produced a change in the mode of participation. The fact that the new mode of participation first appeared in a disreputable form must not confuse the spectator. Yet some people have launched spirited attacks against precisely this superficial aspect. Among these, Duhamel has expressed himself in the most radical manner. What he objects to most is the kind of participation which the movie elicits from the masses. Duhamel calls the movie "a pastime for helots, a diversion for uneducated, wretched, worn-out creatures who are consumed by their worries . . . a spectacle which requires no concentration and presupposes no intelligence . . . which kindles no light in the heart and awakens no hope other than the ridiculous one of someday becoming a 'star' in Los Angeles." Clearly, this is at bottom the same ancient lament that the masses seek distraction whereas art demands concentration from the spectator. That is a commonplace. The question remains whether it provides a platform for the analysis of the film. A closer look is needed here. Distraction and concentration form polar opposites which may be stated as follows: A man who concentrates before a work of art is absorbed by it. He enters into this work of art the way legend tells of the Chinese painter when he viewed his finished painting. In contrast, the distracted mass absorbs the work of art. This is most obvious with regard to buildings. Architecture has always represented the prototype of a work of art the reception of which is consummated by a collectivity in a state of distraction. The laws of its reception are most instructive.

Buildings have been man's companions since primeval times. Many art forms have developed and perished. Tragedy begins with the Greeks, is extinguished with them, and after centuries its "rules" only are revived. The epic poem, which had its origin in the youth of nations, expires in Europe at the end of the Renaissance. Panel painting is a creation of the Middle Ages, and nothing guarantees its uninterrupted existence. But the human need for shelter is lasting. Architecture has never been idle. Its history is more ancient than that of any other art, and its claim to being a living force has significance in every attempt to comprehend the relationship of the masses to art. Buildings are appropriated in a twofold manner: by use and by perception—or rather, by touch and sight. Such appropriation cannot be understood in terms of the attentive concentration of a tourist before a famous building. On the tactile side there is no counterpart of contemplation on the optical side. Tactile appropriation is accomplished not so much by attention as by habit. As regards architecture, habit determines to a large extent even optical reception. The latter, too, occurs much less through rapt attention than by noticing the object in incidental fashion. This mode of appropriation, developed with reference to architecture, in certain circumstances acquires canonical value. For the tasks which face the human apparatus of perception at the turning points of history cannot be solved by optical means, that is, by contemplation, alone. They are mastered gradually by habit, under the guidance of tactile appropriation.

The distracted person, too, can form habits. More, the ability to master certain tasks in a state of distraction proves that their solution has become a matter of habit. Distraction as provided by art presents a covert control of the extent to which new tasks have become soluble by apperception. Since, moreover, individuals are tempted to avoid such tasks, art will tackle the most difficult and most important ones where it is able to mobilize the masses. Today it does so in the film. Reception in a state of distraction, which is increasing noticeably in all fields of art and is symptomatic of profound changes in apperception, finds in the film its true means of exercise. The film with its shock effect meets this mode of reception halfway. The film makes the cult value recede into the background not only by putting the public in the position of the critic, but also by the fact that at the movies this position requires no attention. The public is an examiner, but an absent-minded one.

The growing proletarianization of modern man and the increasing formation of masses are two aspects of the same process. Fascism attempts to organize the newly created proletarian masses without affecting the property structure which the masses strive to eliminate. Fascism sees its salvation in giving these masses not their right, but instead a chance to express themselves. The masses have a right to change property relations; Fascism seeks to give them an expression while preserving property. The logical result of Fascism is the introduction of aesthetics into political life. The violation of the masses, whom Fascism, with its *Führer* cult, forces to their knees, has its counterpart in the violation of an apparatus which is pressed into the production of ritual values.

All efforts to render politics aesthetic culminate in one thing: war. War and war only can set a goal for mass governments on the largest scale while respecting the traditional property system. This is the political formula for the situation. The technological formula may be stated as follows: Only war makes it possible to mobilize all of today's technical resources while maintaining the property system. It goes without saying that the Fascist apotheosis of war does not employ such arguments. Still, Marinetti says in his manifesto on the Ethiopian colonial war: "For twenty-seven years we Futurists have rebelled against the branding of war as antiaesthetic. . . . Accordingly we state: . . . War is beautiful because it establishes man's dominion over the subjugated machinery by means of gas masks, terrifying megaphones, flame throwers, and small tanks. War is beautiful because it initiates the dreamt-of metalization of the human body. War is beautiful because it enriches a flowering meadow with the fiery orchids of machine guns. War is beautiful because it combines the gunfire, the cannonades, the cease-fire, the scents, and the stench of the putrefaction into a symphony. War is beautiful because it creates new architecture, like that of the big tanks, the geometrical formation flights, the smoke spirals from burning villages, and many others. . . . Poets and artists of Futurism! . . . remember these principles of an aesthetics of war so that your struggle for a new literature and a new graphic art . . . may be illumined by them!"

This manifesto has the virtue of clarity. Its formulations deserve to be accepted by dialecticians. To the latter, the aesthetics of today's war appears as follows: If the natural utilization of productive forces is impeded by the property system, the increase in technical devices, in speed, and in the sources of energy will press for an unnatural utilization, and this is found in war. The destructiveness of war furnishes proof that society has not been mature enough to incorporate technology as its organ, that technology has not been sufficiently developed to cope with the elemental forces of society. The horrible features of imperialistic warfare are attributable to the discrepancy between the tremendous means of production and their inadequate utilization in the process of production—in other words, to unemployment and the lack of markets. Imperialistic war is a rebellion of technology which collects, in the form of "human material," the claims to which society has denied its natural material. Instead of draining rivers, society directs a human stream into a bed of trenches; instead of dropping seeds from airplanes, it drops incendiary bombs over cities; and through gas warfare the aura is abolished in a new way.

"*Fiat ars—pereat mundus,*" says Fascism, and, as Marinetti admits, expects war to supply the artistic gratification of a sense perception that has been changed by technology. This is evidently the consummation of "*l'art pour l'art.*" Mankind, which in Homer's time was an object of contemplation for the Olympian gods, now is one for itself. Its self-alienation has reached such a degree that it can experience its own destruction as an aesthetic pleasure of the first order. This is the situation of politics which Fascism is rendering aesthetic. Communism responds by politicizing art.

Aesthetic Theory

THEODOR ADORNO

AESTHETIC REFRACTION IS AS incomplete without the refracted object as imagination is without the imagined object. This has special significance for the problem of the inherent functionality of art. Tied to the real world, art adopts the principle of self-preservation of that world, turning it into the ideal of self-identical art, the essence of which Schönberg once summed up in the statement that the painter paints a picture rather than what it represents. Implied here is the idea that every work of art spontaneously aims at being identical with itself, just as in the world outside a fake identity is everywhere forcibly imposed on objects by the insatiable subject. Aesthetic identity is different, however, in one important respect: it is meant to assist the nonidentical in its struggle against the repressive identification compulsion that rules the outside world. It is by virtue of its separation from empirical reality that the work of art can become a being of a higher order, fashioning the relation between the whole and its parts in accordance with its own needs. Works of art are after-images or replicas of empirical life, inasmuch as they proffer to the latter what in the outside world is being denied them. In the process they slough off a repressive, external-empirical mode of experiencing the world. Whereas the line separating art from

From Aesthetic Theory, *trans. C. Lenhardt (New York: Routledge and Kegan Paul, 1984). Reprinted by* *permission of the publisher.*

real life should not be fudged, least of all by glorifying the artist, it must be kept in mind that works of art are alive, have a life *sui generis*. Their life is more than just an outward fate. Over time, great works reveal new facets of themselves, they age, they become rigid, and they die. Being human artefacts, they do not 'live' in the same sense as human beings. Of course not. To put the accent on the artefactual aspect in works of art seems to imply that the way in which they came to be is important. It is not. The emphasis must be on their inner constitution. They have life because they speak in ways nature and man cannot. They talk because there is communication between their individual constituents, which cannot be said of things that exist in a state of mere diffusion.

As artefacts, works of art communicate not only internally but also with the external reality which they try to get away from and which none the less is the substratum of their content. Art negates the conceptualization foisted on the real world and yet harbours in its own substance elements of the empirically existent. Assuming that one has to differentiate form and content before grasping their mediation, we can say that art's opposition to the real world is in the realm of form; but this occurs, generally speaking, in a mediated way such that aesthetic form is a sedimentation of content. What seem like pure forms in art, namely those of traditional music, do in all respects, and all the way down to details of musical idiom, derive from external content such as dance. Similarly, ornaments in the visual arts originally tended to be cult symbols. Members of the Warburg Institute were following this lead, studying the derivability of aesthetic forms from contents in the context of classical antiquity and its influence on later periods. This kind of work needs to be undertaken on a larger scale.

The manner in which art communicates with the outside world is in fact also a lack of communication, because art seeks, blissfully or unhappily, to seclude itself from the world. This non-communication points to the fractured nature of art. It is natural to think that art's autonomous domain has no more in common with the outside world than a few borrowed elements undergoing radical change in the context of art. But there is more to it than that. There is some truth to the historical cliché which states that the developments of artistic methods, usually lumped together under the term "style," correspond to social development. Even the most sublime work of art takes up a definite position *vis-à-vis* reality by stepping outside of reality's spell, not abstractly once and for all, but occasionally and in concrete ways, when it unconsciously and tacitly polemicizes against the condition of society at a particular point in time.

How can works of art be like windowless monads, representing something which is other than they? There is only one way to explain this, which is to view them as being subject to a dynamic or immanent historicity and a dialectical tension between nature and domination of nature, a dialectic that seems to be of the same kind as the dialectic of society or to put it more cautiously, the dialectic of art resembles the social dialectic without consciously imitating it. The productive force of useful labour and that of art are the same. They both have the same teleology. And what might be termed aesthetic relations of production—defined as everything that provides an outlet for the productive forces of art or everything in which these forces become embedded—are sedimentations of social relations of production bearing the imprint of the latter. Thus in all dimensions of its productive process art has a twofold essence, being both an autonomous entity and a social fact in the Durkheimian sense of the term.

It is through this relationship to the empirical that works of art salvage, albeit in neutralized fashion, something that once upon a time was literally a shared experience of all mankind and which enlightenment has since expelled. Art, too, partakes of enlightenment, but in a different way: works of art do not lie; what they say is literally true. Their reality however lies in the fact that they are answers to questions brought before them from outside. The tension in art therefore has meaning only in relation to the tension outside. The fundamental layers of artistic experience are akin to the objective world from which art recoils.

The unresolved antagonisms of reality reappear in art in the guise of immanent problems of artistic form. This, and not the deliberate injection of objective moments or social content, defines art's relation to society. The aesthetic tensions manifesting themselves in works of art express the essence of reality in and through their emancipation from the factual façade of exteriority. Art's simultaneous dissociation from and secret connection with empirical being confirms the strength of Hegel's analysis of the nature of a conceptual barrier (*Schramke*): the intellect, argues Hegel against Kant, no sooner posits a barrier than it has to go beyond it, absorbing into itself that against which the barrier was set up. We have here, among other things, a basis for a non-moralistic critique of the idea of *l'art pour l'art* with its abstract negation of the empirical and with its monomaniac separatism in aesthetic theory.

Freedom, the presuppostion of art and the self-glorifying conception art has of itself, is the cunning of art's reason. Blissfully soaring above the real world, art is still chained by each of its elements to the empirical other, into which it may even sink back altogether at every instant. In their relation to empirical reality works of art recall the theologumenon that in a state of redemption everything will be just as it is and yet wholly different. There is an unmistakable similarity in all this with the development of the profane. The profane secularizes the sacred realm to the point where the latter is the only secular thing left. The sacred realm is thus objectified, staked out as it were, because its moment of untruth awaits secularization as much as it tries to avert it through incantation.

It follows that art is not defined once and for all by the scope of an immutable concept. Rather, the concept of art is a fragile balance attained now and then, quite similar to the psychological equilibrium between id and ego. Disturbances continually upset the balance, keeping the

process in motion. Every work of art is an instant; every great work of art is a stoppage of the process, a momentary standing still, whereas a persistent eye sees only the process. While it is true that works of art provide answers to their own questions, it is equally true that in so doing they become questions for themselves. Take a look at the widespread inclination (which to this day has not been mitigated by education) to perceive art in terms of extra-aesthetic or pre-aesthetic criteria. This tendency is, on the one hand, a mark of atrocious backwardness or of the regressive consciousness of many people. On the other hand, there is no denying that that tendency is promoted by something in art itself. If art is perceived strictly in aesthetic terms, then it cannot be properly perceived in aesthetic terms. The artist must feel the presence of the empirical other in the foreground of his own experience in order to be able to sublimate that experience, thus freeing himself from his confinement to content while at the same time saving the being-for-itself of art from slipping into outright indifference toward the world.

Art is and is not being-for-itself. Without a heterogeneous moment, art cannot achieve autonomy. Great epics that survive their own oblivion were originally shot through with historical and geographical reporting. Valéry, for one, was aware of the degree to which the Homeric, pagan-germanic and Christian epics contained raw materials that had never been melted down and recast by the laws of form, noting that this did not diminish their rank in comparison with "pure" works of art. Similarly, tragedy, the likely origin of the abstract idea of aesthetic autonomy, was also an after-image of pragmatically oriented cult acts. At no point in its history of progressive emancipation was art able to stamp out that moment. And the reason is not that the bonds were simply too strong. Long before socialist realism rationally planned its debasement, the realistic novel, which was at its height as a literary form in the nineteenth century, bears the marks of reportage, anticipating what was later to become the task of social science surveys. Conversely, the fanatic thoroughness of linguistic integration that characterizes *Madame Bovary,* for instance, is probably the result of the contrary moment. The continued relevance of this work is due to the unity of both.

In art, the criterion of success is twofold: first, works of art must be able to integrate materials and details into their immanent law of form; and, second, they must not try to erase the fractures left by the process of integration, preserving instead in the aesthetic whole the traces of those elements which resisted integration. Integration as such does not guarantee quality. There is no privileged single category, not even the aesthetically central one of form, that defines the essence of art and suffices to judge its product. In short, art has defining characteristics that go against the grain of what philosophy of art ordinarily conceives as art. Hegel is the exception. His aesthetics of content recognized the moment of otherness inherent in art, thus superseding the old aesthetic of form. The latter seems to be operating with too pure a concept of art, even though it has at least one advantage, which is that it does not, unlike Hegel's (and Kierkegaard's) substantive aesthetics, place obstacles in the way of certain historical developments such as abstract painting. This is one weakness of Hegel's aesthetic. The other is that, by conceiving form in terms of content, Hegel's theory of art regresses to a position that can only be called "pre-aesthetic" and crude. Hegel mistakes the replicatory (*abbildende*) or discursive treatment of content for the kind of otherness that is constitutive of art. He sins, as it were, against his own dialectical concept of aesthetics, with results that he could not foresee. He in effect helped prepare the way of the banausic tendency to transform art into an ideology of repression.

The moment of unreality and non-existence in art is not independent of the existent, as though it were posited or invented by some arbitrary will. Rather, that moment of unreality is a structure resulting from quantitative relations between elements of being, relations which are in turn a response to, and an echo of, the imperfections of real conditions, their constraints, their contradictions, and their potentialities. Art is related to its other like a magnet to a field of iron filings. The elements of art as well as their constellation, or what is commonly thought to be the spiritual essence of art, point back to the real other. The identity of the works of art with existent reality also accounts for the centripetal force that enables them to gather unto themselves the traces and scattered parts of real life. Their affinity with the world lies in a principal that is conceived to be a contrast to that world but is in fact no different from the principle whereby spirit has dominated the world. Synthesis is not some process of imposing order on the elements of a work of art. It is important, rather, that the elements interact with each other; hence there is a sense in which synthesis is a mere repetition of the pre-established interdependence among elements, which interdependence is a product of otherness, of non-art. Synthesis, therefore, is firmly grounded in the material aspects of works of art.

There is a link between the aesthetic moment of form and non-violence. In its difference from the existent, art of necessity constitutes itself in terms of that which is not a work of art yet is indispensable for its being. The emphasis on non-intentionality in art, noticeable first in the sympathy for popular art in Apollinaire, early Cubism and Wedekind (who derided what he called "art-artists"), indicates that art became aware, however dimly, that it interacted with its opposite. This new self-conception of art gave rise to a critical turn signalling an end to the illusory equation of art with pure spirituality.

Really Useless "Knowledge": A Political Critique of Aesthetics

TONY BENNETT

IN HIS *IMMANUEL KANT,* Lucien Goldmann cites the early Lukács's view that "the *Critique of Judgement* contains the seeds of a reply to every problem of structure in the sphere of aesthetics; aesthetics need thus only clarify and think through to the end that which is implicitly there to hand." This was precisely what Lukács did in subsequently historicising Kant's conception of the subject and object of aesthetic judgement. The approach adopted here is rather different. The *Critique,* I shall argue, *does* provide a clear statement of "every problem of structure in the field of aesthetics," but less by way of resolving those problems, or anticipating their resolution, than by specifying the conditions that would need to be met were they to be resolved. Viewed in this light, Kant's treatise is most fruitfully read as a commentary on the necessary conditions, properties and requirements of aesthetic discourse.

Before doing so, however, it is necessary to distinguish between aesthetic discourse and discourse of value in order to register a distance from, and resist the gravitational pull of, Kant's transcendental method. By aesthetic discourse, I have in mind the many variants of philosophical aesthetics which exhibit related properties in their attempts to distinguish some unique faculty, lodged within and constitutive of human subjectivity, which would serve as a basis for establishing the potential, if not actual, universality of aesthetic judgement. Aesthetic discourse, that is to say, construes the aesthetic as a distinctive mode of the subject's mental relation to reality. The means by which this is accomplished vary from Kant's transcendental critique of the faculty of judgement to the analysis of the progressive historical construction of a unified subject and object of aesthetic judgement favoured by Hegel and Lukács, to attempts to locate the basis of aesthetic judgement in the biological substratum of the human individual as, for example, in Peter Fuller's work. Whatever the methods used, however, aesthetic discourse exhibits a substantially identical structure: an analysis of the constitution of the subject, whether this be conceived as self-wrought or culturally produced, provides the justification for the view that aesthetic judgement is, ought to be or one day will be universal just as this, in turn, supports the contention that there is a distinctive aesthetic mode of the subject's appropriation of reality. This circularity is an inherent property of aesthetic discourse. Susceptible to neither logical nor empirical demonstration, the existence of a distinctive aesthetic faculty is always ultimately sustained, but entirely intradiscursively, by the projection of a set of conditions in which the subject of value can be represented as universal.

By discourse of value, by contrast, I mean the much more numerous and heterogeneous array of discourses which regulate the social practice of valuing within different valuing communities. Such discourses typically constitute systems for the classification and valuation of persons effected by the means of systems for the classification and valuation of objects and practices. They delimit a set of valued objects and practices and produce, for these, an appropriate valuing subject; that is, a subject marked out from other subjects by his/her ability to recognise the value which such objects and practices are said to embody. This subject is also a *valued* subject, valued precisely because of its ability to correctly apply the rules for valuing which are legislative within a

From Outside Literature *(London: Routledge and Kegan Paul, 1990). Reprinted by permission of the publisher and the author.*

particular valuing community. In this way, the valuing subject functions, ultimately, as the primary valued object also. To the degree that discourses of value address the individual as always-already, either wholly or in part, the valuing subject they produce and require, they constitute a means for the individual's valuation of self as both subject of discernment and ultimate valued object. Their structure is thus narcissistic.

Such discourses are by no means limited to the sphere of artistic practices. Nor, from a sociological point of view, is this necessarily the most important sphere of their operation. As Pierre Bourdieu shows in *La Distinction,* discourses of value may be organised in relation to a wide variety of objects and practices, including sporting and culinary pursuits, for example. Moreover, in Bourdieu's analysis, such discourses, in transforming objects and practices into signs of differentiated social identities, play an important role in relation to more general mechanisms of group formation and group differentiation. They are, in effect, practical social ideologies. As such, Bourdieu focuses on their role in relation to class differences in offering both different modalities for the transformation of economic into cultural capital and supplying the means for the self-differentiation of the bourgeoisie and petit-bourgeoisie from the popular classes as well as from each other. However, discourses of value may also function similarly in relation to national, regional, ethnic or gender differences. Whatever the sphere of their operation, though, they work by constructing an ideal of personality, in both its mental and physical aspects, in relation to which the individual is interpellated as valuing, valued and self-valuing subject.

There are no necessary connections between such discourses of value and aesthetic discourse. In most cases, the two operate in different registers. The rules for valuing as well as the subjects and objects of value which discourses of value propose are legislative and have effects solely within the limits of particular valuing communities. Such discourses are prescriptive, but only for those who occupy or take up the position of the

valuing subject they construct, a position which may be refused since such valuing subjects are identifiably socially specific. Aesthetic discourse, by contrast, is the form taken by discourses of value which are hegemonic in ambition and, correspondingly, universalist in their prescriptive ambit and which have, as their zone of application, those practices nominated as artistic. The position of universal valuing subject which is necessary to such discourse—and, invariably, such a position is produced by generalising the attributes of the valuing subject associated with a socially specific discourse of value—can be refused *to* but not *by* the individual. Such refusals, however, always leave open a route whereby the valuing practices of each and every individual may be conformed to the principles of judgement embodied in the universal valuing subject. This is achieved by the deployment of cultural, and hence remediable, criteria which permit the disqualification of those individuals whose judgements are assessed as being wayward or incomplete from the point of view of the position of the universal valuing subject which such discourse constructs. Such criteria, while maintaining a liberal façade, provide a means of discounting as impertinent any and all aberrant systems of aesthetic evaluation which would otherwise call into question the universalising constructions of aesthetic discourse.

As such, aesthetic discourse rests on two specific conditions. First, there must already be cleared a space within which the construction of a universal valuing subject can be located. It is epistemology which clears this space in securing a general conception of the subject form which enables rules for valuing derived from particular valuing communities to be theoretically represented as universally legislative, either actually or tendentially. This is not merely to suggest that, historically, epistemology provided the surface of emergence on which the problems of aesthetics could become visible, although this is certainly the case. The more important point is that theories of the aesthetic logically presuppose an already elaborated theory of knowledge. The *differentia specifica* of the aesthetic as a specific mode of the subject's mental relation to reality, that is to say, can only be established in relation to some prior conception of the knowledge relation between subject and reality, for it is this which provides the co-ordinating centre of philosophy's theorisation of the mental economy of the subject in supplying a self-supporting point of anchorage in relation to which the characteristics of the other modes of the subject's relations to reality can be specified. Moreover, this knowledge relation must already be secured to provide the necessary conditions for an inquiry into the constitutive properties of the aesthetic, for such an inquiry presupposes a subject that is capable of investigating its own constitution. As Catherine Greenfield has put it, epistemology establishes a conception of "the subject as both the known object of its own introspection and simultaneously the principle which makes such knowledges possible," thereby producing the necessary preconditions for "the proper activity of mind as the study of its *own* contents"—which aesthetics pre-eminently is.

As its second precondition, aesthetic discourse presupposes the existence of the artistic as an identifiably distinct institutional sphere within society for there to be something, on the object side of the equation, for aesthetic discourse to latch on to. To paraphrase Habermas, we might say that aesthetic discourse can acquire momentum and a social purchase only when there exists a "public artistic sphere" produced by the deployment of specific forms of classification and exhibition in such separated exhibition contexts as art galleries and museums.

The combined effect of these two conditioning factors is that, more frequently than not, aesthetic discourse fetishises the object of value in ways which serve as a complement to, and are produced by means of, its universalisation of the valuing subject. This point requires some elaboration. Since it is clear that value is a relational phenomenon produced in the passage between subject and object, it is readily admitted in most forms of aesthetic discourse that beauty neither is

nor can be a natural property of the object. As Kant puts it:

> If we wish to discern whether anything is beautiful or not, we do not refer the representation of it to the Object by means of understanding with a view to cognition, but by means of the imagination (acting perhaps in conjunction with understanding) we refer the representation to the Subject and its feeling of pleasure or displeasure. The judgement of taste, therefore, is not a cognitive judgement, and so not logical, but is aesthetic—which means that it is one whose determining ground *cannot be other than subjective.*

Even so-called objectivist aesthetics, which construe the aesthetic as a distinct set of mental effects produced by those practices nominated as artistic, secure their determining ground in the properties of the subject in assuming a general subject form capable of experiencing or recognising those effects. Once this determining ground has been universalised, however, aesthetic discourse tilts on its axis as the properties of the subject which guarantee the universality of aesthetic judgement are transferred to the object. Value, transfixed in the singular gaze of the universal subject, solidifies and takes form as a property of the object just as, once the universal valuing subject has been constructed, its active, value-constitutive role becomes passive: all it can do is to recognise the value that was already there, secreted somewhere in the dense folds of the object.

David Hume's essay *Of the Standard of Taste* (1757) provides an economical example of many of these regulative procedures of aesthetic discourse, and one in which their association with the exercise of cultural power stands forth particularly clearly. Hume's starting point is to dispute the view that varying judgements of taste should be ranked equally since their claims cannot be adjudicated by appealing to the properties of objects:

> Whoever would assert an equality of genius and elegance between Ogilby and Milton, or Bunyan and Addison, would be thought to defend

no less an extravagance, than if he had maintained a mole-hill to be as high as Teneriffe, or a pond as extensive as the ocean. Though there may be found persons, who give the preference to the former authors; no one pays attention to such a taste; and we pronounce, without scruple, the sentiment of these pretended critics to be absurd and ridiculous. The principle of the natural equality of taste is then totally forgot, and while we admit it on some occasions, where the objects seem near an equality, it appears an extravagant paradox, or rather a palpable absurdity, where objects so disproportioned are compared together.

The ground for demonstrating that the principles of aesthetic judgement are universal is prepared, here, via the initial disqualification of those whose judgements depart significantly from the standards of agreed taste. Moreover, this is justified by an appeal to the properties of the objects compared. This is confirmed by the next step Hume takes in arguing that true and universal principles of taste can only be derived by removing all the exterior, disturbing circumstances which are likely to disrupt the true operation of the finer aspects of judgement or, as Hume calls it, sentiment. The principles of taste, Hume thus contends, are most clearly manifested in "the durable admiration which attends those works that have survived all the caprices of mode and fashion, all the mistakes of ignorance and envy." In short, the classics. The value of these objects is guaranteed by the universality of their acclaim, and vice versa, within what Bourdieu has characterised as "the circular circulation of inter-legitimation" in which judgements of value both consecrate and are consecrated by the "inherently valuable" properties of the objects which they approve. The failure to recognise value where it is thus objectively lodged can therefore, Hume argues, only derive "from some apparent defect or imperfection in the organ." Even where there is no congenital defect, however, the capacity for valid judgement may be unequally developed since different individuals have different opportunities and inclinations to exer-

cise and develop this capacity. It is worth quoting Hume's conclusions on these matters in full since they aptly demonstrate the respects in which the qualification of some subjects of judgement is effected by the simultaneous disqualification of others:

> Thus, though the principles of taste be universal, and nearly, if not entirely, the same in all men; yet few are qualified to give judgement on any work of art, or establish their own sentiment as the standard of beauty. The organs of internal sensation are seldom so perfect as to allow the general principles their full play, and produce a feeling correspondent to those principles. They either labour under some defect, or are vitiated by some disorder; and by that means excite a sentiment, which may be pronounced erroneous. When the critic has no delicacy, he judges without any distinction, and is only affected by the grosser and more palpable qualities of the object: the finer touches pass unnoticed and disregarded. Where he is not aided by practice, his verdict is attended with confusion and hesitation. Where no comparison has been employed, the most frivolous beauties, such as rather merit the name of defects, are the objects of his admiration. Where he lies under the influence of prejudice, all his natural sentiments are perverted. Where good sense is wanting, he is not qualified to discern the beauties of design and reasoning, which are the highest and most excellent. Under some or other of these imperfections, the generality of men labour; and hence a true judge in the finer arts is observed, even during the most polished ages, to be so rare a character: a strong sense, united to delicate sentiment, improved by practice, perfected by comparison, and cleared of all prejudice, can alone entitle critics to this valuable character; and the joint verdict of such, wherever they are to be found, is the true standard of taste and beauty.

The "universal" principle of taste, then, may be held in check by a variety of interior and exterior impediments. They develop to perfection only when the internal organs of sensation are correctly balanced and when exterior circumstances permit their full and unimpeded exercise and progressive refinement. The proof—the only proof—that such principles of taste exist is provided by the few "valuable characters" who manifest them in their fully developed form. Happily, however, everyone (everyone whose judgement is allowed to count, that is) knows who these are: ". . . some men in general, however difficult to be particularly pitched upon, will be acknowledged by universal sentiment to have a preference over others."

The problem Hume is addressing here is clear. Writing against the arbitrary authoritarianism of earlier aristocratic aesthetic prescriptions, his essay articulates the Enlightenment demand that the principles of taste should be arrived at by means of rational and open debate between members of a public who meet as equals. However, the definition of the relevant public, produced by disqualifying the judgements of the congenitally and culturally defective multitude, results in a cultural partiality that is equally arbitrary and authoritarian. The universality of taste turns out, in effect, to be based on the most insubstantial and flimsy of foundations: the consensus of the drawing room. At this point, Hume's analysis is driven into a further contradiction in the respect that the requirements of rationalism require Hume to allow that, within the defined limits of polite society, genuine and irreconcilable aesthetic disagreements may occur:

> But where there is such a diversity in the internal frame or external situation as is entirely blameless on both sides, and leaves no room to give one the preference above the other; in that case a certain degree of diversity of judgement is unavoidable, and we seek in vain for a standard, by which we can reconcile the contrary sentiments.

In brief, once the judgements produced within the bourgeois public sphere have been generalised to equate with the level of the universal, Hume's discourse turns tail on itself, securing a commitment to the principles of rationality necessary to the constitution of the bourgeois public sphere only by sacrificing the possibility that judgement might be represented as universal even in this limited social domain.

Put crudely, the bourgeois public maintains a united front, the illusion of a universality, in face of the masses, conducting its disagreements behind closed—and barred—doors.

Kant's *Critique* is a work of immeasurably greater power and rigour. None the less, in universalizing the rules for valuing that are legislative within civilised society, it accomplishes the same ideological work, albeit that it does so in the laundered sphere of the transcendental method. This "dirty work," moreover, is accomplished only hypothetically, for Kant does not so much found an aesthetic as establish the conditions that would be necessary for doing so. The *Critique* is, in consequence, as Lukács would have put it, "the critical self-consciousness of aesthetic discourse."

Kant's opening question in the *Critique* is whether the faculty of judgement "which in the order of our cognitive faculties forms a middle term between understanding and reason" is governed by independent and *a priori* principles which would constitute it as a "special realm." The existence of this faculty, it is important to note, is presupposed as is its function: that of mediating between and connecting understanding and reason, the subject of cognition and the subject of moral action. Indeed, its existence is required to support the conception of the subject form as a unified trinity of thought, feeling and action. However, the existence of such a faculty cannot, in Kant's view, be proved logically or empirically. "It is only throwing away labour," Kant argues, "to look for a principle of taste that affords a universal criterion of the beautiful by definite concepts. . . ." Moreover, this would defeat the purpose of the exercise since the faculty of judgement itself must furnish the means of specifying its own distinctive properties. Otherwise, if these could be known by concepts, then judgement would be subservient to understanding and would not, Kant contends, constitute a "special realm" within the mental economy of the subject. As for the empirical evidence favouring the view that the sensation of delight or aversion is universally communicable, Kant concedes that this is "weak indeed and scarce sufficient to raise a presumption, of the derivation of a taste, thus confirmed by examples, from grounds deep-seated and shared alike by all men, underlying their agreement in estimating the forms under which objects are given to them."

Kant therefore ostensibly places in brackets the specific application of the faculty of judgement and the particular objects to which it is applied within specific valuing communities, in favour of a transcendental analysis of the principles regulating its exercise no matter what the circumstances of its employment. However, the brackets are soon removed. Kant distinguishes the beautiful from the agreeable and the good, both of which imply a concept of an end and the interest of the subject in that end, as that which pleases without regard to any interest of the subject. "The delight which determines the judgement of taste," he writes, "is independent of all interest." Bourdieu has argued that Kant, in making disinterestedness a defining attribute of the aesthetic, merely rationalises a bourgeois class ethos as manifested in the sphere of taste. This view is based on his empirical studies of different class-based valuing practices. These show, at least in the case of contemporary France, that the premium placed on disinterestedness as an appropriate aesthetic attitude correlates directly with the degree to which a class or class fraction is distanced from the practical need to secure the necessities of life. Indeed, it is a way of *displaying* that distance.

For Bourdieu, then, disinterestedness constitutes a particular form of posturing on the part of the subject which, while serving specific social interests, simultaneously masks those interests as well as its own use in their service. For Kant, by contrast, the quality of disinterestedness provides the means whereby his discussion shifts from the level of a phenomenology of bourgeois taste to that of a transcendental analysis of the faculty of judgement, but only by equating the two. The crucial step in Kant's argument in this respect consists in his contention that: "The beautiful is that which, apart from concepts, is represented as

the Object of a UNIVERSAL delight." It is, however, only within discourses of value governed by the attribute of disinterestedness that beauty is and can be so represented:

> For where any one is conscious that his delight in an object is with him independent of all interest, it is inevitable that he should look on the object as one containing a ground of delight for all men. For, since the delight is not based on any inclination of the Subject (or any other deliberate interest) but the Subject feels himself completely *free* in respect of the liking which he accords to the object, he can find as reason for his delight no personal conditions to which his own subjective self might alone be party. Hence he must regard it as resting on what he may also presuppose in every other person; and therefore he must believe that he has reason for demanding a similar delight from every one.

It is not my purpose to develop a social critique of Kant's aesthetics. None the less, it is worth noting that he hitches his own discourse up into the sphere of universality, which the transcendental method requires, by means of the very slippery toehold provided by the illusions of the subject of a specific discourse of value. It is only the demand for agreement arising from the subject's feeling of disinterestedness in performing judgements of taste which provides the ground for Kant's supposition that there might be a universal, or universalisable, faculty of judgement constituting a special realm. However, my interest lies mainly in Kant's clear perception of the properties of such discourse and of the conditions necessary to sustain it at the level of universality to which it aspires. With regard to the former, Kant is quite unequivocal: universalising discourses of value both fetishise the object of value and deploy a discourse of disqualification in relation to those subjects who do not, or refuse to, conform to their edicts. Of the man who speaks of beauty, Kant says:

> He judges not merely for himself, but for all men, and then speaks of beauty as if it were a property of things. Thus he says the *thing* is

beautiful; and it is not as if he counted on others agreeing in his judgement of liking owing to his having found them in such agreement on a number of occasions, but he *demands* this agreement of them. He blames them if they judge differently, and denies them taste, which he still requires of them as something they ought to have; and to this extent it is not open to men to say: Every one has his own taste. This would be equivalent to saying that there is no such thing at all as taste, i.e. no aesthetic judgement capable of making a rightful claim upon the assent of all men.

Kant, it is important to add, does not provide a warrant for such claims at the level of their empirical application within specific valuing communities. Indeed, he argues that nothing is postulated in such claims but "the *possibility* of an aesthetic judgement capable of being at the same time deemed valid for every one." In his hypothetical deduction of the conditions which must obtain in order to give such claims both a historical and a logical validity, however, Kant is clear that they require a simultaneous universalisation of the object and subject of value, and the identity of the two. They require the former, Kant argues, in the sense that the ideal of the beautiful which regulates the exercise of the faculty of judgement can only be man:

> Only what has in itself the end of its real existence—only *man* that is able himself to determine his ends by reason, or where he has to derive them from external perception, can still compare them with essential and universal ends, and then further pronounce aesthetically upon their accord with such ends, only he, among all objects in the world, admits, therefore, of an ideal of *beauty*, just as humanity in his person, as intelligence, alone admits of the ideal of *perfection*.

It is, then, man, as the ideal of the beautiful, which provides the standard governing our estimation of the aesthetic value of objects. For the moment, in the here and now, this ideal exists as "a mere idea, which each person must beget in his own consciousness, and according to which

he must form his estimate of everything that is an Object of taste, or that is an example of critical taste, and even of universal taste itself." However, it is clear that only the actualisation of this ideal in the world of objects—only, that is, the production of man as the ultimately valued object of whose beauty and perfection all other objects partake and to which they testify—can provide a justification for such claims in finally enabling beauty to be predicated as a concept of the object, now universalised and perfected.

It is equally clear that this universalisation of the object must be complemented by a universalisation of the subject of judgement. Kant thus argues that aesthetic judgements both presuppose and project a *sensus communis:* a common sense on which a yet-to-be-realised unanimity of aesthetic judgement can be founded. "The judgement of taste, therefore," he writes, "depends on our presupposing the existence of a common sense." This is not to suggest that such a common sense actually exists—its status is that of "a mere ideal norm"—but that the demand for agreement which accompanies aesthetic judgement presupposes the possibility of its eventual existence. "The assertion is not that every one *will* fall in with our judgement," Kant says, "but rather that every one *ought* to agree with it." It is in the gap between what is and what ought to be, of course, that discourses of disqualification insert themselves: a *sensus communis* will be produced once the various impediments which inhibit others from applying the faculty of judgement correctly have been removed and once, accordingly, unified subject of value meets unified object of value in a mutually confirming and, no doubt, valuable encounter.

With regard to the likelihood of the production of such a *sensus communis,* Kant is, once again, engagingly, if also revealingly, open:

> Is taste, in other words, a natural and original faculty, or is it only the idea of one that is artificial and to be acquired by us, so that a judgement of taste, with its demand for universal assent, is but a requirement of reason for generating such a *consensus,* and does the "ought," i.e. the

objective necessity of the coincidence of the feeling of all with the particular feeling of each, only betoken the possibility of arriving at some sort of unanimity in these matters, and the judgement of taste only adduce an example of the application of this principle? These are questions which as yet we are neither willing nor in a position to investigate.

Feminist Art Histories and Marxism

GRISELDA POLLOCK

It ought to be clear by now that I'm not interested in the social history of art as part of a cheerful diversification of the subject, taking its place alongside other varieties—formalist, "modernist," sub-Freudian, filmic, feminist, "radical," all of them hot-foot in pursuit of the New. For diversification, read disintegration.

(T. J. Clark, "On the conditions of artistic creation," *Times Literary Supplement*, 24 May 1974, 562)

IN THE ESSAY FROM which this passage is cited, T. J. Clark described a crisis in art history. He began by reminding his readers of a happier time, early in the century, when art historians such as Dvořák and Riegl were counted amongst the great and pioneering historians and when art history was not reduced to its current curatorial role but participated in the major debates in the study of human society. Since that time art history has become isolated from the other social and historical sciences. Within the discipline the dominant trends are positively anti-historical. A review of the catalogue by one of the architects of modernist art history, Alfred H. Barr, Jr., for his exhibition *Cubism and Abstract Art* (1936, Museum of Modern Art New York) published in 1937 by the American Marxist art historian, Meyer Shapiro, provided a still pertinent critique of modernist art history. Shapiro described the paradox of Barr's book, which is largely an account of historical movements and yet is itself essentially unhistorical. Barr, he suggested, provides a linear, evolutionary narrative of individual creators grouped together in styles and schools. History is replaced by mere chronology; the date of every stage in various movements is charted, enabling a curve to be plotted for the emergence of art year by year. Yet connections never are drawn between art and the conditions of the moment. Barr excludes as irrelevant to his story of art the *nature of the society* in which it arose, i.e. the character of the social structures and conflicts, the conditions of social life and exchange and thus the real arena of art's production and consumption. History, if it does make an appearance, is reduced to a series of incidents like a world war which may accelerate or obstruct art, an internal, immanent process amongst artists. Changes in style are explained by the popular theory of exhaustion, novelty and reaction.

In opposition to this kind of art history which forms the backbone of the teaching of nineteenth- and twentieth-century history of art in much of America and Europe today, T. J. Clark has called for, and in his own books begun to lay the foundations for, a critical alternative. The social history of art—informed by a Marxist

From Vision and Difference: Femininity, Feminism and Histories of Art *(London: Routledge and Kegan Paul, 1988). Reprinted by permission of the publisher.*

analysis of society—constitutes a radically new body of art historical work which aims to contest the hegemony of bourgeois modernist art history. True there have been Marxist art historians before; but what is needed now is concerted effort to found a tradition, to produce a radically new kind of understanding of artistic production. Yet in 1974 Clark was fierce in his warnings against other tendencies currently on offer in art history. These he designated as merely pseudo-solutions; themselves proliferating symptoms of intellectual desperation. These novelties, reflecting fashions in related but necessarily distinct disciplines, include literary formalism, Freudianism, film theory and feminism.

As a feminist, I find myself awkwardly placed in this debate. I agree with Clark that one—and a very substantive one too—paradigm for the social history of art lies within Marxist cultural theory and historical practice. Yet in as much as society is structured by relations of inequality at the point of material production, so too is it structured by sexual divisions and inequalities. The nature of the societies in which art has been produced has been not only, for example, feudal or capitalist, but patriarchal and sexist. Neither of these forms of exploitation is reducible to the other. As Jean Gardiner has pointed out, a Marxist perspective which remains innocent of feminist work on sexual divisions cannot adequately analyse social processes: "It is impossible to understand women's class position without understanding the way in which sexual divisions shape women's consciousness of class. . . . No socialist can afford to ignore this question." But it would be a mistake to see a solution in a simple extension of Marxism to acknowledge sexual politics as an additional element. Domination and exploitation by sex are not just a supplement to a more basic level of conflict between class. Feminism has exposed new areas and forms of social conflict which demand their own modes of analysis of kinship, the social construction of sexual difference, sexuality, reproduction, labour and, of course, culture. Culture can be defined as those social practices whose prime aim is signifi-

cation, i.e. the production of sense or making orders of "sense" for the world we live in. Culture is the social level in which are produced those images of the world and definitions of reality which can be ideologically mobilized to legitimize the existing order of relations of domination and subordination between classes, races and sexes. Art history takes an aspect of this cultural production, art, as its object of study; but the discipline itself is also a crucial component of the cultural hegemony by the dominant class, race and gender. Therefore it is important to contest the definitions of our society's ideal reality which are produced in art historical interpretations of culture.

The project before us is therefore the development of art historical practices which analyse cultural production in the visual arts and related media by attending to the imperatives of both Marxism and feminism. This requires the mutual transformation of existing Marxist and recent feminist art history. Marxist art historians' prime concern with class relations is brought into question by feminist argument about the social relations of the sexes around sexuality, kinship, the family and the acquisition of gender identity. At the same time existing feminist art history is challenged by the rigour, historical incentive and theoretical developments of Marxists in the field. Feminist art history in this new form will not be a mere addition, a matter of producing a few more books about women artists. These can easily be incorporated and forgotten as were the many volumes on women artists published in the nineteenth century. Alliance with the social history of art is necessary but should always be critical of its unquestioned patriarchal bias.

Why does it matter politically for feminists to intervene in so marginal an area as art history, "an outpost of reactionary thought" as it has been called? Admittedly art history is not an influential discipline, locked up in universities, art colleges and musty basements of museums, peddling its "civilizing" knowledge to the select and cultured. We should not, however, underestimate the effective significance of its definitions of art and artist to bourgeois ideology. The central figure of art historical discourse is the artist, who is presented as an ineffable ideal which complements the bourgeois myths of a universal, classless Man (*sic*).

Our general culture is furthermore permeated with ideas about the individual nature of creativity, how genius will always overcome social obstacles, that art is an inexplicable, almost magical sphere to be venerated but not analysed. These myths are produced in ideologies of art history and are then dispersed through the channels of TV documentaries, popular art books, biographical romances about artists' lives like *Lust for Life* about van Gogh, or *The Agony and the Ecstasy* about Michelangelo. "To deprive the bourgeoisie not of its art but of its concept of art, this is the precondition of a revolutionary argument."

Feminist interrogations of art history have extended that programme to expose and challenge the prevailing assumptions that this "creativity" is an exclusive masculine prerogative and that, as a consequence, the term artist automatically refers to a man. A useful reminder of this occurred in Gabhart and Broun's introductory essay to the exhibition they organized in 1972, *Old Mistresses: Women Artists of the Past*:

> The title of this exhibition alludes to the unspoken assumption in our language that art is created by men. The reverential term "Old Master" has no meaningful equivalent; when cast in its feminine form, "Old Mistresses," the connotation is altogether different, to say the least.

Gabhart and Broun expose the relationship between language and ideology. But they do not ask *why* there is no place for women in the language of art history despite the fact that there have been so many women artists. In the light of my joint research with Rozsika Parker, I would reply that it is because the evolving concepts of the artist and the social definitions of woman have historically followed different and, recently, contradictory paths. Creativity has been appropriated as an ideological component of masculinity while femininity has been constructed as

man's and, therefore, the artist's negative. As the late-nineteenth-century writer clearly put it: "As long as a woman refrains from unsexing herself let her dabble in anything. The woman of genius does not exist; when she does she is a man."

This is part of a larger question. What is the relationship between this pejorative view of women incapable of being artists—creative individuals—and their subordinated position as workers, the low pay, the unskilled and disregarded domestic labour to which they are so often restricted because such jobs are described as the "natural" occupations of women? Another level of correspondence is the call to biology that is made to support the claim for men's inevitable greatness in art and women's eternal secondrateness. Men create art; women merely have babies. This false opposition has been frequently used to justify women's exclusion from cultural recognition. It is no coincidence that such appeals to "biology" are utilized in many other spheres of women's endeavour to prejudice their equal employment, to lower their wages and to refuse social provision for child care. The sexual divisions embedded in concepts of art and the artist are part of the cultural myths and ideologies peculiar to art history. But they contribute to the wider context of social definitions of masculinity and femininity and thus participate at the ideological level in reproducing the hierarchy between the sexes. It is this aspect of art history that Marxist studies have never addressed.

The radical critiques proposed by Marxist and feminist art history therefore stand in double and not necessarily coinciding opposition to bourgeois art history. Yet to date feminist art history has refused the necessary confrontation with mainstream art historical ideologies and practices. Instead feminists have been content to incorporate women's names in the chronologies and to include work by women in the inventories of styles and movements. Liberal policies within the art history establishment have allowed this unthreatening, "additive" feminism a marginal place at its conferences as a diverting sideline or given it the space for a few odd articles in its academic journals. However, the critical implications of feminism for art history as a whole have been stifled and have not been allowed to change what is studied in art history, nor how it is studied and taught. It is useful to consider a perceptive essay written in 1949 in which the Marxist art historian, Friedrich Antal, pointed out what kind of challenges mainstream bourgeois art history can or cannot accept. He specifically mentioned some of the concessions to new—Marxist—ideals in art history which were then being made. These were accompanied, however, by a profound resistance to anything that posed a fundamental threat to the core of art history's ideology—the sanctity of the artist and the autonomy of art. Thus reference to literature on popular or semi-popular art was tolerated so long as this kind of art was segregated from the general history of stylistic development in the high arts. Discussion of subject matter was possible so long as it was limited to iconography and the reasons for the artist's choice of that subject matter were not given in terms of real, living history. Study of the working conditions of artists could be undertaken so long as it remained detached and its implications were not used in the analysis of the work of "great" artists. Social and political background could even be mentioned so long as no real connection was drawn between it and art. Antal concluded that the last redoubt which would be held as long as possible was "the most deep-rooted nineteenth-century belief, inherited from romanticism, of the incalculable nature of genius in art." Art history has its history as an ideological discourse. Antal's essay clearly specified the ways in which he saw the discipline responding to the challenge of Marxism thirty years ago and his reminder is timely:

> The whole point of view of art historians, of whatever country or training, who have not yet even absorbed the achievements of Riegl, Dvořák, and Warburg (let alone tried to go beyond them) is conditioned by their historical place: they cling to older conceptions, thereby lagging behind some quarter of a century. And

in the same way are conditioned their step by step retreat and the concessions they are willing to make—not too many and not too soon—to the new spirit. Their resistance is all the stronger, their will to give ground, all the less, the greater the consistency and novelty they encounter.

Antal put his finger on the ways in which art history will accommodate what Clark has called a "cheerful diversification." Pluralism can be tolerated. What is refused and cannot coexist is not simply feminist approaches or reference to social context. It is that which fundamentally challenges the image of the world art history strives to create, offering a very different set of explanations of how history operates, what structures society, how art is produced, what kind of social beings artists are. We are involved in a contest for occupation of an ideologically strategic terrain. Feminist art history should see itself as part of the political initiative of the women's movement, not just as a novel art historical perspective, aiming to improve existing, but inadequate, art history. Feminist art history must engage in a politics of knowledge.

My own work on feminism and art history was initially undertaken in a collective of women artists, craftswomen, writers and historians. With Rozsika Parker I have written a book entitled *Old Mistresses: Women, Art and Ideology* (1981). The position from which we worked was in conflict with much existing feminist literature in art history. We do not think that the major issues for feminists in this discipline are the overcoming of the neglect of women artists by the Jansons and Gombrichs. Nor do we think that recording the obstacles such as discrimination against women as explanation of their absence from the history books provides the answers we want. As Rozsika Parker commented in a review of Germaine Greer's *The Obstacle Race* (1979): "It is not the obstacles that Germaine Greer cites that really count, but the rules of the game which demand scrutiny."

We started from the premise that women had always been involved in the production of art, but that our culture would not admit it. The question to be answered is: *Why is this so?* Why has it been necessary for art history to create an image of the history of past art as an exclusive record of masculine achievement? We discovered that it was only in the twentieth century, with the establishment of art history as an institutionalized academic discipline, that most art history systematically obliterated women artists from the record. While most books do not refer at all to women artists, those that do make reference, do it only in order to remind us how inferior and insignificant women artists actually are. Our conclusion was therefore unexpected. Although women artists are treated by modern art history negatively, that is, ignored, omitted or when mentioned at all, derogated, women artists and the art they produced none the less play a structural role in the discourse of art history. In fact, to discover the history of women and art at all means accounting for the way art history is written. To expose its underlying assumptions, its prejudices and silences, is to reveal that the negative way in which women artists are recorded and dismissed is nevertheless crucial to the concepts of art and artists created by art history. The initial task of feminist art history is therefore a critique of art history itself.

Furthermore the art historical literature that does include references to women's art consistently employs a particular cluster of terms and evaluations, so consistently and unquestioningly that it can be called a "feminine stereotype." All that women have produced is seen to bear witness to a single sex-derived quality—to femininity—and thus to prove women's lesser status as artists. But what is the meaning of the equation of women's art with femininity and femininity with bad art? And, more significantly, why does the point have to be stressed so frequently? The feminine stereotype, we suggest, operates as a necessary term of difference, the foil against which a never-acknowledged masculine privilege in art can be maintained. We never say man artist or man's art; we simply say art and artist. This hidden sexual prerogative is secured by the asser-

tion of a negative, an "other," the feminine, as a necessary point of differentiation. The art made by women has to be mentioned and then dismissed precisely in order to secure this hierarchy.

Critically aware of the methods by which art history constructs an image for the artist which epitomizes bourgeois ideals of a masculine persona we can begin to map out a different kind of history for art. Initially we do need to retrieve a knowledge of the consistent but diverse record of women's artistic activity. Then we have to describe the historically specific positions from which women intervened in cultural practices as a whole, sometimes working in support of dominant social ideals, at other times critically resistant, often allied with other progressive forces. Always we need to map the changing definitions of the terms "artist" and "woman." If we lack this sense of the ways in which women have heterogenously *negotiated* their differential position as women in the changing class and patriarchal social relations, any historical account of women, art and ideology which we produce will be devoid of political significance. It will fall back on celebration of individual success or failure, and, fatally, lack a theory of social and ideological transformation.

In this section I want to look more closely at art history itself in relation to the feminist project and discuss some of the lessons to be learnt from related Marxist critiques of art history.

In a useful introduction to his programme for a Marxist art history in his book *L'Histoire de l'art et la lutte des classes* (1973) Nicos Hadjinicolaou identified the obstacles posed by the forms of current art history. These are art history as the history of artists (biography and monographs); art history as part of the history of civilizations (reflection of periods and their intellectual currents); and art history as the history of autonomous aestheticized objects. However descriptively correct, it is hard none the less to characterize any of these methods as historical at all. They do embody, however, bourgeois *ideologies* about how history and thus society functions. In the representation of the historical development of human society which was manufactured after the revolutions of 1848, eighteenth-century arguments that history is a process of contradiction, discontinuity and transformation were replaced by mystifications and what amounted to a denial of history. The bourgeois order had to refute the fact of the drastic social upheavals of which it was born in order to protect its rule from subsequent proletarian challenge. Organic evolution, recurring cycles, or a continuity of the same, all these views serve to make the status quo seem inevitable. The image of the world figured in the bourgeois brain combines therefore both a repression of the real social conditions of its present role, and the necessary repression of any recognizable difference between itself and past societies. This can be accomplished firstly by "modernizing" history, i.e. assuming a complete identity between the present and the past, and secondly by projecting back into the past the features of the present order so that they come to appear as universal, unchanged and *natural*. This has special significance for feminist analyses. Against women the fiction of an eternal, natural order of things is monolithically employed to ratify the continuing power of men over women. The justification for making women exclusively responsible for domestic work and child care is assumed to be the nature of women. Historically produced social roles are represented in bourgeois ideologies as timeless and biologically determined. Feminists have therefore a dual task, to challenge this substitution of nature for history and to insist on understanding that history itself is changing, contradictory, differentiated.

Furthermore art history belies historical scholarship in another way. It often has nothing to do with history at all for it amounts only to art appreciation. Recent critiques of what literary criticism does to the history of literary production are helpful therefore in alerting us to similar historical tendencies in art history. The way in which literature is studied, as Macherey has use-

fully pointed out, does not explain how literature is produced. It aims to teach students how to consume the great fruits of the human spirit. In initiating students into the mysteries of aesthetic appreciation, submission to the inexplicable magic of creativity is instilled. But paradoxically, while literature is being presented as ineffable, the literary critic also strives to explain the hidden meanings and thus to "translate" the work of literature. What usually happens in this operation is that the text is stripped naked, an apparently hidden nugget of meaning extracted through the exercise of sensitive, informed criticism and the whole "translated" in the words of the critic who, while pretending merely to comment upon, in fact refashions the meanings of the work of art in his or her own ideological image (i.e. modernizes it). These dual procedures do not encourage students to ask the important questions—how and why an art object or text was made, for whom it was made, to do what kind of job it was made, within what constraints and possibilities it was produced and initially used? For, as Macherey states: "In seeing how a book is made we also see what it is made *from;* this defect which gives it a history and a relation to the historical."

Literary appreciation and art-history-as-appreciation are concerned with quality—i.e. positive and negative evaluations of artefacts. Careful gradations and distinctions are established between the major and the minor, the good and the bad, the eternally valued and the fashionably momentary. This kind of evaluative judgement has particular implications for women. Women's art is consistently assessed as poor art. Take for instance Charles Sterling's explanation for reattributing a portrait thought to be by Jacques-Louis David to Constance Charpentier (1767–1849): "Meanwhile the notion that our portrait may have been painted by a woman, is, let us confess, an attractive idea. Its poetry is literary rather than plastic, its very evident charms and its cleverly concealed weaknesses, its ensemble made up from a thousand subtle artifices, all seem to reveal the feminine spirit." And James Laver on the same painting: "Although the painting is attractive as a period piece, there are certain weaknesses of which a painter of David's calibre would not have been guilty." Both Sterling and Laver have a norm of good art, against which the women are judged and found wanting. This establishes difference on a sexual axis and a different set of criteria for judging art made by women.

To counter this kind of criticism of women's art, feminists are easily tempted to respond by trying to assert that women's art is just as good as men's; it has merely to be judged by yet another set of criteria. But this only creates an alternative method of appreciation—another way of consuming art. They attribute to women's art other qualities, claiming that it expresses a feminine essence, or interpret it saying that it tends to a central "core" type of imagery derived from the form of female genitals and from female bodily experience. All too familiar formal or psychologistic or stylistic criteria are marshalled to estimate women's art. The effect is to leave intact that very notion of evaluating art, and of course the normative standards by which it is done. Special pleading for women's art to be assessed by different values ensures that women's art is confined within a gender-defined category, and, at the same time, that the general criterion for appreciating art remains that which is employed in discussing work by men. Men's art remains the suprasexual norm precisely because women's art is assessed by what are easily dismissed as partisan or internally constructed values. Feminists thus end up reproducing Sterling's and Laver's hierarchy.

I am arguing that feminist art history has to reject all of this evaluative criticism and stop merely juggling the aesthetic criteria for appreciating art. Instead it should concentrate on historical forms of explanation of women's artistic *production*. For literary and art historical appreciation can be seen as the complement of bourgeois tendencies to "modernize" history. Both efface from the art work or text the signs of its having been *produced*. Stripped of its uniqueness

and historical specificity as production, it is re-clothed in the purely aesthetic values of the bourgeoisie. In one single movement both the historical character of the object and the historically determined ideology of the critic/art historian are conjured out of sight, and with them disappears the visibility of sexual position as a factor in both the production of art and its reception. Feminist art history can expose the derogatory evaluations of women's art, which are used to justify the omission of their art from serious scholarship, as symptoms of the antagonisms of a sexually divided society which masquerade, in this realm, as the exercise of pure judgement.

The insistence upon treating art as production invites us to consider the usefulness to feminist art history of Marxist paradigms. These are plural. There has been considerable development within Marxist cultural theory in the last decades particularly with regard to notions of ideology and representation. But there are also elements of Marxist thinking about art and society to be avoided. In seeking for models of a social history of art within the Marxist tradition, feminist art history should be wary of reproducing its errors. The problems are these: treating art as a reflection of the society that produced it, or as an image of its class divisions; treating an artist as a representative of his/her class; economic reductionism, that is, reducing all arguments about the forms and functions of cultural objects back to economic or material causes; ideological generalization, placing a picture because of its obvious content into a category of ideas, beliefs or social theories of a given society or period.

All these approaches strive, however crudely, to acknowledge the complex and inescapable relations between one specific social activity—art—and the totality of other social activities which constitute the "society" in, for and even against which art is produced. The problem with reflection theory is that it is mechanistic, suggesting at once that art is an inanimate object which merely "mirrors" a static and coherent thing called society. Reflection theory oversimplifies the process whereby an art product, consciously and ideologically manufactured from specifiable and selected materials, represents social processes which are themselves enormously complicated, mobile and opaque. A slightly more sophisticated version of reflection theory is that in which art is studied "in its historical context." History is, however, too often merely wheeled on as background to artistic production. History is conceived of as a lumpen entity, which can be swiftly sketched in as a story which provides clues to the picture's content.

The attempt to place the artist as a representative of a class outlook registers the need to recognize point of view and position in class society as a determination on the production of art. Even so, it involves considerable generalization. For instance in Nicos Hadjinicolaou's book we find the notion that paintings carry a visual ideology. Artists such as David or Rembrandt produced works which can be read as embodiments of the visual ideologies of a particular class or a section, a fraction of a class—art of the rising bourgeoisie at the end of the *ancien régime* for instance. A whole oeuvre or group of works become unitary examples of the singular outlook of a social group via the service of the artist. Secondly this argument tends as a result to reinstate the artist as a special kind of spokesperson—visionary or seer—or "ad-man"—with privileged access to and means of expression of the perspective and concerns of a class. To elaborate the inadequacies of this argument let us apply it to the case of women. Women artists are often treated in feminist art history virtually as representatives of their gender; their work expressing the visual ideology of a whole sex.

An example will illustrate this. I have taught a course on New York painting in the 1950s with special reference to the so-called abstract expressionists. First the general character of the movement and its art was established and then, in order to ensure some engagement with feminist art history, the work of one woman, Helen Frankenthaler, was taken up as a case study. This in effect meant that her work was made to stand for women's point of view in the movement. So the individual producer becomes the representative of an entire sex in a way similar to that in which Hadjinicolaou and Antal placed artists in relation to a class. The individual woman's particular strategies and practices are reduced to a generalization of a sex—i.e. become non-specific and homogeneous. This is of course not to deny that one's position as a woman or within class society profoundly delimits and conditions the production of art.

The third approach—economic reductionism—can be seen precisely as the attempt to insist upon the overall organization of social forces and relations as the determining factor in art-making. But to acknowledge a materialist basis in history, that is, that history is what real people do in concrete social relations, shaped by factors outside their individual control, is not the same thing as saying that knowing how factories are organized helps you to know why such an art is being produced. To know that society has been patriarchal and sexist means that you reject the idea that the oppression of women is divinely ordained, or biologically, psychologically inevitable. (To know that society is capitalist means that you reject the inevitability of wage labour capitalists' profits.) In studying art we want refined understanding of relation to and positions on that knowledge or social experience.

The danger is always of simply shifting your analysis from one set of *causes* to another, i.e. art is the way it is because of economic arrangements. Art is inevitably shaped and limited by the kind of society which produces it; but its particular features are not *caused* by economic structures or organization. They offer some of the conditions of the practice. In application to women the poverty of the argument is obvious since women's position in the basic economic organization of the workplace is easily shown to be mere complement to the kind of exploitation they experience in the home, in sexual relationships, child care, on the streets, as a result of sexual domination that is dispersed across a wide range of social practices.

The fourth problem—ideological generalization—is a response to the reductionism of the third. It is right to see relationships between one area of intellectual culture and others. It is suggested for instance that the historical coincidence of realism in art and positivism in philosophy is in some way a result of new forms of bourgeois ideology. But ideology is a process of basking contradictions; it is itself fractured and contradictory. Referring art to ideology does not sort anything out at all; it merely displaces the necessary study of what ideological work specific pieces of art are doing, and for whom. The parallel in the study of women and art is the way in which what women produce is placed in the category *women's art*. We are of course obliged to introduce the term if only to make known the fact that there is art made by women. But underlying this tactical necessity may be the impulse to imagine that there is such a unitary ideological category as women's art. To treat work by women merely as exemplars of womanness is to reproduce a tautology which teaches us nothing about what being, doing like, thinking as a woman might be.

Whether it be class, race or gender, any argument that generalizes, reduces, typifies or suggests a reflection is refusing to deal with specificity of individual texts, artistic practitioners, historical moments. Art history—Marxist or feminist—must be primarily a historiographical exercise. Society is a historical process; it is not a static entity. History cannot be reduced to a manageable block of information; it has to be grasped itself as a complex of processes and relationships. I suggest that we have to abandon all the formulations such as "art *and* society" or "art *and* its social context," "art *and* its historical background," "art *and* class formation," "art *and* gender relations." All the real difficulty which is *not* being confronted resides in those "*ands.*" What we have to deal with is the interplay of multiple histories—of the codes of art, of ideologies of the art world, of institutions of art, of forms of production, of social classes, of the family, of forms of sexual domination whose mutual determinations and independences have to be mapped together in precise and heterogeneous configurations.

E. The Postmodern Sublime

The recent interest in the aesthetic experience is concentrated mainly on the sublime and that concentration is due, at least in part, to the renewed interest in Kant in the last decade. Our selections in this section bring us into the 1990s and into future debates concerning aesthetic experience and the sublime. With "The Sublime and the Avant-Garde" and "Presenting the Unpresentable: The Sublime," by Jean-François Lyotard, we have a continuation, in many respects, of the ideas of Derrida, Foucault, and Deleuze. In fact, one problem of putting together a book like this one is precisely that of "contextualizing aesthetics." There are so many overlapping methods, themes, and ideas, it is difficult to decide which readings go where. In other words, you should read Lyotard in context with the other writers in Part III because the methods and ideas do crisscross. In addition, Fredric Jameson is a leading Marxist in American academic circles. As a literary critic, however, Jameson also critiques contemporary art and culture. Therefore, our selection from "The Cultural Logic of Late Capitalism" should also be read in context with the other sections, especially those in section D.

Perhaps this newfound interest in Kant actually began in the 1960s, when French philosophers turned away from Hegel and the oversaturation with neo-Hegelianism, and after 1968, in particular, when disillusionment with Marxism caused them to turn once again to Kant. These texts, then, may be said to be the original impetus of the renewed interest in Kant. Kant, however, does not remain unscathed in his newfound popularity. What attracts philosophers to Kant's formulation of the sublime is the paradoxical—according to Lyotard, the *paralogical*—nature of the sublime: terror and pleasure combined in a decidedly pleasurable yet uncomfortable experience. Reason cannot contain or account for the experience, and so contemporary philosophers begin their assault on reason from this paradoxical experience so inadequately theorized, according to contemporary philosophers, by the master, Kant himself.

A good example of the contemporary critique of Kant, connected to the reformulation of the sublime, may be found in Deleuze and Guattari's recent text, *What Is Philosophy?* Like other contemporary philosophers, Deleuze and Guattari wish to show that the philosophical trend since the Enlightenment era of Leibniz and Kant that privileges reason and the categorization of sense in terms of universals is simply one way of looking at the world, often appropriate, in fact, but not absolute. Attempting to think outside the boundaries of reason, rationalized categorical thought, and representation, Deleuze and Guattari theorize that a *plane of immanence* liberates thought to think outside the old categories: "The plane of immanence is not a concept that is or can be thought but rather the image of thought, the image thought gives itself of what it means to think, to use thought, to find one's bearings in thought." The plane of immanence opens up thought to the boundlessness and infinite magnitude that Kant attributed to the sublime.

From Deleuze and Guattari's perspective, Kant's sublime is always already limited by reason's trying to find a symbol for or make reasonable the boundlessness of the experience: "Hence the feeling of the sublime is a feeling of displeasure that arises from the imagination's inadequacy, in an aesthetic estimation of magnitude, for an estimation by reason, but is at the same time also a pleasure." The sublime provokes a futile search for a concept or an idea that can restrict or contain the unboundedness of the object. The "displeasure" or pain results from reason's failure to grasp the experience of indeterminacy; the category of the transcendent, Kant's "transcendental," is then called upon to absorb what reason cannot. Deleuze and Guattari object to immanence becoming immanent to a "transcendental subjectivity": "No longer content handing over immanence to the transcendent, we want to discharge it, reproduce it, and fabricate it itself. In fact this is not difficult—all that is necessary *is for movement to be stopped*. Transcendence enters as soon as movement of the infinite is stopped." For Deleuze and Guattari, finite thought cuts off—by way of the universal or transcendent—our ability to think, see, or read in any other manner than what has already been constituted. To open up the plane of immanence to all strata and not merely to a "transcendental subjectivity" means that we are no longer safe in a preconceived universal or Form. The image of thought is suddenly cut loose from representation and we are adrift, as we also read in section B, in unmapped territory.

It is in this unmapped territory that Lyotard locates the indeterminable and the "unpresentable"—the sublime—in "The Sublime and the Avant-Garde" and "Presenting the Unpresentable: The Sublime." Meanwhile, Jameson locates the postmodern sublime in a more materialist region in "The Cultural Logic of Late Capitalism." Jameson combines the "problem of aesthetic representation already explicitly developed in Kant's earlier analysis of the sublime" with the "relationship to and the representation of the machine" in order to point out that in the technological era what fills us with awe is the "boundlessness" and "terror" of the global network of power that blankets every aspect of our lives. Jameson's unmapped territory is the new postmodern narrative that specializes in "'high-tech paranoia'—in which the circuits and networks of some putative global computer hookup are narratively mobilized by labyrinthine conspiracies of autonomous but deadly interlocking and competing information agencies in complexity often beyond the capacity of the normal reading mind." The presentation of the enormous, awe-inspiring, terrifying and ubiquitous, yet unseen and decentered global network, with its infinite capacity to ferret out the secret, hidden, and private, elicits, according to Jameson, the postmodern sublime.

Likewise, Lyotard understands that technology has had an impact on the aesthetic experience, but does not share Jameson's view that the postmodern sublime is located in the very presentation of technology's power; rather, Lyotard theorizes that the postmodern sublime survives in spite of the technology's power to create, consume, and destroy at a historically unprecedented rate. According to Lyotard, the uneasy relationship that exists among science, technology and capital, and the aesthetic experience, with the "indeterminable" in experience, the "Is it happening?" dislocation that the sublime produces, results from the fact that the former, our culture—the world we live in—does not want the troubling, the loss of control, and the paradox of the experience of the sublime. Lyotard severely criticizes so-called postmodern movements that blend neo- and hyperrealistic themes with "lyrically abstract or conceptual ones on a single surface" because it implies "everything is equal because everything is easy to consume." This taste, Lyotard theorizes, is not Taste, and this "eclecticism panders to the habits of magazine readers, to the needs of consumers of standard industrial imagery, to the sensibility of the supermarket shopper." For Lyotard, the avant-garde artist stands in resistance to the homogeneity of the new postmodern standard of taste: against the rules of technology, against reason, and against the facile ideas of art production, the avant-garde artist presents the unpresentable. In the Introduction to this book we posed the question of whether postmodernism would so thoroughly contextualize the artist in society that she would have nothing to say and no independent voice, only able to articulate the culture of which she is a part. In answering this question in the affirmative (that the artist can resist and critique society), Lyotard's postmodernism is perhaps not completely divorced from modernism.

The Sublime and the Avant-Garde

JEAN-FRANÇOIS LYOTARD

IN 1950–1, BARNETT BARUCH Newman painted a canvas measuring 2.42 m by 5.42 m which he called "Vir Heroicus Sublimis." In the early sixties he entitled his first three sculptures "Here I," "Here II," "Here III." Another painting was called "Not Over There, Here," two paintings were called "Now," and two others were entitled "Be." In December 1948, Newman wrote an essay entitled "The Sublime Is Now."

How is one to understand the sublime, or let us say provisionally, the object of a sublime experience, as a "here and now"? Quite to the contrary, isn't it essential to this feeling that it alludes to something which can't be shown, or presented (as Kant said, *dargestellt*)? In a short unfinished text dating from late 1949, *Prologue for a New Aesthetic*, Newman wrote that in his painting, he was not concerned with a "manipulation of space nor with the image, but with a sensation of time." He added that by this he did not mean time laden with feelings of nostalgia, or drama, or references and history, the usual subjects of painting. After this denial [*dénégation*] the text stops short.

So, what kind of time was Newman concerned with, what "now" did he have in mind? Thomas Hess, his friend and commentator, felt justified in writing that Newman's time was the *Makom* or the *Hamakom* of Hebraic tradition—the *there*, the site, the place, which is one of the names given by the Torah to the Lord, the Unnameable. I do not know enough about *Makom* to know whether this was what Newman had in mind. But then again, who does know enough about *Now*? Newman can certainly not have been thinking of the "present instant," the one that tries to hold itself between the future and

the past, and gets devoured by them. This "now" is one of the temporal "ecstasies" that has been analysed since Augustine's day and since Edmund Husserl, according to a line of thought that has attempted to constitute time on the basis of consciousness. Newman's *now* which is no more than *now* is a stranger to consciousness and cannot be constituted by it. Rather, it is what dismantles consciousness, what deposes consciousness, it is what consciousness cannot formulate, and even what consciousness forgets in order to constitute itself. What we do not manage to formulate is that something happens, *dass etwas geschieht*. Or rather, and more simply, that it happens . . . *dass es geschieht*. Not a major event in the media sense, not even a small event. Just an occurrence.

This isn't a matter of sense or reality bearing upon *what* happens or *what* this might mean. Before asking questions about what it is and about its significance, before the *quid*, it must "first" so to speak "happen," *quod*. That it happens "precedes," so to speak, the question pertaining to what happens. Or rather, the question precedes itself, because "that it happens" is the question relevant as event, and it "then" pertains to the event that has just happened. The event happens as a question mark "before" happening as a question. *It happens* is rather "in the first place" *is it happening, is this it, is it possible?* Only "then" is any mark determined by the questioning: is this or that happening, is it this or something else, is it possible that this or that?

An event, an occurrence—what Martin Heidegger called *ein Ereignis*—is infinitely simple, but this simplicity can only be approached through a state of privation. That which we call

From A. Benjamin, ed., The Lyotard Reader *(Oxford: Basil Blackwell, 1989). Reprinted by permission of the publisher.*

thought must be disarmed. There is a tradition and an institution of philosophy, of painting, of politics, of literature. These "disciplines" also have a future in the form of Schools, of programmes, projects, and "trends." Thought works over what is received, it seeks to reflect on it and overcome it. It seeks to determine what has already been thought, written, painted, or socialized in order to determine what hasn't been. We know this process well, it is our daily bread. It is the bread of war, soldiers' biscuit. But this agitation, in the most noble sense of the word (agitation is the word Kant gives to the activity of the mind that has judgment and exercises it), this agitation is only possible if something remains to be determined, something that hasn't yet been determined. One can strive to determine this something by setting up a system, a theory, a programme or a project—and indeed one has to, all the while anticipating that something. One can also inquire about the remainder, and allow the indeterminate to appear as a question mark.

What all intellectual disciplines and institutions presuppose is that not everything has been said, written down or recorded, that words already heard or pronounced are not the last words. "After" a sentence, "after" a color, comes another sentence, another color. One doesn't know which, but one thinks one knows if one relies on the rules that permit one sentence to link up with another, one color with another, rules preserved in precisely those institutions of the past and future that I mentioned. The School, the program, the project—all proclaim that after this sentence comes that sentence, or at least that kind of sentence is mandatory, that one kind of sentence is permitted, while another is forbidden. This holds true for painting as much as for the other activities of thought. After one pictorial work, another is necessary, permitted, or forbidden. After one color, this other color; after this line, that one. There isn't an enormous difference between an avant-garde manifesto and a curriculum at the Ecole des Beaux-Arts, if one considers them in the light of this relationship to

time. Both are options with respect to what they feel is a good thing to happen subsequently. But both also forget the possibility of nothing happening, of words, colors, forms or sounds not coming; of this sentence being the last, of bread not coming daily. This is the misery that the painter faces with a plastic surface, of the musician with the acoustic surface, the misery the thinker faces with a desert of thought, and so on. Not only faced with the empty canvas or the empty page, at the "beginning" of the work, but every time something has to be waited for, and thus forms a question at every point of questioning [*point d'interrogation*], at every "and what now?"

The possibility of nothing happening is often associated with a feeling of anxiety, a term with strong connotations in modern philosophies of existence and of the unconscious. It gives to waiting, if we really mean waiting, a predominantly negative value. But suspense can also be accompanied by pleasure, for instance pleasure in welcoming the unknown, and even by joy, to speak like Baruch Spinoza, the joy obtained by the intensification of being that the event brings with it. This is probably a contradictory feeling. It is at the very least a sign, the question mark itself, the way in which *it happens* is withheld and announced: *Is it happening?* The question can be modulated in any tone. But the mark of the question is "now," *now* like the feeling that nothing might happen: the nothingness now.

Between the seventeenth and eighteenth centuries in Europe this contradictory feeling—pleasure and pain, joy and anxiety, exaltation and depression—was christened or re-christened by the name of the *sublime*. It is around this name that the destiny of classical poetics was hazarded and lost; it is in this name that aesthetics asserted its critical rights over art, and that romanticism—in other words, modernity—triumphed.

It remains to the art historian to explain how the word sublime reappeared in the language of a Jewish painter from New York during the forties. The word sublime is common currency today in colloquial French to suggest surprise and admiration, somewhat like America's "great," but the idea connoted by it has belonged (for at least two centuries) to the most rigorous kind of reflection on art. Newman is not unaware of the aesthetic and philosophical stakes with which the word *sublime* is involved. He read Edmund Burke's *Inquiry* and criticized what he saw as Burke's over-"surrealist" description of the sublime work. Which is as much as to say that, conversely, Newman judged surrealism to be over-reliant on a pre-romantic or romantic approach to indeterminacy. Thus, when he seeks sublimity in the here and now he breaks with the eloquence of romantic art but he does not reject its fundamental task, that of bearing pictorial or otherwise expressive witness to the inexpressible. The inexpressible does not reside in an over there, in another world, or another time, but in this: in that (something) happens. In the determination of pictorial art, the indeterminate, the "it happens" is the paint, the picture. The paint, the picture as occurrence or event, is not expressible, and it is to this that it has to witness.

To be true to this displacement in which consists perhaps the whole of the difference between romanticism and the "modern" avant-garde, one would have to read "The sublime is now" not as "The sublime is now" but as "Now the sublime is like this." Not elsewhere, not up there or over there, not earlier or later, not once upon a time. But as here, now, it happens that . . . and it's this painting. Here and now there is this painting, rather than nothing, and that's what is sublime. Letting go of all grasping intelligence and of its power, disarming it, recognizing that this occurrence of painting was not necessary and is scarcely foreseeable, a privation in the face of *Is it happening?* guarding the occurrence "before" any defense, any illustration, and any commentary, guarding before being on one's guard, before "looking" [*regarder*] under the aegis of *now*, this is the rigor of the avant-garde. In the determination of literary art this requirement with respect to the *Is it happening?* found one of its most rigorous realizations in Gertrude Stein's *How to Write*. It's still the sublime in the sense that Burke and Kant described, and yet it isn't their sublime any more.

I have said that the contradictory feeling with which indeterminacy is both announced and missed was what was at stake in reflection on art from the end of the seventeenth to the end of the eighteenth centuries. The sublime is perhaps the only mode of artistic sensibility to characterize the modern. Paradoxically, it was introduced to literary discussion and vigorously defended by the French writer who has been classified in literary history as one of the most dogged advocates of ancient classicism. In 1674 Boileau published his *Art poétique*, but he also published *Du Sublime*, his translation or transcription from the *Peri tou hupsou*. It is a treatise, or rather an essay, attributed to a certain Longinus, about whose identity there has long been confusion, and whose life we now estimate as having begun towards the end of the first century of our era. The author was a rhetorician. Basically, he taught those oratorical devices with which a speaker can persuade or move (depending on the genre) his audience. The didactics of rhetoric had been traditional since Aristotle, Cicero, and Quintilian. They were linked to the republican institution; one had to know how to speak before assemblies and tribunals.

One might expect that Longinus's text would invoke the maxims and advice transmitted by this tradition by perpetuating the didactic form of *technè rhetorikè*. But surprisingly, the sublime, the indeterminate—were destabilizing the text's didactic intention. I cannot analyse this uncertainty here. Boileau himself and numerous other commentators, especially Fénélon, were aware of it and concluded that the sublime could only be discussed in sublime style. Longinus certainly tried to define sublimity in discourse, writing that it was unforgettable, irresistible, and most important, thought-provoking—"*il y a à partir d'elle beaucoup de réflexion*" [*hou polle anatheoresis*] (from the sublime springs a lot of reflection). He also tried to locate sources for the sublime in the ethos of rhetoric, in its pathos, in its techniques: figures of speech, diction, enunciation, composition. He sought in this way to bend himself to the rules of the genre of the "treatise" (whether of rhetoric or poetics, or politics) destined to be a model for practitioners.

However, when it comes to the sublime, major obstacles get in the way of a regular exposition of rhetorical or poetic principles. There is, for example, wrote Longinus, a sublimity of thought sometimes recognizable in speech by its extreme simplicity of turn of phrase, at the precise point where the high character of the speaker makes one expect greater solemnity. It sometimes even takes the form of outright silence. I don't mind if this simplicity, this silence, is taken to be yet another rhetorical figure. But it must be granted that it constitutes the most indeterminate of figures. What can remain of rhetoric (or of poetics) when the rhetorician in Boileau's translation announces that to attain the sublime effect "there is no better figure of speech than one which is completely hidden, that which we do not even recognize as a figure of speech"? Must we admit that there are techniques for hiding figures, that there are figures for the erasure of figures? How do we distinguish between a hidden figure and what is not a figure? And what is it, if it isn't a figure? And what about this, which seems to be a major blow to didactics: when it is sublime, discourse accommodates defects, lack of taste, and formal imperfections. Plato's style, for example, is full of bombast and bloated strained comparisons. Plato, in short, is a mannerist, or a baroque writer, compared to Lysias, and so is Sophocles compared to an Ion or Pindar compared to a Bacchylides. The fact remains that, like those first named, he is sublime, whereas the second ones are merely perfect. Shortcomings in technique are therefore trifling matters if they are the price to be paid for "true grandeur." Grandeur in speech is true when it bears witness to the incommensurability between thought and the real world.

Is it Boileau's transcription that suggests this analogy, or is it the influence of early Christianity on Longinus? The fact that grandeur of spirit is not of this world cannot but suggest Pascal's hi-erarchy of orders. The kind of perfection that can be demanded in the domain of *technè* isn't necessarily a desirable attribute when it comes to sublime feeling. Longinus even goes so far as to propose inversions of reputedly natural and rational syntax as examples of sublime effect. As for Boileau, in the preface he wrote in 1674 for Longinus's text, in still further addenda made in 1683 and 1701 and also in the *Xth Réflexion* published in 1710 after his death, he makes final the previous tentative break with the classical institution of *technè*. The sublime, he says, cannot be taught, and didactics are thus powerless in this respect; the sublime is not linked to rules that can be determined through poetics; the sublime only requires that the reader or listener have conceptual range, taste, and the ability "to sense what everyone senses first." Boileau therefore takes the same stand as Père Bouhours, when in 1671 the latter declared that beauty demands more than just a respect for rules, that it requires a further *"je ne sais quoi,"* also called *genius* or something "incomprehensible and inexplicable," a "gift from God," a fundamentally "hidden" phenomenon that can be recognized only by its effects on the addressee. And in the polemic that set him against Pierre-Daniel Huet, over the issue of whether the Bible's *Fiat Lux, et Lux fuit* is sublime, as Longinus thought it was, Boileau refers to the opinion of the Messieurs de Port-Royal and in particular to Silvestre de Saci: the Jansenists are masters when it comes to matters of hidden meaning, of eloquent silence, of feeling that transcends all reason and finally of openness to the *Is it happening?*

At stake in these poetic-theological debates is the status of works of art. Are they copies of some ideal model? Can reflection on the more "perfect" examples yield rules of formation that determine their success in achieving what they want, that is, persuasiveness and pleasure? Can understanding suffice for this kind of reflection? By meditating on the theme of sublimity and of indeterminacy, meditation about works of art imposes a major change on *technè* and the institutions linked to it—Academies, Schools, masters and disciples, taste, the enlightened public made up of princes and courtiers. It is the very destination or destiny of works which is being questioned. The predominance of the idea of *technè* placed works under a multiple regulation, that of the model taught in the studios, Schools, and Academies, that of the taste shared by the aristocratic public, that of a purposiveness of art, which was to illustrate the glory of a name, divine or human, to which was linked the perfection of some cardinal virtue or other. The idea of the sublime disrupts this harmony. Let us magnify the features of—this disruption. Under Diderot's pen, *technè* becomes "*le petit technique*" (mere trivial technique). The artist ceases to be guided by a culture which made of him the sender and master of a message of glory: he becomes, insofar as he is a genius, the involuntary addressee of an inspiration come to him from an "I know not what." The public no longer judges according to the criteria of a taste ruled by the tradition of shared pleasure: individuals unknown to the artist (the "people") read books, go through the galleries of the Salons, crowd into the theatres and the public concerts, they are prey to unforeseeable feelings: they are shocked, admiring, scornful, indifferent. The question is not that of pleasing them by leading them to identify with a name and to participate in the glorification of its virtue, but that of surprising them. "The sublime," writes Boileau, "is not strictly speaking something which is proven or demonstrated, but a marvel, which seizes one, strikes one, and makes one feel." The very imperfections, the distortions of taste, even ugliness, have their share in the shock-effect. Art does not imitate nature, it creates a world apart, *eine Zwischenwelt,* as Paul Klee will say, *eine Nebenwelt,* one might say, in which the monstrous and the formless have their rights because they can be sublime.

You will (I hope) excuse such a simplification of the transformation which takes place with the modern development of the idea of the sublime. The trace of it could be found before modern times, in medieval aesthetics—that of the Victorines, for example. In any case, it explains why

reflection on art should no longer bear essentially on the "sender" instance/agency of works, but on the "addressee" instance. And under the name "genius" the latter instance is situated, not only on the side of the public, but also on the side of the artist, a feeling which he does not master. Henceforth it seems right to analyze the ways in which the subject is affected, its ways of receiving and experiencing feelings, its ways of judging works. This is how aesthetics, the analysis of the addressee's feelings, comes to supplant poetics and rhetoric, which are didactic forms, of and by the understanding, intended for the artist as sender. No longer "How does one make a work of art?", but "What is it to experience an affect proper to art?" And indeterminacy returns, even within the analysis of this last question.

Baumgarten published his *Aesthetica,* the first aesthetics, in 1750. Kant will say of this work simply that it was based on an error. Baumgarten confuses judgment, in its determinant usage, when the understanding organizes phenomena according to categories, with judgment in its reflexive usage when, in the form of feeling, it relates to the indeterminate relationship between the faculties of judging subject. Baumgarten's aesthetics remains dependent on a conceptually determined relationship to the work of art. The sense of beauty is for Kant, on the contrary, kindled by a free harmony between the function of images and the function of concepts occasioned by an object of art or nature. The aesthetics of the sublime is still more indeterminate: a pleasure mixed with pain, a pleasure that comes from pain. In the event of an absolutely large object—the desert, a mountain, a pyramid—or one that is absolutely powerful—a storm at sea, an erupting volcano—which, like all absolutes, can only be thought, without any sensible/sensory intuition, as an Idea of reason, the faculty of presentation, the imagination, fails to provide a representation corresponding to this Idea. This failure of expression gives rise to a pain, a kind of cleavage within the subject between what can be conceived and what can be imagined or presented. But this pain in turn engenders a pleasure, in fact a double pleasure: the impotence of the imagination attests *a contrario* to an imagination striving to figure even that which cannot be figured, and that imagination thus aims to harmonize its object with that of reason—and that furthermore, the inadequacy of the images is a negative sign of the immense power of ideas. This dislocation of the faculties among themselves gives rise to the extreme tension (Kant calls it agitation) that characterizes the pathos of the sublime, as opposed to the calm feeling of beauty. At the edge of the break, infinity, or the absoluteness of the Idea can be revealed in what Kant calls a negative presentation, or even a non-presentation. He cites the Jewish law banning images as an eminent example of negative presentation: optical pleasure when reduced to near nothingness promotes an infinite contemplation of infinity. Even before romantic art had freed itself from classical and baroque figuration, the door had thus been opened to inquiries pointing towards abstract and Minimal art. Avant-gardism is thus present in germ in the Kantian aesthetic of the sublime. However, the art whose effects are analysed in that aesthetics is, of course, essentially made up of attempts to represent sublime objects. And the question of time, of the *Is it happening?*, does not form part—at least not explicitly—of Kant's problematic.

I do, however, believe that question to be at the centre of Edmund Burke's *Philosophical Inquiry into the Origin of our Ideas of the Sublime and Beautiful*, published in 1757. Kant may well reject Burke's thesis as empiricism and physiologism, he may well borrow from Burke the analysis of the characterizing contradiction of the feeling of the sublime, but he strips Burke's aesthetic of what I consider to be its major stake—to show that the sublime is kindled by the threat of nothing further happening. Beauty gives a positive pleasure. But there is another kind of pleasure that is bound to a passion stronger than satisfaction, and that is pain and impending death. In pain the body affects the soul. But the soul can also affect the body as though it were experiencing some externally induced pain, by the sole

means of representations that are unconsciously associated with painful situations. This entirely spiritual passion, in Burke's lexicon, is called terror. Terrors are linked to privation: privation of light, terror of darkness; privation of others, terror of solitude; privation of language, terror of silence; privation of objects, terror of emptiness; privation of life, terror of death. What is terrifying is that the *It happens that* does not happen, that it stops happening.

Burke wrote that for this terror to mingle with pleasure and with it to produce the feeling of the sublime, it is also necessary that the terror-causing threat be suspended, kept at bay, held back. This suspense, this lessening of a threat or a danger, provokes a kind of pleasure that is certainly not that of a positive satisfaction, but is, rather, that of relief. This is still a privation, but it is privation at one remove: the soul is deprived of the threat of being deprived of light, language, life. Burke distinguishes this pleasure of secondary privation from positive pleasures, and he baptizes it with the name *delight*.

Here, then, is an account of the sublime feeling: a very big, very powerful object threatens to deprive the soul of any "it happens," strikes it with "astonishment" (at lower intensities the soul is seized with admiration, veneration, respect). The soul is thus dumb, immobilized, as good as dead. Art, by distancing this menace, procures a pleasure of relief, of delight. Thanks to art, the soul is returned to the agitated zone between life and death, and this agitation is its health and its life. For Burke, the sublime was no longer a matter of elevation (the category by which Aristotle defined tragedy), but a matter of intensification.

Another of Burke's observations merits attention because it heralds the possibility of emancipating works of art from the classical rule of imitation. In the long debate over the relative merits of painting and poetry, Burke sides with poetry. Painting is doomed to imitate models, and to figurative representations of them. But if the object of art is to create intense feelings in the addressee of works, figuration by means of images is a limiting constraint on the power of emotive expression, since it works by recognition. In the arts of language, particularly in poetry, and particularly in poetry which Burke considered to be not a genre with rules, but the field where certain researches into language have free rein, the power to move is free from the verisimilitudes of figuration. "What does one do when one wants to represent an angel in a painting? One paints a beautiful young man with wings: but will painting ever provide anything as great as the addition of this one word—the Angel of the *Lord*? and how does one go about painting, with equal strength of feeling, the words 'A universe of death' where ends the journey of the fallen angels in Milton's *Paradise Lost?*"

Words enjoy several privileges when it comes to expressing feelings: they are themselves charged with passionate connotations; they can evoke matters of the soul without having to consider whether they are visible; finally, Burke adds, "It is in our power to effect with words combinations that would be impossible by any other means." The arts, whatever their materials, pressed forward by the aesthetics of the sublime in search of intense effects, can and must give up the imitation of models that are merely beautiful, and try out surprising, strange, shocking combinations. Shock is, *par excellence,* the evidence of (something) *happening,* rather than nothing, suspended privation.

Burke's analyses can easily, as you will have guessed, be resumed and elaborated in a Freudian-Lacanian problematic (as Pierre Kaufman and Baldine Saint-Girons have done). But I recall them in a different spirit, the one my subject—the avant-garde—demands. I have tried to suggest that at the dawn of romanticism, *Burke's* elaboration of the aesthetics of the sublime, and to a lesser degree *Kant's, outlined a world of possibilities for artistic experiments in which the avant-gardes would later trace out their paths.* There are in general no direct influences, no empirically observable connections. Manet, Cézanne, Braque, and Picasso probably did not read Kant or Burke. It is more a matter of an irreversible deviation in the

destination of art, a deviation affecting all the valencies of the artistic condition. The artist attempts combinations allowing the event. The art-lover does not experience a simple pleasure, or derive some ethical benefit from his contact with art, but expects an intensification of his conceptual and emotional capacity, an ambivalent enjoyment. Intensity is associated with an ontological dislocation. The art object no longer bends itself to models, but tries to present the fact that there is an unpresentable; it no longer imitates nature, but is, in Burke, the actualization of a figure potentially there in language. The social community no longer recognizes itself in art objects, but ignores them, rejects them as incomprehensible, and only later allows the intellectual avant-garde to preserve them in museums as the traces of offensives that bear witness to the power, and the privation, of the spirit.

With the advent of the aesthetics of the sublime, the stake of art in the nineteenth and twentieth centuries was to be the witness to the fact that there is indeterminacy. For painting, the paradox that Burke signalled in his observations on the power of words is that such testimony can only be achieved in a determined fashion. Support, frame, line, color, space, the figure—were to remain, in romantic art, subject to the constraint of representation. But this contradiction of end and means had, as early as Manet and Cézanne, the effect of casting doubt on certain rules that had determined, since the Quattrocento, the representation of the figure in space and the organization of colors and values. Reading Cézanne's correspondence, one understands that his *oeuvre* was not that of a talented painter finding his "style," but that of an artist attempting to respond to the question: what is a painting? His work had at stake to inscribe on the supporting canvas only those "coloristic sensations," those "little sensations" that of themselves, according to Cézanne's hypothesis, constitute the entire pictorial existence of objects, fruit, mountain, face, flower, without consideration of either history or "subject," or line, or space, or even light. These elementary sensations are hidden in ordinary perception, which remains under the hegemony of habitual or classical ways of looking. They are only accessible to the painter, and can therefore only be re-established by him, at the expense of an interior ascesis that rids perceptual and mental fields of prejudices inscribed even in vision itself. If the viewer does not submit to a complementary ascesis, the painting will remain senseless and impenetrable to him. The painter must not hesitate to run the risk of being taken to be a mere dauber. "One paints for very few people," writes Cézanne. Recognition from the regulatory institutions of painting—Academy, salons, criticism, taste—is of little importance compared to the judgment made by the painter-researcher and his peers on the success obtained by the work of art in relation to what is really at stake: to make seen what makes one see, and not what is visible.

Maurice Merleau-Ponty elaborated on what he rightly called "Cézanne's doubt," as though what was at stake for the painter was indeed to grasp and render perception at its birth—perception "before" perception. I would say: color in its occurrence, the wonder that "it happens" ("it," something: color), at least to the eye. There is some credulity on the part of the phenomenologist in this trust he places in the "originary" value of Cézanne's "little sensations." The painter himself, who often complained of their inadequacy, wrote that they were "abstractions," that "they did not suffice for covering the canvas." But why should it be necessary to cover the canvas? Is it forbidden to be abstract?

The doubt which gnaws at the avant-gardes did not stop with Cézanne's "coloristic sensations" as though they were indubitable, and, for that matter, no more did it stop with the abstractions they heralded. The task of having to bear witness to the indeterminate carries away, one after another, the barriers set up by the writings of theorists and by the manifestos of the painters themselves. A formalist definition of the pictorial object, such as that proposed in 1961 by Clement Greenberg when confronted with American "post-plastic" abstraction, was soon overturned by the current of Minimalism. Do we have to have stretchers so that the canvas is taut? No. What about colors? Malevich's black square on white had already answered this question in 1915. Is an object necessary? Body art and happenings went about proving that it is not. A space, at least, a space in which to display, as Duchamp's "fountain" still suggested? Daniel Buren's work testifies to the fact that even this is subject to doubt.

Whether or not they belong to the current that art history calls Minimalism or Arte Povera, the investigations of the avant-gardes question one by one the constituents one might have thought "elementary" or at the "origin" of the art of painting. They operate *ex minimis*. One would have to confront the demand for rigour that animates them with the principle sketched out by Adorno at the end of *Negative Dialectics*, and that controls the writing of his *Aesthetic Theory*: the thought that "accompanies metaphysics in its fall," he said, can only proceed in terms of "micrologies."

Micrology is not just metaphysics in crumbs, any more than Newman's painting is Delacroix in scraps. Micrology inscribes the occurrence of a thought as the unthought that remains to be thought in the decline of "great" philosophical thought. The avant-gardist attempt inscribes the occurrence of a sensory now as what cannot be presented and remains to be presented in the decline of great representational painting. Like micrology, the avant-garde is not concerned with what happens to the "subject," but with: "Does it happen?," with privation. This is the sense in which it still belongs to the aesthetics of the sublime.

In asking questions of the *It happens* that the work of art is, avant-garde art abandons the role of identification that the work previously played in relation to the community of addressees. Even when conceived, as it was by Kant, as a *de jure* horizon or presumption rather than a *de facto* reality, a *sensus communis* (which, moreover, Kant refers to only when writing about beauty, not the sublime) does not manage to achieve stability when it comes to interrogative works of art. It barely coalesces, too late, when these works, deposited in museums, are considered part of the community heritage and are made available for its culture and pleasure. And even here, they must be objects, or they must tolerate objectification, for example through photography.

In this situation of isolation and misunderstanding, avant-garde art is vulnerable and subject to repression. It seems only to aggravate the identity-crisis that communities went through during the long "depression" that lasted from the thirties until the end of "reconstruction" in the mid-fifties. It is impossible here even to suggest how the Party-states born of fear faced with the "Who are we?," and the anxiety of the void, tried to convert this fear or anxiety into hatred of the avant-gardes. Hildegarde Brenner's study of artistic policy under Nazism, or the films of Hans-Jürgen Syberberg, do not merely analyse these repressive manoeuvres. They also explain how neo-romantic, neo-classical and symbolic forms imposed by the cultural commissars and collaborationist artists—painters and musicians especially—had to block the negative dialectic of the "Is it happening?," by translating and betraying the question as a waiting for some fabulous subject or identity: "Is the pure people coming?," "Is the Führer coming?," "Is Siegfried coming?" The aesthetics of the sublime, thus neutralized and converted into a politics of myth, was able to come and build its architectures of human "formations" on the Zeppelin Feld in Nürnberg.

Thanks to the "crisis of overcapitalization" that most of today's so-called highly developed societies are going through, another attack on the avant-gardes is coming to light. The threat exerted against the avante garde search for the artwork event, against attempts to welcome the *now*, no longer requires Party-states to be effective. It proceeds "directly" out of market economics. The correlation between this and the aesthetics of the sublime is ambiguous, even perverse. The latter, no doubt, has been and continues to be a reaction against the matter-of-fact positivism and the calculated realism that governs the former, as writers on art such as Stend-

hal, Baudelaire, Mallarmé, Apollinaire and Breton all emphasize.

Yet there is a kind of collusion between capital and the avant-garde. The force of scepticism and even of destruction that capitalism has brought into play, and that Marx never ceased analysing and identifying, in some way encourages among artists a mistrust of established rules and a willingness to experiment with means of expression, with styles, with ever-new materials. There is something of the sublime in capitalist economy. It is not academic, it is not physiocratic, it admits of no nature. It is, in a sense, an economy regulated by an Idea—infinite wealth or power. It does not manage to present any example from reality to verify this Idea. In making science subordinate to itself though technologies, especially those of language, it only succeeds, on the contrary, in making reality increasingly ungraspable, subject to doubt, unsteady.

The experience of the human subject—individual and collective—and the aura that surrounds this experience, are being dissolved into the calculation of profitability, the satisfaction of needs, self-affirmation through success. Even the virtually theological depth of the worker's condition, and of work, that marked the socialist and union movements for over a century, is becoming devalorized, as work becomes a control and manipulation of information. These observations are banal, but what merits attention is the disappearance of the temporal continuum through which the experience of generations used to be transmitted. The availability of information is becoming the only criterion of social importance. Now information is by definition a short-lived element. As soon as it is transmitted and shared, it ceases to be information, it becomes an environmental given, and "all is said," we "know." It is put into the machine memory. The length of time it occupies is, so to speak, instantaneous. Between two pieces of information, "nothing happens," by definition. A confusion thereby becomes possible between what is of interest to information and the director, and what is the question of the avant-gardes between what happens—the new—and the "Is it happening?," the *now*.

It is understandable that the art-market, subject like all markets to the rule of the new, can exert a kind of seduction on artists. This attraction is not due to corruption alone. It exerts itself thanks to a confusion between innovation and the *Ereignis,* a confusion maintained by the temporality specific to contemporary capitalism. "Strong" information, if one can call it that, exists in inverse proportion to the meaning that can be attributed to it in the code available to its receiver. It is like "noise." It is easy for the public and for artists, advised by intermediaries—the diffusers of cultural merchandise—to draw from this observation the principle that a work of art is avant-garde in direct proportion to the extent that it is stripped of meaning. Is it not then like an event?

It is still necessary that its absurdity does not discourage buyers, just as the innovation introduced into a commodity must allow itself to be approached, appreciated and purchased by the consumers. The secret of an artistic success, like that of a commercial success, resides in the balance between what is surprising and what is "well-known," between information and code. This is how innovation in art operates: one re-uses formulae confirmed by previous success, one throws them off balance by combining them with other, in principle incompatible, formulae, by amalgamations, quotations, ornamentations, pastiche. One can go as far as kitsch or the grotesque. One flatters the "taste" of a public that can have no taste, and the eclecticism or a sensibility enfeebled by the multiplication of available forms and objects. In this way one thinks that one is expressing the spirit of the times, whereas one is merely reflecting the spirit of the market. Sublimity is no longer in art, but in speculation on art.

The enigma of the "Is it happening?" is not dissolved for all this, nor is the task of painting: that there is something which is not determinable, the "There is" [*Il y a*] itself, out of date. The occurrence, the *Ereignis,* has nothing to do with the *petit frisson,* the cheap thrill, the profitable pathos, that accompanies an innovation. Hidden in the cynicism of innovation is certainly the despair that nothing further will happen. But innovating means to behave as though lots of things happened, and to make them happen. Through innovation, the will affirms its hegemony over time. It thus conforms to the metaphysics of capital, which is a technology of time. The innovation "works." The question mark of the "Is it happening?" stops. With the occurrence, the will is defeated. The avant-gardist task remains that of undoing the presumption of the mind with respect to time. The sublime feeling is the name of this privation.

Postmodernism

FREDRIC JAMESON

WE WILL BEGIN WITH one of the canonical works of high modernism in visual art, van Gogh's well-known painting of the peasant shoes, an example which, as you can imagine, has not been innocently or randomly chosen. I want to propose two ways of reading this painting, both of which in some fashion reconstruct the reception of the work in a two-stage or double-level process.

I first want to suggest that if this copiously reproduced image is not to sink to the level of sheer decoration, it requires us to reconstruct some

From Postmodernism, or the Cultural Logic of Late Capitalism *(Durham, NC: Duke University Press, 1991). Reprinted by permission of the publisher.*

initial situation out of which the finished work emerges. Unless that situation—which has vanished into the past—is somehow mentally restored, the painting will remain an inert object, a reified end product impossible to grasp as a symbolic act in its own right, as praxis and as production.

This last term suggests that one way of reconstructing the initial situation to which the work is somehow a response is by stressing the raw materials, the initial content, which it confronts and reworks, transforms, and appropriates. In van Gogh that content, those initial raw materials, are, I will suggest, to be grasped simply as the whole object world of agricultural misery, of stark rural poverty, and the whole rudimentary human world of backbreaking peasant toil, a world reduced to its most brutal and menaced, primitive and marginalized state.

Fruit trees in this world are ancient and exhausted sticks coming out of poor soil; the people of the village are worn down to their skulls, caricatures of some ultimate grotesque typology of basic human feature types. How is it, then, that in van Gogh such things as apple trees explode into a hallucinatory surface of color, while his village stereotypes are suddenly and garishly overlaid with hues of red and green? I will briefly suggest, in this first interpretative option, that the willed and violent transformation of a drab peasant object world into the most glorious materialization of pure color in oil paint is to be seen as a Utopian gesture, an act of compensation which ends up producing a whole new Utopian realm of the senses, or at least of that supreme sense—sight, the visual, the eye— which it now reconstitutes for us as a semiautonomous space in its own right, a part of some new division of labor in the body of capital, some new fragmentation of the emergent sensorium which replicates the specializations and divisions of capitalist life at the same time that it seeks in precisely such fragmentation a desperate Utopian compensation for them.

There is, to be sure, a second reading of van Gogh which can hardly be ignored when we gaze at this particular painting, and that is Heidegger's central analysis in *Der Ursprung des Kunstwerkes* [*The Origin of the Work of Art*], which is organized around the idea that the work of art emerges within the gap between Earth and World, or what I would prefer to translate as the meaningless materiality of the body and nature and the meaning endowment of history and of the social. We will return to that particular gap or rift later on; suffice it here to recall some of the famous phrases that model the process whereby these henceforth illustrious peasant shoes slowly re-create about themselves the whole missing object world which was once their lived context. "In them," says Heidegger, "there vibrates the silent call of the earth, its quiet gift of ripening corn and its enigmatic self-refusal in the fallow desolation of the wintry field." "This equipment," he goes on, "belongs to the *earth,* and it is protected in the *world* of the peasant woman. . . . van Gogh's painting is the disclosure of what the equipment, the pair of peasant shoes, *is* in truth. . . . This entity emerges into the unconcealment of its being," by way of the mediation of the work of art, which draws the whole absent world and earth into relation around itself, along with the heavy tread of the peasant woman, the loneliness of the field path, the hut in the clearing, the worn and broken instruments of labor in the furrows and at the hearth. Heidegger's account needs to be completed by insistence on the renewed materiality of the work, on the transformation of one form of materiality— the earth itself and its paths and physical objects—into that other materiality of oil paint affirmed and foregrounded in its own right and for its own visual pleasures, but nonetheless it has a satisfying plausibility.

At any rate, both readings may be described as *hermeneutical,* in the sense in which the work in its inert, objectal form is taken as a clue or a symptom for some vaster reality which replaces it as its ultimate truth. Now we need to look at some shoes of a different kind, and it is pleasant to be able to draw for such an image on the recent work of the central figure in contemporary visual art. Andy Warhol's *Diamond Dust Shoes* evidently

Vincent van Gogh, *A Pair of Boots,* 1887

no longer speaks to us with any of the immediacy of van Gogh's footgear; indeed, I am tempted to say that it does not really speak to us at all. Nothing in this painting organizes even a minimal place for the viewer, who confronts it at the turning of a museum corridor or gallery with all the contingency of some inexplicable natural object. On the level of the content, we have to do with what are now far more clearly fetishes, in both the Freudian and the Marxian senses (Derrida remarks, somewhere, about the Heideggerian *Paar Bauernschuhe,* that the van Gogh footgear are a heterosexual pair, which allows neither for perversion nor for fetishization). Here, however, we have a random collection of dead objects hanging together on the canvas like so many turnips, as

shorn of their earlier life world as the pile of shoes left over from Auschwitz or the remainders and tokens of some incomprehensible and tragic fire in a packed dance hall. There is therefore in Warhol no way to complete the hermeneutic gesture and restore to these oddments that whole larger lived context of the dance hall or the ball, the world of jetset fashion or glamour magazines. Yet this is even more paradoxical in the light of biographical information: Warhol began his artistic career as a commercial illustrator for shoe fashions and a designer of display windows in which various pumps and slippers figured prominently. Indeed, one is tempted to raise here—far too prematurely—one of the central issues about postmodernism itself and its possible political

Andy Warhol, *Diamond Dust Shoes,* 1980

dimensions: Andy Warhol's work in fact turns centrally around commodification, and the great billboard images of the Coca-Cola bottle or the Campbell's soup can, which explicitly foreground the commodity fetishism of a transition to late capital, ought to be powerful and critical political statements. If they are not that, then one would surely want to know why, and one would want to begin to wonder a little more seriously about the possibilities of political or critical art in the postmodern period of late capital.

But there are some other significant differences between the high-modernist and the postmodernist moment, between the shoes of van Gogh and the shoes of Andy Warhol, on which we must now very briefly dwell. The first and most evident is the emergence of a new kind of flatness or depthlessness, a new kind of superficiality in the most literal sense, perhaps the supreme formal feature of all the postmodernisms to which we will have occasion to return in a number of other contexts.

Then we must surely come to terms with the role of photography and the photographic negative in contemporary art of this kind; and it is this, indeed, which confers its deathly quality to the Warhol image, whose glacéd X-ray elegance mortifies the reified eye of the viewer in a way that would seem to have nothing to do with death or the death obsession or the death anxiety on the level of content. It is indeed as though we had here to do with the inversion of van Gogh's Utopian gesture: in the earlier work a stricken world is by some Nietzschean fiat and act of the will transformed into the stridency of Utopian color. Here, on the contrary, it is as though the external and colored surface of things—debased and contaminated in advance by their assimilation to glossy advertising images—has been stripped away to reveal the deathly black-and-white substratum of the photographic negative which subtends them. Although this kind of death of the world of appearance becomes thematized in certain of Warhol's pieces, most notably the traffic accidents or the electric chair series, this is not, I think, a matter of content any

longer but of some more fundamental mutation both in the object world itself—now become a set of texts or simulacra—and in the disposition of the subject.

All of which brings me to a third feature to be developed here, what I will call the waning of affect in postmodern culture. Of course, it would be inaccurate to suggest that all affect, all feeling or emotion, all subjectivity, has vanished from the newer image. Indeed, there is a kind of return of the repressed in *Diamond Dust Shoes,* a strange, compensatory, decorative exhilaration, explicitly designated by the title itself, which is, of course, the glitter of gold dust, the spangling of gilt sand that seals the surface of the painting and yet continues to glint at us. Think, however, of Rimbaud's magical flowers "that look back at you," or of the august premonitory eye flashes of Rilke's archaic Greek torso which warn the bourgeois subject to change his life; nothing of that sort here in the gratuitous frivolity of this final decorative overlay. In an interesting review of the Italian version of this essay, Remo Ceserani expands this foot fetishism into a fourfold image which adds to the gaping "modernist" expressivity of the van Gogh–Heidegger shoes the "realist" pathos of Walker Evans and James Agee (strange that pathos should thus require a team!); while what looked like a random assortment of yesteryear's fashions in Warhol takes on, in Magritte, the carnal reality of the human member itself, now more phantasmic than the leather it is printed on. Magritte, unique among the surrealists, survived the sea change from the modern to its sequel, becoming in the process something of a postmodern emblem: the uncanny, Lacanian foreclusion, without expression. The ideal schizophrenic, indeed, is easy enough to please provided only an eternal present is thrust before the eyes, which gaze with equal fascination on an old shoe or the tenaciously growing organic mystery of the human toenail. . . .

The waning of affect is, however, perhaps best initially approached by way of the human figure, and it is obvious that what we have said about the commodification of objects holds as strongly for Warhol's human subjects: stars—like Marilyn Monroe—who are themselves commodified and transformed into their own images. And here too a certain brutal return to the older period of high modernism offers a dramatic shorthand parable of the transformation in question. Edward Munch's painting *The Scream* is, of course, a canonical expression of the great modernist thematics of alienation, anomie, solitude, social fragmentation, and isolation, a virtually programmatic emblem of what used to be called the age of anxiety. It will here be read as an embodiment not merely of the expression of that kind of affect but, even more, as a virtual deconstruction of the very aesthetic of expression itself, which seems to have dominated much of what we call high modernism but to have vanished away—for both practical and theoretical reasons—in the world of the postmodern. The very concept of expression presupposes indeed some separation within the subject, and along with that a whole metaphysics of the inside and outside, of the wordless pain within the monad and the moment in which, often cathartically, that "emotion" is then projected out and externalized, as gesture or cry, as desperate communication and the outward dramatization of inward feeling.

This is perhaps the moment to say something about contemporary theory, which has, among other things, been committed to the mission of criticizing and discrediting this very hermeneutic model of the inside and the outside and of stigmatizing such models as ideological and metaphysical. But what is today called contemporary theory—or better still, theoretical discourse—is also, I want to argue, itself very precisely a postmodernist phenomenon. It would therefore be inconsistent to defend the truth of its theoretical insights in a situation in which the very concept of "truth" itself is part of the metaphysical baggage which poststructuralist critique of the hermeneutic, of what I will shortly call the depth model, is useful for us as a very significant symptom of the very postmodernist culture which is our subject here.

Overhastily, we can say that besides the hermeneutic model of inside and outside which

Munch's painting develops, at least four other fundamental depth models have generally been repudiated in contemporary theory: (1) the dialectical one of essence and appearance (along with a whole range of concepts of ideology or false consciousness which tend to accompany it); (2) the Freudian model of latent and manifest, or of repression (which is, of course, the target of Michel Foucault's programmatic and symptomatic pamphlet *La Volonté de savoir* [*The history of Sexuality*]); (3) the existential model of authenticity and inauthenticity whose heroic or tragic thematics are closely related to that other great opposition between alienation and disalienation, itself equally a casualty of the poststructural or postmodern period; and (4) most recently, the great semiotic opposition between signifier and signified, which was itself rapidly unraveled and deconstructed during its brief heyday in the 1960s and 1970s. What replaces these various depth models is for the most part a conception of practices, discourses, and textual play, whose new syntagmatic structures we will examine later on; let it suffice now to observe that here too depth is replaced by surface, or by multiple surfaces (what is often called intertextuality is in that sense no longer a matter of depth).

Nor is this depthlessness merely metaphorical: it can be experienced physically and "literally" by anyone who, mounting what used to be Raymond Chandler's Bunker Hill from the great Chicano markets on Broadway and Fourth Street in downtown Los Angeles, suddenly confronts the great free-standing wall of Wells Fargo Court (Skidmore, Owings and Merrill)—a surface which seems to be unsupported by any volume, or whose putative volume (rectangular? trapezoidal?) is ocularly quite undecidable. This great sheet of windows with its gravity-defying two-dimensionality, momentarily transforms the solid ground on which we stand into the contents of a stereopticon, pasteboard shapes profiling themselves here and there around us. The visual effect is the same from all sides: as fateful as the great monolith in Stanley Kubrick's *2001* which confronts its viewers like an enigmatic destiny, a call to evolutionary mutation. If this new multinational downtown effectively abolished the older ruined city fabric which is violently replaced, cannot something similar be said about the way in which this strange new surface in its own peremptory way renders our older systems of perception of the city somehow archaic and aimless, without offering another in their place?

Returning now for one last moment to Munch's painting, it seems evident that *The Scream* subtly but elaborately disconnects its own aesthetic of expression, all the while remaining imprisoned within it. Its gestural content already underscores its own failure, since the realm of the sonorous, the cry, the raw vibrations of the human throat, are incompatible with its medium (something underscored within the work by the homunculus's lack of ears). Yet the absent scream returns, as it were, in a dialectic of loops and spirals, circling ever more closely toward that even more absent experience of atrocious solitude and anxiety which the scream was itself to "express." Such loops inscribe themselves on the painted surface in the form of those great concentric circles in which sonorous vibration becomes ultimately visible, as on the surface of a sheet of water, in an infinite regress which fans out from the sufferer to become the very geography of a universe in which pain itself now speaks and vibrates through the material sunset and landscape. The visible world now becomes the wall of the monad on which this "scream running through nature" (Munch's words) is recorded and transcribed: one thinks of that character of Lautréamont who, growing up inside a sealed and silent membrane, ruptures it with his own scream on catching sight of the monstrousness of the deity and thereby rejoins the world of sound and suffering.

All of which suggest some more general historical hypothesis: namely, that concepts such as anxiety and alienation (and the experiences to which they correspond, as in *The Scream*) are no longer appropriate in the world of the postmodern. The great Warhol figures—Marilyn herself or Edie Sedgewick—the notorious cases of burnout and self-destruction of the ending 1960s, and the great dominant experiences of drugs and schizophrenia, would seem to have little enough in common any more either with the hysterics and neurotics of Freud's own day or with those canonical experiences of radical isolation and solitude, anomie, private revolt, van Gogh-type madness, which dominated the period of high modernism. This shift in the dynamics of cultural pathology can be characterized as one in which the alienation of the subject is displaced by the latter's fragmentation.

Such terms inevitably recall one of the more fashionable themes in contemporary theory, that of the "death" of the subject itself—the end of the autonomous bourgeois monad or ego or individual—and the accompanying stress, whether as some new moral ideal or as empirical description, on the *decentering* of that formerly centered subject or psyche. (Of the two possible formulations of this notion—the historicist one, that a once-existing centered subject, in the period of classical capitalism and the nuclear family, has today in the world of organizational bureaucracy dissolved; and the more radical poststructuralist position, for which such a subject never existed in the first place but constituted something like an ideological mirage—I obviously incline toward the former; the latter must in any case take into account something like a "reality of the appearance.")

We must however add that the problem of expression is itself closely linked to some conception of the subject as a monadlike container, within which things felt are then expressed by projection outward. What we must now stress, however, is the degree to which the high-modernist conception of a unique *style*, along with the accompanying collective ideals of an artistic or political vanguard or avant-garde, themselves stand or fall along with that older notion (or experience) of the so-called centered subject.

Here too Munch's painting stands as a complex reflection on this complicated situation: it shows us that expression requires the category of the individual monad, but it also shows us the heavy price to be paid for that precondition, dramatizing the unhappy paradox that when you constitute your individual subjectivity as a self-sufficient field and a closed realm, you thereby shut yourself off from everything else and condemn yourself to the mindless solitude of the monad, buried alive and condemned to a prison cell without egress.

Postmodernism presumably signals the end of this dilemma, which it replaces with a new one. The end of the bourgeois ego, or monad, no doubt brings with it the end of the psychopathologies of that ego—what I have been calling the waning of affect. But it means the end of much more—the end, for example, of style, in the sense of the unique and the personal, the end of the distinctive individual brush stroke (as symbolized by the emergent primacy of mechanical reproduction). As for expression and feelings or emotions, the liberation, in contemporary society, from the older *anomie* of the centered subject may also mean not merely a liberation from anxiety but a liberation from every other kind of feeling as well, since there is no longer a self present to do the feeling. This is not to say that the cultural products of the postmodern era are utterly devoid of feeling, but rather that such feelings—which it may be better and more accurate, following J.-F. Lyotard, to call "intensities"—are now free-floating and impersonal and tend to be dominated by a peculiar kind of euphoria, a matter to which we will want to return later on.

The waning of affect, however, might also have been characterized, in the narrower context of literary criticism, as the waning of the great high modernist thematics of time and temporality, the elegiac mysteries of durée and memory (something to be understood fully as much as a category of the literary criticism associated with high modernism as with the works themselves). We have often been told, however, that we now inhabit the synchronic rather than the diachronic, and I think it is at least empirically arguable that our daily life, our psychic experience, our cultural languages, are today dominated by categories of space rather than by categories of time, as in the preceding period of high modernism. . . .

Now we need to complete this exploratory account of postmodernist space and time with a final analysis of that euphoria or those intensities which seem so often to characterize the newer cultural experience. Let us reemphasize the enormity of a transition which leaves behind it the desolation of Hopper's buildings or the stark Midwest syntax of Sheeler's forms, replacing them with the extraordinary surfaces of the photorealist cityscape, where even the automobile wrecks gleam with some new hallucinatory splendor. The exhilaration of these new surfaces is all the more paradoxical in that their essential content—the city itself—has deteriorated or disintegrated to a degree surely still inconceivable in the early years of the twentieth century, let alone in the previous era. How urban squalor can be a delight to the eyes when expressed in commodification, and how an unparalleled quantum leap in the alienation of daily life in the city can now be experienced in the form of a strange new hallucinatory exhilaration—these are some of the questions that confront us in this moment of our inquiry. Nor should the human figure be exempted from investigation, although it seems clear that for the newer aesthetic the representation of space itself has come to be felt as incompatible with the representation of the body: a kind of aesthetic division of labor far more pronounced than in any of the earlier generic conceptions of landscape, and a most ominous symptom indeed. The privileged space of the newer art is radically antianthropomorphic, as in the empty bathrooms of Doug Bond's work. The ultimate contemporary fetishization of the human body, however, takes a very different direction in the statues of Duane Hanson: what I have already called the simulacrum, whose peculiar function lies in what Sartre would have called the *derealization* of the whole surrounding world of everyday reality. Your moment of doubt and hesitation as to the breath and warmth of these polyester figures, in other words, tends to return upon the real human beings moving about you in the museum and to transform them also for the briefest instant into so many dead and flesh-colored simulacra in their own right. The world thereby momentarily loses its depth and threatens to become a glossy skin, a stereoscopic illusion, a rush of filmic images without density. But is this now a terrifying or an exhilarating experience?

It has proved fruitful to think of such experiences in terms of what Susan Sontag, in an influential statement, isolated as "camp." I propose a somewhat different cross-light on it, drawing on the equally fashionable current theme of the "sublime," as it has been rediscovered in the works of Edmund Burke and Kant: or perhaps one might want to yoke the two notions together in the form of something like a camp or "hysterical" sublime. The sublime was for Burke an experience bordering on terror, the fitful glimpse, in astonishment, stupor, and awe, of what was so enormous as to crush human life altogether: a description then refined by Kant to include the question of representation itself, so that the object of the sublime becomes not only a matter of sheer power and of the physical incommensurability of the human organism with Nature but also of the limits of figuration and the incapacity of the human mind to give representation to such enormous forces. Such forces Burke, in his historical moment at the dawn of the modern bourgeois state, was only able to conceptualize in terms of the divine, while even Heidegger continues to entertain a phantasmatic relationship with some organic precapitalist peasant landscape and village society, which is the final form of the image of Nature in our own time.

Today, however, it may be possible to think all this in a different way, at the moment of a radical eclipse of Nature itself: Heidegger's "field path" is, after all, irredeemably and irrevocably destroyed by late capital, by the green revolution, by neocolonialism and the megalopolis, which runs its superhighways over the older fields and vacant lots and turns Heidegger's "house of being" into condominiums, if not the most miserable unheated, rat-infested tenement buildings. The *other* of our society is in that sense no longer Nature at all, as it was in precapitalist societies, but something else which we must now identify.

I am anxious that this other thing not overhastily be grasped as technology per se, since I will want to show that technology is here itself a figure for something else. Yet technology may well serve as adequate shorthand to designate that enormous properly human and anti-natural power of dead human labor stored up in our machinery—an alienated power, what Sartre calls the counterfinality of the practico-inert, which turns back on and against us in unrecognizable forms and seems to constitute the massive dystopian horizon of our collective as well as our individual praxis.

Technological development is however on the Marxist view the result of the development of capital rather than some ultimately determining instance in its own right. It will therefore be appropriate to distinguish several generations of machine power, several stages of technological revolution within capital itself. I here follow Ernest Mandel, who outlines three such fundamental breaks or quantum leaps in the evolution of machinery under capital:

> The fundamental revolutions in power technology—the technology of the production of motive machines by machines—thus appears as the determinant moment in revolutions of technology as a whole. Machine production of steam-driven motors since 1848; machine production of electric and combustion motors since the 90s of the 19th century; machine production of electronic and nuclear-powered apparatuses since the 40s of the 20th century—these are the three general revolutions in technology engendered by the capitalist mode of production since the "original" industrial revolution of the later 18th century.

This periodization underscores the general thesis of Mandel's book *Late Capitalism;* namely, that there have been three fundamental moments in capitalism, each one marking a dialectical expansion over the previous stage. These are market capitalism, the monopoly stage or the stage of imperialism, and our own, wrongly called postindustrial, but what might better be termed multinational, capital. I have already pointed out that Mandel's intervention in the postindustrial debate involves the proposition that late or multinational or consumer capitalism, far from being inconsistent with Marx's great nineteenth-century analysis, constitutes, on the contrary, the purest form of capital yet to have emerged, a prodigious expansion of capital into hitherto uncommodified areas. This purer capitalism of our own time thus eliminates the enclaves of precapitalist organization it had hitherto tolerated and exploited in a tributary way. One is tempted to speak in this connection of a new and historically original penetration and colonization of Nature and the Unconscious: that is, the destruction of precapitalist Third World agriculture by the Green Revolution, and the rise of the media and the advertising industry. At any rate, it will also have been clear that my own cultural periodization of the stages of realism, modernism, and postmodernism is both inspired and confirmed by Mandel's tripartite scheme.

We may therefore speak of our own period as the Third Machine Age; and it is at this point that we must reintroduce the problem of aesthetic representation already explicitly developed in Kant's earlier analysis of the sublime, since it would seem only logical that the relationship to and the representation of the machine could be expected to shift dialectically with each of these qualitatively different stages of technological development.

It is appropriate to recall the excitement of machinery in the moment of capital preceding our own, the exhilaration of futurism, most notably, and of Marinetti's celebration of the machine gun and the motorcar. These are still visible emblems, sculptural nodes of energy which give tangibility and figuration to the motive energies of that earlier moment of modernization. The prestige of these great streamlined shapes can be measured by their metaphorical presence in Le Corbusier's buildings, vast Utopian structures which ride like so many gigantic steamship liners upon the urban scenery of an older fallen earth. Machinery exerts another kind of fascination in the works of artists like Picabia and Duchamp, whom we have no time to consider here; but let me mention, for completeness' sake, the ways in which revolutionary or communist artists of the 1930s also sought to reappropriate

this excitement of machine energy for a Promethean reconstruction of human society as a whole, as in Fernand Léger and Diego Rivera.

It is immediately obvious that the technology of our own moment no longer possesses this same capacity for representation: not the turbine, nor even Sheeler's grain elevators or smokestacks, not the baroque elaboration of pipes and conveyor belts, nor even the streamlined profile of the railroad train—all vehicles of speed still concentrated at rest—but rather the computer, whose outer shell has no emblematic or visual power, or even the casings of the various media themselves, as with that home appliance called television which articulates nothing but rather implodes, carrying its flattened image surface within itself.

Such machines are indeed machines of reproduction rather than of production, and they make very different demands on our capacity for aesthetic representation than did the relatively mimetic idolatry of the older machinery of the futurist moment, of some older speed-and-energy sculpture. Here we have less to do with kinetic energy than with all kinds of new reproductive processes; and in the weaker productions of postmodernism the aesthetic embodiment of such processes often tends to slip back more comfortably into a mere thematic representation of content—into narratives which are *about* the processes of reproduction and include movie cameras, video, tape recorders, the whole technology of the production and reproduction of the simulacrum. (The shift from Antonioni's modernist *Blow-Up* to DePalma's postmodernist *Blow-Out* is here paradigmatic.) When Japanese architects, for example, model a building on the decorative imitation of stacks of cassettes, then the solution is at best thematic and allusive, although often humorous.

Yet something else does tend to emerge in the most energetic postmodernist texts, and this is the sense that beyond all thematics or content the work seems somehow to tap the networks of the reproductive process and thereby to afford us some glimpse into a postmodern or technological sublime, whose power or authenticity is documented by the success of such works in evoking a whole new postmodern space in emergence around us. Architecture therefore remains in this sense the privileged aesthetic language; and the distorting and fragmenting reflections of one enormous glass surface to the other can be taken as paradigmatic of the central role of process and reproduction in postmodernist culture.

As I have said, however, I want to avoid the implication that technology is in any way the "ultimately determining instance" either of our present-day social life or of our cultural production: such a thesis is, of course, ultimately at one with the post-Marxist notion of a postindustrial society. Rather, I want to suggest that our faulty representations of some immense communicational and computer network are themselves but a distorted figuration of something even deeper, namely, the whole world system of a present-day multinational capitalism. The technology of contemporary society is therefore mesmerizing and fascinating not so much in its own right but because it seems to offer some privileged representational shorthand for grasping a network of power and control even more difficult for our minds and imaginations to grasp: the whole new decentered global network of the third stage of capital itself. This is a figural process presently best observed in a whole mode of contemporary entertainment literature—one is tempted to characterize it as "high-tech paranoia"—in which the circuits and networks of some putative global computer hookup are narratively mobilized by labyrinthine conspiracies of autonomous but deadly interlocking and competing information agencies in a complexity often beyond the capacity of the normal reading mind. Yet conspiracy theory (and its garish narrative manifestations) must be seen as a degraded attempt—through the figuration of advanced technology—to think the impossible totality of the contemporary world system. It is in terms of that enormous and threatening, yet only dimly perceivable, other reality of economic and social institutions, that in my opinion, the postmodern sublime can alone be adequately theorized.

Such narratives, which first tried to find expression through the generic structure of the spy novel, have only recently crystallized in a new type of science fiction, called *cyberpunk*, which is fully as much an expression of transnational corporate realities as it is of global paranoia itself: William Gibson's representational innovations, indeed, mark his work as an exceptional literary realization within a predominantly visual or aural postmodern production.

Presenting the Unpresentable: The Sublime

JEAN-FRANÇOIS LYOTARD

IT IS NOT JUST photography that has rendered the profession of painting "impossible"; to claim that it was would be like saying that Stephane Mallarmé's work or James Joyce's were simply responses to the development of journalism.

Painting's impossibility arises from the industrial and postindustrial—techno-scientific—world's greater need for photography than for painting, just as that world needs journalism more than it does literature. The momentum of this world

From Art Forum *20: 8 (1982). Reprinted by permission of the publisher.*

brought with it the decline of the so-called "noble" professions which had belonged to the previous world, as well as the contraction of that earlier world.

Painting won its noble imprimatur, was ranked as a Fine Art, and was awarded almost princely privileges during the Quattrocento. In the centuries that followed it contributed its share toward realizing the meta-physical and political program of visual and social order. Optical geometry, the ordering of colors and values according to a hierarchy of Neoplatonic inspiration, and the pictorial rules that captured and crystalized the heydays of religious or historical legend helped instill a sense of identity in the new political communities—the City, the State, the Nation—by allotting them the fate of seeing all through reason and thus making the world transparent (clear and distinct). The narrative, urban, architectural, religious, and ethical components of these communities were given order on the pictorial plane by the painter's eye, according to Leon Battista Alberti's *costruzione legitima* (broadly, the laws of perspective). In turn, the eye of the monarch registered a well-ordered universe all the way to the vanishing point. Exhibited in the churches and the great halls of seignorial or civic palaces, these representations allowed every member of the community the same possibility as the monarch or the painter for an identity within and mastery over that universe. The modern concept of state—the republic or the democracy—is foreshadowed by this commoner, who in perceptual union with the monarch is a "virtual prince" and who will later become the citizen. The modern concept of culture stems from this public access to historical-political identifying signs and to their collective interpretation. Museums perpetuate this tradition; but more pointedly, a glance into the halls of Congress in Washington, or into the Chambre des députés in Paris, attests to the fact that this classical spatial organization is not limited to museum paintings, but structures the representation of the body politic itself. The extent to which the plans of Greek and Roman public places are paradigms for the modern sociopolitical arena is clear.

Photography achieves this program of meta-political visual and social ordering. It achieves it in both senses of the word: it realizes it, and it concludes it. The know-how and knowledge that were given substance and were transmitted in the school and the studio are now programmed inside the photographic machine. In a single click, an ordinary citizen, whether amateur or tourist, can organize his or her identifying spaces and make a picture that enriches the cultural memory-bank. Improved contemporary instruments free one from the problem of lengthy poses, of focusing, aperture selection, and developing. Thanks to optical, chemical, mechanical, and electronic refinements, the photographic machine makes certain of the skills, experience, and training that were required of the apprentice painter (such as eradicating bad habits, educating the eye, hand, body, and soul, in order to elevate them to a new order) available to the amateur. All the amateur has to do is choose a subject and even there the photographer is guided by customs and connotations, though they can be ignored and the unexpected can be sought—as it often is. Rather than becoming a tedious survey, amateur photography over the course of the nineteenth century became a means of prospecting and discovering, and even of ethnological inquiry. The old political function of painting became fragmented; the painter was an ethnologist of little ethnologies, and the community now had less of a need to identify with its prince, its core, than it had to explore its boundaries. Amateur photographers made field trips; they returned with documents.

Painters had already set themselves to the task of documentation (one thinks here of Gustave Courbet, of Edouard Manet), but they were quickly overtaken in this. Their procedures could not compete: slow professional learning processes, costly materials, lengthy production periods, difficult objects to manage—in short, the cost of the whole endeavor was to be compared to the relatively minimal total cost of making a photograph. Later, Marcel Duchamp concluded that it was no longer the time to paint. With photography, the idea of the industrial ready-made had arrived. Those painters who persisted had to confront photography's challenge, and so they engaged in the dialectic of the avant-garde which had at stake the question "What is Painting?" Painting became a philosophical activity: previously defined rules governing the formation of pictorial images were not enunciated and applied automatically. Rather, painting's rule became the re-evaluation of those pictorial rules, as philosophy re-evaluates philosophical syntax.

Thus avant-garde painters cut themselves off from the public who were already handling well-regulated photographic equipment, and had been leafing through "real" pictures (and seeing them at the movies as well). That public remained convinced that the programs for artificial perspective had to be maintained, and did not understand that it can take a year to make a blank square; in other words, to create nothing (assuming that that's the only form of the unrepresentable).

Thus photography entered the field that had been opened up by the classical aesthetics of imagery, the aesthetics of beauty. Like classical painting of the Renaissance, photography called upon communal taste. The nature of this consensus, however, is profoundly modified in photography, as it is in the whole field of aesthetic objects in the contemporary Western world. Immanuel Kant insisted that consensus as to what is beautiful must remain free; in other words, that it is not regulated *a priori* by laws. The widespread introduction of industrial and postindustrial techno-sciences, of which the invention of photography is only one aspect, evidently signifies painstaking programming, by means of optical, chemical, and photo-electronic processes, of the production of beautiful images. These images immediately bear the stamp of the laws of knowledge. The indeterminate, since it does not allow for precision, will have to be eliminated, and with it goes feeling. The person for whom these beautiful pictures are intended is a consumer of finished products. Photography's infallibility is that of the perfectly programmed; its beauty is that of Voyager II.

Loss of aura is the negative aspect of the hardware involved in producing the machine that produces the photograph. The amateur has to choose a subject, but the look is controlled by the manufacturer. Experience is that mass of affects—of projections and memories—that must perish and be born for any subject to attain the expression of its essence. The body of amateur photography has almost nothing to do with experience and owes almost everything to the experiments of industrial research laboratories. As a result, it is not just beautiful, but too beautiful. Something is inherent in this "too": an infinity; not the indeterminacy of a feeling, but the infinite ability of science, of technology, of capitalism, to realize. The ability of machines to function is, by principle, subject to obsolescence because the accomplishments of the most esteemed capitalists demand the perpetual reformulation of merchandise and the creation of new markets. The hardness of industrial beauty contains the infinity of techno-scientific and economic reasons.

The destruction of experience that this implies is not simply due to the introduction of that which is "well-conceived" into the field of aesthetics. Science, technology, and capital, in spite of their matter-of-fact approach, are also modes of making concrete the infinity of ideas. Knowing all, being capable of all, having all, are their horizons—and horizons extend to infinity. The ready-made in the techno-sciences presents itself as a potential for infinite production, and so does the photograph. In this sense amateur photography, at first glance not much more than the consummation of the machine's image-making capacities, also belongs to the infinite dialectic of ideas in the process of being realized—the state of consuming—and therein it heralds a new condition. The end of experience is no doubt the end of poetics, but it is also the concretization of an objective infinity which continually constructs and deconstructs the world, and one wherein the individual, at whatever level of the social hierarchy, is both voluntary and involuntary subject.

It follows that the definition of a well-realized photographic image, initially linked to the rules of artificial perspective, is subject to revision. Photography enters into that infinite field opened up by techno-scientific research. Its initial function, inherited from the identifying task assigned to painting in the Quattrocento, falls into disuse, as does the general community's previous definition of its identity. In the current state of techno-science and accumulated capital in the developed world, community identity requires no spiritual allegiance, nor does it demand a grand, shared ideology, but it crystallizes instead through the mediation of the total sum of goods and services, which are being exchanged at a prodigious rate. At the edge of the twenty-first-century the search for knowledge, technology, and capital is evident in the very structure of our languages. The traditional function of the state has shifted: it need no longer incarnate the idea of community, and tends instead to identify with its infinite potential to generate data, know-how, and wealth. Within this trend, photography is relieved of the responsibility for ideological identification which it inherited from pictorial tradition, and makes room for research, and, of course, for photographic art. We are past deploring "mechanical reproducibility" in works of art; we know that industry doesn't mean the end of the arts, only their mutation. The question, "What is photography?" draws photographic researches into a dialectic comparable to that of the pictorial avant-garde.

The pictorial avant-garde, as we have seen, responded to painting's "impossibility" by engaging in research centered around the question, "What is painting?" One after another, previous assumptions about the painter's practice were put on trial and debated. Tonality, linear perspective, the rendering of values, the frame, format, the supports, surface, medium, instrument, place of exhibition, and many other presuppositions were questioned plastically by the various avant-gardes. "Modern painters" discovered that they had to represent the existence of that which was not demonstrable if the perspectival laws of *costruzione legitima* were followed. They set about to revolutionize the supposed visual givens in order to reveal that the field of vision simultaneously conceals and needs the invisible, that it relates therefore not only to the eye, but to the spirit as well.

Thus they introduced painting into the field opened by the aesthetics of the sublime—which is not governed by a consensus of taste. Avant-garde painting eludes the aesthetics of beauty in that it does not draw on a communal sense of shared pleasure. To the public taste its products seem "monstrous," "formless," purely "negative" nonentities. (I am using terms by which Kant characterized those objects that give rise to a sense of the sublime.) When one represents the non-demonstrable, representation itself is martyred. Among other things this means that neither painting nor the viewing public can draw on established symbols, figures, or plastic forms that would permit the sense or the understanding of there being, in these idea works, any question of the kind of reason and imagination that existed in Romano-Christian painting. In our techno-scientific industrial world there are no consistent symbols for good, just, true, infinite, etc. There have been certain "realisms," usually academic—bourgeois at the end of the nineteenth century, socialist and nationalist-socialist during the twentieth—that have tried to reintroduce symbolism, to offer the public accessible works of art which will allow it to identify with specific ideas (race, socialism, nation, etc.). We know these attempts always call for the elimination of the avant-garde. For its part the avant-garde, in its prodigious effort of questioning precedents of painting, manages to neglect utterly its "cultural" responsibility for unifying taste and providing a sense of communal identity by means of visual symbols. The avant-garde painter feels an overriding responsibility to the fulfillment of the imperative implied by the question. "What is painting?" Essentially what is at stake in the work is the demonstration of the existence of the invisible in the visual. The task of "cultivating" the public comes later.

That which is not demonstrable is that which stems from ideas and for which one cannot cite (represent) any example, case in point, or even symbol. The universe is not demonstrable: neither is humanity, the end of history, the moment, the species, the good, the just, etc.—or according to Kant, absolutes in general—because to represent is to make relative, to place in context within conditions of representation. Therefore one cannot represent the absolute, but one can demonstrate that the absolute exists—through "negative representation," which Kant called the "abstract." The momentum of abstract painting since 1910 stems from the rigors of indirect, virtually ungraspable allusions to the invisible within the visual. The sublime is the sense that these works draw upon, not the beautiful.

The sublime is not simple gratification, but the gratification of effort. It is impossible to represent the absolute, which is ungratifying: but one knows that one has to, that the faculty of feeling or of imagining is called upon to make the perceptible represent the ineffable—and even if this fails, and even if that causes suffering, a pure gratification will emerge from the tension. It is not surprising to find the term sublime in Guillaume Apollinaire's essays on Modern paintings, in Barnett Newman's writings and painting titles, in texts published by many more recent avant-gardists during the 1960s. The word belongs to the romantic vocabulary.

The pictorial avant-gardes achieved romanticism—in other words, a Modernism (already presaged by Petronius and Augustine) which signifies the weakening of the links between that which can be felt and that which can be understood. But at the same time they were byproducts of a romantic nostalgia, because they looked to their immediate circumstances, to the actual conditions of the artmaking process. Marcel Proust was still a romantic, Joyce less so, and Gertrude Stein even less. Henry Fuseli and Caspar David Friedrich were romantics, and so was Eugène Delacroix; Paul Cézanne less so, the Delaunays and Piet Mondrian barely at all. These last three were already following the experimental imperative (in what they accomplished if not always in what they wrote). Their sublime was fundamentally not nostalgic and tended toward the infinity of plastic experiment rather than toward the representation of any lost absolute. In this, their work belongs to the contemporary industrial, techno-scientific world.

As for Achille Bonito Oliva's "trans-avantgarde" and similar current notions in Italy, Germany, and the United States (including Charles Jencks' post-modernism in architecture—which the reader will kindly not confuse with what I have referred to in the past as the "post-modern condition"), it is clear that under the pretext of consolidating the avant-garde tradition it is in effect squandering it. That tradition can only convey itself through the dialectic of refutation and questioning. Drawing firm conclusions, especially by process of addition, means the end of that dialectic and the encouragement of the eclecticism of consumerism. Mixing neo- or hyper-realist motifs with lyrically abstract or conceptual ones on a single surface is saying that everything is equal because everything is easy to consume. It means establishing and ratifying new "taste." This "taste" is not Taste. Eclecticism panders to the habits of magazine readers, to the needs of consumers of standard industrial imagery, to the sensibility of the supermarket shopper. That kind of post-Modernism, to the extent that it exerts—by means of critics, curators, gallery directors, and collectors—intense pressure on artists, aligns pictorial inquiry to the current state of "culture," and strips artists of their responsibility to the question of the nondemonstrable. That question is, to me, the only one worthy of life's high stakes, and of the world of thought in the coming century. Any denial of that question is a menace—and one that cannot be ignored, as it threatens to relax the tension between the act of painting and the essence of painting, when it is that very tension which stimulated one of the most heroic centuries of Western painting. This menace implies the corruption of painting's honor—which thus far has remained intact in spite of the worst temptations of the state and of the market.

Barnett Newman, *Be I*, 1949

The governing principle of the postindustrial techno-scientific world is not the need to represent the representable, but rather the opposite principle. To turn away from this principle—that infinity is inherent in the very dialectic of search—is absurd, impractical, and reactionary. It is not up to the artist to reinstate a make-believe "reality" which the drive toward knowledge, technology, and wealth will continually destroy in order to replace it with a version considered more viable—and which itself will eventually be replaced. The spirit of the times is surely not that of the merely pleasant: its mission remains that of the immanent sublime, that of alluding to the nondemonstrable. It goes without saying that such a mission causes anguish, but painters are not subject to the question, "How can we avoid anguish?" They are subject to the question, "What is painting?" In addition, they are also subject to the question "How do we communicate our painting to those who are not painters?"—but this does not mean that the two roles are to be confused. To confuse them would be comparable to the philosopher confusing responsibility to thought with responsibility to the public. The responsibility of communicating the meaning of thoughts and paintings belongs to the intellectual. In fact, the question "What is thought?" places the philosopher in an avant-garde position. That is why he dares speak of painters, his brothers and sisters in experimentation.

Bibliography

Aldrich, Virgil. *Philosophy of Art*. Englewood Cliffs, NJ: Prentice Hall, 1963.

Arac, Jonathan. *Critical Genealogies: Historical Situations for Postmodern Literary Studies*. New York: Columbia University Press, 1987.

Aschenbrenner, Karl. *The Concepts of Criticism*. Dordrecht: Kluwer, 1974.

Barthes, Roland. *Camera Lucida: Reflections on Photography*. Trans. Richard Howard. New York: Hill and Wang, 1981.

———. *Image, Music, Text*. Trans. Stephen Heath. New York: Hill and Wang, 1977.

———. *The Pleasure of the Text*. Trans. Richard Miller. New York: Farrar, Straus and Giroux, 1975.

———. *S/Z*. Trans. Richard Miller. New York: Farrar, Straus and Giroux, 1984.

Baxandall, Lee. *Radical Perspectives in the Arts*. Baltimore: Penguin Books, 1972.

Beardsley, Monroe. *Aesthetics*. New York: Harcourt Brace, 1958.

———. *The Possibility of Criticism*. Detroit: Wayne State University Press, 1970.

Bell, Clive. *Art*. New York: Capricorn Books, 1958.

Berleant, Arnold. *The Aesthetics of Environment*. Philadelphia: Temple University Press, 1992.

Blocker, H. Gene. *Philosophy of Art*. New York: Scribners, 1979.

———, and Michael Parsons. *Aesthetics and Education*. Champaign-Urbana: University of Illinois Press, 1993.

———. *The Aesthetics of Primitive Art*. Lanham, MD: University Press of America, 1994.

———, and Zhu Liyuan (eds.) *Contemporary Chinese Aesthetics*. New York: Peter Lang, 1995.

Bloom, Harold, ed. *Deconstruction and Criticism*. New York: Continuum, 1979.

Bosanquet, Bernard. *A History of Aesthetics*. New York: Meridian, 1957.

Bullough, Edward. " 'Psychical Distance' as a Factor in Art and an Aesthetic Principle." *British Journal of Psychology* 5 (1912): 87–118.

Burgin, Victor. *The End of Art Theory: Criticism and Postmodernity*. New York: Macmillan, 1986.

Carroll, David. *Paraesthetics: Foucault, Lyotard, Derrida*. New York: Methuen, 1987.

Collingwood, R. G. *The Principles of Art*. New York: Oxford University Press, 1958.

Cooper, David, ed. *A Companion to Aesthetics*. Oxford: Blackwell, 1992.

Croce, Benedetto. *Aesthetic*. 2d ed. Trans. Douglas Ainslie. New York: Macmillan, 1922.

Dante Alighieri. *The Letters of Dante*. Trans. Paget Toynbee. New York: Oxford University Press, 1966.

Danto, Arthur. *The Transfiguration of the Commonplace*. Cambridge, MA: Harvard University Press, 1981.

Davies, Stephen. *Definitions of Art*. Ithaca, NY: Cornell University Press, 1991.

Debord, Guy. *Society of the Spectacle*. Detroit: Black and Red, 1983.

De Lauretis, Teresa. *Technologies of Gender: Essays on Theory, Film, and Fiction*. Bloomington: Indiana University Press, 1987.

Deleuze, Gilles. *Foucault*. Trans. Sean Hand. Minneapolis: University of Minnesota Press, 1988.

———, and Claire Parnet. *Dialogues*. Trans. Hugh Tomlinson and Barbara Habberjam. New York: Columbia University Press, 1987.

De Man, Paul. *Blindness and Insight: Essays in the Rhetoric of Contemporary Criticism*. 2d ed., rev. Minneapolis: University of Minnesota Press, 1983.

Derrida, Jacques. *Glas.* Trans. John P. Leavey, Jr. and Richard Rand. Lincoln: University of Nebraska Press, 1986.

———. *Margins of Philosophy.* Trans. Alan Bass. Chicago: University of Chicago Press, 1982.

———. *Of Grammatology.* Trans. Gayatri Chakravorty Spivak. Baltimore: Johns Hopkins University Press, 1976.

———. *Positions.* Trans. Alan Bass. Chicago: University of Chicago Press, 1981.

———. *The Postcard: From Socrates to Freud and Beyond.* Trans. Alan Bass. Chicago: University of Chicago Press, 1987.

———. *Speech and Phenomena, and Other Essays on Husserl's Theory of Signs.* Trans. David B. Allison. Evanston, IL: Northwestern University Press, 1973.

———. *Truth in Painting.* Trans. Geoff Bennington and Ian McLeod. Chicago: University of Chicago Press, 1987.

———. *Writing and Difference.* Trans. Alan Bass. Chicago: University of Chicago Press, 1978.

Dewey, John. *Art as Experience.* New York: Minton Balch, 1934.

Dickie, George. *Art and the Aesthetic.* Ithaca, NY: Cornell University Press, 1974.

———. *The Art Circle: A Theory of Art.* New York: Haven, 1984.

———. *The Century of Taste.* New York: Oxford University Press, 1996.

———. *Evaluating Art.* Philadelphia: Temple University Press, 1988.

Dufrenne, Mikel. *The Phenomenology of Aesthetic Experience.* Trans. Edward Casey and Albert Anderson. Evanston, IL: Northwestern University Press, 1973.

Eagleton, Terry. *The Ideology of the Aesthetic.* Oxford: Basil Blackwell, 1991.

Eaton, Marcia. *Aesthetics and the Good Life.* Rutherford, NJ: Fairleigh Dickinson University Press, 1989.

———. *Art and Nonart.* Rutherford, NJ: Fairleigh Dickinson University Press, 1983.

Foster, Hal. *Recordings: Art, Spectacle, Cultural Politics.* Port Townsend: Bay Press, 1985.

———, ed. *The Anti-Aesthetic: Essays on Postmodern Culture.* Port Townsend: Bay Press, 1983.

Foucault, Michel. *The Archeology of Knowledge.* Trans. A. M. Sheridan Smith. New York: Pantheon Books, 1977.

———. *Discipline and Punish.* Trans. Alan Sheridan. New York: Pantheon Books, 1977.

———. *The History of Sexuality.* Vol. 1., *An Introduction.* Vol. 2, *The Uses of Pleasure.* Vol. 3, *The Care of the Self.* Trans. Robert Hurley. New York: Pantheon Books, 1978.

———. *The Order of Things: An Archaeology of the Human Sciences.* New York: Vintage Books, 1973.

———. *Power/Knowledge,* edited by Colin Gordon. New York: Pantheon Books, 1980.

Frampton, Kenneth. *Modern Architecture: A Critical History.* New York: Thames and Hudson, 1985.

Gadamer, Hans-Georg. *The Relevance of the Beautiful and Other Essays,* edited by Robert Bernasconi. New York: Cambridge University Press, 1986.

Gates, Henry Louis, Jr., ed. *The Signifying Monkey: A Theory of Afro-American Literary Criticism.* Oxford: Oxford University Press, 1988.

Gombrich, E. H. *Art and Illusion.* 2d ed. New York: Pantheon, 1957.

———. *In Search of Cultural History.* New York: Oxford University Press, 1969.

Goodman, Nelson. *Languages of Art.* Indianapolis: Bobbs-Merrill, 1968, chap 1. New York: Phaidon, 1963.

———. *Ways of Worldmaking.* Indianapolis: Hackett Publishers, 1978.

Guyer, Paul. *Kant and the Claims of Taste.* Cambridge, MA: Harvard University Press, 1979.

Habermas, Jurgen. *The Philosophical Discourse of Modernity.* Trans. Frederick Lawrence. Cambridge, MA: MIT Press, 1987.

Harvey, Irene. *Derrida and the Economy of Difference.* Bloomington: Indiana University Press, 1986.

Hegel, G. W. F. *Philosophy of Mind*. Trans. William Wallace. New York: Oxford University Press, 1971. Reprinted by permission of Oxford University Press.

Heidegger, Martin. *On the Way to Language*. Trans. Peter D. Hertz. New York: Harper and Row, 1971.

———. *Poetry, Language, Thought*. Trans. Albert Hofstadter. New York: Harper and Row, 1971.

Hermeren, Goren. *Representation and Meaning in the Visual Arts*. Lund: Berlingska, Boktryckeriet, 1969.

Heyl, Bernard. *New Bearings in Esthetics and Art Criticism*. New Haven: Yale University Press, 1943.

Hipple, Jr., Walter J. *The Beautiful, the Sublime, and the Picturesque in Eighteenth-Century British Aesthetic Theory*. Carbondale: Southern Illinois University Press, 1957.

Hirsch, E. D., Jr. *Validity in Interpretation*. New Haven: Yale University Press, 1967.

Horkheimer, Max. *Critical Theory: Selected Essays*. Trans. Matthew J. O'Connell et al. New York: Continuum, 1972.

Hospers, John. *Meaning and Truth in the Arts*. Chapel Hill, NC: University of North Carolina Press, 1946.

Hume, David. *Essays and Treatises on Several Subjects*. London: 1777.

Hungerland, Isabel. *Poetic Discourse*. Berkeley: University of California Press, 1958.

Hutcheon, Linda. *A Poetics of Postmodernism: History, Theory, Fiction*. London: Routledge, 1988.

Hutcheson, Francis. *An Inquiry into the Original of Our Ideas of Beauty and Virtue*. London: 1725.

Huyssen, Andreas. *After the Great Divide: Modernism, Mass Culture, Postmodernism*. Bloomington: Indiana University Press, 1986.

Ingarden, Roman. *The Literary Work of Art*. Trans. G. George. Evanston, IL: Northwestern University Press, 1973.

Jeffers, Jennifer, ed. *Samuel Beckett: A Casebook*. New York: Garland, 1998.

Jencks, Charles. *The Language of Post-Modern Architecture*. New York: Rizolli, 1977.

Kant, Immanuel. *Critique of Judgment*. Trans. J. H. Bernard. New York, 1951.

Kaplan, E. Ann. *Rocking Around the Clock: Music Television, Postmodernism, and Consumer Culture*. New York: Methuen, 1987.

Klotz, Heinrich, ed. *Postmodern Visions: Drawings, Paintings, and Models by Contemporary Architects*. New York: Abbeville Press, 1985.

Koelb, Clayton. *Nietzsche as Postmodernist*. Albany, NY: State University of New York Press, 1990.

Krauss, Rosalind. *The Originality of the Avant-Garde and Other Modernist Myths*. Cambridge, MA: MIT Press, 1985.

Kroker, Arthur, and David Cook. *The Postmodern Scene: Excremental Culture and Hyper-Aesthetics*. New York: St. Martin's Press, 1986.

Lacan, Jacques. *Ecrits: A Selection*. Trans. Alan Sheridan. New York: Norton, 1977.

LaCapra, Dominick. *Rethinking Intellectual History: Texts, Contexts, Language*. Ithaca, NY: Cornell University Press, 1983.

Lang, Berel, ed. *The Concept of Style*. Ithaca, NY: Cornell University Press, 1987.

Langer, Suzanne. *Feeling and Form*. New York: Scribner's, 1953.

———. *Philosophy in a New Key*. New York: New American Library, 1948.

———. *Problems of Art*. New York: Scribner's, 1957.

Langfeld, Herbert S. *The Aesthetic Attitude*. New York: Harcourt Brace, 1920.

Levin, David Michael. *The Opening of Vision: Nihilism and the Postmodern Situation*. New York: Routledge, 1988.

Lyotard, Jean-François. *The Differend: Phrases of Dispute*. Trans. Georges van den Abbeele. Minneapolis: University of Minnesota Press, 1989.

———. *The Postmodern Condition: A Report on Knowledge*. Trans. Geoff Bennington and Brian Massumi. Minneapolis: University of Minnesota Press, 1984.

MacCabe, Colin. *Tracking the Signifier: Theoretical Essays on Film, Linguistics, and Literature*. Minneapolis: University of Minnesota Press, 1985.

Margolis, Joseph. *Art and Philosophy*. Atlantic Highlands, NJ: Humanities Press, 1980.

———. *The Language of Art and Art Criticism*. Detroit: Wayne State University Press, 1965.

Melville, Stephen. *Philosophy Beside Itself: On Deconstruction and Modernism*. Minneapolis: University of Minnesota Press, 1986.

Merrill, Robert, ed. *Ethics/Aesthetics: Postmodern Positions*. Washington, D.C.: Maisonneuve Press, 1988.

Miller, Mark Crispin. *Boxed In: The Culture of TV*. Evanston, IL: Northwestern University Press, 1988.

Miyoshi, Masao, ed. *Postmodernism and Japan*. Durham, NC: Duke University Press, 1989.

Moore, G. E. *Principia Ethica*. Cambridge: Cambridge University Press, 1903.

Mothersill, Mary. *Beauty Restored*. Oxford: Oxford University Press, 1984.

Nietzsche, Friedrich. *The Birth of Tragedy* and *The Genealogy of Morals*. Trans. Francis Golffing. Garden City, NY: Doubleday, 1956.

Osborne, Harold. *Aesthetics and Criticism*. London: Routledge and Kegan Paul, 1955.

———. *Theory of Beauty*. London: Routledge and Kegan Paul, 1952.

Parker, De Witt. *The Principles of Aesthetics*. 2d ed. New York: Appleton-Century-Crofts, 1920.

———. *The Analysis of Art*. New Haven: Yale University Press, 1926.

Pepper, Stephen. *The Basis of Criticism in the Arts*. Cambridge, MA: Harvard University Press, 1949.

———. *The Work of Art*. Bloomington: Indiana University Press, 1955.

Plato, *The Republic*. Trans. Benjamin Jowett. Oxford: Oxford University Press, 1871.

Portoghesi, Paulo. *Postmodern, The Architecture of the Postmodern Society*. Trans. Ellen Shapiro. New York: Rizolli, 1983.

Prall, David W. *Aesthetic Analysis*. New York: Crowell, 1936.

———. *Aesthetic Judgment*. New York: Crowell, 1929.

Ricoeur, Paul. *The Conflict of Interpretations,* ed. Don Ihde. Evanston, IL: Northwestern University Press, 1974.

Rollins, Mark, ed. *Danto and His Critics*. Oxford: Blackwell, 1993.

Ross, Andrew, ed. *Universal Abandon? The Politics of Postmodernism*. Minneapolis: University of Minnesota Press, 1988.

Ruskin, John. *Modern Painters*. New York, 1885.

Said, Edward. *Orientalism*. New York: Pantheon Books, 1978.

———. *The World, the Text, and the Critic*. Cambridge, MA: Harvard University Press, 1983.

Santayana, George. *The Sense of Beauty*. New York: Modern Library, 1955.

Serres, Michel. *The Parasite*. Trans. Lawrence R. Schehr. Baltimore: Johns Hopkins University Press, 1982.

Spanos, William. *Martin Heidegger and the Question of Literature: Toward a Postmodern Literary Hermeneutics*. Bloomington: Indiana University Press, 1979.

———. *Repetitions: The Postmodern Occasion in Literature and Culture*. Baton Rouge: Louisiana State University Press, 1987.

Spivak, Gayatri Chakravorty. *In Other Worlds: Essays in Cultural Criticism*. London: Methuen, 1987.

Sprinker, Michael. *Imaginary Relations: Aesthetics and Ideology in the Theory of Historical Materialism*. London: Verso, 1987.

Stolnitz, Jerome. *Aesthetics and Philosophy of Art Criticism*. Boston: Houghton Mifflin, 1960.

Strong, Tracy B. *Friedrich Nietzsche and the Politics of Transfiguration*. Berkeley: University of California Press, 1988.

Tafuri, Manfredo. *Architecture and Utopia: Design and Capitalist Development*. Cambridge, MA: MIT Press, 1987.

Taylor, Brandon. *Modernism, Postmodernism, Realism: A Critical Perspective for Art*. Winchester: Winchester School of Art Press, 1987.

Taylor, Mark. *Altarity*. Chicago: University of Chicago Press, 1987.

Tilghman, Ben. *But Is It Art?* New York: Blackwell, 1984.

Tolstoy, Leo N. *What Is Art?* Trans. Aylmer Maude. New York, 1899.

Tormey, Alan. *The Concept of Expression*. Princeton, NJ: Princeton University Press, 1971.

Trachtenberg, Stanley, ed. *The Postmodern Moment: A Handbook of Contemporary Innovation in the Arts*. Westport: Greenwood Press, 1985.

Ulmer, Gregory L. *Applied Grammatology: Post(e)-Pedagogy from Jacques Derrida to Joseph Beuys*. Baltimore: Johns Hopkins University Press, 1985.

Vattimo, Gianni. *The End of Modernity: Nihilism and Hermeneutics in Postmodern Culture*. Trans. Jon R. Snyder. Baltimore: Johns Hopkins University Press, 1989.

Virilio, Paul. *Speed and Politics: An Essay on Dromology*. Trans. Mark Polizzotti. New York: Semiotext(e), 1986.

Wallis, Brian. *Art After Modernism: Rethinking Representation*. New York: New York Museum of Modern Art, 1984.

Walton, Kendall. *Mimesis as Make-Believe*. Cambridge, MA: Harvard University Press, 1990.

Weitz, Morris. *Philosophy of the Arts*. Cambridge, MA: Harvard University Press, 1950.

West, Cornell, and John Rajchman, eds. *Post-Analytic Philosophy*. New York: Columbia University Press, 1985.

White, Hayden. *Tropics of Discourse*. Baltimore: Johns Hopkins University Press, 1978.

Wimsatt, William K., and Cleanth Brooks. *Literary Criticism: A Short History*. New York: Knopf, 1957.

Wittgenstein, Ludwig. *Philosophical Investigations*. Trans. C. E. M. Anscombe. New York: Macmillan, 1953.

Wollheim, Richard. *Art and Its Objects*. New York: Harper and Row, 1968.

Wolterstorff, Nicholas. *Art in Action*. Grand Rapids, Mich.: William B. Eerdmans, 1980.

———. *Works and Worlds of Art*. New York: Oxford University Press, 1980.

Yanal, Robert, ed. *Institutions of Art: Reconsiderations of George Dickie's Philosophy*. University Park: Pennsylvania State University, 1994.

Index

Photo Credits

Page 224, Giraudon/Art Resource, NY; **page 225,** Giraudon/Art Resource, NY; **page 232,** Francis Bacon, *Study After Velásquez's Portrait of Pope Innocent X*, 1952, 60¼ × 46½ inches, Purchased with funds from the Coffin Fine Arts Trust; Nathan Emory Coffin Collection of the Des Moines Art Center, 1980.1, photo by Michael Tropea, Chicago; **page 245,** from the collection of the Louisiana Museum of Modern Art, Denmark; **page 246,** Courtesy O.K. Harris Works of Art, New York; **page 247,** Richard Estes, Marlborough Gallery, NYC; **page 323,** The Baltimore Museum of Art: The Cone Collection, formed by Dr. Claribel Cone and Miss Etta Cone of Baltimore, Maryland BMA 1950.302; **page 324,** The Andy Warhol Foundation, Inc./Art Resource, NY; **page 336,** Barnett Newman, Artists Rights Society, NYC.